Physical Education Activity Handbook

THIRTEENTH EDITION

Jerre McManama

Assistant Professor Emeritus,
Ball State University

Lisa Hicks

Chairperson, Department of Kinesiology,
University of Indianapolis

Mark Urtel

Director of Undergraduate Programs,
Department of Kinesiology
Indiana University–Purdue University
Indianapolis (IUPUI)

PEARSON

Boston   Columbus   Indianapolis   New York   San Francisco   Upper Saddle River
Amsterdam   Cape Town   Dubai   London   Madrid   Milan   Munich   Paris   Montréal   Toronto
Delhi   Mexico City   São Paulo   Sydney   Hong Kong   Seoul   Singapore   Taipei   Tokyo

Executive Editor: *Sandra Lindelof*
Development Manager: *Barbara Yien*
Editorial Manager: *Susan Malloy*
Project Editor: *Meghan Zolnay*
Editorial Assistant: *Briana Verdugo*
Text Permissions Project: *Tom Wilcox*
Text Permissions Specialist: *Alison Bruckner*
Managing Editor: *Deborah Cogan*
Production Project Manager: *Elisa Mandelbaum*
Composition, Project Management, and Illustrations: *Integra*
Design Manager: *Marilyn Perry*
Cover Designer: *Riezebos Holzbaur Design Group*
Photographer: *Sycamore Sisters Photography*
Photo Permissions Management: *Donna Kalal*
Photo Researcher: *Ann Armstrong*
Manufacturing Buyer: *Stacey Weinberger*
Executive Marketing Manager: *Neena Bali*
Cover Photo Credit: *GettyImages/MichaelSvoboda*

Credits and acknowledgments for materials borrowed from other sources and reproduced, with permission, in this textbook appear on pp. 493–505.

Library of Congress Cataloging-in-Publication Data on file.

www.pearsonhighered.com

ISBN 10:   0-321-88363-2
ISBN 13: 978-0-321-88363-6

CONTENTS

PREFACE

This handbook was prepared and published in 1951 as the first textbook in the field designed especially for students in physical education service (required) programs. There was a need for a basic textbook for beginners that would include a large variety of physical activities expertly described. For over 61 years, this book has maintained its original purpose: to provide a variety of physical activities for beginners. Information in the text is provided for those who are teaching, who are preparing to be teachers, and who are learning these activities.

Teachers, recreational leaders, volunteer scout leaders, and similar personnel are often called upon to "start the ball rolling," or to teach an activity with which they are not completely familiar. Many teachers have only a few specializations and it would take them too long to master all the present offerings in physical education. Some activities, too, are more familiar to men than to women, and vice versa. Yet, with the changes brought about by Title IX and laws governing participation by special populations, today's teaching personnel must be able to give instruction in a great variety of activities. This is particularly true of individual and team sports such as golf, orienteering, cycling, inline skating, speedball, flag football, field hockey, and soccer.

To meet these needs, the *Physical Education Activity Handbook*, 13th edition, has been written to serve as a teaching and reference tool for physical educators, student teachers, recreational leaders, sports enthusiasts, physical education majors, and all high school and college students who are interested in sports activities and physical fitness. Fifty-six physical activities are described in the 30 activity chapters.

Over time, the classification of activities for curricular purposes has varied. Several activities might fit into more than one classification, depending upon how the individual chooses to participate in the activity. For example, inline skating might be classified as a fitness, lifetime, or individual/dual activity based upon the level of participation. The number of activities based upon the foregoing cross-classification possibilities are as follows: fitness = 12, aquatics = 8, dance = 4, outdoor education = 6, team sports = 10, individual/dual = 21, and lifetime = 27. Because of this extensive variety of activities, some institutions have adopted the *Handbook* as the textbook for all of their teacher preparation physical activity classes. This decision provides a great savings to students, especially with the ever-increasing cost of textbooks and the expanding variety of curricular offerings.

Through all revisions of this textbook, the format for each activity chapter has stayed consistent, with very few changes, which makes it easy to follow and to update information with each succeeding edition. In deciding what changes to make for this edition, we relied on a survey of previous users who expressed their needs and activity interests. In addition, we focused on activities that can be taught to students with varying skill levels and activity interest in order to make the *Handbook* more useful.

Previous users of the *Handbook* will find changes and updates throughout the text, including updated rules, references, modifications for special populations, some new drills, and a complete review of Web sites with corresponding descriptions. Photographs throughout the text have been updated and new photographs have been added to better illustrate skills, drills, and formations. In addition, Chapter 2, *Principles of Physical Fitness*, has been revised reflecting on current fitness data and physical fitness objectives for the next 10 years (*Healthy People 2020*). *Contemporary Activities* which was an appendix in the previous edition is now featured as a chapter (*Lifetime Activities*) and consists of an overview of nine activities which might add variety to existing curricular offerings.

In response to user demand, three new activities have been added. *Zumba®*, *Pilates*, and *Indoor Climbing* are now featured as additions to existing chapters. *Zumba®* reflects a popular trend in aerobic dance concepts. Pilates as an activity offers a holistic approach to fitness of body, mind, and spirit closely associated with many tenants of yoga. Indoor Climbing is a contemporary activity with traverse climbing walls, and it appeals to the elementary school level. Vertical climbing facilities are growing at the secondary level and especially as a popular collegiate and community recreational activity.

In conclusion, the *Handbook* serves as a resource for developing instructional units and lesson plans for a large variety of activities. Each chapter has consistent structural content development and provides ample, detailed information for planning successful instruction. The educator then has a consistent professional resource as a basis for developing and presenting physical activities.

ACKNOWLEDGMENTS

This edition is dedicated to my wife, children, grandchildren, and the many people who would enjoy a lifetime of active participation. —Jerre McManama

Sadly, Jerre McManama passed away as this edition was going to print. He will be missed by all who knew him for his integrity and impeccable character. He and his contributions to the field will be greatly missed. This edition is also dedicated to his memory. —The Publisher

We are indebted to the following professors and instructors who so graciously contributed their knowledge and expertise to the *Physical Education Activity Handbook.*

DR. ARNO WITTIG, Emeritus, Ball State University
Psychological Aspects of Physical Education

DR. GALE GEHLSEN, Emeritus, Ball State University
Mechanical Aspects of Physical Education

DR. LEONARD KAMINSKY, Ball State University
Physical Fitness Principles

JUDY DONAHUE, Ball State University
Aerobic Dance

MARGE HOBLEY, Cornerstone Center for the Arts, and
LEE EDGREN, River Light Yoga
Aerobic Dance

DR. SUNG-JAE PARK, Emeritus, Ball State University
Archery; Team Handball

WILLIAM NICHOLS
Badminton

DEBBIE POWERS, Emeritus, Ball State University
Basketball

SHARON BURGESS, Ball State University
Cycling

TERRY WHITT BAILEY, Cornerstone Center for the Arts
Dance (Square, Social)

YAAKOV EDEN, Emeritus, Ball State University
Western Line Dance

LEANN HAGGARD, 2006 National Dance Educator of the Year, North Central High School
Hip Hop

PENNY JUSTIN
Gymnastics and Tumbling

DALE SCRIVNOR, Emeritus, Ball State University
Golf

DR. RON DAVIS, Emeritus, Ball State University
Modifications for Special Populations

TIM DAVIS, State University of New York–Cortland
Modifications for Special Populations

DR. REBECCA WOODARD, Southwest Missouri State University
Modifications for Special Populations

DR. WARREN VANDER HILL, Emeritus, Ball State University
Angling

KAREN FITZPATRICK, Emeritus, Ball State University
Field Hockey

TERRY HITCHCOCK
Handball and Racquetball

PETER RATTIGAN, Rowan University
Lacrosse

JERRY RUSHTON, Emeritus, Ball State University
Orienteering; Track and Field

PAUL KENNEDY AND CINDY SPALDING, Atlanta's
BohemianSkateSchool.com
Inline Skating

DR. MARILYN BUCK, Ball State University
Softball; Technology and the Future of Physical Education

JOHN WINGFIELD, U.S.A. Diving
Swimming and Diving

PAUL FAWCETT
Swimming; Canoeing and Kayaking

SCOTT B. PERELMAN
Tennis

DR. DAVID PEARSON, Ball State University
Weight Training

LEE EDGREN, River Light Yoga
Yoga

CAROL REED, Ball State University
Skin Diving; Scuba Diving

I would like to thank Jerre McManama, Jr., Roncalli High School, for his assistance in typing and technology plus, Lisa Hicks and Mark Urtel for their professional involvement in this revision. We would also like to thank Jen Buechler and Julie Gallagher for their photographs. Thanks also to Meghan Zolnay and Elisa Mandelbaum at Pearson, for their attention and work in guiding me through this edition. I would also like to thank the reviewers of the edition for their valuable input: Bridget Cobb, University of Texas at San Antonio; Mary Gentry, University of Texas at San Antonio; Britt Johnson, Missouri Western State University; Susan Keith, Angelo State University; Ferman Konukman, The College at Brockport, State University of New York; Wess Meeteer, Concord University; and Jay Thornton, Stephen F. Austin State University.

CHAPTER 1

Considerations for Effective Skill Learning

This chapter will enable you to

- Outline mechanical aspects of basic movement skills
- Outline psychological aspects of learning and performance
- Identify the objectives of physical education
- Discuss the importance of skill assessment and National Standards
- Understand the format of the activity chapters in this book
- Discuss the use of technology in physical education

Nature and Purpose

Physical activity, when planned and taught properly, is "education through the physical." That is, activity serves as a medium through which a total learning experience takes place. Do you recall the first time you ever got up on water skis, jogged a mile or two, or first rode a bicycle? If you have succeeded at some relatively difficult and strenuous physical feat, what happened to your self-esteem as a result? In all likelihood, your achievement created a more positive outlook of yourself. In addition, you may have been encouraged to try other types of activities. Researchers have determined that such experiences improve our total being. In other words, physical activity not only improves our physical health, but also enhances our emotional outlook and even stimulates our intellectual activity and ability. In short, it improves our "wellness" in that it improves us totally.

Effective skill learning focuses on teaching skills, acquiring knowledge, and developing attitudes through movement. Public schools, Boys and Girls Clubs, Scouting programs, and other educational venues recognize the importance of physical activity by making it a part of their curricular plans. School physical education and wellness programs provide students with various opportunities—from assessing fitness levels and appropriate activities that will help overcome personal weaknesses to embarking on lifetime fitness activities (Figure 1-1). Physical activity programs remain a vital part of the total process of "education through the physical" by using games, sports, aquatics, dance, and other vigorous activities to help the individual achieve physical well-being.

We begin by outlining two components of effective skill learning that affect participation and practice in physical activities: the mechanical and psychological aspects of learning a skill. We follow with segments on a quality program's objects and skill assessment pertaining to current educational standards stressing accountability. The section thereafter examines the organizational structure of each succeeding chapter and the relationship of planning and organization to effective skill learning.

Figure 1-1 Some skills provide a lifetime of pleasurable activity.

Finally, we discuss the technological tools that are available to aid in instruction.

MECHANICAL AND PSYCHOLOGICAL ASPECTS

Mechanical Aspects

This section outlines selected positions and movements found in everyday and sport activities. The outline focuses on the mechanical aspects of basic movement skills. It is divided into two sections: The first part lists static and semistatic activities, for which balance considerations are the main concern; the second part lists dynamic activities that depend on force.

This is an overview of the principles of movement biomechanics. Courses on this topic are now part of the professional preparation program for prospective teachers and/or coaches. For this reason, our discussion in this chapter is limited to a brief outline of key concepts. For additional information, see the suggested selections in the interrelated fields of anatomy, kinesiology, and biomechanics in the *References and Further References* section.

BALANCE CONSIDERATIONS

- Standing
- Sitting
- Pushing
- Pulling
- Lifting
- Carrying

FORCE CONSIDERATIONS

- Walking
  - Leg action
  - Arm action
- Running
  - Body lean
  - Stride length
  - Stride frequency
- Jumping
- Leaping
- Catching
- Hopping
- Striking
- Throwing

Psychological Aspects

Psychology is the study of behavior and cognitive processes. As such, it is concerned with all aspects of physical and mental behavior. There are many areas of study in psychology, but in this outline we concentrate on principles that are most relevant for teachers and coaches, particularly those principles that address motivation, learning, personality, and social interaction.

- Motivation
  - Needs and drives
  - Levels of motivation
- Learning
  - Learning—performance distinction
  - Effects of practice
- Reinforcement
  - Positive reinforcement
  - Negative reinforcement
  - Extinction, counterconditioning, and spontaneous recovery
- Shaping
- Modeling
  - Superstitious responding
- Attention
  - Generalization and discrimination
- Overlearning
- Knowledge of results
- Distribution of practice
- Activity versus passive attitude
- Context of learning
- Retention and forgetting
  - Storage
  - Failure to retrieve
- Problem solving
  - Problem-solving sequence
  - Variables affecting problem solving
- Personality and social concerns
  - Personality
  - Social interaction
  - Social expectations
  - Competition and cooperation

This brief outline of psychological principles is sufficient to indicate the need for instructors to be aware of the many variables that may affect learning and performance.

PROGRAM OBJECTIVES

The well-planned physical education program has the potential to contribute to all phases of a student's educational development. Physical education's contribution is unique because it offers movement as the primary medium through which the educational process may occur.

Objectives of Physical Education

Physical educators agree that a sound course will comprise learning in the following three objectives and stress the importance of assessment in each.

Psychomotor Objectives refers to the dual role of skill improvement and fitness development resulting from participation in a physical education or wellness course. For example, in a swimming course, skill improvement refers to one's ability to become a proficient swimmer as a result of planned class instruction and directed skill practice. Fitness development refers to improvement in commonly accepted fitness measures as a result of class participation. In swimming class, a student might notice how easily she can perform the skill as a result of class experiences. This may be an indication that her cardiorespiratory system is strengthening or that the stroke technique has improved (skill development). Whatever the reason, both are desirable traits and constitute important achievement for the student and emphasize the importance of physical education.

Cognitive Objectives refers to the accumulation of knowledge as well as the ability to think and interpret that knowledge. In a fitness walking class, a student hones skills working with times in determining pace-per-mile. He will learn how to compute his target heart rate (and its importance) and determine resting and maximum pulse rates. Pulse rate is closely associated with cardiac anatomy and physiology, which leads to studying appropriate nutrition and diet for a healthy heart. Nutritional study promotes exploration in areas such as the metric system to understand the sodium or fat content of foods, and motivates the student to be a well-informed consumer. Other possible issues to explore in a walking class include appropriate shoe selection, hot or cold weather attire, proper warm-up and cool-down procedures, and learning how to avoid high air pollution levels by scheduling walks at certain times of day.

Affective Objectives deal with the development of traits such as the individual's values, appreciations, attitudes, and interests. How might the affective objective be applied to an activity such as tennis? Perhaps the most obvious example involves calling your opponent's shots as they land in your half of the court. For someone who does not have a background in racquet sports, this responsibility can be quite awesome. But it goes beyond that relatively obvious task. It could involve learning the importance of being an opponent or partner who makes the game a pleasant experience by playing enthusiastically and to the best of one's ability regardless of the conditions. While playing competitively, one's standard of conduct is within both the written word and the spirit of the rules. As a result of participating in tennis, a player acquires habits of loyalty, cooperation, initiative, self-control, and courtesy.

Assessment

Current educational expectations place an importance on student learning and hold schools accountable for student progress. The formation of *outcomes* or *educational standards* identifies what a student should know and be able to do. Activity-based programs needed to join this philosophic framework, so in 1992, the National Standards for Physical Education were developed by the National Association for Sport and Physical Education (NASPE).

This document initially identified 20 outcome statements in five categories (has, is, does, knows, values) defining a "physically educated person":

1. HAS learned skills necessary to perform a variety of physical activities;
2. IS physically fit;
3. DOES participate regularly in physical activity;
4. KNOWS the implications and the benefits from involvement in physical activity;
5. VALUES physical activity and its contribution to a healthful lifestyle.[1]

Many states now use these as a framework for their standards. *Moving into the Future: National Standards for Physical Education* by NASPE in 1995 provided student expectations and sample performance outcomes for grade levels K–2, 3–5, 6–8, and 9–12. This publication lists six revised standards for the "physically educated person," which are located in the technology section of this chapter.

Measurement and evaluation in physical education involves the psychomotor, cognitive, and affective domains. However, the breadth constraints of this textbook do not allow for an in-depth discussion of assessment in all domains. The information is restricted to traditional skill-testing suggestions for chosen activities.

The current trend is toward *alternative assessment*, which refers to any type that differs from traditional, and toward *authentic assessment*, which emphasizes the application of skills in a gamelike setting that also involves cognitive tasks. These two methods require more knowledge and expertise than this activities book can address. There are educational courses and textbooks devoted solely to physical activity assessment and to test and measurement procedures.

Traditional skill testing, addressed in selected chapters, provides suggestions for measuring students' beginning-to-intermediate skill abilities. This method of assessment has limitations but provides the novice teacher with a starting place for objective measurement as opposed to solely subjective, noncriterion-referenced evaluation. Through the years there have been a variety of health-related physical fitness tests, general motor ability measurements, specific sport skill tests, plus motor-fitness assessment for various disabilities. In each study and targeted area being assessed, the procedures and norms are directed at a certain age group. These may not meet the specificities of your teaching situation; however, standardized tests can provide a starting place, with modifications added to meet the various problems confronting your situation and needs.

Selected chapters in this text provide suggestions for addressing Standard One or Standard Four of the NASPE content standards. Standard One states that a physically educated person "demonstrates competence in motor skills and movement patterns needed to perform a variety of physical activities." Standard Four states that the person "achieves and maintains a health enhancing level of physical fitness."[2] Some chapters in this *Handbook* are more lengthy and skill-related, some are allied with selected health-related components, whereas others are of a recreational nature or brief introductions of contemporary activities needing additional resources. Because of the variety of activities, all do not address assessment.

The classification and grouping of activities over the years by the profession has constantly evolved. As an example, most former team sports are now classified as invasion games and field games; individual and dual sports are now net/wall games or target games; physical fitness is health-related fitness; outdoor education and adventure activities is outdoor pursuits; and so on. Regardless of the classification, the assessment in this text falls into activities that are either skill-related, health-related (see Chapter 2 on *Principles of Physical Fitness*), or aesthetic in nature.

SKILL TEST CONCERNS

Experts recommend that no more than 10 percent of a unit length be devoted to formal skill testing. This means that a typical 2-week unit meeting daily for 50 minutes (40 minutes of actual activity due to dressing time) has one day of testing. Factors to consider are which skills to test; age, ability level, and strength of the participants; the facilities and available equipment; the mechanics for administration; and set-up time.

Every skill taught can be skill-tested. So which ones are most important for playing success? Can more than one skill be tested simultaneously? An example might be in volleyball, where the ball handling skills of the forearm and overhand passes are most necessary for beginning and intermediate play. These skills may be tested together by having the student alternate forearm and overhead passes repeatedly to himself, counting each contact over a designated time period.

Age, ability level, and strength are factors that might affect the success of a given test. Using a basketball shooting test as an example, it is easy to see where these factors definitely affect the outcome. A seventh grader shooting 10 jump shots from behind the 3-point arc would have very limited success. Ten free-throws using the set shot is a better choice.

Facilities and equipment availability concerns have a direct effect on the testing procedures and length of time. A tennis forehand half-volley rebound test in a gym with only two end walls available that are padded with mats is not feasible. Similarly, it is impossible to test 30 students with just 10 racquets and 10 tennis balls in one period. Ten available wall spaces, 20 tennis balls, and 10 racquets with 30-second trials per student is a workable testing situation with 30 students.

In the typical class of 20 to 30 students, it is impossible for the teacher to individually administer a test to each student in more than one skill in one period. In a 50-meter pool with eight lanes, the teacher can test eight students at a time using a yes/no checkoff sheet assessing stroke technique factors. Four waves of eight swimming one length at a time make it possible for the teacher to assess each student and even make it possible to assess several different strokes in one period.

The setup procedures and time commitment are important factors. The use of lines for distances/heights, hula hoops or mats for targets, and other devices can aid in solving some of these problems. An example is using common 4-feet by 6-feet folding mats as targets at the back of the badminton court for an underhand clear test (see *Badminton* chapter).

SKILL TEST SUGGESTIONS

Health-related fitness components of body composition, cardiorespiratory fitness, flexibility, muscular endurance, and muscular strength are developed over a more lengthy time than a traditional two- to three-week unit. These fitness components are important objectives for a well-rounded physical education program. However, organized testing should allow enough time, such as a semester or a year, to recognize fitness accomplishments. Health-related fitness units like aerobic dance, weight training, and orienteering need to be distributed periodically throughout the semester or yearly curriculum. Plus fitness targets need to be a major focus in sport skill units to aid in retention or progressive development of each target. It is recommended that the FITNESSGRAM[3] test components be considered for assessment of fitness. This assessment tool has standardized procedures and norms for boys and girls ages 6 to 17.

Traditional standardized skill tests as previously mentioned often do not meet the various situational needs and problems confronting teachers. The American Association for Health, Physical Education, Recreation, and Dance (AAHPERD) has skill test booklets for several activities (www.aahperd.org).[4] *Assessing Sports Skills* also provides a source for skill tests.[5] A review of these tests can serve as a starting point for teachers. However, they will need to modify, create, and manipulate these tests to address individual needs. The following are suggestions to consider.

1. Determine the fewest but most important skills necessary for participation success at the beginning to intermediate level. Where possible, combine more than one skill in the same test. Establish a minimum time limit (e.g., 30 seconds) that allows

for a maximum number of trials in the time allocated for testing (approximately 10 percent of unit length). Eliminate a predetermined number of high and low trial scores and then average the remaining.

2. Predetermine the number of testing stations based upon facilities, equipment, and number of students. Use students to assist in the administration of the test as the participant, counter/recorder, and equipment assistant as needed. Plan a rotation system for changing individual responsibilities and groups. When possible, use the foregoing steps to involve the whole class simultaneously. If not possible, use two different stations to divide the class numbers, such as testing two different skill stations simultaneously or testing one group while the other group is involved in a nontesting activity.

3. The final suggestion is to practice the test periodically throughout the unit as a drill so the students are aware of the procedures and skills.

Tests often are similar in like activities. Many net and wall games (tennis, badminton, table tennis, pickle-ball, handball, racquetball, etc.) involve the use of a racquet to rally an object with the backhand or forehand stroke and initiate play with a serve. Invasion games (soccer, basketball, field hockey, team handball, etc.) include passes, catches, dribbles, and shooting at a target. Some aquatic areas, gymnastics, and dance contain aesthetic characteristics and form. Because of the similarity of activity skill requirements for successful participation, the skills test structure may be comparable. The thought, planning, and organizational process are analogous.

Activity Format

The mechanical and psychological aspects outlined in this chapter plus the fitness principles discussed in the *Principles of Physical Fitness* chapter (Chapter 2) serve as the backbone of each succeeding chapter. Here we provide a detailed discussion of how the chapters are structured and how to use each section. This structure serves as a "cookbook" approach for the teacher to prepare beginning to intermediate classes.

To help the teacher plan and ensure continuity, the chapters follow a specific structural format. Because of differences among the activities and sports, a chapter may not include each element listed in the format. For example, there is no Playing Strategies/Tactics topic in gymnastics or Scoring/Rules for dance. However, the elements as they relate to each activity, and the order in which they are presented, are consistent. References for works cited and sources for additional information (Further References) can be found at the end of the *Handbook*.

CHAPTER FORMAT ELEMENTS AND ORDER

- Chapter Objectives
- Nature and Purpose
- History
- Scoring/Rules
- Equipment
- Suggested Learning Sequence
- Skills and Techniques
  - Learning/Helpful Hints
  - Practice/Organizational Suggestions
- Safety Considerations
- Playing Strategies/Tactics
- Etiquette/Playing Courtesy
- Skill Assessment
- Modifications for Special Populations
- Terminology
- Discussion Questions
- Web Sites

The following sections describe each chapter element in detail.

CHAPTER OBJECTIVES

Objectives identify what the learner will be able to do or know after studying the chapter. They are broadly stated but serve as a model if the teacher wishes to develop additional objectives that specifically cover the information provided in each chapter.

NATURE AND PURPOSE

The Nature and Purpose section provides a brief overview of each activity and its nuances. This section provides a basic foundation as the student starts the activity. In many instances the information offers suggestions or ideas for modifying the activity for participation by both boys and girls.

HISTORY

Knowing how the activity has progressively developed can help the student appreciate the changes that have made it what it is today. When possible, the activity is traced from its origins through important milestone events to its current popularity.

SCORING/RULES

Not all of the 50 activities covered have rules or involve scoring. Where appropriate, the Scoring/Rules section provides the parameters for participation. The section specifies what is expected, allowed and not allowed, and defines the area where the activity takes place. The rules presented define the basics of the activity, along with permitted modifications. They are used as a guide for the students as they practice skills, progress to limited application in modified play, and culminate in actual gamelike conditions.

EQUIPMENT

This section describes the minimum equipment needed for participation and identifies any official specifications and items that the participants need for protection or safety.

SUGGESTED LEARNING SEQUENCE

The Suggested Learning Sequence provides a framework to enable teachers to lead students step by step through each skill the activity involves. This recommended sequence considers how the skills are interrelated and leads students through an orderly progression in which they master basic skills, followed by increasingly advanced ones, and finally to full participation. The strategies and tactics for each skill are discussed as the skill is introduced. Small side-game challenges that incorporate each new skill are also presented. The final part of the sequence integrates all the information and applies it to complete group or team play for participants who have mastered the necessary skills.

SKILLS AND TECHNIQUES

Beginning to intermediate skills are presented with a brief explanation of their purpose and use in the activity. This information, plus the advice in Learning/Helpful Hints and Practice/Organizational Suggestions, provides the basis for progressive skill development.

▶ Learning/Helpful Hints

A mechanical step-by-step analysis in the Skills and Techniques and Learning Hints sections furnishes the participant with a written "picture" of the skill. For many of the skills, an accompanying photograph or drawing illustrates how the action is performed. Knowledge hints are provided to further enhance effective execution of the skill.

▶ Practice/Organizational Suggestions

The Practice/Organizational Suggestions section provides progressive beginning drills and recommendations for practicing each skill. Because of the number of activities covered in the *Handbook*, and the variety of skills possible for each activity, the drills provided are not comprehensive, but are enough to "get the ball rolling."

SAFETY CONSIDERATIONS

Some activities may pose a risk to participants and warrant a special section devoted to safety. For example, the archery chapter provides an extensive list of precautions to ensure safe participation. The Scoring/Rules section may also suggest modifications to enhance safety.

PLAYING STRATEGIES/TACTICS

The Playing Strategies/Tactics section identifies formations, alignments, principles, and other factors that lead to skillful, organized, and controlled play when the student applies the skills in group or team participation. Some chapters offer special suggestions for modified games and small-group drill activities, which also enhance skill development.

ETIQUETTE/PLAYING COURTESY

In some activities—golf and tennis, for example—the conduct of the participants is of prime importance and defines the activity. The Etiquette/Playing Courtesy section defines the code of ethics and provides guidelines for good sportsmanship.

SKILL ASSESSMENT

A reference to the *ASSESSMENT* section previously provides a solid foundation as a basis for the suggested skills tests in selected chapters. Traditional Skill Assessment, addressed in selected chapters, provides suggestions for measuring students' beginning-to-intermediate skill abilities. The information in *Skill Test Concerns* and *Skill Test Suggestions* in this chapter were paramount in the development of the skills tests suggested.

MODIFICATIONS FOR SPECIAL POPULATIONS

The inclusion of special populations in physical activities warrants a need for information and suggestions for modifying activities to meet everyone's needs. The Modifications for Special Populations section provides suggestions for including orthopedically impaired, cognitively impaired, or sensory impaired individuals in the activity with other participants. For activities with a high level of competition involving those with disabilities, this section lists national organizations to contact for further information.

TERMINOLOGY

The Terminology section lists basic terms that help the student understand the activity and develop a professional vocabulary for communication purposes. The terms also provide information that can easily be converted into test questions.

DISCUSSION QUESTIONS

The Discussion Questions section provides a resource for checking the comprehension of material presented. Some of the questions may be used as group discussion topics for a problem-solving approach to learning.

WEB SITES

The list of Web sites greatly enhances researching an activity. Among the offerings described in the listings are links to beginning-to-comprehensive information; skill-specific information; video clips for skill development; equipment sources and prices; history and development; certification programs; and national organizations.

TECHNOLOGY USE IN PHYSICAL EDUCATION ACTIVITY

Technology surrounds us and is part of everything we do. Whenever a computer or other technology source malfunctions, we become painfully aware of our dependence on technology. The increase in technology is also evident in physical education. Schools that have received Physical Education Progress (PEP) grants have devoted large portions of these awards to purchasing heart rate monitoring and fitness assessment devices. Given the obesity crisis in the United States and financial concerns, to remain viable, physical education will need to increase the use of technology even more in the years to come. All physical education teaching majors should receive extensive training in the use of technology.

Hardware advances have provided new tools to enhance the functions of physical educators. Computers have been available for many years, but their capabilities have changed dramatically. A wireless environment is the direction of the future and is present in many areas. Our gymnasiums should be the first areas designated for wireless setup. Teachers can then use laptop computers to access the school network from anywhere in the activity areas, even outdoor facilities.

Handheld computers such as pocket PCs and PDAs provide a means to input and share information from any location. Many of these devices also have wireless and voice recording capabilities and can be put into a pocket or attached to a belt for easy access.

Tablet PCs have been developed to increase the portability of computers in other ways. These devices resemble the monitor of a laptop computer and are detached from the keyboard for use. The individual can write directly on the screen, and the computer will transfer the written text into typewritten material. The devices also have a voice recognition system, so that an individual can speak into the device and it will type what the person has said. The tablet PC is the size of a clipboard and can perform all of the functions of the clipboard, plus many more.

All teaching majors are made aware of professional standards regarding the use of technology, and physical education majors should be no different. Teachers and students in many different areas are now expected to meet these standards. In this section, each use of technology is identified, along with one or more standards that the technology helps to achieve. The standards relate to both physical education content and to technology. These technologies not only will help students meet the standards but also will provide evidence to support that the standards have been met.

NASPE revised its physical education content standards in 2004. For "a physically educated person" the standards are:

Standard 1: Demonstrates competence in motor skills and movement patterns needed to perform a variety of physical activities.

Standard 2: Demonstrates understanding of movement concepts, principles, strategies, and tactics as they apply to the learning and performance of physical activities.

Standard 3: Participates regularly in physical activity.

Standard 4: Achieves and maintains a health-enhancing level of physical fitness.

Standard 5: Exhibits responsible personal and social behavior that respects self and others in physical activity settings.

Standard 6: Values physical activity for health, enjoyment, challenge, self-expression, and/or social interaction.[6]

Technology standards have been developed for students, namely, the National Educational Technology Standards for Students (NETS–S). The Technology Foundation Standards for Students are as follows:

1. Creativity and Innovation
   - Students demonstrate creative thinking, construct knowledge, and develop innovative products and processes using technology.
2. Communication and Collaboration
   - Students use digital media and environments to communicate and work collaboratively, including at a distance, to support individual learning and contribute to the learning of others.
3. Research and Information Fluency
   - Students supply digital tools to gather, evaluate, and use information.
4. Critical Thinking, Problem Solving, and Decision Making
   - Students use critical-thinking skills to plan and conduct research, manage projects, solve problems, and make informed decisions using appropriate digital tools and resources.

5. Digital Citizenship
- Students understand human, cultural, and societal issues related to technology and practice legal and ethical behavior.

6. Technological Operations and Concepts
- Students demonstrate a sound understanding of technology concepts, systems, and operations.[7]

Any discussion of technology use can be organized in a variety of ways. One way is to discuss the various pieces of hardware and software and their use. Another is to organize the discussion around the various responsibilities of physical education teachers and the tools available to enhance each of these roles. This section is organized according to the latter.

The major roles of a physical education teacher are administration, teaching, motivation, and communication. The teaching role is divided into two parts: instruction and assessment. Although instruction and assessment are intertwined in practice, technologies are available to help teachers enhance each function separately.

For years it has been generally accepted that technology saves time. Most people realize that this is not necessarily true, and that technological devices can actually increase the time needed for teaching in some instances. The main purpose for using technology has to be its ability to help users perform their jobs more effectively. So, our discussion of technology focuses on how it enhances teachers' ability to carry out their tasks. Several examples of printouts and other materials for class use are included in this section.

Administration

Administrative functions of physical education teachers include taking attendance, assigning lockers and distributing padlocks, grading, and purchasing equipment, among others.

ATTENDANCE

Many schools have gone to a computerized attendance system. In a wireless environment, a physical education teacher can take attendance on a laptop computer, and it will be sent to the office. In a wired environment, the teacher might have to go to the physical education office and, as a result, leave the class unsupervised while doing so. A variety of software programs, such as PE Manager, have been developed for use on a pocket PC for taking attendance and performing other administrative tasks (Figure 1-2).

PADLOCK DISTRIBUTION

Database programs, such as Access by Microsoft, can store information about students. Instructors can use Access to input locker and padlock information for each

Figure 1-2   Pocket PCs such as the one shown here can be used with software such as PE Manager to take attendance and perform other administrative tasks.

student. The pocket PCs can make the information accessible in areas within the locker room or gymnasium, especially when students need assistance remembering a lock combination. The MasterLock Company has developed a software program called Locker Manager to manage locks and locker information.

EQUIPMENT

A database can also inventory equipment. When new equipment is ordered, it can be entered into the system, and damaged equipment can be easily removed. The result is an equipment inventory that is always current. The database can also include information about the current condition of the equipment and the age of each piece.

GRADING

Schools now use computer systems to record grades. Some of these allow parents to access their child's grades at any time by way of the Internet. Software specific to physical education has been written to accomplish this function. One example is PE Manager. Although it does not allow parents to access their child's grade at any time, it does allow the teacher to easily send a student report to parents by e-mail (Figure 1-3).

Teachers often create tournaments to conclude a unit of instruction and often use the results in grading. Setting up the tournaments and managing them is considered an administrative function. Software such as Tournament Scheduler Pro is available to simplify this process. The user selects the type of tournament, inputs the participants, prints the tournament schedule, and inputs game results. This program can even be used to create certificates for winners, most valuable players, or any other type of recognition desired.

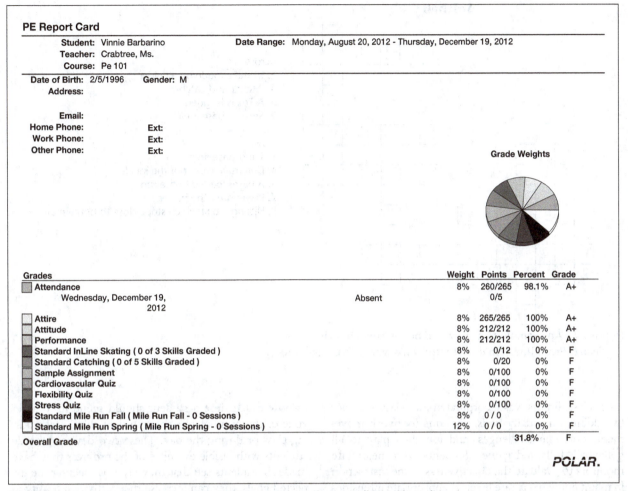

Figure 1-3 A sample grade report from PE Manager; note that not all items have been graded yet.

Instruction

The areas of instruction that can be enhanced by technology include the presentation of information, evaluation of the effectiveness of instruction, motivation of students, and the development of lesson and unit plans.

PRESENTATION OF INFORMATION

Information can be presented by using software such as PowerPoint. An instructor can use PowerPoint to make presentations to the entire class or set it up for students to interact individually. The software allows links to Internet sites and the inclusion of audio and video files. Instructional videos, CDs, and DVDs can also be used. Video can be used to demonstrate the correct performance of a skill or drill. This demonstration can be especially important if the skill has an elevated risk or takes time to replicate several times, such as diving.

Software is also available to assist in presenting related concepts, such as biomechanics, motor learning, and anatomy, to list only a few.[8] Software and Internet sites can also be used to create word games and other materials to enhance instruction (Figure 1-4).

EFFECTIVE INSTRUCTION

Videotaping a lesson for review has been used to evaluate instruction for many years. Other instruction tools are also available; heart rate monitors are one example. The heart rate curves can illustrate the amount of time students spend listening to instruction or waiting. If the goal of a lesson is to increase heart rate to benefit cardiovascular fitness, the printout provides the evidence needed to determine whether the objective has been met.

Can both fitness and skill be developed simultaneously in a traditional physical education setting? Must skill and fitness be separate goals? Heart rate monitors can help answer these questions. In a 1995 study, results from two basic-level volleyball classes were compared. One class was taught in a traditional manner. In the

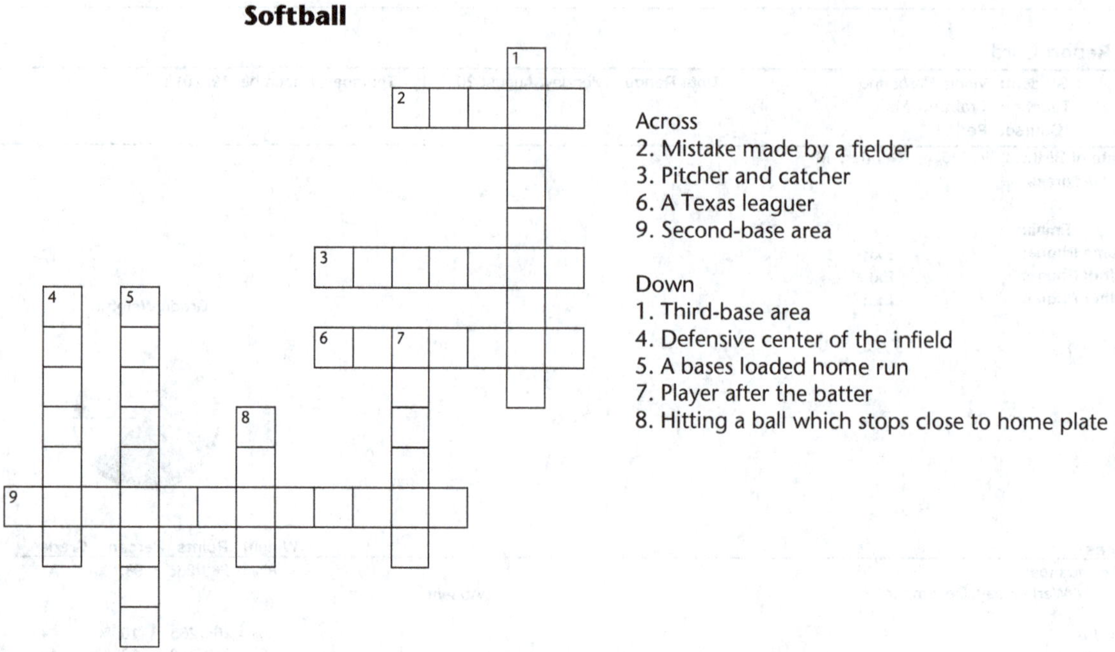

Softball

Across
2. Mistake made by a fielder
3. Pitcher and catcher
6. A Texas leaguer
9. Second-base area

Down
1. Third-base area
4. Defensive center of the infield
5. A bases loaded home run
7. Player after the batter
8. Hitting a ball which stops close to home plate

Figure 1-4   An example of a crossword puzzle created online.
Source: From Puzzlemaker at http://www.puzzle-maker.com

other class, fitness was incorporated into class activities by adding, on a daily basis, vigorous footwork movement, outcome challenges, and modified play to all volleyball drills and games. Students wore heart rate monitors to evaluate the effectiveness of the instruction in maintaining heart rate levels at appropriate intensities and for sufficient durations to achieve cardiovascular gains. Pretests and posttests were administered to measure skill levels, playing ability, and fitness components. Class instruction took place 3 days a week for 8 weeks. Posttests revealed that the classes had no significant difference in skill levels and that each class had improved at the same rate. No difference existed in any other measure except for cardiovascular fitness. In 8 weeks the group who took part in the extra movement showed a significant difference in cardiovascular fitness gains. The study indicated that there is no need to choose just one area—fitness or skill—to emphasize in physical education classes; rather, physical educators can do both simply by incorporating fitness into skill instruction.[9]

A pocket PC or laptop computer can also be used by a class observer to code behaviors of the teacher or students for later review to determine effectiveness of instruction. The best measurement of effectiveness is student learning. Assessment of student learning and the involvement of technology is discussed later in this section.

MOTIVATION

Heart rate monitors and pedometers are particularly effective motivational tools. Teachers establish goals, such as how much time a student should spend in a target zone or the number of steps a student should take during class or during the day. These two devices provide students with visible evidence of the progress they have made. If students see that they are not meeting the expected goals, they can increase their activity intensity in an effort to improve. Students reported that when they wear a pedometer, they are more cognizant of their activity level and may actually seek ways to add steps. Figure 1-5 shows a heart rate curve report for a particular student; the percentage of time the student's heart rate was in the target zone is indicated in the bar graph on the right.

PLANNING

Word-processing programs have made preparing lesson plans, writing tests, and communicating with others easier and more professional. Many teachers create a template for their lesson plans and simply add information for each lesson. With their lesson plans saved to the computer, teachers can easily make modifications to the lesson.

The Internet is an excellent resource for lesson planning ideas and other information used in teaching. The PE Central Web site is probably the best known. The site includes ideas for any age level and many different activity areas. Also included are ideas to assist students with disabilities. Other Web sites provide rules and teaching materials and ideas about specific activities, such as team handball, Ultimate Frisbee, field hockey,

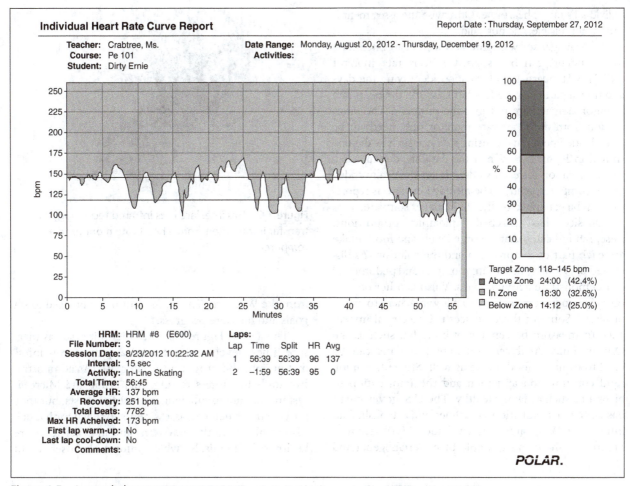

Figure 1-5 A sample heart rate curve report.

tennis, and many more traditional and innovative sport activities. The end of this section lists many of these sites. Listservs are also available for gaining teaching ideas. Two of these are NASPE-Talk and pelinks4u.

E-mail and video conferencing are other ways to get teaching ideas. "Pen pal" relationships among students and teachers throughout the world can provide information about their countries, games, and dances (NETS–S Standards 1, 3, 4, 5). Ideas can be sent and rules taught to broaden knowledge and worldwide understanding. Video conferencing is effective because it allows individuals to see the games and dances demonstrated.

Online courses have become a frequently requested mode of delivery for college and university courses. They are also being used by high schools. Online courses often use heart rate monitors to verify activities, especially those related to fitness. Video cameras can be used to verify performance in all types of activities. By using digital editing, which will be explained in detail later, the student can e-mail visual evidence of performance and other materials requested in class assignments (NETS–S Standards 1, 2, 3, 4, 5, 6; NASPE Standards 3, 4, 6).

TECHNOLOGICAL ASSESSMENT

Technology can be more helpful for assessment than for any other task required of teachers and coaches. The pocket PC and PE Manager and TriFit software allow teachers to record assessments during class and automatically transfer them to the computer and a grading system. The software allows teachers to collect fitness data not only by recording scores but also through the use of timing devices other than the traditional stopwatch. The TriFit software includes software called Cardio Timer. All students can be timed individually at the same time with this software. An entire class can be started at once or individually, and each person's time can be stopped when appropriate by tapping the screen of the pocket PC. Those times are saved and available for further use.

Heart rate monitors can be used in a variety of ways. An obvious use is to determine the effort a student expends during cardiovascular fitness assessments. Monitors can also record test times. If the teacher wants information about a student's actual fitness levels and improvement, then the teacher must monitor the results, using the individual's target heart rate. Otherwise the assessment is simply not reliable, and not valid.

PE Manager software interacts with heart rate monitors. Students can be assigned a heart rate monitor (NETS–S Standard 1). Information identifying the days and time a particular student has class and the heart rate monitor assigned are put into the program. The information from the heart rate monitor only needs to be downloaded periodically, using a device such as the one shown in Figure 1-6. When the data are downloaded, the information for each student is automatically added to the computer, ready to be included in various reports that can be generated by the PE Manager software.

Obesity has reached epidemic proportions. Research indicates that exercise levels and food intake are each part of the problem and the solution. As discussed previously, heart rate monitors and pedometers can demonstrate activity levels. Various other devices measure body composition to allow teachers to assess progress. Some of these devices use electrical impedance to measure percentage of body fat, such as the Omron Body Analyzer. Software programs can be used to evaluate food intake as well. Students can log food consumption and then add the information to programs such as Dine Healthy. The U.S. government has issued new nutrition guidelines and established an interactive Web site at www.ChooseMyPlate.gov.[10] Figure 1-7 shows an example of materials generated

Figure 1-6 This interface uses infrared technology to transfer information from a heart rate monitor to a computer.

from the Web site. This information can be used to set goals and measure progress.

The TriFit (Figure 1-8) and MicroFit systems measure fitness levels and automatically input this information into the program for later use. As administrative tools for fitness testing, the TriFit and MicroFit systems are not as efficient as most field tests, but they provide more detailed assessments for each individual. Also available on these systems and in other tools are health risk appraisals, which inform the user about

Figure 1-7 The USDA's interactive Web site, www.ChooseMyPlate.gov, provides resources to educate individuals about nutritional guidelines.

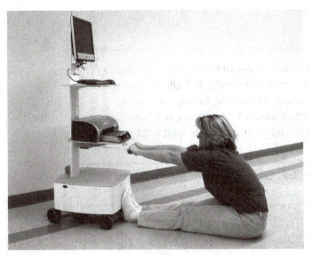

Figure 1-8 The TriFit system is used to measure flexibility.

the effects of the individual's lifestyle choices on life expectancy.

Computerized systems for measuring blood pressure are also available. Students can easily assess blood pressure for one another with the DynaPulse system. Students should learn how to assess each of the fitness measures alone or with the assistance of a partner. Students should be taught to use this information to set goals and monitor individual progress (NASPE Standards 2, 3, 4, 5, 6; NETS–S Standards 2, 5, 6).

Traditionally, skills tests were used to assess sport skill performance. In recent years, there has been increasing interest in assessing game play. Now performance rubrics or checklists are being developed and often used in conjunction with videotapes of the performance. The video clip of a student's performance can become part of the student's electronic portfolio. Digital editing techniques using programs such as iMovie or Adobe Premiere can be used to select one performance from among many to be included in the portfolio.

For secondary, and especially high school students, assessment of sport skills should involve the individual student in the process. Student performances are videotaped, then inputted into an analysis program, such as DartFish. This analysis program allows the student to view his own performance on a split screen beside an ideal performance. The student can then compare performances and create a report as part of an assignment to identify which things the student does well and which areas still need work. The report can also discuss strategies for improving performance. An assignment of this type promotes critical-thinking skills and helps students learn how to take responsibility to learn new sport skills. It is a skill they can use later in many settings (NASPE Standards 1, 2; NETS–S Standards 1, 2, 4, 5, 6).

Technology can also be used to assess student participation, both in and out of class. Heart rate monitors can indicate level of effort; the higher the heart rate, the greater the effort. The percentage of time a student stays in the target zone during class is one measurement of effort. The effort a student puts forth in activities such as the mile run can also be assessed in this manner (NASPE Standard 4; NETS–S Standard 5).

Given the obesity epidemic, it is crucial that students learn to be active outside the classroom and make physical activity part of a healthy lifestyle. Both heart rate monitors and pedometers can be used to measure this activity. In most settings the pedometer is used because it is more cost-effective. FitnessGram/ ActivityGram 8.0 includes a feature to help students record their activity levels. ActivityGram includes an activity log in which students can set goals and record the number of steps or minutes of activity each day (NASPE Standards 3, 6; NETS–S Standards 1, 5). Figure 1-9 is an example of a report that is generated by these programs.

Communication

Technology has enhanced our ability to communicate quickly, particularly through e-mail. PE Manager software has made it much easier for teachers to inform parents of their students' progress. If parents provide an e-mail address, the teacher can create a message to send home to parents and, with it, send their students' class performance information automatically.

E-mail can also be used to inform administrators, faculty, and parents about activities in the physical education classes. Newsletters and information brochures can be created to address many topics of interest, such as weight loss or safe exercises. Students can also write and create such newsletters and brochures for distribution (NASPE Standard 2; NET–S Standards 3, 4, 5, 6).

Today's technology can help teachers and coaches carry out their tasks more effectively. Each individual needs to evaluate how these technological tools can be used to achieve the best results, given their specific circumstances and needs. Initially, everyone needs extra time to learn how to use technology and set up files. Once this is done, the person can expect to save time and increase efficiency. Technology use is not without its problems, however; a teacher who depends entirely on technology functioning correctly at all times will be disappointed and inconvenienced. Anyone using this type of technology should employ back-up systems because all hard drives and other storage devices are subject to system failure at any time.

Technology should never be used simply for the sake of using a "fun toy"; rather, a teacher should use technological tools to enhance teaching and learning. The uses are limited only by the creativity of the teacher.

CARDIOVASCULAR

Cardiovascular fitness is the ability of the heart, lungs and circulatory system to supply oxygen and nutrients to working muscles efficiently, and allows activities that involve large muscle groups (walking, running, swimming, biking, etc.) to be performed over long periods of time. From a health standpoint, cardiovascular or aerobic fitness is generally considered to be the most important of the fitness components.

Cardiovascular Assessment

Protocol: Youth Tests

One Mile Run (mm:ss): 8:20

One Mile Run/Walk

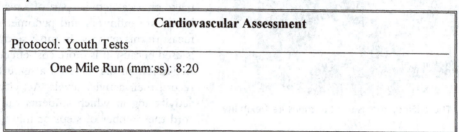

	Exceeds	Healthy Fitness Zone	Needs Improvement
8:20			
time	< 9:00	9:00 - 11:30	> 11:30

REGULAR CARDIOVASCULAR EXERCISE CAN

- Reduce your risk of heart disease
- Lower elevated blood pressure
- Reduce blood cholesterol
- Increase circulation and improve performance of your heart and lungs
- Help you look and feel better

Figure 1-9 A portion of a TriFit report of an individual's health risk appraisal.

Web Sites

The following are some Web sites that provide information about the technological tools described in this section.

www.allprosoftware.com—Includes tournament-building software and statistics software for a variety of sports.

www.dartfish.com—Provides Information on Dartfish, an analysis software used to evaluate individual sport performances or team performances.

www.dinesystems.com—Includes the Dine Healthy nutrition analysis software.

www.dynapulse.com—Details a computerized blood pressure system.

www.fitnessgram.net—Provides information and ordering instructions for FitnessGram/ActivityGram 8.0.

www.ChooseMyPlate.gov—Introduces the U.S. Government's MyPlate and provides the ability to individualize the plate and a nutrition worksheet.

www.pecentral.com—Is the premiere site for physical education lesson planning ideas and a wealth of other information.

www.pelinks4u.org—Contains physical education information as well as information on subscribing to NASPE-Forum, a discussion board for physical education topics and issues.

www.pesoftware.com—Includes software from Bonnie's Fitware and other products for motor learning, biomechanics, and other topics.

www.polarusa.com—Offers heart rate monitors, TriFit system, and PE Manager software and hardware to support each system.

www.puzzlemaker.com—Enables the creation of word puzzles.

CHAPTER 2

Principles of Physical Fitness

This chapter discusses

- Skill-related versus health-related physical fitness
- The need for and benefits of physical fitness
- Components of the pre-exercise program screening
- The principles of exercise training
- Exercise for weight (fat) loss
- Supplemental training programs (interval and circuit training)

If ten people were asked to define physical fitness, it would not be surprising to get ten different answers that are all partially correct. This variation occurs because physical fitness can be categorized into two types—skill-related and health-related—with each type having various components. Skill-related physical fitness includes power, speed, agility, balance, coordination, and reaction time. Prior to 1980, the majority of physical education programs evaluated primarily the skill-related components of physical fitness by using a battery of tests that included sit-ups, pull-ups, shuttle run, 50-yard dash, softball throw, and 600-yard run/walk. However, beginning in 1980, the American Alliance for Health, Physical Education, Recreation, and Dance (AAHPERD) began using a health-related physical fitness test that included a one-mile run/walk, skinfold measurements, sit and reach measurement, and a sit-up test.[1] In 1988, AAHPERD added a pull-up test to the assessment as part of its *Physical Best* program.[2] Health-related fitness includes the following five components:

1. *Cardiorespiratory Endurance*—the ability of the heart, respiratory, and circulatory systems to supply oxygen and nutrients to, and to remove waste products from, the working muscles
2. *Muscular Strength*—the ability of the muscles to exert a force to move an object or to develop tension to resist the movement of an object
3. *Muscular Endurance*—the ability of a muscle to sustain repeated contractions or to maintain a submaximal contraction
4. *Body Composition*—the relative proportion of body fat or fat-free body tissues (muscle, bone, organs) to total body weight

5. *Flexibility*—the ability to move a body part fluidly through a complete range of motion about a joint

This chapter will focus on health-related physical fitness programs specifically related to the cardiorespiratory endurance and body composition components. Information concerning the need for and benefits of health-related physical fitness will be presented. This will be followed by concerns for pre-exercise screening, and then specific types of training programs.

Current Physical Fitness Characteristics

The mechanization of many U.S. industries in the early through mid-20th century decreased the occupational activity level of many individuals. As the technology explosion continued, the automation of products for home and recreation further decreased the activity levels of Americans. This mechanization has led to a substantial number of unfit Americans.

YOUTH

Studies, like data from the National Children and Youth Fitness Study II (NCYFS),[3] conducted in the mid-1980s revealed that a majority of the youth in the United States had low levels of physical fitness. Some specific findings were that 50 percent of the children could not run one mile in less than 10 minutes; 55 percent of girls and 40 percent of boys could not perform more than one pull-up; 40 percent of boys could not reach beyond their toes on a sit and reach test; obesity and superobesity (triceps skinfold > 85th and 95th percentile, respectively) increased 54 percent and 98 percent in youth aged 6 to 11 years old.[4] These data were not surprising given reports that only 19 percent of all high school students were physically active for 20 or more minutes per day 5 days a week, in physical education class; a minority of children had daily physical education; and a majority of physical education class time was spent doing little or no exercise.

The American College of Sports Medicine issued a position stand as early as 1988 on the Physical Fitness in Children and Youth.[5] Among the major points made in this position stand were that youth should have 20 to 30 minutes a day of *vigorous* exercise, programs should promote lifelong exercise behaviors, and recreational and fun aspects of exercise should be emphasized. Recently, some physical educators have developed programs requiring children to wear pulse rate monitors during workouts to ensure that they are of a vigorous nature. Although these types of programs provide important research data, caution is needed to make sure children understand that all physical fitness programs do not need to be highly structured. The challenge to physical educators is to develop creative programs that provide all children with the necessary amount of vigorous exercise in an environment that is fun and conducive to becoming a lifelong activity. Indeed both the 1992 "Statement on Exercise" from the American Heart Association[6] and the current "Physical Activity and Health" report from the Surgeon General[7] recommended that schools offer these types of programs. Six specific objectives set in the "Healthy People 2020" report from the U.S. Department of Health and Human Services are (1) increase to 20 percent the proportion of adolescents who meet current federal physical activity guidelines for aerobic physical activity; (2) increase the proportion of the nation's public and private schools that require daily physical education for all students—elementary 4.2 percent; middle and junior high 8.6 percent; and, high school 2.3 percent; (3) increase to 36.6 percent the proportion of adolescents who participate in daily school physical education; (4) increase by 1.7 states the number of states who regularly schedule elementary school recess in the United States—currently 17 states (the number 7 in 2006); (5) increase to 62.8 percent the proportion of school districts that require regularly scheduled recess; and, (6) increase to 67.7 percent the proportion of school districts that require or recommend elementary school recess for an appropriate amount of time.[8]

ADULTS

Data from the Third National Health and Nutrition Examination Survey (NHANES III) conducted from 1999 to 2001 reported that only 31 percent of U.S. adults participate in any regular physical activity.[9] Twenty-two percent of the population surveyed reported not doing any leisure-time physical activity. Based on findings from these national surveys, the "Healthy People 2020" report made the following specific physical activity

recommendations: (1) to reduce to no more than 32.6 percent the proportion of adults who engage in no leisure-time physical activity; (2) to increase to at least 47.9 the proportion who engage in aerobic physical activity of at least moderate intensity for at least 150 minutes/week or 75 minutes/week of vigorous intensity or an equivalent combination; (3) to increase to at least 24.1 the percent of adults who perform muscle-strengthening activities on 2 or more days of the week; (4) to increase to 20.1 the proportion who meet the objective for physical activity and muscle-strengthening activity.[10]

Data from the NHANES survey of 1999 to 2001 showed that 65 percent of U.S. adults were overweight or obese, up from 56 percent in 1988 to 1994, and 30 percent are obese, up from 23 percent in 1988 to 1994.[11] The data for children ages 6 to 19 years suggest that 16 percent were overweight, a 45 percent increase from just a decade earlier.[12]

These early indicators citing problems continue to grow. Today, slightly more than one-third (35.7 percent) of the adults are considered obese. Facts indicate that obesity affects 17 percent (12.5 million) of the children and adolescents ages 2 to 19, and their weight has tripled from one generation ago.[13]

CONSEQUENCES

The lack of physical fitness has been associated with a number of health problems. The term *hypokinetic disease*, meaning "a condition related to, or caused by, a lack of regular physical activity,"[14] has been used to describe this problem. Specific diseases and health problems associated with inactivity are coronary heart disease, cancer, hypertension, hyperlipidemia, obesity, and low back pain/injury. As early as 1992 the American Heart Association made a major pronouncement when it added physical inactivity as the fourth primary risk factor for coronary artery disease.[15] Prior to this time, the value of exercise as a preventive tool in the battle against heart disease was considered to be of far less importance than getting people to stop smoking, lower their blood cholesterol, or lower their blood pressure. Research evidence has accumulated that now suggests that becoming regularly active is of equal importance as an independent factor to changes in health. Regular exercise may actually be the most important to the population at large. It is associated with beneficial movements in each of the following areas cited by the Center for Disease Control and Prevention. Regular physical activity is one of the most important things that you can do for your health.

It can help:

- Control your weight
- Reduce your risk of cardiovascular disease
- Reduce your risk for type 2 diabetes and metabolic syndrome

- Reduce your risk for some cancers
- Strengthen your bones and muscles
- Improve your mental health and mood
- Improve your ability to do daily activities and prevent falls, if you are an adult
- Increase your chances of living longer[16]

Benefits of Physical Fitness

A regular exercise program will result in numerous physiological adaptations. A summary of some of the physiological changes that occur with aerobic exercise training is provided in Table 2-1. Although most tests of physical fitness emphasize improvements in maximal capabilities (e.g., maximal oxygen uptake is used as the principle measure of cardiorespiratory fitness), the most important benefits to the individual are the ability to perform daily tasks with increased ease and the ability to perform more total work throughout the day. The most generic of definitions of physical fitness suggests it to be the ability to perform daily activities without undue fatigue.[17]

PHYSIOLOGICAL ADAPTATIONS

The beneficial effects of exercise on the cardiovascular system are evident. The heart, which in essence is a muscular pump, becomes stronger and more efficient. Cardiac output, the amount of blood pumped from the heart each minute, is a product of stroke volume and heart rate. The heart adapts to regular aerobic exercise training by increasing the amount of blood it pumps with each beat (stroke volume), thus becoming a stronger, more effective pump. Consequently, at submaximal workloads the heart does not have to beat as often, thus reducing the demand on the heart. One can easily recognize this training effect by simply monitoring the decrease in resting heart rate or the heart rate during a fixed submaximal work task. The body also responds by increasing the total blood volume and the hemoglobin content in the blood. These two adaptations allow the individual to deliver more blood and more oxygen to the working muscles during exercise.

Changes also take place within the muscles themselves. Basically, the "metabolic machinery" of the muscle cell is built up so that it can produce more energy. The muscle can extract more oxygen from the blood, and the enhanced circulation through the muscle helps to remove the additional waste products produced.

The physiological measure of these adaptations is that of maximal oxygen consumption (VO_{2max}). This is also termed the individual's maximal aerobic power or the functional capacity (i.e., the maximal ability of the body to produce energy and thus perform work). Factors such as muscle fiber-type makeup (determined by genetics) and pretraining VO_{2max} level will determine the potential to improve one's maximal aerobic power; however, improvements in the range of 20 to 30 percent are possible following 3 months of appropriate aerobic training. Training will also increase the individual's "anaerobic threshold," the point in metabolism at which lactic acid begins to accumulate in the blood. Lactic acid accumulation, with the resultant decrease in muscle and blood pH, is a key factor associated with fatigue. Increasing the anaerobic threshold allows the individual to work at a higher absolute submaximal workload without fatiguing.

Regular aerobic exercise training can also improve an overfat individual's body composition. Through training, the muscles and bones are stimulated, which helps the body maintain muscle tissue and increase the integrity of bone. At the same time, the increased energy expenditure of training promotes the loss of body fat stores. Exercise for weight loss will be discussed in more detail later in this chapter.

Blood lipids and hypertension are also favorably changed after regular aerobic exercise training. Total cholesterol, low-density lipoprotein (LDL), and especially triglycerides may all decrease, and high-density lipoprotein (HDL) can increase following training. The most consistent effects of training are changes in triglyceride and HDL levels. The lipoproteins serve as carriers of lipids (fats) in blood and have been found to play a major role in the process of developing fatty

Table 2-1   **Physiological effects of training**

At Rest	Increase	Decrease	No Change
During Rest and/or Submaximal Exercise			
Lactic acid accumulation		X	
Heart rate		X	
Stroke volume	X		
Cardiac output			X
VO₂			X
Fat utilization	X		
Ventilatory efficiency	X		
Carbohydrate utilization		X	
During Maximal Exercise			
Lactic acid accumulation	X		
Heart rate	X or		X
Stroke volume	X		
Cardiac output	X		
VO₂	X		
Ventilatory efficiency	X		
Other Changes			
Body fat		X	
Serum cholesterol		X	
Serum triglycerides		X	
Serum high-density lipoproteins	X		
Serum low-density lipoproteins		X	
Resting metabolic rate	X or		X

deposits in walls of blood vessels. Basically, LDL is used to transport cholesterol from the liver to various tissues in the body to serve important purposes, such as the structure of cell membranes. In excess, LDL can promote the development of atherosclerotic plaques within the coronary blood vessels. HDLs, on the other hand, function to transport unneeded cholesterol from the tissues to the liver. Thus, HDLs can prevent the build-up of fatty deposits in the blood vessels. It should be noted that recent evidence suggests that only individuals with unfavorably high total cholesterol and/or low HDL see marked improvement in these lipid concentrations following aerobic training. Training can also help reduce blood pressure in those with borderline hypertension. Thus, the risk of coronary heart disease can be reduced by improving physical fitness.

Reduced Mortality.   Evidence is mounting that physically fit individuals or those who are regularly active have a reduced death rate from coronary heart disease compared with the unfit and inactive population. Findings from the Aerobics Research Institute[18] reported that the largest reduction in coronary heart disease deaths, as well as deaths from all causes, was between the lowest fitness category and those in the moderate fitness category. A follow-up study demonstrated that these same benefits are obtained when previously unfit men improved their physical fitness.[19]

Many of the previous studies on coronary heart disease (CHD) mortality demonstrated favorable effects from moderate increases in physical activity/fitness. Based on these studies, the Surgeon General's report offered the following recommendations.

> Significant health benefits can be obtained by including a moderate amount of physical activity on most, if not all days of the week. . . . Additional health benefits can be gained through greater amounts of physical activity. People who can maintain a regular regimen of activity that is of longer duration or of more vigorous intensity are likely to derive greater benefit.[20]

Thus, it is now clear that health benefits accrue from moderate amounts of physical activity and that regular exercise provides even more benefits (in both health and fitness).

In fact, studies from the Ball State Adult Fitness Cohort,[21] the British Civil Servants Study,[22] and the Harvard alumni[23] suggest that vigorous physical activity/fitness may be most beneficial. Additional research is needed to clarify the threshold levels of physical activity/fitness necessary for optimal health benefits. At the present, it is prudent to advise individuals to engage in at least a moderate amount of activity on a daily basis and, if possible, to include a program of regular exercise.

Psychological and Sociological Values

Regular exercise affects not only the body but also the mental and emotional states. Exercise can serve as an outlet for pent-up emotions through socially accepted channels. Stress, anxiety, and depression may be relieved by exercise, without the ills and side effects of mood-altering drugs. Physically fit individuals speak of their enhanced mental acuity, mental energy, concentration, and feelings of well-being. These feelings have been documented in several studies. In addition, physically fit individuals have an enhanced self-image, a definite sign of excellent mental health.

The late President Kennedy, an exponent of the vigorous life, summed it up in this way:

> Physical fitness is not only one of the most important keys to a healthy body, it is the basis of dynamic and creative intellectual activity. The relationship of the body and the activities of the mind is subtle and complex. Much is not yet understood, but we do know what the Greeks knew: that intelligence and skill can only function at the peak of their capacity when the body is healthy and strong; that hardy spirits and tough minds usually inhabit sound bodies.[24]

In this sense, physical fitness is the basis of all the activities of our society. And if the body grows soft and inactive, if we fail to encourage physical development and prowess, we will undermine our capacity for thought, for work, and for the use of those skills vital to an expanding and complex United States. Thus, the physical fitness of our citizens is a vital prerequisite to the nation's realization of its full potential and to each individual citizen's efforts to make full and fruitful use of her capabilities.

Pre-exercise Screening

Although exercise is a safe activity for most individuals, for some it should be avoided (at least temporarily), and for others some special considerations may need to be followed. To identify those who may have an unfavorable response to exercise, some simple procedures should be followed prior to beginning the physical activity. An essential procedure is a health history questionnaire that asks for items that could present problems during exercise (e.g., heart problems, diabetes, asthma). Many of these questionnaires have been published,[25] and most can use a closed-answer, check-off type response format. However, instructors can construct their own questionnaire to fit their specific program needs.

A second step that is advisable, especially if concerns arise during the health history review, is a medical examination. A medical examination is particularly important for individuals who have been diagnosed with a disease such as diabetes or asthma. Although it is safe and appropriate for these individuals to participate in exercise programs, physicians may have instructions about specific needs or precautions for their patients. A medical examination is also a recommended procedure for sedentary adults before they begin an exercise program.

Finally, the individual's current level of fitness should be assessed prior to beginning the training program. This allows the instructor to design the program to meet the individual's weaknesses and to provide an evaluation of the effectiveness of the training program. As mentioned previously, AAHPERD recommends a battery of tests to assess cardiorespiratory endurance, muscular strength and endurance, body composition, and flexibility of school-age children in the *Physical Best* program. Alternative tests of cardiorespiratory endurance for college-age students are a 1.5-mile run, a step test, and a submaximal cycle test. Likewise, muscular strength can be assessed by weight-lifting tests. These tests are relatively crude markers of cardiorespiratory fitness and have relatively high measurement errors associated with them. At best, they can provide an indication of the student's fitness classification (i.e., poor, fair, average, etc.). For adults, when time and expense are less of an issue, cardiorespiratory fitness can be measured directly during maximal exercise tests. A more complete fitness assessment of these components would include tests of various muscle groups and joints throughout the body. Field test possibilities for each of the five health-related fitness areas are addressed in the *Skill Assessment* section.

When programs are being designed for adults, the guidelines established by the American College of Sports Medicine should be followed for screening individuals.[26] Depending on age and health status, the guidelines provide recommendations for a physical examination and exercise testing before the individual begins an exercise program. Evaluation of individuals' muscular strength can be obtained from weight-lifting tests.

Exercise Programming

Regardless of the type of training to be used, all exercise training sessions should have the same basic structure. The session begins with a *warm-up* period, proceeds with the specific type of training, and finishes with a *cool-down* period. The purpose of the warm-up is to prepare the body for the training session by gradually increasing the heart rate and blood circulation to the active musculature. Walking, calisthenic-type exercises, and stretching are appropriate warm-up activities. Although documentation is lacking, many believe that warm-up activities help prevent injury.

The cool-down helps restore the body to its pre-exercise condition. Initially the cool-down consists of walking, which is then followed by stretching exercises. It is believed that the cool-down is the optimal time for making flexibility improvements because the muscles are warm and the joints are most supple. Although many flexibility exercises are available, a basic routine would include neck rotations, arm pullovers, side stretches, one-legged sit and reach, hip and knee flexion, and ankle rotation.

When designing the training session of the program, the instructor should employ the basic principles of specificity and overload, as well as individualization. The principle of *specificity* states that adaptations to training will be specific to the muscle groups trained, the specific movement patterns and speed of contractions used, and the metabolic energy systems stressed. This principle is most applicable to training for sport; however, it is also important to consider when evaluating improvements in physical fitness. For example, cycling, jogging, and swimming are all appropriate activities to condition the cardiorespiratory systems. However, the 1-mile run/walk test will only accurately reflect cardiorespiratory improvements for those in a jogging program. Those in a cycling or swimming program would have their cardiorespiratory endurance underestimated with such a test. The *overload* principle means that in order for a muscle or system to adapt, it must be stressed beyond a level to which it is normally accustomed. Overload is derived by manipulating the following factors: intensity, duration, and frequency. The American College of Sports Medicine has specific recommendations for training guidelines for healthy adults.[27]

INTENSITY

Intensity refers to the percentage of the maximal capabilities that are being required for the activity. Research has established that for cardiorespiratory improvements, an intensity level of at least approximately 40 to 50 percent of VO_2 reserve must be achieved (note: severely deconditioned individuals will make improvements at lower intensities). Additional improvements are achieved through intensities up to 85 percent of VO_2 reserve. This intensity can be monitored by palpating a pulse rate during the exercise session. Pulse rates of approximately 75 to 85 percent of maximum are the equivalent of 70 to 80 percent of VO_2 reserve. Maximal heart rate can be measured during a maximal exercise test; however, an estimate can be made from the formula of 220 minus age. For example, the training intensity for a 15-year-old would be calculated as follows:

$$(220 - 15) \times .75 = 154 \text{ bpm} - (220 - 15) \times .85 = 174 \text{ bpm}$$

It should be noted that although this equation is widely used, it has a large measurement error associated with it

(95 percent confidence levels $\pm$ 30 bpm).[28] This means that some individuals' "true" target heart rates (exercise intensity) will actually be much higher or lower than that estimated using the age-predicted maximal heart rate formula.

To monitor the intensity of the exercise session, the individual should momentarily stop the exercise (after at least 5 minutes of activity) and immediately count the pulse rate. It is advisable to keep walking or walk in place during this time. The pulse can be palpated using the index and middle fingers at either the radial artery on the wrist or one of the carotid arteries on either side of the neck (Figure 2-1). Some precautions need to be followed if the carotid artery is used. First, it is important to palpate only on one side of the neck (i.e., do not put the thumb on one side of the neck and the fingers on the other side). Also, the individual should not press too hard to palpate the carotid artery because a reflex lowering of the heart rate could occur. The pulse count is taken for a 10-second count (start the count with zero), and the training range can be determined by dividing the training heart rate by 6 (examples: $154 \div 6 = 26$; $174 \div 6 = 29$). The pulse should also be monitored at the end of the training session. Exercising within the training heart rate range will produce optimal physiological adaptations. Highly motivated individuals sometimes have a tendency to train above the training heart rate range (i.e., the feeling that if some is good, then more must be better); however, this should be discouraged because the additional benefits are relatively small and the risk for injury increases at these high intensities.

DURATION

The duration of the program is the amount of time spent in the training part of the exercise session (not including warm-up and cool-down time). The minimum duration necessary to stimulate physiological adaptations is 20 minutes, with further increases seen through 60 minutes of activity. The recommended duration range for most individuals is 30 to 40 minutes.

FREQUENCY

The frequency of the training program refers to how often the training should take place, usually described in terms of days per week. Training needs to be performed at least 3 days per week to derive physiological benefits. Further increases are seen with more frequent training; however, for health-related physical fitness training, more than 5 days per week is of little value. In fact, the body needs rest time between training sessions to make the adaptations. Training 6 to 7 days per week increases the individual's risk for injury. It should be noted that these "off" days do not have to be totally sedentary; indeed, alternative types of physical activities and recreation should be encouraged.

Figure 2-2 shows various combinations of frequency, intensity, and duration that would theoretically derive the same training benefit. The data are hypothesized for a person with a VO_{2max} of 3 L/min. The minimal threshold level as recommended by the American College of Sports Medicine is 1,000 kcal/week.[29] An example of two different combinations to meet the minimal thresholds would be exercising at 55 percent intensity, 5 days per week for 24 minutes per session, or exercising at 85 percent intensity, 3 days per week for 26 minutes per session. It should also be recognized that greater amounts of energy expenditure (i.e., > 1,000 kcal/week) will result in additional training benefits.

INDIVIDUALIZATION

Intensity, duration, and frequency of training are interrelated. This interrelationship allows for designing an exercise program to meet the individual's physical capabilities and psychological perceptions of the comfort of

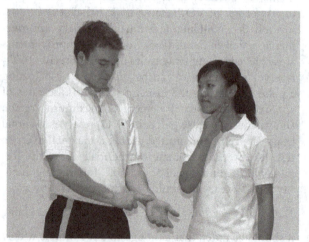

Figure 2-1   Radial and carotid pulse palpation.

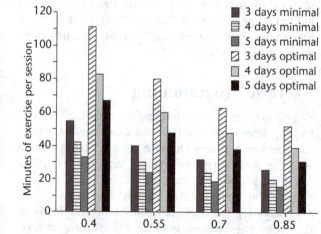

Figure 2-2   Frequency, intensity, and duration of exercise combinations for minimal (1,000 kcal/week) and optimal (2,000 kcal/week) cardiorespiratory fitness.

the exercise program. Also, factors such as availability of facilities, work or school schedules, weather, and medical restrictions can influence the exercise training program. To be effective, regular exercise must become an integral part of one's lifestyle.

If an intensity level of 75 to 85 percent of maximum heart rate (HR max) is found to be undesirably strenuous, the training program can be modified by reducing the intensity level to 65 to 75 percent and either increasing the duration by 5 to 10 minutes per session or the frequency by one day per week.

Individualization can also take place by considering the type of exercise being utilized for the training. Aerobic exercise types are those that use the large muscle groups (i.e., legs or arms and legs) in a rhythmic, dynamic fashion. Activities such as walking, jogging, swimming, cycling, rowing, and cross-country skiing are examples of aerobic exercise types.

A final consideration is the need to begin an exercise program at the reduced intensity and duration and to progress slowly. As one becomes acquainted with the exercise program structure and techniques used, he can gradually increase the intensity and duration of the training session. This helps to reduce injuries at the beginning of the program and also increases the individual's self-confidence. Table 2-2 represents an example of a start-up walk/jog program. Dr. Bud Getchell, the founder of the Adult Fitness Program at Ball State University, has developed protocols for beginning and progressing in programs of walking, running, cycling, and swimming.[30]

Recreational Activities A question that often is asked is whether one can use recreational activities for training. In general, one should "get in shape to play the game, not play the game to get in shape." However, once an acceptable level of physical fitness is obtained, recreational activities can be useful as a supplement to the training program to maintain the desired level. Table 2-3 shows the caloric equivalents of different recreational activities as well as the standard aerobic training modes for comparison purposes. Recreational activities can provide the necessary variety to the training program to make the long-term commitment to regular exercise solid.

Exercise for Weight Loss As mentioned previously, from one-third to one-half of adult Americans are overweight or obese. Body weight is determined by the balance between energy intake and energy expenditure (Figure 2-3). If intake exceeds expenditure, weight will increase, and if expenditure exceeds intake, weight will decrease. Although energy intake is easy to quantify and regulate (increase or decrease food intake), energy expenditure is more difficult to understand, because the body can become more or less energy conservative, depending on how it responds to different stresses.

The goal for weight-loss programs is the loss of excess body fat. Weight can be lost if energy intake is decreased (dieting), if energy expenditure is increased (principally by increased physical activity), or by both dieting and exercising. Intervention programs for obesity have not been successful, as most have concentrated only on the energy intake side of the body weight balance equation. The majority of diet programs require substantial caloric restrictions, which are actually counterproductive to long-term weight loss because they result in a decrease in resting metabolic rate (the largest component of daily energy expenditure). The more successful weight-loss programs use the "exchange" principle for reducing calorie intake. They recommend that individuals exchange their intake of much of the

Table 2-2 **Two-week walking/jogging program**

WALKING PROGRAM

	Mon.	Tues.	Thur.	Fri.
First Week	Walk 20 min.	Walk 20 min.	Walk 24 min.	Walk 24 min.
Second Week	Walk 28 min.	Walk 28 min.	Walk 32 min.	Walk 32 min.

JOG/WALK PROGRAM

	Mon. and Tues.	Thur. and Fri.
First Week	Walk 20 min. Jog/walk ½, ½, ½, ½ Walk 10 min.	Walk 17 min. Jog/walk ½, ½, ½, ½, ½, ½ Walk 10 min.
Second Week	Walk 15 min. Jog/walk ½, ½, ½, ½, ½, ½, ½, ½, ½ Walk 10 min.	Walk 12 min. Jog/walk ½, ½, ½, ½, ½, ½ Walk 10 min.

JOGGING PROGRAM

	Mon.	Tues.	Thur.	Fri.
First Week	Jog 2 miles	Jog 4 miles	Jog 3 miles	Jog 5 miles
Second Week	Jog 3 miles	Jog 4 miles	Jog 2 miles	Jog 5 miles

Note: ½ = 110 yds or 30 to 45 sec. Individual should alternate on the Jog/Walk routine—i.e., jog ½, walk ½, jog ½, etc.

Table 2-3　**Energy requirements of various activities**

		kcal/min.	
Activity		123 lb.	150 lb.
Aquatic Games		7.2	8.7
Archery		3.6	4.4
Badminton		5.4	6.6
Basketball		7.7	9.4
Bicycling		5.6	6.8
Bowling		3.7	4.0
Canoeing		2.5	3.0
Cycling	10 mile/hour	6.5	7.0
Football: Touch/Flag		5.4	6.0
Golf (walking)		4.8	5.8
Handball		7.8	9.5
Hiking		5.5	6.3
Racquetball		7.8	9.5
Running	12 min./mile	8.1	9.9
	11 min./mile	8.7	10.7
	10 min./mile	9.5	11.6
	9 min./mile	10.3	12.7
	8 min./mile	11.6	14.2
	7 min./mile	13.1	16.0
	6 min./mile	15.1	18.5
Skiing: Cross-Country		13.7	15.1
Skiing: Downhill		8.7	10.0
Soccer		7.8	9.5
Softball		3.6	4.7
Swimming		7.2	8.7
Table Tennis		3.8	4.6
Tennis		6.1	7.4
Volleyball		2.8	3.4

Note: A heavier person (150 vs. 123 lb.) must do more work to transport his or her body weight, thus requiring more energy.

dietary fat, which has 9 kcal/gm, for complex carbohydrates (fruits and vegetables), which have only 4 kcal/gm. This essentially reduces the energy intake but still allows the individual to consume *normal* quantities of food. Successful programs also realize that energy expenditure must be increased for long-term maintenance with weight loss. The types of activities used do not really matter; what is important is that the total amount of physical activity be increased. The increased physical activity level actually serves two purposes: (1) It results in an increase in caloric expenditure due directly to the activity, and (2) it maintains or may slightly increase the resting metabolic rate.

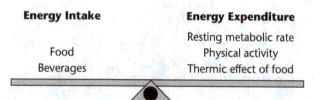

Energy Intake

Food
Beverages

Energy Expenditure

Resting metabolic rate
Physical activity
Thermic effect of food

Figure 2-3　Body weight balance.

Estimates of how much weight should be lost can be made from the following equation:

$$\text{Desired Body Weight} = \frac{\text{Fat-free body weight}}{1 - (\text{desired body fat \%} \div 100)}$$

Note that this equation requires knowledge of the individual's body fat percentage and what percent is a normal or desired body fat. For example, consider a 200-pound man with 25 percent body fat and a goal of 15 percent body fat. The desired body weight would be calculated as follows:

$$\frac{200(1 - 25 \div 100)}{1 - (15 \div 100)} = \frac{150 \text{ lb.}}{0.85} = 175.5 \text{ lb.}$$

Thus, this individual would need to lose 24.5 pounds of fat to achieve his desired body composition. Because 1 pound of fat holds 3,500 kcal, 82,250 kcal must be expended to achieve the desired goal. At first glance this may seem like an insurmountable task. However, success in weight (fat)-loss programs is achieved by using the *long-haul* approach. For example, say this man exchanged one-third of his 133 gm of daily fat intake for carbohydrates; it would result in a daily decrease of 220 kcal/day [44 gm/day × (9 − 4 kcal/gm)]. Additionally, if he began a 4-day-per-week exercise program and expended 300 kcal per session (approximately 2.5 miles of walking or jogging) and increased his daily activity level to expend an additional 100 kcal/day, over a week he would have burned an additional 3,440 kcal, or approximately the equivalent of 1 pound of fat. Thus, it would take him about half a year to attain his goal; however, during this time he likely would also develop lifestyle dietary and exercise habits that will help him maintain his desired body weight over the long term. The exercise training program would also improve total physical fitness. Note that the maximal safe rate of weight loss is 1 to 2 pounds per week. Losing weight more rapidly will involve losing fat-free weight and decreasing resting metabolic rate.

Clothing and Equipment

Essentially the only piece of specialized clothing required for aerobic training is proper footwear. Good exercise shoes provide adequate support and cushioning to protect the feet and reduce the shock of the foot strike to the rest of the body. (Good shoes can take on a force of approximately three times the body weight.) The running/walking shoe industry has gone high-tech with literally hundreds of different shoes available with variable features (outsole, midsole, heel counter, upper, foxing, toe box). One should shop for shoes at a reputable dealer who has personnel that can explain the various features of the shoes and assist in selecting the most appropriate shoe for the individual's needs.

In general, exercise clothing should be lightweight and should fit loosely. Fashionable exercise clothing has become very popular; however, care has to be taken to assure that the clothing is breathable and allows moisture to evaporate from the skin. Seasons will dictate how much to wear. In warm, humid weather, it is important to expose as much body surface area as possible to allow sweat the opportunity to evaporate and thus help keep body temperature down. In cold weather, layering lightweight clothing is most advantageous because this allows removal of a layer (or two) as the body heat production increases. In extremely cold conditions, protecting the extremities is a must. A hat that covers the ears and either gloves or mittens are needed. Additionally, some individuals find using a breathing filter-type mask helps to moisturize the cold, dry air.

One myth is that rubberized sweat suits are helpful for exercise and weight-loss programs. It is true that one can lose a substantial amount of weight in an exercise session by wearing a rubberized suit. However, the weight lost is from body water, *not* body fat, and thus is quickly regained. These suits not only are ineffective for reducing excess body fat, but are potentially dangerous because dehydration can raise body temperature to dangerous levels.

Exercise equipment sales have been tremendous in recent years. Claims that particular machines provide the "best" workout in the shortest period of time have helped fuel sales. As a result of technological advances, computer-aided features such as monitors for heart rate, estimations of caloric expenditure, and interval-type training sessions can be found on some of these exercise devices. Indeed, many of these exercise machines can make the exercise session more enjoyable by adding some variety to the workout. However, the individual must still perform the work (i.e., same specificity and overload principles apply) to achieve the physiological benefits. The other factor to consider is the expense of much of this equipment. Individuals should be counseled to test thoroughly a piece of equipment before purchasing it. Too often an individual purchases a piece of exercise equipment for home use and uses it only for a short period of time before moving it into a closet or out to the garage for storage.

Supplementary Training

Once the major cardiorespiratory adaptations have been made some individuals like to modify their training program for maintenance of the adaptations. One modification is to supplement their regular aerobic training with one or two interval training sessions a week. *Interval training* involves doing repeated cycles of high-intensity exercise followed by a brief recovery period. This type of training is used widely in athletics and can produce excellent fitness benefits. The principal advantage of this type of training is that it allows high-quality training stimulus in a relatively short duration. For aerobic training, work intervals of 0.25, 0.5, and/or 0.75 miles are recommended, with a work-recovery ratio of 1:1 (i.e., if the work interval is 2 minutes, the recovery time is 2 minutes). These distances are run at a pace faster than the average time for that distance based on the individuals' best mile time. For example, if the best mile time is 8 minutes, the average 0.25-mile time is 2 minutes, thus the interval training pace for the 0.25-mile interval run would be less than 2 minutes. A complete description of interval training is beyond the scope of this chapter.[31]

Circuit training involves a series of exercises designed to improve muscular endurance and muscular strength that are completed within a set time frame. The individual moves quickly between each exercise station and then begins the next type of exercise. Some stations may involve aerobic exercise, such as stationary cycling, running, and rope skipping. These types of programs are useful ways to add some variety to the exercise program if it is becoming "stale" and also ensure that the muscular strength and endurance components of fitness are stimulated. A typical circuit could involve two sets of the following exercise stations (1 minute per station):

Station	Activity
1	jumping jacks
2	bicep curls
3	modified sit-ups
4	bench press
5	running in place
6	leg press
7	stationary cycling
8	tricep curls
9	rope skipping or bench stepping
10	leg curls

It is important to remember that the appropriate program structure of beginning with a warm-up and finishing with a cool-down period also applies to these supplemental types of training.

A quote attributable to Hippocrates sums up the value of physical fitness:

All parts of the body which have a function, if used in moderation and exercised in labors in which each is accustomed, become thereby healthy, well-developed and age more slowly, but if unused and left idle they become liable to disease, defective in growth, and age quickly.[32]

Skill Assessment

There are a variety of field tests available for the five health-related components of fitness. Following are lists of possible tests. As previously noted, the norms vary by age.[33–36]

CARDIORESPIRATORY ENDURANCE.   One-mile walk, 1.5-mile run, 5-mile bicycling test, 500-yard swim test, 500-yard water run test, 3-minute step test, 12-minute run/walk test, PACER run.

MUSCULAR STRENGTH AND ENDURANCE.   Modified push-ups, curl-ups, pull-ups, modified pull-ups.

FLEXIBILITY.   Sit-and-reach box test, sit-and-reach wall test, trunk lift, lower back flexibility, hip flexor flexibility, quadriceps flexibility, hamstring flexibility, calf flexibility, shoulder girdle flexibility.

BODY COMPOSITION.   Body mass index (BMI), skinfold assessment, waist-to-hip ratio.

Terminology

aerobic training Exercise training performed at an intensity, duration, and frequency that stimulates adaptations of the aerobic energy system and the cardiorespiratory systems of the body.

body composition The evaluation of the components of the body (e.g., water, muscle, bone, fat), with the determination of percentage of body fat the most common.

calorie A unit of energy.

cool-down A group of activities including walking, calisthenics, and flexibility exercises performed following the exercise training session to gradually return the body to its resting state.

duration The amount of time spent in one exercise training session.

exchange principle A diet modification that substitutes foods of lower caloric value, mainly high carbohydrate foods, for foods of higher caloric value (i.e., foods of high fat content).

frequency The number of training sessions performed in a fixed period of time, usually 1 week.

intensity The percentage of maximal capabilities that are being utilized (e.g., percentage of maximal heart rate).

interval training Exercise training sessions that are characterized by alternating periods of vigorous exercise (work interval) with periods of relief (low-intensity exercise or rest interval).

lipids Substances that are not soluble in water. The most important blood lipids include cholesterol and triglyceride.

lipoproteins A compound formed by combining cholesterol and protein to allow the cholesterol to be soluble in fluid and thus transported in the blood.

overload An exercise training principle that states that adaptations to training will only take place when the activity stresses the body's systems beyond what it is normally accustomed to.

specificity An exercise training principle that states that adaptations to training are specific to the muscle groups utilized, the speed of contractions performed, the movement patterns employed, and the energy systems required to power the activity.

VO$_2$ The volume of oxygen consumed, used as an indirect measure of energy expenditure.

warm-up A group of activities including walking, calisthenics, and flexibility exercises performed prior to the exercise training to prepare the body for vigorous physical activity.

Discussion Questions

1. Discuss the five components of health-related fitness and their specific contributions to fitness.
2. Identify the benefits of physical fitness.
3. Discuss the fitness deficiencies of youth and adults in the United States.
4. Compare and contrast the various testing measures available for assessing the five health-related components.
5. Calculate the estimated maximal heart rate for a 13-year-old student and a 25-year-old adult.
6. Discuss the method for monitoring the training heart rate during and at the end of the exercise bout.
7. Present the factors one needs to consider in determining the frequency of exercise.
8. Discuss the factors involved in weight loss and determining the desired body weight.
9. Compare and contrast interval training and circuit training methods for fitness training.
10. Present the factors participants must consider when selecting proper exercise attire.

Web Sites

http://www.pearsonhighered.com/powers/ Total Fitness & Wellness Companion Web site—provides links to the American Heart Association, American College of Sports Medicine, Web MD, Healthy People, Fitness On Line, and other health-related information, including fitness facts, training, statistics, and topics.

| # Aerobic Dance and Zumba®

This chapter will enable you to

- Communicate the benefits of regular participation in aerobic dance to your students
- Understand both the movement and safety elements that underlie the structure of an effective aerobic exercise class
- Distinguish between high-impact and low-impact movements and know which to use for any given class situation
- Understand the utility and importance of incorporating circuit and interval training in an aerobics class format
- Incorporate all the elements of an effective aerobics class—including safety, appropriate music, and step and movement combinations—in class design
- Understand the growth of Zumba® and the benefits, dance elements, basic rhythms, and variety of class offering

AEROBIC DANCE

Nature and Purpose

Each of the variety of aerobic activities from which to choose has its individual characteristics. The following information identifies these specificities when music, dance routines, and aerobic exercise are combined. Regular participation in aerobic dance improves cardiovascular endurance, yet many other benefits appear concurrently—and all are related to an improved ability to enjoy life. These benefits are both physical and mental; a healthy body, good psychological health, and enjoyment of life are interrelated.

One key to enjoying all the benefits of aerobic dance is an appropriate level of participation. A student can achieve maximum benefits by taking classes 3 to 7 times a week without taking more than one class a day. Resting 1 day out of 7 will not slow the person's progress and may even help sustain freshness and enthusiasm. A second key to enjoying the benefits of aerobic dance is to stay with it long enough to see results. It takes 6 to 8 weeks to establish the habit and to begin seeing both physical and psychological improvements.

The first benefit of aerobics is improved conditioning of the circulatory and respiratory systems, which results in decreased risk of cardiovascular disease, better handling of stress, improved ability to relax, and greater energy and vitality. Regular participants should also benefit from stronger joints, firmer muscles, improved postural alignment, a decrease in body fat, and better digestion. As a student's physical health and physical appearance improve, self-esteem and self-confidence tend to improve as well. In addition, many studies have shown that regular aerobic exercise impacts the body's

systems in ways that alleviate depression. Aerobic dance also develops coordination, balance, and memory.

The informality of most aerobic dance classes promotes social interaction and may lead to the formation of lasting friendships. This aspect also offers significant health benefits; participants are more likely to continue exercising if they take classes with friends, and strong friendship networks foster longevity.

History

The fun of moving to music in a sociable group setting while obtaining a great cardiovascular workout has made aerobic dance one of the most popular leisure activities in the United States. Today's aerobics class, which may feature cardio funk, hip hop, Zumba®, yogaerobics, or slide aerobics, as well as more standard step and arm movements, has an interesting evolution that spans the years since the publication of Dr. Kenneth Cooper's *Aerobics* in 1968.

Cooper's research studies of Air Force personnel in the 1960s determined that the key to human fitness was the ability of an individual to take in and deliver oxygen to the entire body. His studies brought the importance of aerobic conditioning to national awareness. However, his emphasis was on more traditional forms of conditioning such as jogging, cycling, and swimming, which, for many people, seemed to be too much work and too little fun.

Around 1970, Jackie Sorensen, who studied Cooper's Air Force Aerobics Program and who attributed her excellent performance on the 12-minute run/walk test to her years of dance training, began combining her understanding of Cooper's principles and her knowledge of dance. Sorensen created a new form of aerobic movement set to music. This innovation, called aerobic dance, transformed aerobic exercise. Sorenson's aerobic dance was fun and social and it hid the hard work of aerobic conditioning under music and rhythm. Aerobic dance (also called "aerobics") had immediate appeal for many women and men turned off by the undisguised work or competition in other forms of aerobic exercise.

Judi Sheppard Missett is another early pioneer in the evolution of aerobics. Missett, the founder of Jazzercise, Inc., included fitness movements in her jazz dance classes, creating entertaining dance routines that could be followed with little or no explanation.

In the late 1980s, the addition of bench-stepping equipment by former gymnast Gin Miller further enhanced the applicability of aerobic dance to people with many different physical capabilities. Benches not only can allow for variation in the height of the step, creating different levels of intensity, but also provide creative instructors with greatly increased choreographic possibilities.

Today, professional aerobic dance associations are setting standards for instructor qualifications as well as access to professional training. Organizations such as the International Association of Fitness Professionals (IDEA) and the Aerobic and Fitness Association of America (AFAA) provide training, exercise journals, conventions, and workshops, as well as instructor certification.

With each innovation, aerobic dance has become more fun, more diverse in form and style, and more responsive to the increase in knowledge about safe and effective forms of movement. Today, about 25 million people participate in some form of aerobics, enhancing their personal health and contributing to the growth of a multimillion-dollar industry.

The Classroom

The setting in which a class is conducted will impact the success of the class. An ideal aerobics classroom will offer the following:

- A floor that provides traction, resilience, and stability. A hardwood sprung floor is ideal. Carpeted floors provide good traction and shock absorption, but foot-drag on this "slower" surface may increase the likelihood of injury.
- Adequate space for all participants. About 3 to 4 feet of empty space around each exerciser provides room to extend the arms and to move in any direction.
- Floor-to-ceiling mirrors on at least one of the classroom's long walls. Mirrors not only allow participants to see and correct themselves, but also allow instructors to monitor the entire class even while leading with the back turned toward the group.
- Adequate ventilation without drafty areas. A temperature above 60° F but below 70° F is generally comfortable.

- A good sound system and a good collection of music. A wireless microphone is a plus in all but the smallest studios and a necessity in larger rooms.
- Additional equipment such as mats, hand weights, rubber bands, and more, and a storage area where supplies and the sound equipment may be locked away.
- A raised platform for the instructor is helpful in large rooms accommodating many students.

Equipment
SHOES

Appropriate shoes are the most important piece of equipment in any aerobics setting. Shoes should be durable, flexible, and lightweight while providing enough cushion and support to help absorb movements that may generate forces of up to four times the participant's body weight. In general, bigger, heavier people need slightly heavier, sturdier shoes. The shoe should have adequate cushioning, especially under the ball of the foot. It should also provide good support and stability, as well as traction appropriate to the surface in the room. Greater traction is required on hardwood floors, less on carpeted floors. A mismatch in the shoe and the surface increases the likelihood of injury. It is important not to try to substitute running or court shoes for aerobic shoes. The former are not designed to compensate for the stresses of aerobic dance's movement patterns and will not provide the needed safety, support, and traction.

Buying a high-quality, brand-name shoe that is well constructed will save money (and your body) in the end. If you have a limited budget, skimp on outfits, not on shoes. Make sure the shoes really fit. Try at least three different brands in the store, select the best-feeling one, then wear the shoe around a carpeted area in your home for at least an hour. If it doesn't feel good at the end of the hour, return that one and try again.

Many people have feet with high arches, flat arches, or other structural abnormalities and will need shoes designed for their special needs. If aches in the feet, knees, hips, or lower back occur while a student is participating in a class series, suggest that the student may want to consult a podiatrist.

APPAREL

Fashion tends to dictate the look of the clothing, but whatever the current fashion, aerobic apparel should provide mobility, comfort, and porosity. Among current fabric options, cotton fabrics or cotton-Lycra fabrics with high cotton content are desirable because they absorb moisture, allow air to circulate to the skin (thus preventing overheating), and provide good durability. Cotton socks are cooler than wool socks, provide good absorption of perspiration, and also help prevent blisters. In general, T-shirts, knee-length tights, and fitness shorts provide both comfort and mobility. Teachers will want to encourage students to dress in layers, especially if the classroom is cool, and to remove outer layers as the body warms up. Reminding students that they have the freedom to discard the outer layers of clothing then becomes part of the structure of the class.

TEACHING AIDS

A good aerobic dance class can still be taught without any additional equipment, but most classes include some or all of the following (Figure 3-1):

MATS—provide cushioning as well as a sense of personal space. A good mat keeps you from feeling the floor and is also easy to keep clean, transport, and store.

EXERCISE BANDS—add resistance to the strength exercises. Anyone who has a recent or preexisting joint injury, or anyone who develops joint pain during a class series, should not use an exercise band. A wide variety of bands are available.

HAND WEIGHTS—are appropriately used by students working at the intermediate or advanced level. There should be no history of joint injury or disease, such as knee surgery, ligament damage, arthritis, or bursitis.

STEPS (BENCHES)—need to be stable, skid-proof, and of a height that requires a knee-bend of 90 degrees *or less*. Beginners will want to begin on a low (4-inch) bench and progress gradually to higher steps. For advanced workouts, 6- and 8-inch benches are most commonly used, with occasional use of the 10-inch bench.

PULSE READERS—give an electronic reading of the pulse at a glance. Those that clip on the earlobe or slip over the finger are generally unreliable.

HEART RATE MONITORS—are more accurate pulse readers but require wearing a band that wraps around the chest. The monitor electrodes must touch the skin. They are somewhat inconvenient to wear with some clothing.

WIRELESS MICROPHONES WITH HEADSETS—allow teachers to give audible cues without straining their vocal cords. When wireless mikes are used, teachers need to remember that they no longer need to shout to be heard. Amplification should be separate from that used for the music.

Program Fundamentals

A well-designed aerobic dance class is fun, appropriately challenging, and designed for each participant's safety. A good aerobics teacher will incorporate cardiovascular safety and conditioning principles in the structure of the class, monitor the individuals in the class as they work out, and keep the class motivated (as well as safe) by giving clear cues and choosing appropriate music. These are the considerations discussed in this section.

CLASS STRUCTURE

The structure of the class facilitates the body's preparation for and recovery from the cardiovascular conditioning that takes place during the most intense portion of the class.

The warm-up makes the body ready for the demands of the aerobic workout. Warming up seems to shorten the cardiovascular and muscular systems' adjustment to stress, allowing a shift from rest to activity without unnecessary strain on the heart. It is thought that warming up minimizes the risk of inadequate blood flow to the heart during the first bit of intense activity, also helping to prevent cardiac arrhythmias caused by the heart's attempts to provide increased blood circulation. Warming up also facilitates mental preparation.

The *isolation* phase (1–1.5 min.) of the warm-up focuses on exercising one body part at a time with simple movements. It helps to create body awareness and to focus attention on posture and alignment.

The *active warm-up* phase (3–4 min.) involves full body movements such as simple calisthenics, brisk walking, or light jogging. It starts slowly and intensifies, elevating the heart rate and warming the muscles. When light perspiration begins, the participant is ready for more intense activity.

The third phase of the warm-up consists of *static stretching* (1–2.5 min.). The five major muscle groups used during the full-intensity workout are subjected to slow, static stretches lasting anywhere from 10 to 30 seconds. It is important to avoid bouncing to stretch because this actually triggers a reflex that will tighten, rather than loosen, the muscle fibers.

The *aerobic warm-up* (5–10 min.) begins with low- to moderate-intensity movements that are structured into simple routines that stress the use of the large muscle groups. A low-impact approach is usually desirable.

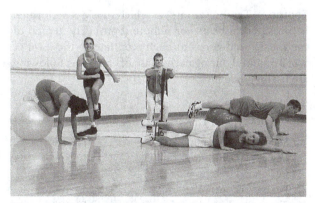

Figure 3-1 Equipment options for aerobics classes. Left to right: fit balls, adjustable slide, jump-stretch bands, and SPRI bands.

The *peak aerobics session* (20–30 min.) may advance to high-impact movement or may increase the intensity of low-impact movements. In this phase students should be in their heart rate zones (defined as 50 to 85 percent of maximum capacity; see Chapter 2) and should monitor the pulse rate periodically to see that they do not drop below or exceed their personal limits.

Aerobic exercise results in the delivery of large quantities of blood to the working muscles. If exercise stops abruptly, the blood tends to pool in the lower extremities. Thus, *cooling down* (15 min.) is an important part of a well-balanced class. The cool-down should last until the heart rate is at or below 120 beats per minute (bpm), which usually takes about 5 minutes. Cool-down is accomplished by keeping the arms below the level of the heart, gradually diminishing the intensity of all movements, slowing movement, and finally shifting to simple locomotion patterns.

Toning and conditioning exercises (5–20 min.) are increasingly a part of most aerobics classes. Typically, exercises targeting the abdomen, chest, arms, buttocks, and thighs are included; frequently resistance equipment is used to add both difficulty and variety. As with every part of class, it remains important to pay attention to participants' body alignment and technique.

Final stretching for flexibility lasts from 5 to 10 minutes, improves or maintains flexibility, and helps prevent muscle soreness. A flexible body is one that is less easily injured and also one that adapts more readily to stress. Deep stretching is facilitated at this time because the muscles are warm and pliable. As in the warm-up, the stretching is slow and static; stretches are held longer; and participants are encouraged to relax into the stretch, rather than straining to achieve an extreme stretch.

Relaxation, even if brief (5–8 min.), is an important part of class. While it helps the body, it also teaches the mind that being able to let go, being able to rest, is as important a human activity as actively moving. It teaches the mind and the body to simply release effort and stress—at least for a short while.

CUEING

Cues are what keeps the class moving. If one wants to be an instructor that students rave about, learn to give good cues. With clear cues, participants have no doubt in their mind when, how, and where to move; without them, the class becomes fragmented, frustrated, and unmotivated.

Good cueing depends on good timing and on a combination of explicit and consistent visual and verbal messages. One must communicate the steps and the arm movements the students are to use *in advance* of their actually performing the movements. This can be done verbally, visually, or both. Because some students

learn best from verbal instructions, and some from visual patterns, a combination of both will provide the strongest teaching style. Typically, cues are given on the last four beats of the measure preceding the one in which the new movement is to begin.

Verbal Cues. Griffith describes five different types of verbal cues. *Footwork cueing* indicates whether one should move the right or left foot; *rhythmic cueing* indicates the correct tempo of the routine; *numerical cueing* involves counting the rhythm, such as one, two, three, and four; *step cueing* refers to the name of the step, such as step touch; and *directional cueing* indicates whether the movement should be forward, back, or to the side. Teachers need to combine cues from all five categories for maximum impact.

Visual Cues. The teacher's body movements are a major visual cue, so one needs to model good technique in all movements. When facing the class, the teacher needs to mirror the movements he wants the class to make. For example, if the class is cued to move left, the instructor will move to the right. A second set of visual cues is the hand signals and other gestures that are used to communicate what the class is to do. Tamilee Webb designed a set of "Step 'Q' Signs" to help teachers communicate with their classes. There are about 10 visual cues that are now widely used. For example, pointing to the eye means "watch me," holding the arm up with the palm facing forward signals "hold or stay." Learning these "Q" signs will help you communicate with all students, especially those who may be hearing impaired.

MUSIC

Selecting music that both inspires students and keeps them moving at an appropriate rate is another creative opportunity for the aerobics instructor. Great music selections make the class exciting. Unfortunately, it doesn't matter how skilled an instructor is if the music does not motivate students to move.

Tempo. Tempo (or rate) at which music is performed is measured in beats per minute (bpm). The tempo of the music used needs to be appropriate to the level of work required during each phase of class. The following are useful guidelines:

Phase/Type of Class	bpm
Warm-up: Floor and step	110–140
Peak workout: Floor only	140–160
Peak workout: Step only	118–124
Peak workout: High impact	144–160
Toning and conditioning	110–130
Flexibility enhancement	100 or less
Relaxation	100 or less

It is wiser to increase intensity by using benches or arm movements rather than by increasing the speed of the music. Music that is too fast may lead students to lose control of their form and their movements.

Movement Groups. Music used in aerobics classes is almost always written in 4/4 meter—four beats to the measure, with the quarter note constituting one beat. In the aerobics world, a phrase of music is almost always 32 beats (or eight measures) long. Usually each phrase is divided into four different movements, each lasting eight counts (or two measures). This makes it easy to match the movements to the music. For example, have the class walk forward for eight counts, moving on the beat, backward for eight counts, slide right for eight counts, and slide left for eight counts, for a total of 32 beats.

Other Considerations. We favor the use of professionally produced CDs that usually have an aerobic side and a toning side, each lasting 45 minutes. There are several music services that provide complete CDs for all segments of an aerobics class. These CDs, available for approximately $20 to $30, give you an accurate bpm count, keep you in step with current music, and save the considerable time it takes to select and mix your own music. By subscribing to a service, you can choose among pop, rock, techno, Motown, funk, 50s, 60s, hip-hop, Latin, and country music, all recorded in aerobic or step format. Having a selection of CDs also provides an easy way to set a theme for the class and to vary themes from class to class.

If you produce your own CDs (or use student-produced CDs), you should preview them carefully. Popular tunes may have offensive lyrics that are not appropriate in a school setting.

Finally, if you use a wireless headset (as we recommend), be sure that the music and your voice are amplified separately. This allows you to keep the music volume up and your voice volume down.

Aerobic Dance Elements

BASE MOVES FOR LOW- AND HIGH-IMPACT DANCE, STEP, RESISTANCE, AND FLEXIBILITY

The footwork patterns known as "base moves" form the choreographic foundation of any aerobic dance class. In low-impact movement, you always have one foot on the floor and you don't do any jumping or hopping. High impact is at a slower pace but involves jumping and hopping. Successfully teaching each individual pattern, then creatively sequencing the base moves, and finally adding other movements to them are some of aerobics' most creative dimensions. Use the guidelines here for selecting and teaching base moves. This will provide a head start in creating a dynamic class that students will find fun and easy to follow.

> **Learning Hints: High Impact**

1. Give students ample time to grasp any base move.
2. Visually determine that most students can perform the move being taught before changing directions or going on to a new movement.
3. Teach the foot movements before adding any arm movements.
4. Be selective. Do not try to put everything you know in any one class. An effective class can be built with four combinations.
5. When beginners and advanced students are in the same class, have the beginners concentrate on the foot movements. Beginners need to master the foot moves before adding the arms.
6. Advanced students may increase the intensity of their work by using higher benches, by using a greater variety of arm movements, or by adding propulsion moves.
7. Vary the level of arm movements to prevent injury to the shoulder girdle. Keep students moving their arms from low to medium to high positions.

BASE MOVES—LOW- AND HIGH-IMPACT DANCE

MARCH/WALK/STEP:

Action: Transfer weight, one foot to the other, without losing contact with the floor.

JOG/RUN:

Action: Transfer weight, one foot to the other; momentary loss of contact with the floor.

STEP TOUCH:

Action: Step right foot to right side; tap ball of left foot next to right foot.

Tip: Weight is not on tapping foot so the foot may be used again.

HAMSTRING CURL:

Action: Step right foot to right side; lift and bend the left leg (heel toward buttocks).

KNEE LIFT:

Action: Step right foot to right side; bend left knee while lifting knee up (perform to front, back, or side).

Tip: Say, "step, knee up; step, knee up."

TAPS (HEEL TAPS, TOE TAPS, SIDE TAPS):

Action: Step right foot to right side; touch left heel in front (do not transfer weight). Step left foot to left side; touch right heel in front (do not transfer weight).

Tip: To get back on the beat, tap both toes (or heels) of both feet.

LUNGES:

> **Action:** Step right foot to right side; extend left leg backward (right leg bends at knee).
>
> **Tip:** As used in aerobic dance, feet are parallel.

SLIDES:

> **Action:** Right foot brushes floor (front, side, or back); momentary loss of contact with the floor as left replaces right.
>
> **Tip:** Uneven rhythm, "long, short."

HOPS:

> **Action:** Lift weight off one foot and land on the same foot.

JUMPS:

> **Action:** Take off on two feet and land on two feet. Momentary or sustained loss of contact with the floor.

JUMPING JACK:

> **Action:** Start feet together, spring up, land feet opening to a straddle position; spring up, landing feet together.

HEEL JACK:

> **Action:** Jump with feet together: jump, extending left heel to left side (left heel should touch floor); jump, landing both feet together. Repeat to other side.
>
> **Tip:** Because weight is even on both feet, this step may alternate or repeat on the same side.

LEAPS:

> **Action:** An aerial movement from one foot to the other; sustained loss of contact with the floor.

KICKS:

> **Action:** Step right foot to right side; extend left leg forward (front kicks).
>
> **Tip:** For a flex kick, bend and then quickly extend the working leg (used in Charleston basic and kick ball-change). For a high kick, move the working leg from the hip. Do not bend the knee.

DANCE MOVES

Aerobics uses movements from the entire dance vocabulary—jazz, ballet, disco, funk, hip-hop, and Latin. Because most of aerobic dance is cued while the students are moving, short phrases are used to identify steps. In the list here are terms generally used in aerobic dance.

GRAPEVINE:

> **Action:** Step right to right, cross left behind, step right to right, touch left next to right.
>
> **Tip:** May end with a jump, both feet together (weight even on both feet). Move can be repeated to same side.
>
> **Cue:** Step, behind, step, touch.

MAMBO:

> **Action:** Step forward right, step in place left, step back on right, step in place left.
>
> **Tip:** This is a rocking step. To alternate leads take three quick steps in place.
>
> **Variation:** Latin-style step on bent knee, smoothly shifting hips.

CHARLESTON:

> **Action:** Step forward with right leg, flex kick or swing left leg forward, step in place with left leg, touch right foot straight back (no weight).
>
> **Tip:** As used in aerobics, do not pivot on balls of feet for each count.

KICK BALL-CHANGE:

> **Action:** Kick right leg forward, step (weight) on ball of right foot (behind left), step left foot in place.
>
> **Rhythm:** Slow, quick, quick.
>
> **Tip:** Use ball of foot with heel lifted; no time to put whole foot down.

JAZZ SQUARE, BOX STEP:

> **Action:** Cross right in front of left, step back on left, step right to right side, touch left next to right in front of right.
>
> **Tip:** Bend knees especially on first step. Difficult step for beginners.

CHA CHA CHA:

> **Action:** (Three small steps in place) Step right in place, step left in place, step right in place. As used in aerobics, not to be confused with the basic ballroom dance step.
>
> **Tip:** Clap three times and say "cha, cha, cha" to help students with rhythm.

PONY:

> **Action:** (Three small steps in place) Step right in place, step left slightly behind right, step right in place.
>
> **Tip:** Variation: Close left beside right or cross left in front of right.

PIVOT TURN:

> **Action:** (As used in aerobics) Step forward right, then turn 180 degrees toward left to face the rear. Step forward right, then turn 180 degrees toward left to face front.
>
> **Tip:** During the turn, make sure your weight is evenly distributed on both feet.

Step

Step aerobics incorporates benches ranging in height from 4 to 10 inches. Step work increases the intensity of any aerobic dance class, as well as expanding the choreographic possibilities. Using step benches is usually fun for both teachers and students. Step benches or platforms are easily incorporated in aerobic dance, circuit training, interval training, and muscular conditioning classes. By giving conditioned athletes higher steps and having beginners work either without a bench or on a low one, students with all levels of skill can be appropriately challenged in the same class.

Warming up is usually done without actually stepping up onto the bench, although the bench can be used as a prop for stretching or calisthenics. Be sure students are thoroughly warmed up and stretched before beginning the step workout.

▶ Learning Hints: Step

1. Be sure students place the whole foot on the step.

2. Students should step softly to avoid unnecessary stress.

3. Students' knees should be slightly bent at all times when stepping up or down.

4. Give students ample time to grasp any base move.

5. Visually determine that most students can perform the move you are teaching before changing directions or going on to a new movement.

6. Teach the foot movements before you add any arm movements.

7. Be selective. Do not try to put everything you know in any one class. An effective class can be built with four combinations.

8. When beginners and advanced students are in the same class, have the beginners concentrate on the foot movements. Beginners need to master the foot moves before adding the arms.

9. Advanced students may increase the intensity of their work by using higher benches, by using a greater variety of arm movements, or by adding propulsion moves.

10. Vary the level of arm movements to prevent injury to the shoulder girdle. Keep students moving their arms from low to medium to high positions.

BASE MOVES—STEP

BASIC STEP:
Position: Start at 6 o'clock.

Action: Right foot up; left foot up; right foot down; left foot down. Cued: "up," "up," "down," "down."

V-STEP:
Position: Start at 6 o'clock and step toward 3 o'clock.

Action: Right foot up wide position; left foot up wide position; right foot down center; left foot down center.

A-STEP:
Position: Face bench and approach from left end (7 o'clock).

Action: Right foot up center; left foot up center; right foot down right end; left foot down right end.

L-STEP:
Position: Face bench and approach from right end (5 o'clock).

Action: Right foot up; left foot up; right foot down (moving sideways off right end 3 o'clock); left foot down tap; left foot up (moving sideways to top); right foot up; left foot down; right foot down tap.

TURN STEP:
Position: Start at 6 o'clock.

Action: Step up onto the bench with a basic step, but as you step down make a quarter turn, ending at 7 o'clock.

UP TAP DOWN TAP:
Position: Start at 6 o'clock and face 12 o'clock.

Action: Right foot up; left foot up tap; left down; right tap.

Cue: "up," "tap," "down," "tap."

KNEE UP:
Position: Start at 6 o'clock and face 12 o'clock.

Action: Right foot up; left knee up; left foot down; right foot down. Reverse. For variety, instead of knee up use hamstring curl, side leg lifts, forward kick, or back kick.

OVER THE TOP:
Position: Start at 6 o'clock and face 9 o'clock.

Action: The footwork is the same as your basic step, but you are moving over the top with your right shoulder toward the long side of the bench.

REPEATER:
Position: Start at 6 o'clock.

Action: A movement that is repeated. For example, right foot up; left knee up three times; left foot down; right foot down.

STRADDLE DOWN:
Position: Stand on top of the bench facing 9 o'clock.

Action: Right foot down (straddling bench); left foot down; right foot up; left foot up.

See Figure 3-2 for the key directional approaches for step.

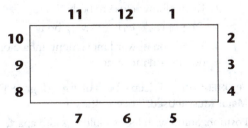

Figure 3-2 Key directional approaches for step.

Resistance

Resistance training is usually part of the aerobic or step training class. Toning exercises can improve muscular endurance and muscular strength and are essential to keeping the body looking taut and fit. While the aerobic portion of class burns fat, resistance training gives the body shape and definition.

Pushing, pulling, or lifting a body part or weight are forms of resistance work. Resistance may be increased in a variety of ways. In the aerobics classroom, this is typically done by adding light weights, resistance tubing, performing the movements more slowly, or using a more difficult body position.

▶ Learning Hints: Resistance

1. It is important to communicate proper body alignment and technique to the student.

2. Always work the large muscle groups before working the smaller muscle groups.

3. Movements should be slow and controlled.

4. Be sure that opposing muscle groups are worked. For example, if one works the gastrocnemius, the tibialis anterior also needs to be worked. They do not need to be in exact sequence but do need to be given equal time.

5. Students should never hold the breath. The exhalation should occur as the muscle is contracted, the inhalation during extension or relaxation.

6. Students should work through the full range of motion, being careful not to hyperextend or lock joints.

7. Always follow resistance training with stretching.

BASE MOVES—RESISTANCE

BICEP CURLS: Biceps—front of arms (Figure 3-3)
Major Muscle Used: Biceps Brachii

Position: Stand with legs shoulder-width apart and arms extended at your side.

Action: Bend the arms at the elbows until the hands come near your shoulders. Return to starting position.

Tips: 1. Keep upper arms stationary; move lower arms only.

    2. Keep elbows close to body.

    3. Do not rock, jerk, or swing body.

    4. Exhale on upward movement, inhale on downward movement.

TRICEP EXTENSION: Tricep—back of arms (Figure 3-4)
Major Muscle Used: Triceps Brachii

Position: Stand with legs shoulder-width apart, knees bent, and one arm extending overhead.

Figure 3-3 Bicep curl: Tubing or free weights.

Figure 3-4 Tricep extension: Tubing or free weights.

Action: Bend the arm at the elbow and lower toward the upper back. Return to starting position. Support the arm with the opposite hand. Hold near the tricep in front of the chest.

Tip: Keep your working arm close to your ear.

FRONT RAISE: Shoulders (Figure 3-5)
Major Muscle Used: Anterior Deltoid

Position: Arms extended downward in front of body.

Action: Raise extended arms up to shoulder level and lower to starting position.

Tip: Do not lock elbow joints or raise arms above shoulders.

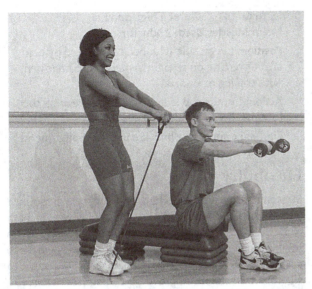

Figure 3-5 Front raise: Tubing or free weights.

Figure 3-6 Chest press: Free weights or tubing.

UPRIGHT ROWS: Shoulders and Upper Back
Major Muscles Used: Deltoid, Trapezius

Position: Stand with feet shoulder-width apart and knees slightly bent. Arms extended downward in front of body.

Action: Pull the hands upward until they reach the chin, elbows extending away from body.

Tips: 1. Keep your hands close together and near your body.

    2. Elbows higher than wrist at the top of the exercise.

CHEST PRESS: Chest (Figure 3-6)
Major Muscle Used: Pectoralis Major

Position: Stand with your feet shoulder-width apart. Elbows extended to sides with forearms pointed upward (elbows bent 90 degrees).

Action: Press the arms together in front of the body. Return to starting position.

Tip: Keep the upper arms lower than the shoulders.

Variation: Point the forearms forward and extend arms forward from chest position (effective with tubing).

PUSH-UPS: Chest and Arms
Major Muscles Used: Triceps Brachii, Pectoralis Major

Position: Begin in the push-up position with hands on the floor, slightly wider than shoulder width, fingers facing forward. Legs are extended backward with weight resting on toes. To modify, rest weight on knees.

Action: Bend elbows to approximately 90 degrees. Then straighten elbows and return to starting position.

Tip: Keep the back straight; do not lock elbows at the top of the exercise.

REGULAR CRUNCH: Abdominals
Major Muscles Used: Rectus Abdominis, Internal and External Obliques

Position: Lie flat on the back with knees bent, feet flat on the floor and shoulder-width apart. Hands may be at sides, across the chest, or placed behind the head for support.

Action: Lift the upper body off the floor while pressing the lower back into the floor. Lower back down to starting position.

Tip: Focus eyes up toward ceiling; lift and curl naturally with the body and neck. Gently press head backward into hands to keep neck in neutral position.

TWISTING CRUNCH: Abdominals and Obliques
Major Muscles Used: Rectus Abdominis, Internal and External Obliques

Position: Assume same position as regular crunch.

Action: Twist and lift the torso to one side as the back is lifted off the floor.

Tip: If hands are placed behind the head, leave one elbow on or near the floor when twisting and lifting with the opposite side of the body.

SQUAT: Buttocks and Thighs (Figure 3-7)
Major Muscles Used: Quadriceps, Hamstrings, Gluteus Maximus

Position: Stand with feet shoulder-width apart, knees slightly bent.

Action: Lower the buttocks to about 90 degrees. Sit backward as though trying to sit on a chair. Keep head and eyes forward.

Tip: Do not round your back.

Figure 3-7 Squat: Arms only or free weights.

4-COUNT LUNGE: Thighs and Buttocks (Figure 3-8)

Major Muscles Used: Quadriceps, Hamstrings, Gluteus Maximus

Position: Head up, eyes forward. Stand with feet together.

Action: Step forward with right foot; left heel should be lifted. Lower left knee toward floor (bending both knees); slowly extend legs. Push off using right foot to starting position. Reverse to left.

Tips: 1. Keep the knee and ankle of forward stepping foot in alignment.

2. Keep back and neck straight.

3. All movement should be slow and controlled.

INNER THIGH LIFT: Inner Thigh and Hips

Major Muscle Used: Abductors

Position: Lie on side with head supported by bent arm or resting on straight arm. Bring top leg over extended bottom leg and relax top knee to floor.

Action: Lift and lower extended leg.

Tip: Do not lower working leg completely to floor.

Figure 3-8   Four-count lunge: Free weights or arms only.

OUTER THIGH LIFT: Outer Thigh and Hip

Major Muscles Used: Abductors

Position: Lie on side with head supported by bent arm or resting on straight arm. Bottom knee bent with top leg extended.

Action: Lift the top leg up and down, keeping the foot parallel to the floor.

Tip: Make sure your hips are in proper alignment.

Flexibility

Stretch Strategy.   Stretching exercises are performed during both the warm-up and the cool-down. In both phases, static stretching is recommended. Warm-up stretches are generally done standing up and are held for 10 to 30 seconds. Warm-up stretches help reduce resistance to vigorous movement, improve psychological readiness to workout, as well as improve the muscle's ability to extend.

Final stretches, performed to maintain or increase flexibility, are held for 30 to 60 seconds. The final stretching is generally easier because the body is warm and the joints are well lubricated. Many of the final stretches are done on the floor and emphasize an increased range of motion. Students should be encouraged to concentrate and relax during each stretch. All major muscle groups should be included—arms, shoulders, chest, back, hips, thighs, and calves; where applicable, the opposite side muscles should be stretched as well. Teachers need to be particularly vigilant about form during final stretching.

▶ Learning Hints: Stretching

1. Avoid partner stretching; it can be dangerous unless performed by a skilled person.

2. Floor stretches are best done on warm, dry surfaces.

3. Breathing is important. Full, deep breathing promotes mental and physical relaxation and helps to slow the heart rate and lower blood pressure.

4. Muscles should be stretched only to a point of tension, not to a point of pain.

UPPER BODY STRETCH MOVES

Upper Body Neck Isolations: Head Turn, Chin to Chest, Head Tilts

Major Muscles Stretched: Trapezius, Sternocleidomastoid

Position: Standing erect, shoulders down, looking forward.

HEAD TURN:

Action: Turn head to right (focus eyes); return to center; turn head to left; return to center.

CHIN TO CHEST:

Action: Slowly lower chin toward chest; hold; return to erect position.

HEAD TILT:

ACTION: Tilt head, right ear toward right shoulder; return to center; tilt head to left shoulder; return to center.

TIPS: 1. Do not "look up" or "break" neck to the back.

2. Do not do neck circles. They may damage the cervical vertebrae.

SHOULDERS:

Major Muscles Stretched: Middle Deltoid, Posterior Deltoid

Position: Standing erect, looking forward.

Action: 1. Shrug shoulders, lower shoulders

2. Shoulder circles backward

    a. Shoulder only

    b. Bend elbow, circling backward

    c. Whole arm circles backward as backstroke in swimming

3. Shoulder circles forward

    a. Shoulder only forward

    b. Bend elbow, circling forward

    c. Whole arm circles forward as freestyle in swimming

ACROSS BODY:

Major Muscles Stretched: Middle Deltoid, Posterior Deltoid, Latissimus Dorsi

Position: Standing erect, with feet in straddle position.

Action: Gently bring left arm across body. Hold and support with right arm. Slowly reverse and repeat.

Tips: 1. Keep the arm close to body, shoulders level. Do not lift arm above chest.

2. Do not hold at elbow or wrist joint. Support above or below.

TRICEP STRETCH BEHIND THE HEAD:

Major Muscle Stretched: Triceps Brachii

Position: Standing erect, with feet in straddle position.

Action: Extend left arm over head. Bend the arm at the elbow and lower toward upper back. Hold left elbow with right hand; press head back slightly to intensify stretch.

Tips: 1. Keep spine long, abdominals pulled in.

2. Do not hold the elbow joint. This may cause undue stress to the joint.

CHEST STRETCH:

Major Muscles Stretched: Pectoralis Major, Anterior Deltoid

Position: Standing erect, feet parallel and directly under hips, knees slightly flexed, and hands clasped behind back.

Action: Clasping hands behind back, pull shoulder blades together to stretch chest.

Tips: 1. Keep abdominals lifted.

2. Keep lower back in rounded position.

UPPER BACK:

Major Muscles Stretched: Rhomboids, Erector Spinae, Trapezius

Position: Feet in straddle position, hands clasped low in front of body, palms facing floor.

Action: Slowly raise clasped hands to front of body (parallel floor) and press palms forward.

Tip: Keep pelvis tipped forward, abdominals tight.

LATERAL:

Major Muscles Stretched: Latissimus Dorsi, Triceps Brachii

Position: Stand with feet shoulder-width apart, feet rotated outward (at 10 o'clock and 2 o'clock); arms reaching toward ceiling; shoulders pressing down.

Action: Looking up at lifted hands, bend right knee, right hand stretching up; hold position. Keeping right hand at that high level, stretch left hand up to meet this level, bending left knee; hold position.

Tip: Keep abdominals lifted, spine long. Keep straight leg rotated outward also.

STANDING CAT BACK:

Major Muscle Stretched: Erector Spinae

Position: Feet in a straddle position, with hands resting on thighs.

Action: Round the back and lift the abdominal muscles. Exhale as the back is rounded.

Tips: 1. Arms may give active support to increase "cat back."

2. May be done in hands-and-knees position on floor.

LOWER BODY STRETCH MOVES

HAMSTRINGS:

Major Muscles Stretched: Hamstrings, Gastrocnemius, Soleus

Position: Standing, with feet shoulder-width apart.

Action: Extend right leg forward; left leg should be bent and right foot should be flexed with heel on floor. Place both hands on left thigh.

Tips: 1. Always place hands on the bent support leg.

2. Keep abdominals tight to avoid low back strain.

STANDING QUADRICEPS:

Major Muscles Stretched: Quadriceps, Iliopsoas

Position: Face wall, left hand on wall for support. Standing on left foot, bend lower right leg behind body. Hold the right foot with the right hand.

Action: Slowly push right foot toward hand and hold.

Tips: 1. Maintain abdominal support and upright posture.

2. Do not compact the knee.

3. May be done lying down on side, arm fully extended on the floor.

4. Support leg should be bent. Avoid hyperextending the leg.

CALF STRETCH:

Major Muscles Stretched: Gastrocnemius, Soleus, Achilles Tendon

Position: Stand with feet together.

Action: Lift right foot and extend right leg backward, slowly pressing right heel toward floor. Left leg should be bent.

Tips: 1. Hands can be placed on the bent support leg.

2. Keep heels of both feet in contact with floor.

3. The knee and ankle of the forward leg should be vertically aligned.

INNER THIGH/OUTER THIGH:

Major Muscles Stretched: Adductors, Abductors

Position: Stand in a wide straddle position with feet parallel. Place hands on floor beneath shoulders.

Action: Lean forward, shifting weight to hands. Straighten right leg as you bend left knee. Reverse.

Tip: Do not bend knees more than 90 degrees.

TOE TAPS:

Major Muscles Stretched: Tibialis Anterior

Position: Feet parallel, one foot apart, knees bent.

Action: Tap toes slowly up and down.

Tips: 1. Both feet may be worked together or one at a time.

2. Deeper bend in the knees allows for greater stretch.

FLOOR STRETCHES

KNEE TO CHEST:

Major Muscles Stretched: Hamstrings, Gluteus Maximus

Position: Lying on back, knees bent, and feet flat on the floor.

Action: Slowly bring your right knee toward your chest. Place hands behind knee.

Tips: 1. Placing hands directly on knee can cause undue stress to knee joint.

2. Contract abdominals and press lower back to floor.

GLUTEAL STRETCH:

Major Muscles Stretched: Gluteus Maximus, Gluteus Medius, Gluteus Minumus, Hip Adductors

Position: Lying on back, with left leg bent and foot on floor, cross your right leg over and rest your ankle on your left knee.

Action: Slowly bring your left knee toward your chest and hold. Deepen stretch by using hands on back of left leg. Hold.

Tip: You can grasp your thigh when pulling your knee to chest.

HAMSTRING STRETCH:

Major Muscles Stretched: Hamstrings, Gluteus Maximus

Position: Lying on back, with knees bent and feet flat on the floor.

Action: Bring the right knee toward the chest and extend the lower leg up. Gently bring the leg closer to the chest and hold.

Tip: The knee of the extended leg should not be hyperextended.

INNER THIGH STRETCH:

Major Muscle Stretched: Adductors

Position: Lying on back, with both legs bent toward chest.

Action: Slowly extend legs overhead. Slowly open and slowly close legs.

Tip: End by returning knees to chest and placing feet on floor.

QUADRICEPS STRETCH:

Major Muscle Stretched: Quadriceps

Position: Lying on side, with head supported by bent arm or resting on straight arm. Both legs extended.

Action: Bend top right leg and grasp foot with right hand. Gently press foot into hand.

Tip: Do not let hips roll forward or backward.

LOW COBRA:

Major Muscles Stretched: Rectus Abdominis, Pectoralis Major

Position: Lying on floor in a prone position (face down). Hands placed beneath shoulders.

Action: Slowly press up, lifting your chest off the floor and arching your lower back.

Tips: 1. Keep hips and elbows on the floor and lower back relaxed.

2. Do not overarch lower back.

3. Do not extend elbows beyond 90 degrees.

CAT STRETCH:

Major Muscle Stretched: Erector Spinae

Position: On hands and knees.

Action: Drop the head, slowly tucking the chin toward the chest, as you curve the spine and contract the abdominal muscles. Hold this position. Return the back to a neutral position.

STANDING STRETCH ROUTINE

Head Tilts
Shoulder Shrugs
Shoulder Stretch (R)
Tricep Stretch (R)
Shoulder Stretch (L)
Tricep Stretch (L)
Chest Stretch (hands clasped behind back)
Upper Back Stretch (hands clasped, in front)
Standing Cat Back
Calf Stretch (R and L)
Quadriceps (R and L)
Hamstring (R and L)
Tibialis Anterior (R and L)
Toe Taps

FLOOR STRETCH ROUTINE

Knee to Chest Stretch (R)
Ankle Flexion and Extension (R)
Ankle Circles (R)
Hamstring Stretch (R)
Gluteal Stretch (right leg resting on left knee)
Knee to Chest Stretch (L)
Ankle Flexion and Extension (L)
Ankle Circles (L)
Hamstring Stretch (L)
Gluteal Stretch (left leg resting on right knee)
Inner Thigh Stretch

Circuit and Interval Training with Aerobic Dance

Circuit and interval training have been around for a long time but have only recently been incorporated into the aerobic dance class. In circuit training, a series of stations is set up and participants move from one station to the next with little or no rest between stations. Stations range in number, but the classic circuit has 9 to 12 stations. Whatever the number, exercises performed at each station are carefully selected and sequenced. Typically, each participant will perform a 15- to 45-second workout of 8 to 20 repetitions. Stations may incorporate exercise machines, handheld weights, calisthenics, resistance bands, or any equipment combination. When a 30-second to 3-minute aerobics station is included, you have aerobic circuit training. Although the research has not yet substantiated the improvement of cardiorespiratory endurance through this type of training, it is enjoyable for both students and teachers. Aerobics stations may be inserted after any number of exercise stations.

Interval training alternates periods of intense work and rest. Typically a student may work at near maximal intensity for 3 minutes and then rest for 3 minutes. Theoretically, alternating work and relief may allow more cardiovascular work to be accomplished in any one training session. Interval training's effect on muscles may lead to more effective use of both fats and carbohydrates, as well as other positive changes in the muscles' blood-carrying capacity and enzyme activity.

It is a good idea to strive for a balance between both of these methods. When used in combination, interval and circuit training have many benefits, including:

- Increased variety and more enjoyment by participants
- The potential for more work in less time
- Improvement in aerobic and anaerobic capacity
- Increased exercise adherence
- Enhanced sports performance

On a practical level, the following approach works well in the aerobics classroom. Alternate cardiovascular and strength stations. One or two exercises may be performed at each station. Students will exercise for 30 to 60 seconds, then rest for 10 to 15 seconds or use that time to move on to the next station. During peak intensity, use music with 120 bpm. Follow the guidelines for appropriate warm-up and cool-down tempos (see Music section, this chapter). Be sure to completely demonstrate the exercise (or exercises) to be performed at each station before starting any activity. Assign students to stations, then begin your group warm-up.

Provide a sign for each station, naming the exercise(s) to be performed there, and any cautions that are appropriate; if you have access to laminating equipment, it is worthwhile to photocopy a picture of the exercise(s), glue it on, and then laminate the entire sign. Signs that are computer generated on 8½-by-11-inch sheets of paper work well. Students may benefit from having color-coded signs that indicate whether they are doing primarily strength or cardiovascular work.

Circuits are easily designed for any class situation. Carefully select the work that you want your students to do, look at the number of students in your class and the size of your room, and decide whether you need to have one or two exercises performed at each station. There must be at least one station for every student. If you have more students than total stations, it is necessary to set up another *complete* circuit. Having empty stations will not disrupt the flow of the class, but having more students than stations is not workable. For example, alternating seven strength stations with seven cardiovascular stations and having students move around the circuit twice will provide approximately 30 minutes of peak-intensity work. With a brief group warm-up, a group cool-down, abdominal work, and brief final stretching, a class can be completed in 45 minutes.

SAMPLE CIRCUIT

This 16-station circuit has proved popular with students. Either one or two complete circuits can be set up in a large classroom, accommodating anywhere from 16 to 32 students (Figure 3-9).

Equipment   (Figure 3-10)

    Resistance tubes or bands
    Hand weights
    Benches
    Stopwatch
    Music with 118–126 bpm

Warm-up. Have students form a circle, moving around the room. Walk, walk on toes, walk on heels, walk backward, easy jog, skip, gallop lead right, gallop lead left, slide, reverse slide direction.

Stations

1. Bench
2. Tricep extension with tube
3. Run
4. 4-count lunge
5. Bench

Circuit Design for 16 Stations

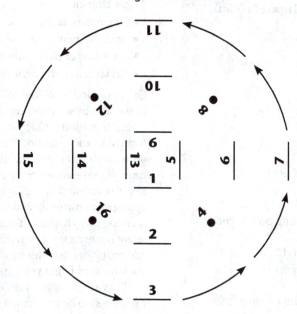

Circuit Design for 32 Stations

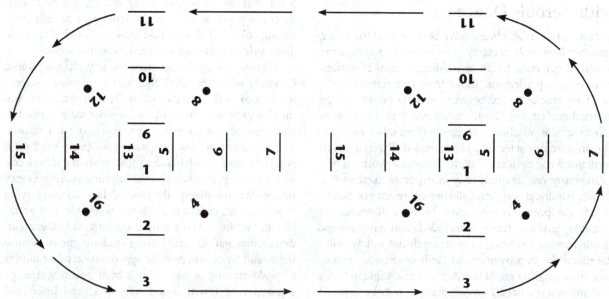

Figure 3-9 Circuit designs.

Figure 3-10 Cardio/resistance circuit.

6. Bicep curl with weights
7. Run
8. Squats
9. Bench
10. Chest press with tube
11. Run
12. 4-count lunge
13. Bench
14. Upright rows with weights
15. Run
16. Squats

When at the run stations (3, 7, 11, and 15), students should travel counterclockwise around the room.

Cardiovascular Cool-down.   Walk around the room.
Abdominal Workout
Final Stretching and Relaxation

Safety Considerations

Although aerobic dance is lively and engaging and provides a lot of fun, teachers also need to keep the safety of all participants uppermost in their minds. The vigilance does not need to show, but it does need to be present if class members are to avoid injury or harm. Here are some useful guidelines.

1. Screen all participants *before* they participate in class. They should obtain a medical history or pre-exercise health risk appraisal.
2. Monitor participants' movements closely while you are teaching. Face the class and teach by mirror image, especially if you do not have a mirror to look in when you turn your back to the class. Students have an easier time following when your back is to them, but these periods should be brief unless you can continue to monitor the entire class by watching their movements in a mirror as you lead. Watch for flailing arm movements and incorrect directional movement that may lead to collision. Also watch

for proper alignment: head up, shoulders back, chest up, buttocks tucked, and knees relaxed.
3. Keep potentially high-risk positions out of your class. These include sustained, unsupported forward flexion in a standing position (forward bends); trunk rotation against a fixed axis; or hyperextension of the neck, elbows, knees, or back. Other exercises to avoid include deep knee bends, the hurdler stretch, double leg raises, straight-leg sit-ups, and side leg lifts while on the knees and either hands or elbows.

Skill Assessment

The major contributions of aerobic dance from the five components of health-related fitness (Chapter 2) are flexibility and cardiorespiratory endurance. The aerobic dance routine consists of two stretch segments for approximately 15 minutes total and a peak aerobic session for 20 to 30 minutes in each individual's target heart rate zone (see Chapter 2 for maximal heart rate calculation).

The lone flexibility assessment suggested is the sit-and-reach test for the lower back-posterior thigh. The test consists of the use of a stretch box. The student sits on the floor with one leg extended so the bottom of the foot is flat against the box. The opposite leg is bent at the knee with the foot flat on the floor 2–3 inches to the side of the extended leg. With one hand on the top of the other, palms down, finger pads on fingernails, the arms are extended over the measurement scale. The student reaches forward, keeping the palms down, and slides the bottom palm forward along the scale on the top of the box four times, holding it for one second on the fourth slide. Repeat with the other side. The FITNESSGRAM has norms for ages 6 to 17.[1]

The aerobic cardiorespiratory test possibilities include the 1-mile walk/run, 20-meter shuttle run, or a walk test for secondary students with norms from the FITNESSGRAM.

ZUMBA ®

Nature and Purpose

Zumba Fitness® describes this program as "an exhilarating, effective, easy-to-follow, Latin-inspired calorie-burning dance fitness-party™."[2] It is basically an aerobic type class set to South American beats with dance elements. However, appeal is the simplicity that lets the students feel the music and does not involve complex cuing with complicated choreography. It provides the workout benefits of any cardiovascular workout.[3] There are eight types of classes involving various age levels and types of physiological targets. The program is known for "zesty Latin music...; the exhilarating, easy-to-follow moves; and the invigorating, party-like atmosphere."[4]

History

Albert "Beto" Perez, an aerobics instructor in Cali, Colombia, accidentally created a dance-fitness craze that today is one of the largest and fastest-growing programs in the world. In the mid-1990s he forgot the aerobic music for his class and quickly improvised by selecting some available salsa and meringue music from his personal collection. The mistake instantly was a hit and focused on "letting the music move you,"[5] replacing the repetitive counting to music as in aerobics.

He brought the class to the United States and in 2001 created a global company with Alberto Perlman and Alberto Aghion centered on a fitness philosophy. They immediately sought a trademark for the word Zumba®. Through infomercial marketing they established a great demand for their videos and the need for qualified instructors. An early target (2003 and 2004) was the Hispanic community. This successful venture led to the development of an instructional academy involving the leadership of fitness experts, educational specialists, and professional choreographers. Additionally, they aligned with several leading national fitness associations and organizations. In 2007, the program expanded its international market. The growth currently consists of more than 12 million people in over 110,000 locations in more than 125 countries.[6]

The Classroom

Refer to the "Aerobic Dance" section of this chapter. Many of the same suggestions apply.

Equipment

SHOES

Footwear is important for the workout, as it is in any type of aerobic floor exercise. A quick review of the shoe section in this chapter provides adequate information. There are shoes specifically designed for Zumba®, and the References and Further References at the end of the book as well as the Resources and Web Sites at the end of this chapter provide contact sources for more information.

APPAREL

A review of the sources previously identified for shoes also provides examples of authentic attire. It is not necessary to wear that specific attire but does add authenticity to the Latin American experience. Cargo and Capri pants are a custom, as well as short leggings and loose-fitting shorts. Loose-fitting baseball-type long sleeve shirts are regularly seen, as well as muscle-type T-shirts for men. Women's upper wear varies from tight to loose-fitting dependent on preference. The main thing is that both are not restrictive of movement.

ACCESSORIES

A lot of equipment is not necessary for Zumba®. There are DVDs and music selections that can be purchased. Toning sticks, similar to low-weight dumbbells, can be used for upper body toning and strengthening. There are video games available for additional variety and fun.

Benefits

Resources indicate a rather long list of observed benefits from participation in Zumba® classes. Some are a direct benefit from any cardiovascular workout, some from rhythmic dance participation, and some from the lively atmosphere and socialization of the activity.

- Increases aerobic threshold
- Lowers blood pressure
- Burns calories
- Lowers body fat
- Boosts metabolism
- Increases bone density
- Interval training workouts (aerobic/anaerobic)
- Increases muscle tone
- Increases muscle strength training targets (arms, abs, gluts, thighs)
- Increases core strength
- Improves muscle tone and body shaping
- Improves balance
- Increases agility
- Improves mobility
- Enhances rhythm
- Improves posture
- Enhances coordination
- Frees inhibitions
- Increases focus
- Provides more stamina

Zumba® Dance Elements

It is a party-like atmosphere consisting of Latin rhythms with easy-to-follow moves. It involves dance and aerobic elements. There is uncomplicated choreography using just four or five steps, which one keeps repeating during a given song.[7] The movement and music include fast and slow rhythms and at times uses resistance training. The elementary level involves steps to four basic rhythms—Meringue, Salsa, Cumbia, and Reggaeton.[8] The class sessions are around one hour in length consisting of approximately 70 percent Latin/International music and 30 percent other more current varieties.[9] Individual instructors at times include additional dance styles such as Mambo, Samba, Flamenco, Soca, Chachacha, hip-hop, Tango, belly dancing, and so on.

The dance steps, body movement, and instructional prompts are available for viewing on the Web. Inclusive sites are listed at the end of this chapter. The variety of music, steps, and workouts are too inclusive for this chapter length format. Visit **www.zumba.com** for more information and to learn how one becomes a licensed instructor.

Following is a brief description of six basic rhythms[10] plus a brief review of the eight varieties of Zumba® classes.[11]

BASIC RHYTHMS

Meringue. It is a faster-paced rhythm said to have originated in the Dominican Republic with suggested ties to Santo Domingo and Haiti. The "basic march" is the most common move.

Salsa. It, too, has a faster tempo with a distinct beat. The salsa has Cuban flavor with a blend of the Caribbean.

Cumbia. Colombia, South America, is cited for the rhythm; however, it has international influences from Europe and Africa. The music is of tropical and Creole descent.

Reggaeton. The reggae style is associated with Jamaica, Panama, and Puerto Rico rhythm and beat. The favored move is the hit known as "Crumping."

Flamenco. It has international influence associated with rhythms from southern Spain and from several other cultures. Upper body movement is strongly involved accompanied with sounds such as clapping, finger-snapping, and so on. Flare and "tude" are projected.

Samba. The Brazilian connection of hip moves danced in a festive atmosphere and mood makes it a popular addition to the workouts.[12]

Additional music and moves can complement the workout at the pleasure of the instructor. Examples might be the Tango, Chachacha, and Rumba presented in the "Dance" chapter of this *Handbook*. One can see the similar historical roots and basic movements that make them a valuable addition to the workouts. Also, hip-hop is presented in the chapter and is an example of other varieties that can make up the 30 percent non-Latin/International music often found in a session.

CLASS VARIETIES

The popularity and excitement of Zumba® leads to a party-like atmosphere of dance-fitness fun. This is the basis found in the variety of targets and program approaches.

Fitness. The original philosophy is targeted with a party-like atmosphere of fitness and fun involving exciting Latin/International beats and dance moves.

Baby Boomers. The program is for older adults with modifications of the moves/pacing and for those just starting a healthy fitness lifestyle. The original music and party atmosphere are incorporated.

Toning. Body sculpting is the target with exercises using toning sticks and exciting Latin Zumba® moves for cardio workout and party atmosphere; and both lead to high-calorie expenditure and strength training targets of the abdominals, gluteus maximus, arms, and thighs.

Aqua. The program combines the aqua fitness workout with the Zumba® philosophy and formula. It leads to toning and a cardio workout through the medium of water that adds challenging fun and safe participation.

Youth. It involves music, dance moves, and high-energy party atmosphere that kids like. The targets are youth ages 4–12, and it focuses on improvement of coordination, self-confidence, and increased metabolism.

Circuit. Sessions use the circuit training philosophy of time intervals of strength exercises integrated with the Zumba® philosophy of dance/fitness moves to Latin music. The results are a short, quick, timed workout that builds strength and boosts metabolism.

Baby Boomer Toning. It combines the two previous programs and original Zumba® dance/party atmosphere with a safe strength training program. The targets are increased bone density and muscle strength with improved coordination, posture, and mobility through light-weight resistance training. It is also applicable for beginners.

Chair Work. It combines the fitness/party with a chair-based choreography. The target is an increased cardio workout in a novel way to strengthen, balance, and stabilize the core. It uses body weight to tone and increase muscle strength while improving muscle definition and endurance.[13]

Visit **www.zumba.com** for complete and thorough information on the types of classes available and on their exact design.

Modifications for Special Populations

ORTHOPEDICALLY IMPAIRED

1. Students using a wheelchair may do a variation of dance movements using the upper body only.
2. Allow students who can push their wheelchairs to move forward, backward, or side to side to the beat of the music.

3. Students using crutches or walkers may be allowed to sit in a standard desk chair.

4. Students with a lower extremity amputation may be allowed to use the back of a standard desk chair for balance.

5. Students with ataxia should be allowed to move with more simple patterns, for example, step forward, step back.

COGNITIVELY IMPAIRED

1. Use key words during directions and not entire phases; for example, "Forward" instead of "Walk forward two beats, rock side to side, and now walk back." Keep your instructions short.

2. Use pictures whenever possible.

3. Allow students to follow at their own rate and pace.

SENSORY IMPAIRED

1. Students with visual impairments might need several physical prompts or "hand over hand" cues, for example, assisting with arm patterns.

2. Students with hearing impairments should be positioned closer to the instructor. You might ask the student with a hearing impairment to teach you specific sign language for the various movements of the dance.

Contact Disabled Sports USA for more information regarding individuals with amputations or other orthopedic conditions: www.dsusa.org. Contact the United States Association of Blind Athletes for more information regarding individuals with visual impairments: www.usaba.org.

Resources

PROFESSIONAL ORGANIZATIONS

Aerobic dance is influenced by factors ranging from shifts in popular taste to new research findings in specialized fields. Professional organizations monitor and evaluate changes and pass the information on to their members. To ensure teaching excellence, membership in one or more professional organizations is highly recommended. Professional organizations set standards of excellence for their members and offer certification programs for those willing to go through an often rigorous certification process. They also offer networking opportunities, workshops, and publications, and frequently sponsor research.

Aerobic and Fitness Association of America (AFAA), 15250 Ventura Blvd.F, Suite 200, Sherman Oaks, CA 91403-3297 www.afaa.com

American College of Sports Medicine, P.O. Box 1440, Indianapolis, IN 46206-1440 www.acsm.org

American Council on Exercise, 4851 Paramount Dr., San Diego, CA 92123 www.acefitness.org

American Aerobic Association International/ International Sports Medicine Association (AAAI/ ISMA), P.O. Box 633, New Hope, PA 18954 www.aaai-ismafitness.com

Aquatic Exercise Association, P.O. Box 497, Port Washington, WI 53074 www.aeawave.com

The Cooper Institute for Aerobic Research, 12330 Preston Rd., Dallas, TX 75230-2299 www.cooperinst.org

IDEA, The Health and Fitness Source, 10455 Pacific Center Ct., San Diego, CA 92121-4339 www.ideafit.com

VIDEOS

There are hundreds of aerobic dance videos. What is right for you and your class? Reviews in journals and magazines help sort the good from the bad, as do previews that some publishers will arrange for teachers in educational institutions (colleges and universities, especially). Another good guide is the Collage Video Specialties' *Complete Guide to Exercise Videos*, published quarterly. Hundreds of videos are reviewed in each issue.

The following questions help you evaluate any video. What are the qualifications of the presenter? How old is the video? Does it provide adequate time for all phases of an aerobics class? Is it appropriate for your group? Does it have heart rate and other safety checks, clear cueing, high motivational value?

Finally, if one learns a routine from a video and then teaches it in a class, one must credit to the class the expert who developed the routine.

MUSIC

It is highly recommended that one use professionally mixed CDs. The following are good sources, and most have 800 numbers. If you decide to mix your own music, remember music copyright laws. Contact the appropriate performing rights society for permission.

MUSIC SERVICES

Music Mixes, P.O. Box 533967, Orlando, FL 32853

Power Music, 560 W. 200 St., Suite 200, Salt Lake City, UT 84101 www.powermusic.com

Dynamix Music Service, 9411 Philadelphia Road, Baltimore, MD 21237 www.dynamixmusic.com

Serenity, 8016 Marion Dr., Maria Stein, OH 45860 www.serenitymusic.com

MUSIC PERFORMING RIGHTS SOCIETIES

ASCAP, 1 Lincoln Plaza, New York, NY 10023
www.ascap.com

BMI, 320 W. 57th St., New York, NY 10019
www.bmi.com

INSTRUCTOR PURCHASE PROGRAMS

Many leading suppliers of fitness footwear and clothing offer instructor discount programs. Contact the following for information about their programs:

Reebok Professional Instructor Alliance, P.O. Box 1245001, 60 North Ronks Rd., Ronks, PA 17572-9987

Nike Instructor Network Program, P.O. Box 4455, Beaverton, OR 97076-4455

Avia Select Instructor, P.O. Box 1823, Beaverton, OR 97075-1823 www.aviaselect.com

Adidas Three Stripe Instructions, P.O. Box 25384, Portland, OR 97298

Rykä Instructor Trainer Alliance, 10200 Swallen, Suite 1, Beaverton, OR 97005 www.rykarita.com

---

Terminology

aerobic Oxygen-using.

aerobic cool-down The period at the end of the aerobics segment of an exercise session in which intensity is reduced to begin lowering the heart rate.

aerobic dance-exercise A method of exercising to music that conditions the cardiovascular system by using movements that create an increased demand for oxygen over an extended time.

agonist A muscle that is directly responsible for the joint movement observed. Also referred to as a prime mover.

alignment The relationship of the body segments to one another. Proper alignment features balanced agonist and antagonist muscle pairs.

anaerobic Without oxygen.

antagonist A muscle that acts in opposition to the action produced by an agonist muscle.

atrophy Wasting of muscle size resulting from disuse.

ballistic stretching A stretch using rapid, bouncing movements. Contraindicated.

basic locomotor steps These are considered to be walking, running, hopping, and jumping.

beats A pattern of strong and weak pulsations that have an even rhythm.

cardiorespiratory fitness (CRF) Related to the capacity of the heart-lung system to deliver oxygen for sustained energy production, CRF is the ability to perform large muscle movement over a sustained period.

carotid pulse An arterial pulse point located in the neck about one inch below the jaw line, next to the esophagus.

concentric muscle action Contraction of muscle that causes the muscle to shorten.

contraindication Any condition that makes any movement, activity, or treatment undesirable.

cueing Hand or verbal signals that identify upcoming movement.

directional cueing A visual or verbal technique that signals the direction in which to move.

exercise intensity The specific level of physical activity at which a person exercises that can be quantified (e.g., heart rate, work, rate of perceived exertion) and is usually reflected as a percentage of one's maximal capacity to do work.

flexibility The possible range of motion around any joint.

footwork cueing A visual or verbal technique that signals which foot to move.

freestyle method Spontaneous choreography by an instructor.

muscular endurance The capacity of a muscle to exert repeated force.

muscular strength The maximum force that can be exerted by a muscle or muscle group.

numerical cueing A visual or verbal technique used by instructors to count the rhythm of the exercise.

rating of perceived exertion (RPE) A scale that correlates the participant's perception of exercise effort with the actual intensity level.

resting heart rate The number of heartbeats per minute after the body has been at complete rest for at least 10 minutes.

rhythm A regular pattern of movement or sound.

rhythmic cueing A visual or verbal technique that indicates the correct rhythm of an exercise or step.

slide aerobics A type of training program in which a lateral movement trainer is used to perform aerobic conditioning movements and exercises.

static stretching A long stretch that holds the desired muscle under tension without pain for at least 15 to 30 seconds.

step cueing A verbal technique that refers to the name of the step in an aerobics routine, such as "grapevine" or "step touch."

step workout A type of aerobic conditioning that incorporates a bench between 4 and 10 inches high.

talk test A method for measuring exercise intensity using observation of respiration effort and the ability to talk while exercising.

target heart rate The number of heartbeats per minute that indicates appropriate exercise intensity levels for each person. Also called training heart rate.

target heart-rate range The exercise intensity that represents the minimum and maximum intensity for safe and effective exercise. Also referred to as training zone.

tempo The rate of speed at which a musical composition is played.

warm-up The early phase of a workout or exercise session designed to ready the body for vigorous motion.

Discussion Questions

1. Identify the various benefits of regular participation in aerobic dance.

2. Discuss the underlying safety and movement elements in the structure of an effective class.

3. What are the differences between high-impact and low-impact movements?

4. Discuss the intensity variables that turn circuit training into interval training.

5. What designs and materials make circuit training more easily understood by the students?

6. Discuss various cueing concerns and how they affect smooth execution of dance steps by students.

7. Identify the various phases of a well-structured class and the suggested time limits for each.

8. What teaching aids might be used to enhance instruction?

Web Sites

AEROBIC DANCE

www.cooperinst.org The Cooper Institute for Aerobic Research—offers training and certification programs for fitness leaders and health professionals.

www.acefitness.org American Council on Exercise—leading provider of certification and education to the professional, commercial, and retail fitness markets.

www.afaa.com Aerobics and Fitness Association of America (AFAA)—offers training, certification, and fitness facts.

www.afpafitness.com American Fitness Professionals & Association—offers health and fitness professionals a variety of certification programs, continuing education courses, and regional conventions.

www.acsm.org American College of Sports Medicine—offers certification and continuing education.

www.ideafit.com IDEA, The Health & Fitness Source—contains information on employment offerings, IDEA events, membership benefits, and products.

www.turnstep.com Turnstep Choreography offers moves, choreography, and ideas, as well as listings of other Internet links.

www.nsca-cc.org National Strength and Conditioning Association (NSCA)—provides certification information.

ZUMBA®

www.zumba.com—A site for learning about the Zumba® program.

www.squidoo.com/100-zumba-workouts—Provides a "related tag" section with fast resources for workouts, routines, programs, videos, music, dress, etc.

CHAPTER 4 | # Archery

This chapter will enable you to

- Identify and demonstrate the 10 basic steps of shooting in target archery
- Identify and demonstrate terms related to the bow and arrow
- Understand the basic terminology associated with target archery
- Identify and describe the rules associated with target archery
- Identify and observe the necessary safety precautions
- Identify the various body movements that might cause faulty arrow flight

Nature and Purpose

Archery is an easy-to-learn activity, and it is possible for people of all ages to develop proficiency in archery skills in a relatively short period of time. As an individual sport, it is relatively inexpensive and can be practiced year-round. The benefits of archery are both physical and emotional.

History

The exact origin of archery is unknown, but the first stone arrowheads were discovered in Africa. This fact suggests that the bow and arrow may have been invented there, perhaps around 50,000 B.C. Pointed flint arrowheads attached to the tip of an arrow bound with feathers to the arrow shaft appeared around 25,000 B.C. Arrow shafts dating from approximately 9000 B.C. were discovered in Germany, and a bow unearthed in Denmark dates from approximately 8000 to 6000 B.C. This early archery equipment was first used for hunting and later became a weapon of war, beginning with the Egyptians around 5000 B.C.

The bow and arrow remained the principal weapon of war for many centuries until the musket was invented in A.D. 1520. Archery soon thereafter became a sport. Henry VIII of England fostered the creation of several archery organizations, and, as a result, archery became a competitive sport. The first published book on archery, *Toxophilis* ("Lover of the Bow"), was written in England by Roger Ascham in 1545. A small group of archers created the Ancient Scorton Arrow contest in England in 1673. Still conducted, this is the oldest continuous archery tournament in existence.

In 1828 the United Bowmen of Philadelphia founded the first and oldest U.S. archery organization, which is still in existence. The National Association of Archery, which later became the National Archery Association, sponsored the first archery tournament in Chicago in 1879. It has continued to sponsor an annual tournament ever since, suspending the event only in war years. In 1971, the National Archery Association formed its College Division to promote archery in colleges and universities. The organization hosts a national tournament annually.

The Olympics initiated archery as an international competition in 1900 (for men), 1904 (for women), 1908 (for both), and again in 1920 (for both). Thereafter archery was discontinued as an Olympic sport until 1972, when it reappeared on the Olympic program, with both genders competing. In 1988, an archery team event was added to the Olympics. The Federation for International Target Archery (FITA), formed in 1931, is the organization responsible for the establishment of archery rules, standards, and meets.[1]

Rules of Target Archery

1. Any bow except a crossbow may be used for competition.
2. Arrows should have a distinctive crest to distinguish each archer's arrow.
3. After the signal to shoot, arrows should be nocked.
4. Arrows that fall from the bow and cannot be reached with the bow from the shooting line are considered to be shot.
5. Only six arrows may be shot at the designated target; if more than six are shot, only the lowest six scores are counted, and any arrow(s) shot at any other target shall not be scored.

6. An archer should shoot from the longest distance first, the second longest distance next, and soforth.

7. Scores are recorded from the highest score to the lowest score.

8. Arrows should be retrieved only after the signal to do so is given.

Scoring

There are five sequential circles of gold, red, blue, black, and white. Each has two equal zones. Sequentially from the gold center circle, the scores awarded are 10, 9, 8, 7, 6, 5, 4, 3, 2, and 1. An arrow that goes completely through the target or that bounces off the target counts 7 points regardless of the part of the target it passes or hits. An arrow that lands on the line between two rings counts as hitting the higher scoring ring. All target archery rounds (competitions) are shot at a regulation 48-inch target face unless otherwise specified.

For physical education classes, a modified institutional round should be implemented to enable a round to be completed within a given time period. For example, the Ball State Round consists of 12 ends: 4 ends each shooting from 20 yards, 25 yards, and 30 yards, and requiring approximately 60 minutes to complete. Each end consists of shooting five arrows. The scoring values of the Ball State Round are 5 points for gold, 4 points for red, 3 for blue, 2 for black, and 1 for white. This gives a maximum total of 300 points (5 arrows × 5 points × 12 ends = 300 points). If a class period is only 45 minutes, a round should consist of 8 ends: 4 ends from 25 yards and 4 ends from 30 yards.

Equipment

Archery equipment as a whole is known as "tackle." The minimum essential tackle for the beginning archer includes (1) a bow of correct length and weight, (2) one dozen matched arrows, (3) a finger tab or glove, (4) an arm guard, and (5) a target. The selection of a proper bow and matched arrows is the most important step for successful archery practice.

BOWS

Bows are constructed of many materials, including wood, fiberglass, or laminated wood core and fiberglass. To overcome the disadvantages of the wooden or fiberglass bow, a laminated (composite) bow was designed. This bow is smooth-shooting and is not subject to changes as a result of weather. Bows are classified as straight, recurved, and compound. The recurved bow has tips that are curved forward. The compound bow consists of a pulley system at the tips connected by cables that positively affect the necessary drawing force. This bow has advanced balancing, weighting, and sighting systems, which increase the cost.

Bow weight refers to the weight in pounds required to bring a bow to full draw. The most important factor in determining bow weight is the individual archer's muscular strength. For the beginner, it is best to start with a bow that is easier to draw and handle rather than using "overbow." The bow weight may be gradually increased as the archer improves shooting technique and develops muscular strength. Table 4-1 shows the recommended bow weights according to the standards established by the Archery Manufacturers Organization.

ARROWS

Arrows are made of wood, fiberglass, or aluminum. The least expensive, wooden arrows, are used by most beginning archers; fiberglass and aluminum arrows are used by more advanced archers. Each type of arrow has its own advantages and disadvantages, but it is important that one select arrows closely matched in weight, length, and stiffness (spine).

A beginner should start to shoot with arrows that are 2 inches longer than the needed proper length in case of an overdraw. To determine the proper length, one should place the nock of the arrow on the center of one's chest and extend arms full length forward, palms facing, so that the point of the arrow extends past the fingertips. When purchasing a bow and arrows, one should seek advice from an expert to determine proper bow and arrows fit.

ARM GUARDS

Arm guards have two main functions: (1) to protect the bow arm from the slap of the bow string; (2) to keep a long sleeve close to the arm so it will not interfere with the bow string. The arm guard is worn on the inside of the forearm below the elbow, near the wrist of the bow arm. The arm guard is usually made of leather with elastic straps to hold the guard on the forearm.

FINGER TABS OR GLOVES

Friction between the fingers and the bow string can produce not only soreness to the fingers but also affect proper shooting. Tabs or gloves will protect the fingers and aid in developing a smooth and consistent release. Many beginners have difficulty using finger tabs or gloves but with a little patience and practice overcome this difficulty.

Table 4-1 **Recommended bow weights**

	Under 20 lb	20 lb	25 lb	30 lb	35 lb	40 lb	Over 40 lb
Children 6–12	X	X					
Teen (girl)		X	X				
Teen (boy)		X	X	X			
Women		X	X	X			
Men				X	X	X	
Hunting							X

TARGET

A target consists of a target face, a mat, and a stand. Ready-made targets can be purchased from a sporting goods dealer. Schools and colleges usually use a 48-inch target face. Target mats are easily made from tightly compressed hay and should measure at least 50 × 50 inches.

Suggested Learning Sequence

Open space with good lighting and a proper backdrop, well-organized lessons, and an emphasis on safety are all important aspects of creating a successful atmosphere for archery. Safety should be stressed from the beginning. Instructions should include the care of the equipment (bow, bowstring, and arrows) and the 10 essential steps for shooting described in this chapter. A good learning sequence is:

A. Introduction

B. Nature of the activity
   1. Archery as a sport and family recreation
   2. Discussion of equipment
   3. Safety

C. Skills and techniques—10 basic steps of shooting

   Static Stage: Practice without arrows
   1. Proper stance
   2. Nocking the arrow
   3. Setting the hook
   4. Holding the bow
   5. Raising the head
   6. Raising the unit

   Dynamic Stage: Practice with arrows
   7. Drawing and anchoring
   8. Aiming and holding
   9. Releasing
   10. Follow-through

   Participants should practice steps 7 and 8 several times before moving to steps 9 and 10.

   The first shooting practice should start from 15 yards, then 20 yards, 30 yards, and so on.

D. Rules and Scoring—Once they have achieved some proficiency in shooting technique, participants can be taught the rules governing target archery and the scoring method.

Skills and Techniques

STRING THE BOW

Push-pull Method

1. Take the bow handle in your left hand with the back of the bow toward you.
2. Holding the left arm in front of the body and angling the bow's upper limb toward the right, place the lower nock against the instep of the left foot, but not touching the ground.
3. Place the right hand on the upper limb just below the upper loop of the bowstring; then keeping both arms straight, pull with the left hand and push with the heel of the right hand, and slide the string into the upper nock with fingers. While stringing, keep your face away from the bow.

Step-through Method

1. Hold the bow in your right hand and the string with the left.
2. Place the back of the lower limb of the bow across the ankle of your left foot.
3. Step through the bow with your right leg.
4. Place the bow handle high on your right thigh.
5. Press the upper limb of the bow forward with the open right hand and slide the string in the nock with the left hand. Always check both notches for proper string insertion and alignment after each stringing.

SHOOTING: THE 10 BASIC STEPS

Archers should always follow the 10 basic steps of the shooting sequence in their proper order. Consistency is key to becoming a good archer. Repeating these 10 steps will help you develop rhythm in shooting and become a satisfied archer. The steps described are for the right-handed person; adjustments are required for left-handers.

Step 1—Establishing a Proper Stance. The stance establishes the foundation of good archery form; the square and open stances are the most commonly used. For both stances, the archer should spread both feet apart (approximately shoulder width) to achieve a comfortable feeling. The archer's weight should be equally distributed and the knees should be locked to maintain balance. Once you decide on a stance—either the square or open stance—you should take the same stance each time you shoot.

1. *Square Stance.* The square stance is recommended for beginning archers because it is natural, easy to establish, and easy to duplicate. In this stance, the archer's feet straddle the shooting line, with both feet parallel to each other, and toes line up with the center of the target. The body should be upright with head turned toward the target (Figure 4-1).

2. *Open (Oblique) Stance.* To assume the open stance, the archer draws the foot nearest to the target back about 4 to 6 inches from the square stance. At the same time, hips and shoulders must also turn so that the body is at about a 45-degree angle to the target (Figure 4-2). The open stance is recommended for advanced archers.

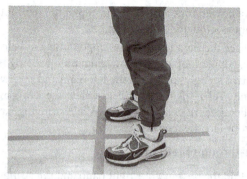

Figure 4-1 Square stance.

Figure 4-2 Open stance.

Step 2—Nocking the Arrow. Nocking the arrow means placing the arrow on the bowstring in preparation for drawing.

▶ Learning Hints

1. Hold the bow with the left hand and the palm of the bow hand facing the ground.

2. With the right hand holding the shaft of the arrow, with index finger pointing upward, slip the nock onto the string at a 90-degree angle with the string. Make a small mark with ink on the string to ensure that the nocking is always done in the same place. If a bow with the nocking point is already fixed on the string, the arrow is usually nicked below the nocking point. After nocking, the archer makes sure there is no gap between the string and the throat of the nock.

Step 3—Setting the Hook. After nocking the arrow, the archer must establish a proper hook. The hook is set using three fingers (index, middle, and fourth fingers) of the archer's right hand. Hook the first three fingers around the string at the first knuckles of these fingers. Hold the arrow lightly between index and middle fingers but do not squeeze the arrow (Figure 4-3). The thumb and little finger of the right hand should be touching each other over the palm. After shooting for a while, relax the thumb and

Figure 4-3 Setting the hook.

little finger. It is important to keep the back of the right hand straight.

Step 4—Establishing a Bow Hold. As in all other aspects of archery, consistency is required in establishing a proper bow hold. First, extend your left arm at the shoulder height toward the target with the left hand in a "handshake" position; then place the pivot point of the bow handle (midsection of the bow) in the V formed by the thumb and index finger. Now the handle of the bow should rest against the base of the thumb, and the other fingers should be placed lightly around the handle. This grip keeps the bow from falling at release of the arrow. Make sure that you do not grip the bow and keep the grip relaxed. Before releasing the arrow, the elbow of the bow arm must be turned down to avoid slapping by the bowstring (Figure 4-4).

Step 5—Raising the Head. Before raising the unit (bow and arrow), the archer's head should be in a natural position with the chin level and the head turned to look directly at the center of the target without any tilt (Figure 4-5).

Step 6—Raising the Unit. At this point, the archer has prepared mechanically for shooting by establishing a proper stance, nocking an arrow, setting the hook, establishing the grip, and raising the head. Now the archer is ready to do the dynamic parts of shooting. The archer raises the entire unit (bow with a nocked arrow) to shoulder height. The bow is now in an upright position facing the target, the bow arm is extended toward the target, and the drawing arm is forming an extension of the arrow. The elbow of the drawing arm is better

Figure 4-4 The bow hold.

Figure 4-5 Note head position.

Figure 4-6 Eyes on target, drawing arm slightly higher than arrow.

3. Keep the elbow of the drawing arm slightly elevated.
4. Now draw the bow by letting your shoulder and back muscles do the pulling with one smooth and deliberate motion.
5. At the full draw, the string should make contact with the center of the nose, lips, and chin.

▶ Learning Hints: Anchoring

1. Anchoring must be done at the same point for each draw. Consistent placement lets the arrow be drawn exactly the same distance and place each time.
2. The index finger of the drawing hand should be under the tip of the jawbone, with the thumb relaxed against the neck (low anchor point).
3. While drawing, take a deep breath, exhale about half of the air, and hold the rest until the arrow has been released (Figure 4-7).

positioned slightly higher than lower in relation to the arrow (Figure 4-6).

Step 7—Drawing and Anchoring. Drawing is the act of pulling the bowstring into the shooting position, and anchoring is the point where the drawing hand is placed. The drawing and the anchoring should be done with one smooth, deliberate motion.

▶ Learning Hints: Drawing

1. Before drawing, keep in mind that the three fingers of the drawing hand are just hooked onto the string at the first knuckles.
2. Relax the drawing hand, giving special attention to relaxing the back of the hand.

Step 8—Aiming and Holding. The three methods of aiming in archery are bow sight, point-of-aim, and instinctive shooting.

1. Shooting with a bow sight is the most accurate aiming technique. The archer should line up the string and bow sight with the center of the target. If the arrow hits high, move the sight up and if low, move the sight down. The sight can also be adjusted left or right.
2. Point-of-aim shooting is aiming at some spot with the point of the arrow. The spot may be in front of, on, or above the target. The selection of the aiming spot depends upon the height of the archer, length

Figure 4-7   Anchoring.

Figure 4-8   Release and follow-through.

of the arrow, and bow weight. When shots are low, move the spot up; when shots are high, move the spot down. String alignment is also important and should be done directly in front of the right eye and lined up vertically with the bow.

3. Instinctive shooting is shooting without a sight or point-of-aim marker. The archer's eyes are focused on the center of the target so the bow arm will adjust itself toward target. Accuracy of this technique depends on the archer's shooting form, eyesight, depth perception, and kinesthetic awareness.

Concentration may be the single most important part of aiming. You should hold your breath and relax a few seconds until the arrow is released. You should also be aware that the sight will oscillate while you are aiming, but make sure it oscillates within the target center.

Step 9—Release.   The arrow should be released with unconscious effort. Simply relax the entire drawing hand and let the string roll off the fingers by itself. No other parts of the body except the drawing hand should be moved. During the release, continue aiming and maintain the contraction of the upper back muscles. Furthermore, let neither the drawing hand move forward nor come off the anchor position to release the string.

Step 10—Follow-through.   Follow-through is the act of maintaining the body position and mental condition assumed at release until the arrow hits the target. The bow arm is pushed slightly forward, and the drawing hand rubs the chin as it moves back behind your neck. During the act of release and follow-through, continue aiming at the target center rather than following the flight of the arrow and continue keeping the tension of the upper back muscles (Figure 4-8).

RETRIEVING ARROWS

To retrieve an arrow from the target, place the palm of your left hand against the target face, with the arrow resting between the index and the middle finger, and push the target face lightly. With your right hand, grasp the arrow by the shaft close to the target and, twisting it slightly counterclockwise, pull the arrow directly backward. If the

arrow goes through the target but the fletchings (feathers) remain inside the mat, go to the back of the target and pull the arrow carefully forward without any twisting motion.

HINTS FOR IMPROVING TECHNIQUE

Upon release, movements of certain parts of the body will cause faulty arrow flights. Be aware of these movements so that you can avoid them.

1. *High arrow flights are usually caused by*
   a. Peeking (looking up to watch the arrow in flight)
   b. Heeling the bow (putting pressure on the low part of the bow handle with the low portion of the bow hand)
   c. Body leaning backward
   d. Overdraw (pulling arrows beyond normal anchor point)

2. *Low arrow flights are usually caused by*
   a. Creeping (letting the drawing hand move forward before arrow is released)
   b. Overhold (maintaining the hold position too long)
   c. String hitting the arm guard upon release
   d. Hunching the shoulder of the bow arm

3. *Arrow flights to the left are usually caused by*
   a. Cupping the drawing hand instead of having the back of the drawing hand relaxed and straight
   b. Bringing the string away from the face (anchor point) to release the arrow
   c. Improper alignment of the bow, body, or string

4. *Arrows falling off the arrow rest of the bow are caused by*
   a. Pinching of the arrow nock with the fingers of the drawing hand. To remedy this, the archer should separate the index and middle fingers to ensure a light touch with the nock, hook the string with the first knuckles of drawing fingers, and use back muscles to draw.
   b. Tight finger tab
   c. Cupping of the drawing hand

Safety

Bows and arrows are weapons capable of inflicting serious injury and should be handled with care. Here are some specific precautions to follow. Remember that the continued enjoyment of archery depends on everyone observing these safety rules.

1. Always check the bow and string to see if it is properly placed at both ends of the string notch before starting to shoot.
2. Shoot only at the target.
3. Do not draw the bow when anyone is between you and the target area.
4. Never allow anyone to retrieve arrows until all arrows have been shot. Varying whistle tones may be used to shoot, retrieve, or for emergencies.
5. Never shoot into the air or in any direction where it might destroy property or endanger life.
6. Always be sure that the area in back of the target is clear or has an adequate backstop.
7. Do not overdraw the bow.
8. Be sure arrows are of the correct length and stiffness for the bow.
9. Do not release a fully drawn bow without an arrow.
10. Obey all commands given for shooting and retrieving arrows.
11. Always wear an arm guard and finger tab to prevent injury.
12. Do not wear bulky clothing or dangling jewelry when shooting.
13. Do not fool around or engage in horseplay on the shooting line.
14. Never run with arrows in your hand; when carrying arrows, keep the pile ends toward the ground.
15. When you have finished shooting, stand behind the other archers until the end has been completed.

Skill Assessment

Archery is classified as a target activity. This type of activity is easy to test because points are awarded for hitting the target. Because of the various student ages, types of targets, and time constraints for testing, the teacher needs to establish the final scoring rules.

Modifications for Special Populations

ORTHOPEDICALLY IMPAIRED

1. Minimal modifications are needed for the student who uses a wheelchair and has good upper body strength and coordination.
2. Students with grasping difficulties should consider commercially purchased assistive devices (e.g., trigger, wrist, and mouthpiece releases).

COGNITIVELY IMPAIRED

1. Individual considerations must be taken into account to determine the appropriateness of archery for students who have low cognitive abilities. Consult with Special Olympics.

SENSORY IMPAIRED

1. Students with visual impairments can be taught to feel the correct way to notch the arrow in the bow.
2. An audio signal could be used as a target.
3. A rope could be tethered to provide the student with a visual impairment with a guide for retrieving an arrow.
4. Students with hearing impairments or who are deaf require minimal adaptations.

Terminology

addressing the target Standing ready to shoot with a proper shooting stance.

anchor point Specific location on the archer's face to which the index finger comes while holding and aiming.

archery golf An adaptation of the game of golf to the sport of archery. Players shoot for the holes and score according to the number of shots required to hit the target.

arm guard A piece of leather or plastic that is worn on the inside of the forearm to protect the arm from the bowstring.

arrow plate A protective piece of hard material set into the bow where the arrow crosses it.

arrow rest A small projection at the top of the bow handle where the arrow rests.

back The side of the bow away from the shooter.

bow arm The arm that holds the bow; this would be the left arm for a right-handed person.

bow sight A device attached to the bow through which the archer sights when aiming.

bow weight Designates the amount of effort (in pounds) needed to pull a bowstring a specific distance (usually 28 inches).

cant The act of holding the bow tilted or slightly turned while shooting.

cast The distance a bow can shoot an arrow.

clout shooting A type of shooting that uses a target 48 feet in diameter, laid on the ground at a distance of 180 yards for men and 140 or 120 yards for women. Usually 36 arrows (6 ends with 6 arrows) are shot per round.

cock feather Now called the "index feather." The feather that is set at a right angle to the arrow nock; differently colored from the other two feathers.

creeping Letting the drawing hand move forward at the release.

crest The archer's identifying marks shown just below the fletchings on the arrow.

draw The act of pulling the bowstring back into the anchor position.

end A specified number of arrows shot at one time or from one position before retrieval of arrows.

face The part of the bow facing the shooter.

finger tab A leather flap worn on the drawing hand to protect the fingers and provide a smooth release of the bowstring.

fletchings The feathers of the arrow, which give guidance to its flight.

flight shooting Shooting an arrow the farthest possible distance.

handle The grip at the midsection of the bow.

hen feathers The two feathers that are not set at right angles to the arrow nock. See *cock feather*.

hold Steadily holding the arrow at full draw before release.

instinctive shooting Aiming and shooting instinctively, rather than using a bow sight or point-of-aim method.

limbs Upper and lower parts of the bow; divided by the handle.

nock The groove in the end of the arrow in which the string is placed.

nocking point The point on the string at which the arrow is placed.

notch The grooves of the upper and lower tips of the limbs into which the bow string is fitted.

overbow Using too strong a bow that is too powerful to allow a bowstring to be pulled the proper distance.

overdraw Drawing the bow so that the pile of the arrow is inside the bow.

petticoat That part of the target face outside the white ring.

pile (point) The pointed metal tip of the arrow.

pinch To squeeze the nock of the arrow.

plucking Jerking the drawing hand laterally away from the face on the release, which will cause arrow flight to the left.

point-blank range The only distance from the target at which the point of aim is right on the bull's eye.

point of aim A method of aiming in which the pile of the arrow is aligned with the target.

quiver A receptacle for carrying or holding arrows.

recurve bow A bow that is curved on the ends.

release The act of letting the bowstring slip off the fingertips.

round The term used to indicate shooting a designated number of arrows at a designated distance or distances.

roving Archery game played outdoors in which natural targets (stumps, trees, bushes, etc.) are selected for competition.

serving The thread wrapped around the bowstring at the nocking point.

shaft The long body part of the arrow.

spine The characteristic rigidity and flexibility of an arrow.

tackle Archery equipment referred to as a whole.

target face The painted front of a target, usually replaceable.

trajectory The path of the arrow in flight.

vane Plastic feather of an arrow.

Discussion Questions

1. Identify the benchmark dates and groups that were important in the development of target archery in the United States.

2. List the sequential 10 steps for shooting.

3. Discuss the items that affect good execution for each of the 10 steps.

4. Because safety is a prime concern in archery, identify specific precautions to be taken.

5. There are certain body movements that will cause faulty arrow flights. Identify the possible causes.

6. Describe the two methods for stringing a bow.

7. Discuss the variables involved in modifying scoring methods.

8. Identify the important considerations when selecting a bow and arrows.

Web Sites

www.usarchery.org USA Archery—includes sections on rules, articles, history, publication links, equipment, a tutorial, and links to other Web sites.

www.archery.org International Federation of Archery—provides information on the history of archery, rules, archery disciplines, and FAQs.

http://nasparchery.com—provides grant information, curriculum guides (elementary, middle, and secondary), lesson plans, instructor resources, equipment, and links.

http://pecentral.org—offers tutorials on bow types, arrows, accessories, shooting tips, and glossary.

CHAPTER 5

Badminton

This chapter will enable you to

- Understand the fundamental techniques in various strokes used in the game of badminton
- Display an understanding of basic strategy in both singles and doubles
- Identify and understand the basic rules for singles and doubles
- Understand basic terminology used in the game of badminton

Nature and Purpose

Badminton has steadily gained worldwide acceptance as a fast-paced competitive game for highly skilled players. At the beginning level, it is usually possible to keep the shuttle in play, which makes the game enjoyable and rewarding for most age groups. Singles, doubles, or mixed doubles may be played; thus badminton is an excellent coeducational activity.

Although courts can be set up outdoors, competitive badminton is generally played indoors where the wind and elements will not affect the shuttle.

History

Historians believe that a game similar to badminton (called *battledore*) was played in China more than 2,000 years ago. However, badminton as it is currently known is believed to have originated from a game called *poona* that was played by English army officers stationed in India during the 17th century. The game derived its current name from the country estate of the Duke of Beaufort, which was called Badminton. During the early 1870s, the game was played at lawn parties, and guests introduced it to others.

By the late 1870s the game had been introduced in the United States by the Badminton Club of New York, which was primarily a social club. The American Badminton Association was formed in 1935 to govern the sport and was renamed the United States Badminton Association in 1978. It became affiliated with the International Badminton Federation (IBF), which was founded in 1934. In 2007 the IBF changed its name to the World Badminton Federation (WBF). Badminton gained Olympic acceptance as a demonstration sport in 1972, exhibition status in 1988, and full membership in 1992.

The IBF established the World Grand Prix Circuit for professional involvement in 1980. The U.S. Open was the highest-paying tournament on that tour,[1] until the WBF organized the World Super Series. Prize money is now estimated to be in the millions of dollars.

Current participation levels in badminton are estimated to exceed 50 million, with most of the top players located in the Far East and Europe.

Rules of Badminton

Rules in all sports constantly evolve, and in 2006 badminton made changes that simplified the scoring system. Over the years there were differing scoring rules for males, females, and mixed doubles. The differences included the number of games in a match, the number of points in a game, and how to arrive at the total points in a game by setting the final score. The new rules established rally scoring, where each serve results in a point regardless of which side served. This scoring method shortened the length of a game. Games are now played to 21 points, and at 20-all the winner is determined by gaining a 2-point advantage. At 29-all there is no 2-point advantage as the winner is the first to 30. Both scoring changes add pressure to the players and excitement to the sport.

1. Toss for serve. Before a match begins, opponents can toss a coin, spin a racket, or toss a shuttle to determine who shall get the choice of "serve" or "side." If spinning a racket, identify a marking on the racket and have one person call the mark. If tossing a shuttle, the proper procedure is for one

person to either hit or toss the shuttle in the air and let it land. The person toward whom the base of the shuttle is pointing gets the choice.

2. Each serve and rally result in a point. A match consists of two out of three games to 21 points. At 20-all, one must win by 2 points, and at 29-all the first side to 30 points is the winner. In each game, the teams change ends at 11 points with a 60-second break. There is a 2-minute interlude between games. The winner of the game serves first in the next game.

3. The serve must be delivered into the diagonal service court and within its boundaries to be a legal serve. Any shuttle hitting the line is in. In singles, the shuttle must land in the long, narrow court; in doubles, it must land in the short, wide court. In doubles, once the serve has been returned, the full court (20 × 44 feet) is played.

4. In both singles and doubles, the server is allowed only one trial to put the shuttle into play. The shuttle may hit the net and land in the proper court and be legal. To start the game, the first serve is always from the right side of the service court. Whenever the server's score is even (0, 2, 4, etc.), the serve is from the right service court, and it is from the left when uneven (1, 3, 5, etc.). The score should always be stated loudly before each serve.

5. In singles games, each player's first serve is made from the right service court. If the server wins the rally, that player next serves from the left service court. If the opponent wins the rally, that player starts service from the right service court. The server alternates service courts each time she wins the rally, serving from the left when her score is uneven or from the right when her score is even.

6. In doubles games, one partner starts on the right side and the other on the left side of the service court. Where the player starts is determined to be that player's even court. There is only one service opportunity per side in doubles. Under previous rules both partners got the chance to serve. When the serving team commits a fault, the service changes to the opponents. The team's score determines which partner will serve and from which side the serve will be initiated.

At the beginning of the game and when the score is even, the server initiates the serve from the right-side court. When the server's score is odd, the serve is initiated from the left service court. The serving side wins the point when it wins a rally. The same server then moves to the opposite side of his team's service court to serve again.

If the receiving side wins a rally, it scores a point and becomes the new serving side. The server who just lost stays in the same court where he last served

and his partner positions in the opposite service court to become the receiver. Players do not change their respective service courts until they win a point when their side is serving. Any errors in service court positioning are corrected as soon as the error is exposed.

7. It is a fault (loss of service or "hand out" for the serving side; or loss of point for the receiving side) when

a. Service is illegal—for example, the shuttle is struck when above the waist, or the head of the racket is higher than the lowest finger of the racket hand when contact is made.

b. Service or played shot lands outside the specified court, passes through or under the net, or hits a player or obstruction outside the court.

c. If server or receiver is standing outside of the proper court upon delivery of the serve or balks in any way before the service. Only the person served to may return the shuttle.

d. The server or receiver steps forward, lifts, or drags a foot during the delivery of the serve.

e. The server misses the shuttle in attempting to serve.

f. A player reaches over the net to contact a shuttle. (The follow-through, however, may break the plane of the net.)

g. A player touches the net with the racket or any part of the body while the shuttle is deemed to be in play.

h. A player contacts the shuttle twice in one swing. (Referred to as a "double hit.")

i. A player fails to return the shuttle to the opponent's proper court. (The opposing player cannot hit, catch, or be struck by a doubtful shuttle and then call it "out.")

j. On a doubles serve, the server's partner unsights the server (does not allow receivers to view the service).

k. In doubles, a shuttle is hit by a player and the player's partner successively.

l. A player prevents or hinders an opponent from making a legal stroke where the shuttle is followed over the net (racket follow-through of the striker).

Equipment

The choice of equipment is important in badminton. High-quality racquets and shuttlecocks (birds) can have a favorable bearing on performance. When purchasing rackets and birds, buy the best you can afford.

RACKET

Badminton rackets are quite light and can be made of wood, aluminum, metal, or synthetic materials such as graphite or carbon. Synthetic rackets are quite popular now because of their extreme lightness and strength.

The price of rackets also varies. There are "playable" rackets that can be purchased from $20 to $35 (excellent for the beginner or physical education classes) and other higher quality rackets for the "competitive" player, ranging from $45 to $150. The racket can be strung with either nylon or gut. Nylon string is sufficient for the beginning player because it usually costs less and lasts longer than gut.

In any case, choosing a racket is a matter of personal preference, and you should use what feels comfortable, not what looks good.

SHUTTLECOCK

The "official" shuttlecock, usually called *shuttle* or *bird*, is made from goose feathers that are placed in a leather-covered cork head. Feather shuttles are quite expensive and can be damaged during play quickly. They are used primarily in high-level tournament competition.

Shuttles are also made of either plastic or nylon. These shuttles last longer and are not as expensive as the feathered bird. There are several types of nylon or plastic birds that are durable and excellent for class play.

BADMINTON COURT

The official badminton court (shown in Figures 5-1 and 5-2) is 44 feet long. The doubles court is 20 feet wide, whereas the singles court is 17 feet wide. The net is 5 feet at the center and 5 feet 1 inch at the posts. A "Half-court" practice/drill arrangement is shown in Figure 5-3.

Overhead clearance is an important factor in setting up a badminton court. Generally speaking, an overhead

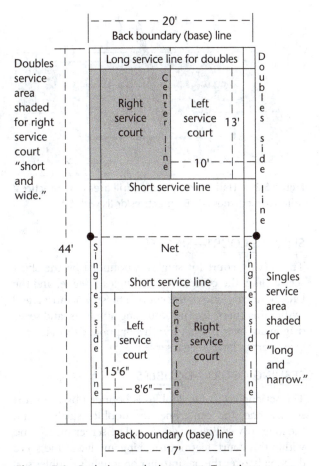

Figure 5-1   Badminton playing court: Top view.

clearance of less than 20 feet would not be considered conducive for playing the game effectively. A clearance of at least 30 feet is required for all national and international competition.

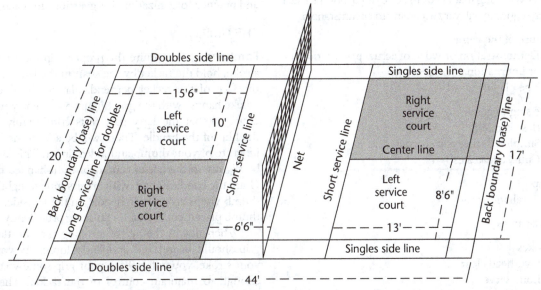

Figure 5-2   Badminton playing court: Side view.

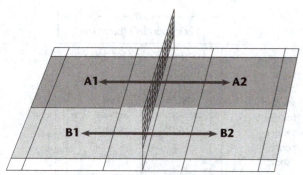

Figure 5-3 "Half-court" practice/drill areas. A1 practices/drills with partner A2; B1 practices/drills with B2.

SERVING COURT—SINGLES

The serving court for singles is bounded by the short service line, the centerline, the singles sideline, and the back boundary line of the court. The server must stand within this court, feet not touching any lines, and serve diagonally over the net into his opponent's singles service court to have a legal serve.

SERVING COURT—DOUBLES

The serving court for doubles is bounded by the short service line, the centerline, the doubles sideline, and the long service line for doubles. The server must stand within this court, feet not touching any lines, and serve diagonally over the net into her opponent's doubles service court to have a legal serve.

Suggested Learning Sequence

After the students have acquired an understanding of the basic strategy, simplified rules, and court courtesies, playing should start immediately. Specific skills will be introduced as the learning sequence progresses. The following outline includes everything that needs to be covered, but the exact teaching sequence will vary according to circumstances.

A. Nature of the game
  1. Demonstration or video of actual play (national or international competition)
  2. The playing court

B. The singles game
  1. Basic strategy
  2. Simplified rules and scoring
  3. Court courtesies

C. Grip
  1. Forehand

D. Play games

E. Strokes
  1. Overhead clear
  2. Long serve
  3. Short serve

F. Introduce intraclass competition
  1. Ladder tournament
  2. Round robin, etc.

G. Strokes (continued)
  1. Smash
  2. Block (forehand and backhand)

H. Footwork and movement
  1. Backcourt
  2. Lateral (blocking)
  3. Forecourt

I. Strokes (continued)
  1. Around-the-head
    a. Clears
    b. Smashes
    c. Overhead drop

J. Grip
  1. Backhand

K. Strokes (continued)
  1. Net clears (forehand and backhand)
  2. Net drops (forehand and backhand)

L. The doubles game
  1. Basic strategy
  2. Simplified rules and scoring
  3. Alignments
    a. Side-by-side (defensive)
    b. Up-and-back (offensive)
    c. Circular rotation (combination of a and b, depending on the situation)

Skills and Techniques

A fundamentally sound badminton player must use many different skills and techniques. In this section we will describe each stroke or skill and give learning hints and practice/organizational suggestions for each.

THE GRIPS

Forehand.   To acquire the proper grip for a forehand stroke, hold the racket by the shaft in the left hand with the face of the racket perpendicular to the floor, and "shake hands" with the grip (Figure 5-4). Slide your hand down so that the fatty part rests comfortably against the butt of the handle. There will be a V formed by the juncture of your thumb and index finger. This V should be slightly to the left of center for right-handed players. Grasp the handle lightly, with fingers spread slightly. The thumb wraps around the handle on the left side. Proper thumb placement is vital for stroking proficiently.

When not in the act of stroking the shuttle, your grip should be relaxed and fairly loose. As you start your stroke, you will tighten your grip somewhat—just enough to maintain control of the racket. The more forceful the shot, the tighter the grip.

Figure 5-4   Forehand grip.

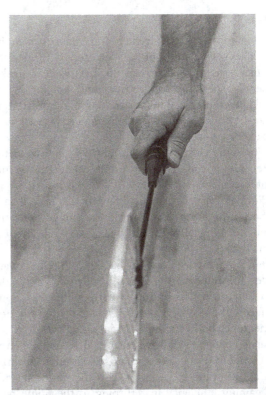

Figure 5-5   Backhand grip. The thumb is farther behind the racket handle.

This same grip may be used for most backhand shots. For our purposes, we will vary this grip only when stroking backhand net drops and net clears. (At the beginning level, asking players to change grips repeatedly during fast-paced volleys can be quite frustrating to most students.)

Backhand.   For backhand net drops and net clears you will move the racket a quarter turn clockwise from the forehand grip, so that your thumb moves farther behind the racket handle (Figure 5-5).

HOME BASE—SINGLES

"Home base" is referred to as the area in the court where a player stands to effectively cover the entire court. In singles, it is in the center of the court—an equal distance to all four corners.

After each shot is hit, the player should attempt to return to home base position as quickly as possible and prepare for her opponent's return. If the player cannot return quickly enough prior to her opponent's return, she should stop, ready herself, and then react to her opponent's return from wherever she is in the court. A player should not be moving at the moment an opponent contacts the shuttle.

THE READY POSITION

Moving efficiently around the court during play is of the utmost importance in badminton. Good movement

Figure 5-6   Ready position: Front.

begins with a proper "ready position." This is the position, or stance, a player should assume prior to maneuvering toward an opponent's return shot. The feet should be spread shoulder width apart or slightly wider, the knees slightly bent, and with weight on the balls of the feet, ready for movement in any direction. A stagger stance, with the racket-side foot forward, is used by most players (Figure 5-6).

FOOTWORK

Efficient footwork is extremely important in badminton. The player must be able to get to the shuttle as quickly as possible to set up for the next stroke. Generally speaking, long strides and lunging action should be emphasized in footwork. Using short steps to cover the court is time consuming and a waste of valuable energy.

For shots close to the net, always lunge with the racket-side foot reaching toward the shuttle at the moment of contact.

For lateral shots, push off with the foot that is farthest away from the shuttle and lunge with the other—pushing off with the right foot while moving to the left.

For shots hit deep into the backcourt, use backward strides. It is important to turn the body sideways to the net when hitting the shuttle, with the nonracket shoulder facing the net. This position will allow full rotation of the upper body and hips in generating power. More advanced players will use a scissors kick (switching the legs) while in the act of striking the shuttle. This motion allows them to push off with the nonracket-side leg, gaining efficiency in returning to the home base position.

THE STROKES

There are five basic groups of shots that should be learned at the beginning level of badminton: serves, clears, smashes, blocks, and drops. Each of these strokes is described, followed by a sixth type: around-the-head shots.

I. Serves. There are two basic badminton serves: the long serve, which is hit high and deep, and the short serve, which is hit low and short. The long serve is used primarily in singles play, and the short serve is used primarily in doubles play. The serving stances and areas are the same in both singles and doubles.

A. LONG SERVE (HIGH AND DEEP). The object of the long serve is simply to move your opponent as far away from the net as possible. In singles play, this would be to the baseline, and in doubles play, it would be to the long service line for doubles.

When positioning yourself, stand approximately 3 to 4 feet behind the short service line and close to the centerline (Figure 5-7). Face your opponent's diagonal service court, stagger your stance (right foot behind the left if you are right-handed) with your weight on the back foot, stand tall, and relax (knees slightly bent).

Hold the shuttle with your fingers and thumb wrapped gently around the feathers and cork base when starting the service (Figure 5-8). Flex the

Figure 5-7 Service stance.

shuttle arm at approximately 90 degrees, and position it across the body toward the racket shoulder. When released, the shuttle is "set out" and dropped away from the body toward your racket side. It should not be allowed to "tumble" (flip end-over-end) or "waver" after it is released because these actions will cause inconsistent flight patterns. The shuttle should be released from approximately shoulder height (refer to Figure 5-7).

Hold the racket in the backswing position, holding the racket head higher than the racket hand. As you release the shuttle to start your serve, your weight shifts forward (to your front foot) and your racket is pulled down and through the shuttle (Figure 5-9). At the contact point, your wrist snaps and the forearm rotates upward and forward in the direction of your serve. Contact point is about knee level. Hips and shoulders

Figure 5-8 Holding shuttle for service delivery.

Figure 5-9 Long serve: After the shuttle is dropped, bring the racket downward and forward.

Figure 5-10 The follow-through position after a vigorous wrist snap and rotation of the forearm.

will rotate toward the net, and the racket arm will finish across the body (Figure 5-10).

The long serve can be described as a basic underhand motion with a vigorous wrist snap and forearm rotation.

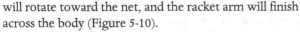

▶ Learning Hints

1. Stand facing the receiver's court in a relaxed, upright, staggered serving stance.

2. Make sure the racket wrist is cocked as much as possible in the backswing position, elbow fairly close to the body.

3. Drop the shuttle before starting the swing.

4. Drop the shuttle in front of and to the side of your body far enough away to force the hitting arm to reach for it slightly.

5. Be as relaxed as possible and try to generate maximum racket head acceleration by snapping the wrist and rotating the forearm at point of contact.

6. Contact shuttle at about knee height.

7. Hit the shuttle up and out.

▶ Practice/Organizational Suggestions

(Figure 5-11)

Get as many shuttles as possible and hit the high, deep singles serve. You can practice serving diagonally

if space permits, or you can practice serving straight across the net using the half-court practice/play variation.

The two keys to look for are height and depth. Hit the shuttle high enough and hit it deeply enough to land in the back alley close to the baseline. Remember, a long serve that is not high enough or deep enough will put you in a defensive situation.

B. SHORT SERVE (SHORT AND LOW). The object of the short serve is to force your opponent to "lift" the shuttle. (Lifting the shuttle—resulting most often from underhand strokes—is considered to be defensive because it will allow the opponent an opportunity to return the "lifted" shuttle downward.)

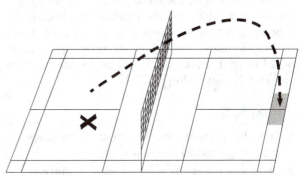

Figure 5-11 Long serve: Trajectory and target zones for singles play.

Figure 5-12   Notice the short follow-through in the direction of the flight.

When positioning yourself, stand approximately 3 to 4 feet behind the short service line and close to the centerline. Face your opponent's diagonal service court, stagger your stance (right foot behind the left if you are right-handed) with your weight on the back leg, stand tall, and relax (knees slightly bent).

The racket is in the backswing position with the racket head being held higher than the racket hand. As you release the shuttle to start your serve, your weight shifts forward (to your front foot) and your racket is "pushed" (rather than pulled as in the long serve) through the shuttle. At the contact point, your wrist remains cocked with the racket arm following through forward (in the direction of your serve)—as if pushing from behind to guide it over the net (Figure 5-12). Contact point is about thigh level. Minimum hip or shoulder rotation is utilized.

The idea is to hit the shuttle so that it will stay low and drop just behind the short service line. Because little power is needed to achieve this, the wrist remains in the cocked position throughout the stroke. The shuttle should reach its maximum height at the net and then immediately start to drop.

▶ Learning Hints

1. Stand facing the receiver's court in a relaxed, upright, staggered serving stance.
2. Make sure the racket wrist is cocked as much as possible in the backswing position, elbow close to the body.

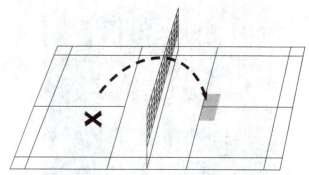

Figure 5-13   Short serve: Trajectory and target zones for singles and doubles play.

3. Drop the shuttle before starting the swing.
4. Drop the shuttle in front of and to the side of your body.
5. Be as relaxed as possible and try to "push" the shuttle rather than "hitting" it.
6. Contact shuttle at about thigh height.
7. Keep the shuttle as low and short as possible.

▶ Practice/Organizational Suggestions

(Figure 5-13)

Get as many shuttles as possible and hit the short, low serve. You can practice serving diagonally if space permits, or you can practice serving straight across the net using the half-court practice/play variation.

The two keys to look for are low clearance of the net and shortness in depth. Hit the shuttle low enough, and hit it short enough, to land just past the short service line. Remember, a short serve that is not low enough will put you in a defensive situation.

Figure 5-14   Singles service return stance: Even court.

Figure 5-15 Singles service return stance: Odd court.

RETURN OF SERVICE—SINGLES. The position for returning serves in singles is approximately 4 feet in back of the short service line (midcourt) and moved slightly to your backhand side in the service court. Your stance will be a slightly exaggerated stagger with the nonracket leg forward (Figures 5-14 and 5-15). Stand tall with the majority of your weight on the forward leg. Hold your racket in front of your body about chin high.

For returning a long serve (high and deep), push off with your forward leg and backstride to position yourself under the oncoming shuttle. To return a short serve (low and short), lunge forward by moving your back leg quickly to the net. As you lunge, reach out with your racket to contact the shuttle at its highest point.

RETURN OF SERVICE—DOUBLES. The position for returning serves in doubles is approximately one foot in back of the short service line and moved slightly to your backhand side in the service court. This position puts you much closer to the net than in the singles return position. Your stance will be a slightly exaggerated stagger with the nonracket leg forward. Stand tall with the majority of your weight on the forward leg. Hold your racket in front of your body slightly higher than the position held for a normal singles return. This stance will allow you a quicker contact time for short serves—the serve that is used most often in doubles play.

The footwork used in returning doubles long serves is the same as that used for returning long serves in singles.

II. Clears. Clears are defensive strokes that allow you time to return to the ready position and regroup and to move your opponent as far away from the net as

Figure 5-16 Overhead clear: Backswing (used for all overhead strokes).

possible. There are two types of clears: overhead and underhand.

A. OVERHEAD CLEAR. Overhead clears are usually taken from a backcourt position. From your home base position, move into a position under and slightly behind the oncoming shuttle. Prepare your racket for the stroke by bringing it back behind the shoulders into what is called the "back-scratching" position: arm bent, elbow parallel to the floor (Figure 5-16).

With your racket shoulder now in line with the shuttle, extend the arm to meet the shuttle at the highest point possible (Figure 5-17). At the moment of contact, your forearm rotates outward, and the wrist snaps quickly, causing the racket head to accelerate and drive the shuttle upward and outward deep into your opponent's court. The racket head will be facing slightly upward at contact. Follow through with the racket arm crossing your body in the direction of your nonracket side (Figure 5-18).

▶ Learning Hints

1. Position yourself under and slightly behind the dropping shuttle.
2. Prepare the racket in the back-scratching position.

Figure 5-17   Overhead clear: Contact.

Figure 5-18   Overhead clear: Follow-through.

3. As you swing upward, rotate the forearm and extend the arm as high as possible, with the racket face pointing slightly upward.

4. At the moment of contact, snap the wrist quickly.

5. Hit the shuttle high (18 to 20 feet) and deep into your opponent's backcourt area.

6. Follow through across your body.

▶ Practice/Organizational Suggestions

   (Figure 5-19)

1. *Straight clears using the half-court area.* Partners hit continuous clears to each other, attempting to get the shuttle into the back alley.

2. *Crosscourt clears.* Partners hit continuous clears diagonally to each other, working on distance and accuracy. Each partner attempts to get the shuttle into the back alley and corner of the singles court.

3. *Side alley clears.* Partners hit continuous clears within the side alley boundaries, working on accuracy and distance.

B. FOREHAND UNDERHAND (NET) CLEAR.   Underhand clears are usually taken from a forecourt position. When your opponent hits a drop shot into your forecourt, or close

to the net, it forces you to "lift" the shuttle and go on the defensive. Hitting an underhand clear in this situation will serve the same purpose as hitting an overhead clear in a backcourt situation. That is, it will allow you time to return to the ready position and regroup, and it will move your opponent as far away from the net as possible.

As the shuttle is dropping toward your forehand side and in the forecourt area, from the ready position take a

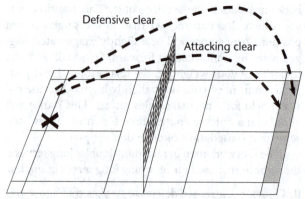

Figure 5-19   Overhead clears: Trajectory and target zones for singles play.

Figure 5-20   Forehand net clear: Contact.

Figure 5-22   Backhand net clear: Contact.

Figure 5-21   Forehand net clear: Follow-through.

Figure 5-23   Backhand net clear: Follow-through.

short first step with your nonracket leg and then a long lunge to the shuttle with the racket leg.

Reach for the shuttle with the wrist slightly cocked and your racket arm in as high a position as necessary to contact the bird at its highest point possible. At the moment of contact, rotate your forearm so that the racket is uncocked explosively up and through the shuttle (Figure 5-20). The follow-through is in the direction that you intend the shuttle to travel (Figure 5-21).

C. BACKHAND UNDERHAND (NET) CLEAR. Change to a backhand grip. As the shuttle is dropping toward your backhand side and in the forecourt area, from the ready position take a short first step with your nonracket leg and then a long lunge to the shuttle with the racket leg.

Reach for the shuttle with the wrist slightly cocked and your racket arm in as high a position as necessary

to contact the bird at its highest point possible. At the moment of contact, rotate your forearm so that the racket is brought explosively up and through the shuttle (Figure 5-22). The follow-through is in the direction that you intend the shuttle to travel (Figure 5-23).

▶ Learning Hints

1. Lunge to the shuttle with your racket leg forward at contact.
2. Contact the shuttle at the highest point possible.
3. Lift the shuttle with a hard, explosive wrist action.
4. Hit the shuttle high (18 to 20 feet) and deep into your opponent's backcourt area.
5. Follow through in the direction you intend the shuttle to travel.

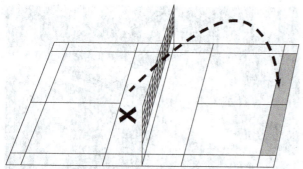

Figure 5-24 Net clear: Trajectory and target zones for singles play.

▶ Practice/Organizational Suggestions

(Figure 5-24)

Straight underhand clears using the half-court area. One player hits overhead drops from the back alley, while the partner hits underhand clears from the net area.

Note: See overhead drop Practice/Organizational Suggestions in Section V, Drop Shots.

D. ATTACKING CLEAR. Attacking clears are used primarily to drive your opponent to the backcourt (farthest point from the net) after she has come close to the net and you think you can "clear" the shuttle over her racket for a winner. They are stroked similarly to the clears discussed previously except that the trajectory is lower. This lower trajectory will cause the shuttle to reach the floor sooner, and in turn put your opponent in a defensive situation (see Figure 5-19).

III. Smashes. The smash is the basic offensive shot in badminton. It is a powerful stroke that is used primarily for getting the shuttle to land on your opponent's side of the court as quickly as possible. However, if the shuttle does not land on your opponent's court and end the volley as expected, it will force him to "lift" the shuttle—putting him in a defensive situation. The smash is a shot that can be tremendously effective.

The body position is similar to the overhead clear stroke, with one exception: The shuttle should be lined up *ahead* of your racket shoulder (Figure 5-25), farther ahead than the contact point of the overhead clear. By the same token, the racket face must be angling downward, as compared with upward for the overhead clear.

You should contact the shuttle at the highest point possible. The higher you contact the shuttle, the greater the angle down to your opponent's court. The greater the angle, the greater the chance you have for clearing the net. Your forearm and wrist will rotate and snap rapidly as the shuttle is contacted. Follow-through is similar to that for the overhead clear.

Unless you have an exceptionally strong smash, this stroke should be used only when you are in the front three-quarters of the court. Remember, smashing from the back alley area forces the shuttle to fly a greater distance to get to your opponent's side of the court. This longer distance will allow your opponent more time to react to your smash and increase his chances of returning the shuttle with some control.

▶ Learning Hints

As far as preparation and motion are concerned, the same learning cues apply to both the overhead clear

Figure 5-25 Smash: Notice that the contact point is forward of the racket shoulder.

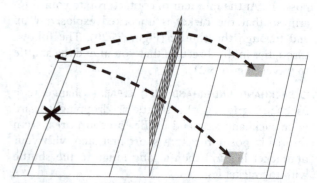

Figure 5-26 Smash: Trajectory and target zones for singles play.

Figure 5-27 Forehand block.

Figure 5-28 Backhand block.

Figure 5-29 High body block.

and the smash. These additional key points apply to smashes:

1. Get into position so that contact can be made ahead of the racket shoulder, which is farther ahead than for an overhead clear.

2. The racket face should be angling downward at contact.

3. A sharp downward angle is just as important as shuttle speed.

▶ Practice/Organizational Suggestions

(Figure 5-26)

Straight smashes using the half-court area. One player hits short, underhand clears while the partner returns them with smashes.

Note: Also see Practice/Organizational Suggestions under Section IV, Blocks.

IV. Blocks.   (Figures 5-27, 5-28, and 5-29)

Blocks are used as a defensive stroke in response to an opponent's smash. They are used primarily for returning a smash in an emergency situation. However, if effectively stroked, a block can also change your defensive situation into an offensive one. (An effective block will force your opponent to return the shuttle with an underhand stroke. This "lifting" action on the part of your opponent may enable you to regain the attack.)

The block shot is best accomplished by trying to get the racket head out in front of your body and to the shuttle as quickly as possible. Use the forehand grip (see Figure 5-27). There is no backswing to this stroke, but merely a slight push of the shuttle to have it rebound from the racket and barely clear the net. The force of your push will depend on the speed of your opponent's smash. The harder the smash, the less the push. A mere rebound off of a stationary racket face—from a powerful smash—is often sufficient to accomplish this stroke. The object is to drop the shuttle over the net shallow in the opponent's forecourt.

▶ Learning Hints

1. Do not try to take the racket back because this stroke does not require a backswing.

2. React as quickly as possible, trying to get the racket head in front of your body and to the shuttle.

3. Try to keep the shuttle low, barely clearing the net.

4. Do not swing at the shuttle. Merely block with a slight push.

▶ Practice/Organizational Suggestions

(Figure 5-30)

1. *Smash and block drill using the half-court area.* One player hits a short, high underhand clear that the partner smashes. The returner attempts to block the smash and get it over the net shallow in the forecourt.

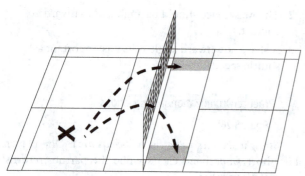

Figure 5-30 Block: Two flight patterns and target zones for blocking.

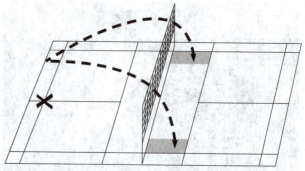

Figure 5-31 Overhead drop: Trajectory and target zones for singles play.

2. *2–1–1 smash and block drill (half-court).* Player (A) hits a short, high underhand clear to start the drill.

Then partner (B) overhead clears,

(A) smashes,

(B) blocks,

(A) -underhand (net) clears, and the drill continues.

Sequence: underhand clear, overhead clear, smash, block, repeat.

3. *3–1–1 smash and block drill (half-court).* Use the same sequence as the 2–1–1 except add in an extra overhead clear to this drill.

Sequence: underhand clear, overhead clear, overhead clear, smash, block, repeat.

V. Drop Shots. There are two types of drop shots: overhead and underhand. Underhand drop shots are taken from the forecourt area, oftentimes close to the net, and are referred to as "net drops." Overhead drops are usually taken from the backcourt area and referred to as simply "drops." Drops are used to force your opponent to come to the net from her backcourt position and to force her to lift the shuttle for her return. They can be described as soft shots that barely clear the net and then drop quickly into the opponent's forecourt area—preferably in front of the short service line.

A. OVERHEAD DROP. Overhead drops are usually taken from a backcourt position. The object is to make your opponent think that you are going to clear or smash, and then execute a soft stroke that gently drops the shuttle over the net. As stated previously, overhead drops are used to move your opponent to the forecourt and to force a "lifting" return of the shuttle. If stroked deceptively enough, overhead drops can put your opponent into such an off-balance position that a decent return from him would be extremely difficult.

The body position used is similar to the overhead clear. The shuttle is contacted in front of the body, but the racket head will slow instead of accelerating at the

moment of impact. As in the smash, the racket face must be angling downward. Follow-through is across your body and toward the non-racket side.

This shot depends to a great extent on finesse and deception. A backswing, stroke, and follow-through similar to the clear or smash are vital in the disguise of this stroke. Remember, *the shuttle is fully stroked and guided*, not pushed from the shoulder or tapped from a stiff, overhead, outstretched arm position.

▶ Learning Hints

1. Get into position so that contact can be made in front of the body.

2. Racket preparation has to be the same as if you were going to clear or smash.

3. Slow the speed of the racket head just before contacting the shuttle.

4. The racket face should be angling slightly downward on impact.

5. Gently guide the shuttle over the net with your wrist action and follow-through.

▶ Practice/Organizational Suggestions

(Figure 5-31)

1. *Continuous straight drops using the half-court area.* One player hits underhand clears while the partner returns them with overhead drops.

2. *2–1 overhead drop drill (half-court).* Player (A) hits a short, high underhand clear to start the drill.
Then partner (B) overhead clears,
(A) overhead drops, and the drill continues.
Sequence: underhand clear, overhead clear, overhead drop, repeat.

3. *3–1 overhead drop drill (half-court).* Use the same sequence as the 2–1 except add an extra overhead clear to this drill.
Sequence: underhand clear, overhead clear, overhead clear, overhead drop, repeat.
Note: Also see Practice/Organizational Suggestions under Net Drop, below.

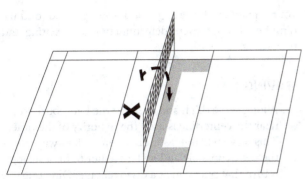

Figure 5-32 Net drop: Trajectory and target zones for singles play.

B. NET DROP. Net (or underhand) drops are hit from the forecourt area and are used to draw your opponent close to the net after she has hit an overhead drop from her backcourt. They are also used to force an opponent to "lift" the shuttle.

Net drops taken on the forehand side are stroked using the forehand grip. Net drops taken on the backhand side are stroked using the backhand grip previously described. The object is to lift slightly or push the shuttle gently over the top of the net so that it falls below the white tape level as quickly as possible. If stroked properly, the shuttle will fall close to the net. This will force your opponent to travel the greatest distance possible from her present position in the court.

Getting to the shuttle quickly is of the utmost importance. The idea is to contact the shuttle as close to the top of the net as possible. The lower the contact point, the more lift you will have to put on your shot. You would rather "push" your drop over the net than "lift" it over. Lifting the shuttle forces you into an uncertain defensive situation. A shuttle that is lifted too softly (not high enough) will result in a bird that does not make it over the net. Pushing and guiding your net drop will eliminate the uncertainty of "lifting."

Lunge toward the shuttle with your racket-side leg. With your arm and racket out in front of your body and as high as necessary to contact the shuttle at its highest point, gently push and guide the shuttle over the net. Have the shuttle barely clear the net so that your opponent will not have a chance to smash it back at you.

▶ Learning Hints

(Figure 5-32)

1. Lunge with the racket-side leg toward the shuttle.
2. Contact the shuttle as near to the top of the net as possible.
3. Gently push and guide the shuttle over the net.
4. Have the shuttle just barely clear the net.

Figure 5-33 Around-the-head: Notice that the contact is on the backhand side of the body.

▶ Practice/Organizational Suggestions

1. *Toss and stroke drill using the half-court area.* One player stands on the short service line and tosses a shuttle over the net while the partner lunges toward the shuttle and net drops. Tosses should be directed to the forehand side for forehand practice, backhand side for backhand practice. The stroker should be in a ready position approximately 2 feet behind the short service line prior to each toss.
2. *Continuous net drops (half-court).* From behind the short service line, one player puts the shuttle into play with a short serve. Each player continues to hit net drops until a missed shot has occurred.
3. *2–1–1 overhead drop and net drop drill (half-court).* Player (A) hits an underhand clear to start the drill.

   Then partner (B) overhead clears,
   (A) overhead drops,
   (B) net drops,
   (A) underhand clears, and the drill continues.
   Sequence: underhand clear, overhead clear, overhead drop, net drop, repeat.

4. *3–1–1 overhead drop and net drop drill (half-court).* Use the same sequence as the 2–1–1 except add an extra overhead clear to this drill.

Sequence: underhand clear, overhead clear, overhead clear, overhead drop, net drop, repeat.

VI. Around-the-Head Shots. Around-the-head shots are used in place of the conventional overhead backhand stroke—a shot usually considered to be weak and defensive. Around-the-heads may be used for overhead clears, smashes, and overhead drops. If stroked properly they can be powerful, attacking strokes. Although this stroke will be contacted on your backhand (nonracket) side, your grip will be a forehand grip.

Position yourself so that the shuttle is in alignment with your nonracket shoulder. The backswing is the same as in other overhead shots, but the contact point will be over your nonracket shoulder (Figure 5-33). Bend at the waist in the direction of the backhand side and extend your racket arm to contact the shuttle at its highest point possible.

The only difference between around-the-head shots and other overheads is that the shuttle is contacted over the nonracket shoulder in around-the-heads.

At the beginning and intermediate levels, it is suggested that around-the-head strokes be strongly emphasized. This encourages more aggressive stroking and also deters players from stroking the weaker backhand shots (clears and drops).

Playing Strategy

There is no set sequence of shots or strategic decisions that one can use to win a volley. However, with sound fundamentals, proficient strokes, and good strategy, you will win many matches.

Basically, shots made from below net level (the white tape), or what is termed "lifted," are considered to be *defensive*, and those made from above the net level, or stroked downward, are considered to be *offensive*.

BASIC STRATEGY

1. Force your opponent to move as far as possible to return a shot.
2. Use attacking strokes whenever you get a chance.
3. Return to "home base" after every shot.
4. Play to your opponent's weakest side—generally the backhand.
5. When in doubt, hit a high, deep clear and hope for a weak return.

SINGLES STRATEGY

The game of singles demands a great deal of determination, hustle, quick reactions, and patience. Outsmarting your opponent by using good strategy and outhustling her through mere determination are exciting and rewarding.

SERVING

1. A long serve (high and deep) to the backcourt area near the centerline is used the majority of the time. This serve will put your opponent as far away from the net as possible and will force her to hit a strong return that puts you at a disadvantage. Directing your serve to the centerline will cut down the angle of return.
2. A short serve can be used if your opponent is standing too deep in her receiving court to return your serve. Or short serves can be used if your opponent has an effective smash from the backcourt area and you want to eliminate a smash return directly off your serve.

RETURN OF SERVICE

1. Return serves with shots that are straight ahead. Crosscourt shots take longer to travel and need to be hit harder because of the extra distance they have to fly.
2. Your service return should move your opponent out of her home base position.
3. Long serves are generally returned with an overhead clear or a drop shot in the near corner.
4. Short serves are returned with an underhand clear or a net drop (push) to the near corner.

THE VOLLEY

1. Move your opponent to the various corners of the court by varying your shot selection. Moving your opponent out of her home base position and to the different corners of the court will increase your chances of forcing a weak return and your opponent losing control of the volley.
2. Move your opponent to the various corners of the court, in diagonal patterns if possible. Moving your opponent diagonally forces her to travel greater distances in covering the court.
3. Force your opponent to lift the shuttle as often as possible. This maneuver will decrease your opponent's chances for returning the shuttle with a strong stroke and increase your chances for staying on the attack (hitting the shuttle downward).
4. Build your game on a pattern of drops and clears. If you are patient, this pattern will eventually force your opponent to hit a weak return. Then use your smash to put the volley away.

5. Take advantage of any weakness your opponent may have. The backhand is usually the weaker side, so direct your shots to that side.

6. In defending a smash, block it to the opposite side of where the smash was originated.

7. If your opponent is moving to cover an open spot on the court when you are about to make your shot, play the bird to the position being vacated. The most difficult maneuver on the court is one that requires a quick change of direction. Retracing your steps demands the utmost agility and speed.

8. Do not play the sidelines too close with your shots. Give yourself about a 3-foot safety variance inside the sideline to reduce your chances of hitting the shuttle out-of-bounds.

9. If late in the game, and you are trailing your opponent, you might want to switch to a more conservative type of play. Direct your shots toward the center portion of the court. This adjustment will increase your chances of staying in-bounds and remaining "in the game." However, you should not become less aggressive in your stroking.

DOUBLES STRATEGY

It must be understood that doubles is a more complex game than singles. It is faster paced and demands considerable strategy and cohesive teamwork for partners to be effective. It is offense oriented, which means that attacking, energy-consuming strokes are used most of the time. With excellently placed strokes and long volleys, doubles can be a very strenuous game.

Serving

1. A short serve (low and short) to the T area (near corner) is used most of the time. This serve will force your opponents to lift the shuttle and will put them in a defensive situation directly off the serve.

2. Long serves (high, but not as deep as the singles long serve) can be used to move a strong forecourt player to the backcourt area, or they can be used to maneuver an opponent who has an ineffective smash to the backcourt. Remember, because long serves in doubles are not allowed to travel as far back into the playing court area, the long serve should be used sparingly.

3. The server's partner should assume a position two feet forward of the long service line and straddling the centerline. This alignment is used in preparation for an attacking strategy (up-and-back).

Return of Service

1. The receiving position in doubles is slightly different for the receiver than in singles. From the doubles receiving position, short serves can be played quickly, which, in turn, increases the possibility of using attacking strokes for short service returns.

2. Rush short serves. As soon as the shuttle is served, step forward with the racket foot and attempt to contact the shuttle while it is still above the net level. Stroke the shuttle downward if possible.

3. Drop returns should be directed to the near corner.

4. A push shot directed to the near side alley, midcourt depth, is an excellent return for a short serve.

5. Return long serves with a smash.

6. The receiver's partner should assume a position 2 feet forward of the long service line and straddling the centerline. This alignment is used in preparation for an attacking strategy.

The Volley. There are three basic alignments used for doubles play. These alignments are generally dependent on the specific situation during the game or volley. There is a defensive alignment, *side-by-side*; an offensive alignment, *up-and-back*; or you can use a combination of these two alignments, called *circular rotation*. Circular rotation depends largely on the situation your team is in (offensive or defensive) during the point being played.

SIDE-BY-SIDE ALIGNMENT. This alignment is considered to be defensive. In this alignment, each partner is responsible for his half of the playing court (Figure 5-34). Whenever your opponents are in control of the volley (using attacking strokes or forcing you to lift the shuttle), the side-by-side alignment is the best strategy to use. With this alignment, it will be harder for your opponents to stroke a smash past you because you and your partner will have the court covered laterally efficiently. This alignment is also easy to understand and learn.

A disadvantage of this alignment is that it allows a team to play to the weaker player. It would be to your advantage, if aligned in this formation, to get back to an attacking (offensive) position as soon as possible. This maneuver can be accomplished by either blocking your

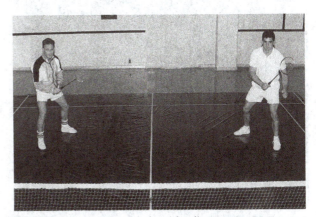

Figure 5-34 Doubles side-by-side alignment.

opponent's smashes to the side alleys or front corners, forcing them to lift the shuttle to you, or net dropping their overhead drops to the front corners, forcing them to lift and assume a defensive alignment. Although the side-by-side alignment is an effective defensive alignment, doubles is an attacking game. Few points can be won directly from defensive strokes or defensive alignments.

UP-AND-BACK ALIGNMENT. This alignment is considered to be offensive. In this alignment one partner is responsible for the forecourt area (sideline to sideline, from the net to the T) while his partner is responsible for the midcourt and backcourt area (sideline to sideline). Both players are situated along the centerline of the court, with one player positioned at the T and the other positioned approximately 2 feet forward of the long service line (Figure 5-35).

Whenever your team is in control of the volley (using attacking strokes or forcing your opponents to lift the shuttle), the up-and-back alignment is the best strategy to use. With this alignment, it will be harder for your opponents to block a smash or net drop effectively, because one partner will have the forecourt covered efficiently. It will also decrease the effectiveness of your opponent's clears in that your partner will have the backcourt covered.

A disadvantage of the up-and-back alignment is that it allows a team to pass or drive a shot down the side alleys of the court.

The net player's (partner at the T) responsibility is to intercept any shot by the opponents before it reaches his partner's midcourt or backcourt area. The net player is also responsible for stroking the shuttle downward, net dropping, or pushing the shuttle back over the net as quickly as possible from the forecourt area in response to an opponent's stroke. The net player should use any stroke that will keep the opponents in a defensive situation, or lifting the shuttle.

Figure 5-35 Doubles up-and-back alignment.

The backcourt player's responsibility is to attack the opponents with strokes that force lifting responses. Smashes and overhead drops used strategically will serve this purpose. He should direct these shots down the centerline or toward the side alleys. The backcourt partner should also direct these attacking strokes to the opponent that is the weaker player.

Remember, the up-and-back alignment is an offensive alignment and doubles is an attacking game. Points can be won directly from attacking strokes with players in offensive alignments.

COMBINATION (CIRCULAR ROTATION). The combination system combines the best of the other two systems, using the side-by-side alignment for defense and the up-and-back alignment for attacking. This system is generally used by advanced players. It takes a great deal of teamwork, practice, and playing time to use this system effectively.

The basic principles are as follows:

1. If the server serves short, the serving team will remain in the up-and-back alignment.

   Reason: A short serve forces your opponents to lift the shuttle, which in turn will allow the serving team to return the shuttle with downward, attacking strokes, keeping that team in an offensive situation.

2. If the server serves long, the serving team will go to a side-by-side alignment. After serving, the server should drop back to his serving side and his partner move to the opposite side.

   Reason: A long serve allows the opponents to return the shuttle with attacking strokes, thereby putting the serving team in a defensive situation.

3. If the receiver of the serve is served short, and he net drops or pushes the shuttle downward back over the net, the receiving team should stay in an up-and-back alignment.

   Reason: The receiving team, with those returns, has just forced its opponents to start lifting the shuttle.

   If the receiver of the serve is served short, and he clears the shuttle, the receiving team should go to a side-by-side alignment.

   Reason: The receiving team has been forced to lift the shuttle. It is now in a defensive situation.

   If the receiver of the serve is served long, his partner should immediately go to the T to play the net, and the receiver should smash or overhead drop the shuttle to force his opponents to lift. With these actions, they have now assumed the up-and-back offensive alignment.

4. On any shot that gives the opponents the advantage and opportunity to smash or overhead drop, the team making the stroke should take up the

defensive side-by-side alignment. The player making the shot should cover the half of the court from which the shot was made.

5. When reverting from a defensive to an offensive alignment, the player taking a backcourt stroke (attacking) that initiates the change will stay in the backcourt back position. The partner will then move to the up position and guard the net from the T. If the stroke that initiates the change is taken from a forecourt position, the player taking that stroke will move to the up position at the net. The partner will then move to the back position in the backcourt.

▶ Learning Hints: Doubles Strategy

1. Attack as often as possible. Hit the shuttle downward and force your opponents to lift the shuttle.

2. When attacking, use the up-and-back alignment.

3. When lifting the shuttle, use the side-by-side alignment.

4. Rush short serves. Attack them if possible.

5. Smash long serves.

6. When opponents are in a defensive alignment, smash or overhead drop toward the centerline.

7. When opponents are in a defensive alignment, play to the weaker opponent.

8. When opponents are in an offensive alignment, direct your shots to the side alleys.

9. When you are in a defensive alignment, revert to an attacking situation as soon as the chance arises.

10. Use clears only in emergency situations. If you must clear, clear to the back corners.

▶ Playing Courtesies

Badminton emphasizes good sportsmanship and playing courtesies. Use good judgment at all times with regard to your own behavior as well as to your attitude toward your opponent. Be cordial and respectful. As in any sport, be a good loser as well as a gracious winner; try to maintain a positive attitude. The following are some courtesies specific to badminton.

1. If your opponent is unknown to you, introduce yourself and shake hands prior to the match.

2. The warm-up period should be gracious and uncompetitive.

3. The server should call the score prior to each serve—server's score first.

4. If in doubt about the shuttle's landing, always call it in favor of your opponent.

5. Inform your opponent of the call as quickly as possible.

6. Never question your opponent's calls.

7. If there is any question of your faulting, be sure to call it on yourself.

8. If a shuttle lands on your side and you are the receiver, pick it up and hit it back to the server so that she does not have to go out of her way to retrieve it.

9. Do not smash at your opponent if the point could be easily won by placing the shuttle elsewhere in the court.

10. Do not stall. Keep the play continuous.

11. If you are the receiver, get ready to receive the serve without any hesitation.

12. Compliment your opponent's exceptional shots.

13. Do not offer playing advice to your opponents.

14. Do not, under any circumstances, throw your racket or the shuttle in anger.

15. Always shake hands with your opponent after the match.

Skill Assessment

The serve and clear are two basic skills beginning to intermediate players need to develop for continuous play. The constraints of time, facilities, equipment, and set-up make it difficult to skill-test more than two techniques taught in a typical 2-to-3-week unit. It is suggested that the short serve and underhand clear be used for assessment. Each test is conducted simultaneously on the same court by three students: a scorer, a bird retriever, and a participant. The participant, with three birds, takes three practice trials and then hits the next nine shots (three at a time) for score. The scorer records the participant's accomplishments, the retriever quickly returns the shuttlecocks, and then the students rotate to their new responsibility.

Short Serve. The participant must serve the bird below a rope stretched 2 feet above the net from side-to-side and over the net, where it lands on a target. The serve is diagonal from the right service court to the opposite right service court. The target, on a 36-by-36 inch poster board, is placed in the front corner of the service area, bound by the short service line and the center line.

You can make the target by drawing lines on poster board. From one corner measure 20 inches along the edge of the board each way, and then draw a line across connecting these two measurements to form a front corner triangle. Next measure 28 inches along the edge of the board on each side and draw a line parallel with the previous one. Finally, measure 36 inches from the top of the board and draw another parallel line. The 36-by-36 inch poster board now has three parallel lines (20 in., 28 in., 36 in.) diagonally across the front half of the board. The target is positioned and secured in the front corner of the service area, with the triangle of the target bound by the short service line and the center line. The front triangle is worth 5 points, the next area is 3 points, the following is 2 points, and any serve that lands legally in the service court beyond the last line is worth 1 point. Zero points are awarded if the serve fails to go between the rope and top of the net. A perfect score is 45 (9 serves worth 5 points).

Underhand Clear.   The participant stands in the middle of the left singles service court on the same side of the net as the short serve participant, with the back foot on a spot 8 feet from the net. The bird is dropped, and with the underhand clear stroke, is hit over the line stretched 2 feet above the net, deep to a target positioned straight across the net to the right-hand singles service area.

The target is two folding mats (4-by-6 ft., or 4-by-8 ft.) with 2-feet folding sections, laid flat lengthwise and side-by-side in the opposite right service court. The first mat butts lengthwise against the baseline and centerline of that court. The second mat is positioned next to the first toward the sideline. The deepest 2-feet section is worth 5 points, the next closest 3, then 2, and finally 1 point for any bird landing legally in the singles court. A perfect score is 45 (9 attempts worth 5 points).

The nine students per court allows for maximum testing and speeds the testing process. Make sure that each person at the court is appropriately positioned to carry out the assigned duties responsibly, efficiently, and quickly.

Modifications for Special Populations

ORTHOPEDICALLY IMPAIRED

1. See modifications discussed in the chapters on handball and racquetball and tennis.
2. Students with grasping difficulties should consider bracing or wrist devices to assist with gripping. The student could have the racket secured to the brace with an ace bandage.

COGNITIVELY IMPAIRED

1. Consult with Special Olympics, and use modifications from the chapters on handball and racquetball and tennis from this text.

SENSORY IMPAIRED

1. Individual considerations must be taken into account to determine the appropriateness of badminton for students who are visually impaired. Students might be able to play a modified game using a tethered shuttlecock.
2. Students with hearing impairments will need minimal modifications. Make sure to face the student, speak slowly, and do not cover your mouth with hand gestures. Also avoid standing in front of a bright light because this may produce shadows on your face.

Terminology

alley The 1½-foot-wide area on each side of the court that is used for doubles. Often referred to as the "side alley."

around-the-head stroke An overhead stroke used when hitting a forehand-like overhead stroke that is on the backhand side of the body.

back alley The area between the doubles long service line and the baseline.

backcourt The back third of the court.

backhand A stroke made on the nonracket side of the body.

baseline The back boundary line of the court.

bird Another name for the shuttlecock.

block A soft shot, used primarily in defense against a smash. Intercepting an opponent's smash and returning it back over the net.

carry Called when the shuttle stays on the racket during a stroke. It is legal if the racket follows the intended line of flight. Also referred to as a throw.

centerline The mid-line separating the service courts.

clear A high shot that goes over your opponent's head and lands close to the baseline.

combination alignment Partners play both up-and-back and side-by-side during doubles games and/or volleys.

crosscourt A shot hit diagonally into the opposite court.

defense The team or player hitting the shuttle upward (lifting), usually from an underhand stroke.

double hit An illegal shot in which the racket contacts the shuttle twice in one swing.

doubles service court The short, wide area to which the server must serve in doubles play.

down-the-line shot A shot hit straight ahead—usually down the sideline.

drive A hard-driven shot that travels parallel with the floor. This shot clears the net but does not go high enough for your opponent to smash.

drop A shot that just clears the net, then falls close to it.

face The string area of the racket.

fault Any infraction of the rules. It results in the loss of serve or in a point for the server.

first serve A term used in doubles play to indicate that the server is the "first server" during an inning.

foot fault Illegal position or movement of the feet by either the server or receiver.

forecourt The front area of the court, usually considered to be between the net and the short service line.

forehand Any stroke made on the racket side of the body.

game point The point which, if won, allows the server to win the game.

hand in The term used to indicate that the server retains the serve.

hand out The term used in doubles to show that one player has lost the service.

home base The position in the center of the court from which the player can best play any shot hit by an opponent.

inning The time during which a player or team holds service.

let The stopping of play because of some type of outside interference. The point is replayed.

lifting the shuttle To stroke the bird underhanded and hit it upward.

long serve A high, deep serve landing near the long service line in doubles or back boundary line (baseline) in singles.

love The term used to indicate zero in scoring.

match A series of games. In badminton, winning two out of three games will win the match.

match point The point that, if won by the server, makes that person the winner of the match.

midcourt The middle third of the court, usually considered to be between the short service line and the long service line for doubles.

net shot A shot taken near the net.

nonracket side The side opposite the hand holding the racket.

offense The team or player that is stroking the shuttle downward (attacking).

overhead A motion used to strike the shuttle when it is above the head.

racket foot or leg The foot or leg on the same side as the hand holding the racket.

ready position The position a player assumes to be ready to move in any direction.

receiver The player to whom the shuttle is served.

second serve In doubles, the term indicates that one partner has lost the serve and the other partner is now serving.

server The player who puts the shuttle into play.

setting Choosing how many more points to play when certain tie scores are reached.

short serve A serve that barely clears the net and lands just beyond the short service line.

shuttlecock (shuttle) The feathered, plastic, or nylon object that is volleyed back and forth over the net.

side alley See *alley.*

side-by-side A defensive alignment used in doubles play. Each partner is responsible for one side of the court, from the net to the back boundary line.

side out When a player or team loses the serve.

smash An overhead stroke hit downward with great velocity and angle. The principal attacking stroke in badminton.

T The intersection of the centerline and the short service line.

underhand A stroke that is hit upward when the shuttle has fallen below shoulder level.

unsight Illegal position taken by the server's partner so the receiver cannot see the shuttle as it is hit.

up-and-back An offensive alignment used in doubles. The "up" player is responsible for the forecourt, and the "back" player is responsible for the midcourt and backcourt.

Discussion Questions

1. Identify the order in which skills and techniques (basic to advanced) should be introduced when there are unit length restrictions.

2. Discuss the mechanical similarities and differences of the overhead clear, overhead drop, smash, and around-the-head strokes.

3. Identify the sport's name changes throughout its history.

4. Discuss the strategies for serving in singles and the counter strategies for returning serves.

5. Discuss the various strategies for the volley in singles play.

6. Identify the strategies for serving in doubles and the counter strategies for returning serves.

7. Discuss the advantages and disadvantages of the three defensive alignments in doubles.

8. Discuss the merits of the basic strategies and learning hints for both singles and doubles.

9. Present the playing courtesies that affect the game.

10. Assess the similarities and differences between the rules for singles and doubles.

Web Sites

www.badmintoncentral.com—provides tips on technique, rules, a forum for addressing techniques with others, and other links.

www.usabadminton.org—provides history, rules, links, badminton facts, and a video library.

www.worldbadminton.com—supplies the laws of badminton, history, a glossary, an extensive list of North American and world badminton organizations, information on training, and badminton news.

www.how-to-play-badminton.com—covers rules, basics, strokes, techniques, and advanced skills.

CHAPTER 6

Basketball

This chapter will enable you to

- Know the playing court, equipment, and basic rules of basketball
- Practice and develop skill in the fundamentals of passing, dribbling, shooting, rebounding, individual offense, and individual defense
- Identify the objectives and strategies of team offense and defense
- Develop practice/organization skills for various skills and techniques

Nature and Purpose

Basketball is an extremely popular game, played in all parts of the world and at every conceivable level. In the United States, the extremes are evident—from rickety backboards attached to garages to multimillion-dollar arenas that hold thousands of spectators. Basketball can be played at a highly organized level or at a neighborhood playground. Children can play on school teams, beginning with elementary school and continuing through college. Highly skilled men and women can earn basketball scholarships to play for colleges and universities. There are amateur tournaments and professional leagues. It is a vital part of school intramural programs, sometimes even played coeducationally. Basketball presents the opportunity to learn ball skills, coordination, agility, and body control; participation in the game can contribute toward maintenance of an individual's total fitness.

This original U.S. sport has broad applications: Large groups can participate at relatively low cost; the game can serve for competitive or recreational purposes; and it has the appeal to make it a popular spectator sport.

Officially, a basketball team is composed of five players. However, in recreational play, two, three, or four players can play a game. The purpose of the game is to score a larger total number of points than the opponent. The score is compiled by shooting the ball through the basket either from the field (called a field goal) or from the free-throw line (called a free throw or a foul shot). The ball is passed, thrown, bounced, batted, or rolled from one player to another. A player in possession of the ball must maintain contact with the floor with one foot (called the pivot foot), unless the player is shooting, passing, or dribbling. Dribbling consists of a series of one-hand taps, causing the ball to bounce on the floor. Physical contact with an opponent can result in a foul if the contact impedes the desired movement of the player.

History

Dr. James A. Naismith introduced the game to a class at the YMCA College (now Springfield College) in Springfield, Massachusetts, in 1892. He had been challenged in 1891 by Dr. Luther Gulich, his superior, to come up with an indoor game that would keep some unruly students busy during the winter. Naismith drew his inspiration from football, lacrosse, baseball, rugby, and soccer.

The game spread rapidly; for example, girls from Buckingham Grade School grasped the concept quickly just 2 weeks after it was introduced. During the first year, basketball spread to all corners of the United States. The first team was organized at the YMCA College in 1892 and played its first game with the 26th Separate Company of the U.S. Army. Colleges and universities are credited with the early spread of basketball, and by 1905 it was firmly entrenched in those institutions' athletic programs. By 1904 the game came under the jurisdiction of the Intercollegiate Athletic Association, which was later named the National Collegiate Athletic Association (NCAA). It adopted its own rules committee in 1905. However, it was not until 1939 that the NCAA sponsored its first national championship, one year after the National Invitational Tournament (NIT) became the first collegiate championship.

As early as 1894, basketball was being played in several foreign countries. The sport grew in international status immediately with the Pan American championship held in 1901. In the 1904 Olympic games, basketball was featured as a demonstration sport, and in 1936 basketball was accepted to the official Olympic sport program. As a result of the game's increasing recognition, the Federation Internationale de Basketball (FIBA) was formed in 1932 to govern international basketball qualifying events for the Olympics.

Professional basketball emerged in 1898 with the formation of the National League. Several professional organizations emerged and merged over the first 75 years of the 20th century, culminating with the formation of the National Basketball Association (NBA) in 1949. It was not until 1997 that the Women's National Basketball Association (WNBA) was established.[1]

Court or Field of Play

The playing area of basketball is called the court. The rectangular court measures a maximum of 94 feet long and 50 feet wide, or a minimum of 74 feet long and 42 feet wide. The baskets are suspended 10 feet above the floor at the endline of each court. The court has three restraining circles and two free-throw areas (Figure 6-1). The court can be modified (made smaller) and the baskets lowered to accommodate younger participants. Basketball can be played on a half-court if large numbers of participants want to play in an intramural, class, or recreational situation.

BASIC RULES

Three at most but sometimes two on-the-court officials regulate a basketball game. The game is divided into 20-minute halves for college and university teams and 8-minute quarters for high school teams. Teams composed of players younger than high school age should have 6-minute quarters. The length of the game in a recreational, class, or intramural situation can be adjusted by shortening the quarters or halves, or by having "running time," wherein the clock does not stop on the dead balls.

There are slight variations of rules between high school and collegiate play, as well as between the men's and women's collegiate games. Nevertheless, there are basic rules of basketball governing play at any level.

PLAYERS

1. Even though only five players per team play at a time, any number of substitutions can be made at any dead ball during the game or during a time-out. Substitutes must report to the scorer and wait to be beckoned onto the court by an official.

2. One of the five players is the designated floor captain and may address the official on matters of interpretation or information. Any player may request a time-out.

SCORING AND TIMING

1. A goal is made when a live ball enters the basket from above and remains in or passes through except on a throw-in. A field goal counts *3 points* if the shot is made by a player situated beyond the 3-point field goal line. There are now two lines with one at 19' 6" and at 20' 6". Various

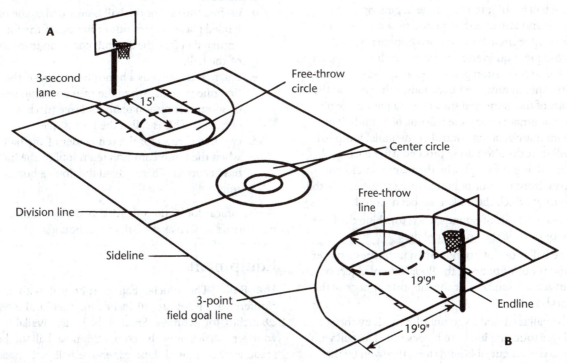

Figure 6-1 The basketball court.

organizations govern the appropriate distance. For a successful 3-point field goal, the player must have one or both feet on the floor and be beyond the 3-point line when attempting the shot. After releasing the ball, the shooter may land on or over the line. Touching the line before the release places the shooter in the 2-point area.

2. A goal from the field other than from the 3-point area counts *2 points*.

3. When a free throw is awarded for fouls, each successful free throw counts *1 point*.

4. If a player mistakenly scores a field goal in the opponent's basket, the goal is counted for the opponent.

5. Each team gets the same number of time-outs per game. Various organizing bodies (NCAA, high school, YMCA, etc.) dictate the number and length of these time-outs. They can vary from 20 seconds to 1 minute. Regardless of the length and time, time-outs can be requested only during a dead ball or anytime by the team in possession of the ball.

6. If the score is tied at the end of regulation time, play continues an extra period. As many extra periods are played as necessary to break the tie.

7. The clock stops each time an official blows the whistle indicating a dead ball (violation, personal foul, out-of-bounds). The clock keeps running after successful field goals.

PLAY

1. The ball is put into play at the beginning of the game and any overtime period by a jump ball in the center circle between two opponents. Each subsequent quarter or half starts with the team entitled to possession given the ball at the center division line. In jump ball situations, other than at the start of the game and start of extra periods, teams will alternate taking the ball out-of-bounds. The team not obtaining control of the initial jump ball will start the alternating process. After each goal, the ball is put into play by the team that did not score from the out-of-bounds area at the end of the court at which the basket has been scored.

2. A player is out-of-bounds when touching the floor on or outside the boundary line.

3. The ball is out-of-bounds when it touches a player who is out-of-bounds, the floor, or any object on or outside a boundary, or the supports or back of the backboard.

4. The ball is caused to go out-of-bounds by the last player touching it before it goes out. The ball would be awarded out-of-bounds for a throw-in by the opposing team. The ball is awarded out-of-bounds

after a violation, successful free throw or field goal, or a common foul until the bonus rule goes into effect.

5. While the ball is alive, an offensive player cannot remain for more than 3 seconds in that part of the free-throw lane between the endline, the free-throw line, and the free-throw lane lines.

6. If two opponents are both firmly holding the ball, or an offensive ball handler is closely guarded by the defense for 5 seconds, a jump ball is called.

7. Violations include causing the ball to go out-of-bounds, double dribbling, running with the ball, kicking the ball (positive act), striking the ball with the fist, interfering with the basket, illegal throw-in (taking more than 5 seconds or stepping on the line), and the 3-second lane rule.

8. Fouls are classified as (1) *personal*—involving pushing, charging, tripping, holding, body contact; or (2) *technical*—involving delay of game, unsportsmanlike conduct, illegal entry, excessive time-outs. For personal fouls, the offender is charged with one foul; a fifth personal foul results in disqualification. The offended player is awarded:

  a. one free throw if the foul occurred during a field goal attempt and the basket was made.

  b. two free throws if the foul occurred during a 2-point field goal attempt and the basket was missed.

  c. three free throws if the foul occurred during a 3-point field goal atempt and the basket was missed.

  d. no free throw, but the ball is awarded to the offended player's team out-of-bounds if the foul occurred before the seventh common team foul of the half.

  e. one free throw plus a bonus free throw if the first one is made, when the fifth common foul or seventh common team foul (see (d)) has occurred. This is called the bonus rule.

  f. two free throws for the remainder of the half when the tenth common team foul of the half has occurred. This is called the double bonus rule.

For technical fouls, the offended team is awarded two free throws as well as the ball out-of-bounds.

Equipment

The Ball. The official ball is spherical with a circumference of 29½ to 30 inches for men and 28½ to 29 inches for women. Smaller balls are available for younger participants. In competition, a ball of high-grade leather is used. Less expensive balls are made of rubber or synthetic materials.

The Basket. The basket consists of a simple metal ring, 18 inches in diameter. A white cord net suspends from beneath the ring. The basket is securely attached to a rigid backboard. Most backboards used in competition are transparent glass and rectangular in shape. However, it is not uncommon for backboards to be fan-shaped and made of solid wood.

Suggested Learning Sequence—Beginners

A. Conditioning and stretching

B. Purpose of the game and general game concepts

C. Basic rules

D. Fundamental skills:
  1. Pivoting
  2. Catching and holding the ball
  3. Passing—chest, bounce, overhead
  4. Dribbling—high speed, low control
  5. Shooting—one-handed set, layup
  6. Rebounding—position, jumping

E. Individual offense:
  1. Cutting—V-cut, front
  2. Driving
  3. Screening

F. Individual defense:
  1. Basic stance and movement
  2. Guarding a player with the ball
  3. Guarding a player without a ball

G. Team play:
  1. *Offense*—basic concepts on how to attack a player-to-player defense
  2. *Defense*—player-to-player
  3. *Other*—jump ball alignment, free-throw alignment

Suggested Learning Sequence—Intermediates

A. Conditioning and stretching

B. Additional rules

C. Review beginners unit

D. Intermediate skills:
  1. Passing—one-hand bounce, baseball
  2. Dribbling—crossover, reverse (spin)
  3. Shooting—free throw, jump shot, layup from various angles
  4. Rebounding—blocking out, outlet pass

E. Individual offense:
  1. Cutting—backdoor (reverse)
  2. Fakes and feints

F. Individual defense:
  1. Defense against a player one pass away and two passes away
  2. Denial defense
  3. Defense against a ball handler

G. Team play:
  1. *Offense*—basic concepts on how to attack a zone defense
  2. *Defense*—combatting picks and screens, zones
  3. *Other*—fast break, in-bounds plays

Skills and Techniques

PIVOTING

Pivoting is the only legal maneuvering a player standing and holding the ball is allowed. One foot (the pivot foot) must be kept at its point of contact with the floor, while the other foot can step in any direction. A good technique for the beginner is to imagine that a spike has been driven through the pivot foot into the floor; this would afford faking movements with the opposite foot, but the spike can be removed only through dribbling, passing, or shooting. Illegally moving the pivot foot or taking too many steps while stopping constitutes "traveling." The result is a loss of possession of the ball for that team.

PASSING

Good passing is necessary to maintain possession of the ball and be able to move into scoring position. The key to an effective offense is accuracy in passing, and passing is the quickest way to move the ball, thus *allowing the offense to catch the defense off balance or out of position.*

Chest Pass. This pass is the most commonly used pass. The ball is held in both hands, the fingers spread on the sides of the ball with the thumbs behind the ball. Held about chest high with the elbows held comfortably at the sides of the body, the ball is released by extending the arms fully, snapping the wrists, and stepping in the direction of the pass. The palms should be facing downward or slightly outward, with the elbow chest high on the follow-through. The chest pass should be received chest high.

Bounce Pass. This pass is a short-distance pass used to avoid a deflection or interception when a player is being closely guarded. It is executed in the same manner as the chest pass except the ball is bounced into the hands of the receiver. The ball should bounce at approximately two-thirds of the distance between the passer and receiver, and should rebound waist high. This pass can also be released with one hand by stepping out with the free foot to either side of a close defender and

A   **B**

Figure 6-2 The overhead pass.

bouncing the ball around him. It is also possible to make this pass directly off of the dribble.

Overhead Pass. This pass is used to pass over a defensive player, usually to a post player or a cutter. The ball is held overhead with both hands, thumbs under the ball and fingers spread on the sides of the ball (Figure 6-2A). The passer steps forward toward the intended receiver and transfers the body weight to the front foot. The arms, which are slightly bent, are brought forward sharply, with a snap of the wrists releasing the ball (Figure 6-2B). This pass is best used by a player who is taller than the defending opponent.

One-Hand Overhead Pass (Baseball Pass). This pass is used most frequently to cover long distances, especially in initiating the fast break. When this pass is thrown with the right hand, the ball is brought back to the right ear, close to the head, with the fingers well spread in back of the ball. The left hand can steady the ball when it is in this position, ready to be thrown. The weight of the body is shifted to the right rear foot as the ball is brought back. The weight shifts forward to the left foot as the right arm is brought forward to release the ball. The ball is released about one foot in front of the body with the wrist snapping forward and downward.

▶ Learning Hints: Passing

1. Passes should be crisp, but not too hard to catch.
2. Use a pass appropriate for the specific situation.
3. Take a step in the direction of the pass.
4. Balance your weight when passing.
5. Do not "telegraph" the pass; be deceptive with your eyes.

6. Aim to hit your receiver between the waist and shoulders.
7. A fake before you pass may cause your defender to move, creating a better passing lane.
8. Put as little spin as possible on the pass.
9. Pass to the side of your teammate away from the defender.
10. Always pass ahead of a running teammate.
11. Learn to catch and pass in one motion.

CATCHING AND HOLDING THE BALL

Possession of the ball is so important that receiving and holding the ball are as essential as passing. A player should attempt to catch every pass regardless of how it is thrown. To help eliminate deflections, a player should cut sharply toward each pass to meet it, with the hands held out in front of the body to provide a target and to maintain balance when moving in any direction to meet the ball. It is also possible to hold one hand up in the air (the hand farther from your defender) to provide a high target for a pass (Figure 6-3). The ball should be caught with the pads of the fingers and brought toward the body to protect it before dribbling, passing, or shooting. If a player must stand for a few moments in possession of the ball, it is best to step back slightly with your free foot, away from your defender, pulling the ball back with you. This places your body between the ball and the defender for added protection.

▶ Learning Hints: Catching and Holding the Ball

1. Provide the passer with a target by holding a hand up or both hands forward.
2. Move to meet passes thrown to you.
3. Have your hands comfortably spread and relaxed when catching.
4. Keep elbows flexed, not stiff, enabling absorption of the impact of the thrown ball.
5. Watch the ball all of the way into your hands.
6. Pull the ball in close to your body for protection.
7. Whenever possible, catch with two hands to ensure control.

▶ Practice/Organizational Suggestions: Passing and Catching

1. Stand approximately 8 feet from a wall. Execute different passes against the wall, concentrating on form and accuracy.
2. With a partner, stand in positions as either two guards, or as a guard and a forward. Pass back and forth, faking before each pass and practicing deception. Add two defenders. Add a cut to the basket after each pass to receive a return pass.

Figure 6-3   Preparing to catch a pass against a defender.

3. To practice the baseball pass, stand 30 feet from a partner. Pass back and forth. To practice this pass on the move, both players position themselves near the backboard. One player rebounds the ball off the board, dribbles toward the sideline, and releases a baseball pass to the other player cutting downcourt. Add defenders.

4. Three-player weave (Figure 6-4): Three players start on the endline approximately 15 feet apart. The player in the middle has a ball. This player passes to a wing and subsequently cuts behind the wing player. The receiver, in turn, passes to the third player and cuts behind this third player.

The three players continue passing and moving downcourt. Vary the passes. Add one, two, or three defenders.

5. Four-corner passing (Figure 6-5): With players in a box formation, one player makes a long pass to the first player in the next line. This player follows the pass and receives a short pass back. The initial player hands off to the same player and goes to the end of that line. Continue with a long pass to the next corner. *Variation:* Add another ball. Start them in opposite corners.

6. Shotgun passing (Figure 6-6): One player stands apart from a half-circle of teammates who are arranged so that two players are just in the peripheral vision of the single player. Using two balls, the half-circle players and the single player pass quickly back and forth.

Key to Maneuvers

Cut	———▶
Pass	−−−▶
Pick or screen	———(
Dribble	∿∿∿

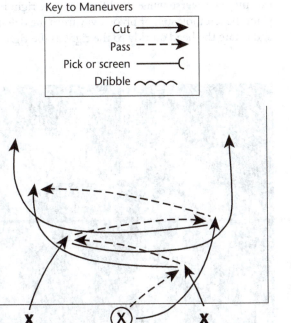

Figure 6-4   Three-player weave.

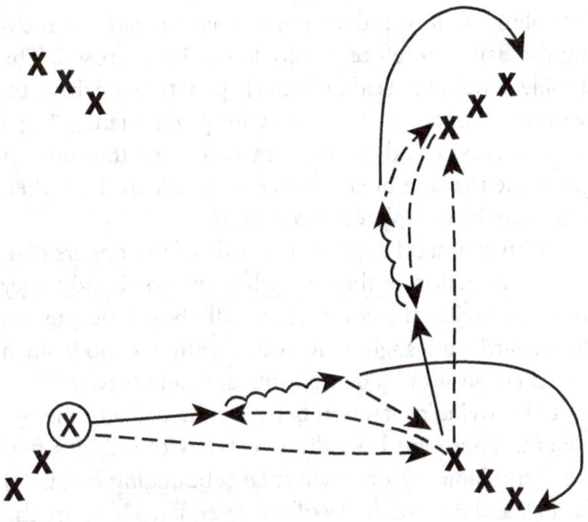

Figure 6-5   Four-corner passing.

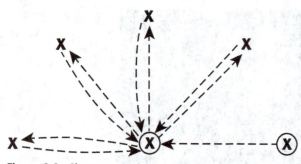

Figure 6-6 Shotgun passing.

7. Reaction pass drill: One partner has a ball, while the other player stands approximately 15 feet away facing away from the partner. The player with the ball calls out the other player's first name, followed by a pass to the player. Upon hearing his name, the player quickly turns and attempts to catch the ball and gain control of it. The pass should vary, making the receiver jump, reach, or stoop to secure every pass.

8. Monkey in the middle: Players form a circle with one player ("monkey") in the middle. Using one ball and any type of pass, a player in the circle attempts to get the ball to any other player in the circle, other than the two players immediately on each side. The "monkey" attempts to touch, deflect, or intercept the pass. If successful, the "monkey" changes place with the passer.

9. Shuttle pass drill: Form two lines in a shuttle formation. The first player in one of the lines has a ball. The first person in the opposite line defends as the player attempts to pass across to the other line. Continue passing between the two lines with the passer each time becoming the next defender.

DRIBBLING

Dribbling is slower than passing as a means of moving the ball. Therefore, it should not be overused. The dribble should be used only to (1) penetrate or drive toward the basket, (2) create a better passing lane, (3) get out of a crowd, and (4) bring the ball down the court. A good rule to remember is never to dribble the ball when a pass can be completed successfully.

With the hand cupped, the pads of the fingers control the direction of the ball, while the wrist and finger flexion provide the force. The ball should be pushed downward and slightly forward, with the body in a crouched position. The opposite arm and forward foot should provide protection between the ball and the opponent. There are basically two types of dribbles that are identifiable by observing the rebounding height of the ball and the proximity of the defender. These are the high-speed dribble and the low-control dribble.

High-Speed Dribble. The high-speed dribble is used when a player is unguarded and moving quickly—leading a fast break, driving to the basket, bringing the ball down the court without opposition. The body is erect, with only a slight forward crouch. The ball rebounds between the waist and chest. The dribbling arm pushes the ball forward and slightly to the side of the body. A full running stride is used, limited only by the dribbler's ability to control the ball.

Low-Control Dribble. This dribble is used when a player is closely guarded or in a congested area. Both the body and the ball should be kept low (Figure 6-7). The ball should rebound knee high and close to the dribbling side of the body. The more frequent contact with the ball allows for control and change of direction when under pressure.

Crossover Dribble. The crossover dribble can be used to change direction. It is effective only if the defender is guarding loosely. The dribbler simply pushes the ball to the floor so that it rebounds across in front of the body to the opposite hand. This crossover must be done quickly and with only one low bounce to avoid an interception. The shoulder opposite the dribbling hand should always be lowered and brought forward to protect the ball. The dribbler can now continue dribbling in the opposite direction.

Reverse (Spin) Dribble. The reverse dribble allows a player to change directions against an opponent who is guarding closely. It provides good protection for the ball but forces the dribbler to turn away from the basket and lose visual contact with teammates (Figure 6-8). To execute the reverse while dribbling with the right hand: plant the left foot, spin or pivot away from the defender, and rotate the head quickly to the right as the right foot

Figure 6-7 Low-control dribble.

A

B

C

Figure 6-8 Reverse (spin) dribble (a three-picture sequence).

swings out past the defender. Only one bounce of the ball is necessary to switch the dribble from the right hand to the left hand. The dribbler then continues dribbling toward the left with the left hand.

▶ Learning Hints: Dribbling

1. Keep your eyes and head up, facing the basket and your teammates as much as possible.
2. Be able to dribble with either hand.
3. Protect the ball with your body and opposite arm.
4. Control the dribble with your fingers and wrist, not the palm.
5. Push the ball; do not slap it.
6. Keep your knees bent for balance.
7. Dribble with the right hand when dribbling to the right, and dribble with the left hand when dribbling to the left, *especially* when being guarded.

▶ Practice/Organizational Suggestions: Dribbling and Ball Handling

(Work to keep your head up during all dribbling and ball-handling drills.)

1. Rotate the ball around the body, starting with the head. Go all the way down around the legs, and back up.
2. Rotate the ball around each ankle—right and left. Rotate the ball in a figure 8 around the ankles in a continuous motion.
3. Dribble the ball around the legs in a figure 8. Keep the ball low.
4. Straddle flip: With the legs shoulder-width apart, hold the ball low in front with both hands. Flip it up slightly between your legs, bringing your hands around behind the legs to catch the ball before it hits the ground. Flip it up again and bring the hands back to the front. Repeat as quickly as you can. *Variation:* Start with one hand in front and one in back on the ball. Flip the ball up, alternating the hands quickly.
5. Dribble the ball around your body while on one knee, both knees, sitting, lying.
6. Standing 2 feet from a wall, tap the ball with the right or left hand high against the wall. *Variation:* Tap two balls simultaneously.
7. Circle keepaway: Within the boundaries of a restraining circle, try to dribble and maintain possession of a ball while another player attempts to steal it. *Variation:* Both players have a ball, trying to dribble *and* steal the other player's ball.
8. On a half-court, try to dribble and maintain possession of a ball while two or three players try to pursue and steal the ball.
9. Dribble tag: On a half-court, with all players dribbling a ball, play "tag." *Variations:* (1) More than one player is "it." (2) Restrict players to use their nondominant hand. (3) Half of the players have a ball, and others try to steal them (legally).

10. Column dribbling drills (players at the endline in three columns): Dribble the full length of the court:
    a. in a zigzag pattern, executing a crossover dribble or a reverse dribble at each corner.
    b. doing a crossover, reverse, or stop on the coach's signal.
    c. going around obstacles in a figure 8 pattern.
    d. against a defender, trying to steal the ball.

SHOOTING

The primary objective of the game of basketball is to score goals. Therefore, all players should be able to shoot. Being able to shoot a variety of shots from varying distances increases the effectiveness of any player.

Point of Aim. There are two targets that can be used in aiming at a basket—the rim or a spot on the backboard for a bank shot. The easiest point of aim for a beginner is the rim of the basket because of its permanent position from anywhere on the floor. The player should concentrate on dropping the ball just beyond the front of the rim. The bank shot is typically used when a player is positioned at a 24- to 45-degree angle on either side of the basket. A spot on the backboard is sighted with the purpose of allowing the ball to hit this spot and rebound into the basket. Selecting the correct spot and judging the force to put on the ball makes this a skill for experienced players. A square box is painted on most backboards to aid in spot selection. In aiming, the brain sights the target, computes the distance, and determines the correct trajectory to put on the ball. It is important for the eyes to be focused on the target before each shot, during the release, and after the follow-through. It is obvious why shooting demands so much practice.

One-Handed Set Shot. This shot is used for most long shots. The feet should be positioned in a forward-backward stride position, with the foot under the shooting hand slightly forward. The ankles, knees, and hips should be slightly flexed, with the weight easily balanced over the feet, and the shoulders square to the basket (Figure 6-9A). The ball is held below the chin (sighting the basket over the ball) or above the forehead (sighting the basket below the ball). It might be noted that the higher the ball is held, the less chance the defense has of blocking the shot. The ball should be held with the fingers, never in the palms of the hands. The shooting hand is behind and slightly under the ball with the fingers spread and wrist cocked (hyperextended). The elbow of the shooting arm should be directly under the ball, making the forearm perpendicular to the floor.

The nonshooting or guide hand is placed on the side and slightly under the ball, with fingers spread. In executing the shot, the legs extend upward while the shooting arm extends toward the basket (Figure 6-9B).

A   B

Figure 6-9   One-handed set shot.

The wrist flexes forward, while the guide hand comes off of the ball. The wrist flexion releases the ball, with the fingertips coming off last, creating a slight backspin on the ball. A proper follow-through should have the guide hand held high, with the palm of the shooting hand facing the floor. The one-handed set shot is used by most players when shooting free throws.

Jump Shot.   The jump shot is an effective offensive weapon because of its high point of release. The initial body position and hand placement on the ball are the same as in the one-handed set shot. The shooter jumps into the air by pushing off with both legs. The ball is brought high above the forehead. At the apex of the jump, the body should be in a near-stationary, balanced position (Figure 6-10). Keeping the eyes focused on the basket, the shooting arm is uncocked and releases the ball with the same action as the one-handed position. Because the force for the jump shot is supplied by the arms and wrist, the range of this shot is limited, as compared with the set shot, which incorporates leg power and arm strength.

Layup.   This shot is one of the highest percentage shots in the game because of the closeness in range. It is used when a player has received a pass close to the basket, or has driven past the defense near the goal. It is best executed on a diagonal in relation to the basket, using the backboard to bank the ball in. At the last dribble, the ball is firmly grasped with the fingers of both hands and carried above the head. When shooting with the right hand, the player should take off with the left foot, while thrusting the right knee upward to achieve maximum height. At the same moment, the ball is set in the

Figure 6-10 Jump shot (a two-picture sequence).

shooting hand and the left hand falls away. The shooting arm and fingers extend upward to "lay" the ball against the backboard. A proficient basketball player will develop the ability to shoot a layup with either hand being the dominant hand—the left hand when on the left side of the basket, the right hand when on the right side.

▶ Learning Hints: Shooting

1. Bend knees to help generate power and provide balance. Keep shoulders square to the target.
2. Keep eyes focused on the target before, during, and after the shot.
3. Keep the shooting arm's elbow directly under the ball.
4. Fingers should control every shot.
5. Use the backboard to bank a shot from an angle.
6. Maintain body balance; try not to lean or fall.
7. The shooting hand should follow through toward the basket after releasing the ball.
8. Backspin on the ball is desirable.
9. A higher arc on the ball results in greater accuracy and a better bounce off the rim if the shot is missed.

▶ Practice/Organizational Suggestions: Shooting

1. Add shooting to passing and dribbling drills.
2. Column shooting drills (two lines of players facing the basket):
   a. One line shoots layups; the other line rebounds. Vary the angles for the layups. Add defensive pressure from the rebounding line.
   b. Same as (a), but use jump shots or set shots.
3. Around-the-world shooting: One player shoots, moving to a new spot after each shot, while another player rebounds and quickly passes to the shooter. *Variations:* (1) The passer-rebounder applies defensive pressure on each shot. (2) Have two rebounders and two balls, so the shooter must move and shoot more quickly.
4. Shuffle and shoot: Using two balls, a player shuffles between two spots, picking up the ball at each spot and shooting. Two rebounders work at rebounding the balls and replacing them at each spot (Figure 6-11).
5. One-on-one: A player passes the ball to a player being guarded. The receiver practices various shots against the defender. *Variations:* (1) The receiver "posts up" to practice hook shots and moves with her back to the basket. (2) The receiver is allowed to use the passer again if she gets stuck.

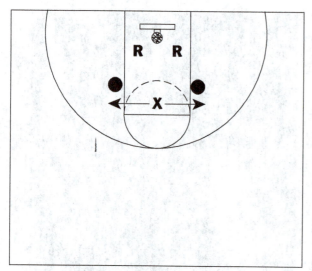

Figure 6-11 Shuffle and shoot.

6. Rebound-pass-shoot drill: Player X shoots from one of the spots, after receiving a pass from the passer. The rebounder rebounds and passes the ball to the passer. In the meantime, the shooter has moved to the next spot, ready to receive the pass there. Use two balls to make the action even more continuous. Vary the shooting spots and passing angle (Figure 6-12).

7. Follow the leader: Each player has a ball. One leader is designated. The leader shoots from various spots, while every player follows her.

8. Competitive shooting: Two teams compete against each other from various shooting spots. *Variations:* (1) Timed shooting. (2) Designated number of completed shots. (3) Least number of misses. (4) First team to finish.

REBOUNDING

Rebounding is gaining possession of the ball after an unsuccessful shooting attempt. Because approximately 60 percent of field goal attempts are missed, rebounding skill is essential to any team. Rebounding is categorized as being either defensive (at the opponent's basket) or offensive (at the team's own basket). The keys to effective rebounding are positioning, aggressiveness, and timing of the jump.

Positioning for the rebound is called "blocking out" or "boxing out" (Figure 6-13). The defensive player has a distinct advantage here, already being closer to the basket. With anticipation and a quick move, however, the offensive player can gain the inside position. Blocking out is done by pivoting to face the basket, putting the opponent behind. It is important here to spread the feet far apart, bend the legs, lower the hips, and hold the elbows out away from the body to create a stable position that does not allow an opponent to get around. Because both the offensive player and the defensive player want the inside position, a player must be aggressive to maintain this desired position. The player that is blocking out must slide and maintain physical contact with his opponent until the rebound is secured.

Once the inside position is attained, a player must observe the ball and anticipate how and where it will rebound off of the rim or backboard. To effectively rebound a ball, jump high and grasp the ball firmly with both hands (Figure 6-14). On the downward move, after getting the ball, spread the legs and hold the ball high and away from the opponents. If it is a defensive rebound, pass (outlet) the ball away from the basket to a teammate near the sideline, or dribble the ball out away from the basket. An offensive rebound should be tipped back up to

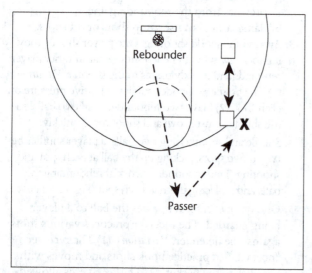

Figure 6-12 Rebound-pass-shoot.

Figure 6-13 Blocking out.

Figure 6-14 Rebounding: Note the blockout by the other player.

the basket, shot back up after landing on the ground, or passed to a teammate in better shooting position.

▶ Learning Hints: Rebounding

1. Work hard to attain or maintain the inside position closest to the basket.
2. Do not get pushed too far under the basket or backboard.
3. Be aggressive.
4. Jumping:
   a. Initiate the jump with the arms.
   b. Explode off of the floor by bending the legs.
   c. Reach high with both arms extended.
   d. Time the jump in order to grasp the ball as high as possible, attempting to keep the ball in line with the forehead.
5. Go for the ball; do not let it merely fall into your hands.
6. Keep a firm hold on the ball, jerking it down and away from any nearby opponents.
7. Land with feet comfortably spread and elbows out.
8. After landing, hold the ball high to keep opponents from getting it.
9. For a defensive rebound, get the ball away from the basket quickly (outlet). For an offensive rebound, try to get an immediate score out of it.

▶ Practice/Organizational Suggestions: Rebounding

1. Standing 20 to 25 feet from a partner, have her toss a ball high into the air toward you. Jump high and grasp the ball firmly with both hands, bringing it down aggressively.

2. Standing in front of the backboard, toss the ball high against the board. Jump and grasp the rebound, concentrating on good rebounding form. *Variations:* (1) Execute an outlet pass after rebounding (defensive rebound). (2) Shoot or tip the ball into the basket (offensive rebound).

3. Second-effort drill: Stand in front of the backboard with a partner holding a ball behind you. On your partner's command, jump high into the air as if rebounding. After you have jumped, the partner tosses the ball against the board, forcing you to spring back up immediately to rebound.

4. Circle blockout: Place a ball in the center of a restraining circle. Align three pairs of players around the outside of the circle—facing each other (one inside player with her back to the ball). On the whistle, the player on the inside turns and blocks out the other player, trying to keep her from touching the ball for approximately 5 seconds. *Variation:* Place a ball on the floor near each pair. Have each player block out her opponent from her ball for 30 seconds (Figure 6-15).

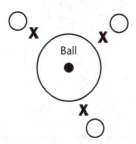

Figure 6-15 Circle blockout.

5. Three-on-three blockout: With three offensive players and three defensive players positioned around the basket, the coach shoots the ball. Both teams attempt to secure the rebound. The offensive player should shoot the ball again or tip it in, while the defensive player should outlet the ball (Figure 6-16).

INDIVIDUAL OFFENSE

To be a good basketball player, a player must always be a threat to the opponents when his team has possession of the ball. He should be able to score when the ball is in his hands as well as move effectively on the floor without the ball in order to free himself or a teammate.

Driving. Driving is a means of getting past opponents by faking them off balance, accelerating, and dribbling hard past them. It is important to dribble with the hand farthest from the defender when driving. Fakes can be executed with the head, ball, or free foot. By holding the ball close to your body, away from the defender, a series of "jab" steps (i.e., stepping forward and back) with the free foot may lure the opponent off balance so that you can drive. It is essential that a player not dribble immediately after receiving a pass. Doing so eliminates the fake and drive—a prime individual offensive weapon.

Cutting. Cutting is sharp, angular movement involving starting, stopping, and changes of direction, which enables a player without the ball to get free from defenders. All cuts should be preceded by a fake in the opposite direction. Cuts can be in front of the defender (front cut) or behind a defender (reverse or backdoor cut). A V-cut is a sharp, angular cut (in the shape of a V) used to clear an area for a pass.

All offensive movement should be purposeful. An offensive player with the ball is constantly looking for open shots, passes, or drives. An offensive player without the ball is cutting and moving to get free or to set a screen for a teammate. Offensive team patterns or plays are a means of regulating and structuring every player's movement on the floor.

Screening. The screen is the use of the body by a player without the ball to block or alter the path of an opponent. The purpose is to free a teammate for a high-percentage shot or pass. The player setting a screen approaches the opponent at the desired angle, plants both feet wide and close to the player, and crosses the arms for protection in anticipation of the contact or collision. The player must avoid leaning or moving the feet because a moving screen is illegal. Following contact, the player rolls to the basket (pick and roll) or moves immediately to an advantageous offensive position to receive a pass.

INDIVIDUAL DEFENSE

Defense involves preventing a team from scoring or, at least, limiting the maneuvering ability of the offensive team. Defense is as important as offense, but is considered less glamorous than scoring baskets. It requires hard work, concentration, and determination. Body balance is the key to good defense. The feet must be ready to move, preventing leaning and reaching with the upper body. It is a general rule (with only a few exceptions) that a defensive player should try to stay positioned between the offensive opponent and the basket. Foot movement is accomplished by sliding, keeping the feet as close to the floor as possible to enable quick shifts in direction.

Individual defense involves guarding a player with the ball (a ball handler) and guarding a player without the ball.

Defense Against a Player with the Ball. Note the fundamental defensive stance (Figure 6-17) of the player: weight low and evenly distributed on the balls of

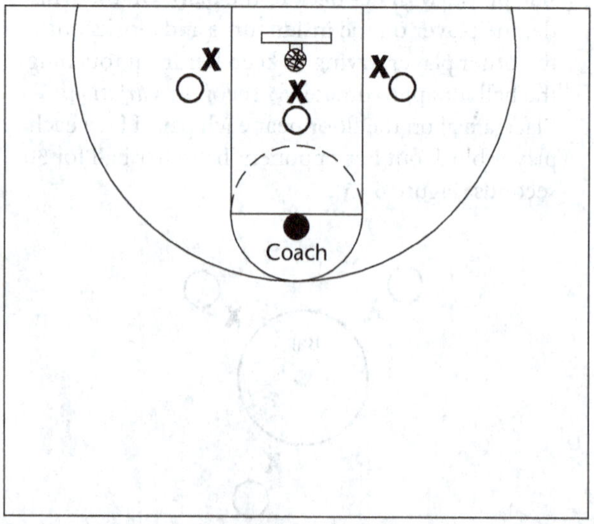

Figure 6-16 Three-on-three blockout.

Figure 6-17 Defensive stance.

the feet, head up, knees flexed, arms flexed, hands relatively close to the body, palms up. The eyes should be focused on the opponent's hips rather than on the eyes or the ball. This prevents being faked out of position. Rather than reaching with the hands, a player should slide the feet to maintain good body position. The arms should extend upward or outward from the body only to deflect a pass or a shot. The distance between the defensive player and the ball handler depends on the quickness and shooting range of the offensive player. Once a player stops dribbling, a close defensive position should be established, with arms extended to prevent passes or a shot.

Defense Against a Player without the Ball.   It makes sense that a player without the ball is not an immediate scoring threat. Thus, in playing defense, a player must work hard to prevent her opponent from *receiving* the ball. She accomplishes this by keeping the player she is guarding and the ball in view at all times. Also, she keeps one arm constantly extended between the ball and her defender to "deny" the pass (Figure 6-18). If her opponent is not close enough to the ball to receive a pass, she may have to open up her body position, using her peripheral vision to keep the ball and her opponent in view. This position allows her to "help out" a teammate who has been beaten by an offensive player. Again, like defending a ball handler, she tries to dictate and thwart her opponent's moves.

▶ Practice/Organizational Suggestions:
Individual Offense and Defense

(Either the *offensive* or *defensive* portion can be emphasized.)
1. Cutting: B attempts to free himself for a pass from A by executing V-cuts, front cuts, or reverse cuts (backdoors). X works to deny the pass (Figure 6-19). Individual offense: After receiving a pass from A, B must do three offensive maneuvers en route to the basket for a shot (jab step, reverse dribble, head fake, etc.). May add a defender.
2. Zigzag: Divide the court into thirds. Staying in her third of the court, the offensive player dribbles in a

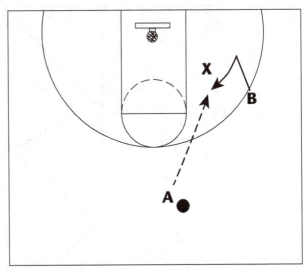

Figure 6-19   Cutting.

zigzag pattern down the floor. The defensive player stays with her, practicing good defensive form and position. *Variation:* The dribbler stops her dribble en route, making the defensive player move closer, straighten, and extend her arms (Figure 6-20).
3. Denial defense: Both defensive players (X) work hard to deny any pass to the player they are guarding. A and B pass the ball back and forth trying to get it to the offensive players (Figure 6-21).
4. Denial in a box: Within a 10- to 15-foot square, X must work hard to deny B from receiving a pass from A (Figure 6-22).

Modified and Lead-up Games

HALF-COURT BASKETBALL

Using the general rules of basketball that govern fouls, penalties, and general playing situations, a half-court game can be played involving two-, three-, four-, or five-person teams. Both teams shoot at the same basket. A throw-in from the center circle is used to start the game and to restart play after each score. If the ball changes hands (after a missed shot, steal, or pass interception), the team gaining possession must take the ball behind the free-throw line before working it in for a shot. Games can be shortened by either time or point limits, with teams rotating to various courts.

▶ Modifications with Instructional Focus

1. Passing-only game with no dribbling (movement off the ball).
2. Game to 3 points with any single player allowed to score only once (helping teammates to score).
3. Tallest players not allowed in the free-throw lane (rebounding and inside game for shorter players).

Figure 6-18   Defense against players without the ball: Note the "help" position of the defensive player.

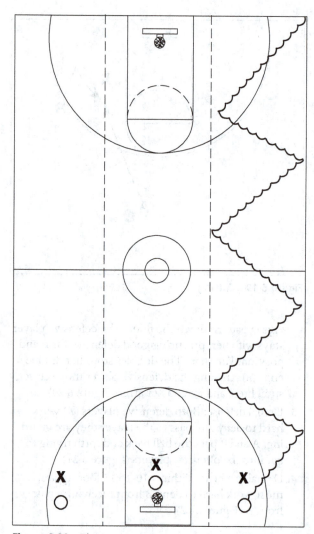

Figure 6-20   Zigzag.

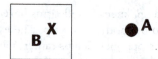

Figure 6-22   Denial in a box.

4. Points awarded for steals or deflections (individual defense).

5. Ten passes completed before a shot is attempted (passing and defense against the pass).

6. On a shot, the ball must bounce before being rebounded (rebound blocking out).

7. Shots made immediately following an offensive rebound are assigned an extra 5 points (offensive rebounding).

8. Offensive team with only one shot per possession (selecting a high percentage shot).

9. A time limit on a player holding the ball (supporting the teammate with the ball).

FIFTEEN-PLAYER BASKETBALL

Fifteen or more players can participate in this continuous-action game. The game begins with three offensive players (Os) working together in an attempt to score against two defensive players (Ds). Once a shot is taken, whether made or missed, every player (Os and Ds) attempts to rebound the ball. The successful rebounder passes the ball out to one of the wing players (Ws) and joins with this player and the opposite wing player to take the ball down the court to attempt to score against the two wing players at the other end of the court who have stepped in to play defense (new Ds). Players who did not get the rebound fill in the wing lines at their end of the court. Play continues up and down the court, with the successful rebounder continually involved in the offense. An intercepted pass by a defender is treated just like a rebound, with that player passing the ball to a wing and getting to continue down the floor on offense. Because there are no distinct teams, no score is kept. If the ball goes out-of-bounds, the player who hustles to recover it gets to pass to the wing and continue as an offensive player (Figure 6-23).

Playing Strategy

TEAM OFFENSE

Offensive tactics in basketball vary according to the defensive tactics employed by the opposing team. Thus, offensive patterns will vary so that the most efficient attack may be developed against the particular defense. Generally speaking, offense is employed against the player-to-player defense and the zone defense.

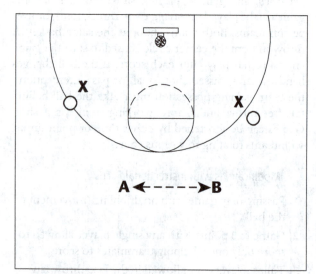

Figure 6-21   Denial defense.

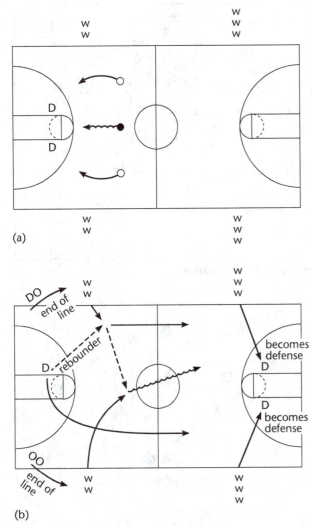

(a)

(b)

Figure 6-23 Fifteen-player basketball.

Offense Against a Player-to-Player Defense. The offense used against the player-to-player defense is a combination of passing and player movement. Even though the offense consists of five players, it is most common for only two or three players to work together for a shot while the others employ decoying or rebounding roles. It only takes one defensive player to falter to enable an open shot for the opposing offensive player. Working together, teammates can do a give-and-go, a backdoor cut, or a variety of screens/picks. These maneuvers employ two or three players and confuse the defense, putting them out of good defensive position. Of course, individual offensive moves such as cutting and driving may be incorporated also (Figures 6-24, 6-25, 6-26, and 6-27).

These maneuvers can be incorporated into set plays or used spontaneously in a freelance situation. Thus, five-player plays are actually a combination of two- and three-player maneuvers.

Offense Against a Zone Defense. The offense used against the zone defense is primarily one of moving the

ball with short, quick passes to force the defensive players out of their assigned positions so that a good shot may be taken. The offensive players move to positions that force the defense to alter their zone and weaken its strength. Even if an offensive player gets past a defender, in a zone defense there is another defender waiting to cover. Therefore, the following principles should guide the offense in defeating the zone defense:

1. Quick passing
2. Outside shooting
3. Penetrate the zone with a dribble or a pass, then quickly pass out to a free teammate
4. Cut through the zone, splitting two defenders
5. Overload one side of the zone with more offensive players than defensive players
6. Dribble sparingly
7. Screen a shifting defensive player

TEAM DEFENSE

The Zone Defense. This style of defense calls for the placement of the defensive players in designated areas in and around the defensive basket to give maximum protection against good shots. The alignments are numbered. The alignment must take into consideration the size, speed, and abilities of the players, as well as the area of the court to be covered. The most common zone defenses are the 2–1–2, the 2–3, the 1–3–1, and the 1–2–2. Each player in zone defense is assigned a certain area on the court to cover and guards any offensive player who comes into that area. The defense shifts in relation to the ball, rather than in relation to the position of the offensive players. The zone defense is valuable in securing rebounds, in cutting off inside shooting against taller opponents, and in protecting players who are tired, weak defensively, or in foul trouble (Figures 6-28 and 6-29).

The Player-to-Player Defense. The principle behind the player-to-player defense is the assignment of each player to guard one offensive player, and thus, the area element that is prominent in the zone defense is eliminated. Instead of shifting as a unit in relation to the position of the ball, each player must follow one player all over the defensive court. This defense takes extraordinary skill, stamina, and teamwork, because any free offensive player is a scoring threat. Because the offensive team will be working screens, picks, and cuts to free a teammate, the defense must communicate and have tactics to avoid such maneuvers. One such tactic involves immediate on-the-floor switching of defensive assignments if an offensive player has gotten free. Another tactic involves defensive players allowing room for each other to slide through picks and screens, enabling them to stay with their assigned players.

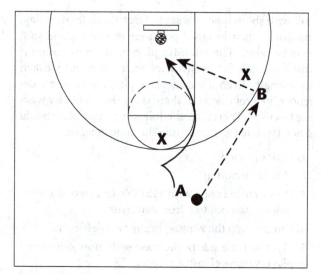

Figure 6-24   Give-and-go.

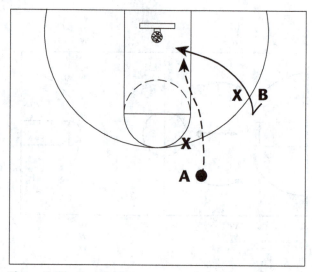

Figure 6-27   Backdoor cut.

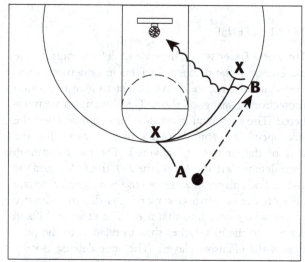

Figure 6-25   Pick (on-the-ball).

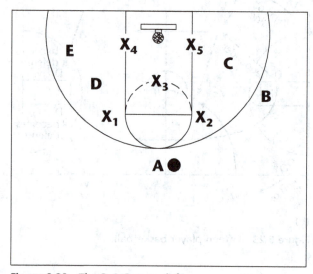

Figure 6-28   The 2–1–2 zone defense.

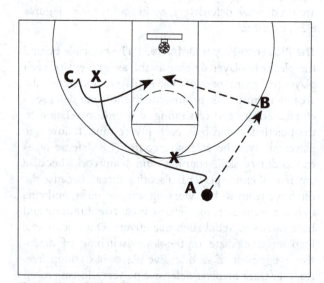

Figure 6-26   Pick (off-the-ball).

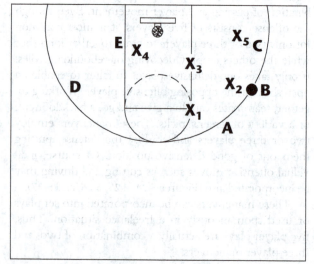

Figure 6-29   The shift of the 2–1–2 zone, with the ball passed to B.

The Pressing Defense.   In recent years, pressing defenses have taken on great significance at all levels of basketball competition. The main objectives are to harass opponents into ball-handling errors, force opponents into changing their game strategy, and force the offensive team to use up valuable time in bringing the ball down the court. The press can be administered full court, half-court, or three-quarters court, and can incorporate zone or player-to-player principles.

Skill Assessment

The most important skills for secondary level students are the pass, catch, dribble, and shot. The constraints of time, facilities, equipment, and set-up make it difficult to separately test each basic skill. It is suggested that two tests be conducted, each combining two skills. One test is passing (chest) and catching (two-hand), while the other is dribbling (dominant hand) and shooting (dominant hand layup). The passing-catching test is against a flat rebound surface, and the dribbling-shooting test is at a goal. Groups of three are involved at each station. There is a participant, a counter, and an assistant. All stations start and stop at the same time and are 30 seconds in length. The participant is tested, the counter records the accomplishment, and the assistant provides another ball if needed. A typical gymnasium has at least four goals and enough flat wall space for four passing stations, allowing for testing of at least 24 students at a time.

Passing-Catching.   For each testing station, mark two targets (24-by-24 in.) on the wall 2 feet apart, with the bottom of each target 3 feet above the floor. A restraining line is 8 feet from the wall. The line may be adjusted according to students' age and upper body strength.

The counter and the assistant are positioned behind the participant who is standing with the ball ready to start at the restraining line. On the command "Go" the participant uses the two-hand chest pass to pass the ball at one target and slide sideways to catch the rebounding ball, which must bounce off the floor. The participant then immediately passes the ball to the other target. This continuous sequence of passing, sliding, and catching continues for 30 seconds. The passer receives 2 points for hitting any part of the target or line and 1 point for hitting the wall space between the targets. No points are given if the ball hits outside either target; a two-hand chest pass is not used; the ball does not bounce off the floor when returning; or the passer steps across the line with one or both feet. The score is the total points accumulated in the 30-second trial. The students rotate in their group of three, changing responsibilities. The number of trials possible depends on the length of class time, the rotation time to the other test (dribbling-shooting), and the speed of recording scores.

Dribbling-Shooting.   A cone is placed for a right-handed student at the right corner of the free-throw line intersecting with the free-throw lane. The counter and the assistant with a ball are located behind the free-throw line in the arc and out of the way. The participant starts at the cone with a ball and on the command "Go" dribbles toward the goal to shoot a layup, retrieves the shot, dribbles quickly back to the cone, and continues the sequence for 30 seconds. The student receives 3 points for making the goal, 1 point for hitting the rim but not making a goal, and 2 points each time the dribbled ball is returned around the cone to continue the sequence. Only one shot per trip is allowed, and no points are given for a complete miss of the goal. The score is the total points accumulated in the 30-second trial period. The three students rotate in their group, changing responsibilities.

Modifications for Special Populations

ORTHOPEDICALLY IMPAIRED

1. Access the National Wheelchair Basketball Association Web site for rules and specific information for wheelchair users at www.NWBA.org.

2. Make sure to discuss spacing issues if you allow the student using a wheelchair to participate on the floor during a game with those who are ambulatory. Wheelchair users need extra space, so you might create a 3-foot rule; that is, no one is allowed to guard the individual using a wheelchair by closer than 3 feet.

3. Students with difficulties grasping and releasing the ball can practice dropping smaller balls into hoops, wastebaskets, or buckets. Use beanbags or other small objects if student cannot grip a small ball.

4. For students with severe limitations, consider using commercial "Near Basketball" games.

5. Consider allowing students without disabilities to shoot from seated position on a bench or chair.

COGNITIVELY IMPAIRED

1. Special Olympics has a well-defined basketball program. Ask for their rule manual.

2. Concentrate on concepts of the game, such as offense, defense, and transition. Allow the students to "travel" if it promotes play. Specific rules of the game will evolve as the unit continues.

SENSORY IMPAIRED

1. Minimal modifications are needed for the student who is deaf or hearing impaired. Consider hand signals for your teaching prompts.

2. Individual considerations must be taken into account to determine the appropriateness of basketball for students who are visually impaired. Consider checking for resources on the game of Goalball at www.usaba.org.

Terminology

backcourt players (guards) Players who set up a team's offensive pattern; usually the smaller players on the team or the best ball handlers.

backdoor An offensive maneuver whereby a player cuts toward the baseline to the basket, behind the defenders, and receives a pass for a field goal attempt.

baseline The endline.

blocking out (boxing out) A term used to designate a player's position under the backboard that prevents an opposing player from achieving good rebounding position.

charging Personal contact against a stationary defender by a player with the ball. This becomes a personal foul against the offensive player.

corner players (forwards) Tall players who are responsible for the rebounding and shooting phases of the team's operation. They usually position themselves closer to the basket than the guards.

cut A quick offensive move by a player trying to get free for a pass.

denial defense Aggressive individual defense where the defensive player works hard to keep the offensive player from receiving a pass.

double foul When two opponents commit personal fouls against each other at the same time. The result is a throw-in for the team entitled as a result of the alternating jump ball process.

dribble Ball movement by a player in control who throws or taps the ball in the air or onto the floor and then touches it. The dribble ends when the dribbler touches the ball with both hands simultaneously, permits it to come to rest while in contact with it, or loses control.

drive An aggressive move toward the basket by a player with the ball.

fake (feint) Using a deceptive move with the ball to pull the defensive player out of position.

fast break Moving the ball quickly downcourt to score before the defense can set up.

field goal A basket scored from the field.

freelance No structure or set plays in the offense.

free throw The privilege given to a player to score 1 or 2 points by unhindered shots for a goal from within the free-throw circle and behind the free-throw line.

give-and-go A maneuver in which the offensive player makes a pass to a teammate and then immediately cuts in toward the basket for a return pass.

held ball Occurs when two opponents have one or both hands firmly on the ball and neither can gain possession without undue roughness. The result is a throw-in for the team entitled as a result of the alternating jump ball process.

inside player (center, post, pivot) Most often the tallest player on the team. This player is situated near the basket, around the 3-second lane area, and is responsible for rebounding and close-range shooting.

jump ball A method of putting the ball into play to start the game or any overtime periods by tossing it up between two opponents in the center circle. In jump ball situations that occur (due to held ball, double foul, etc.) once the game has begun, teams alternate taking the ball out-of-bounds. The team not obtaining control of the initial jump ball starts the alternating process.

outlet pass A term used to designate a direct pass from a rebounder to a teammate, with the main objective being the start of a fast break.

overtime period An extra period of playing time (5 minutes in college; 3 minutes in high school) if the score is tied at the end of the regulation game.

personal foul A player foul that involves contact with an opponent while the ball is alive or after the ball is in possession of a player for a throw-in.

pick A special type of screen where an offensive player stands so the defensive player slides to make contact, freeing an offensive teammate for a shot or drive.

pivot Takes place when a player who is holding the ball steps once or more than once in any direction with the same foot, while the other foot, called the pivot foot, is kept at its point of contact with the floor. Also, another term for the inside player.

posting up A player cutting to the 3-second lane area, pausing, and anticipating a pass.

rebound A term usually applied when the ball bounces off the backboard or basket after a missed shot.

restraining circles Three circles of 6-foot radius, one located in the center of the court and one located at each of the free-throw lines.

running time Not letting the clock stop for fouls or violations, usually used in a recreational situation.

screen An offensive maneuver where an offensive player is positioned between the defender and a teammate to free the teammate for an uncontested shot.

switching A reversal of defensive guarding assignments.

technical foul A noncontact foul by a player, team, or coach for unsportsmanlike behavior or failure to abide by rules regarding submission of lineups, uniform numbering, and substitution procedures.

telegraphing a pass Indicating where you are going to pass by looking or signaling.

throw-in A method of putting the ball in play from out-of-bounds.

traveling When a player in possession of the ball within bounds progresses illegally in any direction (e.g., taking steps with the ball without dribbling).

violation An infraction of the rules resulting in a throw-in from out-of-bounds for the opponents.

Discussion Questions

1. Discuss the origin and historic development of basketball in the United States.

2. Compare the strengths and weaknesses of the three passing techniques.

3. Contrast the two "point of aim" methods for shooting.

4. Contrast the individual defensive positions and strategies when defending a player with the ball or without it.

5. Discuss the offensive playing strategies used against the player-to-player defense and the zone.

6. Compare the zone, player-to-player, and pressing team defensive strategies.

7. Identify the four reasons listed for using the dribble.

8. Discuss the suggested "learning hints" for rebounding.

9. Driving, cutting, and screening are three offensive techniques. Discuss the purpose and techniques of each.

Web Sites

www.coachlikeapro.com—offers extensive information on shooting, offense, defense, play, drills, and practices.

www.ncaa.org National Collegiate Athletic Association—is the site of the regulatory organization for all collegiate athletics, including basketball. Has photos, features, game results, schedules, interviews with players and coaches, and other information.

www.nfhs.org National Federation of State High School Associations—has current news, rules information, sports materials, publications, and resources for basketball.

www.havenport.com/hosa/btlinks.html—provides links to basketball drills, offensive and defensive strategies, and includes J. J. Redick's video on basketball shooting.

www.basketball-plays-and-tips.com—supplies extensive information on basketball fundamentals, drills, plays, training aid, rules, and glossary.

www.nwba.org—complete information on wheelchair basketball rules, skills, history, publications, and links.

CHAPTER 7

Bowling

This chapter will enable you to

- Identify important historical events that contributed to the evolution of bowling
- Select a proper-fitting bowling ball and bowling shoes
- Bowl a game according to the official rules of the American Bowling Congress
- Practice and use the four-step approach and delivery, the straight ball, and the hook ball
- Score a complete game using the appropriate symbols to indicate the line score
- Improve your strategy by converting spares
- Understand the terminology, observe safety rules, and use proper etiquette associated with the sport

Nature and Purpose

Bowling appeals to people of all ages and is easily adapted for special populations. Because a relatively small expenditure of energy is required in bowling, it is not an activity that lends itself to the development of physical fitness. However, participants may bowl for years after more strenuous activities have been abandoned, and fortunately, any person who has a degree of motor fitness can enjoy bowling as a lifetime sport.

The typical bowling center has become an almost 24-hour enterprise. It caters to housewives' leagues in the morning, junior leagues in the afternoon, leagues (separate or mixed) for men and women in the evening, and to late-night and early-morning bowlers who work the second shift. Most establishments are clean and well kept, thus providing suitable entertainment for the whole family.

The modern game of tenpins is played on indoor wooden lanes, 60 feet long from the foul line to the center of the number one pin, and 41 to 42 inches wide (Figure 7-1). The tenpins are set up (or "spotted") in a diamond formation on pin spots 12 inches apart, center to center (Figure 7-2A). A regulation tenpin is 15 inches high, with a diameter of 2½ inches at the base. Pins are constructed of clear hard maple and are usually coated with a plastic outer covering. They must conform to American Bowling Congress specifications. The object of the game is to roll the ball down the lane and knock down all the pins.

The lane is bordered on either side by gutters that prevent an errant ball from moving into an adjacent lane. It is constructed of two types of wood: maple, a hardwood to take the constant punishment of the ball, and pine, a soft wood that aids in gripping the ball. As shown in Figure 7-2B, a lane has several markings, some of which appear to be off the lane (the approach area). All of the marks serve as points of reference for the bowler. The initial sets of dots, found in the approach area, serve as a point of reference for the bowler. The set of points in arrow formation beyond the foul line serve as a point of reference for aiming the ball.

History

A form of bowling may have existed as long ago as 7000 B.C. Archaeological studies of ancient Egyptians provide evidence of implements for playing a game similar to the modern game of bowling. The balls were probably spherical stones without holes for the fingers. The modern sport of bowling probably grew out of a 3rd-century German religious ceremony in which church parishioners set their *Kegel* (a stick like a shillelagh) as a target and attempted to knock it down with a round stone. If successful, the parishioner was deemed free of sin.[1]

Over time, this activity became a recreational one, and early settlers brought it to the American colonies. The game, now called ninepins, became increasingly popular with the colonists, and in 1840 the Knickerbocker Alleys were built in New York City. The game lost favor with government authorities when gamblers began wagering on the outcome of the matches, and in 1841 ninepins was outlawed in Connecticut. To circumvent the laws and keep the game legal, enthusiasts added a 10th pin, thus changing the name of the game to tenpins.

Tenpins soon became popular all over the country, but there was wide variation in the size of the pins, length of the alleys, rules of play, and the general regulations governing the game. The American Bowling Congress (ABC) was organized in 1895 and was given

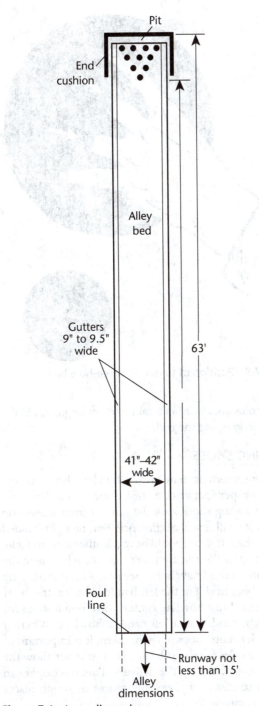

Figure 7-1 Lane dimensions.

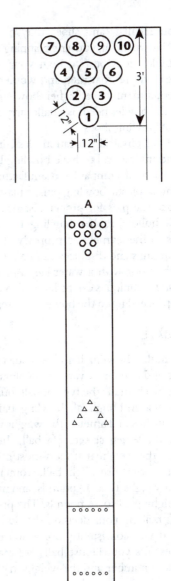

Figure 7-2 (A) Position and number of pins.
(B) Lane markings.

the task of establishing a standardized set of rules governing play, equipment, and tournament competition. The Women's International Bowling Congress was organized in 1916 and was followed soon after by the American Junior Bowling Congress (AJBC).

Professional bowling is governed by two organizations, the Professional Bowlers Association (PBA), established in 1958, and the Ladies Professional Bowlers Tour (LPBT), established in 1981.

Today, millions of people of all ages throughout the United States enjoy bowling. Much of its popularity can be traced to nationally televised professional men's and women's bowling tournaments. Originally, the AJBC sponsored bowlers of high school through college age, but since 1982 the Young American Bowling Alliance (YABA) has taken over that role. The YABA now sanctions leagues and tournaments for bowlers through college age. It is also interesting to note that several colleges and universities have sponsored men's and women's intercollegiate teams for years and host national championships.[2]

Equipment and Facilities

Bowling is one of the few sports that a participant can enjoy without having to buy expensive equipment. For the recreational or occasional bowler, bowling centers provide "house balls," and shoes may be rented for a small fee. However, if you are planning to become a regular bowler, it is best to own your own equipment. Studies indicate that men and women who own their own equipment have higher bowling averages. Basically, all the bowler needs is a ball, carrying bag, and a good pair of bowling shoes.

For a school physical education class, it would be expensive and impractical to have bowling lanes in the gymnasium. Several companies manufacture bowling sets consisting of plastic bowling pins, a plastic sheet on which to place the pins for proper distance and placement, and a hollow rubber bowling ball containing several holes so the learner can properly fit the ball to the hand. Markings and distances can be measured and painted on the floor with a water-based paint for easy removal. Many techniques can be learned in the gymnasium before proceeding to the bowling center.

BOWLING BALL

Choosing a Ball. Bowling balls are made of hard rubber or plastic and come in a variety of colors. The hard rubber ball is black and is the type of ball found in most bowling centers. Although all bowling balls are the same size, 27 inches in diameter, the weight varies from 8 to 16 pounds. When selecting a ball, the beginner should choose the weight that feels most comfortable. Young junior bowlers use a light ball, women generally use a ball that weighs 10 to 13 pounds, and men usually use a ball weighing 14 to 16 pounds. The primary considerations in making your decision should be comfort and control. If you consistently use a house ball, find a ball that best fits you. House balls are marked with an identification number and the weight; try to use the same ball each time you bowl.

Fitting the Ball. It is also important to select a ball equipped with holes that fit your fingers. Balls are drilled with three holes, one for the thumb and two for the third and fourth fingers. If you buy your own ball, the ball is fitted to your hand span. The holes should be large enough for the fingers to slip in and out with ease. The thumb hole should be comfortably loose. The bowler should be able to turn the ball around the thumb without binding, grabbing, or excessive rubbing of the skin.

To determine proper fit, the bowler must decide the type of grip that will be used. There are three grips: the conventional, the semi-fingertip, and the full fingertip. Advanced bowlers use the latter two grips; beginners should use the conventional grip because it is the easiest to control. To determine proper hand span for the conventional grip, place the thumb completely in the thumb hole, keeping the fingers relaxed and spread over the finger holes. As shown in Figure 7-3, the crease of the second joint of the two middle fingers should extend ¼ inch beyond the inside edge of the finger holes. The

Figure 7-3 Position of fingers in three-hole ball.

finger holes are cut at a certain pitch or angle to aid the bowler in grasping the ball.

BOWLING SHOES

Another important item on the bowler's list of equipment is proper footwear. At first glance, both shoes of a pair of bowling shoes look the same. Closer inspection of the soles will reveal a difference. For the right-handed bowler, the left shoe should have a leather sole, to facilitate sliding at the release point, and a rubber heel; the right shoe should have a rubber sole with a leather tip and a rubber heel. For the left-handed bowler, the order is reversed. Most bowling centers have rental shoes for both right-handed and left-handed bowlers. Whether the bowler rents shoes or owns them, it is important to check the soles for any substance that will not allow the bowler to slide during the delivery. Fine sandpaper can be used to clean off sticky substances or rough places that may impede sliding.

For the physical education class, it is important that students wear smooth-soled shoes that enable sliding during the approach and release. Crepe soles or heavy-treaded rubber soles such as used in jogging shoes would be inappropriate.

BALL BAG

The serious bowler and the bowler who owns equipment should have a bag in which to store and carry the ball. Bags come in a variety of materials; those made of plastic, vinyl, or canvas are the least expensive. Many department stores have bags on sale regularly.

Basic Rules

In league or tournament play, two contiguous lanes are used, and the bowling of ten complete frames on these lanes constitutes an official game. Members of contesting teams successively and in regular order bowl one frame on one lane and the next frame on the other lane, so alternating frames until the game is completed. Each player bowls two balls in each frame. If a strike is made on the first ball, the second ball is not rolled (except that in the tenth frame if a strike or spare is made, the player immediately rolls on the same lane the additional balls or ball to which the strike or spare entitles him).

In case of a tie game, each team bowls an extra complete frame on the same lane in which the 10th frame was bowled. The extra frame is bowled and scored in exactly the same manner as the 10th frame. If a tie still exists at the completion of the first extra frame, the teams must change lanes for the additional frames that may be required to determine the winner.

It is a foul if a bowler permits any part of his foot, hand, or arm, while in contact with the lanes or runways, to rest upon or extend beyond the foul line at any time after the ball leaves his hands and passes beyond the foul line. No count is made on a foul ball, and any pins knocked down are immediately respotted. A foul ball counts as a ball bowled by the player. If a player commits a foul that is apparent to both captains and one or more members of each of the opposing teams competing on the same pair of lanes where the foul is committed, and the foul is not seen by the foul judge or umpire or recorded by an automatic foul-detecting device, a foul shall nevertheless be declared and so recorded.

PINFALL—LEGAL

Every ball delivered by the player counts, unless declared a dead ball. Pins must then be respotted after the cause for declaring a dead ball has been removed.

1. Pins knocked down by another pin or pins rebounding in play from the side partition or rear cushion are counted as pins down.
2. If, when the ball is rolling at a full setup or in the attempt to make a spare, it is discovered immediately after the ball has been delivered that one or more pins are improperly set, although not missing, the ball and resulting pinfall is counted. It is each player's responsibility to detect any misplacement of pins and have the setup corrected before he bowls.
3. Pins knocked down by a fair ball that remain lying on the lane or in the gutters, or that lean so as to touch kickbacks or side partitions, are termed dead wood and counted as pins down and must be removed before the next ball is bowled.

PINFALL—ILLEGAL

When any of the following incidents occur, the ball counts as a ball rolled, but pins knocked down do not count.

1. When pins are knocked down or displaced by a ball that leaves the lanes before reaching the pins.
2. When a ball rebounds from the rear cushion.
3. When pins come in contact with the body, arms, or legs of a pinsetter and rebound.
4. A standing pin that falls when dead wood is removed or is knocked down by a pinsetter or mechanical pinsetting equipment will not count and must be replaced on the pin spot where it originally stood before delivery of the ball.
5. Pins that are bowled off the lane, rebound, and remain standing on the lane must be counted as pins standing.
6. If in delivering the ball the player commits a foul, any pins knocked down will not be counted.

BOWLING ON WRONG LANE

When only one player or the leadoff players of both teams bowl on the wrong lane and the error is discovered before another player has bowled, a dead ball shall be declared and the player, or players, will be required to bowl on the correct lane. When more than one player on the same team has rolled on the wrong lane, the game will be completed without adjustment, and the next game will be started on the correctly scheduled lane.

Scoring

All players should learn how to score. It adds to the enjoyment of the game if the player can keep an accurate record of the score as the game progresses. There are 10 numbered boxes on the score sheet to correspond to the 10 frames in a game. At the top of each frame box are two small squares in which to write the number of pins toppled with the first ball and the second ball. Some simple scoring rules must be remembered to score a game accurately.

1. The score that is entered from frame box to frame box is cumulative; that is, it represents the total number of pins toppled up to that point.
2. If a bowler does not get a strike or spare in any frame, scoring is just a matter of adding on the number of pins knocked down in each frame.
3. If all pins are knocked down with the first ball, it is called a *strike*, and a cross (X) is marked in the small square in the upper right-hand corner of the frame box. The strike will count 10 pins plus the number of pins knocked down on the next two successive balls. A score will not be entered in the frame box until those two balls have been rolled.

Frame	1st ball	2nd ball	Total score
1.	7 pins Enter score in first square	2 pins	9 pins
2.	5 pins	3 pins	17—cumulative score of first score of first two frames: 9 + 8 = 17
3.	Strike. Enter (X) in first square		46—2 strikes (20) + 9 pins (see frame five) + 17 = 46
4.	Strike (X)		65—Strike (10) + 9 + 46 = 65
5.	9 pins—add to the two consecutive strikes	Miss (–) no pins	74 (65 + 9)
6.	8 pins	Spare. Enter (/) in second square	89—Spare (10) + 5 pins + 74 = 89
7.	5 pins—add to spare from frame six	4 pins	98—89 + 9 pins = 98
8.	9 pins	(–) no pins	107—98 + 9 = 107
9.	7 pins—a split	(O) no pins, missed converting the split	114—107 + 7 = 114
10.	Strike (X)—Player rolls two more balls, which are also strikes		144—114 + 3 strikes (30) = 144

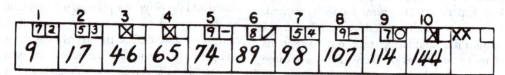

Figure 7-4   Scoring example and score sheet of a complete game.

4. If all pins are knocked down with two balls, it is called a *spare* and is indicated by a diagonal mark (/). The spare will count 10 pins plus the number of pins knocked down on the next ball rolled. A score will not be entered in the frame box until the next ball has been rolled.

5. If the bowler spares or strikes in the 10th frame, then the bowler rolls one more ball if a spare, or two more balls if a strike, and adds that to the total score.

To illustrate scoring, we will score a hypothetical game. The score sheet of a completed game is shown and analyzed in Figure 7-4. Let's review the symbols used and the scoring procedure.

(X) Indicates a *strike*: 10 plus the score of the next two balls.

(/) Indicates a *spare*: 10 plus the score of the next ball rolled.

(O) Indicates a *split*: score will depend on number of remaining pins knocked down by next ball rolled.

(Ø) Indicates a *converted split*: 10 plus the score of the next ball rolled.

(–) Indicates a *miss or error*: no score.

(F) Indicates a *foul*: no score.

(G) Indicates a *gutter ball*.

Suggested Learning Sequence

A. Nature of the game
   1. Equipment
   2. Fitting a bowling ball
   3. Safety: Lane courtesy

B. Techniques. Rules should be introduced early in the learning progression to coincide with specific techniques.
   1. Stance
   2. Approach
   3. Straight ball
   4. Hook ball

C. Scoring. May be introduced as the situation warrants and is most appropriate.

D. Strategy
   1. Pin bowling and spot bowling
   2. Making spares

Skills and Techniques

Bowling is a relatively easy game to learn, but as with all sporting activities, it is important to learn the techniques involved to develop consistency. For the physical education teacher, much of the technique involving the grip, stance, approach, and release can be taught in the gymnasium. The basic skill to be learned is the swing coordinated with a specific number of steps.

THE STANCE

There is no definite or prescribed stance assumed by all bowlers preparatory for the start of the approach. However, there are some important points to remember.

1. Hold the ball with both hands in front of the body. For a man this may be waist high, for a woman a little higher to attain a longer swing for increased speed.

2. Spread the feet slightly apart, weight evenly distributed, perhaps one foot slightly ahead of the other.

3. Most of the weight of the ball should be supported by the nonthrowing hand at this point.

4. Grip the ball with the thumb in a 12 o'clock position for a straight ball or the 10 o'clock position for a hook ball.

THE APPROACH

Bowlers take three to five steps in their approach, but most experts recommend the four-step approach. The beginning bowler should experiment with the delivery and determine which works best. The following discussion centers around the four-step approach for the right-handed bowler. The left-handed bowler will reverse the starting procedure.

In proper execution of the approach, the bowler takes a series of steps in a smooth, rhythmical manner, and ends with a slide and follow-through as the ball is released. The beginning bowler can determine the length of his approach by using the guide dots on the lane at 12 feet and 15 feet as reference points. Starting at the dots near the foul line, with his back to the pins, he walks toward the back of the lane using the number of steps he has chosen for the approach (3, 4, or 5) and adds an extra half step to allow for his slide. Where his last step finishes is his initial starting distance from the foul line.

From this distance, the bowler faces the foul line with his slide foot on or in alignment with the center dot. He can take a few practice approaches without the ball using his desired step pattern and proper arm action with a finishing slide to see if the slide foot crossed the foul line. If necessary, he can adjust his starting position slightly forward or backward according to the finished location of the sliding foot.

After determining the aiming strategy for either spot or pin bowling (see Playing Strategies), the bowler repeats the same procedure with a rolled ball to determine if adjustment to the left or right of the center dot by the starting position of his slide foot is needed. The left or right adjustment is based on a consistent path of the ball toward the head pin. The desired contact for a right hander is the 1-3 pocket.

▶ Learning Hints

Step 1. The push away. Step with the right foot and at the same time push the ball out to an arm's length in front of the body. Do not overextend the push away or loss of balance and direction may result. (Figure 7-5A)

Step 2. The ball moves to the bottom of the arc on the downswing as the left foot completes the second step. (Figure 7-5B)

Step 3. The ball reaches the top of the backswing (shoulder high) as the right foot completes the third step. The ball must swing in a straight line, shoulders square to the foul line. (Figure 7-5C)

Step 4. As the last step is taken, the ball swings forward, the wrist is firm, and the ball is released toward the target. The nonthrowing hand will help serve as a means of balance. The left toe will be pointing at the target. (Figure 7-5D)

If the timing is correct, the ball is released out in front of the body and laid rather than dropped on the lane. The bowling ball, when properly delivered, has a double motion. When first released, it slides and revolves, sliding in the direction toward the pins. After sliding a distance, once it reaches the nonoiled surface, friction increases, and the ball begins to revolve, causing it to hook, roll straight, or back up, depending on the type of ball that is thrown.

▶ Psychological Learning Hints

Closed skill activities allow for advance mental preparation before performing the skill, which can result in a better skill outcome. The bowler should establish a three-step routine when lanes are clear for her to bowl by collecting her ball and stepping onto the lane; preparing for the approach; and relocating for the next ball.

1. The bowler collects the ball from the ball return, wipes off the oil or dust from the ball, dries her hands and applies talc, sights her starting spot and target, and steps onto the back of the lane.

2. Next she slowly walks to her starting spot; sets her feet in a comfortable stance; holds the ball in her chosen starting position; focuses on the chosen target (pins or spot) and visualizes the path the

Figure 7-5 Four-step approach: Note shoulders squarely facing the pins.

ball will take; thinks positively, blocking out any distractions; and takes a deep breath and starts the approach.

3. Finally, she relocates for her next shot. If her ball was a strike, she sits down, relaxes, and refocuses for the next shot. If it was a spare, she stands at the back of the lane for the ball to return and relaxes, concentrating on the new starting position and mapping the route the ball will travel to complete the spare, and repeating #2.

▶ Practice/Organizational Suggestions

1. Allow students to move to the ball rack and demonstrate proper technique for picking up the ball.

2. Pick up the ball and assume a well-balanced stance with ball held comfortably and in proper position.

3. Bellisimo and Bennett recommend a one-step delivery with a ball for slide and release practice.[3] Place students in a position to take the last step. Allow them to take a practice swing with a ball, then allow students to take the last step and delivery. Concentrate on a straight pendulum swing and good follow-through with the hand finishing high.

4. From the designated spot on the floor determined for the approach, try the desired footwork (3, 4, or 5 steps), coordinating the steps and arm swing without the ball and then with the ball.

THE STRAIGHT BALL

Beginning bowlers should concentrate first on perfecting a straight ball before attempting to roll a hook. It is also recommended that a bowler who lacks ball speed continue the use of a straight ball.

▶ Learning Hints

1. Hold the thumb in a 12 o'clock position with the fingers underneath the ball.

2. Maintain the hand position throughout the swing, with no arm rotation during release of the ball.

3. Keep the wrist firm and the palm facing the pins as the ball is delivered; maintain a straight follow-through.

4. Start the ball from the right side of the lane and direct it toward the 1-3 pocket. (Figure 7-6A)

THE HOOK BALL

Most good bowlers use a hook ball; beginning bowlers will want to learn this delivery as soon as possible. To obtain maximum pin action, the ball should strike the pins at an angle, but the angle of the straight ball is limited by the width of the alley. The straight ball revolves forward, but the hook ball revolves at an angle,

thus giving it greater pin splash or action by imparting a revolving action to the pins. This delivery is sometimes called the "handshake" delivery because the position of the hand is similar to that used in an ordinary handshake.

▶ Learning Hints

1. Keep the wrist firm and the thumb in a 10:30 o'clock position.

2. As the ball is released, the thumb comes out first, and the fingers lift and impart a rotational effect to the ball.

3. Release the ball with the V formed by the thumb and forefinger pointing toward the target.

4. Carry the hand upward and forward toward the pins in the follow-through. Do not side-wheel, twist the arm, or intentionally spin the ball. (Figure 7-6B)

There are two other types of deliveries: the curve ball (Figure 7-6C) and the backup ball. However, because of

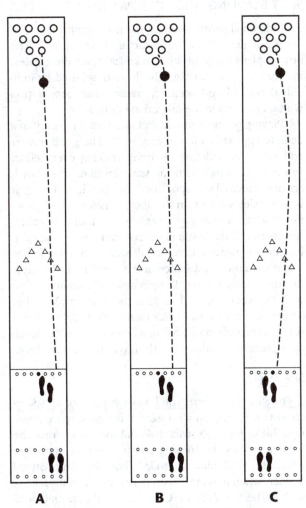

Figure 7-6 Paths of (A) straight ball, (B) hook ball, and (C) curve ball.

the difficulty of controlling them, they are not recommended for the beginning bowler.

1. For the physical education class, use partners. Using a hollow plastic ball, roll a straight ball or a hook to each other. Concentrate on proper wrist and hand position as well as swing consistency.
2. At the lanes, practice the swing first, holding the ball in the correct position. Some experts recommend rolling the ball back and forth between partners to practice the proper release technique.
3. The bowler will continue to roll the ball over the second arrow from the right (right-hander). However, the bowler should experiment with her starting position by moving over one or two boards toward the left to find the most consistent path for her hook (see Figure 7-6).

Playing Strategy

SPOT BOWLING AND PIN BOWLING

An individual sport, bowling has no complicated playing strategies similar to those in team sports. The bowler plans his game so as to knock down the greatest number of pins possible. This is accomplished by individual control and accuracy, rather than cooperation with teammates in the execution of plays.

Playing strategy should include, first, a mastery of a definite approach and delivery style. The good bowler will settle on a definite pattern, making every effort to throw each ball with the same motion. Most bowlers are classified as "spot" or "pin" bowlers. The spot bowler selects a spot on the alley, which is usually a series of seven arrows a few feet from the foul line, and attempts to roll the first ball in each frame over that spot. It is more consistent to roll a ball accurately a few feet to a spot than the full distance of the alley and is the superior method of aiming. The pin bowler looks at the pins while approaching and making the delivery. Whether he prefers throwing a hook or a straight ball, he follows his selected style on all balls and concentrates on developing accuracy with a smooth and rhythmical delivery.

SPARES

To bowl a good score, the bowler must pick up spares consistently. Accuracy is essential for good spare bowling. Unlike rolling a strike ball, the spare may force the bowler to vary the starting position and the spot over which the ball may be rolled. For the right-handed bowler, when pins are left on the right side of the lane—such as the 1, 3, 6, 10 or 3, 5, 6, 9, 10—the starting position should be on the left side of the lane. For pins on the left side, the ball will be delivered from the right side

of the lane. Pins that are left one directly behind another should be hit head-on; otherwise, the bowler runs the risk of having the ball glance off the front pin, thereby missing the rear pin. Conversion of spares will make a marked difference in your scores.

Other Considerations

LANE ETIQUETTE

As in other sporting activities, certain playing courtesies should be extended to your bowling competitors and teammates.

1. Do not talk to or otherwise disturb a bowler who is on the approach and ready to bowl.
2. Do not walk in front of a bowler to secure your ball from the rack when the bowler is ready to bowl. Wait for your ball to return.
3. When bowlers on adjacent lanes are both ready to bowl, the one on the right (as you face the pins) should always be permitted to bowl first.
4. Do not use a ball that is the personal property of an individual unless you have the owner's permission.
5. Be at your post, ready to bowl, when your turn comes.
6. After delivering the ball and noting the result, turn and walk back immediately to the rear of the runway, being careful to stay in your approach lane.
7. Do not argue with the foul line judge over decisions even if you think an unjust call has been made against you.
8. Be punctual when scheduled to bowl. Nothing upsets a team more than having to wait for a late member.
9. Control your temper. Public exhibition of anger disturbs fellow bowlers and detracts from your efficiency.

SAFETY

Bowling is a relatively safe activity. Accidents are few, and good common sense will prevent them from occurring. The following are a few guidelines for safe bowling.

1. With a large class, plan formations well in advance so there is plenty of space between each participant during the approach, backswing, forward swing, and follow-through.
2. Be aware of people around you; swing the ball only on the designated alley.
3. Check to make sure the approaches are free of oily or rough substances that may interfere with the approach.
4. Use a towel to wipe the ball or dry your hands before each roll. A ball can become oily from the lanes, and the oil may get on your hands.

5. When picking up the ball from the rack, always keep your palms perpendicular to the sides of the bowling rack.

6. Be aware of your fellow competitors; make sure the approach area is cleared before rolling the ball.

7. If students are used to set the pins, make sure the pinsetter is clear of the alley before rolling the ball.

Modifications for Special Populations

ORTHOPEDICALLY IMPAIRED

1. Use commercially adapted bowling ramps made from the following: wood, aluminum, or plastic. Consider making your own ramps using carpet roll cardboard cores. The diameter of the core will dictate the size of the ball used in the bowling session; for example, for a 5-inch core, you will use a tennis ball or softball.

2. Use push sticks, either commercial or homemade.

3. Use special bowling balls made with retractable handles.

COGNITIVELY IMPAIRED

1. Minimal modifications are needed. You might use similar adaptations suggested in the

Skill Assessment

Bowling is classified as a target activity and as such the final score provides the assessment outcome. An additional tally for evaluation is the number of total marks (strikes and spares) or the number of marks in a row that the student accumulates. Both approaches can be used for a set number of frames or games. In any event, assessment is best done near the culmination of the unit.

previous section for those with orthopedic limitations.

2. Allow a lot of practice time.

3. Reinforce students with additional tactile and kinesthetic input during delivery.

4. Contact your local Special Olympics office for bowling leagues in your area.

SENSORY IMPAIRED

Use variations on the approach:

1. Mark the pattern of approach with carpet squares or floor tape.

2. Use the ramp previously mentioned; however, ask the student how to reposition the ramp after each delivery. The sighted aide should explain which pins still need to be knocked down, and the student with a visual impairment should be required to adjust the ramp using verbal cues.

Terminology

anchor The person who shoots last on a team.

baby split The 2-7 or 3-10 split.

backup A reverse hook. The ball rotates toward the right for a right-handed bowler and toward the left for a left-handed bowler.

bed posts The 7-10 split.

blow An error; missing a spare that is not a split.

box The same as a frame.

Brooklyn A crossover ball, one that strikes the 1-2 pocket (i.e., crosses over to the other side of the head pin opposite the side it was thrown).

bucket The 2-4-5-8 or 3-5-6-9 leaves after the first throw.

cherry Chopping off the front pin on a spare.

double Two strikes in succession.

double pinochle The 4-6-7-10 split, also known as the *big four*.

Dutch 200 (Dutchman) A score of 200 made by alternating strikes and spares for entire game.

foul To touch or go beyond the foul line in delivering the ball.

frame The box in which scores are entered. There are 10 frames to each game.

gutter ball A ball that drops into either gutter. (Also a channel ball.)

handicap A bonus score or score adjustment awarded to an individual or team based on averages.

head pin The number one pin.

high hit Hitting the head pin full in the face or head-on.

hook A ball that breaks to the left for a right-handed bowler. For a left-hander, a hook ball breaks to the right.

Jersey side Same as a Brooklyn.

kegler Synonym for *bowler*, derived from the German *Kegel* (game of ninepins).

lane A bowling alley.

lane bed Surface on which the ball is rolled.

leave Pin or pins left standing after a throw.

light hit Hitting the head pin lightly to the right or left side.

line A complete game as recorded on the score sheet.

LPBT Ladies Professional Bowlers Tour.

mark Making a strike or spare in a frame.

open frame A frame in which no mark is made; at least one pin remains standing after rolling both balls in a frame.

PBA Professional Bowlers Association.

pocket Space between the head pin and pins on either side (1-3 pins for the left-hander and the 1-2 pins for the right-hander).

railroad Another term for a split. There are several kinds.

sleeper A pin hidden from view.

spare All pins knocked down on two balls.

split A leave, after the first ball has been thrown, in which the number one pin plus a second pin are down, and eight pins remain standing. Indicated by 0 on score sheet.

spot Series of dots or arrows on the alley at which a bowler aims.

spot bowling Method using arrows or dots on the alley as targets as opposed to looking at the pins during the throw.

strike All pins knocked down by the first ball.

striking out Obtaining three strikes in the last frame.

tap When a pin is left standing on an apparently perfect hit.

turkey Three strikes in a row.

WIBC Women's International Bowling Congress.

Discussion Questions

1. Discuss the reasons that bowlers are called *kegler*.

2. Identify the factors one should consider when selecting the appropriate bowling ball.

3. Contrast the differences in scoring a strike and a spare.

4. Discuss the procedures for determining the approach starting point.

5. Compare and contrast the aiming strategies for spot and pin bowling.

6. Identify the etiquette considerations for bowling.

7. Discuss the psychological learning hints that lead to more consistent outcomes.

8. Compare the major differences in the mechanics between the straight ball and the hook.

9. Identify the various symbols used for scoring when manually recording the outcomes on a score sheet.

Web Sites

www.bowlingzone.com—contains multiple categories covering associations and organizations, bowling indices, and collegiate and high school sites.

www.pba.com Professional Bowlers Association (PBA)—covers career bowling.

www.bowlsearch.com—lists multiple sites and provides good instructional information under Expert Tips. Also lists the most popular bowling sites and features a bowling glossary and chat room.

www.bowlersparadise.com—lists bowling videos and books available for purchase and bowling tips.

www.bowlingindex.com—includes bowling news, events, tournaments, instructional tips by Bob Strickland, forums, and more.

www.bowlingball.com—a resource for improving bowling skills.

| # Cycling

This chapter will enable you to

- Identify important historical events in the evolution of cycling
- Use proper hand signals and follow bicycle safety rules
- Discuss the characteristics of various types of bicycles—touring, hybrid, recumbent, mountain, and utility bikes
- Select and fit a bicycle to individual needs
- Select equipment for everyday riding and repair
- Describe and apply the gearing theory to everyday cycling
- Demonstrate techniques for safe and efficient cycling in city and country, including ankling, balancing, body positioning, braking, cadence, emergency stops, group riding, mounting and dismounting, maneuvering, pacing, short radius turning, and straight roadside riding

Nature and Purpose

Bicycling is a wonderful lifetime activity. It can be enjoyed by young and old alike and is a great family recreational pastime. Cycling offers relaxation, fitness, and occasional vacation touring or camping. A bicycle is not only a vehicle for pleasure and sport, but also a means of transportation to work or school—a role it has long played for millions of people throughout the world. Although it is not likely to replace the automobile in this country, the bicycle is relatively inexpensive, durable, and cheap to operate and maintain. It does not use up natural resources nor pollute the atmosphere. This chapter will introduce the fundamentals of cycling. Mountain biking and racing enthusiasts will find additional information on these topics in the Further References section.

History

The bicycle has existed in various forms for centuries. Early bicycles did not look like today's vehicles, but they did perform the bicycle's basic function: providing transportation for the rider under his own power. The ride was uncomfortable; early bikes had a fixed wheel and no seat. By the late 1600s, the bicycle's basic design was much like a scooter with two wheels connected by a board and powered by the rider, who pushed against the ground to propel it forward.[1]

In the next two centuries, many designs appeared, the most significant of which was created by Baron von Dais of Baden in 1817. This bicycle had two wheels of the same size and the front one was steerable. However, it had no pedals; the cyclist propelled himself by using his feet.[2] During this time, the bicycle was a plaything of the wealthy and was not really a form of transportation as it is today.

Over the course of the 19th century, many changes in design were developed that ultimately led to the modern-day bicycle. In 1839, Scotsman Kirkpatrick MacMillan invented the first pedal-driven bicycle; however, the pedals were fixed to the wheel, requiring the rider to pedal the bicycle continuously to move forward. Between 1870 and 1874, two significant inventions by Englishmen appeared: James Starling invented the gear that allowed the wheel to turn faster than the pedal, and H. J. Lawson invented the drive chain, which shifted the drive directly from the pedals on the front wheel to the rear wheel. So, the old style of bicycle—a huge front wheel and small back wheel—became a thing of the past. Later, in 1880, John Dunlop invented the pneumatic tire, making the ride more comfortable. Before this development, bicycle tires were hard rubber, making for a sometimes "bone-shaking" ride.[3]

It was not until 1876, at the Philadelphia Centennial Exposition, that bicycles appeared in the United States. Albert Pope, a builder of horse carriages, attended the exhibit and was intrigued. After visiting bicycle-making shops in England, Pope came back to the United States and, using ideas he found in England and some of his own, set up his own bicycle shop. By the end of the 19th century, Pope had founded the largest bicycle manufacturing firm in the United States: American Bicycle Company.[4] The coaster brake and a 10-speed shifting mechanism were also invented during this period. Then, in 1931, the derailleur system was invented, which allowed gears to change while the rider pedaled.[5] So, in the short span

A

B

Figure 8-1 (A) A racing bike, touring bike, and hybrid bike. (B) A recumbent bike, mountain bike, and utility bike. (Courtesy of B&B Kirks Bicycle Shop, Muncie, IN)

of about 100 years, the principles incorporated into the modern-day design were invented, and the bicycle as we know it today came into being.

In 1880, the League of American Wheelmen was formed to improve riding conditions on U.S. roads, most of which were deeply rutted. The league, made up of thousands of cyclists, more than 150,000 business-men, and governors from several states, petitioned Congress to create the Road Department, which ulti-mately led to a better system of connected and paved roadways.[6] Today, the organization, now known as the League of American Bicyclists, promotes safety and well-maintained roads and advocates for issues concern-ing cycling in communities.

Several developments have made bicycling more popular than ever. First, many communities through-out the United States have reclaimed old railroad beds and developed linear parkways replete with surfaces for walking, jogging, and bicycling. Second, cycling became more popular among U.S. citizens after the Los Angeles Olympics in 1984, chiefly because of the success the U.S. riders acheived in sprint and road racing. Third, in recent years the Tour de France and the success of American rider Greg LeMond sparked worldwide inter-est in cycling. A fourth reason is the increased attention to thrill-seeking sport activities; BMX biking and moun-tain biking have become increasingly popular and have attracted a younger segment of the population. Finally, cycling, as you will see in this chapter, is an excellent lifetime fitness-developing activity for people of all ages.

Bicycles and Equipment

Bicycles come in various models, styles, and colors, and with different components. They are priced from under $200 to over $3,000. Types of bicycles include touring and racing bikes (road bikes), mountain bikes, hybrids, recumbent bikes, and utility bikes (Figure 8-1).

When buying a bike, shop at a local bike store for the best selection, sizing, and service. A dealer will help you choose a bike that is best for you, based on the type of riding you wish to do.

Touring and Racing Bikes. If you want to cycle for fit-ness or for weekend or longer bike trips, choose a touring bike that has multiple gears (10–27). A touring model is durable, with a flexible frame that absorbs shock. It has a wide range of gears for climbing hills, caliper hand brakes, and a padded seat. Dropped handlebars take some weight off the seat and allow a wide range of riding positions. Avoid a racing bike unless you intend to race. Racing bikes are built for speed, with stiffer frames, less shock absorption, a narrow range of gears, and less padding.

Mountain Bikes. If you wish to do a significant amount of trail riding or off-road riding, then the heavier mountain bike is for you. A majority of bikes sold today fall in this category. The mountain bike is also fine for commuting around town or for shorter bike rides on the road. Mountain bikes have at least 18 gears; high ground clearance; fat, knobby tires; upright handle bars; and a sturdy frame.

Hybrid Bikes. If you wish to have a bike that can be used on the road as well as on some trails, then consider a hybrid bike. Hybrids have wider tires than a touring or racing bike, straight, upright handlebars, and larger wheels than a mountain bike. The upright position of the rider on the seat places greater pressure on the but-tocks, arms, shoulders, wrists, and hands. Bicycling on a hybrid can be tiring on a long ride. Although you can ride trails, be advised that the trail should be compact or firm and relatively free of debris.

Recumbent Bikes. If you want a bicycle that places you in a natural sitting position, then consider a recum-bent bike ($650–$2,000). The recumbent is designed to maximize comfort and ride smoothly. The wheels are

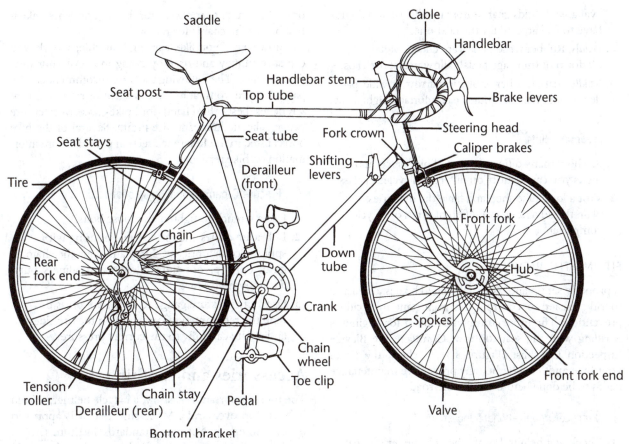

Figure 8-2 Parts of a bicycle.

smaller than most bikes, the handlebars are above or below the seat, and the seat is much larger than a normal seat. Recumbent bikes have become more popular in recent years because of several features: good, broad weight distribution on the back and buttocks; lack of pressure on the shoulders, neck, arms, wrist, and hands; and the comfortable ride. Although the turning radius is generally larger than most bikes, most riders enjoy them during long and extended tours.

Utility Bikes. Utility bikes with heavy frames, upright handlebars, wide tires, and wide padded seats are less expensive, take more abuse, and require less upkeep than other bikes. The one-speed adult cruiser with its balloon tires is easy to handle and gives a smooth ride. It is fine for off-road riding. The three-speed bike has lighter wheels, hand brakes, upright handlebars, and gears that can be shifted when stopped. It is good for commuting around town but is not good for long trips or climbing many hills.

BASIC PARTS OF A BICYCLE

The touring bicycle shown in Figure 8-2 illustrates the basic parts of the bicycle:

1. *Frame*. Heavy frames are welded steel. Better, costlier frames are double-butted, lugged, and brazed

alloy. Frames come in different shapes and sizes and determine the quality of the bike.

2. *Brakes*. Either center- or side-pull hand caliper brakes are good on derailleur bikes. Coaster (pedal) brakes are used on one-speed models.

3. *Wheels* consist of hubs, spokes, rims, and tires, and come in standard, touring, and racing versions.

4. *Tires* come in two basic types. Clinchers are durable and inexpensive (recommended). A liner can be inserted between tire and tube to prevent punctures. Tubulars (sew-ups) are not advised for the general bicyclist. Although thinner and lighter, they are expensive and prone to punctures.

5. *Handlebars* come in raised or dropped styles, and either version can be fitted on any bike. Upright bars allow good vision and are comfortable for many people. Dropped bars take shock off the spine and weight off the seat while allowing a wider range of riding positions. Handlebar padding may be added to reduce road shock, preventing arm and hand soreness.

6. *Crank set* in better bikes is alloy and cotterless (uses bolts or nuts to attach the crank arm to the axle).

7. *Derailleur* is a gear-changing device that lifts and pulls the chain from sprocket to sprocket. If you do not like shifting, click shifting is now widely

available. It finds gears automatically, so you do not have to feel around for the next one.

8. *Pedals.* Rubber tread pedals are cheap. Metal platform or thin cage pedals allow use of toe clips.

9. *Saddle* (seat). Leather or plastic, narrow or wide, padded or not, the seat should be comfortable right away.

▶ Learning Hints

1. See how many different types of bicycle components you can identify on different bicycles in class.

2. Visit a local bike shop and have the owner explain the advantages of different types of bicycle components.

FITTING THE BICYCLE

A properly set up and well-maintained bike is a pleasure to ride, easier to control, and important in accident prevention. The most common problem for beginners is riding with the seat too low. Complete the Bicycle Inspection Checklist (Figure 8-3) to check the fit of your bike and see whether any preventive maintenance needs to be done before you hit the road.

▶ Practice/Organizational Suggestions

1. Check seat height. Locate the bolt (under the seat) that loosens the seat post. Mark on the stem current height, then, if needed, change seat height and set at correct height and tighten bolt.

2. Locate bolts that adjust seat tilt. Loosen and remove saddle, then replace and retighten bolts.

3. Locate quick-release levers for front and rear brakes. Release front lever and squeeze front brakes. Close lever. Recheck front brakes.

4. Locate quick-release levers for front and rear wheels. Loosen front brake, release front wheel, remove. Replace front wheel, center between brake shoes, and close brake lever.

General Maintenance Tips

Regardless of the type of bicycle you have, you must keep it in good working order. Preventive maintenance, tightening loose bolts, and lubricating cables before they rust and stick is better than finding yourself stuck miles from home with a broken bike. If you are not mechanically inclined, consult your local bike shop for a spring tuneup. Then, at least once a month, make the following checks: Investigate rattles and tighten loose bolts. Check tire pressure and inflate to the recommended pressure embossed on the sidewall. Lubricate cables and moving parts with a silicone lubricant, such as WD-40. In addition, spray the chain and clean it off by holding a rag against it as you turn the pedals. If anything is bent

or broken, such as spokes, rims, brakes, or gears, take it to a bicycle mechanic for repairs.

However, if you like learning how things work, you can save money and time by doing much of your own maintenance. The following tools are recommended: tire patch kit, tire irons, adjustable wrench or set of crescent wrenches (best), third hand (for brakes), screwdriver, tire gauge, silicone lubricant, tire pump. Several of the bike books listed in the Reference section provide more information on bike repairs.

▶ Practice/Organizational Suggestions

1. Use a wrench to tighten any loose bolts.

2. Lubricate cables and inside cable housing with spray silicone lubricant. Spray and wipe the chain to clean. Spray pivot points of levers and calipers, but *do not spray bike rims.*

3. Use a tire pressure gauge to check tire pressure. Find the recommended pressure on the tire sidewall and inflate carefully to the correct pressure.

Accessories and Clothing

The most important accessory, a bicycle helmet, should be worn on every ride. Make sure that it is approved by the American National Standards Institute (ANSI) or the Snell Memorial Foundation. It should contain a dense liner made from stiff polystyrene that absorbs most of the impact in a crash. It should fit snugly and be fastened securely with the chin strap.

Toe clips are good because they enable a rider to pull up as well as push down each pedal stroke. However, they do take some getting used to, and must be worn loosely at first so you can get your foot out quickly. Some new safety pedals work like quick-release ski bindings, releasing the shoe with a twist of the foot.

Avoid the "suicide" or "safety" brake levers positioned on the top of handlebars. They decrease braking power and increase the distance needed to stop.

Other recommended equipment includes a lock and chain, water bottle, bike bag, tools, and gloves. Bicycles operated at night must have a headlamp that is visible from a distance of at least 500 feet. New bicycles must have front, rear, pedal, and side reflectors. A patch kit, tire irons, and pump are useful for fixing flats on the road. If you encounter dogs frequently, you may wish to carry dog repellent spray.

Clothing depends on weather conditions. In warm weather, regular or bicycling shorts and a T-shirt are ideal. Also remember to wear a sunscreen with an SPF of at least 15. In cool weather, tights, T-shirts, sweatshirt or jersey, and windbreaker (or warmups) can be layered to keep you comfortable. Gloves are essential, and a stocking cap can be worn under the helmet and pulled down over the ears. If you wear long pants, you

Bicycle Inspection Checklist

Name _____

Bicycle make & model _____

Serial No. _____

Frame size   OK   FIX
Can you straddle frame with both feet flat
on the ground?   ____   ____
(Should be 1- to 2-inch space between
crotch and top bar.)

Saddle

Horizontal adjustment—Nose of the saddle
should be 1 to 3 inches behind a vertical
line drawn through the crank hangar. A   ____   ____
cyclist 5'6" tall would position saddle 1
inch back; 5'10" tall: 2 inches back; and
6'3" tall: 3 inches back.

Vertical adjustment—Sit on bike with heel
on pedal at lowest position. Knee should
be straight, so when toe is on pedal, knee   ____   ____
is slightly bent.

Tilt—Should be horizontal or slightly
downtilted.   ____   ____

Is saddle tight and in good condition?   ____   ____

Handlebars

Vertical adjustment—Top bar should be
level with nose of saddle.   ____   ____

Horizontal adjustment—Place elbow on
nose of saddle. Outstretched fingertips
should just touch center of handlebars.   ____   ____
(Length of stem may need to be changed.)

In line with wheel and symmetrical.   ____   ____

Tight, no horizontal or vertical movement.   ____   ____

Tubing ends plugged, grips tight.   ____   ____

Tire pressure

Check. Correct pressure for this bike is
(Correct tire pressure is embossed on side
of tire.)
Check once a week.

Bolts

Check bolts for looseness. Recheck
monthly.   ____   ____

Hand brakes
Adequate space between lever and
handlebar when engaged? (if not, tighten
cable.)   ____   ____

Cable: Should be taut, with no kinks, rust,
or frayed ends.

Brake shoes: Tight? Openings face rear?   ____

Level with and no more than 1/4 inch from rim? ____   ____
At least 3/16 inch rubber remaining? (Replace if
needed.)

Test operation of each brake separately.
Must hold without catching: Front   ____   ____
                                 Rear   ____   ____

Wheels

Spin each wheel. It should run true (no
wobbles).   ____

Should have no binding or looseness
(bearings).   ____

Centered between forks (and chain stays
in rear).   ____   ____

Rim: Not dented or kinked?   ____   ____

Spokes: All intact and tight?   ____   ____

Tire: Properly seated? Tread?   ____   ____

Derailleurs

Turn bike upside down or have partner lift
rear wheel while you crank pedal and shift
through first the front then rear gears.
(Shift only while pedal is turning!) Derailleur
should shift chain smoothly from one
sprocket to the next without skipping a   ____   ____
gear, catching, or throwing chain off.

Chain condition. (Clean with silicone spray
if dirty.)   ____   ____

Sprocket teeth intact, not bent or broken.   ____   ____

Pedals

Shake and spin to check bearings:
no looseness or binding.   ____   ____

Pedals intact and tight?   ____   ____

Tread intact and tight?   ____   ____

Press down on both pedals at once.
Tight?   ____   ____

Remarks:

_____

G. Robbins, D. Powers, and S. Burgess, _A Wellness Way of Life._
(Dubuque, IA: Wm. C. Brown Publishing Co., 1991), pp. 329–330.

Figure 8-3 Bicycle inspection checklist.

will need pants clips or a rubberband to keep them out of your chain. Rain calls for a rain cape, though a large plastic garbage bag may suffice in a pinch.

Rules of the Road and Safety Considerations

A bicycle is not a toy but a means of transportation. Bicyclists are subject to the same traffic laws as automobile drivers. In most bicycle-automobile accidents, it is the bicyclist who is at fault. Riding on the road requires maturity, knowledge, and ability to follow rules of the road. The police issue traffic tickets to careless cyclists. Rules for safe cycling include the following:

1. Wear an ANSI- or Snell-approved bicycle helmet and brightly colored clothing for maximum visibility in traffic.

2. Obey all traffic regulations, stop signs, stop signals, one-way streets, and traffic control signs.

3. Keep to the right side of the road, drive with the traffic in a straight line, and ride single file. Do not

ride on the sidewalk and do not listen to music while riding.

4. Never hitch a ride on other vehicles or carry other riders or packages that obstruct vision or interfere with proper control of the bicycle.

5. Always use proper hand signals to indicate turning or stopping.

6. Avoid cycling at night, but if you must do so, wear light or reflective clothing and use lights and reflectors on your bike.

7. Watch for doors opening from parked cars, for drain grates, wet leaves, potholes, stones, glass, or other obstacles on the road, and for pedestrians. Cross railroad tracks at a 90-degree angle to avoid catching the wheel in the tracks.

8. Be sure your brakes are operating efficiently, and keep your bicycle in perfect mechanical condition.

9. In rainy weather, caliper brakes lose up to 90 percent of their stopping power. Allow extra stopping distance and do not take corners too fast. Pump the brakes occasionally to wipe water off the wheel rims.

10. Keep alert. Look out for cars pulling out into traffic or turning. Listen for traffic approaching out of your line of vision. Anticipate traffic conditions rather than react to them.

ROAD SIGNS

The cyclist should be familiar with traffic signs and markings. These may be found in a driver's manual. Refer to it for rules specific to your state regarding cycling.

Dogs are potential hazards. If you see a dog at a distance, you can probably outrun it. Water from your bottle might scare it off, or you can stop, keeping the bike between you and the dog. Walk away slowly. Generally, it will leave you alone, but watch it carefully before you get under way again. *Do not try to run over or kick the dog because you may cause an accident or harm the dog.*

GROUP RIDING

When riding as part of a group, the front rider should call and signal (point to) road hazards such as holes, loose gravel, bumps, and so forth (Figure 8-4). The rear rider should call, "Car back," to alert the group when an overtaking car is approaching. When "Car back" is called, all riders should quickly get in single file to allow the car to pass safely. Although experienced riders may draft off each other to cut wind resistance, novice riders should avoid overlapping wheels because a sudden unexpected swerve or bump could cause both to crash.

Ride single file unless traffic is light and you can see and hear approaching traffic well in advance.

Hand Signals. *Always* use hand signals when turning or stopping to alert other drivers to your intentions and allow them time to react appropriately (Figures 8-5 and 8-6). Automobile drivers can anticipate your moves and give you, as a cyclist, more respect and maneuvering room when you use hand signals than when you simply stop without warning or suddenly cut across traffic.

▶ **Practice/Organizational Suggestions**

1. a. Ride a mapped route. Practice braking and signaling before every intersection or stoplight.
   b. Stop or slow. Downshift into a lower gear, signal with the left hand, then squeeze the brakes.

Figure 8-4 Front rider signals road hazard.

Figure 8-5 Hand signal—left turn.

Figure 8-6 Hand signal—stop or slow down.

   c. Make turns. Downshift and slow down before turning. Keep the right hand on or near the brake at all times, make sure traffic is clear both ways, signal the appropriate turn with the left hand, then proceed when safe. Do not brake while turning.

2. Ride route in groups of three to six. Have front rider call road hazards and rear rider call approaching traffic. Switch group positions at intervals so each person rides front and rear. Discuss different road hazards encountered.

3. Before riding a route on which dogs may be encountered, discuss strategies for dealing with them.

Suggested Learning Sequence

A basic learning progression for the beginning cyclist is listed.

1. Bike safety inspection (complete checklist)
2. Rules of the road (signaling, group riding)
3. General practice skills for bicycling
4. Physical fitness
5. Parts of the bicycle and terminology
6. Preventive maintenance and adjustment
7. Bicycle selection
8. Bicycle clothing and accessories
9. Clubs, organizations, racing, touring, bikeways, and so on

Skills and Techniques

MOUNTING AND DISMOUNTING

When mounting, straddle the frame, place one foot on the pedal, raise the pedal to a high position, then push

off and sit down on the saddle. You may dismount from a stationary or moving bike. For a stationary dismount, coast and brake with one pedal high and one low. Stop, then step down first with the higher foot. When both feet are on the ground, swing one leg over the top bar. For a moving dismount, coast with one pedal low, bring the other foot over the frame and downward as you leave the saddle, then apply the brakes and touch the ground.

MOUNTING AND DISMOUNTING WITH TOE CLIPS

After mastering mounting and dismounting, if you wish to ride with toe clips, you will want to practice getting your feet into and out of them. Toe clips keep the ball of the foot firmly centered over the pedal. They may seem more trouble than they are worth at first, but most people who make an effort to use them feel they are indispensable.

Mounting. Practice in an open area where you are not likely to run into anything. You may first wish to use just the clip without the strap. Straddle the frame, place one toe in the clip, push off, and get going a few strokes; then use your unclipped toe to flip the pedal so you can slip your toe into the clip. While you are doing this, you must steer the bike straight.

Dismounting. Use just the clips or keep straps loose. Stop and slide the foot on the higher pedal backward, not sideways, out of the clip. Practice stopping quickly and taking the feet out of the clips without looking at the pedals.

CONTROL AND BALANCE

Cycling on the road requires straight-line riding, ability to maneuver quickly around obstacles, ability to stop quickly without skidding or being tossed over the handlebars, and ability to glance back at traffic without losing balance. To set up a practice course, locate an empty parking lot or other flat surface and use chalk and sponges or empty milk cartons to mark lanes.

> ▶ Practice/Organizational Suggestions

1. *Balance.* Pedal 50 feet slowly within a 2-foot-wide boundary, taking as much time as you can, with feet remaining on the pedals and moving only in a forward direction.

2. *Speed and coordination.* Begin 30 feet before the starting line and pedal quickly through a course that is 8 feet wide but gradually narrows to 2 feet during the 50-foot run.

3. *Steering.* Place sponges 10 feet apart on each side of a 50-foot line. Weave in and out of the line of sponges with both front and rear wheels without knocking over the sponges. Experienced cyclists

steer by leaning the body as well as turning the handlebars.

4. *Left and right spiral.* Follow a spiral to the center without touching any lines on the 2-foot-wide course. This tests left and right turning skill and balance.

5. *Emergency braking.* Caliper brakes are so powerful that they can throw you over the front handlebars if applied forcefully. To brake safely, keep your weight far back in the saddle while applying both brakes simultaneously, just below the point where they skid. Pedal at average speed toward a goal and stop the bicycle 10 feet short of a marked line without skidding.

6. *Evasion.* Set up 12 sponges in the pattern shown in Figure 8-7. Place one sponge, then 4 feet later, two sponges 1 foot apart. Ride around the single sponge, then between the pairs of sponges. A skilled cyclist should be able to quickly skirt an obstacle, yet remain on course.

7. *Checking traffic.* Signaling turns requires that the rider first glance back at traffic without steering off course or losing balance. Ride a straight line in a chalked-off lane, and on signal, look back over the left shoulder and tell your partner how many fingers she is holding up.

8. *Signaling and turning.* Quickly glance back over the left shoulder to check traffic without wobbling; downshift; demonstrate proper signals for turns in both directions or stopping; then execute the maneuver.

GEARING AND CADENCE

When you can skillfully mount and dismount, start and stop, ride a straight line, and make turns, you are ready to use the gears. The purpose of gearing is to be able to maintain a steady pedaling cadence, regardless of terrain, wind, or weather conditions.

There are several gearing errors commonly made by beginners. Many people gear too high and pedal too slowly. They do not feel like they are doing any work unless they are pushing against resistance. This is inefficient and can produce sore knees. It is better to pedal quickly against less resistance in lower gears. Whereas beginners may pedal at a cadence of 60–70 rpm, experienced tourists often maintain cadences of 90–100 rpm.

Second, in climbing a hill, beginners often wait to shift until they are halfway up the hill and pedaling cadence has slowed. To maintain your cadence, downshift in advance of need.

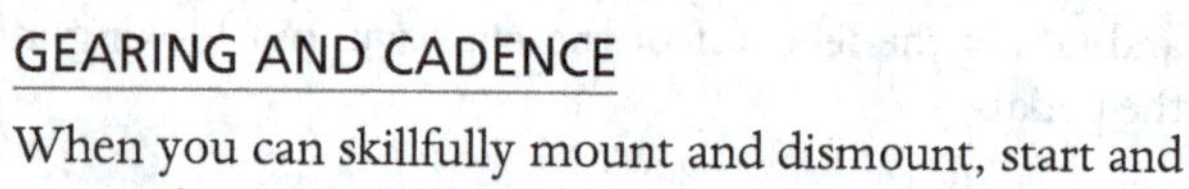

Figure 8-7 Twelve-sponge pattern for practicing evasion technique.

Finally, beginners seldom downshift when approaching stop signs or stoplights. They end up having to stand up on the pedals to get going again. Although it takes practice to coordinate the downshift, signal, and braking, it is more efficient and kinder to the knees to pull away from an intersection in a low gear, upshifting as speed increases.

▶ Practice/Organizational Suggestions

1. *Gearing.* To practice shifting gears:
   a. On a straight road with little traffic, maintain normal pedaling cadence (about 65 rpm) but ease up on the pedal pressure.
   b. Without taking your eyes off the road, move a shift lever slightly forward or back. You will hear a brief rattle, then a click as the chain moves to another sprocket. If the rattling continues, the chain is between gears. Adjust the lever until there is no noise from the chain.
   c. Shift through several gears, using first the left, then the right shift levers, until you can shift into a higher or lower gear by feel.
   d. To achieve the lowest gear, the chain must be on the innermost chainwheels (small front and large rear). In the highest gear, the chain will be on the outermost chainwheels (large front and small rear). Avoid using the large front–large rear or small front–small rear chainwheel combinations. These force the chain to cross at the most extreme angle, producing excessive wear and tear on the chain.

2. *Cadence.* While cycling at a steady cadence, time and count your pedal strokes for 1 minute. How does your cadence compare with the suggested cadence?

3. *Hill climbing.* Ride a course that includes one or more hills. As you approach each hill, keep well to the right. Try to downshift early enough so that you maintain an even cadence as you climb the hill and keep your hands on top of the brake hoods. You can lean forward and either pull on the handlebars with each push of the pedals or practice standing up on the pedals for maximum power. As you pick up speed on the downhill side, get down low and keep your weight well back in the saddle. Pump the brakes on-off to control speed.

4. *Ankling.* Ankling involves applying equal force, with the foot pushing and pulling throughout the pedaling cycle. Adding toe clips and straps enables you to pull on the upstroke as well as push on the downstroke, doubling pedaling efficiency.

▶ Practice/Organizational Suggestion

During part of a ride, concentrate on ankling technique.

Skill Assessment

Cycling requires skill and health-related fitness. The practice suggestions in the Control and Balance section may be used for assessing cycling control. The section Cycling for Fitness includes a suggestion for evaluating improvement in cardiorespiratory fitness from cycling over time.

CYCLING FOR FITNESS

Bicycling offers the benefits of cardiorespiratory activity, plus it is nonimpact. However, the bicycle is so efficient that cycling short distances will not get you in shape. You will have to put in some effort and sustain a training heart rate of 150–160 beats per minute (age 20 and under) if you want to improve your aerobic capacity. The sample workouts below are a good way to begin.

Sample Workout Program

Directions: Ride the recommended number of days and time at your training heart rate; rest one day between rides.

BEGINNING

Weeks

1. Ride 3 days × 15 minutes
2. Ride 3 days × 20 minutes
3. Ride 3 days × 25 minutes
4. Ride 3 days × 30 minutes
5. Ride 3 days × 35 minutes

Intermediate

6. Ride 4 days × 30 minutes
7. Ride 4 days × 35 minutes
8. Ride 4 days × 40 minutes
9. Ride 4 days × 45 minutes

Maintenance

10. Ride 3–5 days × 40–60 minutes

Physical Fitness Evaluation: Take a 5-mile time trial and record your time. After 8 to 12 weeks, repeat the ride and see how your time compares with the first trial.

The route, weather conditions, time of day, and type of clothing worn should be similar on both rides in order to make a valid comparison.

Modifications for Special Populations

ORTHOPEDICALLY IMPAIRED

1. Allow the student using a wheelchair to push the chair manually during the cycling session.
2. Commercial arm-crank and row cycles are available for persons with lower extremity injuries.
3. Use adult tricycles for students with balance deficiencies.
4. Depending on the student's disability, use of a scooter board may be appropriate; for example, the student can push from a prone position using the arms.

5. Use of a stationary cycle is advised if safety or fitness issues predominate.

COGNITIVELY IMPAIRED

1. Safety issues are a concern. Make sure to provide a "biking buddy" for all trips off site.
2. Use adult tricycles for balance.
3. Tandem cycles may be appropriate.

SENSORY IMPAIRED

1. Use of tandem cycles is advised for students who are blind or have a visual impairment.
2. Use of a stationary cycle is advised if safety or fitness issues predominate.

Terminology

ankling Pedaling technique in which the foot applies equal force on both the upstroke and downstroke.

bikeway Paths or roads designated as bicycle routes.

cadence The number of revolutions per minute (rpm) a pedal makes.

caliper brakes Hand brakes.

clincher Common tire and tube combination rim.

coaster brakes Foot-activated internal-hub rear brakes.

derailleur Device that moves the chain from one gear to another.

down tube Part of frame extending from the steering head to the bottom bracket.

granny gear The small chain ring on a triple-chain-ring crank set, which allows the cyclist to climb steep hills more easily.

head tube Tube holding front fork assembly.

presta valve Type of valve that must be unscrewed to allow tire to be filled with air.

saddle Seat.

schrader valve Type of tire valve found on most automobile tires and bike tires in the United States.

seat tube Part of frame extending from the bottom bracket to the seat.

toe clips Metal cages or straps that hold the foot on the pedal.

top tube Part of frame extending horizontally from the head tube to the seat tube.

triple crank The triple chain ring found on most road recreational bikes that allows the rider to change chain position to meet the riding situation.

teve A term that describes a bike wheel that is perfectly straight.

tubular tire (sew-up) Tire glued to rim of wheel.

wheel Includes the hub, rim, spokes, and tire.

Discussion Questions

1. Trace the evolution of the bicycle and the specific changes in design through the first 100 years.

2. Identify the five developments in recent times that have made bicycling popular.

3. Compare and contrast the different types of bicycles.

4. Identify the basic parts of a bicycle and discuss the various components in each.

5. List the tools recommended for general bicycle maintenance.

6. Identify the accessories recommended for safe and comfortable riding.

7. Discuss the important rules of the road when considering safety.

8. List the strategies for mounting and dismounting a bike.

9. Compare and contrast the factors involved when gearing and maintaining cadence while riding.

10. Discuss the factors one should consider when riding in a group.

Web Sites

www.bikeroute.com—offers history about recumbent bikes.

www.bentrideronline.com Bent Rider—offers an online magazine, articles, message board, and terminology.

www.webmountainbike.com—offers trail riding trips, product reviews, terminology, maintenance, mountain bike basics, and tips.

www.railtrails.org Rails-to-Trails Conservancy—provides links to greenways appropriate for cycling, walking, jogging, and in-line skating.

www.ibike.org International Bicycle Fund—includes valuable information on youth bike programs, bike education, safety, bike mechanics, and much more. The fund is an advocacy organization promoting sustainable transportation.

www.usacycling.org U.S. Olympic Cycling—includes Cycling 101, many sites, information about national events, and more.

www.bhsi.org/standard.htm Bicycle Helmet Safety Institute—features everything you want to know about helmets, including statistics, laws, standards, and other links.

www.bicyclinginfo.org Pedestrian and Bicycle Information Center—includes a good practice guide for bicycle education.

www.mountainbike.com *Mountain Bike Magazine*—contains information about bikes, reviews of mountain bike gear, skills, and products.

www.bikeleague.org League of American Bicyclists (formerly the League of American Wheelmen)—contains information about the League's Bicycle Friendly Communities Program; bicycle safety and education; national, state, and local bicycle advocacy; and the National Bike Month Program. Also a valuable source of bicycle fact sheets on many topics (beginning cycling, advanced cycling, riding on the road, commuting, touring, maintenance, tandems, and bike safety PSAs).

CHAPTER 9

Dance

This chapter will enable you to understand

- Country western dance
- Social dance
- Square dance
- Hip-hop dance

Nature and Purpose

Dance can be defined as any patterned, rhythmic movement of the human body in space and time as a means of expression.

Since prehistoric times, humans have had the desire to dance. Today that desire is still with us: People dance (1) for self-expressive purposes; (2) for religious, ritualistic, or ceremonial purposes; and (3) to entertain or please others. Dance will never die because it is constantly being reborn through different dancers, environments, and cultures.

Unlike other art forms, the art of dance is the only art form whose sole necessary tool is the human body. As with other structured or creative physical activities, it is important not only to understand the objectives and basic patterns of dance, but also to practice the skills necessary to achieve a level of proficiency in this highly expressive art form.

This chapter will look at four forms of dance commonly taught in educational institutions: country western, social dance, square dance, and hip-hop. Other popular dance forms such as ballet, tap, jazz, and folk dance are not included because of space limitations.

History

Dance in some form has existed since prehistoric times. At various times in history and parts of the globe, dance has been an expression of war or combat; a religious rite; a formal expression involving complex techniques and artificialities; an informal expression of people's work and play experiences; the attempt to interpret by means of movement the life of earlier peoples; and the attempt to seek novel steps with little artistic, cultural,

or aesthetic value. In these varied purposes, dance continues to fill people's need to give expression through bodily movement. In studying the rhythmic expressions of early cultures, we can find dance in the activities of prehistoric peoples; the aesthetic age of the early Greek civilization, followed by its decline and conquest by the Romans; the medieval period and the influence of aestheticism; the order of the Renaissance with the recognition of individual rights; and on through the dance of today.

In the United States, many of the forces that have affected the development of dance have been those with a direct bearing on the nation's history. The American Indians with their tribal and ceremonial dances, the conservative Puritans, later immigrants bringing the folk dances of their native countries with them, African Americans in the South, and the cowboys of the West are but a few of the groups from which we draw our dance heritage.

Movements Common to All Dances

All forms of dance involve movement. Although dance movement may at times be confined only to the body (nonlocomotor or axial movement), more commonly it requires the use of various forms of locomotion in which the body weight is transferred to the feet or from one foot to the other. All forms of locomotion can be reduced to five fundamental steps: walk, run, leap, jump, and hop. Any other type of locomotor activity is a combination of these basic steps. Closely related to the five fundamental steps are the skip, slide, and gallop, so some sources identify eight fundamental means of locomotion.

Walk. The weight is transferred from one foot to the other, alternately, one foot always being in contact with the ground. The usual foot action is a transfer of weight from the heel to the ball of one foot, during which time the other leg is pushing off, then swinging through to assume its position in the sequence of action.

Run. The speed of the walk is increased, and there is a brief period when neither foot is in contact with the ground. A run is usually a quicker progression than a walk.

Leap. A leap is a spring into the air by means of a strong pushoff from one foot, returning to the ground on the opposite foot. The leap differs from the run in that more energy is needed, and there is a longer period between transfer of weight because of a longer period of suspension in the air. The leap may be done either for height or for distance.

Jump. The body springs into the air by a two-foot takeoff, landing on two feet. Other types of jumps include (1) a single-foot takeoff, landing on two feet; and (2) a two-foot takeoff, landing on one foot. A jump may be made for either height or distance.

Hop. A hop is a spring into the air by means of a strong pushoff from one foot, returning to the ground on the same foot.

Graphic Representation. A walk, leap, jump, and hop are all done to an even beat, sometimes designated as long, and represented graphically as follows:

———   ———   ———

A run can take just as much time but is usually twice as fast and represented as

—— —— ——

In relation to the long beat, it is shown

—— —— —— —— ——

———   ———   ———

and so on. Should the pattern become uneven (long-short), each of the three remaining related forms of locomotion would fit into this rhythm: skip, slide, gallop. The graphic representation would be

——— ——   ——— ——

the total time of which is equivalent to one beat, thus

——— —— ——— ——

——— —— ——— ——

Skip. A combination of a step and a hop, done to an uneven beat in which the step is given the long time value (———) and the hop the short value (——):

step	hop	step	hop	step	hop	step	hop
———	——	———	——	———	——	———	——

Note: Were each part given equal time value, a step-hop would result instead of a skip:

——— —— ——— ——   ——— ——

——— —— ——— ——

step	hop	step	hop

In performing the skip, there is a feeling of elevation resulting from the natural tendency to swing the free leg forward and upward.

Slide. The weight is transferred from one foot to the other by means of a step on one foot followed by a quick drawing up of the other foot, with an immediate transfer of weight to it, resulting in a sideward movement.

Gallop. A gallop is similar to a slide, except the gallop moves forward, and the foot executing the leap is brought up to but not beyond the foot that has completed the step. The leap, a forward movement, is done with slight height; distance is not a factor.

Assessment Common to All Dances

Dance is an art form and has aesthetic qualities. Rubrics with qualifications such as Yes/No; Very Good, Good, Fair, Poor; and so on can be established for assessing traits specific to form such as good posture, moves to beat, weight centered over base, correct patterns, and fluid movement. A sample checklist for alternative assessment and a brief discussion of developing a rubric are presented in the Skill Assessment section of the Gymnastics and Tumbling chapter.

COUNTRY WESTERN DANCE

Brief History

Country western dance has become an integral part of U.S. social dance. Originally this type of dance was called U.S. novelty individual or couple dance. Today it is referred to as country western dance. Country western dancing has expanded its formerly limited repertoire to a broad selection of dance forms and styles, from line dancing to stylized couple dances.

Each country western dance has a sequence of movements, a rhythmic structure, and its own form. Each dance also has subtle differences in the dynamics of performance. For example, the "Texan walk" and "Californian run" are not actual dance steps but rather characteristic ways of traveling across the dance floor. These characteristic ways are the "style" of a dance or a group of dances from one area or people. It is in these different styles that the important differences among country western dances are found.

Executing the style and mannerisms inherent in the dance is as important as being able to dance the steps and pattern sequences. The dancer or student must develop style to achieve the fullest enjoyment of the dance. The following are guidelines dancers can follow to achieve the correct style in a dance or dances:

1. Study the background of the dance.
2. Develop an awareness of the characteristics of different styles.
3. Develop an understanding of the step patterns.
4. Be knowledgeable about the formations and positions.

On a dance floor, dancers must follow certain etiquette. Couples always move in line of dance (counterclockwise) around the floor. There are two imaginary outside lanes on a dance floor. The outside lane is used for couples doing progressive dances. The inside lane is used for couples who do not travel as far. In country western dances, the center of the floor is used for line dancing and stationary couple dances.

Suggested Learning Sequence

1. Vine (Grapevine)
2. Shuffle
3. Strut
4. Jazz box
5. Stomp
6. Stomp up
7. Scuff
8. Triple step
9. Break turn
10. Cha cha
11. Butterfly
12. Hip bump
13. Grapevine
14. Hook step
15. Hook
16. Coaster
17. Paddle turn
18. Rock
19. Kick ball-change
20. Waltz and waltz variations
21. Diamond

BASIC STEPS

Basic steps are any combination of one or more locomotor or nonlocomotor movements. They include the following: break turn, butterfly, cha cha, coaster, diamond, grapevine, hook step, jazz box, kick ball-change, paddle turn, rock, shuffle, strut, triple step, vine, waltz, and waltz variations.

Break Turn. Step forward with one foot, turn a half-turn on the supporting foot, and shift weight to the opposite foot. It is also called a *pivot turn*.

RIGHT BREAK TURN

1. Step right forward.
2. Pivot on right while turning a half-turn to left (counterclockwise); shift weight to left.

LEFT BREAK TURN

1. Step left forward.
2. Pivot on left while turning a half-turn to right (clockwise); shift weight to right.

Butterfly. Butterfly, also known as heel splits and toe splits, is a two-count basic step. Turn heels out and return heels to place.

BUTTERFLY (HEEL SPLITS)

1. Turn heels out.
2. Turn heels in.

BUTTERFLY (TOE SPLITS)

1. Turn toes out.
2. Turn toes in.

Cha Cha. A ballroom basic step. In ballroom, the cha cha has five steps. The last three steps in the cha cha sequence are described here. In a "quick, quick, slow" rhythm, step right to right, step left beside right, step right to right.

RIGHT CHA CHA (IN PLACE)

1 Step right in place.
& step left on ball of left foot beside right.
2 Step right in place.

LEFT CHA CHA (IN PLACE)

1 Step left in place.
& step right on ball of right foot beside left.
2 Step left in place.

RIGHT FORWARD CHA CHA

1 Step right forward.
& step left beside right.
2 Step right forward.

LEFT FORWARD CHA CHA

1 Step left forward.
& step right beside left.
2 Step left forward.

RIGHT BACKWARD CHA CHA

1 Step right back.
& step left beside right.
2 Step right back.

LEFT BACKWARD CHA CHA

1 Step left back.
& step right beside left.
2 Step left back.

RIGHT SIDE CHA CHA

1 Step right to right.
& step left beside right.
2 Step right to right.

LEFT SIDE CHA CHA

1 Step left to left.
& step right beside left.
2 Step left to left.

Coaster. A three-step sequence done in a "quick, quick, slow" rhythm. Step right back, step left beside right, step right forward. Can be done with either foot.

RIGHT COASTER

1 Step right back.
& step left back beside right.
2 Step right forward.

LEFT COASTER

1 Step left back.
& step right back beside left.
2 Step left forward.

Diamond. A basic step that is typical to country western dancing. Point the toes forward, side and back.

RIGHT DIAMOND

1. Touch right toes forward.
2. Touch right toes to right.

3. Touch right toes back.
4. Step right beside left.

LEFT DIAMOND

1. Touch left toes forward.
2. Touch left toes to left.
3. Touch left toes back.
4. Scuff left forward.

Grapevine. One foot steps to the side while the opposite foot steps in front or behind. Example: Step right to right, step left across right, step right to right, step left behind right. Can be done with either foot in any direction.

RIGHT GRAPEVINE (TO RIGHT)

1. Step right to right.
2. Step left across right.
3. Step right to right.
4. Step left behind right.

RIGHT GRAPEVINE (TO LEFT)

1. Step right across left.
2. Step left to left.
3. Step right behind left.
4. Step left to left.

LEFT GRAPEVINE (TO LEFT)

1. Step left to left.
2. Step right across left.
3. Step left to left.
4. Step right behind left.

LEFT GRAPEVINE (TO RIGHT)

1. Step left across left.
2. Step right to right.
3. Step left behind right.
4. Step right to right.

Hook Step. The hook is both a single action movement and a basic step. As a basic step, it is a four-count step. Touch right heel forward, swing right heel across left shin, touch right heel forward, step right beside left. Can be done with either foot.

RIGHT HOOK STEP

1. Touch right heel forward.
2. Hook right in front of left shin.
3. Touch right heel forward.
4. Step right beside left.

LEFT HOOK STEP

1. Touch left heel forward.
2. Hook left in front of right shin.
3. Touch left heel forward.
4. Step left beside right.

Jazz Box. Jazz boxes can be executed in many different ways, and they can take three, four, or five counts. It all depends on the type the dancer is asked to perform in each dance. The basic jazz box is as follows: Step right across left, step left backward, step right to right, step left beside right. It can be done with either foot in any direction.

RIGHT JAZZ BOX

1. Step right across left.
2. Step left back.
3. Step right to right.
4. Step left beside right.

LEFT JAZZ BOX

1. Step left across right.
2. Step right back.
3. Step left to left.
4. Step right beside left.

RIGHT JAZZ BOX WITH A ONE-QUARTER TURN

1. Step right across left.
2. Step left back.
3. Step right to right while turning a one-quarter turn to right (clockwise).
4. Step left beside right.

LEFT JAZZ BOX WITH A ONE-QUARTER TURN

1. Step left across right.
2. Step right back.
3. Step left to left while turning a one-quarter turn to left (counterclockwise).
4. Step right beside left.

Kick Ball-Change. A three-step sequence done in a "quick, quick, slow" rhythm. Kick right forward, step backward on ball of right beside left, step left forward. Can be done with either foot.

RIGHT KICK BALL-CHANGE

1 Kick right forward.
& step on ball of right foot slightly back.
2 Step left forward.

LEFT KICK BALL-CHANGE

1 Kick left forward.
& step on ball of left foot slightly back.
2 Step right forward.

Paddle Turn. A basic step, the paddle turn consists of two actions and two counts. Lead forward, with a given foot and shoulder. During the second action, turn a one-quarter turn.

RIGHT PADDLE TURN

1. Step right forward.
2. Pivot on right while turning a one-quarter turn to left (counterclockwise); shift weight to left.

LEFT PADDLE TURN

1. Step left forward.
2. Pivot on left while turning a one-quarter turn to right (clockwise); shift weight to right.

Rock.   Rock is a two-count basic step. Step in a given direction and follow with a step in the opposite direction.

RIGHT FORWARD ROCK

1. Rock right forward.
2. Rock left back.

LEFT FORWARD ROCK

1. Rock left forward.
2. Rock right back.

RIGHT BACKWARD ROCK

1. Rock right back.
2. Rock left forward.

LEFT BACKWARD ROCK

1. Rock left back.
2. Rock right forward.

RIGHT CROSS ROCK

1. Rock right diagonally forward across left.
2. Rock left back.

LEFT CROSS ROCK

1. Rock left diagonally forward across right.
2. Rock right back.

RIGHT DIAGONAL BACKWARD ROCK

1. Rock right diagonally back behind left.
2. Rock left forward.

LEFT DIAGONAL BACKWARD ROCK

1. Rock left diagonally back behind right.
2. Rock right forward.

Shuffle.   Shuffle is a two-count basic step. It is counted as "1&2" and described as "step together step."

RIGHT FORWARD SHUFFLE

1 Step right forward.
& step left beside right.
2 Step right forward.

LEFT FORWARD SHUFFLE

1 Step left forward.
& step right beside left.
2 Step left forward.

RIGHT BACKWARD SHUFFLE

1 Step right back.
& step left beside right.
2 Step right back.

LEFT BACKWARD SHUFFLE

1 Step left back.
& step right beside left.
2 Step left back.

RIGHT SIDE SHUFFLE

1 Step right to right.
& step left beside right.
2 Step right to right.

LEFT SIDE SHUFFLE

1 Step left to left.
& step right beside left.
2 Step left to left.

Strut.   A stylized walk, the strut leads with the heel or toes and transfers the weight to the whole foot. Usually it takes two counts. The strut can be done with either foot, forward or backward.

HEEL & TOE STRUT

1. Touch right heel forward.
2. Shift weight to right.
3. Touch left heel forward.
4. Shift weight to left.

TOE & HEEL STRUT

1. Touch right toes forward.
2. Shift weight to right.
3. Touch left toes forward.
4. Shift weight to left.

Triple Step.   The triple step is a basic step that has three actions done to two counts. It is counted as "1&2." It is also the basic step for the triple lindy or East Coast swing.

RIGHT TRIPLE STEP

1 Step right in place.
& step left on ball of left foot beside right.
2 Step right in place.

LEFT TRIPLE STEP

1 Step left in place.
& step right on ball of right foot beside left.
2 Step left in place.

Turn.   Turn is a movement that progresses in a circular direction. You can turn a one-quarter turn, a one-half turn, a three-quarters turn, a full turn, or more than a full turn. The type of turn to be executed will be specified in each dance.

Vine.   Vine is short for grapevine. In country western dance, the vine has become a standard for three steps and a fourth action that could be a brush, hitch, hook, kick, scuff, step, stomp, stomp up, or touch.

RIGHT VINE

1. Step right to right.
2. Step left behind right.
3. Step right to right.
4. Do any of the following: brush, hitch, hook, kick, scuff, step, stomp, stomp up, or touch.

LEFT VINE

1. Step left to left.
2. Step right behind left.
3. Step left to left.
4. Do any of the following: brush, hitch, hook, kick, scuff, step, stomp, stomp up, or touch.

RIGHT FORWARD VINE

1–3 Take three steps forward: right, left, right.

4 Do any of the following: brush, hitch, hook, kick, scuff, step, stomp, stomp up, or touch.

LEFT FORWARD VINE

1–3 Take three steps forward: left, right, left.

4 Do any of the following: brush, hitch, hook, kick, scuff, step, stomp, stomp up, or touch.

RIGHT BACKWARD VINE

1–3 Take three steps back: right, left, right.

4 Do any of the following: brush, hitch, hook, kick, scuff, step, stomp, stomp up, or touch.

LEFT BACKWARD VINE

1–3 Take three steps back: left, right, left.

4 Do any of the following: brush, hitch, hook, kick, scuff, step, stomp, stomp up, or touch.

Waltz (Basic). Step right forward, step left beside right, step right beside left. Can be done with either foot in any direction.

Waltz Balance. Step right to right, step left beside right. Step right beside left. Can be done with opposite footwork in any direction.

Waltz Half-Box. Step right forward, step left to left, step right beside left. Can be done forward or backward with either foot.

Waltz Box Quarter Turn. A basic turn in the English waltz. When executing the right turn (clockwise): step right forward, step left to left while turning a one-quarter turn to right (clockwise), step right beside left. When the left foot is the active foot, the turn will be done as follows: Step left backward, step right to right while turning a one-quarter turn to right, step left beside right.

Waltz Half-Turn. The same as in the box turn, except turn a one-half turn.

Waltz Full Turn. Turn a full turn with three steps.

Waltz Twinkle. The twinkle is a basic step used in the waltz. Step right across left, step left beside right, step right beside left. Can be done with either foot in any direction.

SINGLE-ACTION MOVEMENTS

These are the single-action movements: brush, bump, clap, hitch, hold, hook, kick, pivot, scoot, scuff, stomp, stomp up, swing, swivel, touch.

Brush. A movement where the toes or ball of the foot come in contact with the floor. Swing either leg in any direction while touching the floor with the toes or ball of foot. Can be done with either foot in any direction.

Bump. Move a hip in any given direction with an accent.

Clap. Strike hands together in any manner asked for.

Hitch. Lift the knee of the inactive leg, bending knee in a 45-degree angle. For example, step right forward while lifting the left leg with a bent knee. Can be done with either leg.

Hold. Hold a position for a given amount of time.

Hook. Swing the heel across the opposite shin. Can be done with either foot.

Kick. A sharp swinging action of the leg from the knee down. Usually in a forward direction. Can be done with either foot in any given direction.

Pivot. A turning motion on the ball of the foot that has the weight. Step right forward, turn on the ball of the right in any given direction and maintain the weight on the right. Can be done with either foot in any direction.

Scoot. A movement forward on the active foot, similar to a hop without leaving the ground.

Scuff. A movement where the heel comes in contact with the floor. Strike the floor with the heel in a forward motion without a shift of weight.

Stomp. An accented step with a shift of weight.

Stomp Up. An accented step without shifting weight to the active foot. Step right beside the left with an accent, without shifting weight to right. Can be done with either foot.

Swing. A forward or backward movement of either leg or arm.

Swivel. Turning of heel or toes from side to side on the ball or balls of the feet or heels.

Touch. Touch the floor with the heel or toe without shifting of weight. Can be done with either foot in any direction.

SUGGESTED COUNTRY WESTERN LINE DANCES FOR BEGINNERS

Dance	Basic Steps
Arkansas Strut	Strut, jazz box
Barn Dance	Vine
Bartender Stomp	Vine
Boot Scootin' Boogie	Scoot, vine
Canadian Stomp	Vine, jazz box
Celtic Cross	Shuffle, break turn
Country Walkin'	Jazz box, swivels
Cowboy Boogie	Vine, hip bumps
Cowboy Cha Cha	Rock, cha cha, break turn
Cowgirl's Twist	Strut, swivels

Cruisin'	Rock, cha cha, break turn, vine
Electric Slide	Vine
Lazy Shuffle	Shuffle, rock
Pure Country	Vine, coaster
Rebel Strut	Break turn, shuffle
Rocky Mountain Scramble	Vine, diamond
Ski Bumpus	Shuffle, break turn, kick ball-change
Tush Push	Hip bumps, shuffle, rock
Waltz Across Texas	Waltz and variations

SOCIAL DANCE

Brief History

Social or ballroom dancing began in the United States at the time of World War I with the introduction of many new forms of couple dances. The Charleston was followed by a series of "jitterbug" dances and the Latin American rhythms that were performed to big swing bands. Rock-and-roll music influenced an individual type of dance that led to performances of disco. Novelty and fad dances seem to fill a need at a particular time and may reflect changing trends in music. They may stimulate interest and participation, but they seldom last long enough to merit a place in the repertory of traditional social dances. The following discussion focuses on basic elements used in social dance.

DANCE POSITIONS

Closed. In waltz, fox-trot, and polka dances, partners face each other, standing toe to toe, looking over each other's right shoulder, the man facing the line of direction. With his style arm (left), the man's left hand holds the woman's right hand at about shoulder height; arms are relaxed and slightly bent at elbows. With his lead arm (right), the man's fingers are closed and on the woman's back slightly above her waist. The woman's left hand is placed on the man's right shoulder.

In Latin dances (tango, samba, merengue), rumba, mambo, and cha cha cha, the man's lead arm (hand on partner's back) should be above the small of the back, and the elbow should be slightly higher than in the aforementioned closed dance position. The man's style arm (left) is also placed higher when performed.

Semi-Open. From the closed position, partners turn slightly away from one another, looking in the line of direction—man's right and lady's left sides are near each other.

Open. From semi-open position, partners turn apart so that both are facing in line of direction.

Reverse Open. Partners turn so that both are facing in reverse line of direction—man's left and woman's right sides are near each other. Man's right arm and woman's left arm may hang down at side.

LINE OF DIRECTION

In general, couples move about the floor in a counterclockwise circle known as the line of direction (LOD). Couples may, however, move forward, backward, or sideward within this pattern; and there are many new dance steps in which the couples dance in much the same spot.

Style and Etiquette

Every dance is performed with a certain style. The particular dance form, its tempo, and rhythm determine the style with which a particular dance is executed.

A man asks a woman to dance in a simple and direct way: "May I have the next dance?" or "Will you dance with me?" are the two customary approaches. It is polite to escort the woman to and from the floor and to thank her for the dance. Usually a man may cut in on a couple at a private party, but at a public dance, cutting in is not condoned. Dancers should always be courteous and well mannered on the dance floor.

HOW TO LEAD AND FOLLOW

The man must indicate his steps and lead sufficiently in advance so that the woman can follow with confidence. He does this primarily with his upper torso, shoulders, and right arm and hand. The right hand becomes the steering rudder. The woman's principal method of following is to remain relaxed so that her partner may guide her easily.

Suggested Learning Sequence

There is no set sequence for learning basic social dance patterns. The teacher might consider the interests and ages of the students, variety in rhythm, available music, and then select the order of dances that best fits the students. The following dances are described later in detail:

Fox-trot	Rumba
Waltz	Cha cha cha
Tango	Jitterbug

All steps indicated as slow (S) use two beats of the music, and all steps indicated as quick (Q) use one beat of the music. Unless otherwise indicated, the steps described are for the man's (or lead) part; the woman's is opposite. For example, the man's "forward left" would mean the woman's "backward right."

FOX-TROT (4/4 TIME)

The fox-trot is a U.S. ballroom dance first introduced by Harry Fox to ragtime music in a 1913 musical. A fox-trot may vary in tempo, but for beginning students, a slower version is more appropriate. Although it began as a trotting dance, the fox-trot developed into the smoother, gliding dance that is performed today.

Magic Step. Basic Rhythmic Pattern: S S Q Q

1. Closed position
   Fwd left-S
   Fwd right-S
   Side left-Q
   Close right to left-Q

   Lead Cue:
   Lift right arm, lean forward

2. Semi-open position
   Side left-S
   Cross right over left-S
   Side left-Q (return to closed position)
   Closed right to left-Q

   Lead Cues:
   Pressure with heel of right hand
   Pressure with fingertips of right hand

3. Turn-under
   Man's part same as semi-open position
   Lady's part:
   Side R: start to turn under R arm-S
   Complete turn under R arm onto L foot-S
   Side R-Q (return to closed position)
   Close L to R-Q
   Lady's right and man's left hands are released
   during turn

Box Step. Basic Rhythmic Pattern: S Q Q

   Fwd L-S
   Side R-Q
   Close L to R-Q
   Back R-S
   Side L-Q
   Close R to L-Q

WALTZ (3/4 TIME)

The waltz is the oldest form of ballroom dance, and it is credited as being the first of its kind to be performed in the basic closed-couple dance position. It was not accepted when first introduced in the United States; however, composers such as Johann Strauss, von Weber, and Franz Shubert gave the waltz a dignified grace through their smooth and flowing musical styles.

It is important to note that the heels stay off the ground when performing this dance pattern.

Basic Rhythmic Pattern: Q Q Q

1. Box step
   Same as fox-trot except each step is Q

2. Crossover
   Do one-half box
   Cross R over L (semi-open position)
   Slide L (return to closed position)
   Close R

Lead Cues:
   Pressure with heel of right hand
   Pressure with fingertips

TANGO (4/4 OR 2/4 TIME)

Some scholars believe the tango is derived from the "milongo," a dance that originated in Andalusia, Spain; others feel that the tango's roots lie in an Iberian gypsy dance resembling flamenco. Regardless of its beginnings, the tango is characterized by low, lingering steps followed by quick directional changes.

Basic Rhythmic Pattern: S S Q Q S

1. Basic step (closed position)
   Fwd L-S
   Fwd R-S
   Fwd L-Q
   Fwd R-Q
   Draw L to R, weight remaining on R-S

2. Semi-open position
   Side L-S
   Cross R over L-S
   Fwd L-Q
   Side R-Q
   Draw L to R-S

Lead Cues:
   Pressure with heel of right hand
   Pressure with fingertips

RUMBA (4/4 TIME)

The rumba came to the United States in the late 1920s from Cuba. This Latin American dance was originally performed by African slaves living in South America. One of the main characteristics of the rumba is the smooth lateral swaying of the hips, a movement known as Cuban motion.

Basic Rhythmic Pattern: Q Q S

1. Box (closed position)
   Side L-Q
   Close R-Q
   Fwd L-S
   Side R-Q
   Close L-Q
   Back R-S

2. Cuban walk
   Walking forward or backward in the Q Q S rhythm

CHA CHA CHA (4/4 TIME)

The cha cha cha, which is a combination of the swing and mambo, became popular during the 1950s. The cha cha cha has Mexican, Afro-Cuban, and American influences, and was probably named after the three quick rhythmic sounds that the feet make when executing the steps. Like the rumba, the cha cha cha uses Cuban motion.

Basic Rhythmic Pattern: S S Q Q S

1. Basic step (closed position)

   Dancing toward each other with hands held:
   Fwd L-S, Back R-S
   Back L-Q, Back R-Q
   Back L-S, Back R-S
   Fwd L-S, Fwd R-Q
   Fwd L-Q, Fwd R-S

2. Cross-step

   Cross L-S (reverse open position), man's L and lady's R hands joined
   In place R-S
   Side L-Q, Close R-Q, Side L-S
   Cross R-S (open position), man's R and lady's L hands joined
   In place L-S
   Side R-Q, Close L-Q, Side R-S

JITTERBUG (4/4 TIME)

The jitterbug evolved from the lindy hop, a U.S. novelty dance that was named after the famous pilot Charles Lindbergh in 1927. As the movement of the lindy hop evolved into more exaggerated hopping sequences, viewers remarked that the dancers looked like "jittery bugs," thus giving the jitterbug its name.

Basic Rhythmic Pattern: S S Q Q

1. Basic step (closed position)

   Touch L, then take weight on L-S
   Place R, then take weight on R-S
   Back L-Q (semi-open position)
   Fwd R-Q (return to closed position)

2. Basic turn

   Man's part same as basic step
   Lady's part:
   Start to turn to R under R arm on R foot-S
   Complete turn under R arm on L foot-S
   Back R-facing partner-Q
   Fwd L-Q
   Start to turn to L under R arm on R foot-S
   Complete turn under R arm on L foot-S
   Back R-facing partner-Q
   Fwd L-Q

Lead Cues:
   Pressure with heel of right hand
   Pressure with fingertips

▶ **Practice/Organizational Suggestions**

Because leading and following are basic elements for partner dances, the teacher should introduce them by using a simple dance walk. Today's young persons are not accustomed to dancing in contact with a partner, traveling on a dance floor, or following a definite basic step. The teacher, therefore, should try to begin in a fundamental manner.

Using a free formation, the student should learn the basic step of any social dance without a partner. The teacher, prior to presenting the foot pattern, might have students clap hands to the music that will be used for the dance because being able to recognize the underlying rhythm is essential. The basic step pattern should be performed next with partners, all couples moving in line of direction. While the individuals keep dancing, the teacher may give verbal cues in relation to position, rhythm, or step pattern. If necessary, individual assistance may be continued through additional demonstration or dancing with the student. Students may receive extra ideas or be encouraged to create variations with partners learning together.

SQUARE DANCE

A Brief History

Although square dancing originated in 17th-century England with the English country dances (as well as the French contra dances), square dance has been labeled "America's folk dance." (Note: Some scholars believe that the dances of the American Indians are the true U.S. folk dances.)

The early New England colonists brought with them these pompous and precise line dances in which the couples faced each other. However, as U.S. square dance evolved, the less rigid and the more recreational and social these dances became. In fact, square dancing was one of the most popular and satisfying forms of social recreation because it was something in which all generations could participate and enjoy.

The "caller" was introduced to U.S. square dance in the early 19th century. The caller enabled dancing participants to execute the basic patterns without having to memorize the dances. Square dance calling requires a good deal of practice, understanding, voice control, and ability to handle large groups. Anyone who attempts calling must have a distinct and pleasant voice, a sense of timing so that the calls will immediately precede the figure and produce continuity in the dance, and a thorough knowledge of the dance figures.

Although there have been radical changes in the calls, style, and music of contemporary square dance, the basic patterns and figures have been standardized, making it possible to enjoy this popular recreational art form all over the United States and abroad (Figure 9-1). Today, this popularity has created avenues in the competing commercial market for professionally trained callers, square dance retreats and vacations, and square dance clothing and accessories.

Figure 9-1 Square dancing has become a popular recreational art form in the United States and abroad.

Suggested Learning Sequence

Honor	Couple promenade
Shuffle	Grand right and left
Forward and back	Star left (right)
Do-sa-do	Pass through
Seesaw	Ladies chain
Allemande left (right)	Right and left through
Swing	Square positions
Promenade single file	Half promenade

These steps, terms, and figures are described next, along with a few other important square dance terms, in alphabetical order. The number of counts usually used to fully execute the figures and steps are also indicated where appropriate.

SQUARE DANCE TERMS, FIGURES, AND STEPS

ALLEMANDE LEFT. Man gives his left hand to the woman on his left. With left hands joined, they shuffle around one another (exchanging places) and then both return to place. This figure is sometimes followed by an allemande right, in which the man executes the same figure but with his partner. More frequently, the allemande left is followed by a grand right and left (eight counts).

CIRCLE LEFT (OR RIGHT). Three or more dancers circle to the left or right, as directed. Hands are joined with elbows comfortably bent so that the hands are above the elbows, man's palm up, woman's palm down (16 counts for a full circle, eight counts for half).

CORNER. The person to the man's left or the woman's right is the corner person.

COURTESY TURN. The man takes the woman's left hand in his left, then places his right hand in her right, which is at her back, waist high. Turning counterclockwise, the man backs up and the woman walks forward one-half turn.

DO-SA-DO. Do-sa-do is a French term meaning back to back. Two dancers face each other and advance, passing right shoulders. Each person slides behind the other person passing them, then moves backward into place (eight counts).

FORWARD AND BACK. The persons or couples designated move four steps into the center of the circle, then move four steps backward out of the circle (eight counts).

GRAND RIGHT AND LEFT. In a square or circle formation, the partners face and take right hands. Men going counterclockwise and then women clockwise, each partner moves ahead, giving the left hand to the next person and pulling by, giving the right hand to the next person and pulling by, giving the left to the next, and stop. In square formation, the original partners will now be facing each other and ready for the next call (16 counts).

HONOR. The men bow while the women curtsey to their partners (or to the "corner" person, depending on the call). "Honor your partner" is an acknowledgment of your partner, usually at the beginning of a dance.

LADIES CHAINS

1. *Two Ladies Chain.* With couples facing each other, men stand still as the women shuffle forward, take right hands, pull by them, then give the left hand to the opposite man, who completes a courtesy turn (eight counts).

2. *Four Ladies Chain or Ladies Grand Chain.* In square formation, all four women start right and move clockwise to their opposite man, who gives them a courtesy turn (eight counts). Partner: The woman on the man's right, the man on the woman's left. Sometimes partners are changed temporarily before returning to the original partners.

PASS THROUGH. Two facing couples move forward, pass right shoulders, and remain facing in the same direction until the next call.

PROMENADE

1. *Couple Promenade.* The most commonly used promenade in square dancing is the couple promenade. Standing side by side, couples join left hands, then join right hands on top of their left hands. The couple then moves forward in a counterclockwise direction.

2. *Half Promenade.* Two couples, indicated by the call, use a couple promenade position to move counterclockwise and exchange positions in the square (eight counts).

3. *Promenade Single File.* Dancers face counterclockwise and move one behind the other.

RIGHT AND LEFT THROUGH. With couples facing, each person gives a right hand to the person opposite them and pulls by. The left hand is immediately given to the partner, and each couple does a courtesy turn (eight counts).

SEESAW. Two dancers face and pass left shoulders. Each slides to the left while back to back, then backs up to original position (eight counts).

SEPARATE. Each dancer turns his back on his partner, then they move in opposite directions. This movement is followed by a directional call.

SHUFFLE. A walking pattern in which the feet alternately slide in short, smooth steps along the floor in time with the music. A shuffle step is executed in an even rhythm, unlike the boisterous skip or hop of the early square dances, which is now regarded as an unacceptable style.

SQUARE POSITIONS. A square is an arrangement of four couples who stand facing the center in a square formation. The couples are numbered consecutively to the right, beginning with couple number 1, whose backs are closest to the music or caller. Couples 1 and 3 are the "head couples"; couples 2 and 4 are the "side couples."

STAR LEFT (OR RIGHT). If couples or ladies star, those involved touch fingers of the designated hand, elbows bent, and shuffle forward. If men star, each turns the designated side toward the center of the star, and with an overhand grip, takes the wrist of the man in front of him. Dancers move around the circle to return to their original positions (eight counts).

SWING. This is a modified social dance position in partners. The man's left arm is extended to the side, his right arm around the woman's waist. The woman puts her right hand in the man's left, her left hand is on the man's shoulder. They stand to the side so that right hips and right feet are in line with one another and almost touching. Using the right foot somewhat as a pivot, they push with the left foot so that partners circle about in place, in a clockwise direction. As the swing is performed, partners look at each other and lean away, which results in a quick, vigorous turn (eight counts).

▶ **Practice/Organizational Suggestions**

1. The most common mistake made by the inexperienced square dance teacher is selecting a specific square dance and then directing the dancers to walk through the basic movements and figures of the dance. The movements from these dances require a great deal of practice and probably cannot be performed with music, resulting in uninteresting drills more than an enjoyable dance. Basic calls should be taught in a single circle. This method enables the teacher to see quickly all dancers, to use music immediately, and to eliminate the necessity for a specific number of students for squares. A simple dance to music can begin, for example, with

   Honor your partner
   Honor your corner
   Join hands, circle left, circle right
   Walk into the middle
   Come right back

2. When the movements can be done effectively, teach a do-sa-do, seesaw, swing, allemande left, and a couple promenade. All calls may be combined then in varied sequence or in the following manner:

   Face your corner, do a do-sa-do
   Seesaw your partner
   Join hands, circle right
   Circle left
   Face the center, go forward and back
   Allemande left your corner
   Allemande right your partner
   Swing your corner

Swing your partner and promenade
Go single file
Face the center
(Repeat)

3. A grand right and left may be taught by designating a certain number of hands until a new partner is reached. For example, a right hand to the partner would be "one" and a left to the next would be "two." Any number may be chosen, but seven hands enables the dancers to learn the principle involved and eliminates the confusion of counting a large number of hands. Once the grand right and left is mastered, an allemande left with the corner may precede this figure. These movements are ready to be combined with those already learned.

4. The group of dancers may then move smoothly from the single circle formation to a double circle with partners facing. One may direct calls already acquired to make dancers comfortable in this new formation, for instance,

Honor your partner
Do-sa-do your opposite
Swing your partner
Circle left, circle right
Allemande right your partner
Allemande left your opposite
Do-sa-do your partner
Seesaw your opposite
Swing your partner

5. In the double-circle formation, star left and right and pass through may be taught rapidly. This permits dancers to work with different couples while being at ease with the basic calls. Two ladies chain and right and left through may be added to the figures. All basic calls except the grand right and left and the promenades may be combined to music.

The teacher will be able to teach the square formation using previously taught calls and may add more advanced figures as the selected dances require. Many of these are performed to music that has a familiar melody; therefore, the callers may choose to sing their calls. Happy dancing!

SELECTED SQUARE DANCES FOR BEGINNERS

Big Daddy
Buffalo Girls
Gentle on My Mind
If You Knew Susie
Little Ole Winemaker
Little Red Wagon
Marina Just Because
Oh, Johnny
Ragtime Banjo Ball
Winchester Cathedral

HIP-HOP DANCE

A Brief History

Michael Jackson gave us a sneak peek of break dance (and the movements that would later become the hip-hop style) when he first performed his robot dance on television in 1974. His dancing brought about a large following, including many break dance pioneers. Though break dance's popularity eventually faded in the 1980s, it was followed by the hip-hop dance style that swept mainstream youth culture in the 1980s and beyond. It is now most recognizable for the "popping and locking" that is done to a strong rhythmic beat. All parts of the body can capture the hip-hop beat. Even though the style developed in New York and on the West Coast, it can be traced back even farther to African tribal movements where the lock, freeze, pause, and pop are demonstrated in the basic fundamental movements of the villagers as they celebrate life, death, poverty, and prosperity. Taking those same movements and refining them to the music of today demonstrates that there really is nothing new under the sun. Dances are cyclic, and students (and teachers) can enjoy the exercise and dance excitement that high energy hip-hop provides.

MUSIC SELECTION

Music selection can be tedious with this genre of dance. The choices may be slim of appropriate music for the primary grades, middle school, and high school ages; however, it is possible to find music that is not only full of wonderful bass beats but has lyrics that can be played for all levels. A music search should be done first to produce a workable CD for the classroom. There are Web sites that have clean, downloadable versions of popular tunes and computer programs are available that will allow one to "cut and paste" together just the right beats for a successful hip-hop unit for every classroom. The time invested in finding the right music will launch this unit into a popular form of exercise for the students.

Suggested Learning Sequence

The following progression builds a knowledge base for learning hip-hop dance by incorporating basic rhythmic movement skills to music that motivates. The selections listed cannot be done in one class time, so mixing and matching is suggested to come up with the right combination to inspire and motivate the students. All these movements should be covered in a hip-hop unit:

Swing and stretch
Isolations (head bone's connected to the neck bone)
Styling
Pop it, punch it, and kick it
Corner-to-corner and back and front

Hip-hop line dance
Freestyle
Cool it down

SWING AND STRETCH. The warm-up can be anything fun that gets the body moving. Stationary stretches that follow the beat and have downward number progressions are good because the students know what is coming. *Example:* Start with eight overhead reaches with the right arm, reverse to the left. Then repeat the sequence with four, two, and one overhead reaches on each side.

ISOLATIONS (HEAD BONE'S CONNECTED TO THE NECK BONE). Popping and locking are terms used with hip-hop, but really they are the street names for isolations. These movements start at the head and work down to the feet. Done in a stationary position, the movements give students a chance to warm up each part of their bodies. *Example:* Start with isolating movements: down, look side-to-side, tip head to side (ear-to-shoulder), gently roll and circle head. Next explore the body's ability to move independent parts, an essential skill in hip-hop dancing. Do rib contraction and expansion (the start to "popping") and move the ribcage side-to-side.

STYLING. Form a large circle to do the locomotor part of the class. The circle is the time to get the heart rate climbing and to get moving in the free and relaxed style. Students should swing arms in opposition to the feet (right arm forward when the left foot is forward) as they walk with an attitude. *Example:* Have students side-step (face center with seven side-steps to the right and touch, and then reverse), walk backward, cross over step, step-kick, step-hop, drag to the side, and reverse.

POP IT, PUNCH IT, AND KICK IT. Kickboxing movements to current music mimics the high-energy street dance movements that freestylers use. Take the basic moves for arms and legs and put them to popular songs to give students a broader vocabulary of movement. Keep the movements relaxed, large, and "rubbery."

CORNER-TO-CORNER AND BACK AND FRONT. The corner-to-corner and back and front movements involve exploring all the areas of the room. *Example:* use *attitude walks*—high and low, turns, knee-drops, glide and slide (looks like a speedskater), step-hops—to travel the room.

HIP-HOP LINE DANCE. Line dances can be two-walled or four-walled, and may involve four to six steps that are repeated facing each new wall. Having students choreograph dances will allow them to explore isolations, styling, corner-to-corner, and other movements they have seen performed on television or learned from friends. Line dance choreography assignments should include parameters on acceptable music and appropriate movements.

FREESTYLE. This part of the class is a wonderful opportunity for the students to dance at the same time and "show what they know." The teacher can call out "arms only" or "just use slide and glide" or "let's do a partner challenge." Freestyle can also be a reward at the end of class for hard work during the period—a "show-off" time.

COOL IT DOWN. Every dance unit needs to have time at the end of class sessions for cooling down. A nice ballad by a current recording artist allows the students to do slow, sustained stretching of the muscles that have worked so hard throughout the class. Stretches can be student- or teacher-led.

▶ Learning Hints

Hip-hop dance is wildly popular with students of all ages, so a well-thought-out unit produces a challenge for the teacher and students to choreograph movements that may be difficult at first but achievable through experimentation and good humor. Persistence in learning the basic movements and a willingness to explore the suggested activities will bring extremely satisfying results. Should the students know more than the teacher, that's okay! The teacher can become the student, yet also guide and direct the goals of the class. Nothing is wrong when learning hip-hop. All movements are encouraged and then expanded on through careful instruction. The key words for this unit should be "relaxed" and "fun," and the teacher should remain positive and upbeat.

The Best Dance Moves in the World ... Ever is a great resource for more than 170 new and classic moves using various body part movements and steps that can be incorporated into a hip-hop unit. Limited pictures and instructions provide valuable information for understanding the movements.[1]

Skill Assessment

A dance unit will be most successful when formatted as a structured opportunity to learn the movement possibilities of the body in terms of the various ways the head, arms, upper body, lower body, and extremities can move. The body can move in smooth ways, sharp ways, straight, curved, up, down, narrow, wide. Rubrics may be established for the range of movement achieved for each part of the body. Students can divide into groups to do original choreography that can be shared in the form of an in-class performance. A list of expectations including music selection, movement quality, originality, use of floor space, participation of each student, and levels will give the students goals for their choreography. Students can self-assess, peer-assess, or the grade can be a teacher-only assessment.

Modifications for Special Populations

ORTHOPEDICALLY IMPAIRED

1. Keep movement patterns slow, and avoid quick changes for students with movement difficulties, such as students with cerebral palsy, muscular dystrophy, or spina bifida.
2. Keep tempo of music moderate.
3. Emphasize concepts of high, low, soft, hard, rough, smooth, and so on, and have students interpret movements.
4. Minimal modifications are needed in square dance for students using a wheelchair, such as a larger work area.

COGNITIVELY IMPAIRED

1. Follow suggestions for the orthopedically impaired.
2. Keep concepts and movement patterns simple.

SENSORY IMPAIRED

1. Use peer teachers and paraprofessionals for students who are blind or have a visual impairment.
2. Individual considerations need to be made to determine the appropriateness of dance for students who are deaf or have a hearing impairment.

Discussion Questions

1. Discuss the reasons why humans have always desired to dance.
2. Identify the many ways that dance has existed since prehistoric times.
3. Dance requires various forms of locomotion in which body weight is transferred to the feet or from one foot to the other. Identify the common movements.
4. Discuss why "style" in country western dance is important.
5. Compare the etiquette differences between line dancing and stationary couple dancing in country western dance.
6. Discuss why social (ballroom) dance has outlasted fad dances.
7. Identify the traits a square dance caller must possess.
8. Hip-hop dance is a contemporary art form. Discuss the reasons for its popularity.
9. Does dance contribute to cardiorespiratory health? If so, is it aerobic or anaerobic exercise?

Web Sites

COUNTRY WESTERN DANCE

www.sapphireswan.com/dance/—provides links to several country western dance sites. The two "Let's Dance" selections provide an extensive listing of dances.

www.cwdi.org—Country Western Dance Information—serves as a resource guide to country western dance information. The dance resources selections on the site are beneficial to the learner.

www.youtube.com/watch?v=ljpf6_35k1c—features actual dance tutorial.

SOCIAL (BALLROOM) DANCE

www.dancetv.com—features ballroom dancing, with tutorials on the waltz, fox-trot, and swing, plus a section on dance tips.

SQUARE DANCE

www.dosado.com—Provides more than 40 square dance selections, as well as details on other dance forms.

HIP-HOP DANCE

www.hip-hop-dance.net—offers access to hip-hop lessons, live video moves, music, culture, shoes and apparel, newsletter, and blog.

CHAPTER 10 | Field Hockey

This chapter will enable you to

- Identify the field markings
- Describe the basic rules of the game
- Analyze and demonstrate the techniques of holding the stick, dribbling, the hit, fielding, various passes, the tackle, the dodge, the penalty corner, the free hit, defense hit, and push in
- Identify and describe the common goalkeeping techniques
- Describe basic offensive and defensive tactics
- Understand and use the basic terminology

Nature and Purpose

Field hockey is recognized as one of the most popular sports throughout the world. In the United States it has been played predominantly by women; however, men do play in various locations.

The game is played by two teams of 11 players usually designated as forwards, midfielders (links), defensive backs, sweeper, and goalie. The forwards are offensive players and therefore must be quick, possess good stickwork and ball control skills, and shoot well. The midfielders serve as links transforming the game from defense to offense. Midfielders must be in good physical condition to play both offense and defense; they must be good playmakers to set up the forwards and sure tacklers to stop the offensive thrust of the opponent. Defensive backs must be aggressive and possess good marking skills in addition to being strong tacklers. The sweeper, the last line before the goalie, directs play and shores up the defense. Sweepers must have patience, good fielding skills, and a "nose" for the ball. The last link in the defensive chain is the goalie, who must have catlike reflexes and be aggressive. Although some players are by nature offensive or defensive, an emphasis should be placed on total team offense and defense.

Field hockey has changed significantly in recent years. Although a traditional 5–3–2–1–G alignment is still used, most teams are moving to a style of play that is more characteristic of soccer. Spectators may expect to see a variety of system alignments (e.g., 3–3–3–1–G, 4–2–3–1–G) being employed by a team based on the talents of individual players (Figure 10-1).

Goals count one point and can be scored only if an attacker's stick touches the ball inside the striking circle. The official game is played in two halves with time out between halves, at which point the teams change ends.

Whether played by all boys, all girls, or on a coeducational basis, it is important to emphasize the rules of play, particularly those governing the hockey stick. Emphasis should also be placed on the wearing of shin guards and other protective gear.

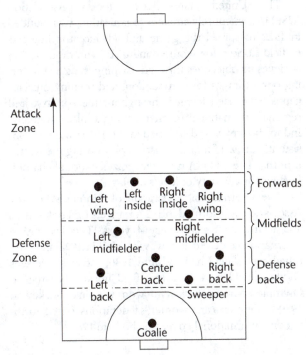

Figure 10-1 Starting alignment of 4–3–2–1–G. Note team balance (depth), possible passing routes, and opportunities for 2-on-1 or 3-on-2 situations.

For coeducational play, any or all of the following rule modifications may be made:

1. Use a larger, softer rubber ball rather than the official field hockey ball (especially in youth hockey).

2. Alternate positioning of girls and boys on the field to encourage participation and passing to one another.

3. Reduce the size of the field and the number of players (six on six) so the emphasis is on skill rather than on speed or strength.

4. Involve both boys and girls in specialty situations, such as penalty corner plays (i.e., boys push out and girls stop and hit) and penalty strokes.

5. Eliminate the hit and allow only a push.

6. Eliminate the flick when shooting at goal.

History

Field hockey is thought to be one of the oldest sports. Figures with hockey sticks appear in early Greek art and Egyptian hieroglyphics. In England, where the game has existed for centuries, it is a popular men's sport, with the women's game somewhat less popular. In the United States, field hockey has been played principally by women. It was introduced in 1901 by Constance Applebee, an Englishwoman, at a Harvard summer session. The Harvard community accepted the game with great enthusiasm, and Applebee was asked to teach it at several eastern women's colleges.

The United States Field Hockey Association (USFHA), an entirely amateur organization, was founded in 1922 to spread the game and advance the interests of field hockey for women and girls. The organization achieves its objectives through teaching the game, offering opportunities for competition, and training officials. Clubs have been formed throughout the country, and regional and national tournaments take place annually. Indoor hockey was developed in the 1950s and has consistently grown for enthusiasts to play during the winter months. The USFHA now recognizes national championships for a variety of levels of play.

The International Federation of Women's Hockey Association was formed in 1927. It meets for conferences and tournament play every 4 years. The Federation Internationale de Hockey was founded in 1924 and governed men's field hockey until 1930; today it oversees Olympic field hockey. Men's field hockey became an Olympic sport in 1908, and women's field hockey in 1980.[1] The men's and women's federations joined, forming one international governing body in 1981.

Playing Field

The field is about the size of a football field, 100 yards long and 60 yards wide, with a goal at each end (Figure 10-2). Goal posts are 4 yards apart and 7 feet high, joined by a crossbar. The posts and crossbars should have a square front and be painted white. The goal is usually enclosed with a net or screening.

The striking circle is placed on the field by starting with a straight line drawn 16 yards in front of the goal and 4 yards long. This line is continued to the end line by quarter-circle arcs of a 16-yard radius with the goal posts as centers.

Basic Rules

The following rules may require modification for coeducational play and perhaps additional rules for safety. Suggested modifications include the requirement of protective eyewear; the elimination of the goalie (for safety reasons and to save the expense of goalie gear); and the elimination or modification of dangerous skills such as the full-swing hit. Additionally, the field size and number of players can be modified to accommodate the involvement of more students in a limited space.

FOULS

1. Taking part in the game without a stick.

2. Using the rounded side of the stick.

3. Advancing a ball off the body. Note: Only the goalkeeper is permitted to kick the ball or block the ball with the body. The goalie is not penalized if the ball

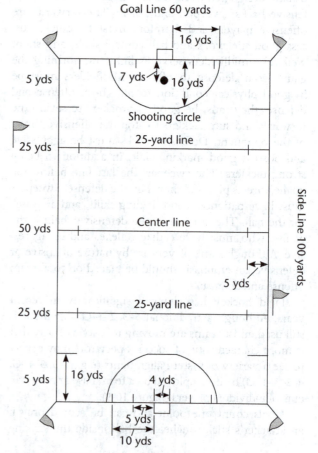

Figure 10-2 The hockey field.

is deflected off the body, provided it is not dangerous to another player and the goalie contacts the ball within the striking circle.

4. Hitting the ball in a dangerous manner (i.e., into a player at close range, a hard hit that rises, or a ball that is hit on the fly).

5. Using the stick in a dangerous manner (i.e., following through into another player, tripping, or slashing).

6. Obstruction: placing the body (feet, shoulder, or any part) between an opponent and the ball. A player may not obstruct an opponent from playing the ball by shielding the ball with her body or stick. If a player keeps moving with the ball, obstruction can be prevented.

7. Stick obstruction: interfering with an opponent's stick (i.e., strike, hook, hold).

8. Pushing, charging, shoving, tripping, or in any way interfering with an opponent.

PENALTIES FOR FOULS

A. Outside the circle. A free hit is awarded to the team fouled against on the spot of the foul.

B. Inside the circle

1. Foul by the attack—a defense hit that is outside the circle and 16 yards out from the end line. This also applies when the foul occurs outside the circle but within 16 yards of the offensive goal. The 16-yard distance is designated by a hash mark on the sideline.

2. Foul by the defense

a. A penalty corner is awarded to the attacking team.

b. A penalty stroke is awarded if the foul stopped a sure goal or was flagrant.

OUT-OF-BOUNDS PLAY

In all cases, the line is considered "in the field of play" whether it be the circle, side end, or goal line. The umpire must decide which team touched the ball last because there is no provision in the rules for coresponsibility (off two sticks).

A. Over the sideline. A hit-in (hit or push) by a member of the team opposite that of the player who last touched the ball before it crossed the sideline.

B. Over the end line but not between the goal posts

1. Off the attack—a defense hit

2. Off the defense

a. When the ball is unintentionally hit over the end line—a long hit

b. When the ball is intentionally hit over the end line—penalty corner

c. Over the end line between the goal posts

i. A legal goal when the ball was touched by the stick of an attack player inside the striking circle. Play resumed by a center pass on the center line. The goal counts even if the ball was last touched by the stick or person of the defense.

ii. When the ball was not touched by a stick of the attack player inside the circle and

(a) was touched by a stick of the defense—a long hit is awarded.

(b) was last touched by a stick of the attack player—a defense hit is awarded.

Equipment

THE BALL

The official ball is hard and slightly larger than a baseball. For class purposes, a seamless polyurethane ball is most practical.

THE STICK

The hockey stick ranges from 26 inches (youth sizes) to 38 inches in length and generally weighs from 16 to 23 ounces. The thin portion above the heel has a wrapping (usually fiberglass, although other materials are used) around the wood to give greater strength to this critical area. The blade is generally made of mulberry wood and is somewhat shorter today than it used to be. The left side of the blade is flat and is used for contact with the ball. The right side of the blade is rounded and may not be used for contact with the ball at any time (Figure 10-3).

When selecting the stick, keep in mind that the handle should be comfortable, thin, and strong. The stick should be light enough to facilitate technique and ease of control. To determine the suitable stick length, the individual should stand, grasp the stick as for a hit, and swing it in front of the body. The stick should "feel" comfortable and should not hit the ground behind the ball at contact. For elementary age physical education classes there are junior hockey sticks available that are shorter and lighter than typical adult sticks.

PROTECTIVE EQUIPMENT

Shin guards are wise protection for all field players. The padding should cover the ankle bone as well as the shins. Mouthguards and protective eyewear are strongly suggested for all players.

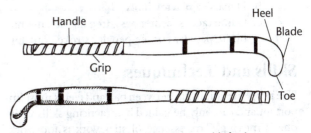

Figure 10-3 The hockey stick, right and left views.

Goalkeeper's pads should cover the leg from the thigh down. In addition to pads, kickers are worn to provide padding over the goalie's field shoe. Required protection for goalies also includes a helmet with a face guard and throat protector. Chest, shoulder, groin, arm, and elbow pads are also encouraged.

Suggested Learning Sequence

There are numerous ways to arrange the sequence of skill development for field hockey. In the one proposed, dribbling and passing skills are introduced early along with teaching students to move into space and use support passing to beat a defender. Fielding should be taught with the push pass and hit so that students can stop a ball coming toward them. As a general guide, it is best to introduce a technique along with its definition, a rule that may apply, and some strategy involved.

A. Nature and purpose

B. Conditioning aspects—plan drills and exercises that might be related to movements found in field hockey. Emphasize all areas of fitness, particularly upper body (forearm, wrist) strength, agility, speed, and flexibility.
   1. Circuit training with stickwork
   2. Footwork and acceleration moves

C. Basic game concepts
   1. Field of play
   2. Use of equipment
   3. Playing courtesies

D. Skills and strategy—introduce rules and terminology as well as combination skills and strategies at most appropriate times.
   1. Skills
      a. Gripping the stick
      b. Dribbling
      c. Push pass and fielding
      d. Hitting
      e. Reverse sweep
      f. Flicking
      g. Dodging
      h. Tackling
      i. Goalkeeping
   2. Tactics and strategy
      a. Offensive playing hints and passing combinations
      b. Defensive playing hints
      c. Game tactics: center pass, free hit, defense hit, hit-in, penalty corner, penalty stroke, long hit

Skills and Techniques

The proper relationship between ball and feet is most important and can only be gained by practicing skills while one is moving. The essence of stickwork is footwork.

Make the feet assume the proper relationship to the ball, not the ball to the feet. Be able to see the ball while also scanning the field for open space and passing options.

GRIPPING THE STICK

There are three basic grips used in field hockey. The fundamental position is used for the basic dribble as well as hitting, pushing, and fielding. A grip change is required for reverse stick contact on the ball, as in the Indian dribble. A third grip is used in defensive play when using the jab.

1. *Fundamental position.* With the heel of the stick resting on the ground in front of the body, allow the top of the handle to fall into the fingers of the left hand. This grip is basically a handshake position on the stick. Place the right hand 6 to 8 inches below the left. Grip the stick easily so the V formed by the thumb and index finger of both hands is in line with the top of the stick (Figure 10-4).

2. *Indian dribble grip.* A slight variation of the fundamental grip occurs when the player executes an Indian dribble or any reverse stick action of the ball. In this grip, the left hand slides right slightly. To assure correct positioning, place the stick flatside on the ground; reach down and place the V of the left hand on top of the stick (Figure 10-5). The right hand assumes its normal positioning. This grip allows the left hand to rotate the stick over the ball. The right simply acts as a sleeve allowing the stick to rotate in it.

3. *Defensive grip.* Slide the left hand slightly left from the fundamental position. In this grip, the V of the left hand comes on the handle when the flat side of the stick is up (Figure 10-6).

> ▶ Learning Hints

1. Hold the stick firmly but comfortably.
2. Adjust grip appropriately according to the skill executed.

DRIBBLING

In the dribble, the fundamental grip position is used with the body in a crouched position for running. The stick is on the ball, which is in front of the body and slightly off to the right side (Figure 10-7). The arms are relaxed and away from the body, with the right arm extended beyond the left. The ball is moved forward by the stick as the player begins to run. The feet should stay behind the ball; a change of direction is initiated by accelerating the feet in that direction. The ball should be kept close to the stick unless a player is in open field, in which case the ball can be pushed slightly ahead.

Figure 10-4 A Fundamental grip. Note the handshake positioning to the stick with V of left hand on side when toe is up.

Figure 10-5 Assuming correct positioning for the Indian dribble grip. Note the V of left hand is on rounded side of stick.

Indian Zigzag Dribble. This dribble is generally used in crowded areas and before attempting to move around an opponent. The ball is positioned in front of the body and is rolled over on alternate sides by the use of forehand and reverse stick taps (Figure 10-8). This movement uses the Indian dribble grip. The zigzag motion with the stick around the ball allows the dribbler to disguise the dribble with faking moves, making it difficult for the opponent to tackle.

▶ Learning Hints

1. Keep the feet behind the ball.
2. Stay low and reach out for the ball.
3. Keep the stick close to the ball. Move the ball by accelerating with the feet.

▶ Practice/Organizational Suggestions

1. Begin by moving in a straight line—push the ball ahead with an emphasis on footwork and ball control. Concentrate on staying low by bending at the knees and keeping the head up. As they dribble, have the students call out the number of fingers held up by the teacher.
2. Move on diagonals and into open space with a change of direction. Emphasize that the feet initiate the action when changing direction.
3. Practice the Indian dribble stationary, then in a straight line, with direction change and around cones.

4. Make a grid area and have 6 to 10 students dribble around each other on it. Encourage dribbling into open space. Place cones on the grid and see how many cones the students can dribble to in one minute.

FIELDING THE BALL

The ball should be fielded or controlled when it comes to a player before it is passed or played. A "two-touch" sequence is used when fielding and passing. The first touch stops the ball, and the immediate second touch advances the ball. The right hand slides further down the stick (Figure 10-9).

▶ Learning Hints

1. Line the body up behind an approaching ball in a low position.
2. Let the ball come to the stick. Absorb the ball by having a "soft" right hand. Control deflections.
3. The left hand angles forward to trap the ball in the stick. Second touch the ball with pass or dribble.

▶ Practice/Organizational Suggestions

1. Have a partner roll a ball to a player with a stick. Emphasize lining up, absorbing, and trapping the ball.
2. Have a partner field a ball pushed or hit from another.

Figure 10-6 Defensive grip. Note the V of left hand is on flat side of stick.

Figure 10-7 Dribble position. Ball is on the stick in front of the body. Player's eyes scan ahead.

A B C

Figure 10-8 Zigzag dribble. Forehand action on the ball (A), stick rolls over ball (B) with reverse stick action (C).

Figure 10-9 Fielding the ball. Left hand angles forward as right hand absorbs the ball.

Figure 10-10 Push pass positioning. Left shoulder in direction of pass and low positioning.

3. Introduce fielding on the move, that is, shuttle passing, passing down the field with a partner.

4. Introduce a passive defender and play two-versus-one keep-away. Later, as proficiency in fielding is gained, add an active defender.

5. Add passing drills that encourage give-and-go passing, i.e., player A receives a pass from player B, A passes back to B, cutting to receive and hit on goal.

PUSH PASSING

The push pass is used for short, accurate passing or shooting when there is no time or necessity to hit the ball. The pass can be executed quickly off the dribble or after receiving a pass. There is no backswing on this skill because the stick stays on the ball as it is pushed forward. The approach on this skill involves starting with the left shoulder and foot forward in the direction of the pass, and the body in a low position (Figure 10-10). The ball should be contacted opposite the left foot.

▶ Learning Hints

1. With the body in the correct approach position, extend the arms out away from the body to push the ball forward. Let the wrists snap as the skill is completed.

2. The left side of the body initiates the action of this skill. Transfer the body weight from back to front foot, and finish with the head over a bent left knee.

3. Both hands need to push through and away from the body toward the intended direction of the pass.

▶ Practice/Organizational Suggestions

1. In a stationary position, push pass with a partner. Emphasize arm extension and follow-through.

2. Pass the ball off the dribble to a partner, as in a shuttle formation.

3. Move into give-and-go passing and keep-away as presented in steps 4 and 5 for fielding.

HITTING

The hit is used for passing and shooting, and with proper execution will be quicker and harder than the push pass. Use the fundamental grip position but bring the hands together at the top of the stick. The stick swings in a perpendicular plane with a hip to hip pendulum-like motion in the direction the ball is to travel. The ball should be contacted opposite the left foot. On the backswing and follow-through, the toe of the stick is up (Figure 10-11). This is primarily a left-sided skill. A straight left arm pulls the stick through, with a weight transfer onto the front (left) foot. To ensure an accurate hit, allow the hands to guide the stick in the direction of the pass.

▶ Learning Hints

1. Bring hands together (fundamental grip position).

2. Transfer the weight to front foot. Initiate a left arm pull.

3. Let the arms swing freely.

4. Follow through with arms to intended direction of pass. Right hand helps guide the stick as the left arm pulls through.

Figure 10-11 The hit. Note the backswing and the beginning of weight transfer.

Figure 10-12 Reverse sweep. Knees are bent with hands and stick close to the ground.

3. The follow-through carries the stick low and close to the ground as it wraps around the body.

▶ Practice/Organizational Suggestions

1. Practice the sweep in a stationary position with a partner. Emphasize hand and stick position. To help keep the body low, start with the left knee on the ground.
2. Pass the ball off the dribble by pulling the ball left and passing to a target.
3. Dribble toward goal, and pull and shoot with the reverse sweep.

FLICKING

There is no backswing on the flicking skill, which is executed like the push pass. In the flick, the ball is slightly in front of the body so the stick can be placed under the ball. The left hand brings the top of the stick back and behind the right hand, which causes the stick face to open. Therefore, when the stroke is executed, the ball will rise with the height, depending on the angle of the stick. The flick is used as a technique for lifting the ball over a defender's stick, for penalty strokes, and for shooting. The flick is especially valuable for shooting at close range, since the ball comes off the ground. It is possible to execute the flick with a moving ball, but it is more difficult.

▶ Learning Hints

1. The stroke and follow-through are executed like the push pass.
2. Angle the stick by bringing the left hand back behind the right. This opens the stick face up and causes the ball to lift up.

▶ Practice/Organizational Suggestions

1. In a stationary position, practice the flick with a partner or into the goal.
2. Flick the ball to goal off a dribble.
3. Practice penalty strokes.

▶ Practice/Organizational Suggestions

1. Let the arms swing the stick in a pendulum fashion. Assume a relaxed and freely flowing arm position. Practice left arm swings.
2. Hit to a fence (or rebound board) and follow through with the stick to the fence.
3. In a stationary position practice the hit with a partner. Add hitting on the move (i.e., shuttle, passing down the field, dribbling, and hitting on the goal).

REVERSE SWEEP

The reverse sweep is used in the game as a technique to pass or shoot when the ball is on the left side of the body. The approach involves moving the right shoulder and foot forward in the direction of the pass. The grip has the hands sliding so the Vs are on the flat side of the stick. On the backswing the stick and hands are close to the ground. Contact is made with the ball in front of the right foot with the shaft of the stick coming through the back of the ball (Figure 10-12). On the swing the toe of the stick comes through ahead of the hands, with a quick wrist action that brings the stick low and around in a sweeping motion on the follow-through.

▶ Learning Hints

1. Backswing is low with hands and stick close to the ground and knees bent.
2. Keep the body low, and let the arms, with an exaggerated wrist snap, swing through to ball contact off the right foot.

DODGING

The dodge is used when a player in possession of the ball wishes to evade an opponent who is approaching from the front. Because this technique is so useful, players should learn a variety of dodges and body fakes. It is particularly important for beginners to learn how to dodge, thereby avoiding the natural tendency to move directly into an opponent—which is illegal. Teachers should introduce dodging at an early stage in the unit and provide for continued practice.

Nonstick Side Dodge. The player in possession of the ball sends the ball ahead and close to the nonstick side of the approaching opponent. The player runs to the stick side of the opponent. In other words, the ball goes right, and the player goes left (Figure 10-13A). This dodge (which is sometimes called Y dodge) is easily executed and successful because it is played to the opponent's nonstick side. However, control of the ball is important because possession is temporarily lost.

Reverse Stick Dodge. Before the opponent can reach the ball, the player in possession pulls the ball with a reverse stick action laterally to the right. After this move, the player accelerates forward by the opponent (Figure 10-13B). The advantage of this dodge is it also goes to the nonstick side of the opponent, but with the player remaining in possession of the ball at all times. However, it is a more difficult dodge to execute.

Pull Left Dodge. On this dodge, both the ball and player go to the left of the approaching opponent. Shortly before the ball is within reach of the opponent, the player pulls the ball laterally to the left past the opponent's stick (Figure 10-13C). On completion of this move, the player should accelerate forward by the opponent. During this dodge, the ball remains in the player's possession; however, the timing must be accurate and the ball must be played laterally left, not diagonally, to avoid the opponent's stick.

▶ Learning Hints

1. Execute the dodge just before the opponent is within reach of the ball. Remember that both players are moving, thus this point will be considerably farther away than expected.
2. Keep the ball in control on the dodge to assure player possession.
3. Execute the dodge right off the dribble. Accelerate by the defender and cut in behind the defender to eliminate opponent recovery.
4. On lateral pulls, turn the feet and run with the ball. Avoid side stepping.

▶ Practice/Organizational Suggestions

1. Practice dodge moves against a cone or a stationary defender. Be sure to emphasize lateral pulls as needed and footwork.
2. Dodge a passive defender who is standing but may use a stick to reach. Encourage early dodging by going against a defender who is using an ice hockey stick to extend the reach. The player must dodge before getting within a stick's reach of the opponent.
3. Carry this into one-versus-one play with an aggressive defender.

TACKLING

The tackle is a technique used in attempting to take the ball away from an opponent. The key to becoming an accomplished tackler is preparation and patience.

In the preparation, a defender must establish a basic athletic stance: feet shoulder-width apart, knees flexed slightly, head up with eyes watching the ball, and feet moving. The stick is down low to the ground and extended toward the ball in a shadowing fashion (Figure 10-14). As the opponent approaches, the defender should establish an overplaying position (to the left of the opponent), which forces the opponent to dribble into the defender's stick side. If the opponent dribbles to the right, the defender must quickly move the feet to constitute forcing the opponent right. If the opponent does get to the nonstick side (left) of the defender, the tackle must be made with a reverse stick, which is more difficult.

The defender's feet must be moving and giving with the opponent before a tackle can be made. This

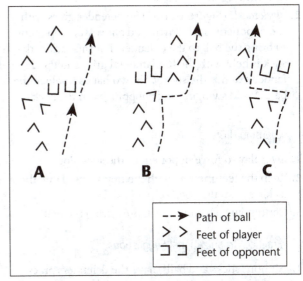

Figure 10-13 Diagrams of dodges: (A) nonstick side dodge, (B) reverse stick dodge, (C) pull left dodge.

Figure 10-14 Defensive positioning. Note the stick is down, with player in a balanced position using the jab grip.

shadowing will allow the defender to be patient and find the opportune time to steal the ball from the opponent. Caution must be made to avoid overcommitment and lunging, which makes the defender susceptible to being beaten with an opponent's dodge.

There are two basic approaches to tackling:

1. *Jab tackle* (Figure 10-15). As the defender retreats with the opponent, extend the stick with the left hand to jab under the ball. If the attempt is unsuccessful, resume the position of two hands on the stick and attempt again. Fake jabs may be successful in confusing the opponent.

2. *Block tackle* (Figure 10-16). The defender gives with the opponent, stick down, and allows the opponent to bring the ball to the defender. For this tackle, the stick is held with the fundamental grip, and the defender extends the stick with two hands to block the ball. Avoid swinging and chopping with the stick.

▶ **Learning Hints**

1. Overplay to force opponent to the stick side.
2. Keep the feet moving with the opponent. Time the tackle so it is unexpected.
3. Continually jab and retreat, pressuring the ball.

▶ **Practice/Organizational Suggestions**

1. Without sticks and balls, have the defenders practice footwork against an opponent.

Figure 10-15 Jab tackle.

2. Have a defender move with an opponent who is dribbling straight ahead with the ball. The defender may not tackle but should watch for the appropriate time to tackle. The defender can also make jab fakes.

3. Allow a defender to make a tackle against an opponent moving at half speed. Incorporate block and jab tackles.

4. Move into one-versus-one play with the defender tackling an aggressive dribbler. After the defender tackles and assumes possession, accelerate away from the opponent. Can also build in a passing option after possession is gained.

GOALKEEPING

Goalkeeping requires skills different from those of other positions. The goalkeeper must be agile, quick, and have good concentration and anticipation. The goalie is well protected with a helmet, gloves, pads for the legs, and padded kickers that go over the regular field shoe. Pads to protect the chest, throat, groin, and elbows are recommended. The goalie has the privilege of using the feet for stopping and directing the ball and may also stop the ball with the hand and other parts of the body, as long as it is not batted or deflected in a dangerous manner.

Stance. A basic athletic stance with a few modifications describes the goalie stance. The feet are shoulder-width apart, weight evenly distributed on the balls of the feet, legs slightly flexed, a slight lean forward, the arms hanging in front with the forearms parallel to the ground. Grasp the stick with palms facing out; the blade will be up and slightly pointing away from the right goal post. The head should be up, watching the ball.

Goalkeeping Principles. The goalkeeper is the last line of defense. There are three important principles to follow and practice.

1. To defend the goal line, the goalkeeper moves with small steps and drop steps in a triangular movement

Figure 10-16 Block tackle.

Figure 10-17 Goalkeeper blocks the ball off the foam kickers. The body is low with the head over the ball on contact.

from the post to a point position 3 to 4 yards in front of the goal and back toward the opposite post. This allows the goalkeeper to narrow the angle to goal and thereby eliminate shooting space.

2. The goalkeeper should be set when a shot is made. This readiness will allow the goalie to react to the shot. If moving on the shot, the goalie could be caught off balance and unable to change direction to react to the ball.

3. The goalkeeper should line up with the ball; that is, the ball should be in line with the goalkeeper and the goal line.

Technique. The beginning goalkeeper should meet the ball with legs together and "give" on impact so the ball drops almost dead. It is then cleared with the inside of the foot or the toe, hard and accurately, to a space away from the opponent (usually along the sideline) or to a teammate ready to receive and relay the ball up the field. On the kick to clear the ball, the goalie must have the head over the ball and hold a balanced position. After contact, the knee follows through upward to bring the foot back into place alongside the other. With more experience, the goalie may learn to step out and redirect the ball with one foot, especially a well-directed shot that is impossible to get behind with two feet. The stick is used only for emergency clears.

With the development of foam kickers and leg guards, the technique of goalkeeping has changed. Because of the high rebound effect that the foam equipment offers, goalkeepers will go right into blocking the ball with the foot or leg to clear the ball out (Figure 10-17). Contact is made with the ball in front of the body, with the foot moving flat along the ground. Body weight will transfer into ball contact, and it is still most important for the head to be over the ball.

▶ Practice/Organizational Suggestions

Students should always wear protective equipment when practicing goalkeeping or in a scrimmage.

1. Conduct reaction drills. Roll balls to the right, straight on, and to the left one at a time but quickly after each goalie clear. Emphasis is on getting behind the ball and maintaining balance and control.

2. Practice the application of basic goalkeeping principles by having a player push or hit on goal. Use caution to avoid players hitting when close to the goalie; instead, encourage players to use the more accurate push pass rather than the hit.

3. Place a goalie in the goal area with a three-on-three or five-on-five scrimmage situation. Emphasis should be placed on clearing the ball into space away from the rushing attack.

Modified Games

SIDELINE HOCKEY

Using a grid area, divide the group into two teams and number off each side. Each team protects a line. Call out a number, and the player from each side with that number approaches a ball in the middle. The players compete one against one, trying to score by pushing the ball across the line of the opposing team. Repeat after a score. Develop the passing game by increasing the number of participants.

KEEP-AWAY

Divide into teams of three, four, or five and have teams work to keep the ball from each other through passing. Every three completed passes score a point. For beginners, it may be best to give the advantage to the team with the ball (i.e., three versus one, four versus two, five versus three).

SIX ASIDE

On a half-field, play six players against six attacking a goal. The smaller number of people participating will allow more touches on the ball for each player.

Playing Strategies

Invasion games have the same basic strategies for cohesive team and individual play. (A comprehensive discussion of similar team strategies for offense and defense are identified in the Soccer chapter.)

OFFENSIVE STRATEGY

Once the ball is in a team's possession, the players on that team must advance the ball toward the goal. Advancement is executed by dribbling and through a series of passes. No matter which formation is used, the following principles must be employed if the attack is to be successful.

1. *Movement in space.*
   a. Players with the ball—a player in possession should move the ball into free space. This movement should result in the drawing of a defender, in which case the player should look for further options.
   b. Players off the ball—the responsibility here is for a player off the ball to move into a helping position for the player with the ball. These players are in a "support" role and need to position themselves in open space where the ball can be passed. A player standing behind a defender is considered in "dead space" where a teammate will have to pass through the defender in order to make the pass.
2. *Passing.* The ability to execute an accurate and well-paced pass to a teammate is the essence of field hockey. Passing includes the responsibilities discussed previously of moving the ball to open space and support play. Teams that employ a hit-and-chase style of play will have minimal opportunities to establish a cohesive offensive plan. The team having the ability to make accurate, precise passes and maintain possession of the ball will have the most scoring opportunities and will control the tempo of the game.

   At any time during a game, a player should have two to three avenues available to execute a pass if the team has established good field balance and depth (i.e., relationship of forwards, midfielders, and defense). Considerable practice time should be allowed for passing in combinations of two, three,

or four players. Drills should be developed that include two-versus-one, three-versus-two, or four-versus-three situations where the passer and players without the ball must confront and get around a defender.
3. *Scoring ability.* The team that wins is the team scoring the most goals. A constant offensive pressure employed by all members of the team will usually result in more scoring opportunities. Players must be able to get shots off quickly and accurately, and follow up on rebounds.
4. *Individual ball control.* Although creating space and passing are the most essential elements of the game, there are circumstances in which an offensive player must be able to get by a defender (one versus one) while carrying the ball. Successful dodging, acceleration, and stick and body fakes while maintaining tight ball control are necessities in developing success in the one-versus-one situation.

DEFENSIVE STRATEGIES

Once the ball is in the possession of the opposing team, all players on the team without the ball must focus on defensive strategy. Defense involves total concentration on the game and an awareness of the offensive players in the vicinity. Various strategies are employed in the game involving player to player, zone play, and a combination of both. In general, though, a good defender must understand the following concepts.

1. *Pressure on the ball.* The first responsibility on defense is to provide constant pressure to the player in possession of the ball. When applying this pressure, it is important to channel the offensive player to a specific direction. In most instances, this should result in forcing the opposing player to the strong side or stick side. An exception would occur with left-side defensive players, who generally would channel the opponent to the sideline.
2. *Marking.* The second responsibility on defense is to apply pressure on the opponent most likely to gain possession of the ball. Being able to mark an opponent without the ball in order to prevent that player from receiving a pass or to decoy that player is good defensive strategy. In such a situation it is important to know the position of the ball and the location of your own goal. The defensive player should stand ball side and goal side of the opponent when marking.
3. *Covering.* If an offensive player gets behind a defender assigned coverage, then another defender must be prepared to move in and accept the responsibility. The sweeper is most frequently found in a covering role. Once the opponent moves past a

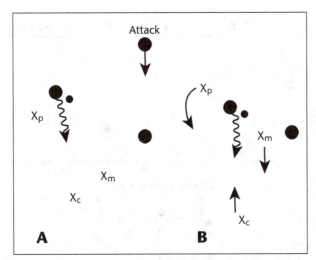

Figure 10-18 Defensive roles: (A) X_p pressure player with the ball; X_m marking ball side, X_c covering goal side; (B) when X_p is beaten and X_c moves to pick up the free offensive player while X_p recovers.

defender, it is important for that defender to switch into an unoccupied position (to cover) or to recover and catch the attacker (Figure 10-18).

4. *Transition.* Being able to switch from offense to defense without a moment's delay is going to save valuable yards. It may also make the difference in regaining possession of a ball momentarily lost and turning it back to your advantage. The reverse is also true in changing from defense to offense. On changing possession, the defense needs to accelerate immediately into space, looking for passing options.

SITUATIONAL GAME TACTICS

Center Pass. From the middle of the 50-yard line, the game is started with a center pass at the beginning, at halftime, and after a goal.

Formation. Both teams line up in any manner on their own respective halves. All opposing players must be 5 yards away.

Execution. The ball must be hit or pushed at least 1 yard in any direction. Emphasis should be placed on an accurate, well-paced pass.

Penalty Stroke. The penalty stroke is awarded to the attacking team when a foul (intentional or unintentional) is committed by the defending team inside the circle and a sure goal is prevented, or for a flagrant foul inside the circle.

Formation. The penalty shot is taken at a point 7 yards from the center of the goal line. Aside from the shooter and opposing goalie, the remaining players must remain outside the circle behind the 25-yard line until the ball is played.

The play. The goalkeeper should be in a ready position on the goal line, not leaving the goal line or moving the feet until the ball is played. The player (on the 7-yard spot) taking the penalty shot must use a flick or a push (no backswing allowed). The referee asks the goalie, then the shooter if each player is ready and then whistles for the play to begin. The shooter has 5 seconds in which to execute the stroke and is allowed one stride to the ball before shooting. Faking or any other deceptive moves by either player are not allowed. After a successful goal, the play is restarted by a center pass. If the try is unsuccessful, the defense is awarded a free hit from the 16-yard area.

Penalty Corner. This formation is awarded as an advantage to the attacking team. It occurs when the defense fouls in the circle or when a defender intentionally sends a ball out-of-bounds over the end line.

Formation. The ball is placed on the end line 10 yards from the nearer goal post on either side of the goal, according to the choice of the attacking team. A member of the attacking team hits the ball out to a designated teammate on the circle. At different play levels, rules vary as to whether the ball must be stopped in or outside the circle. However, to score, the ball must be hit from inside the circle. Other attacking players arrange themselves around the circle and, when the ball is hit, move in to rush the shot and play any rebounds. Additional players need to back up the forwards to provide support in case the ball is missed or is hit out of the circle by the defense (Figure 10-19A).

The defending team has five players (including the goalie) who start with sticks and bodies behind the end line. No player may be nearer than 5 yards to the player hitting the ball out. These players may move as soon as the ball is hit. Usually a zone formation (Figure 10-19B) is used to defend against the initial shot. The other six members of the defending team are behind the 50-yard line, and may not cross it until the ball is hit out.

The zone formation usually involves a rusher who pressures the initial shot. This player must approach in a stick-to-stick position (defender on attack) to avoid being hit with the shot. A trailer also follows out stick-to-stick but behind the rusher in case that individual is beaten. A cover moves by the goalie to assist with any rebounds and to get the ball out of scoring range. The goalie moves out from the goal line to narrow the angle and play the shot. Last, but certainly not least, is a post player who positions on the goal line (to the goalie's nonstick side) to stop any shots that may get past the goalie. Once support from other players is available, the defense moves into marking position on the opponents.

The play. The designated offensive player pushes or hits the ball along the ground to a teammate, who must stop the ball. After the stop, the ball should be hit to goal or passed to another teammate to hit to goal. In circumstances in which field hockey is played on artificial turf, a corner frequently involves a stick stop. In this case, after the ball is hit out, a teammate stops the ball for a second player to hit immediately. A variety of alignments and plays can be developed to assist in getting a shot off to goal. However, the success of a corner basically lies in a good initial pass, consequent stop, and hard, accurate hit to goal.

Free Hit.   A free hit is awarded to the opposite team when a foul is committed anywhere on the field, except inside the circle (in which case a defensive hit or penalty corner is awarded according to the circumstances).

Formation. For a free hit outside the circle, the ball is placed on the spot where the breach occurred and is usually played by a midfielder or defensive player of the team fouled against. However, a forward can also play the ball, especially if the player can resume play quickly and help gain an advantage. For any free hit, all opposing players must stand 5 yards away. Within a team's offensive 25 yards, teammates must be 5 yards away as well. The ball must be motionless before the hit can be taken.

The play. The player taking the free hit may hit or push pass the ball, and the ball must move at least 1 yard. In high school play, the ball may also be lifted, but in college play, the ball must remain on the ground. After taking a free hit, a player may not play the ball again until it has been touched by another player. When possible, a free hit should be taken quickly, so as to take full advantage of the penalty before the opposing team gets placed to block the play. A free hit should be passed to a teammate or into open space for a teammate to run immediately onto the ball.

Defense Hit.   A defense hit is awarded to the defending team when an attacking player hits the ball over the end line or commits a foul within the attacking 16-yard area.

Formation. The ball is placed 16 yards from the end line exactly opposite the spot where it left the field of play (and should be outside the circle). It is usually taken by a defensive player in whose area the ball is placed. The ball must be motionless, and all opposing players must be at least 5 yards away.

The play. The ball is put in play as for a free hit.

Hit-in.   When the ball has completely rolled over the sideline by one team, the opposing team is awarded a hit-in.

Formation. The ball is placed on the sideline and can be hit or pushed in by any member of a team. The hitter may have the feet in bounds or over the sideline as the hit-in is being executed. The defending team must remain 5 yards away from the ball.

The play. Successful execution will result when the hit-in is made quickly because the defenders are 5 yards away. Once the whistle blows, indicating the out-of-bounds, the hit or push may be executed without

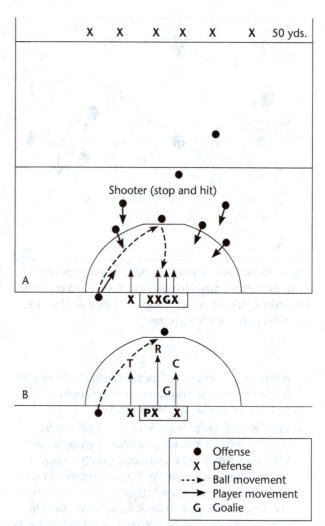

Figure 10-19   (A) Formation for penalty corner; (B) defensive zone alignment with rusher, trailer, cover, post, and goalie.

another whistle to start play. The premium is on getting the ball to the point where it crossed the line and getting it in play. Once the ball is hit by the player, it cannot be played again by the same player until it is touched by another player.

Long Hit.   A long hit is awarded to the attacking team when the ball is hit unintentionally over the end line by a defending player.

Formation. The ball is placed 5 yards in from the sideline. Any team member may hit or push the ball into play, and opposing team members must position themselves 5 yards away.

The play. The player taking the hit will try to direct the ball onto a teammate's stick or try to hit the ball across to the goal mouth if an opening is available. Note: A team cannot score directly off of a long hit. The defending team will attempt to block the hit with one or more players, while other players attempt to deny the ball to the opponent.

Skill Assessment

The most important skills for beginning to intermediate students are the pass, the field, and the dribble. Time constraints, facilities, equipment, and setup issues make it difficult to test each basic skill separately. It is suggested that all three skills be combined into one test. The recommended test requires a flat rebound surface and a ball of the size and composition meeting player ability, rebound (distance/speed), and playing surface factors. The test involves three individuals—a participant, counter, and assistant. The participant is tested and the counter records the score while the assistant provides aid to the counter. Each alternates responsibilities. After taking two 1-minute trials in a turn, the participant's final score equals the most points accumulated during one of the two trials. The wider the wall space, the greater the number of students that can be tested at one time.

Pass/Field/Dribble Test. The width of the target rebound surface is 10 feet and the length of the course is 30 feet. It is recommended that multiple testing stations be 10 feet apart along the wall.

Each course has three cones set 10 feet apart from each other in a zigzag pattern. The first cone is 10 feet from the rebound surface on the imaginary extension line of the left side of the target area. The next cone is 20 feet from the rebound surface on the opposite side (right side) of the imaginary extension line. The final cone is 30 feet from the rebound surface on the imaginary extension line of the left side of the target area.

The participant starts on the right side of the target area at a spot directly across from and opposite the first cone (10 feet from the wall). On the command "Go," the student passes the ball to the wall, fields the rebound, and turns to dribble around the outside of the first cone to her left. The dribbler rounds that cone and continues back across the course diagonally to the next cone (20 feet from the wall), rounding it on the outside. The dribble is continued diagonally to the last cone (30 feet from the wall), where the participant rounds the outside of the cone and speed-dribbles straight back toward the wall and the first cone. On reaching the first cone, the dribbler turns the ball around the outside of the cone and back across to the starting spot. From the starting spot, the participant passes the ball against the wall, fields it, and repeats the same pattern for 1 minute.

The score for one trial is the total number of passes to the wall (one per trip), traps (one per pass), and number of cones rounded (four per trip). After each trip, the sequence is restarted immediately and points are accumulated until the time expires. The final score is the total accumulation of points from passes, traps (field the ball), and cones rounded during a 1-minute trial.

Modifications for Special Populations

ORTHOPEDICALLY IMPAIRED

Individuals who use wheelchairs will have to play in a gymnasium. Floor hockey is the recommended modification for students with movement difficulties. Contact Special Olympics for the rules of floor hockey.

1. Students using power wheelchairs can have a stick secured to their wheelchair in a low position (e.g., an Ace bandage wrapped around the armrest to secure the stick).
2. Students can play floor hockey using a 6- to 8-inch Nerf ball.

COGNITIVELY IMPAIRED

1. Follow suggestions for the orthopedically impaired.
2. Keep concepts and movement patterns simple.

SENSORY IMPAIRED

1. Use peer teachers and paraprofessionals for students who have visual impairments.
2. Individual evaluations should be made to determine the appropriateness of field hockey for students who are blind or have a visual impairment.
3. Minimal modifications are needed for students who are deaf or hard of hearing.

Terminology

advancing Foul committed when the ball rebounds from a player's body (i.e., kicked).

center pass Technique used to start a game, at halftime, and to restart play after a goal.

covering A back-up defensive position used to support a teammate who is beaten or to pick up a free player moving into attack position.

defense hit Term used to denote how play is resumed when the attacking team hits the ball over the end line or commits a foul within the attacking 16-yard area. The ball is placed 16 yards from the end line opposite the spot where it left the field or the foul was committed.

dodge Play used to evade an opponent while maintaining control of the ball.

dribble A skill used to move the ball on the field while maintaining constant control.

fielding Controlling an approaching ball before it is passed or played.

flick A skill that causes the ball to lift off the ground in a controlled fashion. Useful for shooting, lifting the ball over an opponent's stick, and in penalty strokes.

foul Infringement of rules. Penalty may be a free hit, penalty corner, or penalty stroke.

free hit A method used to restart play following certain infringements of rules. It is taken by a player on the team fouled against.

hit A skill used to pass the ball that provides power and distance. This skill involves backswing into the ball.

long hit A method used to restart play after the ball is hit unintentionally over the end line by the defending team.

marking Guarding an opponent without the ball, which is performed with ball side–goal side defensive positioning.

nonstick side A player's left side, which is not easily defended by the stick.

obstruction A foul made by placing the body between the opponent and the ball so as to interfere with the opponent's effort to play or reach the ball.

penalty corner The play awarded to the attacking team for a foul by the defense inside the circle or when the defense intentionally hits the ball over the end line.

penalty stroke A shot awarded to the attacking team when a defensive player commits a foul to prevent a sure goal or flagrantly fouls the opponent in the circle.

push back Technique used to start a game, at halftime, and to restart play after a goal.

reverse stick Turning the stick over to play a ball on the left.

stick side A player's right side, where the stick can easily be extended to play the ball.

tackle A skill used to dislodge the ball from an opponent.

Discussion Questions

1. Discuss the methods for modifying field hockey for coeducational play.

2. Identify the major forces that aided in the development of field hockey.

3. Discuss which skills are of primary importance to teach when some skills must be eliminated because of unit length restrictions.

4. Identify the key principles for advancing the ball.

5. Discuss the basic concepts for defensive success.

6. Present each of the deadball game situations and identify the specific formations and possible plays for each.

7. Identify the strategies for field area factors from soccer that also relate to field hockey.

8. Discuss the defensive principles of soccer that are identical in field hockey.

9. Discuss the team offensive principles of soccer that are identical in field hockey.

10. Present the styles of play from soccer, both offensive and defensive, that also relate to field hockey.

Web Sites

www.usfieldhockey.com—Offers information about the history of field hockey, camps and grants for field hockey, and international events. Offers links to national and international organizations and clubs.

www.fieldhockey.com—Offers field hockey news, updates on rules, information on coaching/teaching, umpiring, and links to more sites.

www.planetfieldhockey.com—Excellent site for drills for goalkeepers, defenders, forwards, team, indoor play, and skill development.

www.nfhca.org—provides drills, practice plans, rules information, and videos.

CHAPTER 11 | Football: Touch and Flag

This chapter will enable you to

- Identify historical events in the evolution of touch and flag football
- Discuss the key points of the games of touch and flag football
- Identify the differences in equipment, rules, and strategy between flag football and touch football
- Describe the rules governing play
- Analyze and demonstrate the various skills and techniques, including the stance, passing, catching, blocking, tackling, and kicking
- Describe the offensive and defensive strategies used
- Take proper safety precautions
- Use the basic terminology associated with the game

Nature and Purpose

TOUCH FOOTBALL

The object of touch football (and its variation, flag football) is to advance the ball over the opponent's goal line without being "tackled." Points are awarded for a touchdown (6 points), a point after touchdown (1 point or 2 points, depending on where the attempt takes place), and a safety (2 points).

Informal games of touch football are often played in areas any size large enough to give the players running and passing room. In schools and recreation leagues in which the game is played on an organized basis, a regulation football field equipped with goal posts and yard lines is used. A regulation football is used, but players are not required to wear the heavy official football equipment because tackling is not permitted. Runners are stopped by a touch with one or both hands instead of a tackle. The fact that expensive equipment is not needed makes this game appropriate for use in recreational programs and in schools that do not have funds available for outfitting a regular football team.

The game retains most of the fundamentals of regular football, which gives it a popular appeal in the fall, when sport pages are filled with news about forward passes, touchdowns, and long runs. An official touch football team is usually composed of 7 players, but variations (from 5 to 11 players) may be used with little rules adaptation. The game provides an opportunity for the individual interested in football to duplicate in a relatively safe situation many of the skills used by widely publicized members of the gridiron game. Most present-day versions of the game resemble regulation football to the extent that names of positions of players, running and passing plays, punting, first downs, and scoring are used. The tackling element is eliminated in favor of the touch, and in most versions of touch football certain limitations are placed on blocking. In many cases, no limitations are placed on eligibility of pass receivers, making it possible for any player to receive a forward pass. This factor makes the game more interesting to players on the line of scrimmage, who seldom have an opportunity to score or handle the ball in regulation football.

FLAG FOOTBALL

Flag football is a variation of touch football in which cloth or plastic flags are worn on both hips by all players. In lieu of a touch, the flag is detached or stripped from a belt (worn by all players) by the defensive player. Flags are generally 12 to 15 inches long and 2 inches wide and are attached to the belt by an adhesive substance such as Velcro or by plastic snaps (Figure 11-1). A different colored flag is used by each team.

The basic rules governing flag football are similar to those used in touch football. Holding an opponent or holding onto the flag to prevent detachment are common infractions in flag football and must be closely regulated. Some contend that use of the detachable flag in lieu of the one- or two-handed touch tends to minimize roughness in team play. Officiating is easier in flag than in touch football because detachment of the flag is readily discernible, whereas there may be arguments regarding the touch.

From a strategic standpoint, flag football would appear to orient itself better to all-around offensive and defensive strategy because of the increased difficulty in detaching a flag. Teams will be more prone to include a

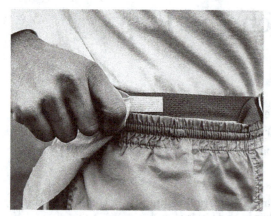

Figure 11-1 Flag and belt worn in flag football. Flag is attached by Velcro.

balanced running and passing attack; defenses will have to be designed to prevent both strategies.

To minimize hazardous play in flag football, the following precautionary measures are suggested:

1. Eliminate the blocking, tackling, or holding of the ball carrier by a defensive player attempting to secure the flag.

2. Defensive players must maintain contact with the ground when attempting to secure the flag—no jumping or diving.

3. The ball carrier may not employ a straight-arm or use body contact against a defensive player to prevent him from securing the flag.

History

Flag and touch football are an outgrowth of regular football, which was first played in the United States around the middle of the 19th century; in fact, flag and touch football have been around nearly as long as tackle football. The first intercollegiate football game was played between Princeton and Rutgers in 1869, and since that time the sport has developed steadily in the United States. Young boys and men who did not have an opportunity to play on organized teams were interested in the game and began to use many elements of regular football, such as kicking, passing, and running with the ball, in informal games on sandlots and playgrounds.

Flag football has grown steadily, not only in the number of players but also in the increased number of coeducational leagues that have been formed in many college and university intramural programs. Today flag football has extended outside educational institutions. The United States Flag and Touch Football League was formed in the late 1980s and regularly holds a national tournament. The International Women's Flag Football Association organizes and promotes flag football for women. Other organizations have formed around the

country as well as sponsor leagues and national tournaments; however, there is no one unifying organization for flag and touch football.[1]

There is no standardized set of official rules used throughout the United States. There are regional variations in rules, but it is usual for interested groups to agree on certain fundamentals. The NFL Youth Football Network publishes a set of rules that are used in programs it sponsors. The National Intramural-Recreational Sports Association (NIRSA) has published a recommended set of rules that most colleges and universities use in their programs, although many programs have made some modifications. The U.S. Flag and Touch Football League also has published a set of rules.

Basic Rules

As mentioned, there are many sources of rules for flag and touch football. Although there may be some variations, generally they are very similar. When playing flag football, however, the rules for blocking, fumbling, and tackling must be strictly enforced. In flag football, any ball carrier without two flags is considered tackled. The rules for this section have been adapted from the campus recreation program at Ball State University, Muncie, Indiana.

PLAYING FIELD AND EQUIPMENT

PLAYING FIELD. An official touch football and flag football field is 40 yards wide by 100 yards long, including the end zones (Figure 11-2). The field is divided into four 20-yard zones and two end zones, each 10 yards deep.

GOALS. Goal posts are not a necessity; points after touchdown are gained by running or passing.

UNIFORM. No special uniform is required. The use of football helmets and football pads is prohibited, although athletic shoes or soccer shoes with molded rubber cleats may be used. Players are not allowed to wear jewelry, pants or shorts with pockets, bandannas or hats, or tear-away pants at any time during a game.

BALL A regulation leather or rubber-coated football can be used. It is recommended that a junior-sized football be used by younger children.

FLAGS. Flags should measure 12 to 15 inches in length and 2 inches in width. They can be made of cloth and tucked in the elastic top of the gym trunks if belts are not available.

LENGTH OF GAME. A game consists of two 22-minute halves with a 5-minute intermission. There is a running clock that is stopped for time-outs, injuries, and

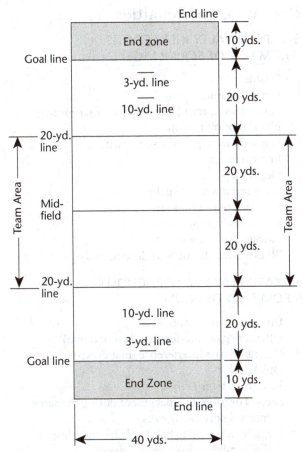

End line

End zone   10 yds.

Goal line

3-yd. line

10-yd. line   20 yds.

20-yd. line

Team Area   20 yds.   Team Area

Mid-field

20 yds.

20-yd. line

10-yd. line   20 yds.

3-yd. line

Goal line

End Zone   10 yds.

End line

← 40 yds. →

Figure 11-2 The touch and flag football field.

the last 2 minutes of each half. There is a 25-second play clock, and teams are allowed two time-outs per half (60 seconds).

OVERTIME. If a game is tied at the end of regulation play, teams will have four downs from the 10-yard line to score. An interception results in loss of ball possession. A coin flip determines who will go first. Time-outs from regulation play do not carry over.

FORFEITS. If a team is not ready to play within 10 minutes after the scheduled starting time, the opponents are awarded the win on a forfeit. A team refusing to resume play after an order to do so by the referee forfeits to the opponent.

TIME-OUT. As mentioned, each team is allowed two time-outs per half. Time-outs are also taken under the following conditions:

1. When ball goes out of bounds
2. After a score is made
3. While a penalty is being enforced
4. At the discretion of the referee

SCORING. Scoring is the same as in regulation football:

touchdown	6 points
safety	2 points
point after touchdown	1 point from the 3-yard line; 2 points from the 10-yard line

PLAYERS AND OFFICIALS

PLAYERS. A team consists of seven players, although fewer or more players may be used by mutual consent. The offensive team must have at least three players on the line of scrimmage when the ball is put in play.

SUBSTITUTES. Any number of substitutions may be made at any time during the game. Substitutes must report to the referee.

OFFICIALS. Officials consist of a referee, an umpire, and linesmen.

PLAYING REGULATIONS

STARTING THE GAME. A toss of a coin by the referee determines which team has the choice of kicking off, receiving, or goals. The loser of the toss has the choice of remaining options. Privileges of choice are reversed at the beginning of the second half.

FLAGS. Flag belts must be worn at all times by all players. Flags need to be properly fastened. No flag should hang directly in the front center of a player. Penalty yardage is assessed for flags that are not fastened properly and are worn incorrectly. Flag belts may not be the same color as shorts.

PUTTING THE BALL IN PLAY. The ball is put in play at the start of the game, after a score, and at the beginning of the second-half period by a placekick from the kicker's 20-yard line. Defensive team members must be 10 yards away when the ball is kicked, and members of the kicking team must be behind the ball. If the ball does not go 10 yards, it must be kicked again. If the ball goes out of bounds after 10 yards, the opponent has a choice of beginning play where the ball went out of bounds or on their own 20-yard line. If the ball is kicked into the end zone and the opponents elect not to run it out, play begins on their 20-yard line.

FUMBLED BALL. A fumbled ball at any time is dead and belongs to the team that fumbled the ball at the point of the fumble, the down and point to be gained remain the same. A fumbled forward pass is ruled as an incomplete pass.

DOWNED BALL. In touch football, the ball is dead and the player downed when an opponent touches him with one hand or two hands simultaneously somewhere between his shoulders and his knees. In flag football, the ball is downed or player tackled when one flag is detached from the belt or the ball carrier loses a flag.

FIRST DOWNS. A team has four chances to move the ball from one 20-yard zone to the next. If a team does not advance the ball from one zone to the next in four downs, the ball goes to the opponents at that spot.

PASSING. The following regulations govern passing:

1. All players on both teams are eligible to catch passes.

2. Forward passes may be thrown from any point back of the line of scrimmage, and lateral passes may be thrown from anywhere on playing field.

3. Any number of passes may be thrown in a series of downs.

Other Important Rules

1. All offensive players (except the player in motion if that player is parallel to the line of scrimmage) must come to a complete stop before the ball is snapped.

2. There must be a 2-yard separation between the center and the person receiving the snap; no direct snap is allowed.

3. One foot in-bounds is required for a catch. The line is out-of-bounds.

4. An interception of a conversion try and return will result in 2 points.

5. All punts are a protected scrimmage kick. Neither team may advance beyond its respective scrimmage line until the ball is kicked. All scrimmage line rules apply.

6. A team must inform the official of the decision to punt or go on the fourth down. Once a team makes this decision, it can be changed only if the team calls a time-out or if a foul occurs prior to or during the down.

7. The ball carrier may jump or spin to avoid deflagging but may not dive through another player to gain additional yardage.

8. If the ball carrier's flag belt comes off without being pulled, a one-hand touch between the knees and the shoulders will mark the player down.

9. If a flag belt falls off momentarily after being touched or grasped, the runner is downed where the deflag was attempted.

10. No player may stiff-arm or flag guard.

11. Mercy rule: If a team is ahead by 17 points or more with 2 minutes left in the second half, the game is over.

Partial List of Penalties

5-YARD PENALTY INFRACTIONS (FROM LINE OF SCRIMMAGE)

Offside
Delay of game
Fewer than three players on line of scrimmage
Illegal motion or shift
Illegal forward pass (loss of down)
Encroachment
Illegal snap
Equipment worn illegally
Free kick out-of-bounds
Intentional grounding
Blocker leaves their feet
Blocker's hands not held close to body

10-YARD PENALTY INFRACTIONS (FROM SPOT OF FOUL)

Unsportsmanlike conduct
Offensive pass interference (loss of down)
Defensive pass interference (first down)
Quick kick
Kick catch interference
Second or more encroachment during the same interval between downs
Illegally secured flag belt (and ejection), loss of down offense, first down defense
Spiking, kicking, or throwing the ball during a dead ball (possible ejection)
Tripping or clipping
Roughing the passer
Illegal screen blocking
Flag guarding or stiff-arm
Illegal substitution

COED 5-YARD PENALTY INFRACTIONS

Advancement through the line of scrimage by male runner
Two consecutive male-to-male pass completions

Flagrant violations of rules should result in automatic disqualification of the players who commit them.

Rules for Coeducational Flag Football

Coeducational flag football is becoming an increasingly popular game. Many variations and modifications can be used. Modifications can be found in *Rules for Coeducational Activities and Sports*, published by the American Alliance of Health, Physical Education, Recreation, and Dance, 1977 and 1980. Some of the following may be considered in coeducational play:

1. A touchdown thrown or caught by a female player scores 9 points.

2. The number of men and women on the field may differ by no more than one player.

3. An eight-versus-eight lineup may be allowed (at least six players are required).

4. A male player cannot advance the ball through the line of scrimmage.

5. Mercy rule: If a team is ahead by 23 points with 2 minutes left in regulation play, the game is over.

6. Two consecutive plays involving a male quarterback throwing to a male receiver are not allowed. After a male-to-male completion, the next play is "closed," and a female player must catch or complete a pass; a rush by a female player does not count.

7. After a completion or catch by a female player, the next play is "open," and male-to-male completion is allowed.

8. Violation of a male-to-male completion results in a 5-yard penalty from where the quarterback released the ball and in loss of down.

Suggested Learning Sequence

A. Nature and purpose of touch or flag football

B. Conditioning aspects—plan drills and exercises that might be related to movements of touch and flag football.

C. Basic game concepts
   1. Field of play
   2. Equipment
   3. Safety
   4. Playing courtesies

D. Rules/coeducational rules—rules should be introduced when appropriate and at a time that relates to a specific skill or strategy. This does not mean that all rules must be discussed at one time.

E. Skills and techniques—skills should be taught in combinations whenever possible; the sequence that skills are taught is up to the individual preference of the instructor.
   1. Stances
      a. 3-point stance
      b. Upright stance
   2. Ball carrying
   3. Passing and receiving
      a. Pass patterns
   4. Kicking
      a. Punting
      b. Placekick
      c. Kickoff
   5. Blocking
   6. Tackling
      a. Touch
      b. Flag detachment

7. Centering
   a. Short snap (between the center and quarterback)
   b. Long snap

F. Strategies—offensive game concepts as well as defensive game concepts should be introduced as early as possible so that skills can be practiced within the context of a game.
   1. Offense
      a. T-formation
      b. Shotgun formation
      c. Single wing
   2. Defense
      a. Pass defense—pass rush
      b. Running defense

G. Game play

Skills and Techniques

The techniques and fundamental skills associated with touch football and flag football are identical to regular football in most instances. There are two areas, however, in which touch and flag football differ from the parent game; these are in tackling and blocking. The tackle in touch football refers to a one- or two-handed touch between the shoulders and knees, whereas the tackle in flag football refers to the detachment or stripping of a flag by an opponent from a belt that circles the waist. In both touch and flag football, players cannot leave their feet when blocking. There are other skills that all players must work on because the skills will be used regardless of the position played.

STANCES

The stance will vary according to the position played and the function of either the offense or defense. Generally speaking, the 3-point stance is used by the players on the line on offense and defense and sometimes by the offensive backs. The upright stance may be used by linebackers, defensive backs, and sometimes, the offensive backs (Figure 11-3).

▶ Learning Hints—3-Point Stance

1. Feet are shoulder-width apart, one foot slightly ahead of the other in a heel-toe relationship.

2. The supporting arm hangs vertically, the back is nearly horizontal, the head is up looking ahead, the weight is on the support hand.

3. The free arm rests on the knee of the forward leg.

▶ Learning Hints—Upright Stance

1. Foot position is much the same as in the 3-point stance.

Figure 11-3 Stance. The people on the line are in a 3-point stance; the backs are in an upright stance.

2. Hands are placed just above the knees, the back is slightly bent at the waist, the head is up, and the player is focused downfield.
3. Weight is on the balls of the feet.

BALL CARRYING

Because of the rules governing play, most players have an opportunity at one time or another to carry the football. The effective ball carrier is one who can start quickly, change direction, dodge, side-step, and execute fakes that will throw the defensive player off stride. It is important that the ball carrier follow the blockers in order to elude the defensive players.

▶ Learning Hints (Figure 11-4)

1. Carry the ball in outside arm away from the defensive player.
2. Place one end of the football in the armpit, and hold the other end in the palm of the hand with fingers spread comfortably around the end to provide a firm grip.

▶ Practice/Organizational Suggestions

1. Align a ball carrier facing a defensive player standing 10 yards away. On the signal, have the ball carrier run toward the defensive player, changing ball position as the defensive player changes direction.

2. For the same type of formation, have the ball carrier run toward the defensive player using a series of fakes to try to avoid being tackled.
3. Using a blocker, have a ball carrier try to set up the block on the defensive player by following the interference and setting up a series of fakes.

PASSING

The forward pass assumes an important role in touch football and flag football because rules permit everyone to be an eligible receiver. A good passing attack will loosen up the defense and allow the running game to

Figure 11-4 Proper way to carry a ball.

become more effective. There are two types of passes commonly used: the forward pass and the lateral pass. The lateral pass may be thrown in an overhand motion or it may be "pitched" to a player in an underhand motion. The lateral, which cannot be thrown forward, adds much interest and excitement to the game because it can be used anywhere on the field.

▶ Learning Hints—Forward Pass

1. The ball is gripped by the hand on the top; the thumb is opposite the middle finger; the other fingers are spread on the laces (Figure 11-5).
2. As the ball is brought up behind the ear, plant the rear foot, step with the opposite foot in the direction of throw as the arm is brought forward.
3. The wrist is snapped downward and the palm of the throwing hand is rotated outward as the ball is released, thus giving the ball a spiral motion.

▶ Practice/Organizational Suggestions

1. Place players opposite each other and throw ball back and forth. Begin at a distance of 10 yards and gradually move farther away.
2. After you have reviewed certain pass receiver patterns, have players form two lines. Next have a player center the ball back to the quarterback, with receivers going out for a pass. First begin with short passes and then progress to longer passes.
3. Use the same formation as in item 2, but add two defensive linesmen; force quarterback to throw on the run. Another variation is to add two defensive backs and attempt to complete a pass.

RECEIVING

Pass receivers should become adept at eluding their opponents by dodging, faking, and using a change of pace that enables them to move past the defensive player. It is important for the pass receiver to focus in on the ball as soon as it leaves the passer's hand, watching all the way to his own hands. Some basic fundamentals must be remembered.

▶ Learning Hints

1. Palms face out, thumbs toward the incoming pass. Catch the ball with the hands and pull into the body.
2. On passes above the chest, thumbs are turned in; below the waist, thumbs are turned out (Figures 11-6 and 11-7).
3. As the receiver moves away from the passer, fingers are extended, thumbs are turned out; give with ball on contact.
4. On passes caught over either shoulder, the thumbs are turned out; the arm on the ballside (nearest the body) is held below the shoulder; the forearm is held at eye level (Figure 11-8).

▶ Practice/Organizational Suggestions

1. Form two parallel lines and have passes thrown above chest and below chest to pass receivers.
2. Two lines, passer drops back and throws pass over the receiver's head for over-the-shoulder catch.
3. Two lines, receivers practice pass patterns and catches. Add defensive backs as a variation.

Figure 11-5 Proper grip for a forward pass. Note that the middle finger and thumb are opposite.

Figure 11-6 Catching the ball above the waist, with thumbs turned in.

Figure 11-7 Catching the ball below the waist, with thumbs turned out.

Figure 11-8 Catching the ball over the shoulder.

head-on approach and the soccer-style instep kick, which is described in the chapter on Soccer (Chapter 20). Some key points to remember for the traditional kick:

1. Assume a stance five to seven steps behind the spot of the kick. Approach the ball.

2. The nonkicking foot is placed approximately 2 feet behind and a foot to the side of the ball.

3. With the head down and eyes on the contact point, the body leaning forward, the right leg follows through with a definite leg snap coming at the contact point.

4. The ball is contacted just below the center of the football; extend the leg at impact.

KICKING

The kicking game consists of kickoffs to begin play, punting, and placekicks.

▶ Learning Hints—Punting

1. The punter stands 13 yards behind the line of scrimmage, awaiting the center snap; the kicking foot is slightly ahead of the nonkicking foot, arms are relaxed, palms open and up, and the trunk is slightly flexed.

2. Follow the ball into the hands; the ball is held in the hand of the kicking foot toward the end and underneath. The other hand is placed on the ball with laces up to the front and side. The ball should be slightly tipped, nose downward just below the chest.

3. The kick and step is a step with the right foot, a hop with the left, and a follow-through with the right leg. The kicking foot may finish above the head.

4. The ball is released with the nonkicking hand after being guided to the correct position of the foot by the kicking hand prior to release.

KICKOFFS. Practice and timing are essential in executing the correct form for the placekick during a kickoff. There are two types of placekicks, the traditional

BLOCKING

Because the player is not permitted to leave the feet in executing a block, he must become adept at maintaining balance while retaining a position between the defensive person and the ball carrier. It is important to try to maintain contact with the defensive player and draw her away from the ball carrier. The blocker is not allowed to hold the defensive person, so the hands must be held in close to the body at all times.

▶ Learning Hints

1. Assume a 3-point stance opposite your opponent; the initial steps are short, choppy steps to the opponent.

2. The body is in a semi-crouch position, the shoulder and forearms make contact with the opponent's midsection, and the head is placed between your opponent and the ball carrier.

3. Drive your opponent away from the ball carrier; again, use short, choppy steps.

▶ Practice/Organizational Suggestions

1. Form two parallel lines 2 yards apart. On the signal, block right or block left; the blocker attempts

to maintain contact on a blocking position for 3 to 4 seconds.

2. With a center, a ball carrier, defensive player, and offensive player, on signal the ball carrier runs behind the blocker and cuts right or left, depending on the direction of the block.

TACKLING

Tackling is the term used to denote the touching of a ball carrier to stop play or, in flag football, the detachment or stripping of the flag to stop play. An important point to remember is that, for the tackle to be valid, both feet of the tackler must be on the ground. A legal touch is between the shoulder and knee of the opponent. The game may be played using a one-hand touch or it may be increased in difficulty by making it a two-hand touch game (Figure 11-9). In flag football, one flag must be detached from the belt (Figure 11-10). Body balance, control of body movement, and speed are important factors to practice.

CENTERING

The center plays an important part in touch and flag football. The center snap is executed at longer range and at still longer range on punts. Note that in touch or flag football, if the center snaps the ball on the ground before getting to the receiver, it is a dead ball.

▶ Learning Hints—Short Snap (Figure 11-11)

1. With feet more than shoulder-width apart, bend at the knees, keeping weight centered over feet and keeping the feet balanced.

Figure 11-9 Tackling: A two-handed touch above the waist.

2. Keep wrists slightly cocked, placing the hands on the front half of the ball, with fingers apart and parallel to each other (Figure 11-11A).

3. Head is looking up at the person who will be blocked.

4. Quarterback stands 2 to 4 yards behind the center with the hands up at chest level, waiting to receive the pass backward.

5. Extend arms through the legs, releasing the ball toward the quarterback's hands (Figure 11-11B).

▶ Learning Hints—Long Snap

1. With feet shoulder-width apart, bend at the waist, flexing the knees and keeping arms hanging comfortably in front. Weight may be forward and head lower than the buttocks.

A

B

Figure 11-10 Tackling, flag football style (A). The tackle shown on the right (B) is illegal; the ball carrier's hand may not protect the flag.

Figure 11-11 The short snap.

2. Sweep arms toward the receiver, with a wrist snap to impart a spiral motion on the ball.

▶ Practice/Organizational Suggestions

1. Pair up in two lines, with centers assuming position for short snaps to the quarterback. Using the quarterback's hands as a target, try to hit the target at chest height on the release 8 to 10 times.

2. Pair up with a partner, and practice long snaps with 5 to 7 yards between the snapper and the punter. Try to hit the punter's hands 8 to 10 times with the snap, and then change partners.

3. Combine a short snap with a pitch to a running-back or with a pass to a receiver.

Strategy for Touch or Flag Football

OFFENSIVE STRATEGY

Touch football permits the use of a wide range of offensive plays because of the emphasis on passing and the fact that everyone is eligible to receive a pass. In arranging the offensive strategy, a team should plan a signal system that will denote the kind of play to be used (pass, run, punt), who is to carry the ball, and where the ball is to go. Plays should be kept as simple as possible. Numbers may be employed to represent the type of play, the player executing the play or carrying the ball, and the side of the line where the play is to go. The line may be numbered with odd numbers on the left side and even numbers on the right (Figure 11-12). The backs may be numbered: 1—quarterback, 2—right halfback, 3—fullback, and 4—left halfback. Thus, after the ball has been centered, the signal "Run 14" indicates

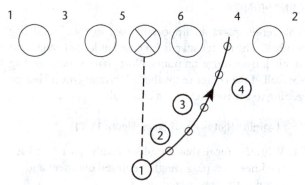

Figure 11-12 Numbers for offensive holes.

a running play through the number 4 hole, with the number 1 back carrying the ball.

Offensive strategy should combine running and passing plays to create confusion for the defense. It is not good strategy to constantly employ all passing plays or all running plays. Keep the defense guessing; attempt running plays on second down with a lot of yards to go for first down.

OFFENSIVE FORMATIONS. There are several formations that can be created by the offense as long as three people line up on the line of scrimmage before the ball is snapped. Three common formations used in touch football and flag football include (1) the T-formation, (2) the shotgun formation, and (3) the single-wing formation (Figure 11-13).

▶ Learning Hints—Offensive

1. Keep the defense guessing by varying running and passing plays.

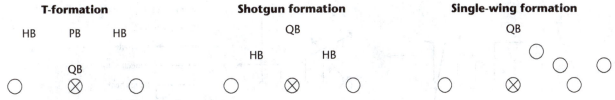

Figure 11-13 Types of offensive formations.

2. If the defensive secondary plays deep, use many of your players in short passing patterns. When the defensive team draws in, use the deep pass.

3. If you receive a long penalty, do not try to make it up on one play; use a run and perhaps some short passes.

4. Change your cadence occasionally to pull the defensive team offside.

5. Use a quick kick on third down to get your team out of a defensive hole.

Let your field position help dictate the type of plays you will use (Figure 11-15)—long passes are dangerous near your own goal line; plays involving deception are best in the vicinity of midfield; use quick hitting or pass plays near your opponent's goal line.

DEFENSIVE STRATEGY

Teams should agree on a plan for the pass and the run defense. For a passing defense, certain players on the line of scrimmage should be assigned to rush the passer, while other players drop back to help the defensive backs cover possible receivers. Generally a person-to-person assignment is made for the deep pass receiver, while a zone defense is employed by the remaining defensive players to watch for the short pass receivers. Figure 11-14 illustrates four types of pass patterns.

▶ Learning Hints—Defensive

1. Assign rushers to contain the passer or runner inside, not allowing the ball carrier the opportunity to break outside the defensive containment.

2. Learn to recognize the opponent's formations and most effective players; set up your defenses accordingly.

3. Listen to see whether an opponent is continually using the same cadence; occasionally time your rush to the cadence.

4. Defensive backs should not turn their backs on the pass receiver; learn to run backward or sideward so that you can always see the ball and the pass receiver.

5. Use different pass rushers to confuse the offense; send in linebackers at times as an element of surprise.

Safety

Observe the following safety precautions to minimize the incidence of injuries.

1. Do not wear any equipment with sharp or projecting surfaces that may injure teammates or opponents. This includes rings, belt buckles, and watches.

2. Use rules that prevent leaving the feet in executing the block.

3. Declare the ball dead on all fumbles.

4. See that the playing area is smooth and free from holes and projecting objects that may prove a hazard.

5. Use competent officials who enforce the rules and eliminate rough play.

6. Be sure adequate treatment is available for players in case of injury during play.

7. Players who wear glasses should wear a headband or eyeglass guard.

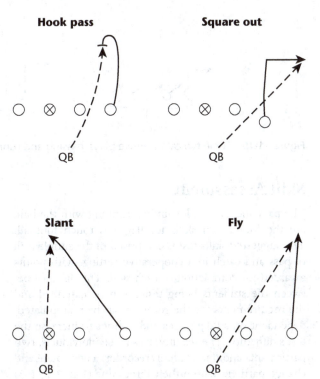

Figure 11-14 Types of pass patterns.

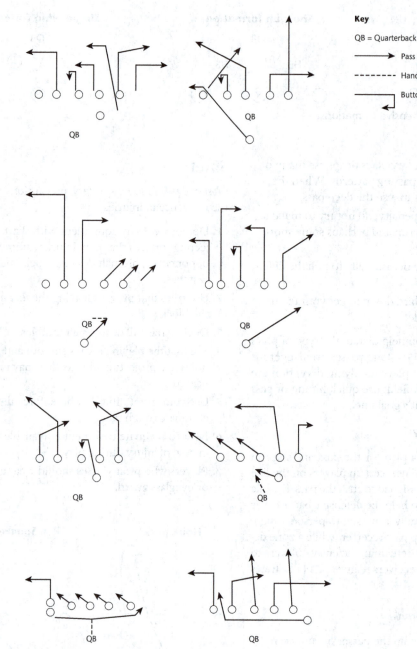

Key

QB = Quarterback

———→ Pass route

- - - - - Handoff or toss

⌐   Button hook

Figure 11-15 Some typical offensive plays, passing and running.

Skill Assessment

The pass and catch, plus limited running with the ball, are the foundation skills for flag and touch football. The suggested skills test is comprised of the simple drill of pass and catch in a cooperative setting, with points awarded for completion of each skill. The distance between the students being tested can be extended and the requirements for the receiver can be manipulated, dependent on student ages and abilities to increase the test's difficulty. The test involves three individuals: two participants and one counter/recorder. They rotate and change partners within their threesome (1–2, 2–3, 1–3) so that each has two turns. The participants alternate throwing and catching during a turn until each has thrown 10 times. As a result, they each have a score for that turn before changing partners and responsibilities. This simple throwing and catching drill can be practiced occasionally throughout the unit to enhance and check skill development, extend difficulty, and promote consistent scoring.

The two participants face each other 10 yards apart. The student with the ball throws a catchable (1 point) overhand pass to the receiver above the waist (1 point). No points are awarded on the throw if it is below the waist or uncatchable (subjective judgment by the counter/recorder). The receiver is awarded 5 points for catching any thrown ball (high or low), an automatic 2 points for an uncatchable pass from the thrower, or 0 points for a dropped catchable pass. The scoring system leads to the pair performing to the best of their abilities for their own and their teammate's success. The final individual point total is the better of the two turns. A class of 30 students can be tested quickly with 10 footballs.

The difficulty of the test can be increased by extending distance; the receiver with his back turned to the passer and not turning around until the passer calls "Hike!"; or the receiver with back turned and performing a "jab step" (left or right) before turning around when the passer calls "Hike!"

Modifications for Special Populations

ORTHOPEDICALLY IMPAIRED

1. For students using wheelchairs, games need to be played on the gymnasium floor, and a foam rubber football is recommended. Students without disabilities could play while positioned on a scooter. For students with functional upper body skills, no modifications are needed for throwing and catching. Forward passes to students using motorized wheelchairs would be considered complete if the football struck any part of the wheelchair above the waist area (e.g., chair arms, seat back).

2. Students using crutches, canes, or walkers should be able to participate on an outdoor or indoor field. These students could be positioned as defensive linemen and coached to raise their assistive devices to block forward passes. Quarterbacks would not be allowed to move when throwing against this defense.

COGNITIVELY IMPAIRED

1. Concentrate on teaching the concepts of the game (e.g., offsides, line of scrimmage, offense, defense, first downs).

2. Make sure to use some means of designating team players in play demonstrations (e.g., green and red pennies).

3. Stationary lead-up games might be helpful (e.g., stationary passing relays the length of the field).

4. Reduce the size of the playing area and the number of players per team.

SENSORY IMPAIRED

1. Minimal modifications would be needed for students who are deaf or hearing impaired. You will need to develop some visual system for stopping play (e.g., cue cards, waving a towel, or hand signals).

2. Individual considerations must be taken into account to determine the appropriateness of football for students who are visually impaired or blind. You might consider using a "double pass" system, in which the student who is blind or visually impaired is required to pass the ball to a sighted teammate before the defensive rush could occur. The sighted player would then be considered the second quarterback, who must continue the play.

Terminology

backs Players who ordinarily carry or pass the ball on offense. Stationed behind the linemen.

backward pass Play in which the ball is thrown or passed in any direction except toward the opponent's goal. Any player may make a backward pass.

balanced line An offensive formation that has an equal number of linemen on each side of the center. Line is unbalanced if more linemen are on one side of center than the other.

block Action of offensive linemen and backs in which they use their bodies to ward off defensive players from the ball carrier.

bootleg play An offensive play in which a back fakes handing the ball to a teammate, conceals it on his hip, and turns in the opposite direction.

brush blocking Momentary blocking by an offensive player.

button hook A forward pass play in which the receiver runs toward the defender, turns, and runs back toward the passer to receive the pass.

clipping A blocking action in which a player throws her body across the back of the leg(s) of a player not carrying the ball. This move can cause injury, and is a personal foul.

cross-buck An offensive play in which two backs cross paths in moving toward the line of scrimmage, one faking to receive the ball and the other actually taking the ball.

cut-back An offensive maneuver in which the back starts wide and then cuts back toward center of the line.

end around An offensive maneuver in which one end wheels around, takes the ball from a teammate, and attempts to run for a gain.

fair catch A player may make a fair catch on a kickoff, return kick, or kick from scrimmage by raising his hand clearly above his head before making the catch. He may not be tackled, and must not take more than two steps after receiving the ball. The ball is put in play from the spot of the catch by a free kick or scrimmage.

flanker An offensive maneuver in which a player lines up nearer the sideline than a designated opponent.

flat pass A forward pass that travels chiefly in a lateral direction and is usually thrown with a flat trajectory.

forward pass An offensive play in which the ball is thrown toward the line of scrimmage.

handoff An offensive play in which one back hands the ball off to another back who attempts to advance the ball.

lateral pass An offensive play in which the ball is passed sideward or backward to the line of scrimmage.

line of scrimmage An imaginary line, or vertical plane, passing through the end of the ball nearest a team's goal line and parallel to the goal lines. Thus, there is a line of scrimmage for each team, and the area between the two lines is called the neutral zone. Any player of either team is offside if she encroaches on the neutral zone before the ball is snapped.

naked reverse An offensive play in which the ball carrier takes the ball from another back and attempts to advance without benefit of backfield blockers.

neutral zone The imaginary line that passes between the lines of scrimmage for each team. Either team is offside if it moves across the neutral zone before the ball is snapped.

offside When an offensive or defensive player is ahead of the ball before it is snapped. (The penalty is 5 yards.)

safety A score made when a free ball, or one in possession of a player defending his own goal, becomes dead behind the goal, provided the impetus that caused it to cross the goal was supplied by the defending team.

screen pass An offensive maneuver in which a wave of eligible receivers converge in area where a pass is to be thrown.

shotgun offense A formation in which the quarterback lines up 5 to 6 yards behind the center. Usually one or both halfbacks may line up 1 to 2 yards on either side of the quarterback and 1 yard in front of the quarterback.

shovel pass An offensive maneuver in which a pass is thrown, underhand, usually forward to a back behind the line of scrimmage.

touchback When the ball becomes dead behind the opponent's goal line legally in possession of a player guarding his own goal, provided the impetus that caused it to cross the goal line was supplied by an opponent. No points are scored on the play, and the ball is put in play by a scrimmage at the 20-yard line.

Discussion Questions

1. Trace the historical events that influenced the evolution of touch and flag football.

2. Identify the rule modifications that aid in minimizing hazardous play in flag football.

3. Discuss the rule modifications for coeducational flag football.

4. Identify the three types of formations suggested and discuss their strengths and weaknesses.

5. Identify the four types of pass patterns and discuss their strategic purposes.

6. Discuss the suggested safety precautions for minimizing the incidence of injuries.

7. Discuss the various methods for defensive coverage of receivers.

8. Present various offensive strategies for enhancing play.

9. Present various defensive strategies that aid in cohesiveness of play.

Web Sites

www.americanfootballassn.com American Football Association—offers complete rules, a glossary, and other information.

www.aftfl.com American Flag and Touch Football League—includes league information, links to other football sites, rules, and more.

www.usftl.com United States Flag and Touch Football League—features newsletters, history, a rule book, and membership information.

www.nirsa.org/Content/NavigationMenu/Sports/FlagFootball/flag_football.htm National Intramural-Recreational Sports Association (NIRSA)—provides links to a list of flag football regional and national flag football championship information, flag football rules interpretations, and an online flag football officials course.

www.americanyouthfootball.com—coaches resources, performance/training ideas, books, videos, and links.

www.usffa.org United States Flag Football Association—features the rule book, history/evolution, and women's participation.

www.coachflagfootball.com—provides drills, practice plans, instruction book, plays, and tips.

CHAPTER 12

Golf

This chapter will enable you to

- Identify historical events contributing to the evolution of golf
- Identify the parts and features of a golf course
- Identify the various clubs and other equipment and how to use and care for them properly
- Describe and, after practice, execute the following skills: grip; stand; swing (irons and woods); pitch, chip, and sand shots; putting; and various golf exercises
- Identify and carry out the courtesies associated with the sport
- State and interpret the major official rules of golf

Nature and Purpose

One of the greatest advantages of golf lies in the age range of its participants. Both young boys and girls and mature men and women can play golf. More children are playing at younger ages; in recent years the United States Golf Association has sponsored Junior Golf Programs (ages 9 to 17). Many private and public golf courses have extensive instructional programs for the junior golfer and sponsor golf tournaments all summer long. Most public and private clubs have set aside specific playing times for the juniors in order to encourage participation.

Golf may be played by strokes or by holes. The objective is to play a ball from a teeing area to a hole, a prescribed distance from the tee, in the fewest strokes possible. An official round is 18 holes. In stroke play, the winner is the person taking the fewest number of strokes over an entire 18 holes of play. Each hole receives a rating of par determined by the length of the hole (Figure 12-1). In match play, or play by holes, the winner is the golfer who wins the greater number of holes despite the final total in strokes. Stroke play is considered more exacting, because each shot is of equal value, whereas in match play, a loss of two or more strokes on a hole may be recouped by a one-stroke victory on a later hole.

Golf is one of the few sports that allows a handicapping system among participants. Handicapping is a means of equalizing competition among golfers of differing abilities. The player with the lower average score is required to give strokes to the higher average golfer. In stroke play, the higher average player subtracts these strokes from his total to get a *net* score. This is compared with the other player's *gross* or total score

to determine the winner. In most handicap play, the strokes are usually computed in relation to the difference between par and the average score of the player. Thus, many can compete in a tournament on a handicap basis. In match play, the strokes are subtracted from the higher average player's score on holes designated as the most difficult. That is, a handicap of 5 would allow the player to subtract one stroke from his score on the five most difficult holes.

History

The game of golf as it is played today originated in Scotland in the early 14th century. However, the origin of the game has been ascribed to many peoples and lands. A game that involves striking a ball or pellet with a knobbed stick is probably as old as the spirit of play.

For men	
Par 3	Up to 250 yards, inclusive
Par 4	251 to 470 yards, inclusive
Par 5	471 yards and over

For women	
Par 3	Up to 210 yards, inclusive
Par 4	211 to 400 yards, inclusive
Par 5	401 to 575 yards, inclusive
Par 6	576 yards and over

Figure 12-1 Directions for computing par on a golf course.

In 1754, the first rules to govern golf were established by a committee at the Royal and Ancient Golf Club of St. Andrews in Scotland. In 2004, the club delegated responsibilities for administering the rules of golf to a group of companies formed for that purpose, called the R & A. The R & A and the United States Golf Association (USGA) govern the rules by which golf is played today. There were 13 original rules, some of which remain in the rules of today's game. St. Andrews has come to be considered almost a shrine among lovers of the game. Built in 1552, it is still considered one of the world's most outstanding and historic courses.

Golf was introduced in the United States around 1885, although there is evidence that it was played in Canada as early as 1873. The first golf club in the United States, St. Andrews of Yonkers, New York, was established in 1888. John G. Reid, called the "Father of American Golf," introduced it to his friends at Yonkers at this time. Play took place in a cow pasture, and the course consisted of six holes from 150 to 250 yards long. Because the players had no lease from the owner to use the land, it was not long until they were forced to move to another site. The first permanent clubhouse was established at Shinnecock Hills Golf Course in Westchester County, New York.

The United States Golf Association was established in December 1894. Two annual championships were set up: one that was open to anyone, and one that was only for amateur golfers. These still exist as the U.S. Open and the U.S. Amateur Golf Tournaments. Anyone is eligible for the Open, including players who teach the game and professionals, but the Amateur is restricted to members (amateurs) of any club associated with the USGA. There are two U.S. national amateur tournaments played each year, one for men and the other for women.

Golf is now played worldwide. Notable matches between world players include the Ryder Cup, played every 2 years, in which professional players from the United States compete against players from Europe; the President's Cup, played every 2 years, in which professional players from the United States compete against players from around the world; the Walker Cup (men amateur players); the Solheim Cup (U.S. women professionals competing against women from around the world); and the Curtis Cup (U.S. women amateur players competing against European women amateurs). The professional men's "Grand Slam" of golf consists of the Masters Tournament, the U.S. Open, the British Open, and the PGA Championship. The professional women's "Grand Slam" of golf includes the Kraft Nabisco Championship, the U.S. Women's Open, the Weetabix Women's British Open, and the McDonald's LPGA Tournament.

Golf is played at all age levels, and many outstanding young players, such as Michelle Wie, have added interest to the tournament fields as they compete with professionals. The Byron Nelson Invitational Golf Tournament made history in 2003 when it invited outstanding woman professional Annika Sorestam to play in a formerly all-male professional tournament, the first woman to do so.

The two primary professional organizations governing golf in the United States include the Professional Golfers of America (PGA) and the Ladies Professional Golf Association (LPGA). In 1981, the men's professional circuit became known as the Tournament Players Tour.

Many opportunites are available for anyone wishing to play golf. It has become a popular sport in high schools, colleges, and universities. Tournaments exist for almost every level of golfer, and there are tours for junior golfers who wish to hone their skills and perhaps seek a career in golf.

The Course

The course is the whole area within which play is permitted, and it is the duty of authorities in charge of the course to define its boundaries accurately. Most courses consist of 18 holes; however, there are many 9-hole courses. Golf scores are based on 18 holes of play, with the par usually varying between 70 and 72. Each hole consists of many common components and some not so common components (see Figure 12-2).

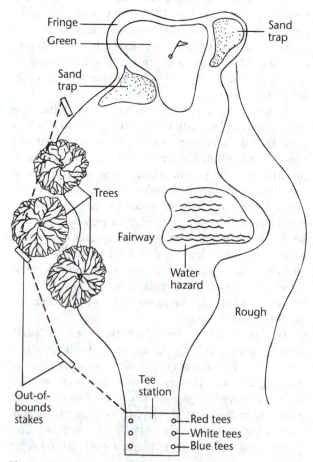

Figure 12-2 A typical layout of a hole.

A player tees a ball on a wooden tee in the teeing area, in line with or no more than two club lengths behind the tee markers. Generally there are three sets of markers on a tee: the farthest from the hole are for championship play; the middle markers are generally for men; and the markers closest to the hole are where women may initiate play. From the tee, the golfer hits to a fairly well groomed area called the fairway and, from there, hits to a closely cut area of the hole called the green.

Generally the area to the right and left of the fairway where the grass is long and other obstacles may be found is known as the rough. Most courses include obstacles such as sand traps, bunkers, water hazards, out-of-bounds, and trees placed in strategic positions to penalize a poor shot made by a golfer. There are specific rules governing play that the golfer must understand when confronted by one of these obstacles. These are discussed later under Rules of Golf.

Scoring

Figure 12-3 represents a typical scorecard. The golfer will note the yardage given for each hole, dependent on the set of markers from which play is initiated. Also included is information on the course rating, the par designation for a particular hole, as well as the hole's difficulty as expressed in men's or women's handicap. Thus, the hole having the men's handicap designation of 7 (hole number 6) means that it is the seventh hardest hole on the course. If the golfer had a handicap of 7, he would be given a deduction of 1 stroke from his score to equalize the competition. In this example, the golfer would also receive a stroke deduction on holes 7, 11, 2, 13, 1, and 12.

The par designation is the number of strokes that an expert would take to play a hole. It is usually the number of shots from the tee to the green plus two strokes for putting. Thus, an expert playing a par four hole would take two shots to reach the green and two putts to hit the ball into the hole. Sometimes a golfer will hit a ball from the tee into the hole in less than par. A score of 1 under par is a birdie, 2 under par is an eagle, 3 under par on a par 5 is a double eagle, and 2 under par on a par 3 is a hole in one, the golfer's dream.

Rules of Golf

The rules of golf have been developed and are periodically upgraded by two coordinating bodies—the USGA and the Royal and Ancient Golf Club of St. Andrews, Scotland. The rules undergo continual study and are revised by these two bodies every 4 years. The USGA publishes a rule book each year and offers it for sale at a minimal cost. It is strongly recommended that serious students obtain a copy. A booklet titled *Easy Way to Learn Golf Rules* is available at a minimal cost from the National Golf Foundation.

LOCAL RULES

In constructing the rules that uniformly govern all golf play in the United States, the USGA recognizes that certain local conditions such as climate, variable physical conditions, and characteristics of golf courses may necessitate modifications of the rules. These modifications are termed Local Rules and are designed to protect the golf course and make the game more enjoyable. A player is responsible for becoming acquainted with the Local Rules before playing. Sources of information concerning Local Rules include the golf professional, the

HOLE	1	2	3	4	5	6	7	8	9	OUT	10	11	12	13	14	15	16	17	18	IN	Total
Championship BLUE	440	545	250	350	175	385	420	385	480	3430	520	440	525	420	205	350	385	185	405	3435	6865
Men's WHITE	365	515	245	325	160	380	415	350	455	3210	450	420	510	405	150	325	380	180	395	3215	6425
PAR	4	5	3	4	3	4	4	4	5	36	5	4	5	4	3	4	4	3	4	36	72
Men's handicap	5	3	13	15	17	7	1	11	9		12	2	6	4	18	14	10	16	8		
Won + Lost - Halved O																					
Women's YELLOW	360	490	245	320	160	365	410	350	440	3140	440	405	510	405	150	320	370	175	395	3170	6315
PAR	4	5	4	4	3	4	5	4	5	38	5	5	5	5	3	4	4	3	4	38	76
Women's Handicap	5	1	17	9	15	7	11	13	3		4	10	2	16	18	12	8	14	6		

SCORE CARD

COURSE RATING 70.5

DATE _____ PLAYER _____ ATTEST _____

Figure 12-3 Score card.

score card, the golf course bulletin board, and players familiar with the golf course.

The USGA limits the extent to which Local Rules may modify the USGA rules. Players should refer to the USGA Rules of Golf Appendix to familiarize themselves with the limitations.

SUMMARY OF IMPORTANT GOLF RULES

1. A player may have a maximum of 14 clubs in the golf bag at any one time. The penalty for exceeding the maximum is (1) *match play*: one hole for each hole at which the breach occurred (maximum per round: two holes) or (2) *stroke play*: two strokes for each hole at which the breach occurred (maximum: four strokes per round).

2. A player must tee up her ball between the tee markers or anywhere in the rectangle two club lengths behind them. Violation of the rule is a two-stroke penalty.

3. An intentional swing at the ball must be counted as a stroke, even if the player "wiffs" it.

4. A ball is considered lost outside of a hazard if not retrieved in 5 minutes. The player must hit the ball from the previous spot and take a one-stroke penalty.

5. A ball must be played as it lies except as provided for in the rules.

6. Loose impediments such as leaves or sticks (anything of nature lying around) may be removed outside of a hazard, so long as the ball does not move.

7. For relief from artificial obstructions, drop the ball within one club length of the point of nearest relief without penalty, but no closer to the hole. See rule book for exceptions.

8. If a player hits a ball out-of-bounds, the player must take a one-stroke penalty and play the ball from the original spot.

9. When a ball is hit into a water hazard, the player may drop a ball behind the hazard, keeping the spot at which the ball crossed the hazard between herself and the hole. The penalty is one stroke.

10. A player, while in the act of putting on the green, whose ball hits another player's ball or the flag stick, is assessed a two-stroke penalty. Putting from off the green is not considered a putt.

Equipment

CLUBS

A set of golf clubs consists of woods, irons, and a putter (Figure 12-4). The beginner may not wish to invest in a complete set of expensive clubs and can initially get along with less expensive clubs. A minimum set should

contain two woods, four irons, and a putter. The recommended choices would be a driver and a number 3 wood, the 3, 5, 7, and 9 irons, and a putter. While it is possible to obtain a full set by gradually adding the missing clubs, such as the number 4 and 5 woods and the 2, 4, 6, and 8 irons, as well as the sand wedge, a better plan is to play with the basic set until a fairly high level of skill is reached. A new entry into golf club design is the *hybrid*, or *rescue club*, which is a combination of a fairway wood and a long iron. The head is smaller, and the shape may be like that of a fairway wood or a large long iron. The shaft is shorter than a fairway wood, and it can typically have a loft of 18 degrees to 26 degrees. The hybrid club generally takes the place of a long iron because it can more easily get the ball into the air and, depending on the loft, can hit it as far or farther than the long iron.

When the player reaches a fairly high skill level, a golf professional should be consulted to fit the player with a completely matched set of 14 clubs. The most popular 14 clubs are the driver, numbers 3 and 5 woods, numbers 2 through 9 irons, a pitching wedge, a sand wedge, and a putter. A set of clubs may cost anywhere from around $75 to more than $1000. Generally the beginning golfer can purchase a starter set for approximately $100 to $175.

The Putter. The putter is a golf club carried by all golfers; it is used primarily on the putting green to hit the ball into the cup. Today there are as many putter designs as there are golfers. The putter comes in various sizes, shapes, and colors. According to the noted golf instructor Dick Aultman, the key points to look for when choosing a putter are first, that the putter when soled flat on the ground allows you to look directly over the putting line; second, that it should be simple to aim, and thus, that it be easy to control.[1]

CHOOSING CLUBS

Golf clubs are precision instruments and vary in design for men, women, and children. A golfer's shotmaking ability is affected by many factors directly related to the construction of the golf club. Among these factors are swingweight, length of the club, shaft flexibility, clubhead design, and the grip.

Swingweight. Determined by a swingweight scale, swingweight is the relationship among the weights of a club's component parts—grip, shaft, and head. Scales to measure swingweight may be found in most pro shops. Swingweights are usually designated by the symbols C and D followed by a number ranging from 0 to 9. Women usually use a lightweight club that has a swingweight of C4 to C7; stronger women might use a C9 or even move to the D classification. Men's clubs start at D0; an average male golfer would use a swingweight of D0 to D4. Children's clubs are generally lighter.

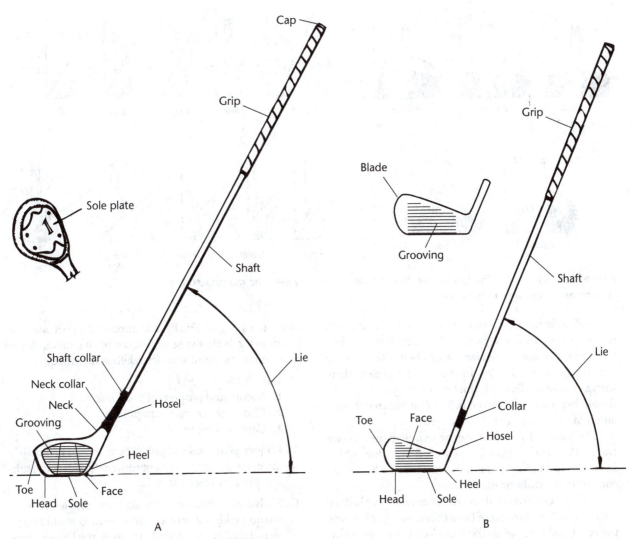

Figure 12-4 Parts of (A) a wood club and (B) an iron club.

Club Length. An important point to remember is that the higher the *number* of the club, the shorter the club's *length*. The woods have the longest shafts while the 9 iron, pitching wedge, and sand wedge have the shortest shafts.

In addition, shorter clubs have a more sharply angled club face (greater degree of loft). The combination of club length and club loft determine in part the distance a golf ball can be hit under normal conditions. If a golfer can execute a good shot each time, there is an approximate 10-yard difference between each club used. Figure 12-5 indicates the degrees of loft of specific clubs.

Women's golf clubs are 1 to 2 inches shorter than men's clubs, and children's clubs are shorter still. Some companies make fully matched sets of junior clubs, but they are quite expensive.

Shaft Flexibility. Matching the correct shaft flexibility to a golfer's swing is important. Most men golfers should use a golf club with a shaft flexibility rating of R, meaning regular. This shaft is also recommended for stronger women players. An S shaft means *stiff* and

should be used by stronger male players. Most women golfers will use a golf club with an L (lady)-rated shaft because these shafts have more flexibility.

Clubhead Design. In recent years significant advances have been made in clubhead design in both woods and irons. The topic is too extensive and technical for discussion here. Almost any golf clubs can be used to get you started. When your skill level increases, you can consult a local golf professional for the latest clubhead information.

Grip. Grips are generally made of synthetic rubber, although other materials such as leather or cord also are used. The standard size grip put on the club in the factory can be changed to accommodate different hand sizes. A good general rule is, "If it feels right, it probably is."

BALLS AND TEES

Golf Balls. Golf balls come in a variety of types and a wide price range. Beginners do not need to buy the most expensive ball.

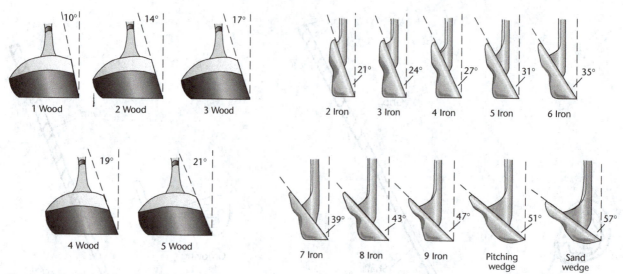

Figure 12-5 Club lofts. The loft of any club will vary a few degrees. The manufacturers' recommendations are shown here.

Golf balls have two kinds of covers. Balata is a soft rubber cover that damages easily but is preferred by better golfers because they claim it has better feel. Surlyn is a sturdier cover made of plastic; some golfers claim surlyn-covered balls can be hit farther. Beginning golfers should use a surlyn-covered ball at first but may have a different preference as skill develops.

The inside of a golf ball can be manufactured in two ways: (1) a small rubber core covered by a thin rubber string wound tightly around the core; (2) with a center consisting of synthetic material.

Today there are two, three, and even four-piece balls on the market. The three-piece has a thin extra layer between the cover and core, while the four-piece has a core within a core. Professional golfers use a ball specifically geared toward their game, where the rate of spin, hardness, and launch angle match their needs. The scientific development of all golf equipment continually makes advances.

Tees. The best tees are made of wood and come in various lengths; the standard is $2^{1}/_{8}$ inches. Tees made of other materials should be avoided.

Suggested Learning Sequence

Golf can be taught a number of different ways and from various starting points. Many of the skills can be learned and practiced indoors as well as outdoors. The availability of space and equipment (clubs, balls, screens, rugs, or mats) are important factors to consider. For beginning golfers, audiovisual aids can play a significant role in the learning process, for they reinforce many of the concepts explained during the initial stages of instruction. Another point to remember is that psychomotor and cognitive material is much better learned when presented together at the appropriate time. For example, etiquette and the rules governing play on the putting green are more meaningful during a lesson on putting than during a lesson devoted

to the rules of golf. Finally, it is important to become proficient in the basic swing techniques before attempting to move on to the more advanced skills and techniques.

A. Introduction to golf
   1. Nature and purpose of the game
   2. Choosing the right equipment
   3. Care of equipment

B. Etiquette and rules of golf. These should be introduced as deemed most appropriate for learning during different class intervals.

C. Skills and techniques. Golf skills are best learned starting with the shorter clubs. Putting should be introduced early. As skill increases, the longer clubs can be introduced with the wood clubs coming last. Chipping can be introduced following putting and full swing fundamentals.
   1. Putting. Grip, stance, alignment, pendulum stroke, lag putting, short putts, reading greens, rules, and etiquette.
   2. Preswing fundamentals. Grip, club face alignment, body alignment, stance, target selection, and strategy.
   3. Full-swing techniques. Takeaway, backswing, downswing, follow-through, balance, and tempo.
   4. Special shots. Chipping, pitch and run, and sand trap shots.
   5. Strategy of golf. Best taught on the golf course during play, or as deemed most appropriate for learning.

Skills and Techniques

PRESWING FUNDAMENTALS

It is important to have a good understanding of the preswing fundamentals. These fundamentals—grip, club face alignment, body alignment, stance, and target

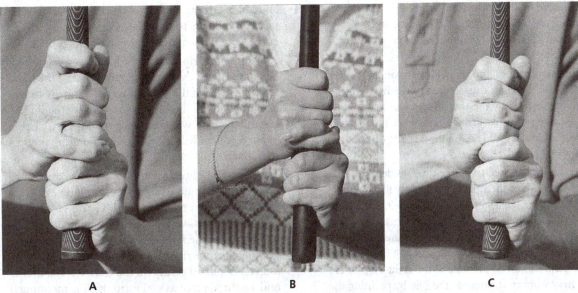

Figure 12-6 Types of grips. (A) Overlapping, (B) interlocking, and (C) the 10-finger grip.

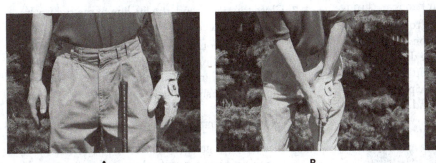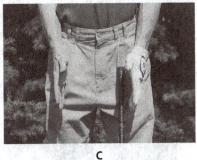

Figure 12-7 Assuming a grip.

selection—should be mastered before proceeding with the swing fundamentals. These fundamentals should be reviewed before every practice session and before playing a round of golf. Should a swing problem occur during a round of golf, a review of these fundamentals most often will solve the swing problem.

The following directions for all fundamentals are for the right-handed player. Substitute left for right and right for left in the skill analysis when instructing the left-handed player.

THE GRIP

The correct grip is the most important fundamental skill to be learned by golfers of any skill level. It can determine in great part the path of the ball and consequently the directional flight of the ball. There are three types of grips used in golf: the overlapping (or Vardon) grip, the interlocking grip, and the 10-finger grip (Figure 12-6). The overlapping grip is the most commonly used. In this grip, the little finger of the right hand overlaps the index finger of the left hand. The interlocking grip is used by the golfer who has small hands and short fingers. In this

grip, the little finger of the right hand *interlocks* with the index finger of the left hand. Both grips have the advantage of having the hands work as a unit because the hands are joined together. The 10-finger grip, used frequently by beginning junior golfers, enables the golfer to take a strong hold, but there is a tendency for the hands to slip apart at times.

When assuming a grip, the golfer should not think that because the grip is uncomfortable it is incorrect. However, the grip should not feel like a vise; rather it should feel firm yet somewhat relaxed. Tenseness in the grip will cause a restricted swing; the golf swing should flow.

▶ Learning Hints—Overlapping Grip (Right-handed Golfer)

1. A good golf grip starts by using the same hand position used when standing erect. As you stand erect with your arms hanging freely from your sides, notice how both hands turn slightly inward (Figure 12-7A). Extend your left hand and arm as though to shake hands. Close the thumb next to the first finger. The

line formed by the thumb and first finger should be pointing toward the right eye. The back of the left hand should be pointing in the direction you want the ball to travel.

2. Extend your right hand in the same manner as before. Close the right thumb next to the first finger. This line formed by the thumb and first finger should also point toward the right eye. The palm of the right hand should be pointing in the direction you want the ball to travel.

3. Extend both hands at the same time, as described previously. Place the right hand slightly forward of the left hand. (The right hand will be below the left hand when gripping the club.) The palms of your hands should be facing each other (Figure 12-7B). The lines formed by the thumb and first finger of each hand should be pointing at the right eye. Later you may want to strengthen the grip by pointing the lines toward the right shoulder, as most women golfers do. You may want to weaken the grip by pointing the lines toward your nose if your hands are strong.

4. Using a 7 iron or a 5 iron, attempt to grip the club. Be sure the sole of the club is flat on the ground and the club face is pointed toward the direction you want the ball to travel. Place the left hand on first, using the correct hand position. Grip firmly with the last three fingers of the left hand. The thumb

and index finger grip with less pressure. Use both palm and fingers to hold the club firmly and securely, but do not squeeze too hard. (Figure 12-7C).

5. The left-hand grip, for a right-handed golfer, should have the end of the club cross the palm of the hand from the base of the index finger, diagonally to the heel of the hand (Figure 12-8A). Closing the fingers around the club will ensure a good firm grip. Left-handed golfers will use the same grip using their right hand.

6. The right-hand grip is mainly a finger tip grip. First place the two middle fingers on the club next to the index finger of the left hand (Figure 12-8B). Use only fingertips. Overlap the little finger between the index and middle fingers of the left hand. The index finger of the right hand is formed like a trigger finger and placed gently on the club. Let the thumb find a natural place as you form the line mentioned previously. The palm of the right hand covers the left thumb but does not touch the golf club.

7. Close the right hand; the life line of the right palm should be placed over the left thumb.

8. The palms should face each other; the line formed by the index finger and thumb of the right hand should also point toward the right eye; the club face should be square to the line of flight.

▶ Practice/Organizational Suggestions

1. Place class in groups of two. One student works on acquiring a correct golf grip aided by the second student.

2. Grip with the left hand only. Hold the 7 iron at arm's length using only the left arm and hand. Remove all of the fingers from the club except the index finger. The club will be held with only this finger and the base of the hand.

3. Have the student helper attempt to pull the club from the golfer's grip. The club should not come out easily, if at all. If the grip is incorrect, the club will be difficult to hold at arm's length and can be removed easily by the student helper.

4. Correct right-hand position must be observed by a qualified instructor.

5. Grip aids can be purchased and placed on a dowel rod. Grip aids come premolded for both right- and left-handed golfers. Normal, strong, or weak grips are also available. Home practice with a grip aid will speed learning (Figure 12-9).

THE STANCE AND ADDRESS

The stance and address first involve assuming a good grip. Next, the feet, hips, and shoulders are properly aligned along with the club face. The stance is completed with two bends and a tilt. The first bend is in the waist,

Figure 12-8 (A) Left-hand grip—fingers and palm. (B) Right-hand grip—two middle fingers.

Figure 12-9   A grip aid helps place hands in perfect grip.

the second bend is at the knees, and the right shoulder is dropped to form a tilt.

Although there are three styles of stances, the square stance is used by most golfers for most all shots (Figure 12-10). The open stance is used for special shots, such as a sand trap shot. The closed stance is usually used to compensate for certain types of body builds. The open and closed stances can produce altered ball flight patterns, such as a slice or a hook.

▶ Learning Hints

1. Always choose a target before attempting the address and stance. Stand in line with the ball, select a target, and draw an imaginary line from the ball to the target. A second imaginary line must be drawn parallel with the first line. These two lines must run parallel and not converge.

2. After securing a correct grip, place the club face on the target line, with the bottom of the club face at a right angle to the line.

3. The second line is used to align your feet, hips, and shoulders at a right angle to the club face. The feet, hips, and shoulders should be pointing in the same direction.

4. In a good stance the arms will hang freely from the shoulders and straight down. Standing too far from the ball will cause a poor swing plane, and poor shots will result.

Ball position is determined somewhat by experimentation. As a general rule, the golf ball will be placed near the inside of the left heel for all fullswing shots. You may need to move the ball nearer the center of your stance for the shorter clubs. Place the ball right of center for special shots or unusual circumstances (Figure 12-11).

SWING

The swing is a long, large elliptical circle. The radius of the circle is the firm left arm and the club. The left arm, wrist, and hand must be in control from the takeaway,

A

B

C

Figure 12-10   Three types of stances: (A) square stance, both feet turned out and toes on a line parallel to the line of flight; (B) open stance, forward foot slightly open and dropped behind the back foot; (C) closed stance, back foot slightly open and dropped behind the front foot.

through the backswing, especially at the beginning of the downswing, and on into the follow-through. Any undue influence by the right arm or hand will distort the swing circle and ruin the shot.

Swing the club back and up as far as you can, maintaining your balance. The right knee should remain inside the right foot during the backswing. The wrists will fall into a cocked position, with the thumbs under the

Figure 12-11 Ball positions.

shaft. This will occur near the top of the backswing. You will have turned your back to the target, but your head has remained steady. Your right elbow will be pointed downward.

Start the forward swing by replacing the left heel in the original address position. You should strive for the feeling of stepping into the shot. Your left heel may not come off the ground for all clubs, but the feeling of stepping into the shot is the same for all clubs. As you step into the shot, you must keep your head positioned behind the ball. Avoid anxiety and an urge to let the right shoulder take over the swing.

The wrists will remain cocked during the beginning of the downswing and will uncock automatically at the end of the swing.

During the forward swing, you should have a sensation of the right side working underneath the left side, causing a bowing action in the waist. With the irons, you should feel as though you are swinging down and through, and with the woods, you should feel a more level swing.

The entire swing lasts but a short time and does not require complicated thought processes. If you follow the previous description of a golf swing with good tempo, you will have the sensation of swinging the club through the ball and down the target line. The swing will finish as you face the target, with most of your weight on the left foot. The right foot will turn up on the toes. Your hands will finish high, and the weight will be equally distributed between the outside of the left foot and the right toes.

Although we frequently think of the adage "practice makes perfect," the truth is that "practice makes permanent." Therefore, haphazard practice is worse than no practice at all. Plan your practices well, concentrating on one phase of the swing at a time. Remember that you will probably get worse as your mind and body attempt to learn or relearn this new skill. Be patient and give yourself time to succeed.

▶ Learning Hints (Figure 12-12)

Takeaway. The takeaway is the act of moving the club away from the ball. The length of the takeaway is determined by how far the club moves away from the ball yet remains close to the ground. The longer the club, the longer the takeaway. The speed of the takeaway also determines the overall tempo of the entire golf swing.

1. With the left hand, wrist, and arm in control, start moving the club straight back away from the ball. Do not pull the club inside the target line. The club will eventually begin an inside route as the club rises from the ground and is lifted into the backswing.

Backswing. This is not really a swing, but the act of turning and lifting the club into position.

1. With the left arm still in control, begin coiling the body as you lift the club upward. The left shoulder will begin turning to a behind-the-ball position.

2. As the club reaches waist level, you should see the left arm still firm and in control. The right elbow has begun to hinge. The left knee has begun to turn inward. The right leg is still braced, with the knee turned inward to prevent a lateral sway and loss of balance. The head has also begun to rotate slightly, but does not move laterally.

At the top.

1. The club should be horizontal for the longer clubs, near horizontal for shorter clubs. The left side is still in control. The thumbs are under the shaft to support the club.

2. Sometime during the backswing, usually near the finish, the wrists move to a cocked position. This action should happen naturally and is caused by the speed of the backswing.

3. Your back should be turned to the target. The head will have continued to rotate but with no lateral movement. The right elbow is pointing toward the ground.

4. The right leg has remained in the braced position. The left knee has turned inward, and the left heel may have been pulled off the ground.

Downswing.

1. The initial movement is made by replacing the left heel. A feeling of stepping into the swing should occur. As you step into the swing, the hips will begin to slide on a line parallel with the target line.

2. With the left side still in control, you should pull the club on a downward angle. You will attempt to swing down and through the ball.

3. The right side is active as it works under the left side. You will feel a bowing sensation in the waist.

4. The wrists will uncock naturally; correct timing of the wrist cock will be obtained by practice.

Figure 12-12   Swing sequence: (A) address position, (B) takeaway, (C) at the top of backswing, (D) beginning downswing, (E) downswing, (F) follow-through, (G) near top of follow-through, (H) completion of follow-through.

5. The head must remain behind the ball. Swing the club beyond your face before you allow head movement.

Follow-through. The follow-through is a reaction to all that has gone on before. If all has gone well, the hands will finish high, and you should be facing the target. You will be equally balanced between the outside of your left foot and the toes of the right foot.

▶ Practice/Organizational Suggestions

Many warm-up exercises can be used that approximate the rhythm and pattern of a full swing. In addition, golf is a target game and therefore a target should be selected and used as a reference in all drills.

A. Without a ball or club

1. Assume a golf stance and grip, arms hanging straight down from shoulders, knees and waist bent slightly. On command, pivot and swing to a position with arms horizontal to the ground. Stop and check for correct balance and body position. Continue on to the top of the backswing and stop. Execute a downswing, stopping at a point where the ball would be struck. Finally, finish the swing. Each stop should be examined for correct body balance and position. Peer assessment is beneficial to both individuals.

2. With a towel rolled and grasped at either end, assume a stance, then execute a golf swing. (A golf club can be used.) Make sure weight is kept inside the rear foot on the backswing. Avoid excessive lateral movement.

B. With a club and ball

1. Assume a golf stance, noting the position of the left foot. Next, place left foot next to right foot. From this position, execute a backswing and come to a stop. The downswing is started by lifting the left foot from the ground and beginning to step this foot toward its original position. At the same time, begin to pull downward with the left arm. Complete the swing by replacing the left foot in its original position. Correct

execution will teach the sensation of weight transfer in the golf swing. Practice this drill without a ball first until control is gained. Add the ball to the drill only after the student has good balance and control.

2. To learn control of the clubface, choke down on a 7 iron, put feet together, and practice hitting balls. When a majority of the balls are flying toward the target, try a regular grip or move to a longer club. This drill can be used with any club, including the woods.

3. Stand on the left foot only, using only the right toes for balance. Hit balls toward a target from this position. This drill simulates body position at ball contact.

4. Peer assessment in each of the forgoing drills is beneficial.

Suiting Clubs to Shots

WOODS

The woods are used for the longest shots in golf. The driver, the longest club, is used for shots from the teeing ground on the longer holes. The first shot on every hole may be teed.

The 3 and 5 woods are also used for distance. They may be used for teeing off, but their primary use is from the fairway. They do not afford as much distance as the driver, but are more accurate. A near-perfect lie is necessary when using a wood from the fairway or rough. If in doubt as to the lie, it is best to use an iron.

LONG IRONS

The 2, 3, and 4 irons are considered the long irons. They produce less distance than the woods but are more accurate. Most long par 3 holes require a long iron for the first shot. These clubs are good for fairway and rough shots. They can also be substituted for a wood in a bad lie situation.

Some golfers find the long irons too difficult to use. A 7 wood can substitute for the 2 and 3 irons, leaving room for an extra club.

MEDIUM IRONS

This name applies to the 5, 6, and 7 irons. Remember, as the number becomes higher, so does the flight of the shot produced. Increased height gives less distance and less roll, but more accuracy.

Medium irons are versatile and can be used for several different kinds of shots. Par 3 golf holes of medium length require a medium iron for the first shot. On any hole, the medium irons should be considered as you near the 150-yard marker. A medium iron is a good choice from a fairway bunker with a large front lip. Near the green, if you desire a shot to land on the green and roll toward the hole, a medium iron works well. From deep rough, these clubs can get you back in play.

When first learning the golf swing, the medium irons are an excellent choice as the clubs with which to begin. Most golf drills require a medium iron.

SHORT IRONS

This category includes the 8, 9, and pitching wedge (10 iron). These are the most accurate of all the irons and are used inside the 150-yard marker. Because the shots will fly much higher, you can expect less roll. You may now shoot more toward a specific target, such as the green or the hole, rather than a landing area.

During your practice sessions, learn how far the shortest club in your set will travel with a full swing under normal circumstances. On the golf course, once you are located at a distance that requires less than a full swing, adjustments will have to be made.

To curtail distance, first open your stance slightly. This will help shorten the backswing. Choking down on the club can also reduce distance. Narrow the stance in conjunction with the short irons for shorter shots. See "Chip Shot" and "Pitch Shot" for further ideas.

Special Shots

The short approach shots discussed in this section—the pitch, chip, sand shot, and putt—are frequently called the golfer's scoring strokes. A high percentage of shots taken during a round of golf consists of these four types; therefore, the more proficient you become, the lower your scores will be. One of the key elements in these shots involves "feel"; consequently, the shots must be practiced frequently to develop a comfortable feeling. Most of these shots, with the exception of a fairway sand shot, are executed near the green or on the green itself.

PITCH SHOT

The pitch shot is characterized as a high-flying, minimum-roll type of shot. This shot is generally executed with a high-lofted iron such as the 8, 9, or pitching wedge. Less than a full swing is required.

The pitch shot is a good choice for a golfer faced with a hazard, sand or water, blocking the entry to the green. Many golfers use the pitch shot as a substitute for the chip shot, even though it is more difficult (Figure 12-13).

▶ Learning Hints

1. Assume a square or open stance. Use your normal grip.

2. Move the feet closer together (Figure 12-13A).

3. Play the ball slightly left of center.

4. Pick the club up early in the backswing by cocking the wrists (Figure 12-13B).

Figure 12-13 Pitch shot: (A) takeaway, (B) wrists cocked in backswing, (C) hands ahead of the clubhead, (D) follow-through.

Figure 12-14 Chip shot: (A) hands ahead of ball at address, (B) clubhead low, wrists not cocked, (C) clubhead low on follow-through.

5. Swing down and through, making sure the hands do not stop at ball impact (Figure 12-13C).

6. Shift the weight slightly to the left foot, and avoid trying to scoop the ball in the hitting area. The arms, hands, and club generally reach waist high at the finish (Figure 12-13D).

CHIP SHOT

The chip shot is characterized as a low-flying, maximum-roll type of shot. Generally, the ball will be in the air one-third of the time, rolling two-thirds of the time. Any club—5 iron through pitching wedge—may be used. More lofted clubs produce less roll.

Most instructors suggest that the beginning golfer select one club, 7 or 9 iron, to develop the necessary experience. Because the chip shot is largely roll, the shot must be treated much like a putt. Select a landing spot, then read the green to the hole (Figure 12-14).

▶ Learning Hints

1. Narrow stance, square or slightly open.

2. Normal grip. Some golfers prefer a putting grip.

3. Play ball left of center. Hands, head, and weight center must be in front of ball. This position deflofts the club, allowing maximum roll.

4. The arms, hands, and club act as one unit and move back in a small arc in the backswing. With a right-handed golfer, the weight remains on the left foot (Figure 12-14A).

5. The arms, hands, and club are brought forward on the downswing, the butt of the club is kept ahead of the hands and arms through the hitting area. Make sure to accelerate the movement through the hitting area (Figure 12-14B). Do not stop the swing by punching at the ball, but continue the swing and freeze the hands at the end of the swing slightly ahead of the front leg.

Figure 12-15   Sand shot: (A) club face open, stance open, (B) wrists cocked, (C) club face open, (D) club splashes ball out.

6. The follow-through is generally the same length as the backswing (Figure 12-14C).

▶ Practice/Organizational Suggestions

1. Experiment with different clubs at 10-yard intervals, starting 10 yards from the green.

2. Hit chip shots over a barrier, such as your golf bag.

3. Hit chip shots onto a practice green. Notice how far the ball rolls when using different clubs.

4. Practice both chip shots and pitch shots with the same club. Note how changes are made to produce each shot.

SAND SHOT

The sand shot is usually a difficult shot for the beginner to master because sand does not have the firmness of the fairway and the ball does not set up as it does on grass. A specially designed club called a sand wedge is used to execute the shot. Again, the element of "feel" can determine success. Getting out of a sand trap requires various strategies. With traps that are flat, near the green, and with no lip, the beginner might try putting the ball out of the trap, provided the ball is not buried. For shots with a low lip near the green, the golfer may try a chip shot. However, for shots in a deep trap and with the ball buried in the sand, the golfer must execute an explosion shot. Remember, a golfer may not ground a club in a trap without incurring a penalty.

▶ Learning Hints

1. Address the ball with an open stance. Wiggle the feet into the sand to secure a good foothold and prevent slipping.

2. The ball is played right of center. Preshift some weight forward prior to the swing, but maintain your head position behind the ball during the entire swing. Open the club face slightly.

3. Cock the wrists early in the backswing, much like the pitch shot. Focus on a spot an inch or so behind the ball.

4. Explode the clubhead onto the spot behind the ball. You must hit sand—not the ball.

5. Be sure to keep the clubhead traveling through the sand, under the ball, and into a good finish (Figure 12-15).

In most school settings, the school may have a long jump pit containing sand that can be used for practicing sand shots. When teaching a unit in golf, set up various stations far enough apart that students will not hit anyone with a swing or ball. As an alternative to a long jump pit, consider using a large sandbox filled with 4–5 inches of sand, making sure that it is large enough to allow the students to asssume a proper stance with the club.

1. Draw a line or use a flat marker and place a ball 2 inches in front of the line or marker. Splash the ball toward the target. Set up targets 5 feet, 10 feet, and 15 feet away and practice hitting the shot to the targets.

2. Vary the depth of the ball in the sand, and with the same swing, use a pitching wedge instead of a sand wedge to get the ball out of the trap.

3. Bury a 1-foot-long two-by-four 2 inches beneath the surface of the sand. Place the ball over the two-by-four and practice splashing the ball out of the sand without hitting down into the wooden board.

THE PUTT

Putting is probably the most important phase of the game, and too often one of the most neglected. Concentration and confidence are two of the primary requirements for good putting, and can be gained best through practice of fundamental techniques. Forms of putting differ widely, but basic fundamentals are much the same.

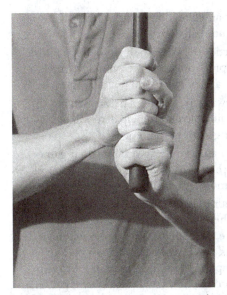

Figure 12-16 Putting grip. Note overlap of index finger.

A   B

Figure 12-17 Putting stance: (A) front view, (B) side view.

▶ Learning Hints

1. Grip the club with your fingers, palms facing each other and in line with the putter face. All five fingers of the bottom hand grip the club. Overlap the index finger of the top hand (Figure 12-16).

2. Any stance that is comfortable and allows you to place your eyes directly over the ball is acceptable.

3. Both elbows most often are bent to allow you to stand close to the ball. You must also crouch down slightly for comfort. However, some individuals elect to putt with straight arms and stand more upright, thus allowing the arms and shoulders to work efficiently as one unit in a pendulum swing.

4. Play the ball left of center. The putting stance may seem awkward at first, but give it a chance (Figure 12-17).

5. Keep the backswing low. Use your arms to initiate the backswing, with little or no wrist break.

6. Return the forward stroke along the same line, keeping the putter face square to the intended putting line.

The Sweetspot. The sweetspot is the name given to an $1/8$-inch-wide vertical area located on the face of the putter. The most successful putts occur when the sweetspot strikes the center of the ball. Missing the sweetspot toward the heel of the putter will cause the loss of distance and some control. Missing the sweetspot toward the toe of the putter will cause even more loss of distance and even more loss of control.

Of all putting fundamentals, striking the sweetspot to the center of the ball ranks as the most important. Regardless of which putting style you choose or change to later, striking the sweetspot to the center of the ball will always be your number-one goal.

Finding the Sweetspot. To find the sweetspot, using your thumb and first finger, hold your putterhead in front of your face, putter face facing you. Using a golf ball, begin dinging the putter's face. Find the area that will allow you to drive the putter straight back and forth with no gyrations or shaft vibrations. Note the spot. Make a line on top of the putter to align with this sweetspot. Some putters already have a line marked for you; this line may or may not be correct.

The Putting Stroke. The putting stroke can be described as a sweeping motion. There should be no lower body movement. Your head should also be kept still until the putt is well on its way. The amount of wrist break depends on the individual. Generally, the closer to the hole, the less wrist break needed to putt. Be sure to keep your hands moving with the putt. Many beginners stop the hands at ball impact causing mis-hit putts.

Finally, learn to read the greens. A putt seldom rolls perfectly straight to the hole unless it is a short putt. Because no green is perfectly flat, study which way the ball will turn and to what degree. The most important factor in reading a green is judging distance. Misjudging distance and missing the sweetspot are the main causes of missed putts.

Judging distance on a putt must include factors along with distance. How fast the ball will roll on a green can be affected by the grass length. Greens are mowed early each day and are much faster early in the morning after being mowed. Soft greens are usually slower than hard greens. A putt traveling downhill will roll much farther than one going uphill. In some areas, the grain of the grass is a factor to be considered. Because putting can account for nearly half or more of your total strokes, be sure to devote plenty of time to developing your putting skills.

You can use a large piece of smooth carpeting, artificial grass carpeting, or commercially made putting carpet to practice your putting stroke.

1. Work with a partner. Have your partner stand behind you as you putt the ball and check the alignment of your head, feet, arms, and the putter head as it moves through the ball.

2. Place the balls in a circle around the cup at varying distances and practice putts of various lengths.

3. Using two clubs lying parallel to each other slightly farther apart than the width of the putter head, putt the ball. Make sure the putter head does not hit the clubs as you stroke through the ball. You can also use four to five sets of tees in this drill in place of the clubs.

4. Place five golf balls 2 feet apart in a single line. Try to hit the second ball to the first, then the third ball to the first, and so on, to get the feel of stroking putts of varying length.

5. Place an object underneath a carpet so that the player has to hit a downhill or uphill putt from various distances.

Helpful Hints

1. Always select a target when planning any shot or putt. Stand at least 10 feet behind the ball, plan your shot, then choose a club.

2. During the swing, concentrate on ball contact and direction rather than distance.

3. Know what club to use from 150 yards. Generally, men can add or subtract 10 yards and women 7 yards when choosing clubs for other distances.

4. For downhill shots, use a lofted club, wide stance, and play the ball back in the stance.

5. For uphill shots, use a less lofted club than normal, wide stance for balance, and play the ball forward in the stance. In both uphill and downhill shots, adjust your shoulder position and swing to match the contour of the hill.

6. For sidehill shots with the ball above your feet, take more club than normal, but choke down and swing easy. Expect the ball to travel in the direction of the contour of the hill.

7. For a sidehill shot with the ball below your feet, take more club than normal and plan to use a short, easy swing. This is one of the more difficult trouble shots in golf.

8. Consider weather conditions when planning shots. A golf ball will fly farther in warm, dry air. Consider the velocity and direction of the wind and how it will affect your ball flight.

9. Do not practice the swing before you hit a normal shot. Use a practice swing after you have made a poor swing, and only if it will not delay play.

10. A practice swing may be used before playing an unusual or difficult shot to help determine how the normal swing must be altered.

11. Immediately after you play, analyze your game. Decide which part of your game needs the most practice or more instruction.

12. Most amateur golfers make three mistakes: They underclub themselves, then overswing, and finally overestimate their ability. Try to play within your own abilities and when in trouble, get back in play. Avoid attempting the miracle shot. It is better to accept a score of one or two strokes over par on a hole, rather than a very large score made by using poor judgment.

▶ Practice/Organizational Suggestions—Indoor Work

Sometimes the teacher is confronted with situations that will not allow outside practice and is forced to teach indoors. With a little ingenuity and the use of typical types of equipment found in most physical education departments (track hurdles, gymnastic mats, badminton nets, hoops, balance beam, rope circles, waste baskets, portable pitching net, tires, goal cage), it is possible to continue the unit without interruption. Many of the following suggestions can be organized into stations for practice. Plastic, hard rubber, foam rubber, or other softer synthetic practice balls should be used in most situations for safety reasons. Most equipment catalogs will have a listing of such equipment. Many carpet stores are willing to donate carpet samples for use as teeing areas and carpet remnants for use in putting, chipping, and pitching stations.

The most important phase of station work inside is to recognize the space required for stations, the type of golf ball (plastic or real) required for the station or skill being used, and the position of the student in relation to the station setup and to other stations. Care must be taken to ensure a safe area where students are not in line with clubs during a swing. Consideration should be given to using mats that are propped up or tied up to a wall for stations where golf balls are being chipped or pitched or where a full swing (without a golf ball) is being practiced.

1. There are several instructional videos that can be used when the class is forced to stay indoors because of weather.

2. Worksheets can be developed to help students understand terminology normally associated with golf.

3. Rainy-day weather is a perfect time to review the basic rules governing golf. Situations can be

4. Divide the gymnasium into stations to practice putting, the full swing, the chip, and the pitch shot.

5. From a mat, the pitch shot can be practiced, using a mat draped over a track hurdle. Rolled-up mats can be used as obstacles for the golfer to pitch over.

6. From a mat, the chip shot can be practiced by extending a net between volleyball or badminton standards and having the students keep the chip under the net.

7. Putting can be practiced on large carpet remnants. Be sure to ask for pieces of carpet that have a close nap so the surface nearly approximates the feel of putting on a green.

8. A miniature putt-putt course can be developed in the gymnasium by using a variety of equipment as obstacles.

9. With a mat, the full swing can be practiced, with a partner offering corrections as the teacher leads the students through a swing. Careful attention must be given to placing the partner behind and far enough away so as not to be in direct line with the swing. Swing toward a wall that has been padded or draped with netting.

10. The teacher can develop cue cards for the non swinging partner to observe key points as the golfer is practicing the swing using peer-teaching assessment.

11. A variety of contests using targets (hoops, rope circles, cardboard circles, baskets, etc.) can be implemented to help students practice various beginning skills.

12. Stations can be set up with defining conditions typically involved in golf that would involve the student in making the correct rules or etiquette interpretation.

Safety Considerations

Golf can be a dangerous game if you do not pay attention to your play and the play of others. Whether golf is being played in a class situation, on a practice range, or while playing a round, observe basic safety rules:

1. Never hit a shot until you are sure those in front of you are out of your range. If you hit another player, you may be liable for injuries.

2. Never swing a club, especially on the tees, unless you are sure no one is standing close to you.

3. If the warning "Fore" is given, do not turn to see where the ball is coming from; doing so can be dangerous. It is best to cover your head for protection and turn away from the direction of the warning.

4. In the event of a thunderstorm, it is not wise to remain outdoors. Seek shelter in a closed building protected against lightning. Large or small unprotected buildings, respectively, are alternatives. If you must remain outdoors, keep away from open spaces and hilltops, isolated trees, wire fences, and small shelters in exposed locations. You may also seek shelter in caves, depressions or deep valleys and canyons, the foot of a cliff, or a dense stand of trees. Holding umbrellas overhead in exposed places is dangerous.

5. Never practice in an area where others are playing. Most golf courses have special practice areas.

6. Never hit practice shots while playing a round. It not only wastes time but also is dangerous.

7. Only one person should hit at a time. The person farthest from the hole should play first.

8. Knowing and applying the rules of golf and golfing etiquette will increase your safety on a golf course.

9. Carry a towel and wipe hands dry, particularly on hot, humid days and rainy days.

10. Know the distances of specific clubs and distances you can hit the ball.

IN CLASS—RULES FOR THE TEACHER

1. Plan the lesson well in advance, checking such things as formation, target areas, and methods of retrieval.

2. Allow no one to swing a club unless instructed to do so.

3. Provide plenty of space between golfers.

4. If stations are used, provide for adequate distance between groups.

IN CLASS—RULES FOR THE STUDENT

1. Do not retrieve a golf ball until asked to do so; never step out of line to pick up a "muffed" shot.

2. Do not walk too closely behind other golfers who are swinging their golf clubs.

3. If working with a partner, stand in front and to the side of your partner, not behind.

4. Listen to instruction and follow prescribed rules.

Etiquette and Playing Courtesies

Because golf is a polite game with a well-defined code of ethics, it is important for every golfer to observe common courtesies while on the course.

IN GENERAL, WHILE PLAYING THE COURSE

1. Be polite at all times; know the rules of golf so decisions can be made quickly without causing undue delay.

2. Be aware of the local rules and regulations that govern play on a course.

3. Do not hit practice shots between regular shots—it is an infraction of the rules.

4. Abstain from obscene language, loud talk, and club throwing.

5. Plan ahead and be ready to play your next shot without undue delay. The player farthest from the flag stick shoots first.

6. Do not talk, move around, stand too close or directly in line of a shot when another player is preparing to shoot.

7. Never play a shot until the group ahead is completely out of range.

8. While looking for a lost ball, do not unduly delay the play of others. Allow a group playing behind you to go through by signaling them to do so, and do not resume play until they are out of range.

9. After each shot, pick up the divot or loose grass and replace it with your hand in the divot mark. Pat it down with your foot.

10. Fill holes made in bunkers and smooth the sand after playing from a trap. Be sure to rake all sand traps before leaving them.

11. Keep pull carts and motorized carts off the green area.

12. Yell "Fore" if a ball is in danger of striking another person.

13. The person having the honor (lowest score on the preceding hole) tees up first.

14. Notify your partners when you wish to change a golf ball.

ON THE PUTTING GREEN

1. As soon as a hole has been completed, the player should leave the green. Do not total the scores and record them on the green.

2. Allow the person farthest from the hole to putt first.

3. When lifting a ball on the green, mark it with a coin.

4. Never lay a bag of clubs down on the green.

5. Do not throw the flag stick off to the side. Always lay it down gently, away from all play, and replace it when the hole has been completed.

6. Do not damage the hole with the stick or by standing too close to the hole.

7. Repair ball marks on the green.

8. Do not drag your feet or in any way scuff the green.

9. Do not walk in the putting line of another person's intended line. Always walk around the outside of the green.

Skill Assessment

Most experts agree that the putter and medium irons (5, 6, and 7) are the most important clubs to learn to use. The putter is important because golf is designed such that a good round requires that half of the 72 strokes are putts (18 holes × 2 putts per hole). The medium irons are recommended because they are an excellent choice of club for beginners learning the full golf swing. The two recommended skills tests use these two types clubs. Both tests are intended for indoor testing; however, the medium-iron test could easily be set up and conducted outdoors crosswise on a football field.

Putting Test.   The putting surface can be a flat smooth length of carpet, artificial grass carpet, or commercially made practice putting carpet. The carpet should be at least 2 feet wide and 10 feet long, with a 4½-inch diameter "hole" made of paper taped in the middle at 9 feet. Four to five putting stations, with three students per station, will involve approximately half of an average class. The remaining students, if space is available, will be at the medium iron test or practicing their skills.

The first student putts three regulation balls for practice and the next seven for score. The second student immediately measures each putt for score, collects the ball, and tells the result to the third student, who records it on a score sheet. Students rotate responsibilities until all have completed their turn.

The student's score is the sum of the seven putts measured in inches. Each putt is measured to the nearest inch from the edge of the hole to the ball. Any ball that goes off the putting surface (carpet) past the hole is recorded as an automatic 12 inches. Any ball that touches the hole during its roll is recorded as a zero (except if it rolls off the surface, which counts as 12). The lower the total sum in inches of the seven putts, the better one's score.

Medium Iron Test.   The minimum area required for the medium iron test is 45 feet wide by 60 feet long. An additional 20 feet in length is optimal. The total number of testing stations depends on the size of the indoor space. One basketball court is approximately 55 feet by 94 feet of playing surface, which easily provides one station lengthwise. However, two stations are possible sideways on one basketball court with just a few additional feet available on the sidelines of the court. A facility with two basketball courts side-by-side, which is quite common at the secondary level, offers additional station options. If more stations are available, the testing time quickens.

A single station consists of two side boundary lines 45 feet apart, a baseline connecting the sidelines, and an end line 60 feet from the baseline, forming a rectangle (45 ft. × 60 ft.). The sidelines should extend 10 feet or more past the end line, thus providing an imaginary, unending sideline for scoring purposes.

The rectangle is divided into nine sections by criss-crossing lengths of rope. Two ropes 45 feet long, 20 feet apart and parallel with the baseline, are stretched across the width of the rectangle. These two ropes should be fastened to the surface. Then, two ropes 70 feet (or more) in length are stretched the length of the now trisected rectangle. These two ropes are placed 15 feet inside the two sidelines and are parallel to each other, 15 feet apart. They are fastened to the surface as well. Ten feet (or more) of the two long ropes extend past the 60 feet end line, thus providing an imaginary, unending line for scoring purposes. The aforementioned extension of the two sidelines and the two 70 feet (or more) vertical ropes form three additional unending scoring areas, for a total of 12 sections. A target (cone) is placed in the center of this distant middle area for sighting and for a challenge.

Two groups of four students (eight total) per testing station are suggested. The ball is placed on a piece of smooth carpet or practice mat that is located just outside the baseline of the area in the middle (approximately 22 ft. from both sidelines). One participant from each group, using plastic golf balls, alternates shots with the other participant until both complete 10 attempts. The participants take three practice shots with the next seven being for score. One score recorder and two ball shaggers also are in each group. Group members rotate responsibilities.

The score for each shot is based on where the ball first lands and the point value for that area. A ball landing on any line is the higher score. Because lofted ball distance and accuracy are important factors for a good

medium iron shot, the point values on the 12 areas reflect this. The flighted shot is initiated from the middle of the baseline with three vertical columns of points possible and three areas in each of the four horizontal rows (12 areas total). Facing the length of the rectangle, row 1 point values are 1-1-1; row 2 values are 2-4-2; row 3 values are 4-6-4; and row 4 values are 8-10-8. These last three areas extend indefinitely, as previously explained and shown in the example grid (Figure 12-18).

The middle area of the trisected space is the highest value because of the importance of accuracy and distance toward the target cone. The far-left and far-right areas of each row across have identical values. A missed ball on the swing receives no points, and a topped (nonlofted) ball that rolls forward receives one point.

Modifications for Special Populations

ORTHOPEDICALLY IMPAIRED

1. Allow students who use wheelchairs to play from their chairs, using a standard position for striking (e.g., perpendicular to the ball). Reposition striking position to accommodate the swing (e.g., facing the green and striking with one arm if necessary).

2. If outdoor facilities are not accessible (e.g., terrain is rough or the student's orthopedic condition is too severe) develop an indoor putting course. Use carpet remnants for greens and tees, and boards for side rails.

3. Modify the length of the club.

COGNITIVELY IMPAIRED

1. Keep the concept of the game simple. Do not stress various club selections for various conditions; suggest that a student select a driver for the tee, an iron for the fairway, and a putter for the green.

2. Refer to item 2 under Orthopedically Impaired.

SENSORY IMPAIRED

1. Allow students who are blind or have a visual impairment to "feel" someone complete a golf swing.

2. Allow students who are blind or have a visual impairment to pace off the distance on the putting surface to the hole.

3. Minimal modifications are needed for individuals who are deaf or have a hearing impairment.

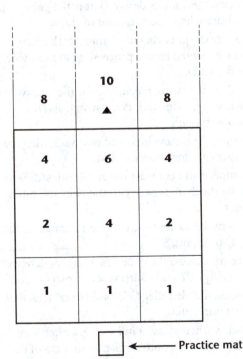

Figure 12-18 Example grid.

Terminology

ace A hole in one.

address The position taken by a player when preparing to start a stroke.

apron The area immediately surrounding the green.

banana ball A slice.

aest ball tournament Competition in which the better score of a partnership on each hole is used as the team score.

birdie The score of one under par on a hole.

bogey A score of one over par on a hole (U.S. rules). In countries playing the British rules, a bogey is the score an average golfer should make on a hole; on easier holes, par and bogey might be the same score.

casual water Temporary accumulation of water that is not recognized as a hazard on the course.

course rating The comparative difficulty of a specific course. Usually computed by a committee of a local association to have uniform handicapping for all courses within a district.

divot Sod cut with the clubhead when executing or attempting to execute a shot.

dogleg A hole that has a sharp bend in the fairway.

driver Number 1 wood.

eagle A score for a hole played in two strokes under par.

fairway The course between the teeing ground and the putting green, exclusive of hazards.

flag Banner on top of the flagstick identifying the cup.

fore A warning cry to anyone of a stroke about to be played or one that has been played.

go to school Learning the roll of a green by watching a previous putt over the same area.

ground under repair Any portion of the course so marked that includes material piled for removal or a hole made by a greenskeeper.

hazard Any bunker, water hazard, or lateral water hazard.

hole Small cup sunk into the green, into which the golf ball is hit. The hole is $4\frac{1}{4}$ inches in diameter and at least 4 inches deep.

honor The side entitled to play first from the teeing ground is said to have the honor. This is usually determined by a coin flip on the first tee. Once play begins, the player having the lowest score on the previous hole is said to have the honor thereafter.

hook A ball in flight that curves from right to left (for a right-handed golfer).

lie The position of the ball on the playing ground. Also refers to the angle of the clubhead.

loft The slope given to the face of a golf club to aid in knocking the ball in a high curve.

loose impediments Natural objects not fixed or growing and not adhering to the ball, and including stones not solidly embedded; leaves, twigs, branches, and the like, dung, worms, and insects, and casts or heaps made by them.

match play Competition in which the winner is decided by the number of holes won.

mulligan Permitting a second hit of a badly played ball—usually on a tee shot. (Not permitted under the rules but by mutual agreement in friendly matches.)

obstruction An artificial object erected, placed, or left on a course and not an integral part of the course.

par The standard score for a hole.

pull-shot To hit a ball straight, but to the left of the target (for a right-handed golfer).

push-shot To hit a ball straight, but to the right of the target (for a right-handed golfer).

rough The unmowed terrain on either side of the fairway.

scotch foursome A competitive round in which two partners play the same ball, taking alternate shots.

slice A ball in flight that curves from left to right (for a right-handed person).

stroke play (medal play) Competition in which the winner is decided by the total number of strokes taken from a specific number of rounds, not by individual holes won, as in match play.

summer rules Playing the ball as it lies from tee through green.

teeing ground The starting place for the hole to be played.

trap A hazard, technically known as a bunker.

waggle Body or club action prior to starting the swing.

wedge A heavy iron club that is used to loft the ball high into the air. It is also used for special situations, such as getting out of heavy grass or sand.

winter rules The privilege of improving the lie of the ball on the fairway of the hole being played.

Discussion Questions

1. Contrast the differences between stroke and match play.

2. Trace the origination of golf and its introduction to the United States.

3. Discuss the various design factors the golfer must consider when selecting a set of clubs.

4. Discuss the preswing fundamentals that need to be mastered before proceeding to the swing fundamentals.

5. Analyze the swing mechanics for the takeaway, backswing, at-the-top, downswing, and the follow-through.

6. Discuss the factors involved when selecting the proper club for a specific shot.

7. Compare and contrast the similarities/differences of the mechanics between the chip and pitch shots.

8. Present the various factors that might affect the distance on a putt.

9. Cite and discuss the code of ethics that define common etiquette and courtesy when playing golf.

10. Discuss the identified "Helpful Hints" and how they affect one's play.

11. Discuss when to use a full swing, a pitch-shot, a chip-shot, or a putt in relation to areas of the course.

Web Sites

www.pga.com Professional Golfers' Association of America—provides details on up-to-date tour happenings, and sections that cover instruction, fitness, golf equipment, rules, and a host of other topics.

www.randa.org Royal and Ancient Golf Club—contains rules of golf, etiquette, and definitions; discusses golf around the world.

www.mrgolf.com/primer.html—is a primer about golf etiquette.

www.lpga.com Ladies PGA Tour—contains biographies of players, tips for improving your game, history, and information about junior golf programs.

www.golf.com *Golf Magazine's* Web site—covers a broad spectrum of golf topics developed by the editors; includes a section on rules, instruction, junior golf, women's and men's golf.

www.golfdigest.com *Golf Digest*—includes good feature articles on the various aspects of golf, has interactive swing sequences of players, provides equipment reviews, and more.

www.usga.org U.S. Golf Association—contains an information section about rules, including modified rules for golfers with disabilities, animated rules of golf, and rule quizzes.

http://golf.about.com—includes articles and resources covering tips for beginners, equipment, rules of golf, handicaps, history of golf, golf tips, fitness and health, women's and junior golf, terminology, and tips on golf basics.

www.pgaprofessional.com—contains golf tips, articles, information about golf schools, books, videotapes, a free book for beginners on the ABCs of golf, and a section called "Ask the Pro."

www.golfcircuit.com/instruction/—contains significant information about all phases of golf and a section on golf rules made easy.

www.1st-beginners-golf-swing-tips.com—Free instruction and tips for the beginning golfer.

www.nagagolf.org National Amputee Golf Association—is a good source of information for amputees wishing to play golf.

www.ajga.org American Junior Golf Association—Contains latest information for serious golf-minded juniors on tournaments, tournament results, outstanding players, and the latest news in junior golf.

CHAPTER 13

Gymnastics and Tumbling

This chapter will enable you to

- Understand gymnastics as a competitive sport
- Identify the various events that comprise competition in gymnastics for men and women
- Appreciate the importance of acquiring safety attitudes and habits in gymnastics
- Understand how to introduce a tumbling or gymnastics unit in the classroom
- Identify basic body positions, grasps, and moves used in beginning tumbling and gymnastics

Nature and Purpose

Many people find it hard to think of gymnastics as a sport. It does not have the same tangible, competitive aspect that spectators see in other sporting events. We cannot yell "defense" or "get the ball," nor can we measure the performance of the gymnast with a stop watch or measuring tape. Gymnastics is the performance of a routine on a piece of apparatus. The routine is a combination of stunts and moves that have been practiced and improved over a period of time. The gymnast is actually competing against himself, trying to improve on the last performance. The sport of gymnastics involves individual effort; however, the gymnast's score is added to that of his teammates to obtain a team score.

One reason it is difficult for the uninformed spectator to grasp the concept of gymnastics is the lack of a scoreboard or clock to watch during a performance. In gymnastics it is not only *what* is performed but also *how* it is performed that is important.

Gymnastics, like figure skating and diving, is judged by qualified individuals. Although judging may sometimes seem too subjective, there are specific guidelines that judges must use in scoring. A judge is considering the difficulty, the execution, and the composition of the routine. These three aspects are fundamental in scoring, but other areas also enter into a score—among them, amplitude, creativity, elegance, risk, and so forth.

All parts of the body benefit in the sport of gymnastics. It promotes strength, agility, flexibility, coordination, kinesthetic sense, and balance. Furthermore, mastery of a stunt or routine develops more than the physical aspects; it also improves the participant's self-image.

History

Gymnastics may have originated 7,000 years ago in Egypt, where acrobats performed before the nobility. The name comes from the Greek *gymnos*. Gymnastics as a sport may have originated in Greece; records of Sparta indicate that the city's men and women placed great emphasis on gymnastic activities. The unique type of gymnastics practiced by the Greeks centered on the idea of working *with* apparatus, rather than *on* it.[1]

Modern gymnastics began in Germany. Johann Basedow (1723–1790) was the first teacher of organized gymnastics, which were included as a part of regular schoolwork. His idea that gymnastics make a significant contribution to the general education of the child was further promoted by Johann Guts Muths (1759–1839), who wrote the first book of gymnastics, *Gymnastics for Youth*. Muths is commonly referred to as the "Great-Grandfather of Gymnastics."

Frederick Jahn (1778–1852) presented a plan in Germany to promote national strength and unity through Turnverein organizations. His plan was partially the result of the Napoleonic victories over the Germans. The military defeat prompted Jahn to develop a *plan* for building national fitness and pride for the German people. He also invented such equipment as the horizontal bar, side horse, and parallel bars. His contributions brought him the title of "Father of Gymnastics."

The development of gymnastics in the United States received its principal impetus from European immigrants. The most prominent agency promoting this development was the Turnverein organization. In 1865, the American Turners established the Normal College of the American Gymnastics Union, with a mission to train future gymnastics teachers. In 1869 the YMCA added gyms and educated a generation of physical education instructors who taught gymnastics.

Gymnastics as a competitive sport dates only as far back as the 1850s. It was in Switzerland that the first gymnastics competition was held. The International Gymnastics Federation was formed in 1881. The first international competition was held in 1884 in Germany. Gymnastics was one of nine sports of the first modern Olympics in 1896. It was not until 1928 that the women competed.[2]

The first national men's championship in the United States took place in 1897 and was sponsored by the Amateur Athletic Union (AAU). In 1931, the first women's championship took place. By 1938 the National Collegiate Athletic Association (NCAA) held a men's championship, and the first for women took place in 1982. The U.S. Gymnastics Federation was formed in 1963 and is currently recognized as the national governing body by the International Olympic Committee.[3]

The Participant

As in other sports, size may determine the future and success of a gymnast. However, in gymnastics someone small in stature is more likely to succeed than the usual stereotyped 6'5", 220-pound athlete. This does not mean that a tall gymnast will be unsuccessful, but generally a gymnast is shorter than 5'10".

Today's gymnast must be above average in strength for height and weight. Flexibility is another needed physical attribute. Also required are a good kinesthetic sense (awareness of where one's body and body parts are in space) and a sense of balance. In addition, a well-developed sense of timing along with good coordination are important.

Cardiorespiratory endurance does not play as vital a role in gymnastics as in other sports; however, a gymnast must have muscle endurance. A gymnastic routine may last only from 1 to 2 minutes, but the abdominal or quadricep muscles may be contracted throughout that time. Also, a gymnast must have muscle power to be able to use the body and muscle groups with explosive force. Timing plays a part with the burst of energy, but unless the strength is there to call on, the gymnast may end up on the floor.

Along with the physical attributes, there are psychological aspects to be considered. The participant is individualistic, self-motivated, confident, and self-assured. The sport involves perseverance and a drive for perfection. The gymnast is subject to taking risks but not to the extent that safety is sacrificed.

Gymnastics is a team sport, but as a member of a team, a gymnast is also competing against teammates. As previously mentioned, a gymnast is actually competing against herself, always striving to perfect the routine.

The individual's score will not only determine her place among the competitors, but also will be added to the team scores to determine its final standing.

The Competition

The gymnastics meet is an event in which more than one thing is happening at once. In large meets, all pieces of equipment may be worked simultaneously. Judges will be at every station, and the gymnasts rotate to each station to perform.

On a smaller scale, for instance, a women's college meet, the balance beam and floor exercise may be judged at the same time by different sets of judges. Later, the uneven parallel bars and vaulting are judged. There are usually two judges per event at these meets. One set of judges may score the balance beam and uneven bars, while the other set will judge the floor exercise and vaulting.

At a meet, the judges watch and score the performance. The average of scores is flashed (open scoring) or a runner will take the score to the scorer's table (closed scoring) where it will be tallied. Individual gymnasts' scores are added together to form a team score. A gymnast may score differently on each piece of equipment. For instance, he may be first on the pommel horse and third in vaulting.

The "all-around" event comprises a total of the scores of a gymnast who competed in every event. The gymnast who wins the all-around is considered the top gymnast of the meet. A gymnast who does not compete all-around is called a specialist and may work only the floor exercise and vaulting. In most countries gymnasts are always all-around. Only in the United States do we continue to have gymnastic specialists, and many argue that this system enables more people to participate.

Each piece of equipment or event is unique, requiring a different strength from the gymnast. For example, a performer on the still rings would require more upper body strength than someone working floor exercise. However, the gymnast who specializes on rings may not be as flexible as the floor exercise specialist. The balance beam requires the athlete to have some dance background and a good sense of balance, while vaulting centers more on the gymnast's speed and explosive power. The all-around gymnast is able to compete in all areas at the meet.

The Rules and Judging

In 1968 the Fédération International Gymnastique (FIG), or International Gymnastic Federation, published a Code of Points, which has been the basis for the rules in gymnastics. It is not possible to state the universal rules. The National Federation of State High School Associations establishes the rules for high schools whereas U.S.A. Gymnastics sets the rules for clubs and college.

Unless otherwise agreed on by the teams involved, the men's gymnastic competition has six events and the women's has four events. The following is a list of events, but the order of competition varies according to each organization.

Men	Women
Floor exercise	Floor exercise
Horizontal bar	Balance beam
Parallel bars	Uneven parallel bars
Pommel horse	Vault
Rings	
Vault	

For both men and women, there is also the all-around event, which is the total of either the men's six events or the women's four events.

To qualify as a judge, one must be certified. Certification involves passing a written test, attending workshops, and paying a fee. A judge must be aware of the rules of the meet and the sport of gymnastics. He must watch the performance with complete concentration and be as objective as possible. Judges consider three major areas when scoring a gymnastic routine:

Difficulty (what has been performed). Most stunts have been given a difficulty value that the judges have learned.

Composition (the way the routine is put together). Each event has certain requirements that must be incorporated in a routine.

Execution (how the routine is performed). This area makes up the greatest part of a judge's score sheet.

Depending on the level of competition, the judge may have a point with which she may judge risk, elegance, amplitude, and so on. Usually deductions are made on the floor exercise area each time the gymnast goes out of bounds. Deductions are also made for falls, spotting, and not meeting time requirements on balance beam and floor exercise.

Another aspect of judging usually seen in private clubs is *compulsory routines*. This is a routine that is constructed for each piece of equipment at different skill levels. A gymnast learns the routine for her skill level and competes against other gymnasts at the same level, performing the same routine. As the gymnast becomes more skilled, she may move to harder "class levels" and learn more difficult compulsory routines. When judging this type of competition, the judge has also learned the routine and is aware of the specific deductions.

Routines used in the Olympics or in intercollegiate meets are those constructed by the gymnast, called *optional routines*. These routines contain certain difficulties, but each is as different in composition as each gymnast.

Suggested Learning Sequence

A. Stretching, sit-ups, and push-ups

B. Introduction—nature and purpose

C. Basic rules and safety conditions

D. Fundamental skills

1. Tumbling
   a. Forward roll
   b. Backward roll
   c. Tripod balance
   d. Headstand
   e. Prone headstand
   f. Kip (neckspring)
   g. Cartwheel
   h. Round-off
   i. Back walkover
   j. Front walkover
   k. Headstand and forward roll
   l. Tinsica
   m. Valdez
   n. Back handspring
   o. Elementary combination

2. Pommel horse
   a. Feint
   b. Front support and swing
   c. Single leg circle forward
   d. Simple travel
   e. Elementary combination

3. Vaulting
   a. Squat vault
   b. Straddle vault
   c. Front vault
   d. Rear vault
   e. Stoop vault
   f. Thief vault
   g. Handspring vault
   h. Elementary combination

4. Rings
   a. Inverted hang
   b. Nest hang
   c. Forward single leg cut
   d. Backward double leg cut dismount
   e. Elementary combination

5. High bar
   a. Backward hip circle
   b. Knee circle
   c. Kip
   d. Squat dismount from support
   e. Elementary combination

6. Parallel bars
   a. Forward hand walk
   b. Hip roll
   c. Corkscrew mount
   d. Flank dismount
   e. Elementary combination

7. Uneven parallel bars
   a. Back hip pullover
   b. Mill circle
   c. Pop-up
   d. Straddle sole circle
   e. Elementary combination

8. Balance beam
   a. Squat mount
   b. Chassé
   c. Back shoulder roll
   d. Arabesque
   e. Leap
   f. Forward roll
   g. Cartwheel dismount
   h. Elementary combinations

Skills and Techniques

Basic gymnastics terms refer to body positions used in many of the events. A simple understanding of the basic body positions helps performance. Following are the positions a gymnast uses when performing different stunts in a routine:

1. *Tuck*—The knees and hips are bent, and the head is in a chin-down position.
2. *Pike*—The legs are straight, but the torso is bent at the hips.
3. *Layout*—The entire body is straight.
4. *Puck*—This position is a combination of tuck and pike. There is only a slight bend in the knees.

Different grasps are used when working the pieces of equipment. Grasps are generally changed a number of times in a routine.

1. *Over grasp*—The palms of the hand are on top of the bar (Figure 13-1).
2. *Under grasp*—The palms of the hand are under the bar (Figure 13-2).
3. *Mixed grasp*—One hand is in an over grasp and the other hand is in an under grasp.

The following are specific terms for the way the body moves in gymnastics:

1. *Somersault*—A rotation around a horizontal axis. The somersault could be in the tuck, pike, or layout position.
2. *Twist*—A rotation around a vertical axis. Again, it can be done in different body positions or in combination with a somersault.
3. *Kip*—A skill involving the flexing of the body and then finishing in the extended position. It is done quickly and is used in all events.

Figure 13-1 Over grasp.

Figure 13-2 Under grasp.

4. *Extension*—The opposite of the kip. The gymnast extends first and then achieves the move because of flexion. A good example of the use of extension would be a back handspring.

To help the beginning gymnast master some elementary combinations, a learning series (Practice/Organizational Suggestions) is given at the end of each apparatus and tumbling section.

Men's Gymnastics

Although both women and men vault and work floor exercises, the way they perform in these areas is completely different. First we will describe the six men's gymnastics events and then the four women's events.

POMMEL HORSE

The pommel horse is 64 inches long and 14 inches wide. It stands 45½ inches tall, with two handles extending up from the leather body. The height of the handles is 4¾ inches, which makes the overall height 50 inches. The pommel horse is divided into three sections: The left end, as you face it, is called the neck; the middle is called the saddle; and the right end is called the croup. All three areas must be worked in a routine, without hesitations or stops, or deductions are made by the judges. The pommel horse requires a great deal of upper body strength and balance and is considered by many to be the most difficult men's event. This is one event in gymnastics in which a spotter seems only to be in the way. Because of the scissor and leg circles, there is a greater chance of the spotter being injured than the performer.

> ▶ Learning Hints

Feint. A feint is used on the pommel horse primarily to initiate movement. A feint helps the gymnast gain momentum to perform a stunt. In the move, the gymnast swings one or both legs in the direction opposite to which the stunt is performed. Many think of a feint as an extra swing or pumping action. In competition, a feint is considered unnecessary movement, and its use would result in points being deducted.

Front Support and Swing (Figure 13-3). The gymnast jumps to a front support with hands in an over grasp on the pommels. The arms are straight, and the body is straight, with the legs spread wide apart. The swing is initiated from the hips, going side to side. The entire body moves side to side so the swing encompasses the shoulder joint as well as the hips. The gymnast tries to attain as much height as possible on the swing. There is a slight shift of weight as the body swings from pommel to pommel.

Single Leg Circle Forward (Figure 13-4). This move can most easily be learned by placing the right hand on

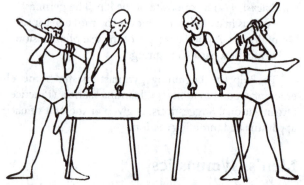

Figure 13-3 Front support and swing.

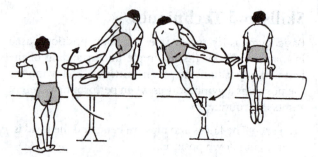

Figure 13-4 Single leg circle forward.

the pommel and the left hand on the neck of the horse. Jump to a straight arm support and immediately begin the move. Bring the right leg to the left between the horse and the left leg, twisting the hips slightly and leaning on the right arm. Bring the right leg over the neck of the horse and under the left hand, which regrasps the pommel (neck of the horse) after the left leg passes under it. Continue the right leg circling by passing under the right hand and over the croup. This sequence is considered one circle. It should be rhythmic and repeated, making continuous clockwise circles. Correct timing of this movement helps with the momentum and support, making it much like a pendulum swinging.

Simple Travel-Through.   Though this is called a simple travel, it is anything but simple and requires a lot of practice to master. Begin by placing the left hand on the neck and the right hand on the left pommel. Jump to a front support. Swing the left leg forward, cutting away the left hand and replacing it. Swing the right leg forward; now both legs are forward. The right hand is between the legs, with the left hand balancing on the neck. Swing the left leg back and shift the weight to the right hand and the pommel. The left hand regrasps the left pommel. Both hands are now on the pommel. Swing the right leg back and regrasp the right pommel again by shifting weight. This travel is repeated. Swing the left leg forward and under the left hand, which replaces itself on the pommel. Swing the right leg forward, and again the right hand is between the legs. Swing the left leg back and shift the body weight to regrasp the right pommel with the right hand. Swing the right leg back and shift the right hand off the pommel to the croup. At this point, the performer can dismount, having performed a simple travel. When the gymnast is moving from the neck to the pommels, it is considered an uphill travel; moving from the pommels to the croup is considered downhill.

▶ Practice/Organizational Suggestions

Jump to front support, single leg circle forward, simple travel, dismount.

VAULTING

The pommel horse may be used in this event. Remove the pommels and tape the holes to prevent any injury to the fingers. The horse is placed with the croup nearest the vaulter at a height of 53 inches. The male gymnast's hands must land only in the middle area of the horse to prevent a 0.5-point deduction in competition.

When working with a beginning gymnast, it is advisable to lower and turn the horse sideways. Women gymnasts vault with the horse in this position, and it is much less intimidating to a beginner. The horse can be lowered to a height comparable with the gymnast's skill level.

The other piece of equipment used in vaulting is the spring board or reuther board. It is placed in front of the horse, and the gymnast hits the board with both feet to initiate the takeoff over the horse. The preflight is the time between hitting the board and touching the horse. The vault is performed and then the after-flight begins until landing. All three phases of the vault are judged. The run to the board is not judged. Judging begins with the board takeoff. Vaults are illustrated in Figures 13-5 and 13-6 with the horse turned sideways to decrease difficulty for beginners.

▶ Learning Hints

Flank Vault (Figure 13-5).   The flank vault is so named because the side (flank) of the body passes over the horse. The flank vault is performed by swinging upward from the board and swinging the body and legs to the right over the horse. The right hand is cut away and the left hand leaves the horse just before landing. The gymnast lands facing forward. To spot this vault, the spotter is on the side opposite the passing legs. The spotter helps support and keep the arm of the vaulter stationary by grasping above the elbow. The spotter moves with the gymnast as he passes over the horse.

Front Vault.   As with the flank vault, the front vault is so named because the front of the body passes over the horse. On takeoff, the body makes a quarter turn to the left. The legs swing up to the right so that the front of the body passes over the horse. The right arm supports most of the weight, and the left arm pulls out to counteract the legs. The right arm leaves the horse just

Figure 13-5 Flank vault.

before landing. The gymnast lands with his left side to the horse. The spotter again stands away from the legs and helps support the shoulders.

Rear Vault (Figure 13-6).   The rear of the body passes over the horse. On takeoff from the board, the hands hit the horse and the body quarter turns to the right as the legs are swinging sideward. The rear of the body passes over the horse, while the legs are parallel to the floor. The right hand leaves the horse on the quarter turn, and the left hand releases as the body passes over. The right hand reaches for the horse on the landing for stability. The gymnast lands with the right side toward the horse. The spotter grasps the arm closest to him (away from the legs), moves with the gymnast, and releases the arm when the vault is being completed.

The Thief Vault.   The thief vault is different from most vaults because it doesn't use a 2-foot takeoff. The takeoff is from one foot; as the other foot swings upward, the takeoff foot joins it. Both legs pass over the horse, followed by the rear. The hands touch the horse as the body passes over in a sitting position. The hands give a downward and backward push. Two spotters are used for the thief vault: One spotter stands on the vaulter's side to support the gymnast's shoulder and arm in case it is needed; the other spotter stands on the board side of the vault to help prevent a fall backward in case the vaulter does not clear the horse.

Figure 13-6 Rear vault.

RINGS

In competition the rings are called still rings. The performer not only controls his body movement but also that of the rings. It is important in a learning situation to have plenty of mats below the ring station. Women lack the upper body strength to compete on the rings; however, the stunts listed here can be taught to both men and women because they do not rely on a great deal of upper body strength.

▶ Learning Hints

Inverted Hang (Figure 13-7).   Jump to grasp the rings and at the same time flex the arms and tuck the knees to the chest. Lean back with the upper body and stay in a squat position until the head is down, arms are straight, and the inverted position is attained. Extend the legs, using the ropes to stabilize the body if needed, then bring the legs together. The inverted hang can be done in a squat position or a straight position. To return to a starting position, simply flex at the hips and slowly bring the upper body forward. One or two spotters on each side of the performer grasp the performer's wrist, and with the other hand assist by lifting up and back if needed. Once the inverted hang has been attained, remain near the performer to steady him by placing a hand in front and back.

Nest Hang (Figure 13-8).   Jump to hang and bring the feet up to the rings in a tuck position. Hook the feet through the rings and then push the body through the arms by arching the back. Raise the head. Return by reversing the process. Spotting is done by grasping the performer's wrist and supporting his midsection in case the feet slip out of the rings.

Forward Single Leg Cut and Catch.   Attain an inverted squat hang and straighten legs. The position is an inverted pike with the legs parallel with the floor. Both legs are going to move quickly forward, with the left leg straddling out to cut away the left hand from the ring. Regrasp the ring with the left hand as the legs move down to a hang. The performer keeps the arms slightly

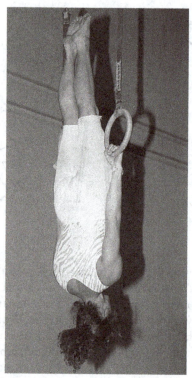

Figure 13-7 Inverted hang.

Figure 13-8 Nest hang.

flexed and bears the weight on the right arm before releasing the left. Keep the ring as still as possible on the release and look for the ring on the regrasp. The spotter supports the performer's upper back and hips after he has reached the pike position. The spotter can help by lifting, once the "cut" has been made, so the performer can regrasp the ring.

Backward Double Leg Cut Dismount. The rings must be high enough so that the performer cannot reach the floor in a hang. Momentum is the key to successfully completing this dismount. In a hanging position, arch and flex the body to gain some momentum and then raise the legs up and back over the head, bending at the hips. As the feet approach the arms, straddle the legs and look back with the head. Release the rings and raise the chest as the momentum carries you to a stand. For the beginner, two spotters are advisable. The spotter on the left side uses his right hand under the performer's shoulder and the left hand on his back. It is important to support the shoulder, especially if momentum is lost or the performer releases the rings too soon.

▶ Practice/Organizational Suggestions

Swing to an inverted hang, nest hang, forward single leg cut and catch, backward double leg cut dismount.

HIGH BAR (HORIZONTAL BAR)

The high bar is perhaps the most exciting piece of equipment to watch the male gymnast work. It has constant

motion and moves quickly so that the spectator is often left wondering, upon completion of a routine, what the gymnast actually did! The steel bar is 7 feet, 10½ inches wide and is 8 feet, 4⅜ inches off the floor. A routine flows with no stops or pauses. The stunts performed on the high bar are much like the stunts performed on the women's uneven bars. If there is no high bar available, the top bar of the unevens can be used to learn beginning moves. Spotting of the performer on the high bar is virtually impossible without a spotting belt attached to the ceiling with pulleys. Spotting without a belt means that the spotter is in a position to catch the performer when difficulty arises.

Chalk (magnesium carbonate) is used when working the high bar to prevent the performer from slipping when hands are sweaty.

▶ Learning Hints

The following movements can be spotted by lowering the bar. These are beginning moves with which the student can attain success.

Backward Hip Circle (Figure 13-9). Jump to a straight arm support, hands in an over grasp. Cast the legs back by flexing at the hips, lifting the heels backward (legs straight and toes pointed) toward the ceiling. As the body comes back to the bar, the head and upper body drop back, and the momentum helps the hips circle around the bar. Keep the hips next to the bar. The spotter or spotters are next to the performer. If standing on the performer's right side, the spotter helps secure the performer's arm with his left hand and uses his right hand to help guide and lift the performer's hips as he circles the bar.

Figure 13-9 Backward hip circle.

Knee Circle. Jump to a front support and then lift the right leg over the bar and between the hands. Sit on the right leg while changing hands to an under grasp. Circle the bar with the knee by moving in a forward motion, first raising the hips so the bar is placed in the bend of the knee. Once in position, lift the head and chest to begin the forward motion. Circle the bar and return to the sitting position on the right thigh. The arms cannot collapse in the circling motion, and the head and chest remain up. The spotting for this act requires almost as much technique as the stunt itself. The spotter or spotters stand beside the performer. If the spotter is on the performer's right side, he uses his right hand to reach under and around the bar to grasp the performer's wrist. The grasp used is inverted, and the knuckles will be facing the spotter. The left hand helps support and lift the performer on the back as he circles the bar. The

performer may want to chalk the back of the knee to prevent chafing.

Kip (Figure 13-10). There are many variations of a kip (glide kip, drop kip, reverse kip, etc.). The kip can be used as a mount, a stunt within a routine, or a connecting move between stunts. A kip requires strength, but the key is timing. It usually takes a lot of practice to master. Stand facing the bar with hands in an over grasp. Jump, flexing the hips, and bring the ankles forward. As the body swings slightly forward, prepare to whip the legs out and downward. The reaction to the whip with the legs is an upward motion; bear down with the arms and end in a front support. The spotter is on the performer's side and has a sense of timing to assist with the kip. The spotter on the right side of the performer places his left hand on the performer's back

Figure 13-10 Kip.

and the right hand on his calves. The spotter moves with the performer, helping lift the legs, and after whip, lift lower back.

Squat Dismount from Support.   From a straight arm support, cast the legs back and tuck the knees to the chest. At the same time, move the feet between the arms and over the bar. Land facing forward in a standing position. Once the momentum is established from the cast, the body continues forward with the head up. The spotters are on either side of the performer in front of the bar he is going to squat over. The spotter's one hand grasps the performer's wrist and her other hand grasps his upper arm. Spotters need to move with the performer on the dismount.

▶ **Practice/Organizational Suggestions**

Jump to front support, backward hip circle, squat dismount from support.

PARALLEL BARS

Only men compete on the parallel bars, but there is no reason why women cannot successfully learn to work the parallel bars, too. The parallel bars are wooden bars measuring 11 feet, 6 inches in length, and they are adjustable in height from 5 feet, 7 inches to 5 feet, 9 inches and in width from 18 to 20 inches. Many beginners lower the bars and adjust the width according to the length of their forearm and hand.

▶ **Learning Hints**

Forward Hand Walk.   Jump to a straight arm support between the bars and move one hand at a time down the bars in a walking motion. Keep the head up and do not let the shoulders depress or sag. Take short hand steps and transfer the weight to the opposite arm on each movement. The spotter grasps the performer's thigh under the bar to support or lift if the performer becomes fatigued.

Hip Roll.   Sit in a straddle seat position in the middle of the bars and place both hands in an over grasp on the right bar. The right hand is the hand closest to the right leg. Lower the upper body and bring the head and shoulders under the right bar. At the same time lift the right leg, maintaining the straddle position, and roll across the hips on the left bar. Still in the straddle position, roll across the right thigh as the left leg crosses over to the right bar. The upper body lifts as the motion ends in a straddle seat, facing the opposite direction from which he started. The spotting for this is done from underneath the bars at the shoulders to support the performer, and another spotter may be helpful in guiding the leg placement.

Corkscrew Mount (Figure 13-11).   This is a fun mount to teach beginners. The name matches the

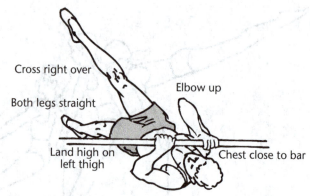

Figure 13-11   Corkscrew mount.

movement of the body, and the success rate is great. Stand facing the middle of one side of the bars. Grasp the near bar with the right hand in an under grasp and the left hand in an over grasp. Jump, lifting the legs toward the far bar, landing on the back of the left thigh. Begin turning over the bar with the right leg extended and moving downward toward the bar where the hands are grasped. As the legs are twisting, the chest and head stay near and under the grasped bar. When the legs are straddling the bars, the upper body rotates, and the left hand releases to grasp the far bar. Push up with both hands to finish in a straddle seat. Spotting, like the hip roll, is done from under the bar, but this time the spotter supports the performer's hips. Again, it may be helpful as a teaching aid to have another spotter helping to guide the performer's legs.

Flank Dismount.   Jump to a straight arm support. The body is between the bars. Begin swinging. When the legs are forward, lean on the left arm and release the right hand. Pass the body over the bar, making a quarter turn and pushing off with the left hand to land with the back toward the bar. The spotter stands to the outside and slightly behind the performer. The spotter grasps the performer's left arm at the wrist with his left hand and above the elbow with his right. As the performer dismounts, the spotter helps guide him over the bar.

▶ **Practice/Organizational Suggestions**

Corkscrew mount, hip roll, flank dismount.

FLOOR EXERCISE

The floor exercise mat is 42 feet by 42 feet and at least 1-inch thick. The floor exercise event is the longest of the men's events, lasting 1 minute and 30 seconds. Along with tumbling, the performer displays strength, agility, and balance. The routine moves smoothly and covers all the corners and area of the mat. (Tumbling dominates the floor exercise routine and will be covered later in this chapter.)

Women's Gymnastics

Women's competitive gymnastics consists of four events. Two events are timed (balance beam and floor exercise) and must be completed in the allotted time to avoid score deduction. Both balance beam and floor exercise require dance and tumbling. The uneven parallel bars are similar to the men's horizontal bar. The use of two bars reduces the need for upper body strength on the part of the woman gymnast. The uneven bars require circling moves, changes of direction, and changes in hand grips. Lastly, the vault is performed with the vault positioned sideways. The run and takeoff are like the men's vault. The women's performance centers on dance and the ability to perform difficult moves with ease. Unlike the men's gymnastic performance, a woman gymnast does not display strength throughout her routines.

UNEVEN PARALLEL BARS

This event is done with two parallel bars at different heights. The top bar is 7 feet, 6½ inches above the floor, and the lower bar is 4 feet, 11 inches high. The width between the bars can be adjusted out to 2 feet, 9⅞ inches. Routines are constructed to flow smoothly without stops or pauses.

▶ Learning Hints

Back Hip Pullover (Figure 13-12).   Stand between the bars with the hands shoulder-width apart in an over grasp. Keeping the shoulders and chest close to the bar, kick one leg forward, up and back over the bar. As the first leg travels up, the second leg joins it, and the head drops back. Pull the hips back over the bar and end in a straight arm support. The spotter stands on the side of the bar opposite to the performer. The spotter on the performer's right places her left hand on the performer's lower back and helps lift the legs with the right hand.

Mill Circle (Figure 13-13).   The mill circle is much like the knee circle performed on the horizontal bar. The difference is that the knee is not bent during the stunt. Sit astride the bar with both legs straight, the bar resting on the front of the back thigh and hands in an under grasp. Keeping the bar in place on the back thigh, lift hips up and thrust the chest forward with the head up. Remaining in this position, circle the bar and finish in the starting position. The spotter stands on the same side of the bar as the back leg of the performer. If the spotter is on the performer's left, she uses her left hand to reach under the bar and grasp the performer's wrist in a reverse grip. As the performer circles the bar, the spotter helps lift the hips with the right hand.

Pop Up.   Pop up is an elementary transition from the low bar to the high bar. Jump to a long hang on the high bar, hands in an over grasp. Place the left foot on the low bar, with the knee bent. The right leg is straight, toe pointed on top of the low bar. The move is much like a back hip pullover. As the left foot pushes off the lower bar, the head drops back and the arms pull the hips to the high bar. The right leg joins the left as they circle the high bar, ending in a straight arm support on the high bar. Keep the hips close to the high bar and attempt to lift them up and over the bar. The spotter stands on either side of the performer. The spotter helps lift the

Figure 13-12   Back hip pullover.

Figure 13-13 Mill circle.

hips up and back over the bar. On completion, the spotter grasps the calves of the performer to help steady the straight arm support.

Straddle Sole Circle Underswing Dismount (Figure 13-14). Stand between the bars facing out. Grasp the bar in an over grip and jump up, placing

the soles of the feet on the bar outside of the hands. The arms and legs remain straight as the body swings downward. The arms pull against the bar to keep the feet on while circling under the bar. As the height of the swing is reached, the feet release from the bar and extend outward to land. The body follows in an arched position. The spotter is located at the outside of the low bar. Because of the straddle position, the spotter reaches in for the upper body after the feet have passed. The spotter helps lift the upper body on the landing and follows the completed move.

▶ **Practice/Organizational Suggestions**

Back hip pullover, mill circle, straddle sole circle underswing dismount.

BALANCE BEAM

The balance beam is 3⅞ inches wide, 196 inches long, and 47¼ inches above the ground. The gymnast is required to work from end to end on the beam, using tumbling, dance, and poses. The event is timed and the routine must be completed in 1 minute and 30 seconds to avoid penalty. A deduction is also made for each fall, and the gymnast is allowed only 10 seconds to remount the beam after a fall.

▶ **Learning Hints**

Lower the beam when teaching beginning students, or use lines on the floor.

Squat Mount. Place the spring board at a right angle to the beam. Stand on the board with the hands

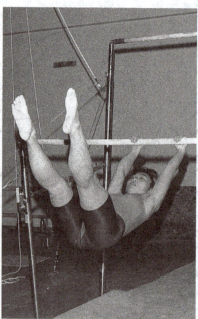

A   B   C

Figure 13-14 Straddle sole circle underswing dismount.

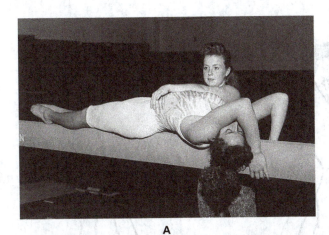

A

B

C

Figure 13-15 Back shoulder roll.

shoulder-width apart on the beam. Jump from the board, pressing down on the beam. At the same time, raise the hips and tuck the knees to the chest, placing the feet on the beam. The spotter stands on the opposite side of the beam and grasps the performer's upper arms to prevent her from falling forward.

Back Shoulder Roll (Figure 13-15).   Lie back on the beam and drop the head to one side. Bring the legs back over the head to the beam, bending one knee to place on the beam. The hands move to the top of the beam and both hands push up. End in a knee scale. The spotter is on the opposite side of the performer's head. Facing the direction of the roll, the spotter grasps the performer's hips and guides them until the knee scale is attained.

Forward Roll.   Standing on the beam, bend at the waist and extend the arms to grasp the beam. Lower the upper body to the beam by bending the arms. Tuck the head by pressing the chin to the chest. Raise the hips, roll to the back of the neck, and continue forward. Allow one leg to bend, and place the foot on the beam as the other leg extends forward. Complete the roll by coming to a stand. The spotter stands to one side of the beam and guides the performer's hips. Follow the performer until she is balanced.

Leap.   The leap is the transfer of weight from one foot to the other with neither foot touching the beam during the transfer. A leap is actually an isolated running step. The beginner may be hesitant to leave the beam for much height. Arms are out to the side at shoulder level for balance. Try to spot the end of the beam with the eyes and not look directly down. Spotters are on either side of the beam with the near arm extended toward the performer. The performer can then use the spotter's arms for balance when needed.

Chassé (Figure 13-16).   The right leg is in front of the left and remains in front throughout. Step forward with the right leg and bring the left leg from behind to take its place. The weight shifts from the right to the left as the right leg is replaced with the left. Continue again, stepping forward with the right, and repeat. Spotter again walks along the side of the beam as the performer travels down the beam.

Arabesque (Figure 13-17).   This stunt is generally considered a momentary balance or pose. Step forward on one leg and lift the other leg to the rear as high as possible. Chest and head are raised by arching the back. Extend the arms to the side. The arms may be changed to different positions; be creative. Use spotters on either side of the beam if needed.

Cartwheel Dismount.   In order to do a cartwheel dismount, the performer should first be able to do a good cartwheel on the floor. Stand approximately one step back from the end of the beam. Execute a cartwheel, placing the hands at the end of the beam. Legs travel overhead and land together, much like a round-off (see "Tumbling"). The performer ends facing the beam for better balance. Keep arms straight, and push off to land. The spotter may want to stand on a bench or a stable chair to approximate the performer's height. Stand on the side of the beam at the performer's back when the cartwheel is performed. If the performer is placing her right hand down first, the spotter will cross her arms with the right arm on top and grasp the performer's waist. The spotter moves with the performer, and as the

Figure 13-16 Chassé.

Figure 13-17 Arabesque.

cartwheel is done, the spotter's arms uncross and end with the left over right. Reverse when spotting is on the other side.

▶ Practice/Organizational Suggestions

Squat mount, leap, forward roll, cartwheel dismount.

VAULTING

When teaching a beginner to vault, begin with the run and hurdle step. A teacher may want to first use the takeoff board without the horse. The student can run, use the two-foot takeoff, and land on a layer of mats. The hurdle step precedes the two-foot takeoff. The hurdle is a step onto one foot in front of the board and a 2-foot jump onto the board. The takeoff from the board is explosive. With practice, the run and takeoff become second nature, and the gymnast concentrates on the actual vault.

For women's vaulting, turn the horse sideways, remove the pommels, tape the holes to prevent injury, and adjust the height to 45 inches.

▶ Learning Hints

Squat Vault (Figure 13-18). The lead-up to a squat vault is a squat mount onto the horse. After leaving the spring board, tuck the knees to the chest and place the hands on the horse. Land in a squat position on top of the horse. As soon as the student masters the squat mount, she can try the vault. The performer will again draw the knees to the chest, but as the hands land on the horse, she pushes downward and keeps the head and chest up. Next she passes over the horse in the squat position to land facing forward. The spotter is on the far side of the horse, ready to grasp the performer above the elbows if she should need assistance.

The Straddle Vault. The lead-up to the straddle vault is the straddle mount. After hitting the spring board, straddle (spread the legs) and land in a straddle position

Figure 13-18   Squat vault.

Figure 13-19   Stoop vault.

on top of the horse. The head is up, with the feet and hands in contact with the horse. The spotter is in front of the performer on the opposite side of the horse, grasping the upper arms, to prevent the performer from falling forward. The vault is done the same way as the mount, only the hands push downward and the performer clears the horse. The head remains up, and the hips travel in a forward motion over the horse. The spotter is in front of the performer, ready to grasp the upper arms if the performer should catch a toe while passing over the horse. If the performer clears the horse, the spotter moves quickly out of the way.

Stoop Vault (Figure 13-19).   This vault is much like the squat vault except the legs are kept straight. The hips are raised high enough to clear the feet between the hands. The head is up, and again the performer is pushing down against the horse with the hands. As the hips travel forward, the chest lifts upward to prepare for the landing. The spotter stays to the side to assist by grasping the performer's upper arm.

Handspring (Figure 13-20).   The handspring is a more difficult vault to master than the previous vaults because the performer needs a great deal of momentum to accomplish it properly. The performer must have a good approach and takeoff. The hips bend slightly on the takeoff as the hips and legs pass overhead. The arms remain straight, and the head is aligned between the arms. There is a push on the horse that actually originates from the shoulders to the hands. The contact with the horse is short and explosive. The after-flight is approximately the same distance as the preflight. The spotter stands on the far side of the horse. Beginners should have spotters on each side ready to grasp the performer's shoulder and upper arm to prevent the arms from folding. Sometimes a spotter can also stand between the spring board and horse, lifting the vaulter's hips to attain the needed height.

FLOOR EXERCISE

Floor exercise for women is similar to the men's event in that the same equipment is used and the routine lasts no more than 1½ minutes. However, requirements for the women's floor exercise are considerably different. The women's routine is choreographed to music, which must be instrumental only. Women must show dance skills, tumbling, and acrobatic skills, and they must work on the floor level sometime in the routine. The difficulties required in the composition of the routine may be derived from a gymnast's dance skills as well as from her tumbling. Beginning tumbling skills in floor exercise will be covered in the tumbling section.

TUMBLING

Tumbling does not require the use of apparatus. Mats of different thicknesses are used as the tumbling stunts become more difficult or in the learning process of a certain skill. Most tumbling stunts require some courage and determination to accomplish; thus a student can gain self-confidence by mastering these new skills. Tumbling also increases balance, agility, coordination, and flexibility. Tumbling units can incorporate partner stunts, pyramids, and tumbling routines for variation.

The squad method of teaching a tumbling unit has been highly successful. Six to eight students on each mat is the preferred number. The mats are placed in a three-sided square or horseshoe formation, with the demonstration mat at the open side. The teacher can demonstrate or have a student demonstrate a skill and then let the class practice the skill. Always explain and show spotting techniques.

Teachers can be creative in their methods of teaching tumbling. The important thing to remember is that

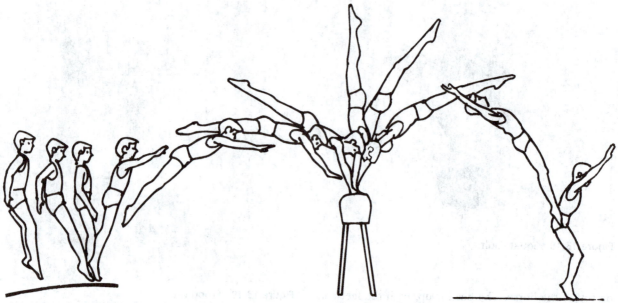

Figure 13-20 Handspring.

each student should feel successful. The stunts introduced must be challenging and yet not too difficult, so the majority of students can master them by the end of the unit.

▶ Learning Hints

Forward Roll (Figure 13-21). The forward roll is one of the basic skills in tumbling. Squat and place the hands, shoulder-width apart, on the mat. Next, tuck the chin to the chest, bend the arms and raise the hips. The back of the head touches the mat as the body continues to roll until the feet touch the floor. Lift the arms to extend into a stand. The hands *do not* touch the mat again. Some students find it helpful to grasp the shins and tuck more tightly on the roll. The spotter assists by placing one hand on the head (not the neck) and the other on the upper legs. The hand on the head keeps the chin tucked, and the hand on the upper legs assists with the roll.

Backward Roll. The backward roll is another basic skill and is sometimes more difficult to master than the forward roll. Start in a squat position. The hands begin on the mat, but as the backward roll starts, they move upward to the shoulders, fingers pointing back and palms up. It is essential that the chin be tucked. The hands reach back and are placed on the mat beside the head, under the shoulders. As the hips come over the head, the hands push off the floor. Remain tucked, never allowing the knees to touch the mat, and land on the feet. The spotter may have a more difficult time helping the student complete the backward roll. If possible, try to lift the hips as the roll begins. Many students will roll backward crooked. This usually indicates they are not pushing evenly with both hands at the same time.

Tripod Balance (Figure 13-22). Place the hands, shoulder-width apart, on the mat. The head is placed on the mat to make the third point of a triangle with equal sides. The balance is done on the roof of the forehead, not the crown of the head. Raise the hips and place the knees, one at a time, on the elbows. Balance. The spotter is behind the student to steady her at the hips.

Headstand. The headstand can be done out of the tripod balance. Straighten both legs slowly, with toes pointed. Once the balance is achieved, return to the tripod slowly. The spotter stands behind the student, making sure that the balance is maintained by steadying the legs. This stunt is readily adaptable to a uniform count so that everyone can try it at once, for example,

1. Hands down
2. Head down
3. Legs up (tripod forward)
4. Headstand
5. Legs down
6. Head up

Make sure that students are far enough apart that a loss of balance will not cause an injury.

Prone Headstand. Begin in a prone position, lying flat on the mat with the hands placed under the shoulders, fingers pointing forward. Pressing down with the hands, lift and bend at the hips. Keep the legs straight and raise the hips as if a string attached to the ceiling is pulling them up. Drag the feet along the mat. At the same time, place the forehead on the mat. Once the hips are overhead, raise the legs into a headstand. Once balance has been achieved, reverse the procedure, or roll

Figure 13-21 Forward roll.

Figure 13-22 Tripod balance.

out of the headstand by tucking the chin to the chest and rolling. The spotter stands behind the student and helps maintain balance. If the student has trouble lifting the legs off the floor, pull the hips slightly toward the spotter. Continue to spot at the hips when the student returns to the starting position.

Kip (Neck Spring) (Figure 13-23).   Lying on the back, flex at the hips and bring the legs straight back so the

knees are over the face. The hands are beside the head under the shoulders (same position as a backward roll). The hips begin to move slightly forward toward the floor and just at the off-balance moment, the legs snap upward and backward. Simultaneously, the hands push against the floor, and the feet come under the body to land on the mat. The hips must be kept high, and the legs remain straight on the whip. The spotter must have a feel for the timing of this stunt to help the student effectively. The spotter kneels on the student's left side and places the left hand on the small of the back and the right hand on the upper arm. The spotter helps the student feel the slight movement forward before the whip by lifting at the small of the back on the whip and continuing to lift with the right hand as the student stands.

Cartwheel.   The cartwheel (Figure 13-24A) is a basic move in tumbling. The student can visualize the spokes of a wheel when performing this move. The cartwheel is performed to either side (usually there is a preference). Stand with the right side to the mat. The legs are spread slightly more than shoulder-width apart, and arms are overhead. Bend sideways, placing the right hand (straight

Figure 13-23   Kip (neck spring).

A

arm) on the mat, and at the same time raise the left leg up, followed by the right, as the left hand goes down onto the mat. The left foot follows, and then the right foot arrives. As the feet are landing, the hands are coming off the mat. As with a wheel, the spokes (hands and feet) move in a straight line and hit the floor in an even count. The cartwheel can be modified by beginning facing the mat and bending forward instead of sideward. The hand and foot placement are the same. The spotter (Figure 13-24B) always stands to the student's back to avoid being struck by her legs. If the student is going to her left, the spotter grasps the student's hips with the left arm crossed over the right. The spotter moves with the student, lifting at the hips as needed. Hand placement is reversed if performed to the right.

Round-off.   The round-off should be attempted after the cartwheel has been mastered. The round-off is done from a short run. Perform as if doing a cartwheel, and as the legs are overhead, snap together and quarter-turn the trunk. The legs snap down together, and the hands push off the floor together (mule kick). End facing the direction from which the stunt was started. The hands and feet are not in contact with the floor at the same time. It is difficult to spot a round-off because the student must learn to snap down and push off. If the cartwheel has been sufficiently mastered, there is little chance of injury. Verbal cues will be the greatest aid to the student in learning a round-off.

Back Walkover (Figure 13-25).   This stunt requires back flexibility. Stand with hands stretched up overhead,

B

Figure 13-24   (A) Cartwheel. (B) Spotting the cartwheel.

abdomen pulled in, and the torso stretched. One foot is pointed in front of the body, and all the weight is on the back foot. Stretch up and look back, keeping the arms on either side of the head. As the head and shoulders move

Figure 13-25 Back walkover.

back and down toward the floor, the support leg may bend slightly, the pointed toe lifts off the floor and travels back. The legs remain split and move over the inverted torso to the floor. As the first foot lands, the hands push off the floor. The spotters may kneel or stand. If there is only one spotter, the spotter stands on the side of the forward leg, placing the closest hand on the student's back and the other hand on the back of the lead leg as it goes over.

Front Walkover. The front walkover requires even more flexibility than the back walkover and therefore is considered by many to be more difficult. Essentially, it is the reverse of the back walkover. Stand with the hands overhead and one foot pointed forward. Place the hands on the mat, shoulder-width apart. The weight transfers to the front foot as the back leg raises behind and upward. The leg continues to travel overhead, and the legs are in a split position. The back leg becomes the lead leg, or the leg that will contact the floor first. As the foot lands, the hands push off the floor. There is no period of flight. The leg that is still moving through the air drives downward and forward, with the upper body trailing behind. The spotter supports the student throughout the walkover. It may be easiest for the spotter to kneel beside the student, supporting the shoulders with one hand and the small of the back with the other.

Handstand to Forward Roll. To achieve a handstand, place the hands shoulder-width apart on the mat and kick one leg back and up overhead. The other leg quickly raises upward to join the first. The head remains

aligned with the rest of the body, ears next to the arms. A tight, straight body makes maintaining a balance easier. After the balance is maintained, shift the shoulders to the back to create a loss of balance. At the same time, tuck the chin to the chest and slowly bend the arms, lowering the upper body toward the floor. As the back of the head contacts the floor, begin the roll by tucking the legs to the chest. Finish the roll to a stand. The spotter stands to the side of the student, moving slightly to the back as she kicks to the handstand. Spotting at the legs helps the student attain balance. When the roll begins, the spotter makes sure the student is leaning off balance in the direction of the roll before the head begins to lower toward the ground. The spotter helps control the momentum of the roll by controlling the legs of the student.

Tinsica. The tinsica is a cross between a cartwheel and a front walkover. It is advisable to be able to do both before trying the tinsica. Begin with the hands overhead and the preferred foot forward. Place the same hand down on the mat in front of the foot that is forward. As the back leg rises, the other hand is placed ahead of the hand on the mat. The back leg continues overhead, followed by the forward foot, which has pushed off. The legs remain spread apart and walk out of the stunt, one leg landing at a time. Visualize doing a front walkover on a balance beam with the hands and feet landing in a cartwheel-type rhythm. The hands and feet arrive at four different times, moving forward in a straight line. The spotter kneels and supports the student's back and upper body at the shoulder, moving and lifting with the student as the tinsica is being attempted.

Valdez (Figure 13-26). Sitting on the floor, extend the left leg and bend the right knee, placing the right foot close to the buttocks. The right hand is placed on the floor behind the buttocks, with the fingertips pointing away from the body. With a vigorous push off the right

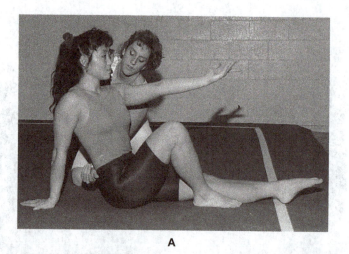

A

B

C

D

Figure 13-26 Valdez.

foot, swing the left arm back from the shoulder (backward and upward) and place the left hand on the floor. The legs remain split as they proceed overhead, finishing as if doing a back walkover. The right hand, which is on the floor, executes a half-turn during the inverted period. This usually happens naturally as the valdez is being performed. The spotter kneels beside the student on the side of the extended leg and places the hand nearest the student's back on the lower back and the other hand on the extended leg's upper thigh. As the push-up and back is made by the student, the spotter lifts and guides the leg back and over.

Back Handspring (Figure 13-27).   This tumbling stunt should be taught with two good spotters. Stand with the feet shoulder-width apart and the arms extended in front, shoulder level. Lower backward as if to sit in a chair. When balance is lost, push against the floor with the legs and vigorously swing the arms up and back, stopping beside the head. The head looks back when the arms begin the move

upward; however, it is best not to overemphasize this aspect to prevent the student from traveling straight back. The motion is explosive, and the body is extended as the hips thrust upward. The back arches slightly as the hands reach for the mat. When the hands hit the mat, they push off and the legs snap down after having passed through the overhead inverted position. The spotters stand on either side of the student. The spotter on the student's right places her left hand on the student's lower back and right hand on the back of the upper thigh. The spotter on the student's left reverses the hand placement. The spotters are careful not to lift the student through the handspring but rather to provide support. To master the back handspring, the student must "feel" the sense of timing that is needed. The spotters can help by providing the security needed in attempting a backward tumbling move.

▶ Practice/Organizational Suggestions

Prone headstand, tripod, forward roll, cartwheel, handstand, forward roll, round-off.

Figure 13-27   Back handspring.

Safety Considerations

The nature of tumbling and gymnastics makes safety a major concern of those supervising the program. It is recommended that the participant warm up before beginning any work on the equipment. Warming up helps prevent muscle pulls and strains and makes an individual aware of his body's limitations. Stunts often require assistance (spotting), which aids in safety. The facility, equipment, and area organization can also assist in providing a safe environment.

SPOTTING

The purpose of spotting is to aid the gymnast in mastering a stunt safely. This aid can be manual or via the use of a spotting belt.

A participant should not attempt a new stunt without having performed the progressions and lead-ups and without the confidence and ability required to succeed. The spotter should be used only as assistant or teaching aid, not as a guarantee of protection from injury.

Manual manipulation—the use of hands or body to assist the performer—is a valuable learning tool for students. A good spotter can apply just the right amount of support and protection. Of course, it helps if the spotter has also tried the stunts, but that is not always necessary. A person can be an excellent spotter without ever having trained as a gymnast.

The Spotting Belt.   The "hands-on" method of spotting seems preferable to the spotting belt, but for hazardous stunts, the belt is a necessary safeguard. The belt fastens around the performer and has ropes on either side that are attached with hooks that swivel. The spotters stand on either side of the performer and hold the ropes. Depending on the stunt, the spotters move and lift with the ropes to assist or secure the performer. With the belt, it is much harder to attain the feel of the stunt, and the timing may not be as precise, but safety is always assured.

There is also an overhead spotting belt, which is attached to the ceiling through pulleys. Only one individual assists the gymnast. The overhead belt can be helpful on the balance beam, high bar, and floor exercise (if it can travel). The spotter *must* have experience with

this type of spotting method because it requires a good sense of timing for both the gymnast and the spotter.

FACILITY AND EQUIPMENT

Proper facility and equipment is important in providing a safe environment. Most schools use the gymnasium, which has plenty of space and overhead clearance. Equipment cannot be too close to existing walls or other pieces of equipment. For example, there must be ample distance for the run and preflight in vaulting, as well as for the after-flight of the vault. The high bar and uneven parallel bars need overhead clearance. A low ceiling limits the use of these pieces of equipment.

Gymnastic equipment is expensive and must be kept in good repair, not only for safety reasons, but to prolong its life. Individuals need to be instructed in how to adjust settings and properly move the equipment. It is a good idea to show those involved how each piece is set up and to have safety checks done on each piece of equipment before performing.

Those responsible must continually emphasize that the gymnasium and equipment may not be used without proper supervision. No one should be allowed on the equipment at any time without prior permission from the instructor, coach, or supervisor.

ORGANIZATION

To provide a safe, controllable learning environment the teacher can organize the class into squads. By dividing a class into groups and then instructing by either rotation or at each station, the teacher can make sure a safe teaching progression of skills is used.

Teach the lead-ups and fundamentals of each skill before progressing. Teaching basics first not only makes it easier for participants to learn and master the more difficult skills but also makes their execution safer. Injuries mainly result from the individual's lack of understanding the skill he is executing. Mind and body cannot work together unless they both have a basic understanding of the skill. This understanding can be accomplished only through lead-up and mastery of elementary progressions. The responsibility ultimately lies with the teacher's knowledge of these progressions. The "Further References" section provides resources for enhancing one's knowledge of proper progressions for the stunts and apparatus.

Skill Assessment

There are many ways of evaluating a gymnastics or tumbling unit. The instructor can compose a short routine that all students must perform, or the students can compose their own routines, which must include certain identified stunts. The instructor can evaluate certain predetermined skills at the end of the unit or may find it beneficial to have a testing day every three or four days following practice of a given skill. On testing day, a student may choose to be evaluated on mastered skills. The more skills mastered by the end of the unit, the better the evaluation.

Gymnastics and tumbling are classified as aesthetic physical activities. Evaluating and judging the performance is based on *how* it is performed. Checklists requiring a Yes or No response identifying the mechanics necessary for quality skill attainment are often used. A thorough verbal description or picture of a stunt provide the step-by-step sequence for a checklist. The following is a sample evaluation for using the forward roll using skill information from the text as a reference.

FORWARD ROLL CHECKLIST

Directions: The student performs a forward roll three separate times. View each roll from a different perspective to better see the performance, then circle either Yes or No to indicate whether the student consistently does or does not perform each step of the skill.

Preparation:

Yes	No	**1.**	Full squat position in a tuck
Yes	No	**2.**	Hands on the mat, shoulder-width apart, and directly below the head
Yes	No	**3.**	Knees together between the arms
Yes	No	**4.**	Chin tucked to the chest
Yes	No	**5.**	Weight equally on toes and hands

Execution:

Yes	No	**1.**	Arms bent and hips rocked forward
Yes	No	**2.**	Pushed off with the toes
Yes	No	**3.**	The back of the head touched the mat first
Yes	No	**4.**	Pushed with the hands
Yes	No	**5.**	Rolled in tucked position until the feet contacted the mat

Follow-Through:

Yes	No	**1.**	Extended the arms straight in front of the body parallel to the floor
Yes	No	**2.**	Weight was forward with head above the knees
Yes	No	**3.**	Extended and straightened the knees
Yes	No	**4.**	Both feet planted flat on the floor and stable
Yes	No	**5.**	Stood straight up with arms fully extended above the head and shoulders

More Yes than No answers quantifies the quality of the performance. Each teacher then sets their own level of expectations (norms).

Modifications for Special Populations

ORTHOPEDICALLY IMPAIRED

1. Create obstacle courses using gym mats draped over classroom chairs, balance beams, and similar apparatus, and allow wheelchair users to travel the course out of their wheelchairs. Emphasis should be placed on traveling over, under, around, and through the course. (Consult with the adapted physical educator or physical therapist before removing the student from the wheelchair.)

2. Students using canes or crutches should be able to participate in upper body activities (e.g., parallel bars).

COGNITIVELY IMPAIRED

1. Contact the Special Olympics for their gymnastics units.

2. Contact Adventures in Movement for the Handicapped, Inc., in Dayton, Ohio. (See Paciorek and Jones, 2000, listed in Further References.)

3. Make sure all students with Down syndrome are screened for atlantoaxial syndrome. Screening can be completed with an X-ray study of the C_1/C_2 vertebrae.

SENSORY IMPAIRED

1. Use peer teachers for blind students.

2. Contact the United States Association of Blind Athletes in Muskogee, Oklahoma. (See Paciorek and Jones, 2000.)

Terminology

amplitude The extent or degree to which a skill or routine is performed.

balance (inverted) The body weight is supported by the hands, upper arms, head, or forearms in an inverted position, with the shoulders above the point of support.

dismount A stunt that moves the performer from the apparatus to a stand on the floor. Also the last moves of a floor exercise routine.

grasp The placement of hands on a piece of apparatus with the thumb and fingers wrapped around.

hang A position on a piece of apparatus in which the weight is borne by the hands, knees, and so on, with the shoulders below the base of support.

kinesthetic sense The self-awareness of one's body parts.

layout The entire body is straight.

mixed grasp A grasp in which one hand is in an over grasp position and one hand is in an under grasp position.

mount A stunt that moves the performer from a stand on the floor to the apparatus. Also can be the first moves of a floor exercise routine.

over grasp A grasp in which the palms of the hand are on top of the bar.

pike The legs are straight, with the body bent at the hips.

puck A combination of the tuck and pike, bent at the hips with a slight bend in the knees.

roll A rotation of the body in contact with a surface.

routine A combination of stunts in a series. A routine begins with a mount, followed by stunts, and ends with a dismount.

seat A position on a piece of apparatus in which the weight is borne by the thighs or buttocks: *Straddle seat*—legs apart with the weight borne evenly. *Side seat*—legs are together with the weight borne by the buttocks or legs on one side of the apparatus.

somersault The rotation of the body in the air around the horizontal axis.

stand A fixed position, with the body weight supported by the feet.

support A position on a piece of apparatus in which the weight is supported by the hands or arms, with the shoulders above the base of support.

tuck The knees and hips are bent, with the head in a chin-down position.

twist The rotation of the body around the vertical axis.

under grasp A grasp in which the palms of the hand are under the bar.

Discussion Questions

1. Compare and contrast the differences and similarities in the evaluation of gymnastics and tumbling to other activities.

2. What nationality is credited with the development of modern gymnastics? Who were some of the noted individuals, and for what are they known?

3. What are the benefits of participating in gymnastics? What special physiological attributes does the gymnast possess?

4. Identify the various safety considerations that affect good instruction of gymnastics and tumbling.

5. Discuss instructional methods that affect good teaching of gymnastics and tumbling.

6. Discuss ways for evaluating a gymnastics routine.

7. Discuss the various ways to evaluate a tumbling unit. Identify your favorite method and explain your rationale.

8. Identify and discuss the common faults that students have in executing the forward roll.

9. Identify and discuss the basic body positions that aid skill performance when executing different stunts in a routine.

10. Identify and discuss the specific terms for the way the body moves in gymnastics.

Web Sites

www.usa-gymnastics.org USA Gymnastics Online—offers information on events, athlete biographies, member services, games, and more.

http://gymnastics.about.com—provides gymnasts, coaches, and fans useful material to improve involvement in and understanding of the sport.

CHAPTER 14

Handball and Racquetball

This chapter will enable you to

- Identify important historical events that contributed to the evolution of handball and racquetball
- Select equipment necessary to play handball and racquetball
- Identify and put into practice the rules governing handball and racquetball
- Identify and develop the basic skills, namely the forehand stroke, the backhand stroke, the serve, and the back wall shot
- Employ the basic strategy necessary to play the game
- Identify and put into practice necessary safety considerations for a successful game of handball or racquetball

Nature and Purpose

Handball and racquetball are related competitive sports in which the hand (or a racquet) is used to serve and return the ball. In their principal variations these games can be played by two opponents (as a singles game), by three opponents (as a cutthroat game), or by two opposing pairs of players (as a doubles game). In this chapter, all that is said about handball also applies to racquetball, unless otherwise stated.

Although the game can be played on one or three walls, the four-wall enclosed court provides the greatest challenge to skill and the most competition. Primarily the four-wall game will be discussed, but most of its related description applies to the other variations of the game.

The first side scoring 21 points wins the game (in racquetball, first side to reach 15 points), and the first side winning two games wins the match. The third game, or tie-breaker, is usually played to 11 points. There is no tie score nor requirement to win by two points, as in some games.

A player may use either the right or left hand for hitting the ball (or holding the racquet), but only one hand at a time may be used to play the ball, and the ball must be struck only once in each instance.

History

HANDBALL

The game of handball originated in Ireland around the 10th century; since that time it has been a popular sport around the world. Championship tournaments were held in the 1800s; John Cavanagh of York was the outstanding player during this early period. William Braggs of Tipperary followed Cavanagh and is credited with developing the technique of imparting "English" to the ball, that is, making it hop and curve on rebounds.

During the 1800s, several Irish handball players immigrated to the United States and were surprised to find that there were no courts in their new country. Phil Casey, one of these Irish players, began developing an interest in the game around Brooklyn, and in 1887, after winning the handball championship of the United States, he arranged a 21-game series with John Lawlor, champion of Ireland. A side bet of $1,000 was placed on the match. The first 10 games were to be played in Cork and the remaining 11 in the United States. Lawlor won 6 of the first 10 games, but Casey won 7 straight when the series was resumed in the United States, thereby becoming the world champion. He is known as the "Father of Handball in America."

One of the greatest players of modern times was Joe Platak, who won the singles championship of the United States nine times between 1935 and 1945. He was recognized by many authorities as the greatest handball player in history.

The U.S. Handball Association, the governing body for handball in the United States, also has rules for one-wall and three-wall handball, a game that is played in many colleges, universities, and public schools around the country.

RACQUETBALL

Racquetball developed later than handball and paddleball but has reached popularity worldwide. Paddleball was originated by Earl Riskey at the University of Michigan in 1930. Because the game was played in a regulation handball court, Riskey adapted handball rules with some minor modifications. Although paddleball is still played, it evolved into a game first using a wooden racquet and later a racquet with strings. Racquetball as we know it today can be attributed to Joe Sobek, a tennis player who wanted something to do in the winter, so he developed racquetball as an alternative activity.[1]

Since the early 1950s, racquetball has become a popular sport and is played throughout the world. During the 1970s, the sport experienced a boost in popularity with the development of racquetball centers throughout the United States. By the 1980s, racquetball had become one of the fastest-growing sports in the United States. By the start of the 21st century, there were more than 8 million participants worldwide.[2]

Many colleges and universities offer racquetball as a physical education class. It is also popular as a good aerobic fitness activity. Because players are continually moving, racquetball contributes to cardiovascular fitness, muscular strength, endurance, and flexibility. Racquetball is governed in the United States by the U.S. Racquetball Association.

Playing Area and Equipment

Court.   The standard four-wall handball court is 40 feet long × 20 feet wide × 20 feet high (Figure 14-1). An outdoor single-wall court is 34 feet long × 20 feet wide × 16 feet high (Figure 14-2). The four-wall court is divided into a front court and a back court of equal dimensions by a line called the *short line*, running parallel to the front wall. Five feet in front of the short line is another parallel line called the *service line*. The area between the short line and the service line is called the service zone. Eighteen inches from and parallel with each side wall a line is drawn to form a box, termed the *service box*, where the partner of the serve (in doubles) must stand while the ball is being served. Three feet from and parallel with each side wall is the drive serve

line. A player can drive serve to the same side of the court on which he is standing as long as his racquet does not break the plane of that drive serve line.

The racquetball court has a *receiving line*, which is marked as a broken line parallel with the short line. The back edge should be 5 feet from the back edge of the short line.

Ball.   The handball is made of rubber, has a diameter of 1⅞ inches, and weighs 2.3 ounces. In racquetball a seamless rubber ball is used that is 2¼ inches in diameter and weighs approximately 1.4 ounces. If one-wall handball is to be played in a physical education class, it would be advisable to use the racquetball ball.

Gloves.   The rules of handball require that gloves be worn. This is for protection and to keep perspiration off the ball. In racquetball, gloves are not required by the rules; however, many players prefer to wear them for a better grip and reduced slippage due to perspiration.

Racquet.   The racquetball racquet length must not exceed 22 inches. There should be a thong attached to the bottom of the racquet handle that should slip over the player's wrist to secure the racquet to the wrist. The racquet frame may be of any material judged to be safe; popular types are made of aluminum, steel, fiber glass, graphite, or a combination of materials. The strings of the racquet must be gut, monofilament, nylon, graphite, plastic, or a combination of these. Whatever the material, it should not leave a mark or deface the ball. The frame comes in three sizes—regular, midsize, or full-size. Racquet prices range from $20 to $200. For physical education classes, a less expensive solution is to use wooden paddle racquets that cost much less.

Eyeguards.   Eyeguards should be required of all racquetball players. Guards are available in various price ranges and styles.

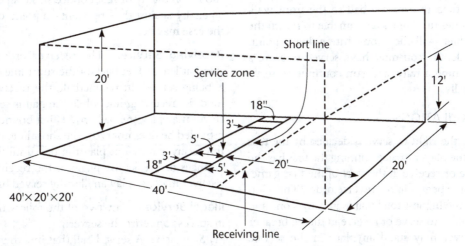

Figure 14-1 Four-wall handball court. The dotted line behind the short service line is for racquetball (receiving cue).

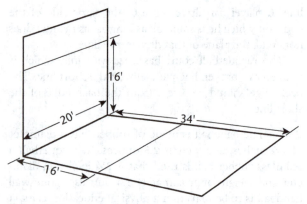

Figure 14-2   One-wall handball court.

Basic Rules

A strong point in favor of handball is the simplicity of the rules governing the game. Any person can become familiar with the basic rules in one or two class sessions. In 1958 the Amateur Athletic Union, the U.S. Handball Association, and the YMCA agreed on a unified set of handball rules that would be applicable throughout the country. In 1959 these rules were adopted by the Jewish Welfare Board. A summary of the latest rules is given here.

THE GAME

In the act of serving, the server drops the ball on the floor (between the short and service lines) and strikes the ball on the first rebound in such a manner that it will first hit the front wall and on the rebound land on the floor back of the short line, either before or after striking one of the side walls, but in front of the back wall. After the ball is legally served, one of the receiving team players returns the ball by striking it either on the fly or on the first bounce so that it will strike the front wall before striking the floor, either directly or after having struck one or both of the side walls, back wall, ceiling, or any combination of these surfaces. The receiving side then returns the ball to the front wall, and play continues until one side is unable to return the ball legally, which will then constitute either a point, handout, or sideout. You must have served to score a point after winning a rally, and you continue to serve until losing a rally.

PLAYING REGULATIONS

The choice for the right to serve is decided by the toss of a coin, and the player or side winning the toss has the option to serve or receive at the start of the first game. The second game begins in the reverse order. The team or player with the highest total points in games one and two has the option to serve or receive in the tie-breaker game. The server may stand anyplace in the service zone. When the server or serving side loses the rally, she or they become the receiver and the receiver the

server; they alternate in this fashion in all subsequent services of the game. The serve must be made within the service area; stepping on the line, but not beyond, is permitted. In racquetball, however, you may step over the service line, provided that some part of both feet remains either on or inside the service line. The server may not step over the short line until the ball passes the short line as it rebounds from the front wall.

When serving the ball, the server must let it bounce on the floor and strike it on its first rebound from the floor. If the server attempts to hit the ball on this rebound and fails, the server is out. The server may not bounce the ball more than one time in the service zone in making a service. Violation of this rule retires the server. A server may not serve until the opponent has had a fair opportunity to get placed. The server's partner, in doubles, must stand within the service box with her back to the side wall, both feet on the floor, until the ball passes the short line on its return from the front wall.

If a player's partner is hit by a served fly ball while standing in the service box, it counts as a "dead ball" without penalty, but it does not eliminate any short or long fault preceding this service. If a player is hit by a served ball on the bounce, it is a short ball. If the served ball should pass behind the partner and strike the floor back of the short line, it is a dead ball.

In doubles, the side starting each game is allowed one handout only. After that, both partners are permitted to serve. Players in doubles must follow the same order of service throughout the game. It is not necessary for players to alternate serves to their opponents.

If a ball is swung at and missed, it may be played again, provided it is hit before bouncing twice on the floor. If a player swings at and completely misses the ball, and if in her or her partner's attempt to again play the ball there is an unintentional interference by an opponent, it will be a hinder. If the completely missed ball should on the fly or first bounce strike an opponent, it is a penalty against the opponent—a point, or handout, as the case may be.

Receiving Service.   The receiver or receivers must stand at least 5 feet back of the short line while the ball is being served. In racquetball, the receiver stands behind the receiving line while the ball is served. The receiver may play the ball on the first bounce or volley it, provided he does not cross the short line. In racquetball, the receiver may not play the ball until the ball either bounces or breaks the plane of the receiving line. The receiver may not play an illegally served ball.

Illegal Service.   Any two of the following fault serves in succession retire the server:

1. *Short serve.* A served ball that hits the front wall and fails to strike the floor back of the short line on the fly.

2. *Three-wall serve.* A served ball that hits the front wall and two side walls before striking the floor.

3. *Long serve.* A served ball that hits the front wall, side wall, and back wall before striking the floor.

4. *Ceiling serve.* A served ball that hits the front wall, then the ceiling before striking the floor.

5. *Foot fault.* The server steps beyond the short line or over the service line in the act of serving.

6. *Screen serve.* A served ball that first hits the front wall and on the rebound passes so closely to the server, or server's partner in doubles, that it prevents the receiver from having a clear view of the ball.

7. A served ball that hits the ceiling, floor, or side walls before striking a front wall.

8. *Crotch ball.* A served ball that hits the front and side wall, or front wall and floor, or front wall and ceiling at the same time.

9. A served ball that hits the front wall and rebounds back to hit the server.

Note: In racquetball, items 7, 8, and 9 are out serves. The server gets only one attempt.

Suggested Learning Sequence

A. Introduction
 1. Origin and development
 2. Equipment
 3. Safety

B. Rules and procedures of play
 1. Playing area
 2. Scoring
 3. Serving
 4. Hinders

C. Skills and techniques
 1. Forehand shot (sidearm stroke)
 2. Overhead stroke
 3. Overhead ceiling shot
 4. Back wall shot
 5. Backhand shot (racquetball)
 6. Service
   a. Forehand serve
   b. Drive serve
   c. Lob serve
   d. Z serve
 7. Kill shot

D. Playing strategy

Skills and Techniques

FOREHAND OR SIDEARM STROKE

The forehand stroke is the primary offensive stroke in handball and its mastery is essential to achieve a winning game. The most efficient stroke occurs at knee

Figure 14-3 "Cocked" position, forehand.
Note: eye guards are required for racquetball.

height and is similar to the motion of bending over to skip a flat stone across a body of water or throw a sidearm pitch in baseball.

▶ Learning Hints

1. Position your body as if you were a baseball batter, facing the side wall.

2. Raise the striking hand to the height of your ear in a "cocked" position (Figure 14-3).

3. As the ball is struck, step forward with the front foot, shifting weight from back to front foot (Figure 14-4).

4. Simultaneously with the step, drop your striking shoulder, rotate your body to enable your forearm and hand to move forward in a plane parallel with the floor.

5. Contact the ball at the vertical center of your body.

6. The wrist moves past the elbow in a snapping motion.

7. The ball is struck by the hand at the base of the fingers or in the "sweet" part of the racquet.

8. Follow through ahead of the front knee.

▶ Practice/Organizational Suggestions

1. Stand facing the side wall in a ready position. Bounce the ball in front of you easily, striking the ball as it rebounds at about knee level. Start a series of practice shots near the short line, then move back 5 feet and hit a series, then back 5 feet more, and so on.

Figure 14-4 Contact point, forehand stroke.

Figure 14-5 Overhead "cocked" position.

2. Stand facing the side wall (5 feet away) in a ready position. Toss the ball easily against the side wall so that the ball will rebound up from the floor into a striking position for a forehand shot.

OVERHEAD STROKE

The overhead stroke is used to strike the ball at eye level or higher and is similar to a baseball catcher's throw or a quarterback's pass in football.

▶ Learning Hints

1. Position toes toward the side wall and open shoulders to the front wall.
2. Weight is on the rear foot.
3. Bring cupped hand to the ear, cocked (Figure 14-5).
4. Weight shifts to the front foot as the arm moves up and forward.
5. Ball is struck above and in front of the head.
6. Ball is struck by the fingers with a wrist snap.
7. Follow through in the direction you wish the ball to take (Figure 14-6).

▶ Practice/Organizational Suggestions

1. Stand in a ready position deep in the court. Bounce the ball vigorously on the floor so that it rebounds up into a striking position for the overhead.
2. From a position deep in the court, throw the ball high against the front wall so that it bounces high to you, returning it with an overhead stroke. Move your body as soon as possible to the striking position.

Figure 14-6 Overhead follow-through.

OVERHEAD CEILING SHOT

The overhead ceiling shot, fundamental to racquetball, can be used effectively as either an offensive or defensive strategy. It can be hit with the side arm, forehand, backhand, or underhand strokes; the overhand ceiling shot is described here. The motion is similar to a tennis serve, the objective being to hit the ceiling first, the front wall, and the floor, and then land deep in the court.

▶ Learning Hints

1. The body should be facing the side wall, with shoulders open to the front wall.

2. The weight is on the rear foot and will transfer forward as the contact and follow-through are executed.

3. The racquet arm is cocked, elbow up, and racquet dropped behind.

4. The nonhitting arm should be pointed upward, overhead, almost pointing to the ball.

5. As the racquet arm snaps upward, the ball should be contacted at the midline of the body. Too far behind will cause the ball to hit the ceiling directly overhead and too far forward will cause the ball to hit the front wall.

6. Follow through in the direction you wish the ball to take.

▶ Practice/Organizational Suggestions

1. Throw the ball against the ceiling to get the feel of the ball rebounding off the ceiling, then against the front wall and the floor.

2. Toss the ball overhead, using the same drill as 1; gradually increase the force at point of contact.

3. Repeat drill 2 and begin placing the ball in different parts of the court, trying to hit the ball consistently to the corner of the back court.

BACK WALL SHOT

The back wall shot, unique to handball and racquetball, rebounds from the front wall to the floor and then off the back wall before the opponent can get into position to play the ball. If you want to become an above average player, you have to learn to play this shot successfully. The stroke most applicable for the back wall shot is the forehand stroke in which the forearm is swung parallel with the floor. This stroke offers a balanced and powerful method of hitting the ball.

▶ Learning Hints

1. Face the back wall or the area of the back wall that the ball is in.

2. Move the ball toward the front wall.

3. As the ball rebounds from the wall and begins to descend, pivot on your right foot (for a right-hand shot) and turn your body, stepping toward the front wall.

4. Lock hand and arm above the ear.

5. Strike the ball at the vertical midpoint of your body.

6. Let the ball drop as low as possible.

7. Follow through in the direction you want the ball to follow.

▶ Practice/Organizational Suggestions

1. Facing the back wall, toss the ball against the back wall, letting it bounce toward the front wall from the floor. Move with the ball, positioning yourself for a back wall shot.

2. Facing the back wall, toss the ball against the floor to the back wall, but before it bounces on the floor, position yourself for a back wall shot.

BACKHAND SHOT

Although the handball player needs to develop both hands equally well in playing both sides of the court, the racquetball player must learn to use the backhand shot. The backhand shot is a mirror image of the forehand shot, but the stroke is much shorter and uses more wrist snap.

▶ Learning Hints

1. Position your body by facing the side wall (opposite side of the forehand stroke).

2. Rotate the racquet in your hand one-eighth of a turn toward the front wall.

3. Cock the racquet back near the ear, with pelvis turned (Figure 14-7).

4. As the ball is struck, step forward with the front foot, shifting the weight from the back leg to the front leg.

Figure 14-7 Backhand "cocked" position.

Figure 14-8   Backhand position on contact.

5. Simultaneously with the step, bring the racquet forward and contact the ball in line with the front foot, but away from the body using a level swing (Figure 14-8).

6. As the ball is struck, uncock the wrist, snapping the ball toward the front wall using a full follow-through.

▶ Practice/Organizational Suggestions

1. Standing at midcourt, facing the side wall, bounce the ball easily into the backhand hitting area. Hit a series of shots from this area, back up 5 feet, hit another series, back up another 5 feet, and repeat.

2. Stand at midcourt, facing the side wall. Toss the ball easily into the floor to the side wall so it will rebound into the striking area for a backhand shot. Repeat this series from deeper in the court.

SERVICE

The service, the beginning stroke of each point, must be placed successfully in order to continue the point, but the service can also be an offensive weapon if developed to its potential. You may serve from anywhere in the service area, the most advantageous spot being in the center, so that you may direct your serve to either side. You must drop the ball into the serving zone and strike it on the first rebound, causing the ball to strike the front wall and rebound over the short line and land on the floor.

Drive Serve.   The drive serve is a low, hard serve placed so that it returns close to the side wall and drops dead in the back corner; or a low, hard serve that strikes the floor and wall just behind the short line. If possible,

the drive serve should not rebound off the back wall, thereby giving your opponent a back wall shot. The drive serve should be struck with the same techniques described in the forehand stroke.

Lob Serve.   The lob serve is a high ball placed on the front wall, which permits the ball to return in an arc, hugging the side wall, and striking the floor a few feet past the short line in such a manner that the ball rebounds again and drops gently into the corner. The lob serve may be struck with either an underhand or an overhead stroke, the underhand stroke being generally easier to develop in the beginning.

Z Serve.   This serve is named from the z pattern formed by the ball. Standing near the left wall of the service area, serve the ball so that it strikes the extreme right side of the front wall about a racquet's distance from the corner, approximately 4 feet above the floor. It should then strike the right wall, angle past in front of the server, strike the floor, and finally strike the left side wall from which it spins off nearly parallel with the back wall (Figure 14-9). The z serve should be struck with a low forehand, almost an underhand stroke. The z serve also could be executed from the right side of the service area.

KILL SHOTS

A "kill" shot is placed so low that there is little or no possibility of a return. Generally hit with a forehand stroke, a kill occurs not when the player hits "down" on

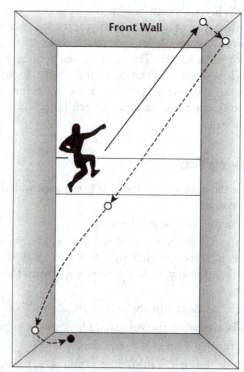

Figure 14-9   The z serve.

the ball but when he lets the ball drop to knee height or lower before contacting it with a powerful stroke. Kills can either be front wall kills or corner kills. The front wall kill is stroked straight ahead, hitting so low on the front wall that the ball bounces twice before the opponent can hit it. The corner kill is hit low, but is aimed toward either corner formed by the front and side walls. The ball should strike either the front or side wall, and then it immediately will carom into the side or front wall, producing an angled return that is low and considerably slowed by the ball striking the two wall surfaces.

Safety Considerations

1. Dress properly for the game. Always wear rubber-soled court shoes to ensure firm footing.

2. Always warm up thoroughly before beginning competition.

3. Do not play a dead ball, because your opponent may turn and get struck in the face.

4. Do not deliberately hit an opponent with the ball in the hope that he will call a hinder on the play. You may both get hurt, and ill feelings will develop.

5. After you play the ball to the back court, keep your eye on the ball by protecting your face with your shoulder or looking through your racquet.

6. Allow your opponents room to make the play. Do not crowd or you may be struck.

7. Wear eyeguards at all times.

Playing Strategy

Handball and racquetball are games in which a premium is placed on analyzing the opponent's strengths and weaknesses. Some players are unable to use their left hand with much effectiveness in handball, or they have not developed a strong backhand shot in racquetball. When facing such an opponent, a player should direct a majority of the shots so the opponent is placed at a disadvantage. Players should vary their strategy by employing fast balls alternated with lobs (high, soft shots) in sufficient frequency to get the opponent off balance. The change of pace is particularly effective on the serve, and many good players use it to their advantage. In playing doubles, partners should agree on the area that each is to cover and assign the areas so each player may take advantage of her strong points.

Players should work for a desirable position on the court. It is usually good strategy to maintain a position in the well—near middle of the court and close enough to enable one to play low balls and corner shots. By skillfully placing shots, a player can keep an opponent in such a position that the opponent will be at a disadvantage in returning crosscourt angle shots. Think ahead and make the first play a forerunner to a second or third

play that will result in an error by the opponent, or afford the opportunity to place a passing or kill shot. An opponent who persists in playing close to the front wall can be driven out of position by high lob shots that go overhead but do not strike the back wall with sufficient force to rebound any distance. In the final analysis, a careful scrutiny of your opponent's style of play is the first step in planning a campaign that will be most effective. Identify the opponent's weak points and take advantage of them.

Helpful Hints

HANDBALL

1. Practice "kills" alone. Play the ball around an imaginary opponent and work on the various arm strokes.

2. If your hands swell from playing, soak them in hot water before entering the court, which helps to minimize the swelling.

3. Gloves are worn by a majority of handball players. Your enjoyment of the game will be increased if you wear a pair of gloves that fit your hands well. Always hang gloves up to dry after using them.

4. Do not rush the ball. Wait for it, and you will not only save energy but also play a better game.

5. Control is more desirable than speed.

6. Serve each ball so that it is difficult for the opponent to return. Try to get several ace serves in each game.

7. A ball hit close to the floor has less bounce and is more difficult to return. The forehand stroke is best for this shot; practice regularly on this play.

8. Watch good players and pattern your play after those who have mastered the game.

9. As a playing courtesy, the opponent is entitled to a fair and unobstructed opportunity to play the ball.

10. If there is any doubt about a play, it is advisable to play the point over.

11. Take advantage of short balls—take the front court.

12. Establish a pattern sequence of shots and then change it.

RACQUETBALL

1. "Think" your serve before serving; you have 10 seconds—use them.

2. Back out of the serving zone as soon as the ball crosses the short line, keeping your eye on the ball the entire rally.

3. Remain in a set position until you see if your shot will be a forehand or a backhand; then turn facing the correct side wall and move to properly align yourself to take your shot.

4. Return to center court. Try to place your shots to keep your opponent out of center court so you can remain there.

5. Place the ball away from your opponent.

6. Try to get the ball to take two bounces before reaching the back wall.

7. Hit with 80 percent power for control.

8. Running around the forehand and backhand will pin you against the side walls.

9. Your shoulder level should equal the ball height.

10. Let any ball at chest level in center court go past you and play it off the back wall.

11. Keep your opponent away from the front wall—hit shots deep.

12. Keep your opponent on the run—hit to open spaces.

13. Exploit your opponent's weaknesses, such as the backhand.

Skill Assessment

The recommended skill test can be used for both handball and racquetball with minimal adjustments for age or strength variables. The most important skill in these games is the ability to consistently keep the rebounding ball in play.

Rebound Test.   A flat surface 20 feet wide and at least 15 feet high is desirable. An official handball or racquetball court is ideal but limits the number of students that can be tested simultaneously. A large, flat front wall, with no side walls, where several stations can be set up side by side is more practical. Set up a station every 20 feet.

Each station accommodates three to four students. One is tested, another is a counter/recorder, and the remaining student(s) provides extra balls and retrieves errant ones. Each group establishes a rotation order for the various responsibilities.

Put a 20-foot restraining line across the station parallel with the front wall at a specific distance from the wall. The line's distance is adjustable dependent on age, strength, or whether handball/racquetball is being tested. The suggested starting distance is 20 feet from the wall, which coincides with the short service line on a regulation court. The participant stands behind the restraining line, drops the ball to the floor, and hits it to the front wall. The others in the group stand behind the participant to assist. The rebounding ball is continuously hit to the wall and replayed. There are no restrictions on the number of times the ball bounces before being rehit. However, the fewer the bounces, the quicker the ball can next be contacted, which results in a better score. The participant must stay behind the restraining line at all times.

The score is the total number of times that the participant legally contacts the wall with the ball in 30 seconds. The ball must hit within the 20-foot-wide area. Each participant receives one 30-second practice trial before the first trial for score. Students rotate responsibilities after each trial. The total number of trials depends on the length of testing time, number of testing stations, and number of students. A student's final score is the sum total of all trials; every student must have the same number of trials. This same process can be used periodically throughout the unit as a challenge-type drill, which prepares the students for the procedures prior to the final skill testing.

Modifications for Special Populations

ORTHOPEDICALLY IMPAIRED

1. Follow rules from the Wheelchair Racquetball Association, and allow students who use wheelchairs two bounces before a return shot is required.

2. For students with movement difficulties, tether a ball to an assistive device, such as a walker or crutch.

3. Use a larger-size ball or one made of different material (e.g., Nerf ball).

4. Use Velcro strapping to secure a racquet to the player's hand during play.

5. Instead of a racquet, use a fat paddle-type board secured to the player's hand.

6. Commercial extension devices are available for students who have amputations or grip limitations.

7. Serve from anywhere in the service area.

8. The ball may bounce any number of times, but the player may swing only once. The ball must be struck before it crosses the short service line on its way back to the front wall.

COGNITIVELY IMPAIRED

1. Reduce the court size and responsibility for court coverage.

2. Use one-walled courts or stations in the gymnasium.

3. Refer to item 3 in Orthopedically Impaired.

SENSORY IMPAIRED

1. Individual considerations determine the appropriateness of handball or racquetball for students who are blind or have a visual impairment. Set up a lead-up game in which the

student rolls or throws an audio ball against a wall to practice movement and appropriate positioning. Make audio balls by placing small bells inside whiffleballs.

2. Minimal modifications are needed for students who are deaf or have a hearing impairment. To enhance instruction, use sign language, videos, and pictures.

Terminology

ace A service that completely eludes the receiver.

back wall shot A shot made from a rebound off the back wall.

box See Service box.

ceiling shot A shot striking the ceiling first, then the front wall.

crotch shot A ball simultaneously striking two surfaces—two walls or a wall and the floor—is not good.

cutthroat A three-person game in which the server plays against the other two players, with each player keeping an individual score. Not played in official competition.

drive shot A power shot against the front wall that rebounds fast, low, and in a straight line.

fault An illegally served ball, given a second attempt.

handout The loss of service by the player on a doubles team who is the first server on that team.

hinder Accidental interference or obstruction of the flight of the ball during play. Point is played again.

kill A ball directed to the front wall in such a way that it rebounds so close to the floor that it is impossible to return.

passing shot A placement driven out of opponent's reach on either side.

rally Continuous play of the ball by opponents from the serve until the ball is dead.

receiving line A broken line parallel with the short line on a racquetball court. The back edge of the receiving line is 5 feet from the back edge of the short line.

run-around shot Ball that strikes one side wall, the rear wall, and other side wall.

safety zone A 5-foot area bounded by the back edge of the short line and receiving line. The zone is observed only during the serve in racquetball.

screen A hinder because of an obstruction of vision by opponent.

server Person (or persons, in doubles) in the "hand-in" position and eligible to serve.

service box Area within the service zone bounded by the side wall and a parallel line 18 inches away; denotes where server's partner must stand in doubles when the serve is being made.

service court The area in which the ball must land when returning from the front wall on the serve.

service line The service line is parallel with and 5 feet in front of the short line. The front line of the service zone.

service zone The area where the server must stand when serving the ball. Located between the service line and the short line, usually 5 feet wide and extending across the court.

shoot To attempt kill shots.

short line A line on the floor parallel with front wall and equidistant from front and back walls. Serve must carry over this line on its return from the front wall.

side-out The loss of serve by a player or team.

thong Strap attached to the bottom handle of the racquetball racquet, worn around the player's wrist.

volley To return the ball to the front wall before it bounces on the floor.

z ball A defensive shot that strikes three walls before touching the floor. The ball strikes the front wall, a sidewall, and then the opposite side wall.

Discussion Questions

1. Compare the evolution of handball and racquetball.

2. Discuss the similarities of the two sports.

3. Identify the strategy for the three types of serves presented.

4. Discuss the safety considerations for both sports since the players are in a small restrictive area.

5. The back wall shot is a skill unique to both sports. Discuss the learning hints which aid in the development of the shot.

6. Discuss how scrutinizing your opponent's style of play might affect your playing strategy.

7. Discuss how racquetball contributes to health-related fitness.

8. Present the similarities/differences of four-wall, three-wall, and one-wall games, and how the rules then change.

Web Sites

www.ushandball.org U.S. Handball Association—includes instructional resources, handball links, racquetball and fitness, terminology, rules for four-wall and one-wall play, how to create draw sheets, and court specifications.

www.racquetball.org U.S. Racquetball Association—provides information on the history, tournaments, and rules of racquetball.

www.internationalracquetball.com International Racquetball Federation—includes a listing of events worldwide, players' rankings, and official rules.

www.howtoplayracquetball.org – features pictured tutorials, instructional videos, shots, serves, and equipment needed.

CHAPTER 15

Hiking, Backpacking, and Camping

This chapter will enable you to

- Identify the equipment required for hiking, backpacking, and camping
- List the specific areas to consider when planning a camping trip
- Efficiently locate and pack items within a backpack
- Construct an extensive list of items to take on a trip
- Identify safety considerations for planning a trip
- Understand outdoors etiquette for leaving natural resources beautiful for future generations

Nature and Purpose

Hiking, backpacking, and camping are fun-filled activities enjoyed by thousands of people throughout the world. The wide variety and large numbers of trail systems and parks provide people an opportunity to experience nature's many wonders. The activities can take place in many different environments—the heat of the desert, the coolness of the mountains, and the snow of winter. Hiking can be done on mountain trails, through urban settings, on the network of rails-to-trails systems in the United States, through the forest and woods, through neighborhoods—in other words, hiking can be done almost anywhere.

Generally, hiking refers to walks that are taken for exercise or for pleasure, whereas backpacking refers to an activity that requires the hiker to take along (i.e., carry on one's back) everything necessary for an overnight stay.[1] The benefits far outnumber the dangers. By following some simple rules, wearing proper attire, being able to read a map and a compass, and learning a few other rules of the road, the hiker can minimize potential dangers and look forward to a lifetime of adventure and pleasure.

As the participant gains more experience and increases the length of the trips, she may want to consider extended overnight camping. This requires additional skills and equipment and more extensive planning. Both *recreational* and *organized* camping involve group activities such as hiking, campfire cooking, and other activities that pertain to the natural environment.[2]

History

For centuries humans have walked through the wilderness, carried their essentials on their backs, prepared their meals over fire, and sought shelter from the elements. Over time, these activities have evolved from a means of survival to today's structured outdoor recreational pursuits.

Camping connotes leaving one's comfortable indoor way of living to enjoy a more simple outdoor life enjoying nature, typically at a campsite. Camping developed along two routes. *Recreational* camping refers to simply spending one or more nights outdoors at a campsite.[3] *Organized* camping usually has a mission or goal such as the promotion of trust; the fostering of compatibility; or, the encouragement of accomplishment. This type of camping is more defined and has a directed experience with a purpose to educate. With youth organizations such as the Scouts, the education is a key ingredient to the outdoor experience.[4] Both types of camping imply participation in a variety of activities such as hiking, cooking over a campfire, and a wide assortment of other outdoor activities involving the natural environment.

The history of organized camping is traced to the northeastern United States, where early proponents focused on educational and philosophical theories. Frederick William Gunn is credited with organizing the first camping trip in 1861, when he took a group of students on a 2-week trek. They hiked to their destination, camped out, and participated in such activities as swimming, fishing, playing games, cooking their own food, and telling stories around the campfire. This Gunnery Camp, credited as the world's first organized camp, took place over 12 seasons.[5] Today, probably thousands of groups and organizations sponsor camping trips.

In recreational camping, individuals or small groups attempt to escape the urban life and live in the natural environment. Recreational camping has expanded rapidly. The state and national park systems cater to this type of camper. Camping equipment and establishments devoted to serving recreational campers have become big business. Education about the outdoors has continually expanded and has earned a place in the school curriculum. The philosophy of organized camping—to educate and increase socialization through a camp experience—has led many individuals to become recreational campers in their leisure time.

The information in this chapter provides guidance for developing both educational curricula and individual skills and knowledge for recreational pursuits.

Equipment

The types of equipment needed for hiking, backpacking, and camping will vary according to many factors, including, but not limited to, the length of the trip (day hike or overnight hike, weekend to week-long trek or longer), the temperature, the type of environment, the type of terrain, and the time of year. The beginning to intermediate-level hiker, backpacker, or camper should consider the following types of basic equipment.

FOOTWEAR

Without doubt, the most important equipment is well-fitted footwear. Although tennis or running shoes may be comfortable to wear, they are not appropriate for hiking. Hikers should wear boots made of leather, fabric, or both (Figure 15-1). The type of boot depends on the terrain, the distance the hiker wishes to walk, and the weight carried in the backpack. Boots have a hard sole to protect the hiker from sharp rocks and uneven surfaces. They are also designed to support the ankle (i.e., to prevent twisting). The weight of the boot is also an important consideration. Although a heavier boot may appear to be stiffer and therefore offer more protection, over a long, strenuous hike, its weight can quickly tire the backpacker. Some boots intended for longer, more rugged hiking are made entirely of leather and serve to give support and maximum protection. Boots that are insulated and extend over the ankles are used for backpacking in snowy terrain. For day hikers moving over moderate terrain, a boot made of a combination of leather and fabric is lighter and more comfortable. All-fabric boots are most often used for moderate hikes on fairly smooth, consistent surfaces where protection is not as necessary.

As with all equipment, it is best to try on the boots or to consult an expert who can help ensure a proper fit. Boots can cost from $50 to $300. Spend as much as you can afford; remember that footwear is the most important piece of equipment.

Socks are also essential footwear. There is a wide variety to select from, but a good combination is a mid- to heavyweight wool-blend sock with a lightweight polyester sock underneath.

Figure 15-1 High-top hiking boots and a low-cut hiking shoe.
Courtesy of www.TheExtremeOutfitters.com

CLOTHING

The type of clothing depends on many factors: the temperature, type of terrain, type of environment (the woods, the desert, mountains, heavy underbrush, etc.), and the intensity of the experience. Hiking is a physical activity, and as the hiker becomes more active he will generate more heat—even on cooler days. A simple rule is to dress in layers, that is, to wear layers of clothing that can be taken off as the hiker becomes warmer and added when the hiker becomes colder. Fabrics that are worn next to the body should "breathe," that is, allow heat and air to escape and allow moisture to evaporate. Cotton does not breathe well; in fact, it retains moisture. Some experts recommend wearing three layers. The first layer should be a synthetic material (polypropylene) worn next to the body. The second layer should be a pile or fleece covering that serves to keep the hiker warm if necessary or helps to wick moisture away from the body. The final layer should be a breathable shell, such as Gore-Tex, or a fabric that is windproof and waterproof and helps to protect from the elements.[6]

The hiker must also be aware of conditions of the hike. For example, even in warm weather, long pants might be necessary to protect legs from the underbrush, insect bites, or thorns. For day hikes on a fairly flat terrain with a consistent surface, shorts, a light T-shirt, and a light pair of hiking boots may be sufficient. In other words, the hiker must know something about the route and the prevailing conditions to determine the type of clothing to wear.

BACKPACKS

Selecting the proper backpack can be a bewildering experience. Backpacks come in many different sizes and shapes; some come with an external frame to which the backpack attaches, whereas others come with an internal frame that is sewn into the backpack (Figure 15-2). Generally, the external-frame style is used for trail hiking. The frame keeps the backpack away from the body

Figure 15-2 Backpacks with internal and external frames.
Courtesy of www.TheExtremeOutfitters.com

and allows air to circulate. However, the backpack itself may not move with the body, causing a loss of balance if the hiker decides to move off-trail. Backpacks with built-in frames are used in off-trail hiking and move more easily with the body. However, this type of pack is difficult to fit and needs more adjustment.[7]

Beginners should consult an expert for help selecting a backpack. Before buying the backpack, the beginner should try it on, place the weight that might normally be carried in it, and walk around with it on the back. Other features to look for include enough pack space to carry necessary items, adjustable straps to allow weight to be carried high on the shoulders, some type of padded hip belt that allows weight to rest on the pelvis, and a padded back for a more comfortable fit.

Other important pieces of equipment depend on the distance traveled. A person who is backpacking should carry a first-aid kit, well-marked maps and routes developed for the area, and the equipment discussed in the next section. Other miscellaneous equipment to consider are a flashlight, a compass, a mirror, waterproof matches, sunglasses, sunscreen, a pocketknife (Swiss

Army knife), water equipment (canteen and purifying tablets), rope, a candle, spare batteries, a whistle, and insect repellent. Most camping books provide recommended checklists of equipment for the beginner as well as the advanced backpacker.[8]

Daypacks.   An excellent heavy-duty daypack with several pockets costs between $30 and $100. These are suitable for short hikes.

CAMPING EQUIPMENT

The extended hiking and backpacking experience calls for camping equipment. The beginner's basic items, in addition to equipment already identified, include a sleeping bag, tent, and cooking equipment.[9] Campers should choose items with the features they will need based on the number of participants, type of camping, and length of the trip. Beginners should restrict the initial trip to one or two nights.

Sleeping Bags.   The type of sleeping bag to select depends on the type of camping and on personal needs. Campers should consider style, temperature, comfort, types of fill, and cost limitations. Bags are divided into three categories: four-season heavy-duty, three-season all-purpose, and summer lightweight. How the bag is going to be carried is another style consideration. The compactability and weight are important features. Most bags have temperature and comfort ratings. The lower the rating, the cooler the sleeping comfort a person requires. The length, width, and foot space are other considerations. The two most common bag shapes are the barrel and mummy. The barrel bag is roomy, suited for warmer climates, and, because of more fabric fill, is both bulky and heavy. The mummy bag is lighter, more compact, fitted to body size, and provides neck and head insulation.

Bags usually consist of either synthetic or down fillings. A variety of synthetic fibers are available, each with strengths and weaknesses. Any reputable outdoor outfitter can explain these factors. The synthetic bag, in general, is less compact, less expensive ($60 to $150), and less durable, but it is better in wet conditions than is a down-filled bag. Down bags are more expensive ($200 and up), compressible, lightweight, and warm.[10] Sleeping pads are available for additional comfort but add to the transportation problem, especially if the camper is also backpacking.

Tents.   Tent selection is important. The major considerations are the temperature and usage. Tents fall into four categories: three-season, summer screen, convertible, and mountaineering. Size requirements, which depend on number of people, height, equipment storage, and inside cooking needs, are key considerations in selecting the tent. The prices range from $100 to $500. Other features, such as weight, color, rain-fly, ventilation, and interior storage/hanging hooks, also should be considered. An inexpensive waterproof ground cloth under the tent floor helps keep it dry and clean.

For overnight stays, campers also must consider their water and food needs. Both are discussed in more detail later in the chapter. Foods should be selected according to their weight, calories, nutrition, and portability. Water for drinking, cooking, and washing is needed for short trips of one to two nights. Many camping facilities provide a source of clean, drinkable water, but a person who camps in a wilderness area without facilities will have to treat water by boiling, chemical methods, or filtration. Next, the camper must consider how to prepare food. If the camper will be cooking by campfire or stove, he or she will need appropriate cookware. Choices depend on the portability of the items and the expertise of the camper.

Considerations

Before considering hiking or backpacking, the hiker should possess a moderate level of physical fitness, including cardiovascular fitness, muscle strength and endurance, and flexibility. In other words, some physical preparation is necessary before the person embarks on day-long and longer treks. Likewise, campers need to prepare and practice skills before the trip. The beginner should practice setting up the tent, both to develop the skill and to make certain that the necessary tools and equipment are available. Building a campfire is a skill that needs to be learned and practiced prior to the trip, as is the use of cooking stoves. Hikers and campers also need to practice water purification techniques and compass/map reading skills.

This unit provides an excellent opportunity for interdisciplinary planning. If you are a teacher and are considering this a unit of instruction, then look for opportunities to engage in a multidisciplinary experience with other teachers in the school. The physical educator can help prepare students to become fit and teach them about how to set up a tent and campsite; the health teacher can teach basic first aid; the consumer science teacher can teach students about types of fabric to wear, food, nutrition needs, and cooking on the trail; the geography teacher can teach students how to read maps and provide information about the terrain they will encounter; and the life science teacher can contribute information about the environment, the vegetation, and the animals.

Suggested Learning Sequence

The content provided is for beginners who are just starting these activities. Never travel alone, and start your experiences at state parks or government-run facilities with mapped trails and predetermined campsites. They usually provide established sites, fresh water, fire pits, and often toilet facilities. Always check with the proper authorities prior to the trip for detailed information, costs, and necessary permits. This research will help you determine what items you will need to select, assemble, and pack. Taking several 1- or 2-night trips provides valuable experience for future lengthier excursions.

A. Introduction to hiking, backpacking, and camping with basic requirements

B. Skills and strategies
 1. Moderate fitness preparation
 2. Trip planning
 3. Hiking
 4. Backpacking
 5. Sleeping system
 6. Clothing
 7. Water
 8. Food
 9. Cooking
   a. Fire sources
     i. Stove
     ii. Campfire
   b. Cooking over fire
   c. Cookware
 10. Light sources
   a. Flashlights
   b. Lanterns
 11. Human waste

C. Safety and first-aid supplies

D. Etiquette

Skills and Strategies

FITNESS PREPARATION

The terrain and distance requirements dictate physical preparation. The beginner needs to start slowly, with shorter distances and smoother terrain. Another consideration is the amount of weight to carry in the backpack.

A 2-week walking/jogging program, as outlined in an earlier chapter (Chapter 2, *Principles of Physical Fitness*), is sufficient preparation for novice hiking. Beginners should practice on a surface that is similar to the trails that will be covered. Walking on concrete is not recommended. If the hike will cover hills, then the hiker should practice specific leg muscle exercises to help alleviate sore muscles and body posture stress.

Leg lunges described in an earlier chapter (Chapter 28, *Weight Training*), help in training for climbing as well as correcting body posture. Another recommended exercise is to wear a backpack containing the approximate weight that will be carried on the hike, and to alternate stepping up and down on a stair step, keeping the back upright.

Take walks similar in length to the hike, and use a walking stick with the correct arm actions when walking or climbing hills. Wear the same footwear you will wear on the trip. Make sure not to wear new boots for the first time on the trip. Also, wear two pairs of socks while training.

PLANNING THE TRIP

The novice hiker, backpacker, or camper needs to start slowly. A primitive backcountry trip is not recommended. For the most comfortable and simplest experience, select a state park or government-run facility. Spending a couple of nights during mild weather conditions is another wise choice. An added feature of these parks is that they often offer activities such as canoeing, horseback riding, fishing, and swimming.

Car camping, in which the participants and camping gear are transported to the actual base campsite, is another suggestion for novices. This choice makes it easier to select the amount and type of gear, offers more storage options, and provides emergency transportation if needed.

A group experience has several benefits. It provides more people to share in the multitude of responsibilities for the planning and success of the venture. The following are responsibilities that might be assigned: transportation, site selection, contact and permits, sleeping gear, cooking gear and cleaning supplies, food selection and preparation, campfire preparations and care, first-aid kit, recreational activities, and water supply. The size of the group determines how these areas might need to be combined.

The final and most important planning decision is the selection of all gear. Specific gear is identified and discussed in each of the following sections, along with packing suggestions. Construct a checklist for each section to make sure that all items are identified specifically and not left to chance (see First-Aid Kit section later in this chapter for an example). Many of the book references and Web sites listed at the end of this chapter offer such checklists.

HIKING

The first decisions for the hiker are footwear and clothes. An additional consideration is full-length gaiters that cover the lower leg and strap around the boot. They keep stones and dirt from getting into the boot or shoe. If secured tightly, they might even keep water from the boot when you ford shallow streams. The gaiters also protect the lower leg from brush scratches, especially if you wear shorts.

The novice needs to hike in a group setting. Regardless of the group size, hikers need to stay on the trail so that the environment is not disturbed. State parks usually have established paths of a variety of lengths and difficulties from which to select. Start with the easier ones, but still carry short-term (half-day or less) essential equipment, such as sunscreen, bug repellent, pocketknife, water bottle, adhesive bandages, snack, compass, and whistle. Always let others know your route and estimated time limits.

Participants who walk in the woods need to learn map reading and compass skills. Practice these before going on the trip; they could be life-saving. The Orienteering chapter of this book provides instruction on these skills.

BACKPACKING

As discussed previously, the hiker/camper in most cases needs to be able to carry most of his or her equipment. The two most common styles of backpack are the internal and external frame; see the Equipment section at the beginning of this chapter. They are used for overnight treks (Figure 15-2). The daypack is not appropriate for overnight stays.

Packing.   Backpack preparation takes skill, strategy, and practice. The internal- or external-frame styles have specific differences to consider. Distributing weight along the center of gravity is important for comfort and ease of movement. Locating specific equipment items appropriately helps achieve this objective and allows easy access to items needed quickly.

In the internal-frame pack, locate the heavier items closer to the middle of the body. Because of the frame inside, it is harder to reach items immediately. The external-frame pack provides outside pockets that allow for easier storage and quicker location of items. The tent and sleeping bag are the bulkiest items to carry.

The tent is heavy and is usually located near the top, regardless of pack style. It can be split into separate parts—rain-fly, poles, and tent body. The tent body is strapped at the top, the poles are tied to the sides, and the rain-fly is easily stuffed in any available area. The compressed sleeping bag is attached to the bottom of the pack along with sleeping pad/mattress because both are lightweight.

It is good strategy to keep some equipment easily accessible. Rain gear, water bottle, first-aid kit, and toilet paper are such items. A hip belt on the pack with holsters provides easy access for items such as sunscreen, adhesive bandages, bug repellent, flashlight, pocketknife, compass, and medication. Always store water and fuel outside the bag. Clothing, food, cookware, and personal gear are packed inside the bag. If you are taking a stove and water filter, store them in outside pockets on an external-frame pack. Store them near the top of an internal-frame pack. The objective is to travel as lightly as possible yet have all the essential equipment for a successful trek. The loaded backpack should weigh no more than one-fourth of your body weight.[11]

Mounting the Pack.   Rest the backpack on the ground with the hip belt unfastened. Face the backpack, and grasp both shoulder straps. With a stride stance and bent knees, lift the pack and rest it on the thigh of your forward leg. Let go of the shoulder strap on the side of the forward-striding leg. Put that arm through the opposite shoulder strap loop, and pivot so that your back rests against the pack with that shoulder strap looped securely on that shoulder. Release the grip of that shoulder strap, straighten both legs, and put the newly freed arm through the other shoulder-strap loop. Grasp both straps with your hands at shoulder level, and make sure that the straps are seated securely and properly on each shoulder. Clasp and tighten the hip belt around your waist. Repeat this technique several times for practice. Make sure that you do not strain your back during this exercise.

SLEEPING CONSIDERATIONS

A good night's sleep is essential for hiking, backpacking, and camping. Three considerations lead to an enjoyable trek: site selection, sleeping bag selection, and tent selection.

Site Selection. Car camping and public camp sites provide a comfortable start for the novice outdoor experience. They offer easy storage of large items, such as an ice chest or food, and easy access to fresh water, toilets, fire rings, picnic tables, and established hiking trails.

Choose a level and smooth spot for the tent. Ideally, find a location that is high and dry, so that water drains; is close to the water source; is close, but not too close (because of odor), to toilet facilities; provides morning sun and afternoon shade; and offers visually pleasing surroundings. If the site is not assigned by the park, choose an area away from other groups.

Sleeping Bag Selection. Sleeping bag selection was discussed previously in the Equipment section. An additional piece of equipment to consider, which promotes comfort, is the sleeping pad (Figure 15-3). It provides softness and insulation from damp and cold surfaces.

The choices fall into two basic categories: inflatable and foam. Some inflatable pads are self-inflated; others must be inflated by mouth or pump. The biggest disadvantages of the self-inflated type are its cost and fragility. The novice camper needs to seek professional assistance based on his or her individual needs before selecting an air mattress. Not all foam pads are the same; they vary in water absorption, weight, thickness, compressibility, and cost. Again, seek professional assistance because these choices are important for comfort and must be based on individual requirements.

Tent Selection. There are many types of tents to choose from; the various shapes and features are presented in more detail to aid in the selection process.

- *A-frame.* This type of tent is often referred to as a "pup tent." It is easy to set up. It has a support in the middle and is stable and roomy.

Figure 15-3 A sleeping pad adds comfort for sleeping in a bag.
Courtesy of www.TheExtremeOutfitters.com

- *Modified A-frame.* This type offers more room and more stability. Some are free-standing.
- *Dome.* This is probably the most popular type of tent, shown in Figure 15-4. It is roomy, free-standing, and stable, especially in the wind. There is ample headroom. The drawbacks are that it is heavy, bulky, provides poor ventilation, and is higher priced.
- *Pyramid/Tepee.* This type is primarily restricted to temperate climates because it must be staked. Some have detachable floors. Frost and condensation accumulate inside.
- *Hoop/Tunnel.* This style is quite popular because it is lightweight, compact, and provides ample floor space for its size. It is not good in windy conditions.

Also, consider a tent that is equipped with a rain-fly and vestibule. The rain-fly protects the doorway from rain. The vestibule extends over the opening and provides valuable covered space for storing items, such as wet or muddy gear, in a place other than the interior surface of the tent. A ground cloth placed under the floor of the tent protects it from moisture. A thick but lightweight piece of plastic serves the purpose.

Figure 15-4 The popular free-standing dome tent. Courtesy of www.TheExtremeOutfitters.com

Figure 15-5 High and low gaiters protect the lower leg. Courtesy of www.TheExtremeOutfitters.com

Practice setting up the tent several times before the trip. Also, practice taking it down, packing it, and attaching it to the backpack for carrying. In both instances, double- and triple-check that all support pieces, such as poles, stakes, and ropes, are present.

CLOTHING

The pros and cons discussed in the Equipment section regarding wearing breathable fabrics, layering, rain gear, and weather conditions also apply here. The prime issues for selecting clothes are type, weight, bulkiness, comfort, and amount.

Following is a list of clothing suggestions for the recommended one- to two-night experience.

1. *Footwear.* Boots and running/walking shoes.
2. *Socks.* Two pairs each of a lightweight polyester sock and a mid- to heavyweight wool.
3. *Shirts.* One synthetic shirt for daytime wear, and one cotton shirt for sleeping. Depending on the temperature, the daytime shirt should be cargo-style, with long sleeves and pockets for carrying small items.
4. *Pants.* A cargo-style pant of thin cotton provides several pockets. Many styles have zippers that allow them to be converted into shorts if needed. To protect the lower leg, gaiters (low or knee-high) provide scratch-proof covering (Figure 15-5). Additionally, gaiters keep stones from getting into boots.
5. *Jacket.* A light fleece jacket provides warmth, and it dries quickly when wet.
6. *Rain gear.* A rain- and wind-resistant suit is a must. A lightweight, inexpensive poncho offers additional protection. Plastic garbage bags are another inexpensive choice.
7. *Hat.* Either a baseball cap or fly-fishing hat provides warmth and protection from the weather.

Keep in mind that clothes must either be worn, carried, or packed, and they must be appropriate for the anticipated weather conditions.

WATER

Water is needed for drinking, preparing meals, washing cookware, brushing teeth, bathing, and washing clothes. Some of these do not apply to a 1- or 2-day experience. For example, is it absolutely necessary to bathe or to wash clothes? The beginning experience of car camping at a public campsite also alleviates some of the water source and use problems.

The safest water sources, in order, are piped spring water, spring water, stream water, river water, and lake water. The safest choice, actually, is to bring your own with you, but this is not practical for an extended stay. At a public park, fresh water may be transported to the campsite by using a 5-gallon container, which may be stored in the car. Bottled juices or sports drinks can also be used.

The camper can never be too confident in the purity of the water source and should never count on only one source. Boiling water for 15 minutes is one recognized method of purification. Another is the use of chemicals, such as chlorine or iodine in the form of tablets, liquid, or crystals. These treatments need more advanced knowledge and practice before using. A third method for water treatment is to use a filtration system. These systems vary and are more costly. They are not recommended for the novice camper. When purchasing a water purification system, seek professional advice; see Figure 15-6 for two examples. Make sure that you know the type of water source you'll be using and how to use the selected purification method before setting off on the trip.

Figure 15-6 Two methods of water purification are chemical and filtration systems.
Courtesy of www.TheExtremeOutfitters.com

Figure 15-7 Small stoves, lightweight cookware, and dried foods simplify meal preparation.
Courtesy of www.TheExtremeOutfitters.com

COOKING

Initial camping treks usually reveal interests and needs on which campers can base future experiences. Food selection and preparation are areas where it is best to start simple. The fire source for cooking and the type of cookware can be a complex choice; by taking several practice trips, campers can learn which is most appropriate for them.

Fire Source. Food can be cooked either by stove or campfire. Using a stove involves a variety of important decisions and choices that are difficult for the beginner. A campfire is a simpler choice for the tenderfoot, and it provides a gathering place that enhances the camping experience.

STOVE. Stoves vary in the number of burners, use of gas or liquid fuel, weight, amount of time to boil water, and cost. Before purchasing a stove, seek advice from an experienced salesperson about the strengths and weaknesses of each stove. Explain your anticipated needs and your previous experience. Always practice assembling and lighting the stove in advance.

CAMPFIRE. Whether you will use a campfire for cooking or just for atmosphere, you need to follow specific steps. Check for fire restrictions in advance. Locate a spot where there was already a fire or an existing fire ring. Build the fire a minimum of 10 feet away from other flammable materials, tents, and overhanging trees. Keep the fire small so that you conserve wood and keep it in control.

To collect wood and tinder, use a folding saw, small axe, or knife. Before attempting to start the fire, have the following items available: dry matches or lighter, tinder, kindling or newspapers, sticks the size of your thumb or slightly larger, at least four logs from deadwood the size of your forearm, and water. Construct a fire ring with rocks, if one is not already available, to contain the fire.

FOOD

Plan the menu for each meal in advance of the trip. Consider day-hike meals that involve lightweight, nutritional snacks involving only simple preparation, and base camp meals, which can be more elaborate. A storage cooler with ice can hold a variety of food options and will keep food protected for up to 2 days. Choose foods based on their nutrition value, calories, weight, and portability.

Be sure to balance proteins, carbohydrates, and fats, keeping in mind that caloric expenditure will be higher because of added exercise. A large portion of the food choices need to be light in weight for packing and transporting purposes (Figure 15-7). For the novice camper, freeze-dried meals can meet these needs. The drawback is that this type of food is more expensive and definitely requires a water source for preparation.

For a variety of nutritious lightweight choices, consider nuts, dried beans, dried salami, jerky, cheese, peanut butter, dried fruit, raisins, powdered eggs, powdered milk, energy bars, pastas, rice, dry cereal, instant-cook cereal, granola, trail mix, bread, candy bars, hard candy, power bars, powdered soups, "tubes" (such as jelly, cheese, and peanut butter), and crackers.

The ice cooler furnishes storage for larger perishable items for breakfast or evening meals, such as dairy, meats, and fresh produce. Canned food offers more choices, but cans tend to be heavy.

Prepare to start the fire by collecting dry pine needles and twigs from the base of trees or by wadding newspaper into a ball. Place these items in the center of the ring, and build a small tepee over them with small twigs. Light the needles or newspaper. As the fire starts, slowly place finger-sized twigs in the same tepee shape. If the fire is dying, gently blow across the base. Gradually add larger sticks and then logs, keeping the same tent shape. Never leave the fire unattended.

Another method, especially if the wood is damp, is to gather sticks about 1 inch in diameter and 1-foot long. Lay two sticks parallel with each other about 6 inches apart. Continue this process, crisscrossing the previous sticks until there are at least three layers. Stuff kindling (dry needles or newspaper) in the open end of each level. Light the kindling with matches.

Equally important is learning how to safely extinguish the fire. First, separate the materials by using a long stick to spread them out. Gradually pour on water, being careful to avoid the steam. Next, stir with a stick and add water as needed to extinguish the fire. Check under the fire ring rocks for embers, and pour water on them. Make sure that the fire is completely out.

Cooking over Fire. Coals provide a consistent cooking temperature. Place stones that are large enough to sit above the coals in a triangle so that you can place the cookware securely. The higher above the coals, the less the heat, so provide a variety of stone sizes to adjust the temperature as needed. Cover a pot with a lid to reach boiling point more quickly.

Another method is to place two Y-shaped supporting sticks securely in the ground and hang a pot above the flames from a crossbar supported by the sticks. Make sure that these sticks are placed wider than the fire. In this method of cooking, the flame of the fire needs to maintain a consistent height below the pot for an even temperature. The fire needs continuous stoking with wood to achieve the necessary strength.

Cookware. The amount and type of cookware, like other previous decisions, depends on the size of the group and ease of transportation. Food choices and cleaning methods also figure into this decision.

Cookware can be made of aluminum, stainless steel, titanium, or any combination of these materials. Each has its advantages and disadvantages. Aluminum is lightweight but is not durable. Stainless steel is more durable, and titanium costs the most. Cast iron is the most durable, but the weight makes it prohibitive when transportation is a concern. At a minimum you will need a pot with a lid that can also be used as a frying pan or eating bowl. Many lids have a detachable handle, and many pots have a hanging handle. For group camping, a larger pot plus a bowl and spoon for each person will be needed. A griddle is useful for cooking bacon, eggs,

pancakes, and such, but it may be prohibitive because of size and weight. If a griddle is used, a spatula or fork is also necessary. A long-handled skillet is another useful item. A nonstick surface makes for ease of cooking and cleaning. Aluminum foil is another item that can be used to contain and cook food, and it is disposable.

Biodegradable soap and water are most often used for cleaning. Small plastic wash tubs are also useful. Many public sites have a designated place to dump dirty water. If one is not available, do not dump wastewater near water sources such as rivers, lakes, or streams. Nylon scrubbers and steel-wool pads are lightweight materials for cleaning. In remote areas, grass may be used to scrape out cookware, and sand or pinecones may be used for scrubbing with a water rinse. In these cases, use boiling water to sterilize the cookware every few days.

LIGHT SOURCES

The campfire is a light source, but it is stationary. Moveable sources of light, such as flashlights or lanterns (Figure 15-8), are also necessary. In choosing lights, consider the specific needs for the trek and the weight limitations.

Flashlights. A flashlight is a must, especially away from the base camp. Flashlights come in a variety of styles. Consider those that have an adjustable beam focus to meet varying needs. The weight and size are other considerations. Choose batteries according to ease of purchase, staying power, units of candlepower, and size/weight. Heavy-duty lights with a 6-volt battery might be appropriate for the base camp, but not for the trail.

Lanterns. Like flashlights, lanterns come in an almost endless variety: large and small; battery-powered, gas-fueled, and propane fueled; lightweight and heavy

Figure 15-8 Candle, battery, and gas- or propane-fueled lantern sources provide light.
Courtesy of www.TheExtremeOutfitters.com

duty. Determine your specific needs, and then consult a professional outfitter for recommendations. It is always a good idea to try several lanterns at the store before making a final purchase.

HUMAN WASTE

It was previously suggested that the beginning camper select a public camping site, such as a state park. One reason is the availability of toilet facilities. However, toilet facilities are not always available on a hike.

Plan ahead by carrying some toilet paper in a resealable plastic bag, an empty bag, and a small shovel. Locate a flat, open site 150 feet or more away from water sources, the hiking trail, or other people. Dig a hole 6 to 8 inches deep with the shovel or with a sharp stick. Deposit the fecal matter in the hole. Place the soiled toilet paper in the empty, resealable plastic bag. Cover the hole with dirt. Carry the soiled toilet paper in the sealed plastic bag, and immediately dispose of it after the hike at the public campsite toilet facilities. If this is not feasible, then carefully burn the paper in small amounts within a fire ring, but only as a last resort.

Safety Considerations

Plan for emergency situations in advance of the trip. This text cannot adequately cover all situations with specific detail, so it is recommended that advanced training and knowledge be part of the preparation for the trip. Refer to the comprehensive references section at the end of the book. Additionally, Red Cross training for cardiopulmonary resuscitation (CPR) and first aid provides skills that might be needed on a hiking, backpacking, or camping trip. The following sections discuss the basics of first-aid kit equipment, what to do if a hiker gets lost, safety concerns about weather conditions, and encountering living nature—animals, creepy/crawly hazards, and plants.

FIRST-AID KIT

Although you can prepare your own first-aid kit, purchasing a preassembled kit is usually a better choice. Kits prepared especially for wilderness activities are available from camping outfitters (Figure 15-9). CPR and first-aid training should also be taken. Suggested items to include in a kit are listed below; in making your choices, keep in mind that weight is always a prime consideration.

Bandaging

Sterile gauze pads
Adhesive bandages (various)
Moleskin
Tape
Elastic wrap

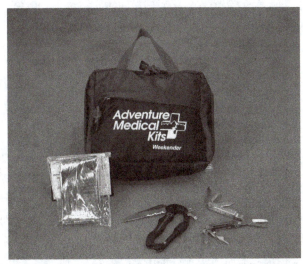

Figure 15-9 Safety equipment should include a first-aid kit, lightweight thermal blanket, and multipurpose tools. Courtesy of www.TheExtremeOutfitters.com

Medicating

Pain relief medication
Antacids
Antihistamines
Decongestants

Treating

Antibiotic ointment
Tincture of benzoin
Calamine or Caladryl lotion
Anti-itch ointment
Sunscreen
Snake-bite kit
Ice pack

Other

Needle
Safety pin
Scissors
Tweezers
Pocket knife
Matches
Flashlight (and batteries)
Duct tape
Sunglasses
Whistle
Mirror
Fire starter
Water purification pills

GETTING LOST

It is wise to provide an itinerary for others in the group and give a copy to the park ranger. Identify the trail or area where you plan to be, and estimate how long you expect to be away. A knife, matches, whistle, compass, water, energy food bars, poncho, and jacket can be especially useful if you get lost.

If you get lost, stay where you are and do not wander. Electronic devices such as cell phones and very high frequency (VHF) radios are invaluable aids. Stay calm, and build a fire. A fire is the most noticeable signal, especially at night, or if it is smoky, during the daylight. Green wood and boughs supply fuel that produces heavy smoke. Build three fires 100 feet apart in the shape of a triangle to send a distress signal to aircraft; choose a location on a hill or in an open clearing. Holding both arms above the head is also a distress signal to aircraft, as is reflecting light off a mirror.

Use a whistle to signal for help. Blow the whistle three times at 5-, 10-, and 15-minute intervals to signal distress. Of course, you can yell for help, but the whistle is shriller and carries greater distances.

If nightfall is approaching, gather a lot of wood before dark to fuel a fire all night for warmth and for signaling. Build a lean-to shelter for protection from moisture. The many resources listed in the Further References section provide specific information on building a variety of structures. Collect dry pine needles or leaves to build a bed for protection from ground moisture. Drink water to avoid hypothermia. Stay as warm and as dry as possible.

WEATHER

The main safety concerns for mild weather travel are electrical storms, hypothermia, and hyperthermia. In an electrical storm, seek a low valley, stay away from tall trees, stay away from metal (tent poles, frames of backpacks, etc.), and avoid bodies of water.

Hypothermia can result if you get wet or cold and then are unable to get warm. Hyperthermia can result if you get too hot and cannot cool down. Seek first-aid information so that you can recognize the symptoms and treat these conditions. Red Cross manuals or *The Ultimate Survival Guide* listed in the Further References section provide the necessary information.

ENCOUNTERS WITH LIVING NATURE

Animals. Storing food properly and keeping a clean camp are the main measures for avoiding animals. Check with the rangers or park attendants before the trip to find out what kinds of animals are prevalent in the area.

When car camping, store all food in the car. Other items, such as salt, pepper, candy, toothpaste, and lotions, also attract animals. A cooking stove and cookware may carry a scent that attracts animals. Collect trash properly; keeping it and all other items in the vehicle overnight leads to a less dangerous and more

restful night's sleep. It is dangerous to keep any scented items in the tent.

When you are in a more remote setting, store food and trash by hanging these items from a high tree branch. Select a limb that is approximately 15 to 20 feet high and that extends 10 to 15 feet out from the tree. Attach a bag full of food items to a long rope, and throw the rope over the limb. Pull the rope until the bag almost touches the limb. Next, attach a second bag of equal weight as high as possible to the dangling rope. Take a long stick to push the second bag up until both bags are about equal distance (approximately 10 feet) above the ground and near the end of the extending limb. A thin extended limb is best because it will not support a large animal.

Safety from bears is a serious consideration. Beginning campers should select areas where this is not a concern. Before addressing these problems, the camper needs to obtain more advanced knowledge and skills. Several books and Web sites are listed at the end of the book that can provide complete instruction for dealing with the bear problem.

Snakes. Contact park rangers in advance of the trip to determine the types of venomous snakes found in the area. Study the markings and habits of these snakes in advance. Red Cross training is a necessity, as is having a snake-bite kit available. Heavy hiking boots, full-length gaiters, and heavy long pants help provide lower leg protection from bites.

Creepy-Crawly Hazards. Spiders, ticks, and mosquitoes present concerns for the camper. There are three types of venomous spiders in the United States. Before the trip, get to know their markings and habits, and learn to recognize the signs and symptoms of their bite. Be able to provide first-aid care and address medical needs. Red Cross training is advised.

Ticks are a concern during the late spring and summer months. The most serious problem is the possibility of contracting Lyme disease from certain species. In advance of the trek, study how to recognize ticks, remove them, treat their bite, recognize symptoms of further problems, and provide treatment. Again, Red Cross training is recommended, as well as consulting the sources listed at the end of this book.

To prevent a tick from getting on the skin, wear long pants and tuck them into the socks. Wear a hat or other head covering. Wear light-colored clothing to help spot ticks. Always inspect the skin closely after hiking in the woods. Use tweezers to extract any ticks that are attached to the skin. Follow Red Cross protocol for examination of the skin and for treatment.

Mosquitoes are more a nuisance than a threat. Several types of repellents, with varying chemical ingredients, are available. Read labels carefully to identify potent ingredients and precautions. As with ticks, it is best to avoid mosquitoes as much as possible. They like the scent of lotions and dislike breezy conditions. Long sleeves and pants are the best protection. Make sure to keep the tent entrance covered at all times. Include anti-itch cream in the first-aid kit.

Plants.   Be able to recognize poisonous plants. Before the trip, study the leaf shapes and textures. Skin exposure is a primary concern, but just touching clothing brushed by these plants can irritate some people's skin. The smoke from burning wood that has been in contact with poisonous plants can also cause irritation. Calamine or Caladryl lotion from the first-aid kit can help alleviate the irritation.

Etiquette

The primary rule of both trail and camping etiquette is "Leave it the way you found it or even better." The following list offers suggestions to help the hiker and camper keep natural resources beautiful for future generations.

1. Stay on the trail.
2. Walk in small groups—single file.
3. Leave wildlife alone.
4. Do not collect souvenirs.
5. Do not use electronic noise devices.
6. Wear muted colors.
7. Locate your campsite at least 150 feet from other campers, water sources, the trail, or toilet facilities.
8. Pack out what you pack in, or dispose of items through accepted camping procedures.
9. Do not wash clothes or cookware in natural water sources.
10. Use existing fire rings when possible.
11. Do not dig unnecessary holes or trenches.
12. Do not litter.
13. Keep campfires small.
14. If burning trash is necessary, burn only paper.
15. Use a hole or trench for human waste.
16. Keep loud noise to a minimum.
17. Use only fallen deadwood for a campfire.
18. Use a camp stove to conserve nature's wood sources.

Skill Assessment

Hiking, backpacking, and camping, referred to as outdoor pursuits in the activity classifications identified in an earlier chapter (Chapter 1, *Considerations for Effective Skill Learning*), do not fit into a traditional individual specialized skill test structure. An outdoor pursuits unit stresses learning more in the cognitive and affective domains than in learning individual specialized skills (psychomotor). Thus, no skill test is presented.

It is suggested that this unit be organized by assigning specific groups specific tasks required in planning a group overnight hiking, backpacking, and camping excursion. For example, one group prepares safety considerations for the trip. They might prepare a checklist for a first-aid kit and gather the necessary items; discuss and prepare a handout covering dos and don'ts if lost; research weather concerns and preparation for inclement weather; and identify procedures for dealing with animals, snakes, plants, and other natural hazards.

A rubric can be developed for assessing the cognitive and affective domains. However, as previously stated, assessment in this textbook relates specifically to individual specialized skills tests. Development of a rubric for alternative assessment in the cognitive or affective domains requires research in test and measurement textbooks.

Modifications for Special Populations

ORTHOPEDICALLY IMPAIRED

1. Some park facilities have paved surfaces for wheelchair hiking accessibility. For additional information and suggestions, contact Adaptive Sports Association, P.O. Box 1884, Durango, CO 81302, www.asadurango.com.

COGNITIVELY IMPAIRED

1. Peer students might be needed to assist with hiking, backpacking, or camping outings.
2. Make sure students have developed good cardiovascular fitness prior to engaging in hiking and backpacking.
3. Try to hike on level surfaces as much as possible.

SENSORY IMPAIRED

1. Students who are visually impaired or blind can be tethered to their sighted peers when hiking. Make sure to provide training sessions for the sighted peers beforehand.
2. Students who are visually impaired or blind can, with practice, assist in many camping duties, such as setting up the tent, building the fire ring, and cleaning the cookware.
3. Students who are deaf or have a hearing impairment will need minimal modifications. Make sure to maintain eye contact with these students during any trips through wooded areas.

Terminology

A-frame A basic tent shape in which the cross section resembles the letter A.

backcountry Off the beaten path, where amenities are not available.

barrel bag A sleeping bag constructed for warmer climates that is roomy but bulkier and heavier than a mummy-style bag.

bivouac A site where a tent is set up.

burn time The length of time a camp stove or lantern will burn given its capacity of fuel.

campsite The area for sleeping and building a fire.

checklist A list of important items for taking on a trek.

daypack A small backpack that holds enough gear for a one-day outing.

dome A free-standing tent shape in which the poles create a dome by curving over each other.

double-walled tent A tent made of dual-construction fabric that provides insulation by trapping a pocket of air between the layers.

external-frame pack A backpack supported by a rigid frame on the outside of the pack.

fire ring A ring of stones or other nonflammable material to protect a fire from spreading to other areas.

four-season tent A tent that is designed to handle any condition and for all seasons.

free-standing Tents that do not require stakes or support lines to stand erect.

gaiters Lower leg protectors against the elements and terrain.

ground stakes Anchors that hold a tent to the ground.

hip belt The main adjustable support device on a backpack; often has storage pockets or clips.

internal-frame pack A backpack supported by stays on the inside of the construction.

modified dome A dome tent that has been designed for specific weather elements.

mummy bag A close-fitting, shaped, hooded sleeping bag that conserves body heat.

pole sleeves Fabric tunnels on the outside of a tent for inserting the poles.

purifier A water system that removes contaminants and microorganisms with a combination of specialized filters.

rain-fly A covering that helps keep the tent dry and protects it from wind.

single-walled tent A single-fabric construction tent that is lightweight and chemically treated against water leakage.

stuff sack A small sack with draw cords for storing and carrying items.

three-season tent A tent recommended for use in summer, spring, and fall.

topographical map A map that identifies land features, roads, and distinguishing structures.

tunnel tent A low-profile tent that is long and rounded in the shape of a tunnel.

two-way zipper A set of zippers running toward each other on the same slider.

ultralight tent A tent weighing 5 pounds or less designed for one or two people; it can be carried in or on a backpack.

vestibule An area outside of a tent often created by extending the rain-fly.

Discussion Questions

1. What considerations should the hiker or camper take into account when selecting clothing and footwear?

2. Identify the criteria the hiker or camper needs to consider when selecting a backpack.

3. Compare the advantages and disadvantages of the types of tents available for overnight camping.

4. Discuss the variety of needs one must consider when cooking is a part of the camping experience.

5. Discuss how responsible hikers and campers follow the motto "Leave it the way you found it or even better."

6. Safety is an important consideration in the wilderness. Discuss safety factors, in detail, and present preplanning ideas for each.

7. Discuss plans for staying hydrated during a wilderness trek.

8. Identify the ways human waste might be disposed of safely and in consideration of the environment.

9. Discuss plans and actions for a lost camper.

Web Sites

www.thebackpacker.com—offers a beginner's corner, backpacker directory, articles, a question-and-answer section, trail database, and more.

www.backpacking.net—serves as repository of resources useful for year-round backcountry safety and enjoyment for the modern backpacker; promotes ultralight backpacking and hiking, featuring lightweight backpacking equipment; and provides information on backcountry outdoor gear.

www.americanhiking.org American Hiking Society—offers information about trail conservation and policy, events around the country, information about the National Trail Endowment, and more.

www.backpacker.com *Backpacker Magazine*—provides articles, technique suggestions, gear information, and much more.

www.gorp.com/gorp/activity/hiking.htm Great Outdoors Recreation—offers information on where to hike, trail finders, how to hike, gear, Web links, and discussion boards.

| # Lacrosse

This chapter will enable you to:

- Identify the similarities and differences of the playing field in women's and men's lacrosse
- Analyze and demonstrate the techniques of the scoop, carry, throw, cradle, and dodge
- Describe the rules of the game for men's and women's lacrosse
- Describe basic offensive and defensive tactics
- Understand and use the basic terminology

Nature and Purpose

Lacrosse is a fast-paced invasion team game that is considered to be the oldest North American sport. The modern game involves passing (throwing) and catching a small, dense rubber ball using a lacrosse stick or *crosse*, to shoot and score in a 6-feet by 6-feet goal. The stick is used to pass, catch, scoop, carry, dribble, and tackle, as well as to check opponents and their sticks when rules allow. Lacrosse is generally played on an outdoor field roughly the size of a soccer field and has several unique rules that set it apart from other team sports. The men's and women's outdoor games differ from each other in the type of equipment, contact rules, field dimensions, and components.

History

Lacrosse is an ancient game that began with the American Indians of the northeast. The violent nature of the original game can be surmised from the American Indian name for the game, *baaga àdowe* (Ojibway for "bump hips"). In early American Indian life lacrosse served several purposes. The sport was used to resolve intertribal conflicts, to train young warriors, and as a religious ritual or celebration. The games involved 100 to 1,000 men playing on fields from 500 yards to miles in length, with games lasting up to three days.[1] Game objects varied from balls to pieces of bone connected with a leather thong. The name *lacrosse* was coined by French missionaries who saw American Indians playing the game. Jesuit missionary Jean de Brebeuf brought knowledge of the game to Westerners after seeing Iroquois playing it in 1636. The lacrosse stick was named *crosse* based on its similarity to a bishop's crozier; the game's name is a contraction of the phrase *le jeu de la crosse* ("the game of the hooked stick").

In 1856, a Canadian dentist, Dr. William George Beers, founded the Montreal Lacrosse Club and devised rules for the modern game.[2] He shortened the length of the game and reduced the number of players to 10 per side. The first competitive game was played in 1867, when Upper Canada College lost to the Toronto Cricket Club, 3–1. By the early 1900s the game had spread to high schools, colleges, and universities. Lacrosse was included in the Olympics as a medal sport in 1928 and 1932.[3] The modern women's game began when the men's game was exported to Europe. The headmistress of St. Leonards School in Scotland, Louisa Lumsden, adapted the rules for women in 1890, and soon the women's game was introduced in the United States.

Lacrosse was an outdoor sport until the 1930s, when Canadian hockey arena owners developed *box lacrosse*, a game that is played on an ice hockey rink that has been covered and converted into an indoor arena. This venture was so successful that box lacrosse emerged as the dominant form in Canada; however, the outdoor game has made a comeback. In 1987 the Eagle Pro Box Lacrosse League (now National Lacrosse League) formed professional clubs in cities throughout Canada and the United States. In 2001, Major League Lacrosse (MLL) was founded with 6 teams, and by 2007 had grown to 10 teams.[4]

In recent years the popularity of lacrosse in schools has grown exponentially. According to the U.S. Lacrosse National Federation of High Schools, lacrosse is currently the fastest growing high school sport.

Men's Lacrosse

PLAYING FIELD

Field dimensions are 110 yards long by 60 yards wide (Figure 16-1). Goals measure 6 feet by 6 feet and use a rugged mesh netting similar to an ice hockey goal. The goal is in the center of a circle, or crease, 18 feet in

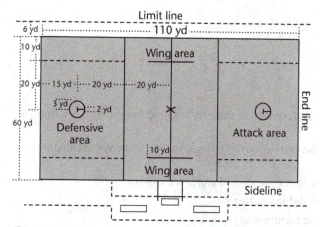

Figure 16-1   Men's lacrosse field with dimensions in yards.

diameter. The area behind the crease is referred to as "X." As in ice hockey, an attackman positions himself at X during offensive set-ups so he can retrieve the ball after a shot goes out-of-bounds. In lacrosse, normal out-of-bounds rules apply (possession goes to the other team); however, if the ball goes out-of-bounds behind the goal, possession goes to the player nearest the point at which it went out-of-bounds.

EQUIPMENT

Each player carries a *crosse* or lacrosse stick measuring 40–42 inches long ("short crosse"), or 52—72 inches long ("long crosse"). The goalie is allowed a stick 40–72 inches long. On all crosses the head must be at least 6.5 inches at the widest part and at least 2.5 inches wide at its narrowest (see Figure 16-3).

A goalie's crosse head can measure up to 15 inches. This head is much larger than those carried by the other players and is helpful in blocking shots on goal. A team may have only four long crosses on the field. Often the three defensemen carry long crosses, but the long crosses can be distributed among all positions. Modern sticks typically have a shaft of aluminum, titanium, or alloy, with a required plastic or rubber cap at the bottom. The modern stick head is a hard plastic frame strung with string or leather mesh. The strings in the "pocket" are called shooting strings and accuracy or "v" strings. The strings are either mesh or woven. Goalies prefer the mesh, which keeps rebounds at a minimum. Likewise, the mesh strings are better for beginning players.

Lacrosse players are required to wear helmets and gloves (similar to ice hockey gloves). Men often also wear shoulder pads, elbow pads, and mouth guards. Other protective gear includes rib pads and cups.

Both men's and women's games use a dense rubber ball, typically yellow in color, with specific bounce characteristics. It must be 7.75–8 inches in circumference and weigh between 5–5.25 ounces.

BASIC RULES

Men's lacrosse is a contact sport. It involves two teams of 10 players each: a goalkeeper ("goalie"), three defensemen, three midfielders, and three attackmen. Players are allowed anywhere on the field, excluding the goal circle, as long as there is no offside violation (see offside).

PLAY

Games consist of four 15-minute quarters (four 12-minute quarters for high school games). Time runs continuously, with no stoppage for a dead ball. Stoppages occur at the discretion of the referee for delays such as injuries or a long ball out-of-bounds. The game is usually controlled by a referee and an umpire. In addition, a third official, or field judge, may be used. Quarters and restarts after a goal begin with a face-off. The ball is placed on the ground and the face-off opponents' sticks are laid down next to it. Face-off men tussle for the ball, either attempting to get possession or trapping it under the stick and then flicking to one of their midfielders. Midfielders must start from behind the restraining line, 10 yards from the sideline, and run in on the whistle. Attackmen and defensemen have to wait behind their restraining line until a player from the midfield has possession of the ball.

Players must scoop the ball from the ground with their crosse. They may run carrying the ball in their stick, and pass or throw the ball to other players or to the goal. Players are allowed to kick the ball and may also cover it with the crosse as long as the ball is not kept out of play.

Scoring. A shot can be made from any part of the field. The whole ball must cross the goal line or break the plane of the line to count. The body of the attacker may not enter the crease and his crosse may not break the plane of the goal crease during a shot or its follow-through.

Offside. At all times a team must have three players in its attack half between the end line and centerline and four players in its defensive half. Because players on one team cannot crowd the offense's goal, the game is more open and free-flowing as well as generally high scoring.

Out-of-bounds. A ball thrown or carried out-of-bounds goes to the opposing team, which can throw it in or run it in from the sideline. If a ball goes out-of-bounds over the end line after a shot on goal, the *nearest player* to the ball on its exit gets the ball. Thus, offensive teams with a player in the X can maintain possession of the ball after a missed shot on goal.

Substitutions. Players may be substituted during suspended play after the ball goes out-of-bounds or during play, as in ice hockey. One player may be substituted at a time; players must be exchanged at a special substitution area by the center of the field. There are no limits to substitutions and players may reenter the game.

Fouls and Penalties. Body and stick checks are legal in men's lacrosse; however, there are limitations on contact. An opponent may be legally bodychecked if he is in possession of the ball or within 5 yards of a loose ball. Contact must be made above the knees, from the front or side of the opponent. A player may also use their stick to check their opponent's stick. A gloved hand is considered part of the stick and may be checked, but no other body part may be checked with the stick. Similar to ice hockey, rule violators must spend a prescribed amount of time in a penalty box. The penalized team plays a man down until he returns.

Fouls are categorized as personal fouls or technical fouls. *Personal fouls* are more serious and include illegal body checks, slashing (downward slashing action of stick), unnecessary roughness, tripping, and unsportsmanlike conduct. Most personal fouls result in a 1-minute suspension. However, suspension time can be 1 to 3 minutes, based on what the referee believes was the intent or severity of the foul. *Technical fouls* are less serious and result in removal from play for 30 seconds if the offending player's team does not have possession of the ball. Technical fouls include interference, pushing, holding, offside, and stalling. Players must stay in the penalty box for the full time allotted, unless a goal is scored, at which time they may leave the box for all except expulsion fouls and unsportsmanlike conduct, for which the full time must be served.

The *alternate possession* rule is used for "neutral" infractions, such as simultaneous fouls or the ball getting caught in a player's uniform or crosse for more than 4 seconds. A coin toss at the start of the game decides which team gets possession of the ball first in such a situation; possession alternates after that.

A *slow whistle* is used when a defending player commits a violation against an attacking player in possession of the ball close to the goal. The referee will drop a flag but not blow the whistle until the scoring play is over. At that point, either a goal is scored or the attack is over and the ball has left the area, in which case the infraction will be called.[5,6]

Women's Lacrosse

PLAYING FIELD

The women's field did not have specified boundaries until 2005. The playing area is 120–140 yards long by 60–70 yards wide, with a 6 feet by 6 feet goal (Figure 16-2). The goal is in the center of a circle or crease 18 feet in diameter. Goals are set 100 yards apart. Surrounding the goal area is a 12-meter fan, a half-circle centered on the goal line. In addition,

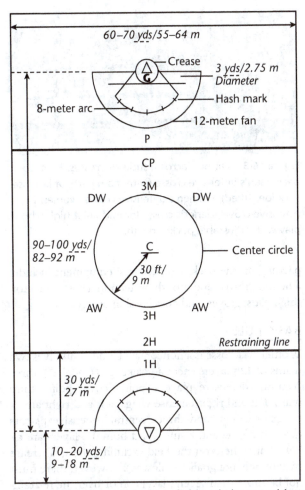

Figure 16-2 Women's lacrosse field and player positions.

there is an 8-meter arc of about 80 degrees, a center circle of 30 feet radius, and a restraining line parallel to the goal line and 30 yards in front of each goal. In women's lacrosse, if the ball goes out-of-bounds, possession goes to the player nearest the point at which it went out-of-bounds. If two players are equal distance from the out-of-bounds ball, the game reconvenes with a *throw* from the referee.

EQUIPMENT

Each player carries a *crosse* measuring 36–44 inches long. The stick shaft can be made of aluminum, fiberglass, or wood; the head made of wood or plastic; and the pocket material made of gut, leather, or nylon. The head is strung with 4–5 thongs, with 8–12 cross-stitches; webbing is not allowed. The pocket is shallower than on the men's crosse, with the maximum depth allowed at 2.5 inches (Figure 16-3). The head is 10–12 inches long and 7–9 inches wide. The goalie is allowed a stick 36–48 inches long. The head of the women's goalie crosse may be larger than those of other players and may have webbing. In addition to eye protection, women wear mouthguards and sometimes close-fitting gloves with

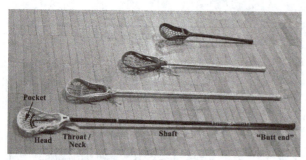

Figure 16-3 Various lacrosse sticks or *crosses. Front to back:* men's defensive crosse (with main parts of lacrosse stick identified); women's defensive crosse; women's offensive crosse; generic crosse for middle or high school play with adjustable pocket depth.

padding on the back. Goalkeepers' equipment includes a helmet, throat and mouth protection, chest protector, thigh pads, gloves, and possibly shin protectors.

BASIC RULES

Women's lacrosse is a noncontact game. It involves two teams of 12 players each: a goalkeeper ("goalie"), three "central" defensive players (point, cover point, third man), left and right defense wings, left and right attack wings, a center, and three "central" offensive players (first home, second home, third home). Players are allowed anywhere on the field excluding the goal crease (where only the goalie is allowed); however, there must not be more than seven players on or over the restraining line (Figure 16-2) in a team's offensive end, and no more than eight players over the restraining line in a team's defensive end.

PLAY

Games consist of two 30-minute halves (two 25-minute halves for high school games). Time runs continuously, with no stoppage for a dead ball. Stoppages occur at the discretion of the referee for delays such as injuries or a long ball out-of-bounds. Halves and restarts after a goal begin with a draw. The ball is placed between the stick heads of opposing centers. Sticks are held over and in line with the centerline. The referee calls *ready* and the centers try to get control of the ball. Wings and other players must be outside the center circle for the draw. Players must scoop the ball from the ground with their crosse. Players may run carrying the ball in their crosse and pass or throw the ball to other players or to the goal. Players are not allowed to kick the ball or cover it with their crosse.

Scoring. A shot can be made from any part of the field; the whole ball must cross the goal line or break the plane of the line to count. The body of the attacker may not enter the crease and the crosse may not break

the plane of the goal crease during a shot or its follow-through. The ball may not be shot deliberately at the goalie. If the goal crease is violated or the ball does not cross the line, the goalie gets to place the ball in her crosse and pass it out of the crease within 10 seconds.

Offside. At all times, a team must have three players in its attack half, between the end line and centerline, and four players in its defensive half.

Out-of-bounds. When a ball or player goes out-of-bounds, players *stand* and the other team gets the ball 13 feet from the spot it went out-of-bounds. For a deflected shot, the nearest player gets the ball.

Substitutions. Players may be substituted during suspended play after the ball goes out-of-bounds, after a goal, at halftime, or during play. One player may be substituted at a time; players must be exchanged at a special substitution area by the center of the field. Players may reenter the game; there are no limits to substitutions.

Fouls and Penalties. Body and stick checks are illegal in women's lacrosse. A cross check is allowed whereby a defender makes stick to stick contact with their opponent to dislodge the ball. Fouls are categorized as *major fouls, minor fouls,* or *goal crease fouls.*

Major fouls include (1) dangerous/rough stick checks; (2) slashing or stick to body contact; (3) holding the ball too close (preventing stick check); (4) reaching the stick across an opponent from behind; (5) blocking a player's movement without letting her leave the area; (6) blocking "free space to the goal" (cone-shaped area close to the goal between ball carrier and goal posts/goal line); (7) staying in the 8-meter arc longer than 3 seconds if not closely guarding an opponent (one defender per attacker); (8) blocking a player's movement or pushing through a defender with the body when carrying the ball; (9) holding the stick dangerously close to the opponent's head or neck area.

Minor fouls include (1) covering a ground ball with stick or foot; (2) checking an opponent's empty stick; (3) guarding one's own stick with hand or elbow; (4) playing the ball off the body (with the exception of the goalie within the crease); (5) touching the ball with the hand; (6) throwing the crosse; (7) stepping into the center circle prior to the whistle on the starting or center draw; (8) playing with an illegal crosse.

Goal crease fouls include field players entering the goal circle with any part of their body or stick, and goalies (1) playing the ball outside the goal crease with the hand; (2) returning to the crease from outside it while carrying the ball; (3) allowing the ball to stay in the crease for more than 10 seconds; (4) placing one foot outside the goal circle while dragging the ball inside the crease; (5) scoring a goal with a stick that does not comply with field stick specifications.

Penalty for major and minor fouls: A "free position" is awarded for these violations. On the referee's whistle, players must stand. The fouled player is awarded the ball and all other players moved 13 feet away. For a major foul, the offending player is moved 13 feet *behind* the player awarded the ball. From the free position the player may carry, throw, or shoot the ball (except for *indirect* offenses—see the following section for minor fouls) on restart, which is a signal and whistle from the referee.

Penalty for major fouls inside the 12-meter fan: For a major foul committed by the defense within the fan, the offensive player is awarded a free position from the spot of the foul. All players and their crosses, except the goalie, are moved out of the penalty lane (direct pathway to the goal between player awarded free position and goal).

Penalty for minor fouls inside the 12-meter fan: For a minor foul committed by the defense within the 8-meter arc, the offensive player is awarded an *indirect* free position from a spot on the fan nearest the point of the foul. All players remain where they were (from the stand), so long as they are 13 feet away, or they must move to a distance 13 feet away. The offending player is placed 13 feet behind the offended player. Another player must contact the ball before it can be shot on goal from an indirect free position.

Penalty for major fouls inside the 8-meter arc: For a major foul committed by the defense within the arc, the offensive player is awarded a free position from the nearest hash mark on the arc. All players and their crosses, except the goalie, are moved out of the 8-meter arc penalty lane (direct pathway to the goal), and the player committing the offense is placed 13 feet behind the offended player. If the foul occurs to one side of the arc, the player takes the free position from that line, 8 meters from the goal, and all players are removed from the penalty lane.

Throw: If the game is stopped because of a neutral situation, such as the ball getting caught in a crosse or a player's uniform, two players being equally close to the ball when it goes out-of-bounds, or simultaneous fouls, a *throw* occurs. One player from each team stands 3 feet apart from the other, on their defensive sides, and 6 yards from the referee. All other players must be 13 feet away from the team representatives. The referee blows the whistle and throws the ball upward, just above head height, between the two players. On the whistle they can run for the ball and their teammates may move also.

A *slow whistle* is used for women's lacrosse in the same manner as the men's game.[7,8]

Suggested Learning Sequence

A. History and purpose
B. Crosse, ball, and other equipment; safety rules
  1. Scoop
  2. Carry—left and right hand
  3. Cradle—left and right hand
  4. Throw; catch; throw/catch combinations; modified games
  5. Throwing and catching on the run
  6. Shooting—overhand
C. Dodges:
  i) "bull";
  ii) face;
  iii) roll
D. Individual defense
E. Games: one on one; two on two
F. Basic strategy: triangular play, shape, movement
G. Three on three—one on one marking
H. Shooting—sidearm
I. Intermediate strategy: offensive width and depth; defensive delay, contraction, and expansion
J. Games: six on six; seven on seven
K. Full-sided games; field positions (optional)

Skills and Techniques

GRIP

The lacrosse grip can vary depending on whether the player is carrying, cradling, receiving, or defending. The basic grip involves holding the (short) crosse at the bottom of the shaft with the nonthrowing hand and at the top of the shaft, just below the head of the crosse, with the throwing hand. The throwing hand should hold the shaft in the fingers, with a relaxed grip, allowing for an effective cradle. When holding the stick comfortably in front of the body and slightly over to the throwing side, the inner edge of the head should be facing the player, with the open pocket facing to the nonthrowing side and slightly inward. This position will enable the player to receive, carry, cradle, and throw the ball with relative comfort without changing grip. Lacrosse is an ambidextrous game—left- or right-handed carries can be made with one or both hands.

In a two-handed carry, a right-handed carry means the right hand is on top.

▶ Learning Hints

Have students practice left and right one- and two-handed grips. Those comfortable with a left-handed grip can play on the left side of the field.

SCOOP

The scoop is necessary to retrieve a ground ball quickly by scooping it into the crosse. To scoop the ball from the ground, the player gets into a low position, with one foot in front of the other, the body turned slightly sideways. Bending forward, the player holds the stick low to the ground, pointing down slightly. The head of the crosse should slide on the ground under the ball.

A   **B**

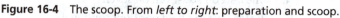

Figure 16-4   The scoop. From *left to right*: preparation and scoop.

For a right-handed carry/scoop, the right foot should be forward (Figure 16-4). For a left-handed carry/scoop, the left foot should be in front. In preparation for an effective and safe scoop, the crosse should be close to the body and the end of the stick should be angled slightly away from the body so that the player does not "spear" herself with it.

▶ Practice/Organizational Suggestions

Have students practice the scoop without, then with a ball. Have them practice left and right handed. Make sure they get the crosse low and the tip of the head on the ground under the ball. Have them practice scooping and carrying the ball (the area around a ground ball may be crowded during play).

CARRY

In the men's game, the ball is often carried in the stick without a cradling action—on the side away from potential defenders—because the men's crosse has a deeper pocket and the ball stays more easily in it. To carry the ball when being guarded and to carry effectively in the women's game with the ball in a shallower pocket, players should learn the cradle.

CRADLE

The cradle is used to travel with the ball when being guarded and to keep the ball buried in the pocket. In an *upright cradle*, the player moves the stick, held vertically, across the body from left to right shoulder, at the same time rotating the head 180 degrees so that the back of the pocket faces the shoulder at the end points of the cradle action (Figure 16-5). The upper hand creates most of the cradling action by moving the stick across the body and rotating it with a flexion and extension of the wrist, or

"rolling" action of the hand. Proper, relaxed grip enables a player to rotate the stick quickly and easily for an effective cradle. In a *front cradle*, the action of the upper hand is similar, but the stick is held horizontally, so the movement of the stick is vertical (upward and downward) on the carry side of the body. Rotation of the head is again 180 degrees, so as to keep the ball in the pocket.

▶ Practice/Organizational Suggestions

If indoors, players may stand with their backs to a wall and move their crosses across their bodies from shoulder to shoulder. The faces of the stick heads should tap the wall each time the sticks pass from throwing to nonthrowing side, and the backs of the stick heads should tap each time the sticks pass from nonthrowing to throwing side. Have students practice without, then with a ball standing, walking, and running. Have them practice left- and right-handed cradles.

THROW

A throw (not to be confused with the referee throw in a game) is how the ball is passed from player to player in lacrosse. The three types of throws are overarm lever, overarm punch, and sidearm.

Overarm lever: Bring the crosse behind the shooting side shoulder by moving the throwing hand back and the nonthrowing hand forward; pocket should be facing up. Bring the throwing hand through in an overhand throwing action while stepping forward with the nonthrowing side (contralateral) foot. For a basic throw, the nonthrowing hand should finish near the thigh of the contralateral leg, the throwing hand should snap through as when throwing a ball with the hand, and the crosse pocket should face the target (Figure 16-6). For a more advanced throwing action,

A   B   C

Figure 16-5 The cradle. Note the shallowness of the women's crosse pocket.

and for greater speed and distance in the throw, the nonthrowing hand should pull in toward the shoulder of the throwing arm, the throwing wrist snap through a little more, and the crosse follow through until parallel with the ground (i.e., more follow-through).

Overarm punch: This throw is appropriate when being closely guarded because it can be performed quickly and in a restricted space. The throw is similar to the overarm lever, but the head is brought back only to the shoulder and the follow-through may be slightly shorter, with or without the snap follow-through.

For both overarm throws, the grip should adjust slightly so that the throwing hand moves around until the palm is facing the back of the crosse.

Sidearm throw: When a player is guarded by a defender whose crosse is in front of the passer's throwing side to block a pass, the thrower can switch hands and throw from the opposite side (difficult to do quickly) or make a sidearm throw. The throw begins in similar fashion to the overarm throw, but then the throwing hand drops to the throwing side, the lower hand comes up, and while the throwing hand sweeps around in a sidearm throwing action, the nonthrowing hand draws up and sharply toward the opposite shoulder (Figure 16-7). The grip for sidearm throws is similar to that for the cradle, so the thrower will not need to change grip if shooting from a cradle.

▶ Practice/Organizational Suggestions

Have players practice the techniques by throwing a ball, overarm and sidearm, to a partner or target. Also have players attempt the action of the nonthrowing hand. Next, have players use just the stick to get the overarm and sidearm action. Finally, have players throw the ball using the crosse to a target if indoors or a fence if outdoors. Progress to having players throw from a run. A defender can be added to make the thrower decide which type of throw to use.

CATCH

The catch is made with the hands in a similar position and grip as used in the cradle. The proficient catcher will catch the ball and smoothly transition into a cradle. The receiver should move into position behind the incoming ball so that it is on their stick side. The upper hand should turn out and the arm extend to reach the face of the crosse head toward the incoming ball. As soon as the ball hits the middle of the pocket, the receiver makes the crosse give and absorb the force of the ball by moving toward the body, as the other hand assists by moving away from the body. After the catch is made the player should move immediately into the upright cradle position (Figure 16-8).

A catch may be made above or below the shoulders, or on the backhand side. The key is to maneuver the

Figure 16-6 Overarm throw.

Figure 16-7 Sidearm throw/shot.

crosse so that the pocket faces the incoming ball. This maneuver may be done by lowering the stick, extending it to the side, or moving it across the body, and rotating the upper hand inward for a backhand catch. Other options for backhand catches are to switch hands or to slide to the side to make the catch a regular forehand catch.

▶ Practice/Organizational Suggestions

It can be useful to have players catch a soft ball with one hand above the waist, below the waist, and to the forehand and backhand sides. A stick can then be added. Have players catch from stationary and then moving positions. Ultimately, have partners move, throw, and catch to each other and play small-sided keep-away games of throw and catch.

SHOOTING

Shooting in lacrosse uses throwing—in this case, at the goal. Sidearm throws around defenders or overarm throws should be aimed at the upper or lower corners of the goal, as the goalie, usually in the middle of the goal, can use a larger stick and any part of the body to defend against the shot. Throwing action is similar to the overarm lever, overarm punch, and sidearm throws.

DODGES

Players in invasion sports such as lacrosse, soccer, field hockey, and basketball need three individual offensive skills to beat a defender: change of speed, change of direction, and fakes. One, two, or all three of these skills can be used at one time. Beginning players can master a *bull dodge*, while more proficient players should master the *face dodge* and the *roll dodge*.

Bull dodge: In the men's game, the bull dodge is a powerful burst of speed from the attacker forcing his way past the defender. However, the essential bull dodge is simply a change of speed. The attacker approaches the defender at a slow to medium pace, then quickly puts on a burst of speed that even a quick defender may not immediately react to, giving the attacker a few steps advantage if timed well.

Face dodge: A burst of speed may not be enough for an attacker to elude a defender. In addition to speed, the ball carrier can use a change of direction. A fake can be as simple as stepping toward one side of the defender as if intending to go by him on that side, then quickly changing direction to the other side. In addition to the change of direction, the ball carrier can use a fake with the head or the crosse. If done with the crosse, a *face dodge* is the result. The attacker approaches the defender and brings the ball over to one side, in the direction they appear to be heading. As he changes direction to the other side, the attacker brings the ball around—across the face—in a cradling action, to the opposite side, and passes to the defender on that side. The crosse and ball will therefore be shielded from the defender. Alternatively, the ball carrier can fake a throw to one side of the defender, but quickly pull the ball in with a cradle, then complete the face dodge to the other side (Figure 16-9).

Roll dodge: A roll dodge involves aggressive stick checking in the men's game or overguarding in the

A   B   C

Figure 16-8 The catch. From left to right: preparation, contact give, cradle movement.

women's game. As the attacker approaches the defender, whose stick is up ready to check or prevent a throw, she steps toward the defender with the foot opposite the throwing hand so that the crosse is away from the defender. The attacker then quickly pivots on the ball of that foot, rolling away from the defender and her crosse (i.e., back to the defender), and completes the dodge running with a burst of speed behind the defender. If executed properly, the ball carrier will shield the ball through the entire maneuver (Figure 16-10).

▶ Practice/Organizational Suggestions

Dodges can be practiced initially with an obstacle such as a cone. Both offensive and defensive skills can be practiced in pairs for maximum repetitions of both. Partners face each other about 11 yards apart and move toward each other, with the defender taking up a defensive position (see Defending). The offensive player practices dodges against a passive defender, then a more active defender. This sequence requires the offensive player to make decisions based on what the defensive player does—for example, where she places the crosse. Offense and defense can be practiced in combination with throw and catch: After three throws from 11–16 yards, the players move toward each other, the attacker being the one with the ball. They then practice

individual offense and defense. By using an odd number of throws and catches, the players will alternate playing offense and defense. For all three dodges, the key is to keep the ball away from the opponent.

DEFENDING

Individual defense in lacrosse is similar to other invasion sports such as basketball or soccer. The difference is that the defender has a crosse that can be used to dislodge the ball. In the men's game several types of checks are allowed. In the women's and high school interscholastic games, only poke checks or stick checks are allowed. In physical education classes, older students can be allowed to use a poke check at the discretion of the teacher, if protective eyewear is used and supervision is tight. However, a nonchecking version of the game is preferable in most situations.

Positioning: The defender should approach the ball carrier quickly and then slow down as he moves into a defensive posture. He must not block the attacker's path by rule, but if he gets in position quickly enough for the attacker to see him, the attacker must move around him. This movement gives the defender the opportunity to force the attacker away from the goal or toward a sideline or other defender (double-team), by angling his body away from the goal or toward the trap.

A

B

C

Figure 16-9 Face dodge.

crosse through the "sleeve" of the upper hand, which controls the direction.

Stick check: In the women's game, the attacker's stick may be checked with a short chopping action of the defender's stick. The check must be short and at the stick, not the hands; a slashing action is not allowed. In fact, any action the referee rules potentially dangerous is not allowed and will be a foul.

Both types of check, if done properly, and if the defender is in good "ball side–goal side" position and defensive posture, will not over commit the defender. If unsuccessful the defender can still move with the attacker and attempt to prevent him from scoring or passing, or dispossess him of the ball.

▶ Practice/Organizational Suggestions

Pairs of students can practice defensive skills along with offensive skills for maximum repetitions of both. The offensive player can be initially more passive to allow the defender to get into position or to poke check the ball. Later have students practice offense and defense in combination with throw and catch: After three throws from 11–16 yards, the players move toward each other, the attacker with the ball. The defender (without the ball) can then practice defense.

Poke check: The crosse can be used to block a throw or check the ball out of the attacker's stick. In the poke check, the defender shoots her stick toward the head of the ball carrier's stick (it must not travel in a direction toward the attacker's head). The action is similar to that of a billiard stick, where the lower hand pushes the

Figure 16-10   The roll dodge.

Playing Strategies

ATTACK/OFFENSE

Attackmen score most of the goals. The three attackmen in the men's game use short sticks. They need good stickhandling with both hands and to be able to maneuver around opposing defensemen using long sticks. They also need to be able to set up in a fast or slow break formation when midfield or defensemen create breakaways. Often this formation will look like an L shape, with two attackmen on one side of the goal line extended (GLE) and the third moving back and up on the side of the midfielder or clearing defender. To delay a fast break, attackmen must be ready to be the first line of defense if they turn over the ball. In the women's game, the "home" players are responsible for playing offense in the zone in front of and a little wider than the 12-meter fan around the goal (first home), in front of the goal (second home), and in front of center (third home). The attack wings play on their side of the offensive half of the field and create width in attack as well as depth. They set up triangular offense shapes and pass options with the home players.

MIDFIELD/WINGS

Men's teams have three midfielders, or "middies." They can move anywhere in order to play offense and defense. There are defensive and offensive middies. The defensive middie can use a long crosse. Teams can substitute players quickly to have defensive or offensive (three short crosses) formations in midfield. Some teams use specialized face-off middies who take face-offs and are then quickly substituted. In the women's game, teams have two attack wings and two defense wings. They provide width in attack and defense and quick lateral transition opportunities for offense and defense. In addition, the center can provide transition in the middle of the field and assistance to both attack and defense wings. The center should be a player who can cover a large area of the field effectively without tiring.

DEFENSE

In the men's game, defensive players have long crosses. The defensemen use their crosses to throw checks in an attempt to dislodge the ball from an attacking player's crosse. Three defensemen and a midfielder with a long crosse per team are allowed on the field at any time. In the women's game, the defensive players are the defense wings (DW), point (P, closest to goal), cover point (CP, between P and 3M), and "third man" (3M, farthest from goal). These players cover the middle of their defensive half unless the play is close to their goal, in which case they can play close one-on-one defense against the attack. Or with the help of a center, these players can play a tight zone around the goal area, creating a "box"

around the goal and covering the player in their quarter of the box (as a "chaser," chasing the ball). The points and defense wings are also key players in a fast break, moving into the space to the right or left of the goalie to receive a quick pass to begin a fast counter attack.

GOALKEEPERS

The goalie's job is to stop the ball from crossing the goal line. Goalies also direct team defense as they are in the best position to see the defensive part of the field. Goalies need to be tough to use their bodies to defend the goal, and assertive to guide defensive cover. Goalies are often team leaders or captains. Although their crosses are unwieldy for throwing, a good goalie can begin a fast break attack after saving a shot.

▶ **Practice/Organizational Suggestions**

Scooping, throwing, catching, and cradling can be taught right away. These skills can be practiced individually and in pairs. Small-sided games (two on two, three on three) of keep-away can be played. To give the possession team an advantage at the outset, groups of four can play three on one and groups of six can play four on two. Rotate the defenders after every minute or so, so that everyone gets an equal amount of time on offense and defense. Begin with passive defense and work up to safe body checking (by position; no contact) and stick checking if players have eye protection. With younger students (elementary school level), stick checking is not appropriate, even with eye protection.

Invasion games like lacrosse can be taught using 10-yard by 10-yard grid squares, marked on a field with painted lines or by cones for corners. Partners, two on two, or three on one activities can be played in each grid square, and three on three or four on two activities can be done in two or four squares joined together, depending on available space. For strategic skills such as making cuts, passing into space, moving to space, and using shapes (triangles) to create passing options, activities can be set up quickly in grids (see Figure 16-11 A–D).

For shooting, targets against the wall indoors or against a fence outdoors can be used so that the ball is somewhat contained. Mini goals or pop-up goals can be used to help players shoot low at the corners. Shooting can be done from a static position, then moving/cradling, and finally moving around obstacles or defenders. For example, a line of four to six players can face three cones, weave around them, and then shoot from 3 yards or more away from the goal. For more advanced practice, players can practice different dodges around each cone. Cones can also be replaced by passive or semi-active defenders, with the players rotating positions after each shot. For full field practice, paired players can move up the field from defense to goal at a distance of 10–15 yards from each other, finishing with a shot on goal.

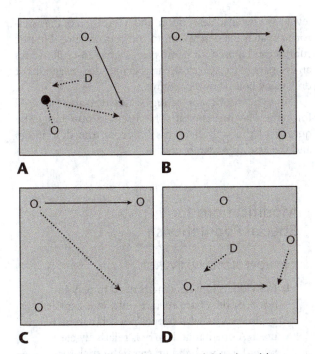

Figure 16-11 Skill development activities in grids: A. *Cut:* Ball attacker moves left then cuts to the right as defender moves to cut off the pass. B. *Passing to space* (open corner drill): Ball handler passes to open corner, off ball player moves to space to receive. Communication between players, pacing and timing of the throw, and movement should be emphasized. C. *Moving to space:* Similar to B, but this time the ball handler passes to either player then runs to the space. D. *Shape/passing options:* Offense moves around grid maintaining triangular shape (make sure players do not just "rotate"). As the defender moves to cut off a pass to one player, the other can move into the space to collect the pass. The triangular shape maintains offensive width and depth, with two passing options.

Key: O–offense; O.–ball carrier; D–defense;
→ path of ball; ... path of player

Modified Games

Small-sided keep-away games mentioned in the skill development activities section of this chapter are effective for applying throwing and catching techniques and are suitable for practicing scooping and cradling skills.

Zone lacrosse can be played with a relatively large group on one field or indoors. Divide the field or court into three zones (offense, midfield, defense) and two wings of 3–5 yards width, divided at the halfway line. Put small goals near the ends of the field with a crease. Use a soft lacrosse ball or tennis ball, soft sticks, and safety eyewear. Have players wear pinnies to differentiate teams. Three or four players from each team play in each zone, as well as a defensive wing and offensive wing for each team in each wing zone. Thus, there are 11 to 14 players

<u>Assessment:</u> Lacrosse Carry, Cradle, Dodge and Shoot; <u>Type:</u> Holistic rubric; <u>Protocol:</u> Set up four cones about 6 feet apart with the last cone 5 m from the goal. <u>Player:</u> weave in and out of the cones using cradle and at least one face dodge. Shoot at the goal immediately after passing the last cone. Perform as quickly as possible. Start facing the opposite direction of the goal, between cones.

<u>Assessor:</u> Move the cones a little each time; evaluate according to the rubric levels below.

Pre Control Level (Beginner or Initial Stage)—Score 1*

- Student is unable to repeat movements in succession; one attempt does not look like another attempt to perform the same movement
- Student uses extraneous movements that are unnecessary for proficiently performing the skill
- Student seems awkward and does not come close to performing the skill correctly
- Correct performances are characterized more by surprise than by expectancy
- The ball seems to control the student rather than the other way around

Control Level (Advanced Beginner or Elementary Stage)—Score 2

- The student's movements appear less haphazard and appear to conform to their intentions
- Movements appear more consistent, and repetitions are somewhat alike
- The student's attempt to combine one movement with another or perform the skill in relation to an unpredictable object (moved cones) is usually unsuccessful
- Because the movement is not automatic, the student needs to concentrate intensely on what he or she is doing

Utilization Level (Intermediate or Mature Stage)—Score 3

- The movement is somewhat automatic and is performed successfully with concentration
- Even when the context of the task is varied (cone weave), the student can still perform the movement successfully
- The student can execute the skill the same way constantly
- The student can use skills in combination with other skills (carry, cradle, dodge and shoot) and still perform it appropriately

Proficiency Level (Advanced or Lifelong Utilization Stage)—Score 3

- The skill has become almost automatic, and performances in a similar context appear almost identical (over repeated tries)
- The student is able to focus on extraneous variables (cones), the flow of travel—and still perform the skill intended
- The movement often seems effortless as the student performs the skill with ease and seeming lack of attention
- The movement can be performed successfully in a variety of planned and unplanned situations (different cone placement) as the student appears to modify performance to meet the demands of the situation

Figure 16-12 Lacrosse skill assessment for cradle, carry, dodge and shoot—holistic rubric. For examples of additional skill assessments, visit www.rubrician.com.

on the field or court at a time, 22 to 28 total. Players must stay in their zones, but they can pass the ball across zones (one zone only). The idea is for teams to move the ball from defense, to midfield or wing, to offense, and score. On scoring, the scorer retrieves the ball from the goal and gives it to the instructor on the sideline/halfway area and collects a point for the team. The instructor then restarts with a *throw* to the midfield. After a minute or two, more balls can be added—up to three, or even six, depending on the maturity level of the players, the size of the playing area, and number of players. For safety reasons, players must make eye contact with teammates before passing. For advanced players, middies may move up or back one zone, as long as an offensive or defensive player switches zones with them, and vice versa. This switching helps players understand the offside concept in the men's game.

A good game to play after three-on-three games is six-on-six lacrosse. It can be played on a half-field or a 2 by 3 grid (10 yard by 10 yard grid squares) area. Goals can be a cone or minigoal; there are no goalies. Play using offensive and defensive triangular shapes can be emphasized, which will maintain a game shape similar to the women's game, or games can be played with two defense players, two middies, and two offense players, as in the men's game. One-on-one defense should be enforced to spread the field, prevent crowding the ball, and allow players to match up with opponents of similar size and ability.

The *seven-a-side lacrosse* game is a variant of the full-sided women's game and can be played indoors or outdoors. It can be an effective lead-up game to the full-sided game, or a "regulation" game for physical education classes in middle or high school. Teams have one defender, one attacker, and one center. Goals are modified versions of a basketball backboard and goal, tilted forward at 45 degrees. A minigoal or small target can be used for a modified version. The field has a goal crease and center circle. Play starts with a throw from the center circle (only the throwing player is allowed in the circle for the throw; he has 10 seconds to throw the ball). There are essentially no goal area rules (if using a minigoal, a rule that players or crosses cannot enter the goal crease can be enforced), and players can play anywhere. One-on-one defense is advisable, and teams should be encouraged to keep a balanced distribution on the field of play.

Skill Assessment

Assessments for lacrosse can include skill tests or game play assessment. There are three types of assessments: skill checklist, holistic, and small-sided game play assessment. Skill checklist (descriptive) assessments break down skills by critical elements. The assessor determines whether each component is present or not.

Holistic rubrics provide a full description of a skill based on levels of skill performance. Each performance level has a detailed description, and it is the job of the assessor to match the description to the performance. Holistic rubrics can be used for game play. Figure 16-12 illustrates an assessment for a lacrosse carry, cradle, dodge, and shoot drill, using holistic rubric scoring.

Analytic rubrics or rating scales can also be used for game play assessment. The assessor must judge the quality of the skill elements based on the descriptors and the assessor's own expertise.

Modifications for Special Populations

ORTHOPEDICALLY IMPAIRED

1. Individuals in wheelchairs need to play indoors or on a hard surface outdoors. Smaller, generic sticks with deeper pockets can be used. A one-handed carry is relatively easy, with the other hand grasping the stick for throws and catches. Use a lighter ball, such as a foam ball or soft lacrosse ball.

2. A shorter stick/crosse can be used by individuals who need assistance walking. A crosse can be strapped or taped to one arm, or a scoop or short-handled (modified) stick can also be used.

COGNITIVELY IMPAIRED

1. Throwing and catching games without a stick (see *Practice/Organizational Suggestions* for throw and catch) will help students grasp the concept of passing.

2. Scoops can be used as a lead-up to crosses. A lighter ball should be used with scoops.

3. Small-sided games will keep the movement concepts less complicated and increase the amount of contact with the ball.

SENSORY IMPAIRED

1. Instructors should assess the safety of lacrosse activities for students with vision impairments. A buddy can be used to "see" for students who are visually impaired.

2. A small cut can be made in a tennis ball or hollow rubber ball and a bell inserted as a noisemaker to help students who are visually impaired track its location.

3. For students with auditory impairment, minimal adaptations are needed, but visual communication should be emphasized for strategic and safety reasons.

Terminology

attackmen The three players in the men's game who play around the goal.

ball stop Foam rubber strip at the bottom of the crosse head that keeps the ball in the pocket.

blocking In the women's game, movement into a ball carrier's path without giving her time to change direction, thus incurring contact.

body check Legal movement of a defender in the women's game causing the player to change direction, slow down, or pass.

bridge Part of a wooden crosse, made of gut, that connects the throat and open side of the head to the wooden side of the head.

charge Occurs when a ball carrier pushes through an opponent using the body—illegal in women's game.

clear Throwing or running the ball from defense to the attack area.

cradle Movement and rotation of the crosse head laterally or vertically to protect and seat the ball in the pocket.

crease The circle around the goal. With the exception of the goalie, no player, or crosse, is allowed in the crease.

crosse Lacrosse stick.

cut Sharp-angled movement of an offensive ball player toward goal or to get clear for a pass.

defensemen The three players in the men's game who play in the defensive third.

dodge Individual offensive techniques to beat a defender, such as bull, face, and roll.

ground ball Loose ball on the field.

gut The woven material of the pocket on a wooden stick made of thinner gut than the bridge.

handle The part of the stick grasped by a player. Also called the *shaft*.

head The "throwing" end of a crosse, usually made of plastic, containing the pocket.

holding Technical foul in the men's game caused by grabbing or hindering a player with the crosse.

home The offensive players in the women's game (first, second, and third; first is closest to goal).

interference Technical foul in the men's game caused by preventing movement of a player not in possession of the ball or within 5 yards of a loose ball.

midfielders ("middies") The three designated central players in the men's game who play both defense and offense.

offside Technical foul in the men's game caused by a team having fewer than three players in its offensive half, or fewer than four players in the defensive half of the field.

pocket Strung part of stick head that holds the ball in the crosse.

point, cover point, third man Defensive players in the women's game (point is closest to goal).

sidewall The side of the crosse head.

slashing Reckless or dangerous swinging movement of stick at or across opponent's body.

stand A unique rule of women's lacrosse. On the referee's whistle, players immediately stop and remain in their positions until play restarts.

stick check A controlled check of the opponent's stick to dislodge the ball. It must be made on the stick only (not hands) in the women's game.

thong/lead Strips of leather or synthetic material set vertically in the pocket.

throat The part of the crosse where the head meets the handle.

Discussion Questions

1. Identify the skill progressions recommended for lacrosse.

2. List four critical skill cues each for throw, catch, and cradle.

3. Describe the major differences between the rules in the men's and women's games.

4. Describe the major differences between the field and equipment in the men's and women's games.

5. What are the general roles of defensemen, middies, and attackmen in the men's game?

6. What are the general roles of home, wing, point, cover point, and third man players in the women's game?

7. Should physical education classes use men's or women's rules and equipment? Why?

8. Describe small-sided activities that can be used to teach basic tactics of offense and defense in lacrosse.

9. Lacrosse is an invasion team sport. What other team sports are invasion games and therefore use similar offensive and defensive strategies?

Web Sites

www.insidelacrosse.com *Inside Lacrosse*—contains news of professional, men's and women's collegiate, high school, and club lacrosse and features discussion forums and blogs.

www.uslacrosse.org U.S. Lacrosse—provides information from the national governing body of lacrosse, including news of men's and women's collegiate, high school, and club lacrosse programs, sport development, and science/research.

www.iwlca.org—provides drills, tactics books, and clinic videos.

CHAPTER 17 | Orienteering

This chapter will enable you to

- Identify historical events contributing to the evolution of orienteering
- Identify the parts of a liquid-filled compass and how it works
- Use fundamental topographic map-reading techniques and skills
- Use basic compass techniques and skills
- Navigate an orienteering course using a topographic map and a liquid-filled compass
- Identify the basic terminology necessary to understand the activity and sport of orienteering

Nature and Purpose

Orienteering is a cross-country activity in which the participant uses topographic map-reading skills and follows directions by compass or other means to navigate over unfamiliar terrain. The skills of orienteering can be used to enjoy many outdoor pursuits, such as camping, backpacking, hiking, cross-country skiing, fishing, and hunting, or for competing in the sport of orienteering. Called "the thinking sport," competitive orienteering requires great mental acuity, problem solving, and decision making, along with cardiorespiratory fitness because the orienteer can cover distances from 2 up to 10 miles in navigating an orienteering course. With today's back-to-nature interests, orienteering skills can be valuable to people of all ages in improving environmental awareness and self-reliance in the out-of-doors.

Participants can take part in orienteering as a recreational activity or competitive sport. In competitive orienteering, courses with various degrees of difficulty are set up to allow for differences in skill levels; therefore, all participants can achieve success. For many, just completing the course can be a satisfying experience.

Orienteering is an excellent coeducational activity. The environmental setting makes for social acceptance. Because outstanding physical ability is not a limiting factor, girls often achieve the same success as boys.

History

Throughout the world, particularly in the Scandinavian countries, orienteering rivals soccer as the most popular sport. One would expect to find thousands of spectators at an event at any one time. The roots of orienteering can be traced to Scandinavia in the 19th century. In its beginnings, it was probably used as a part of military training. Orienteering has a relatively young history in the United States. As in Scandinavia, orienteering got its start in the United States as a military exercise; the U.S. Marine Corps used orienteering as part of its military training in the mid-1960s.

In Sweden in 1919, Captain Ernst Killander of Stockholm organized many meets, attracting many people to events that featured walking, running, and compass reading. Later, in the 1930s, the Kjellstrom brothers, Alvar and Bjorn, invented the protractor-type, liquid-damped magnetic compass. This development enabled the orienteer to simplify movement and navigation on land.[1] In 1941, the first orienteering events in North America were held at Dartmouth College and continued through 1943. Bjorn Kjellstrom of Sweden moved to the U.S. in 1946 and started events for the Boy Scouts sponsoring and supporting events through the 1950s and 1960s.[2]

The first U.S. championship was held at Southern Illinois University in 1970. A world championship competition takes place each year. In the team event, the U.S. Marine Corps participants have accorded themselves quite well. Today, many of the events and the largest number of clubs can be found on the East Coast. The U.S. Orienteering Federation oversees many events and clubs in the United States.

COMPETITIVE ORIENTEERING

Point-to-point or cross-country orienteering is the most common type of competition. This event requires competitors to navigate through a prescribed series of control points shown on a topographic orienteering map (Figure 17-1), with all competitors visiting the controls in the same order. At the start of the event, competitors receive a clue card (Figure 17-2). The clue card identifies the control

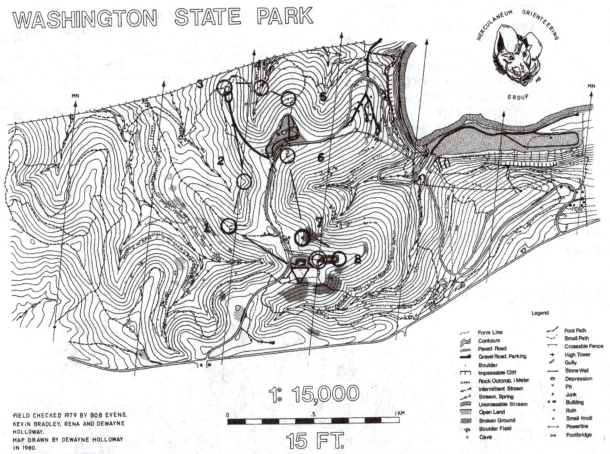

Figure 17-1 Topographic orienteering map showing a white course used by beginning orienteers. Map courtesy of the St. Louis Orienteering Club and Dewayne Holloway.

markers by letter code and describes a prominent feature in which the control marker has been set. The competitors leave the starting line at equal intervals of time, for example, 1-minute intervals, so that the event becomes for each a contest of route selection and physical skills, with the time to complete the course determining the order of finish. To ensure that each competitor has visited the control markers, a code or punch is located at each control and must be marked on a competitor's scorecard (Figure 17-3). In competitive orienteering, courses of different levels of difficulty are set up to allow for the differences in navigational and physical skill abilities of the contestants. These courses are designated by colors: white, yellow, orange, green, red, and blue; white and yellow are for the novice, orange and green for the intermediate, and red and blue for the advanced orienteer. Course difficulty is determined by the number of controls, distance between the controls, and the difficulty of the placement of the controls in the field. For example, compare the distance between controls and the total distance of the red course shown in Figure 17-4 with the

distances of the white course shown in Figure 17-1. The red course is obviously much more difficult.

Equipment

Maps. The most essential item of equipment for successful orienteering is the map. For children just beginning, a map of a schoolyard, local park, or forest preserve, drawn to scale, is sufficient; however, for the advanced orienteer, large-scale topographic maps showing selected artificial and natural features are necessary. These topographic maps, usually drawn on a scale of 1:24,000, are produced by the U.S. Geological Survey (USGS) of the Department of the Interior. Recently, more accurate and highly developed orienteering maps have been produced. These maps, usually drawn on a scale of 1:15,000 and developed from current aerial photographs, have been accurately field checked and printed in the standard international orienteering colors: blue (water features), black (artificial features), green (vegetation features), brown (contour features), and yellow (clear areas). Although colored maps are more meaningful and precise, black-and-white maps can be successfully used and are less expensive.

Day 1 White Course 2.7 km

1	(WA)	The trail junction
2	(WB)	The re-entrant (head)
3	(WC)	The trail junction
4	(WD)	The re-entrant
5	(WP)	The junk
6	(WE)	The fence corner
7	(WF)	The depression
8	(HW)	The earth bank

Follow streamers to finish

Figure 17-2 Competitor's clue card for the white course. Courtesy of the St. Louis Orienteering Club and Dewayne Holloway.

ROSE ORIENTEERING CLUB CONTROL CARD

Name

Course   Class

Finish

Start   ○○

Elapsed

11	12	13	14	15	16	17	18	19	20
1	2	3	4	5	6	7	8	9	10

Figure 17-3 Competitor's scorecard. Courtesy of the Rose Orienteering Club.

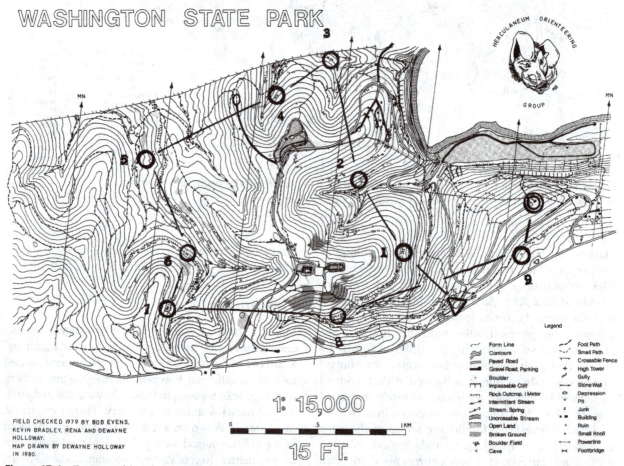

Figure 17-4 Topographic orienteering map showing a red course used by advanced orienteers. Map courtesy of the St. Louis Orienteering Club and Dewayne Holloway.

Orienteering maps provide the following important information to the orienteer:

1. *Map scale.* Each map contains a certain scale that is proportional between a distance on the map and the actual distances in the field. For example, a scale of 1:15,000 on a topographical map means that one unit of distance on the map equals 15,000 units of actual distance in the field. A bar scale representing map distance is located in the margin of the map.

2. *Directions.* The top of an orienteering map represents geographic north; therefore, the other cardinal directions are south (the bottom), east (the right),

and west (the left). Most orienteering maps will have the magnetic-north lines already drawn on the map. These lines, called the declination lines, represent the degree difference between the magnetic north direction and true north direction. The angle of declination on USGS topographic maps can be found in the margin.

3. *Elevation features.* A topographic map is distinguished from a planemetric map (roadmap) in showing the shape and elevation changes of the terrain by brown contour lines. Each of these lines represents a constant elevation, in feet or meters, above sea level. The space between each line on a topographic map represents a vertical distance, called the contour interval. The contour interval is given below the bar scale at the bottom of the map sheet. In areas of the United States with little elevation, the contour interval will be 5 to 10 meters (or feet) to more accurately represent the land features, whereas contour intervals of 10 to 20 meters (or feet) are found in more mountainous areas.

4. *Other map features.* Other important artificial or natural features, such as power lines, roads, trails, bridges, buildings, fences, boulders, cliffs, streams, lakes, marshes, or ponds are also shown on the map. These features are either drawn to actual scale or displayed symbolically with the description of each symbol found in the map's legend (see Figure 17-1).

Compass. The second most essential item of equipment for successful orienteering is the compass. The protractor-type compass with the liquid-filled housing (Figure 17-5) is the most widely used compass in orienteering because it permits the orienteer to take a bearing and measure its distance quickly and accurately. The parts of the compass and their basic function are as follows.

1. *Base plate.* The transparent rectangular plate on which the compass housing is mounted is called the base plate. The front edge and one of the side edges are marked off in inches and millimeters for measuring map scale or distance.

2. *Compass housing.* The degree markings are found on the outer rim of the rotating compass housing. Each mark represents 1 degree, and they are numbered in intervals of 20. (It should be noted that 0 and 360 degrees coincide and are both north.) Once the compass is set correctly, the degree bearing is taken at the index pointer on the rim of the housing.

3. *Orienting arrow.* Located inside the compass housing is the orienting, or north-seeking, arrow. Its function is to assist in orienting the compass. The compass is oriented by holding it in such a way that the orienting arrow is lined up with the magnetic needle, both of which will be pointed north.

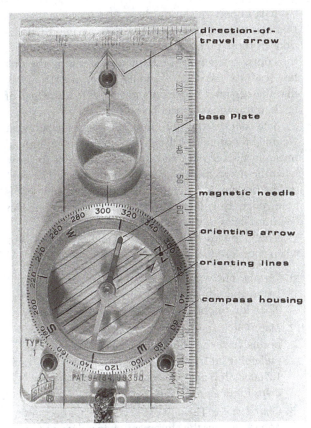

Figure 17-5 The protractor compass.

4. *Magnetic needle.* The free-floating needle located inside the compass housing is called the magnetic needle. The north end is painted red and always points to magnetic north unless affected by a metal object.

5. *Orienting lines.* Located inside the compass housing and running parallel with the orienting arrow are the orienting lines. These lines assist in determining declination by setting them parallel with the magnetic lines on the map, with north on the compass pointing to north on the map.

6. *Direction-of-travel arrow.* At the upper end of the base plate is located the direction-of-travel arrow, which is used for determining the direction of travel when the compass is oriented.

Suggested Learning Sequence
WHOLE METHOD

The direct, or whole, method is recommended for teaching younger children and novice orienteers. In this method, beginners walk or run an orienteering course in the field with suitable terrain as their first introduction to orienteering. The only preliminary learning prior to this field work is a knowledge of map symbols, an understanding of how to "orient the map," and the ability to map read by using the thumb—the first basic skills of orienteering.

It is important during these first learning sessions that orienteering courses be set that are good illustrations of those points that are to be learned. Therefore, the course-setter must understand that during the first few sessions, the courses should be set in such a way that the beginner needs only to follow roads, edges of fields, trails, and other similar objects.

The course-setter must never be enticed to set what we might normally call "good" controls but instead must always keep in mind that the purpose is to show what the map symbols and definitions mean. The control points should be typical for the symbol and definition. All controls should be so distinct that no one can be uncertain as to what is meant.

The following factors must be carefully attended to when course-setting:

1. *Terrain.* There must be lots of trails, open country, roads, and similarly distinct and easily read features. Then it is important to make proper use of these.
2. *Map.* The map should be drawn according to the norms, have the correct colors, be easily read, and preferably be 1:15,000, although it is possible to use 1:24,000. (It is a good idea to enlarge the normal maps for beginner courses.)
3. *Control choice.* The aim of the control has been mentioned. Besides the aforementioned points, the control should be such that even without a compass, the novice can match the map with the terrain and find the control.
4. *Route choice.* Route choice, as we usually mean it, should not be introduced at the novice level. There are lots of things that must be learned before you start on route choice. "Route choice" that comes in a later part of the course means only that the novice, for example, chooses the correct path at a path junction.
5. *Orienting the map.* The controls and the legs between controls should be such that the novice can always match (orient) the map with the terrain without using the compass. It is important that the novice be taught always to have the map oriented. Map positioning is the most important point in the entire course, and should be introduced in the beginning.

After these basic techniques and skills are mastered and confidence gained, more advanced techniques and skills, such as a knowledge of contour lines, map scale, handling a compass, measuring distance, use of attack points, off-aiming, and pace counting, may be introduced.

PART-WHOLE METHOD

While the "whole" method of teaching is often used with children and novice orienteers, the most widely used and accepted method of teaching is the "part-whole method." In this method, the basic and advanced techniques and skills of using the map, compass, and map and compass together are taught in a classroom/field setting before the orienteer attempts to navigate an orienteering course. An orienteer using this method should start with a novice yellow or white course (such as the one shown in Figure 17-1), gradually progressing to an intermediate orange or green course, and then to a more advanced blue or red course (such as in Figure 17-4)—once the basic orienteering skills and techniques are mastered.

Skills and Techniques

Map Reading.   Because the map is the primary tool for navigation in orienteering, it is essential to teach basic map-reading techniques and skills first.

1. *Orienting the map.* Orienting the map simply means keeping the map turned so that north on the map corresponds to north in the field, regardless of the direction the orienteer travels. Orienting the map can be done either by inspecting the surroundings and aligning the terrain features with those on the map or by using the compass. The steps in using the compass to orient the map are as follows:
   a. Set the compass dial at 360 degrees. Then place the compass on the map with the edge of the base plate parallel with one of the magnetic north lines, making sure the direction-of-travel arrow points north.
   b. Rotate the map and compass until the magnetic needle is over the orienting arrow. The map is now oriented with respect to magnetic north.
2. *Map reading by thumb.* In using this technique, fold the map so that it can be easily held and read, with only the immediate area in which you are orienteering showing. Then place the tip of the thumb on the map corresponding to the place in the field where you are standing and pointing in the direction you will travel. As you travel along, move the thumb to the place on the map corresponding to the location in the field where you have traveled. This technique helps keep you oriented, allowing you to easily analyze and check the terrain features that lie ahead.

Compass Reading.   The compass can be used with a map or by itself. For the beginning orienteer, the steps in taking a bearing and traveling with the compass by itself should be taught first. These steps are as follows:

1. Stand facing the direction of the intended destination. With the direction-of-travel arrow pointed in this direction, turn the compass housing until the north end of the orienting arrow is lined up with the north end of the magnetic needle.
2. Once the compass is set, pick out a prominent feature, such as a tree or hilltop, in line with the direction-of-travel arrow. Travel to that feature, take another bearing, and continue toward the desired destination.

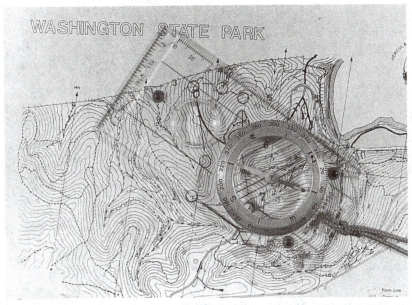

Figure 17-6 The first step in taking a bearing with compass.

Additional Procedures.   Taking a bearing and traveling with a compass and map involve additional procedures and should be done with precision. Three basic steps are used in this process:

1. Put the edge of the base plate from the present place of location to the intended destination, making sure the direction-of-travel arrow is pointing in the direction of travel (see Figure 17-6).

2. Turn the compass housing until the orienting lines are parallel with the magnetic lines and the orienting arrow is pointing north on the map (see Figure 17-7). When magnetic north lines are not present, the orienting lines can be set parallel with the meridian lines—the lines running true north to south. In this case, the declination (angle of difference in degrees between true north and magnetic north) must be added or subtracted to the final bearing. This degree difference is given in the margin on topographic maps. To decide whether to add or subtract, think of the rhyme "East is least and West is best." If the angle of declination is *east*, the degree of declination is *subtracted*; if the declination is *west*, it is *added*.

3. The final important step is to turn yourself until the north end of the magnetic needle points to the north end of the orienting arrows (Figure 17-8).

Safety Considerations

Although orienteering is a relatively safe activity, there are some precautions that must be followed:

1. Orienteers should be cautioned to avoid potentially dangerous obstructions and features shown on the map, such as cliffs, rock faces, barbed wire fences, or deep rivers and streams.

2. The orienteer should be instructed to wear protective clothing when heavy brambles, briar patches, or thick vegetation exist in the terrain.

3. Before embarking on a course, a safety bearing should be given that will lead the orienteer to a large catching feature such as a road or trail in the event he becomes lost or totally disoriented.

Competitive Strategies

In competitive orienteering, the orienteer must know special techniques and skills to select the fastest and least tiring route between control points.

1. *Pace counting*. Pace counting involves a two-step approach:
   a. In step one, the orienteer measures the distance on the map by using the marked edge of the compass and the map bar scale.
   b. Step two involves measuring the distance in the field by pace counting. In pace counting, you count your double step, or each time the same foot hits the ground. This technique can be practiced by measuring an exact 100 yards or 100 meters over different terrain and counting the number of double steps taken in covering this distance.

2. *Attack points*. Sometimes called secondary controls, these are large, prominent features such as a cliff, building, bridge, trail junction, or other features near the control that can easily be found and identified on the map. Finding an attack point makes the final approach to the control much easier.

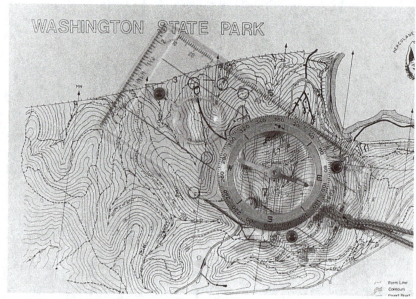

Figure 17-7 The second step in taking a bearing with compass.

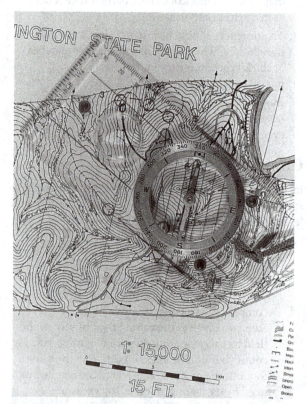

Figure 17-8 The third step in taking a bearing with compass.

4. *Handrails*. Linear features running parallel with the direction of a control point or an attack point are called handrails. These can take the form of natural features such as a stream, the edge of a field, or a ridge or artificial features such as a road, trail, fence, or power line. Handrails are used by the orienteer as a natural guide to follow toward the control point.

5. *Catching features*. Long features running crosswise to the orienteer's direction of travel are called catching, or collecting, features. These features can assist the orienteer in navigation, as upon reaching the catcher, the orienteer needs only to turn in the proper direction and follow it until the attack or control point is reached. These catchers include the same linear features described as handrails.

6. *Aiming off*. When control or attack points are located on linear features such as roads, streams, fences, and so forth, the orienteer aims off, that is, sets the compass toward a point 40 to 60 meters to the right or left of the control point rather than right at it, so that upon arriving at the linear feature, the orienteer knows exactly which way to turn, right or left, to find the control point.

Skill Assessment

The instructor sets a course and the students navigate it using a map and compass. The course can be set up on the school grounds or in the gym. The course should challenge both mental and physical skills. Assessment is based on finishing time.

3. *Checkpoints*. After finalizing the route, the orienteer should visualize certain prominent features (checkpoints) she will see along the way that will indicate she is on the correct route.

Modifications for Special Populations

ORTHOPEDICALLY IMPAIRED

Work on special "searches" within the gymnasium using maps and other coded documents. Designate each wall in the gym a color and have the students follow the colored map; for example, travel to the yellow wall, then the green wall, and find the hidden treasure.

COGNITIVELY IMPAIRED

Have the student work on making a special compass to learn north, south, east, and west; for example, color code the directions.

SENSORY IMPAIRED

1. Use peer teachers and paraprofessionals for students who are blind or have a visual impairment.
2. Use visual cues, for example, posters and notebooks, for students who are deaf or have a hearing impairment.

Terminology

aiming off A technique in which the orienteer purposely aims to one side of a control point so that he will know which way to turn.

attack point A large, prominent visible feature both on the map and in the field, from which the final approach of attack to the control can be made.

bearing Sometimes called an azimuth, it is a direction measured in degrees from north with a compass.

cardinal points The four basic directions on a compass: north, south, east, and west.

catching feature A long natural or artificial feature running perpendicular to the orienteer's direction of travel.

contour interval The vertical distance in height between contour lines on a topographic map.

control Marker of two colors—usually red and white or orange and white—placed in the field before the orienteering meet starts; used for locating control points on the map.

control description A word description for the location of a control point.

declination The degree difference between the magnetic north direction and the true north direction.

handrail Linear features running parallel with an orienteer's direction of travel that are used to navigate to a control or an attack point.

magnetic north The direction to the magnetic north pole located north of Hudson Bay.

map symbols Designs found in the legend on a map used to indicate landscape features.

meridians Real lines on the map or imaginary lines in the terrain running true north to true south.

orienteering The skill or the process of finding your way in the field with map and compass combined.

orienting the compass Turning the compass until north on the compass is the same as north in the field.

orienting the map Turning the map until north on the map corresponds to north in the field.

pace counting Method used to measure distance in the field by counting each time the same foot strikes the ground.

scale A proportion between a distance on the map and the actual distance in the field.

topographic map A map showing elevation changes by means of contour lines.

true north Geographic north (the North Pole).

Discussion Questions

1. Discuss the reasons that orienteering is called "the thinking sport."
2. Trace the roots of orienteering.
3. Discuss the rules involved in competitive cross-country orienteering.
4. Identify the important information that orienteering maps provide and discuss each in detail.
5. Identify the basic functions of the various parts of the compass and discuss each function.
6. Contrast the differences between the whole method and part-whole method in teaching orienteering.
7. Discuss the techniques of orienting the map and map reading by thumb.
8. Present the steps for taking a bearing and traveling with the compass, as well as the three additional procedures that should be done with precision.
9. Discuss the strategy techniques that aid the orienteer in selecting the fastest and least tiring route between control points.
10. Identify safety precautions.

Web Sites

www.us.orienteering.org U.S. Orienteering Federation (USOF)—offers information on books, competition, clubs, equipment, and Web sites.

www.orienteering.org International Orienteering Federation—provides news and information.

CHAPTER 18

Recreational Sports

This chapter will enable you to understand and take part in

ANGLING

Nature and Purpose

Angling is fishing for sport. More specifically, it is the use of the skill of casting to catch fish. Angling has increased steadily in popularity, and today countless people of all ages engage in the sport. More than 30 million fishing licenses are issued in the United States each year, and millions of people fish without a license. With so many participants, it is quite possible that more money is spent on angling than on any other sport. Anyone can enjoy this lifetime recreational activity, wherever fish and water are to be found.

The basic skill in angling is casting. Even though this is a relatively simple skill, few master it because they neither learn under proper guidance nor take the time to practice the skill once acquired.

There are two types of casting: fly casting and bait or spin casting. There are some similarities between the two, but they employ different tackle and different techniques. In *fly casting*, a longer, more flexible rod is used, the line is controlled from the hand, and the light fly is propelled entirely by the weight of the line. The technique of fly casting makes it possible to use small, light "lures" (i.e., artificial flies) and to cast with a great deal of precision and accuracy. *Bait* or *spin casting* requires a shorter, less flexible rod. The weight of the bait or lure achieves distance, and the line is controlled at the reel.

History

Fishing with line and hook was probably originated by the Egyptians. They used a crude line of woven animal hair and a sharpened bone for the hook. Other cultures devised methods of catching fish, but it is not known when and where fly casting originated, although some records indicate that the Macedonians used long rods with wool attached to a hook. The modern reel with free-running spool geared to four revolutions to one turn on the handle was invented by George Snyder, a watchmaker of Paris, Kentucky, between 1800 and 1810. Izak Walton, the Englishman who published *The Compleat Angler* in 1653, is considered the patron saint of anglers because, more than anyone else, he originated and advanced the sport of angling.

Although there are many types of fishing, fly fishing's popularity has increased in the United States because of the movie *A River Runs Through It*. Fly fishing was brought to the American colonies by the English during the 18th century. Early rods were made of a long branch with a fixed line. Later, split bamboo rods were invented, which were lighter and provided the angler greater flexibility in casting.

Today, no matter what the style of fishing an angler engages in, he can choose from sophisticated rods and reels because of modern materials. Rods are lighter, measuring in ounces of weight, and more specific for the type of fish. Angling has increased in popularity over the years, from bass fishing to trout fishing, and from fishing in rivers and lakes to the ocean.

As the numbers of anglers have increased, so has the concern for maintaining the environment for generations to come. Organizations such as Bass Anglers Sportsman Society, Trout Unlimited, and the Federation of Fly Fishermen have become active in educating youth about good conservation practices and stream, river, and lake maintenance. These organizations have produced programs and designed curricula to teach youth not only about fishing but also about maintaining the environment that supports fishing.

Equipment

FLY-CASTING TACKLE

The beginner should enlist the assistance of an experienced fly fisher to help select the proper equipment. This should not be a difficult task because most fly fishers are willing to provide basic instruction as well as other information about getting started in this recreational activity.

Rod. The most important piece of equipment is the rod. Fly rods come in different lengths and have different actions. An 8½- or 9-foot graphite rod with a medium to fast action is probably the best choice for the beginner.

Reel. A single-action fly reel is recommended. This reel should have an adjustable drag (a mechanism that increases or decreases the resistance on a line once a fish is hooked), an interchangeable spool, and the capacity to hold enough backing line to play the fish. Figure 18-1 shows fly-casting as well as bait- and spin-casting reels.

Line. The beginner should closely follow the manufacturer's recommendations of line size for the rod. Fly lines are usually constructed of a core of braided dacron or nylon fibers covered by a plastic or other synthetic coating. They come in various tapers (thicknesses) and weight. To balance an 8½- or 9-foot rod properly, select a weight-forward floating line in a 6 or 7 weight. These lines would be listed as a WF6F or WF7F on the manufacturer's box.

BAIT- OR SPIN-CASTING TACKLE

Once again, the advice of an experienced bait or spin caster is invaluable and will save the beginner a great deal of time in getting started.

Rod. The beginner should select a rod that is 5 to 6 feet long and has a medium action. Most rods are constructed of fiberglass, graphite, or some combination of the two.

Figure 18-1 Types of reels. Top left, fly reel; bottom left, bait reel; two spin-casting reels on the right.

Bait-Casting Reel. The beginner should select a "level-wind" reel, meaning that the line is wrapped evenly on the spool. The reel should fit the length and action of the rod.

Spinning Reel. Spinning reels are divided into two general classes. In the *open type*, the spool on which the line coils has no cover, leaving the spool and line fully exposed. In the *cone type*, a cone covers the spool and line to protect the line from dirt and to prevent its being touched by lures, twigs, weeds, and other foreign objects. The line passes through a hole in the center of the cup, directly in front of the axis of the spool shaft.

The action of the reel spool is the basic difference between the spinning, spin-casting, and standard bait-casting outfit. The spool of a spinning reel does not rotate to release the line on the cast or to respool it during the retrieve. On most reels, it advances and recedes as the line is being coiled on, to spool the line uniformly—but it never rotates. On the cast, the line slips off the exposed end of the spool. This action can best be visualized by thinking of a spool of thread. If one end of the spool of thread is held firmly in one hand and the thread end is grasped by the other hand and stripped off straight over the opposite end of the spool, the action would be similar to that of the spinning line leaving the reel. The spool also remains stationary on the retrieve. A metal "finger" rotates around the spool, picking up the line and placing it back around the spool.

Line. Generally speaking, a light to medium monofilament line is recommended for the beginner. When putting the line on a spinning reel, follow the manufacturer's instructions carefully to avoid twisting the line. Usually, a braided monofilament line is used for the bait-casting (level-wind) reel because many anglers feel it is less likely to backlash.

Skills and Techniques

The ability to cast the line onto the water is the most important skill the angler must learn. Indeed, developing a good casting stroke is the key to success in any type of fishing. As the various techniques are described in this section, you will notice some similarities in the use of the fly rod, bait-casting rod, and spinning rod; however, there are important differences. Reference will be made to the positioning of the casting arm in relation to the hands on a clock. Most of the movements center on the 10 o'clock and 2 o'clock positions. Therefore, if you think of the movement in terms of the hands of a clock face, you should have relatively little difficulty in understanding the action of the arm and rod in the learning sequence.

FLY CASTING

There are two important things to remember when learning to fly cast: First, the right hand will grip the handle and become part of the execution of the cast, and second, the left hand must control the feed of the line as the cast is being made. After sufficient practice, the sequence and action of the two hands will become smooth and rhythmic. (Left-handed individuals should reverse the described procedure.) Another key point for the beginner to remember is that the cast is primarily a result of the action of the hand and the forearm and less of the wrist.

To practice the cast, begin by pulling 15 to 20 feet of line from the tip of the rod and placing it on the ground in front of you. Grip the rod on the handle, with the thumb placed on top in line with the rod. Wrap the fingers comfortably around the handle. Bend the wrist until it becomes a parallel extension of the forearm. The stroke itself is best executed between the 10 o'clock and 2 o'clock positions. The greatest problem for novice fly casters is using their wrist too much, resulting in a casting action like a "buggy whip" (Figure 18-2).

▶ **Learning Hints**

1. Begin by lifting the rod tip up, and then rapidly accelerate from the 10 o'clock to 1 o'clock position. The space between the wrist and handle opens slightly.

2. Stop the rod at the 1 o'clock position and let the line drift behind the shoulder. Wait until the line is almost completely unrolled, then begin the forward cast.

3. Accelerate the rod forward to the 10 o'clock position, stop quickly, and allow the line to unroll forward. The line should land softly on the surface as you complete the follow-through.

4. Because the basic principle of fly casting is to cast ("roll" and "unroll") loops of line, the beginner should watch the back cast to be certain that these loops are rolling and unrolling properly. Indeed, fly casting is a recreational skill that requires the caster to apply equal power to *both* the back cast and the forward cast. Even more specifically, a proper forward cast is impossible to execute after an incorrect back cast.

▶ **Practice/Organizational Suggestions**

The left hand plays an important role in the cast because it feeds line to the rod on the forward cast or draws line from the reel during a false cast.

1. Take slack and grasp the line between the thumb and forefinger and strip (draw) it from the reel. Repeat this action two or three times to form additional coils.

2. At the end of the forward cast, release the line from the coil in the left hand, releasing the loop nearest the ends of the finger first. It is important to keep the loops separated.

3. As soon as sufficient line is drawn for the length of the cast, complete the cast, releasing the loops of line. The release of these loops of line into the cast is called "shooting the line" and is usually done to add distance to the cast.

BAIT CASTING

The grip for bait casting is different in that the thumb must be placed on the spool flange for the conventional type and the reel turned sidewise so that the handle points straight up. The index finger should grip the finger trigger, while the other fingers grasp the handle firmly but not rigidly.

In fishing, a good caster learns to cast from any position and with either hand. In target casting, which is the only method of learning accuracy, the caster may stand directly facing the target or slightly sidewise, with the right side (if casting right-handed) toward the target and the right foot slightly advanced. The arms should be held in a relaxed, "natural" position, with the elbow at or near the side. Align the target by looking at it through the top of the rod tip.

The overhead casting action has two parts: the backward motion and the forward motion. Each is equally important.

▶ **Learning Hints**

1. Stand comfortably; keep the elbow clear of the body, while the forearm becomes an extension of the rod.

2. Bring the rod up quickly and stop at the 2 o'clock position; the weight on the lure will bend the rod further back.

3. With no hesitation, bring the rod swiftly to the 10 o'clock position, and ease the thumb off the line on the spool.

4. While the lure is in flight, gently apply pressure with the thumb, braking the spool, and allow the rod to follow through in the direction of the line of flight. Brake the spool to a complete stop as the lure reaches the surface of the water. Shift the rod to the left hand to retrieve the plug. Then grasp the handle of the reel with the right hand and begin to reel in the line. The method of retrieving depends on the type of bait being used. Often the manufacturer supplies printed instructions on proper manipulation so the angler may secure the best results from each type.

SPIN CASTING

Remember that there are two types of spinning reels: the open and the closed cone type. The cast for both is made in the same manner as with the bait-casting outfit. The only difference is in the control of the line during the cast. With the closed-type reel, the thumb button is pressed then released at the 10 o'clock position, and the left hand helps to feather the line and eventually brake it. With the spinning outfit, the caster places pressure upon the line between the forefinger and the rod grip *after* the line has left the spool.

In starting the cast, hold the line (ahead of the reel) firmly against the rod grip with the forefinger of the hand with which the cast is made. While holding the line securely, release the pick-up bail or finger and move aside so that it will not interfere with the line during the

Figure 18-2 Overhead fly cast (sequence). (A) Beginning position. (B) 10 o'clock position. (C) Rod stops at 1 o'clock position. (D) Finishing position. Note that the wrist is firm, not fixed, throughout the cast.

cast. This motion is done by turning the handle slightly in reverse, by pressing a release button, or as required for the particular make of reel. Release the pressure on the line at the same time and in the same manner as you would release the thumb pressure on the spool with a bait-casting outfit. During the flight of the lure, exercise control by decreasing or increasing the index finger pressure on the line against the cork grip.

As with the conventional rod and reel, the beginner should start with the direct overhead cast until he acquires proficiency with the new outfit.

▶ Practice/Organizational Suggestions

The beginning angler must not only learn accuracy and form but also develop a "feel" for the casting technique she is learning. Distance is secondary in the beginning. Use a dummy lure (no barbs) when practicing. *Teaching note*: In all instances, whether dealing with beginners or more advanced anglers, make sure there is adequate space between participants. Single line formations with two or three arms' length between participants are safest.

1. Pick up the rod and practice the forearm and wrist action without casting.

2. For a class, place a series of plastic hoops at a standard distance and have students hit the target. As students gain proficiency, move the hoops to varying distances, designate high scores for those hoops farthest away and lower scores for those that are nearest to the angler. Promote both individual and team competition.

3. Because many people fish from a boat, bring a bench or low-backed chairs to class so students can practice each method of casting from a sitting position.

Safety Considerations

1. *All* anglers should carry or have access to a first-aid kit at all times. Hooks, whether on flies or lures, occasionally end up in one part or another of an angler's body!

2. Anglers must be constantly aware of the dangers of being in the sun too long. Use a sunscreen or sunblock, and wear a hat (which is also good to ward off hooks on errant casts) and polarized sunglasses—for safety and to see fish.

3. Anglers often, probably too often, fish in places where there are lots of insects, especially of the flying variety. Be certain to carry appropriate repellent.

4. Using waders in unknown waters or wearing them in a boat is hazardous, so the angler must avoid such risks.

Skill Assessment—Skish

Skish is a dry-land game designed to improve one's skill in casting with regular bait- or spin- and fly-casting tackle. It is an excellent way for all casters to master the skills of accuracy and the control of distance.

BAIT CASTING

Bait-casting rules call for the plug not to exceed ⅝ ounce, and the line must be no smaller than 9-pound test. Ten targets, rings not to exceed 30 inches, are randomly scattered with distances unknown to the caster. The closest target is not less than 40 nor more than 45 feet from the casting box (4 × 4 feet), and the farthest one should not be more than 80 nor less than 70 feet away. Each target has its own casting box. The contestants move from box to box, taking two casts at each target (Figure 18-3).

Scoring: Score 6 points for a perfect cast on first trial; 4 points for a perfect cast on second trial. The cast must fall within the target to score. In the event of a tie score, the student having the greatest number of points on initial casts is declared the winner.

FLY CASTING

Fly-casting rules for regular fly-casting tackle require a fly tied in approved dry fly style, with the hook broken off back of the barb. Five targets are placed at distances unknown to the casters, between 20 and 40 feet from the casting boxes.

First Round.   The caster starts with fly in hand and no slack in the line and is given 2½ minutes at each target to make three casts.

Scoring: Score 5 points for a perfect cast on first trial; 3 points for a perfect cast on second trial; and 2 points for a perfect cast on third trial. The maximum score is

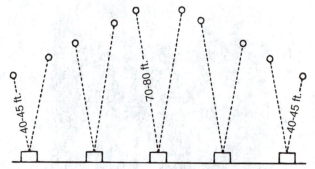

Figure 18-3   Skill testing set-up or skish game using 10 targets and 5 stations.

50 points. (On water, the fly must rest on the water until the judge calls for the score.)

Second Round.   The time limit is 1½ minutes (90 seconds) for each target. The caster roll casts until a "perfect" has been scored on all five targets or until the official calls time. Time begins when the fly drops on the surface. Each perfect score counts 5 points, with a possible score of 25.

Third Round—with Fly.   The time limit is 1 to 1½ minutes. The caster starts with fly in the hand and no slack in the line. To begin, the caster extends the line to the nearest target by false casting; time begins when the fly drops on the surface as a measured cast. The student makes two casts, without false casts, at each of the five targets from left to right, stripping the necessary line and shooting it to reach each target.

Scoring: Score 3 points for a perfect cast on first trial; 2 points for a perfect cast on second trial. The maximum possible score is 25 points. In case of a tie, the caster having made the greatest number of initial perfects is declared the winner.

Modifications for Special Populations

ORTHOPEDICALLY IMPAIRED

Modifications must be considered for several aspects of fishing: baiting the hook, holding and casting, reeling, and removing the catch. Several adaptations can be made for grasping the rod (see chapters on handball/racquetball and tennis). Electronic devices exist to help casting and reeling; the simplest modification, however, is to eliminate these tasks and use a simple "cane pole" arrangement.

COGNITIVELY IMPAIRED

Minimal modifications are needed.

SENSORY IMPAIRED

Minimal modifications are needed.

Terminology

back cast Drawing the rod back; the initial movement in the cast.

backing line Thin braided line put on the reel before the fly line to fill up the spool and for insurance against a fish making a long run.

backlash A faulty casting technique that results in a tangling of the line.

bait casting The throwing and placing of a lure and line from the rod and reel.

dry fly fishing Casting a surface fly so that it resembles an insect on the water.

false cast A fly-casting cast in which line is held in the air and not allowed to fall to the surface. Usually used to increase the length of a dry cast or to cause a fly to change direction.

ferrules The connections between the sections of the rod.

fly Natural or synthetic materials tied on hooks.

fly casting Throwing a line with an artificial lure by means of a fly rod.

forward cast The last movement forward with the rod that throws the lure or the fly to the desired spot.

guides Small loops on the rod through which the line is run.

leader The strong, transparent material that connects the line to the hook or lure.

level-wind reel A reel that has a carriage that distributes the line evenly on the spool.

lure Artificial or natural bait used to attract fish. One or more hooks are attached to the lure.

net A device to take the fish safely out of the water.

power stroke The brief time in fly casting between the backward and forward cast when the caster applies power.

reel The mechanism that winds or unwinds the line.

reel seat The part of the rod handle to which the reel is attached.

rod tip The top end of the rod.

roll cast A fly cast in which line is rolled out over a surface without using a back cast.

shoot Feeding out extra line during a fly casting forward or backward cast. Also used to increase the distance of a cast.

spinner Artificial lure that spins when it is drawn through the water.

spoon Artificial lure shaped something like a spoon.

strike When a fish grasps the lure or fly; the angler's response is to set the hook.

tackle Fishing gear; usually refers only to the rod and reel.

thumbing Controlling the speed of the cast by means of thumb pressure on the reel.

Discussion Questions

1. Compare the similarities and differences between fly casting and bait or spin casting.

2. Discuss the equipment (rod, reel, and line) needed for fly and bait casting.

3. Discuss the sequential skill steps needed when practicing fly casting and the learning hints that will facilitate skill acquisition.

4. Discuss the sequential skill steps needed when practicing bait casting and the learning hints that will facilitate skill acquisition.

5. Identify precautions that aid in making angling safe.

Web Sites

www.tu.org Trout Unlimited—includes up-to-date articles about environmental issues, conservation issues, and more.

www.flyfisherman.com *Fly Fisherman* magazine—includes articles on a variety of topics such as conservation, tying, and skill building.

www.outdoorreview.com—offers resource for fly fishing equipment, articles, listing of fly shops worldwide, and much more.

www.flyanglersonline.com—provides fly fishing 101, information on tying, animated film clips of tying knots, chat rooms, and a fly fishing forum.

www.fedflyfishers.org Federation of Fly Fishers—offers comprehensive information.

www.womensflyfishing.net—features tips for fishing, books, links, and suggestions for disabled fly fishers.

www.about-flyfishing.com—contains many resources concerning fly fishing, including a beginner's corner, fly tying, articles about kids and fly fishing, newsgroups, clubs, associations, and more.

http://fishing.about.com—includes a variety of articles about fishing with family, fishing tackle, getting started, and ice fishing.

Nature and Purpose

Floor hockey is a fast-moving noncontact game. The constant strategic repositioning and end-to-end transitions demand cardiorespiratory endurance. Hand-eye coordination is necessary for the player to manipulate the puck, ball, or similar object, using a stick to dribble, receive, pass, and shoot. The continuous motion requires quick reaction time, foot speed, and agility.

The strategies are similar to those of many goal-scoring games. The object is to pass or dribble toward the opponents' goal; maintain control of the puck, keeping it wide on the court; center it in front of the goal for a teammate; and score by shooting it directly into the goal or from rebounds.

Floor hockey is an adaptable game. The rules can be adapted to the size and markings on the court; the age, gender, abilities, and number of the participants; and the types of equipment available. Additionally, the skills transfer to other activities that involve striking.

History

Games involving a stick and ball can be traced to ancient times. Early Greeks played a game similar to hockey more than 2500 years ago. Centuries later, the French played a game called *hoquet*, and the English played one called *hokay*. The Irish developed *hurling*, whereas American Indians participated in stick-and-ball games.[1]

Most authorities agree that floor hockey is a direct descendant of ice hockey with modifications. The roots of floor hockey trace back to the 1950s. The first indoor game was introduced in Battle Creek, Michigan, in 1962.[2] The game was presented to physical education teachers, coaches, and athletic directors and spread quickly across the United States.

In the 1970s, floor hockey spread across the ocean and was first played in Sweden under the name of *floorball*. A plastic ball was substituted for the puck. Floorball is traced to a similar game called *bandy* from northern Europe. It rapidly spread throughout Europe during the 1980s, at which time several national organizations formed.

In 1986 the International Floorball Federation (IFF) was organized. The first European championships were held in Zurich in 1994, and the first world championships were hosted by Sweden in 1996. Both championships alternate men's and women's tournaments every other year.[3]

Court, Equipment, Players

Floor hockey can be modified to meet the specifics of the environment. Following are some suggested modifications.

THE PLAYING AREA

The court usually consists of an area the size of a basketball court. The markings on the basketball court may be used for establishing rule requirements. For example, use the boundary lines to determine when the puck is out of play. However, allow the puck to rebound off of the surrounding walls if this is feasible in the facility. This provides for more continuous action with limited stoppage of play.

1. In side-by-side court play, side boundary lines may be used to determine out-of-bounds. When the puck goes out-of-bounds, restart play immediately with a player taking an indirect free hit with the nearest defender at least 10 feet away.

2. When it is necessary to use end lines, restart of play can be similar to soccer. The offensive player places the puck at the corner of the court with an indirect free hit. If it is the defensive team's restart, a defensive player places the puck on the end line where it went out-of-bounds and restarts with an indirect free hit.

3. Other basketball court markings may be used. Use the center line or center circle to start play or restart following a goal or end of a period of play. Each team is in its own half of the court outside the center circle. One player from each team is in the center circle, and the puck is dropped between them in a face-off. To maintain balanced positioning, use the center line to restrict certain players from moving out of a given area.

4. Use the width of the basketball 3-second lane (12 feet) as the sides of the crease and put a line parallel with the end line 6 feet in front of the goal connecting the 3-second lane lines. Place the front of the goal on the end line centered in the 3-second lane.

EQUIPMENT

When preparing a floor hockey unit, instructors must consider the length and construction of the stick; indoor or outdoor use; puck or ball limitations; goal sizes and construction; safety equipment; and playing area border dividers. Most physical education catalogs provide detailed selection information. Following is a brief overview of each area.

Sticks.   The suggested length of the stick depends on age of the player: for ages 5 to 7, 30 inches; for ages 8 to 12, 36 inches; ages 13 to 15, 42 to 45 inches; ages 16 and older, 48 to 52 inches. Most sticks consist of a shaft, blade, and butt-end separately attached. There are a few one-piece molded models. The shaft may be made of wood, aluminum, polyethylene, PVC, polycarbonate, or fiberglass-reinforced. Most blades are fiberglass-reinforced polyethylene. There is a blade made of urethane foam that is safe yet durable for elementary and middle school ages. Consider the material, construction method, age of participants, and indoor/outdoor use when selecting a stick.

Puck/Ball.   The object used as a puck varies depending on the abilities of the participants, desired speed of play, and facility environment. The size of the puck varies from $2\frac{5}{8}$ to $3\frac{7}{8}$ inches and the ball from $2\frac{5}{8}$ inches in diameter to 3 inches. The larger the object, the easier for the younger, less experienced player. The puck shape and type of construction determines speed of play and control. Most pucks are made of polyethylene for durability. The ones that are air-filled with a hollow core are faster and less controllable. A pellet-filled puck shaped like a donut with rounded edges stays on the floor and is slower, allowing for more control. These flat pucks can slide under bleachers, however, and stop play. A puck-ball, which is flat on one side and rounded like a whiffle ball on the other, also is available. It travels more slowly and does not become stuck in small places. A beanbag may also be used.

There are a variety of floor hockey balls from which to choose. As with the puck, the particulars of the situation dictate choice. One choice is a dense foam ball 3 inches in diameter, which does not bounce and is safe to use. Another option, the poly-ball, rolls smoothly and has limited bounce. Or consider a ball 2⅝ inches in diameter with a soft vinyl composite construction; this type of ball leads to slower play, is excellent for young children, is safe, and can be used indoors and outdoors. A ball made of super high-density plastic with virtually no bounce and 3 inches in diameter is also suitable for both indoor and outdoor play. A double-stitched vinyl-covered beanbag ball may also be used.

Protective Gear. The type of safety equipment selected depends on the level of competition, the size and strength of the participants, and modified rules for limiting possible injuries. The choices are protective eye goggles; mouth guard; hand protectors made of high-impact plastic, which slide on the stick; and goalie equipment, such as helmet with or without face guard, leg pads, blocker-glove, and catch-glove.

Goal. Goals may be made from PVC or steel and are either folding or nonfolding. The size usually is 54 inches wide by 44 inches high by 24 inches deep, or 72 inches wide by 48 inches high by 24, 30, or 36 inches deep. Nets are attached. Plastic cones may be used as goals at lower levels of play to lower costs. Cones range in height up to 36 inches; a 50-inch telescoping model cone has attachments at the top for a crossbar or rope.

Border Panels. Border panels can be used to divide playing areas or restrict the puck from going under bleachers. In either case, the outcome is keeping play continuous. The panels are made of either plastic or high-density foam with a wide base for stand-alone stability. The panels are easily attached to each other and can be used for other activities, for example, as bowling lanes.

PLAYERS

The standard number of players is six: a goalie and five other players. Larger court sizes might allow for adding more players per team. In any case it is strongly suggested that players be restricted in where they are allowed to go on the court. These restrictions provide for constructive, continuous, and coordinated play.

The following are suggestions for a six-player game:

1. One goalie, restricted to the already recommended crease (12 feet wide by 6 feet deep). No other players from either team are allowed in the crease.
2. Two forwards, allowed only in the offensive half of the court.
3. Two defenders, allowed only in the defensive half of the court.
4. One center, allowed to cover the entire court.

Basic Rules

Floor hockey has yet to emerge in the United States as an activity that is highly regulated by a consistent set of rules. The activity draws from its similarities to ice hockey, with adjustments and modifications made to meet the specific conditions of the playing area, age, gender, ability levels, number of participants, equipment, and so on. Choose from among the following rules, or further modify them to meet specific needs.

SCORING

Score a goal when the whole puck/ball is propelled, only by the stick, across the goal line, between the uprights, and below the crossbar.

FOULS AND PENALTIES

The penalties for infractions vary according to the severity of the infraction. The following is a list of possible infractions classified as major fouls (severe) or minor fouls (less severe), along with a suggested penalty for each. A detailed definition of each foul is found at the end of this section under Terminology.

Major Fouls

1. Slashing
2. Roughing
3. Tripping
4. Hooking
5. Charging
6. Cross-checking
7. Checking

Minor Fouls

1. High stick
2. Goalie violations
3. Obstruction
4. Crease violations
5. Illegal hands
6. Trapping
7. Slap shot
8. Sliding
9. Out-of-play
10. Offside
11. Icing
12. Stick lifting
13. Kicking
14. Illegal grip

Major Foul Penalty. The player is given a 2-minute penalty, and play restarts with an indirect free hit for the opponents at the point of the foul.

Minor Foul Penalty. Play restarts with an indirect free hit at the point of the foul.

Indirect Free Hit. Play restarts following a foul or out-of-play puck at the point of infraction. It is an uncontested hit with the opponents at least 10 feet away in all directions. The player taking the free hit cannot recontact the puck until someone else touches it. A goal cannot be scored directly from the first contact of the puck on the free hit. If the defense last touches the puck as it goes out of play over their end line, the offense restarts play with a free hit at the corner of the court nearest where it went out.

Penalty Shot. A free shot at goal is awarded when, in the opinion of the referee, a player is prevented from scoring because of a foul. There are two recommended methods for taking the penalty shot. In the first method, the puck is placed on the penalty line (basketball foul line). The player taking the penalty shot has 5 seconds to dribble toward the goal to shoot. If the shot is missed or blocked by the goalie, play restarts with a face-off at the center line. In the second method, the puck is placed on the front edge of the basketball foul circle, which is 14 feet from the goal line (basketball end line). The player taking the penalty shot immediately shoots on goal, and the goalie—with both feet on the goal line—may not move until the shooter contacts the puck. If the shot misses or rebounds, play is restarted at the center line with a face-off. All players except the shooter and goalie stand on the sideline in both penalty shot methods.

Offside. It is a violation for forwards or defenders to move out of their designated area. If this occurs, play is restarted with an indirect free hit by the offended team at that spot on the floor.

Crease Violation. Play is restarted with a face-off for any crease violation (see the Players section) by either team. The face-off takes place at the basketball foul line or at least 20 feet from the goal. Players are never allowed to play the puck back to their goalie in the crease.

Out-of-Play. See Indirect Free Hit.

LENGTH OF PLAY

The length of the game depends on individual desires or needs. It is played in periods, usually three.

Suggested Learning Sequence

A. Nature, purpose, and history of floor hockey

B. Playing area, equipment, safety, and player responsibilities

C. Skills and techniques.
1. Grip and stance
2. Dribbling, stick handling, and dodging
3. Forehand/backhand passing, tackling, fielding/receiving, and shooting/goalie skills
4. Individual offense and defense (tackling)
5. Rules of the game introduced starting with individual fouls

D. Modified games, with group offensive/defensive strategies

E. Team rules, including face-off, indirect free hit situations, and penalty shot

F. Full-game play

Skills and Techniques

The fundamental skills for floor hockey are the grip, stance, dribbling, stick handling, dodging, passing forehand/backhand, fielding/receiving, individual defense (tackling), shooting, and goalie skills. Because the game of floor hockey is primarily a passing, receiving, and shooting game, it is essential that players master the technique of controlling the puck and keeping it close to the stick. Long and destructive hitting of the puck and excessive dribbling lead to uncontrolled play.

GRIP AND STANCE

Hold the stick at all times with both hands and keep the blade as selected rules dictate: either on the floor or not higher than the ankle. Place the nondominant hand (left hand for a right-handed person) in a hand-shaking grip at the top of the stick and the dominant hand similarly gripping at least 12 inches below the top hand (Figure 18-4). A visible strip of tape at this point ensures that the bottom hand is not allowed to slide higher (minor foul), which may lead to dangerous stick action. The player needs to learn to carry the stick on the right side of the body (right-hander) with this gripping action.

▶ Learning Hints

1. Hold the stick firmly but comfortably.
2. Lean forward, with the heel of the blade on the floor on the dominant side of your body and your feet spread wider than the shoulders. This stance forms a triangle base.
3. Run around the area in the front-leaning position. Never allow the blade to rise above the ankle.

DRIBBLING AND STICK HANDLING

In the dribble, the fundamental grip, stick, and crouched running position are used to control the movement of the puck around the area. Passing is the first option; dribbling is used to avoid a defender or

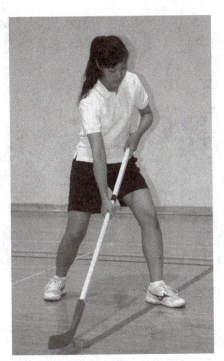

Figure 18-4 Forehand push-pass.

relocate for a shot. Stick handling refers to moving the stick and the puck in a variety of positions while maintaining control.

▶ Learning Hints

1. Keep the puck on the blade in front of your body and slightly off to your dominant-hand side (refer to the positioning for Field Hockey—see Figure 10-10).
2. Extend your dominant arm with the stick and move the puck forward as you run.
3. Stay low and reach out for the puck.
4. Keep your feet behind the stick and puck while you move.
5. Stay low and keep the puck in front.
6. Keep the puck close to the blade, always within reach.
7. Alternate contacting the puck with both sides of the blade to change directions, pass, or shoot.
8. Keep your head up, with your eyes focused ahead of the puck when you look to pass to a teammate or avoid a defender.

▶ Practice/Organizational Suggestions

Refer to dribbling drills 1, 2, and 4 of the Field Hockey chapter.

DODGING

Refer to Dodging in the Field Hockey chapter for an explanation of the skill.

▶ Learning Hints

1. Execute the dodge just before the opponent is within reach of the puck.
2. At the last moment, push or pull the puck to one side of the defender, depending on the direction you wish to go.
3. Keep the puck in control on the dodge to ensure you remain in possession of the puck.
4. Attempt to keep your body between the puck and the defender when you change directions.
5. Pass or shoot as soon as possible following the dodge around the defender.

▶ Practice/Organizational Suggestions

1. Players spread out in a restricted area, each with a puck, and dribble. On command, dodge an imaginary defender.
2. Place cones randomly in a restricted area and have each student with a puck shuttle forward and backward throughout the course, dodging each cone as they approach it.
3. Spread hula hoops throughout a restricted area. A defender stands with at least one foot in the hoop. Have the dribblers shuttle forward and backward, dodging each defender who is attempting to contact either the puck or the stick of the dribblers.
4. Have students work in pairs. In these pairs, a dribbler attempts to continuously dodge a defensive partner, who passively backpedals. Once the dodging dribbler gets around the defender, the role is reversed. Continuously change roles.

PASSING FOREHAND AND BACKHAND

The most common pass, and most accurate, is the forehand push-pass from the dominant side of the blade. The backhand pass is used when the puck is on the back of the blade. Both are used for short passing situations. The same techniques are used for shooting or long passing by lifting the stick higher but never higher than the waist.

▶ Learning Hints—Forehand

1. Grip the stick as previously described.
2. Keep your feet in a wide stance, with the front foot pointed toward the target (refer to Figure 10-10 in Chapter 10 on field hockey).
3. When pushing the puck forward, keep it slightly forward of the middle of the stance. For more power, start with the puck at the back of the stance.
4. Do not backswing; the puck contacts the front of the blade.

5. Keep your shoulders perpendicular to the target, with your front shoulder slightly pulled back in an open position for your upper body.

6. Transfer weight to your front foot as that side of the body initiates the action.

7. The arms and stick act as one with a pushing action toward the target.

8. Snap and roll your wrists over during the follow-through for added force. The blade is still close to the floor, facing down toward the floor.

9. The blade ends up 1 to 2 feet above the floor upon finish.

▶ Practice/Organizational Suggestions—Forehand

1. Stand sideways to the wall at approximately 10 feet and pass the puck at a designated target (cone), keeping track of the number of successful hits. Gradually move farther away from the wall to increase difficulty.

2. Dribble toward the wall, and then turn sideways to repeat the foregoing drill.

3. See Fielding/Receiving suggestions detailed in the Field Hockey chapter for additional partner drills.

▶ Learning Hints—Backhand

1. Grip the stick (Figure 18-5) as previously described.

2. Reverse the stance from that for the forehand because the front foot and dominant lower hand, arm, and shoulder lead the action toward the target. The puck is on the back of the blade.

3. Repeat the motion and actions of items 3 to 8 for the Learning Hints—Forehand.

▶ Practice/Organizational Suggestions—Backhand

1. Same as those for the forehand.

FIELDING/RECEIVING

Refer to the Fielding section in the Field Hockey chapter for an explanation of the skill.

▶ Learning Hints

1. Position the feet parallel to the approaching puck.

2. Watch the puck all the way to the blade of the stick.

3. Keep the blade touching the floor and perpendicular to the approaching puck.

4. Make initial contact forward of the front foot, and pull the stick backward to absorb the force of the puck.

5. Have a relaxed grip on the stick, especially with the bottom hand.

Figure 18-5   Backhand pass.

6. The harder the pass, the more "give" with the stick is necessary.

7. Attempt to keep the puck in contact with the blade on initial contact, with minimal rebound for immediate passing or shooting opportunities.

▶ Practice/Organizational Suggestions

1. Refer to fielding drills in the Field Hockey chapter.

TACKLING

Refer to the Tackling section in the Field Hockey chapter for an explanation of the skill.

▶ Learning Hints

1. Overplay the opponent to his stick side.

2. Keep your feet moving and backpedal while faking until the puck is too far off the opponent's blade.

3. Time the contact with the blade when the puck is not on the opponent's blade.

▶ Practice/Organizational Suggestions

1. Refer to tackling drills in the Field Hockey chapter.

SHOOTING

The drive and flicking are used to shoot on goal. The drive is used for power from a greater distance from the goal. Flicking is a finesse shot close to goal whose purpose is to lift the puck high to the corners. It is possible to flick a moving puck, but it is easier when it is stationary after it has been fielded.

▶ Learning Hints—Drive

1. The basic technique is the same as the technique for the forehand pass.

2. The backswing and follow-through are higher. At no time is either the stick or puck above the knee or waist, whichever height is used as a rule.

▶ Practice/Organizational Suggestions

1. Use drills 1 and 2 for forehand passing but from a greater distance.
2. Place three players single-file on the end line, 10 feet away from the goal. The first two in line have a puck. Place three other players single-file opposite the end line players, starting at 15 feet. The first baseline player passes the puck straight to the player on the opposite line, who fields the puck and then drives the puck on goal. The third end line player retrieves the puck and moves up in line as the first passer shuttles to the end of the shooting line. The shooter shuttles to the end of the passing line. Continuously repeat the sequence, shuttling back and forth between lines.
3. Repeat drill 2 without the shooter fielding the puck but instead driving it immediately from the pass.
4. Repeat drill 2 with the shooting line gradually farther from the end line.
5. Repeat drill 2 with the passing line parallel to the shooting line and at the same distance from the goal.

▶ Learning Hints—Flick

1. Use the same grip as for the forehand pass.
2. Use the same stance and body position as for the forehand pass.
3. Contact the puck in front of the lead foot so that you can place the blade of the stick under the puck.
4. With no backswing, use your top hand to bring the stick back fast and behind the bottom hand. This action causes the blade face to open, lifting the puck upward in a flicking action.

▶ Practice/Organizational Suggestions

1. Refer to forehand pass and drive drills. On the drive drills, have the lines closer together—never more than 10 feet apart—moving closer to 6 feet just outside the crease.

GOALKEEPING

Goalkeeping requires skills different from those of other players. The goalkeeper must be agile, quick, have good concentration, and be able to anticipate other players' movements. The goalie may use equipment to avoid injury. The goalie has the privilege of using the feet to stop or direct the puck when defending the goal. The hands may be used also to stop the puck if modified rules allow. However, the hands may not be used to pass the puck out of the crease.

GOALKEEPING PRINCIPLES

1. Refer to the Field Hockey chapter.

▶ Learning Hints

1. Stance—refer to the Stance section in the Field Hockey chapter.
2. Meet the shot with legs together and "give" when the puck makes contact with the stick so that the puck drops almost "dead."
3. Clear the puck with a forehand push-pass to a teammate, or push it hard to the side of the goal when a teammate is not open.
4. If hands are used to catch the puck, drop it to the floor and use the clearing technique in item 3.

▶ Practice/Organizational Suggestions

1. Refer to the goalkeeping drills in the Field Hockey chapter. A goalkeeper may also be used in the shooting drills for the drive or the flick.

Modified Games

Keep Away. See this game in the Field Hockey chapter.

Sideline Hockey. See this game in the Field Hockey chapter.

Square Hockey for Goalkeeping. The court is formed by a square of approximately 40 feet by 40 feet. Two teams of equal numbers (10 to 12) defend two connecting sidelines surrounding the whole court. Number off each player from both teams. Randomly call two or three numbers aloud; these players become the court players who attempt to capture the puck and score. The remaining players on the sidelines become goalies, working on goalie skills. It is a score when the court players get the puck across either of the opponents' two sidelines. Repeat by randomly calling different numbers following a score.

Six-Goal Hockey. Use cones to make goals centered on each end line (one centered on each end line—for two total end line goals) of a regulation court and two equidistant on each sideline (four total sideline goals), for a grand total of six goals surrounding the whole court. Six teams consist of three players—a goalie and two court players. The object is to score on any of the other five goalies. Each of the six teams starts with a puck. To score, a team may use any of the pucks that it captures. Following a score by any team, play immediately restarts after the players on each team rotate, with a new player in the goalie position.

Three-on-Three Half Court. Two forwards and a center attempt to score on a goalie and two defenders. Play starts at the center line, with the offense in control of the puck. The offense attempts to move and pass to score on the goalie. The two defenders and goalie attempt to intercept the puck and gain control. It is a score if the offense, which has superior numbers (3-on-2), scores a goal or if the defense is able to gain control of the puck and get it past the center line under their control. When a score is made, all players on both teams rotate to a new position on their team. Teams change from offense to defense, and vice versa, after three rotations.

Playing Strategies

Offensive.   Refer to the Field Hockey chapter.

Defensive.   Refer to the Field Hockey chapter.

Skill Assessment

The skills necessary at the beginning to intermediate levels are identical to those for field hockey. Refer to the Skill Assessment section of the Field Hockey chapter and use the same procedures for testing floor hockey.

Modifications for Special Populations

Refer to the Field Hockey chapter.

Terminology

backhand Shooting or passing with the back of the blade. The bottom hand pulls the stick forward.

body contact Incidental or accidental body contact, which is not penalized.

center The player who is allowed to move the length of the floor in a game and who plays both offense and defense.

charging The use of the body over distance to gain speed and force before contacting an opponent.

checking Illegal contact between two players (body-to-body, stick-to-stick, or stick-to-body); any type of contact that is deemed hazardous.

clear Getting the puck out of your defensive zone to prevent your opponents from scoring.

crease The area in front of the goal in which only the goalie is allowed.

cross-check Using the stick sideways across the body of an opponent when making contact.

defenders The players who cannot go past the center line into the offensive area and who play defense.

dribble (also known as "stick handling" or "puck handling") The use of both sides of the blade to control and move the puck.

face-off The start or restart of play when an official drops the puck between the sticks of two opponents, who try to hit it to one of their teammates or in the direction of their goal.

fielding/receiving The absorption of the puck's speed on the blade of the stick so that it is immediately under control.

forehand Shooting or passing with the front of the blade. The bottom hand pushes the stick forward.

forwards/wings (Right and Left) The players who cannot go past the center line into the defensive area and who play offense with the center.

goal Each score is worth 1 point. A goal counts when the whole puck crosses the goal line between the uprights and below the crossbar. A puck kicked or hit by the hand into the goal is not a score.

goalie/goalkeeper The player who is allowed to stop the puck with the hands, feet, or stick. This player attempts to block all shots on the goal and works with the defenders to prevent the opposing team from scoring.

goalie violation Illegal use of the hands to stop the puck (modified rule), to reach for a puck outside the crease, or to leave the crease. When modifications allow for catching the puck with the non-stick hand, the goalie is allowed to hold it for only 3 seconds.

high sticking The lifting of the blade above the waist during the backswing or follow-through.

hooking Illegal use of the hockey stick to "hook" another player.

icing A player on the defensive side of the floor sends the puck down the length of the floor and it crosses a designated line without being touched by a teammate (modified rule).

illegal grip The bottom hand slides higher than the restrictive tape on the stick—this encourages a full swing, and is dangerous.

illegal hands The use of the hand to play the puck. Rule modifications may allow the goalie to use the nonstick hand to stop the puck.

indirect free hit The restart of play following a foul or when the puck goes out of play. Opponents must be at least 10 feet from the puck, and the player taking the free hit may not recontact it until someone else touches it.

kicking The illegal use of the feet (by any player other than the goalie) to play the puck.

major foul A severe foul; the penalized player must sit out of the game for a designated period of time.

minor foul The type of foul that is noninjurious; results in restart of play with an indirect free hit.

obstruction The illegal use of the body to shield an opponent from playing the puck.

offside Movement of players out of the designated areas assigned to their position.

out of play The puck leaves the playing area or is located where it is not playable.

penalty shot A free shot at goal when—in the opinion of the referee—a player was prevented from scoring because of a foul.

poke check The use of the stick to move an opponent's stick or to take the puck away.

power play A team with all its players (full strength) having an advantage over the team charged with a penalty, playing with fewer players (short-handed).

receiving/fielding *See* fielding.

roughing Play that endangers other players; results in a penalty. Examples: making contact with the goalie, pushing, blocking with the body, and any major foul.

short-handed A team playing with fewer players because of a player's serving a penalty.

slap shot An illegal shot that involves swinging the stick backward, slapping the puck, and using a follow-through that brings the stick high above the waist.

slashing Deliberately hitting an opponent's arms or hands with the stick.

sliding Deliberately sliding on the floor.

stick handling The use of the stick to maneuver the puck with finesse.

stick lifting Lifting the blade of the stick too high (off the floor or above the ankle) when moving around the playing area without the puck. Limiting lifting aids in preventing stick injuries to players.

trapping Using the hands or feet to trap the puck on the floor.

tripping Intentionally tripping an opponent with the stick.

wrist shot or flick Using a flicking motion with the stick to move the puck. The stick remains in contact with the floor, with no backswing or follow-through. This is the best shot for speed and accuracy.

Discussion Questions

1. Trace the evolution of floor hockey.
2. Compare the strategies used in floor hockey and other goal-scoring games.
3. Identify and discuss the differences between major and minor fouls.
4. Discuss the various adaptations that may be implemented in a unit on field hockey.

Web Sites

www.usafloorball.org—provides basic information about the game, history, national associations, and international federation.

FLYING DISC

Nature and Purpose

Today, there are many varieties of activities that incorporate a flying disc. Ultimate Frisbee, disc golf, freestyle, double disc court, guts, field events, and discathon are a few of the games that have official rules for participation or national organizations. Many new flying disc activities are created regularly by people who enjoy throwing the flying disc.

Presented in this section are one team activity, ultimate Frisbee, and one individual activity, disc golf. The Web sites listed at the end of this section provide additional details on these two disc sports and links to a wide variety of disc activities.

History

The flying disc traces its origins back to the Frisbie Pie Company and its predecessor, the Olds Baking Company in New Haven, Connecticut. The actual disc was either a pie or cookie tin, which was turned upside down and tossed. Students at Yale University played an early version of a flying disc game in which the thrower would signal the receiver by calling "Frisbie."

Walter Frederick Morrison, the son of an inventor, is credited as the first to develop metal pie tins for commercial purposes following World War II. He eventually turned to plastic to manufacture a disc that would be used as a toy. The original was a flop, but in 1951 he developed an improved model. Eventually this was purchased by a toy company and called Wham-O's Pluto Platter. Because the activity was slow to catch on, the Wham-O company decided to distribute the disc throughout the United States. While visiting Harvard University's campus, distributors first heard the term *Frisbie.* The students said they had been tossing pie tins for years and called it Frisbie-ing. The company borrowed the term and spelled it *Frisbee.* Ed Headrick is credited with the development and patent of the modern Frisbee and with marketing the disc, millions of which have been sold.[1]

ULTIMATE FRISBEE

Nature and Purpose

Ultimate Frisbee is a noncontact team game consisting of throwing and catching the disc continually without holding it too long and without running with it. The objective is to score a goal by catching a thrown disc while in the end zone of the field. The opponents gain possession of the disc on a turnover, which occurs when a pass is knocked down, is incomplete, is intercepted, or is out of bounds. The disc is immediately put back in play with a throw from the spot where the infraction occurred. The strategies of the game are similar to those of football, soccer, and basketball. The participant needs good hand-eye coordination, speed, quickness, and agility. The spirit of the game embraces sportsmanship, fair play, player respect, self-officiating, and the joy of playing.

Rules

Ultimate Frisbee rules are easily modified to meet the needs of the participants.

Players. A team consists of seven people: handlers, mids, and longs.

Field. The area is a rectangle with a playing surface of 70 yards by 40 yards and end zones at each end 20 yards deep.

Start of Play. A throw-off initiates play, and the members of both teams throwing the disc must be on their own goal line. A throw-off is repeated after each score and after each period.

Scoring. A point is awarded for catching a throw in the opponent's end zone.

Disc Movement. The player in possession has 10 seconds to throw the disc while the defender loudly counts the seconds. The player with the disc may not run but attempts to complete a pass, after establishing a pivot foot, in any direction.

The receiver must take no more than two steps to establish a pivot foot for the next throw. If the receiver wishes to avoid stopping when catching the disc, he must throw it before taking a third step and may not change direction, increase speed, nor purposefully bobble it to himself, which constitutes traveling.

Possession Change. Possession of the disc changes to the defending team if the disc is intercepted, blocked, dropped, or goes out of bounds. With the possession change, the defender (marker) must be no closer to the thrower than one disc diameter, and there may be only one defender. The new thrower establishes a pivot foot, may not pivot into the defender, and must throw before 10 seconds have elapsed. Stalling to restart play is not allowed; in such cases, the defender, who immediately starts the 10-second count, calls, "Delay of game."

Contact. No contact is allowed, and picks/screens are illegal.

Fouls. Any contact with another player results in a foul. If it is a foul of the player in possession, play immediately resumes.

Length of Game. There are two 24-minute halves with a 5-minute overtime period.

Equipment

The disc comes in a variety of sizes and weights. The team captains may choose the disc. Protective gear is allowed, provided it is not dangerous to others. No cleated shoes are allowed. A team is required to wear uniforms of the same color.

Skills and Techniques

All the disc activities revolve around throws, including grips and catches. It is important for beginners to focus first on the various ways to grip the disc and afterward on throwing. Developing good grip technique is an often overlooked factor of playing the game well.

GRIPS

Backhand Beginner. The thumb rests on top of the disc, the index finger runs along the rim, the middle finger extends toward the center, and the remaining two fingers grip under the rim. Alternatively, the middle, ring, and little fingers can grip the rim, producing more power.

Backhand Power. The thumb is on top of the disc, and all fingers grip the rim tightly. The position of the thumb can vary from along the edge of the rim to pointing toward the center of the disc (Figure 18-6).

Backhand Hybrid. This grip is a combination of the two foregoing grips. The difference is that the middle finger flexes toward the disc, so that the top of the finger applies pressure to support the disc.

Backhand Thumber. The thumb is under the disc, and all four fingers are on top.

Forehand Beginner. The thumb is on top of the disc, the index finger is underneath pointing toward the middle, the middle finger is along the inside of the rim, and the remaining two fingers are clenched toward the palm, with no clutching on the disc (Figure 18-7).

Forehand Power. The thumb is on top of the disc, the index and middle fingers together are pressed hard against the rim, and the remaining two fingers are clenched toward the palm, with no clutching on the disc. One alternative is to curl the index and middle fingers slightly rather than extend them fully. Another alternative is to place the side of the middle finger against the rim rather than pressing the pads of the index and middle fingers against the rim. This position promotes a palm up follow-through.

Forehand Hybrid. The thumb is on top of the disc, the index finger is bent slightly and pressed firmly on the rim, and the middle finger is extended also on the rim. These two fingers are no longer parallel because the index finger is bent. The remaining two fingers are clenched toward the palm, with no clutching on the disc.

Forehand Thumber. The thumb is under the disc and all four fingers are on top.

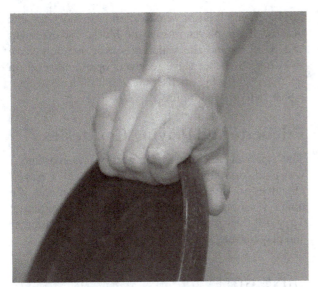

Figure 18-6   Backhand power grip.

Figure 18-7   Forehand beginner grip.

THROWS

Throws may be made using a variety of grips. A basic throwing strategy is to step forward with the foot opposite the throwing hand or arm. The difference between the backhand and forehand throws is the point where the hand or arm starts the throwing action. The backhand throws are across the body, with the disc starting on the opposite side of the throwing hand or arm, which is coiled across the chest (Figure 18-8).

BACKHAND THROW
STRATEGIES (RIGHT-HANDED)

Air Bounce.   The air bounce is a slower throw that hangs in the air, allowing the receiver to run under it.

Inside Out.   The path starts to the opposite side of the body and curves back to the other side. To start the throw, the thrower tilts the outside of the disc down.

Reverse Curve.   The path starts to the nonthrowing arm side and curves back toward the opposite side. To start the throw, the thrower tilts the inside of the disc down.

Blade.   The outside of the disc is tilted down but is released so that it goes high into the air above defenders, curving to the left of the thrower.

Scooper.   The grip on the disc is like holding a hammer. The arm is in an overhand vertical position moving slightly forward, releasing the disc with all wrist action.

CATCHES

Sandwich Catch (Pancake).   Use two hands to catch the disc, with one hand on top and the other on the bottom. Alternating hands on the disc is an advantageous strategy.

C-Catch.   Form a C with the thumb and fingers, and close them to grasp the disc. The fingers are up for catching high throws, whereas the thumb is up when receiving low throws.

▶ Practice/Organizational Suggestions

Start 5 to 10 yards apart with a partner when initially practicing grips, throws, and catches. Gradually increase the distance as skill improves. Increasing the distance results in less accuracy and more movement of the disc, so safety in aligning the players becomes a greater concern. Additionally, as the disc moves greater distances, the receiver has more opportunity to run and catch, which compounds the difficulty of the game. By requiring the players to stop within three steps of the catch and to restructure the time before the next throw, the instructor can foster the players' application of skills to competition level. A final step might be to add defenders, more teammates, and restrictions for field size in a game of keep-away.

Playing Strategies/Tactics

In offensive play, the basic individual strategies for Ultimate Frisbee are similar to those of many field games. The strategies include quick passes, becoming a receiver after passing, fast cutting, avoiding "bunching," maintaining balance among teammates, maintaining control of the disc, and moving the disc upfield toward the goal.

OFFENSIVE FORMATION AND STRATEGIES

The "stack" is an often-used formation in which the players line up near the middle of the field in a line parallel with the sideline and in advance of the thrower.

Figure 18-8   Backhand throw.

The player closest to the thrower positions herself 15 to 20 yards ahead, with each succeeding player about 5 to 10 yards ahead of each other. The players closest to the thrower are called *handlers*, those in the middle are *mids*, and the ones toward the end of the stack are *longs*. This formation, because of its alignment, provides open areas to either side for passes to be thrown.

The tactics are for the players to systematically run back toward the thrower and make a cut to an outside open space, starting with the one closest to the thrower. Timing when to cut and when the next player starts is important. A cutting player who does not receive the pass rejoins the stack after clearing the area.

Offensive and cut strategies include gaining the most yardage possible with each throw; moving the disc to a better position on the field; maintaining possession; starting long cuts when close to thrower, not from the top of the stack; staying away from a deep cutter so that one defender cannot cover two players; and clearing the deep area.

Strategies to improve scoring opportunities include having the good handlers use the give-and-go, designating one person as the scorer near the end zone, and assigning the fastest players to long cuts. End zone scoring failures usually result from too many cuts or no cuts, not from great defensive efforts.

DEFENSIVE STRATEGY

A person-to-person defense is most often used at the beginning levels of play. There are three positional tactics for the defender. First, face the receiver, attempting to stay at least 3 yards away, and focus solely on the player. Second, position to the open field side of the receiver and attempt to see the disc and receiver at all times. Third, face the thrower while glancing over the shoulder at the receiver. Another possible alternative for a defender covering a deep receiver is to play behind that player in an attempt to assist a teammate who has lost his player. It is not wise to attempt to block the disc because if the player misses the block, the opponent will be open and the teammates will therefore have to switch. Switches leave receivers open and result in quick passes by the offense, making it difficult to reestablish defensive continuity.

Etiquette and Playing Courtesies

The spirit of the game embraces sportsmanship. A win-at-all-costs attitude is not acceptable in a player. One does not attempt to circumvent the rules and take unfair advantage. Players are expected to self-officiate: They call their own fouls. Players respect one another and play for the joy of the game.

DISC GOLF

Nature and Purpose

Disc golf involves throwing the disc with power and accuracy, using the nuances of golf. The objective is to cover the course in the fewest number of throws. Play starts with a throw from the tee area, is followed by succeeding throws from where the disc comes to rest, and concludes when the disc is thrown into the above-ground target. The course, consisting of 9 or 18 holes, often includes trees, water, and other obstacles, which add difficulty to the activity. However, because of the adaptability of the game, a course can be set up in open areas. The activity appeals to all ages, sexes, ability levels, and the physically challenged.

Scoring and Rules

Scoring (Same as Golf).   The score for each hole is determined by the total throws it takes to complete the hole, plus any penalties. The final score for the course is determined by comparing each player's score to par. Par for each hole depends on the difficulty and usually ranges from 3 to 6.

Penalties (One Stroke Assessment Each).   A disc that goes out of bounds is placed 1 yard from where it went out (penalty stroke). A disc that comes to rest above the ground (e.g., in a tree or bush) is placed directly below (penalty stroke). If the lie is unplayable or unsafe, the disc is placed at a spot 5 yards from the original location but not closer to the hole (penalty stroke). A *falling putt*, where the player steps past the disc marker without the body momentarily stopping, is illegal (penalty stroke).

Order of Play.   On the first hole, the order for throwing is determined by the names listed on the scorecard. All succeeding throws on that hole are by the player farthest from the hole. On succeeding holes, the first throw from the tee is determined by the best score on the last hole. If the score is tied, the order is the same as that for the previous hole.

Throws. The lie on each throw is marked at the spot where the disc comes to rest. On the *drive* and *approach* shots, the player must not step in front of the marker before the disc is released. Any throw within 30 feet of the target is considered a *putt*. The player must not step in front of the marker on the putt until balance is demonstrated (penalty stroke).

Equipment

One of the advantages in disc golf is that little equipment is needed and the necessary equipment is inexpensive. A player needs only one disc. However, it is an advantage to have two available. One disc may be used to mark the lie and is available if the original disc is lost or damaged. Advanced players carry different types of discs, which are designed for the drive, approach, and putts. The disc for golf is different than the traditional Pluto Platter in that it is thinner with sharper edges. The target (hole) may be a post, tree, basket, or official target. The official target is an upright pole with a basket suspended by chains. When the disc hits the suspension chains, it falls into the basket. There are several official targets on the market.

Skills and Techniques

The basic skill is throwing. The throws require power and accuracy. The layout of the course often demands various flight paths to navigate dog-legs and hazards. A reference to the skills section on Ultimate Frisbee in this chapter describes various grips and throws. The beginner needs to master the backhand throw before attempting other more advanced varieties.

BACKHAND

The backhand grip is the key to good throws. The thumb is on top of the disc near the edge. The index finger is under the rim edge of the disc. Most of the pressure is supplied by the thumb and index finger in a pinching action. The other three fingers are under the disc and are used to help make the grip stable or change the angle.

In the drive and approach throws, the body stands sideways to the target, with the throwing shoulder pointing toward the target. The feet and shoulders are in a straight line to the target.

The backswing starts with a slight flexion of the knees. The disc is at chest level as the straight throwing arm reaches backward across the body as far as possible. That arm is parallel to the ground. The wrist cocks, so that the disc touches the inside of the throwing arm like a coiled spring. The nonthrowing arm is extended backward in a straight line pointing away from the target. The pulling action of the straight throwing arm

leads with the elbow as the coiled wrist leads the disc. The arm continues forward rapidly as the wrist uncoils (snaps), releasing the disc. Simultaneously, the lower body unwinds and the upper body rotates as the arm extends. The torso twists outward vigorously as the feet stay stationary on the follow-through.

▶ **Learning Hints**

1. The harder the thumb and index finger pinch, the harder the throw.
2. Practice throwing using only the thumb and index finger as the grip.
3. Do not bend the throwing arm.
4. Make a complete throwing action without stopping short.
5. Do not release the disc too late.
6. Do not let the nose of the disc be in an up-leading position.
7. Arm speed and wrist snap are the most important factors for distance.
8. If the disc leads the wrist, the throw will be to the side of the dominant arm.
9. Snap the wrist like a whip.

PUTT

The putt is the most important throw. The grip is the same as in the drive or approach throws. The only difference is the foot position, which provides an open stance. The stance is 45 degrees from the line to target as the front foot drops, allowing the upper body to more closely face the target.

▶ **Learning Hints**

1. Check body alignment.
2. Focus on a specific spot on the target.
3. Visualize the throwing action.
4. Develop a consistent pattern for the putt, and do not deviate.
5. Make the swing automatic; groove it.
6. Wind from the side is not important unless you are throwing a curve. A front wind causes the disc to rise, and a wind from the back causes it to drop.

Playing Strategies

1. Visualize the shot before throwing the disc. Look for any potential hazards or obstacles. Visualize the flight over or around these elements.
2. When a disc lands in a bad spot, throw it out into an advantageous area in preparation for the next throw. Attempting to take risks often leads to a bad score. Another option is to take a stroke penalty and move

the disc 5 yards from the trouble spot for an open throw.

3. Do not gamble by attempting a putt that is too long. Lay up with the throw, placing it close to the target. The long putt often leads to worse problems.

4. Master the backhand first. Later, learn new throws that help you get out of tough spots.

Etiquette and Playing Courtesies

Disc golf is a polite game, just like regular golf. Refer to the chapter on Golf for an extensive list of courtesies.

Skill Assessment

Distance and accuracy are skill factors in flying disc activities. Basketball courts (50 ft. × 84 ft.) provide markings suitable for skill testing both factors. The jump-ball circle (4 ft. dia.) and center circle (12 ft. dia.) provide two natural targets for accuracy. A disc thrown from the corner of the court to the circles shows ability to throw for a distance.

A group of three students gathers at a corner of the court. In each group of three there is a participant, scorer/recorder, and a retriever. The participant takes three practice throws and then seven trials for score. The scorer/recorder marks the score and the retriever returns thrown discs to the participant. They rotate responsibilities until each student has thrown for score. The disc thrown backhand in the air at the target receives the assigned score where it first hits the floor. A disc landing on a line between scores receives the higher point evaluation. The jump-ball circle is worth 5 points, the center circle 3 points, and any other flighted thrown disc outside the circles scores 1 point.

Terminology

ULTIMATE FRISBEE

air bounce A throw aimed downward, which results in the disc's being buoyed by a cushion of air.

backhand A throw across the body, where the disc is gripped with the thumb on top and fingers underneath.

blade A forehand throw that goes high in the air and curves to the left of a right-handed thrower.

check Restarting play following a stoppage where the marker touches the disc before the thrower is allowed to pass it.

end zone The area on the field where a score is made if the disc is caught by the team attacking that end.

forehand A throw where the arm starts on the dominant side of the body and makes a sidearm action.

hack A foul.

handler A team's primary thrower.

marker The defensive player who guards the thrower.

mid A receiver who cuts for shorter passes rather than deep.

receiver The offensive player who is in the act of catching the disc or not in possession of the disc.

stack An offensive strategy where players position up and down the field in a vertical line.

strip An illegal act by the marker attempting to touch or touching the disc while in thrower's possession.

thrower The offensive player in possession of the disc or who has just released it.

throw off The lining up of the offensive team in their own end zone and throwing the disc to the opponents, which initiates play.

traveling Throwing the disc before establishing the pivot foot when changing from marker to thrower.

turnover A pass that is incomplete, knocked down, intercepted, or out of bounds, which results in loss of possession.

DISC GOLF

Refer to the Golf chapter for additional terms.

ace A hole in one.

birdie A score that is 1 under par.

casual A hazard that is not designed as part of the course, such as standing water.

clear A term indicating that a hole is ready for play.

lie The spot where the disc comes to rest and where the next throw is taken.

mandatory A flight path that is designed as a path that must be followed on a hole.

mini A small disc used to mark the lie.

par A score that is required in order to complete the hole.

putt A throw made from within 30 feet of the target.

roller A disc that advances by rolling.

safari golf Players make up different holes from an existing course.

taco A term for a warped disc that has been damaged by hitting a hard object.

tee pad The area on each hole that is designated as the place to begin.

worm burner A disc that takes a down angle, resulting in a premature landing.

Discussion Questions

1. Discuss the origin and development of the flying disc.

2. Define and discuss the "spirit of the game" in Ultimate Frisbee and how it differs from most team games.

3. Compare and contrast the similarities in strategy of Ultimate Frisbee and football, soccer, and basketball.

4. Discuss how the disc used in disc golf is different than those used for other disc activities.

5. Discuss the playing strategies for disc golf that lead to a better score.

Web Sites

www.discgolf.com—provides history, products, course design, promotional assistance for educational groups at various levels, rules, other disc games, and additional links.

www.usaultimate.org—provides information and links concerning Ultimate Frisbee.

www.wfdf.org World Flying Disc Federation—provides official rules for all forms of flying disc activities (ultimate frisbee, disc golf, double disc court, freestyle, guts, field events, and discathon).

www.ultimatehandbook.com—addresses beginner, intermediate, and advanced skills and knowledge. Other highlights are history, drills, rules, media, glossary, and other links.

HORSESHOES

Nature and Purpose

Horseshoe pitching has been popular for a long time, both as a recreational and a competitive sport. The formation of the National Horseshoe Pitchers Association (NHPA) in 1921 gave rise to chapters in nearly every state as well as Canada. The NHPA sanctions local and regional meets for men, women, boys, and girls. A world tournament is held each year for men and women, as well as junior boys and girls world championships.

The game is played by pitching horseshoes toward a metal stake some 40 feet (30 feet for women and juniors) from the pitching point. Points are scored for shoes landing closest to the stake, provided the shoe is not farther than 6 inches from the stake. A ringer (shoe that encircles stake) counts 3 points. The winner is the player who first scores 21 points (informal play) or 40 points (official tournament competition). Players alternate in throwing shoes, with the player who scored one or more points on the previous pitch throwing first. In singles play, the players move from stake to stake after each throw, but in doubles, one partner is stationed at each stake and makes all throws from there.

History

The origin of the game of horseshoes is unknown, although historians have established that horseshoes came from the game of *quoits*, a modification of the Grecian game of discus throwing.[1] Other historians have found evidence that a form of horseshoes was played in Europe around 200 B.C.

Colonists brought the game with them to America; it became a popular pastime of soldiers in both the Revolutionary War and the Civil War. It was said that the soldiers in the Union camp used the plentifully available mule shoes to play.[2]

In the first tournaments, games were played to 21 points. The horseshoes did not have a standard weight or configuration, and the height of the stakes was only 6 inches, a far cry from the modern game.

The NHPA is the present-day organization that evolved from other organizations to govern the sport. The NHPA has presided over many changes since the 1920s: Stakes were raised from 14 to 15 inches; shoe weights were standardized to 2 pounds 2 ounces; the distance between stakes changed from 38 feet to 40 feet; and game points changed from 21 points to 40 points.[3]

Horseshoes are enjoyed by people of all ages and both sexes. It is estimated that 15 million enthusiasts enjoy pitching horseshoes in leagues, tournaments, recreation settings, and at picnics or in the backyard.

Playing Area and Equipment

THE COURT

The official horseshoe court (Figure 18-9) is a minimum of 6 feet wide and 46 feet long, with 1-inch metal stakes placed 40 feet apart (30 feet for women and juniors). The stakes are centered in a pitcher's box measuring 6 feet by 6 feet. An extended platform of an additional 10 feet should extend beyond the pitcher's box in each direction to allow for pitching at shorter distances. For informal recreational games, the distance between stakes may be arranged to fit the available space. If courts are to be built on a school ground, it is advisable to build backstops behind each pitcher's box to prevent the horseshoes from rebounding into a student. In schools that lack the space or do not wish to build permanent courts, temporary ones can be built in a place of convenience.

HORSESHOES

Horseshoes may be bought at local hardware stores, discount department stores, or they may be specially ordered from a number of companies approved by the NHPA. For schools, several physical education and recreation equipment companies sell either official metal shoes or indoor and outdoor rubber horseshoes that are used with wooden stakes. An official shoe should not exceed 7¼ inches in width and 7⅝ inches in length, and it should weigh no more than 2 pounds 10 ounces. The opening should be no more than 3½ inches from point to point.

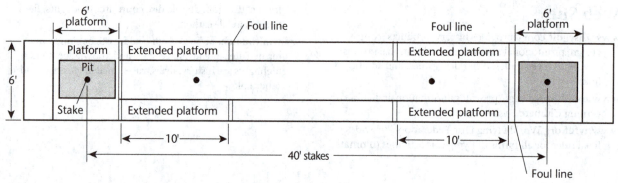

Figure 18-9 Typical horseshoe court (NHPA dimensions).

Basic Rules

The NHPA establishes the official rules of horseshoe pitching. The simplified rules follow.

1. A game is divided into innings, and each contestant pitches two shoes in each inning. The length of the game is determined before play begins. There are two options: (1) the game can be played to a predetermined point limit (40 points is suggested); or (2) the game can be played by a predetermined number of shoes. An even number of shoes must be thrown. In the event of a tie, an extra two innings may be played.

2. The choice of the first pitch to start the game is decided by the toss of a horseshoe or a coin.

3. A shoe that has left the pitcher's hand is ruled a pitched shoe.

4. A pitcher's opponent must stand behind the person in action and may not interfere with the pitch in any way.

5. A contestant may not walk to the opposite stake or be informed of the position of the shoes until the inning is completed.

6. Shoes thrown when a foul has been committed are considered shoes pitched; however, they may not receive any point value. Fouls may be assessed for the following:

   a. Illegal delivery of a shoe
   b. Failure of the opponent to stay behind the pitcher, or interfering in any way while the opponent is in the act of pitching
   c. Touching thrown shoes before a measurement has been made
   d. Thrown shoes that strike part of the pitcher's box or land outside the foul lines and that then rebound into the box
   e. Stepping on or over the foul line

7. Ties are broken by pitching an extra inning(s).

SCORING

1. The shoe nearest to the stake scores 1 point, provided it is within 6 inches of the stake.

2. Two shoes closer than opponent's shoe score 2 points.

3. One ringer scores 3 points, and two ringers, 6 points.

4. A player having two ringers to one by his opponent scores 3 points.

5. All shoes equally distant from the stake count as ties, and no points are scored.

6. A leaning shoe has the same value as that of a shoe lying on the ground and in contact with the stake.

Skills and Techniques

Players must stand behind the foul line on the pitching platform when pitching. Most players assume a starting stance with the pitching arm closest to the stake and in a position that permits a forward step in the act of delivery of the shoe. The number of turns that the shoe takes in flight usually determines the style of grip to be used. Regardless of the grip used, there are several factors common to all pitches:

1. The shoe should be held parallel with the ground, with calks down.

2. The rotation of the shoe should be clockwise.

3. The open end of the shoe should face the stake when landing.

There are four standard methods of delivery, so the beginner should do some experimenting to determine which method is best.

1. In the single-turn delivery (Figure 18-10), the open face of the shoe is directed toward the stake.

2. In the one-and-one-quarter-turn delivery (Figure 18-11), the open end of the shoe faces the pitcher's left and the thumb is across the top.

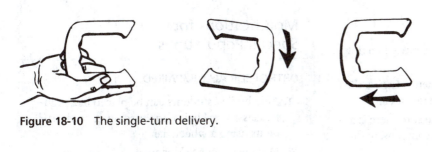

Figure 18-10 The single-turn delivery.

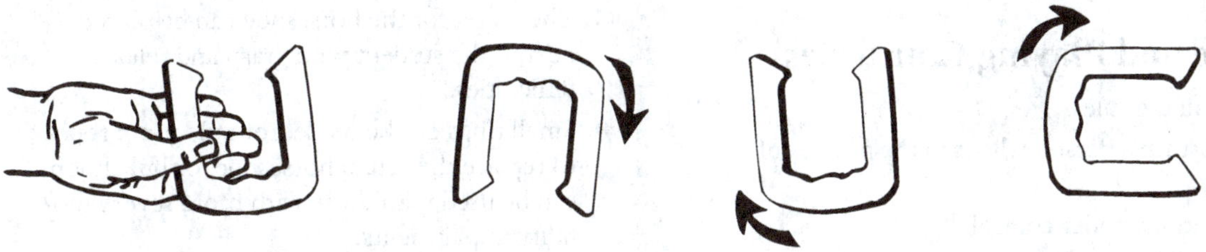

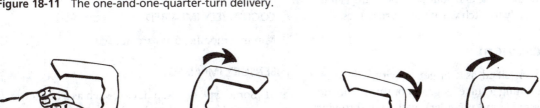

Figure 18-11 The one-and-one-quarter-turn delivery.

Figure 18-12 The one-and-one-half-turn delivery.

Figure 18-13 The one-and-three-quarter-turn delivery. Two different grips are illustrated.

3. In the one-and-one-half-turn delivery (Figure 18-12), the open end of the shoe faces the pitcher.

4. In the one-and-three-quarter-turn delivery (Figure 18-13), the open end of the shoe faces the pitcher's right and either of two shoe-holding methods may be used.

▶ Learning Hints

1. With weight evenly distributed on both feet in the stance, step off on opposite foot, knees bent, eyes on the target, shoulders square to target.

2. While you lean forward slightly, keep your arm straight and let it fall down and back and retrace the same arc on the forward swing. The pitch must be smooth and rhythmic.

3. At the release, extend your body and arm, giving proper lift, and roll your forearm to turn the shoe.

▶ Practice/Organizational Suggestions

1. Experiment with deliveries; usually the one-and-one-quarter-turn delivery is best for a beginner.

2. Practice the step and throw without a horseshoe, and then add the horseshoe. Partners should check to see that arc is straight, shoulders are square, and delivery is rhythmic.

3. Juniors and school-age children might start closer to the stake and work their way back to 30 feet.

Safety Considerations

1. Stand well away from the pitching court when not involved.
2. Be aware of people around you when swinging the horseshoe. Pitch only in the designated area.
3. If setting up courts for a class, make sure there is adequate distance between courts to compensate for erratic throws of beginners.

Etiquette and Playing Courtesies

1. Observe all the rules.
2. Do not disturb a person who is in the process of pitching.
3. Keep emotions under control.
4. Be aware of the game and your position in the game so you are ready to pitch when your turn comes.

Skill Assessment

Horseshoes is classified as a target activity, which requires skill in hitting a stake. A group of three students (participant, scorer, and recorder) alternates throwing two horseshoes at the stake and changing responsibilities. Each receives a total of eight throws for score following two practice throws. The participant throws two horseshoes, the scorer determines the point assessment, and the recorder writes down the score. The points are 6 for a ringer, 4 for a leaner, 2 for a shoe within 6 inches of the stake (width of a shoe), and 1 for a shoe in the pit.

Modifications for Special Populations

ORTHOPEDICALLY IMPAIRED

1. Able-bodied students can be placed in a regular classroom chair if mainstreamed with students using a wheelchair.
2. Distances can be shortened.
3. The target for the horseshoe can be placed next to the student with grasp and release difficulties.
4. Small rings can be made from old jump ropes to replace the actual horseshoe, or hula hoops can be used with those with more severe mobility impairments.

COGNITIVELY IMPAIRED

Minimal modifications are needed.

SENSORY IMPAIRED

1. Some type of audio device, such as a buzzer or bell, can be placed as the target and positioned inside of a hula hoop. Blind or visually impaired students can toss bean bags instead of horseshoes inside the hoop.
2. No modifications should be needed for the deaf or hearing impaired.

Terminology

calks Raised areas on the heels and toes of one side of the pitching shoe. They tend to make the shoe less likely to skid when they strike the surface of the pit area.

double ringer Two successive thrown shoes that encircle the stake by the same player in the same inning.

flipped-up shoe Flipping a shoe in the air to determine which player takes the first pitch. Instead of calling heads or tails, a player calls smooth or rough.

heel The ends of the prongs on each side of the open end of the shoe.

inning The pitching of two shoes by each player.

leaner (also **hobber**) Shoe that leans against a stake.

pit The area in which the shoe lands.

pitcher box The area that includes the pitching platform and the pit.

ringer A shoe that encircles the stake.

toes Two extensions at the open end of the shoe.

Discussion Questions

1. Discuss the origin and development of horseshoes.
2. Compare and contrast the four standard methods of delivering the horseshoe.
3. Identify how point values of thrown shoes are determined.
4. Identify the reasons why a thrower might be assessed a foul.

Web Sites

www.horseshoepitching.com National Horseshoe Pitchers Association of America—offers sections on how to pitch horseshoes, court materials, backyard courts, court construction, game etiquette, and more.

PICKLEBALL

Nature and Purpose

Pickleball is a fast-paced, fun-filled game for individuals of all ages. Developed first as a recreational backyard game, it has found popularity among racquet enthusiasts and in physical education programs. Combining the court markings and dimensions of badminton, skills associated with tennis, a net that is 3 feet high, solid wooden racquets, and a plastic whiffle ball, the game can be played in a singles or doubles format. The premium is on ball placement rather than strength or size of the players. For this reason, pickleball can be played as a school or recreational activity by boys and girls and men and women. The winner of the game is the first player or team to reach 11 points; however, an individual or team must win by a margin of 2 points.

Pickleball can be played in a number of venues; the surface of the court must be hard enough so that the plastic ball will bounce. Therefore, it is not unusual to see pickleball courts set up inside a gymnasium or on a concrete or blacktop playground surface. Official pickleball equipment can be purchased at a reasonable price from a number of physical education equipment suppliers or from Pickleball, Inc. The square-headed paddles can be made from a good-quality plywood, a piece of nylon for a safety strap, and wooden handles. Whiffle balls the size of a baseball or softball may also be used, and generally the smaller the ball, the quicker the game. A badminton net strung across a series of wooden standards 36 inches high will meet the requirements of the net needed for the game. Because the equipment is relatively inexpensive, pickleball is an attractive game not only for class but also for recreation and intramural tournament play.

The game uses skills associated with tennis. Some physical education instructors use the game as a good skill developer for the forehand and backhand drives, lobs, and volleys. Because the player has to bend his knees to get low enough to stroke the ball properly, it is a good developer for this element of tennis. The game is played on a court with the same dimensions as a badminton doubles court. Although the service areas retain their markings, the pickleball court has a nonvolley zone 7 feet on either side of the net. For the gymnasium that has a permanent badminton court painted on the floor, the short service area may serve as the nonvolley zone.

Most important of all, it is a safe game not requiring size or strength to enjoy. The person who has difficulty with tennis, racquetball, or handball because of the speed of the ball will find greater success with the moderately paced pickleball game.

History

Pickleball is a hybrid activity that includes elements of badminton, tennis, and table tennis. Played on a court typically the size of a badminton court with a net that is positioned much like a tennis net, it evolved from a backyard game developed by William Bell, Congressman Joel Pritchard, and Barney McCallum of Washington in 1965. It is probably the first sport to be named after a family pet. When the game originated, Pritchard's dog, Pickle, would lie near the court watching the ball go back and forth. When a ball was hit off the court, Pickle would chase it and run off with it. Thus, in his honor, the game was called pickleball.[1]

Pickleball has evolved into a popular game played in backyards and in many junior and senior high schools, colleges, and universities. The United States of America Pickleball Association (USAPA), established in 1984, is the governing body.[2] Today, thousands of people enjoy this popular activity.

Equipment

PADDLE

The official pickleball racquet is generally made of hardwood or a good-quality plywood. The squared-off head should not exceed 8 inches in width nor 15½ inches in length. A racquetball paddle, any strung paddle, or paddle with holes is not legal. A cord should be attached to the butt-end of the handle for safety purposes; the wrist should be inserted through the cord so the paddle does not come off during play (see Figure 18-20B).

BALLS

The official perforated ball used in pickleball is 3 inches in diameter. Various sizes of whiffle balls may be used in a physical education class. Generally, the larger the ball, the slower the game. For smaller children, the larger ball is easier to strike and to "watch" into the hitting area.

NET

A badminton or a tennis net may be used. Wooden standards may be constructed and strung across a gymnasium floor to make up several pickleball courts for class play.

Basic Rules

1. *Court.* The size of the court is 20 by 44 feet for both doubles and singles. The net is hung at 36 inches on ends and hangs 34 inches in the middle. When laying out a court, allow adequate space—3 to 5 feet at each end and 1 to 2 feet at the sides—from the court

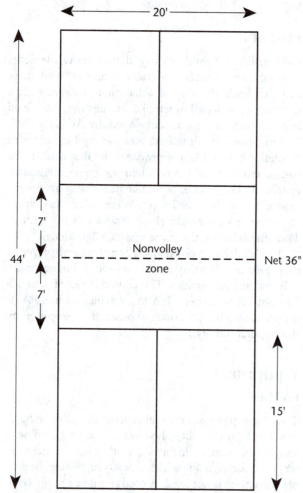

Figure 18-14 Official pickleball court. Note the nonvolley zones.
Courtesy of Pickleball, Inc., Seattle, WA.

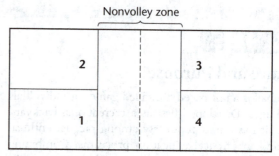

Figure 18-15 Position of players at net when volleying.
Courtesy of Pickleball, Inc., Seattle, WA.

boundary lines for player movement (Figure 18-14). However, it should be noted that many families play pickleball with little or no back and side court and enjoy the game.

2. *Serve.* The player must keep one foot behind the back line when serving. The serve is made underhand. The paddle must pass below the waist. The server must hit the ball in the air on the serve. Bouncing the ball before hitting it is not allowed. The service is made diagonally cross-court and must clear the nonvolley zone. Only one serve attempt is allowed, except if the ball touches the net on the serve and lands in the proper service court; then the serve may be taken over. At the start of each new game, the first serving team is allowed only *one* fault before giving up the ball to the opponents. Thereafter, both members of each team will serve and fault before the ball is turned over to the opposing team. When the receiving team wins the serve, the player in the right-hand court starts play.

3. *Volley.* To volley a ball means to hit it in the air without first letting it bounce. All volleying must be done with player's feet *behind* the nonvolley zone line (Figure 18-15). *Note:* It is a fault if the player steps over the line on his volley follow-through.

4. *Double-bounce rule.* Each team must play its first shot off the bounce. That is, the receiving team must let the serve bounce, and the serving team must let the return of the serve bounce before playing it. After the two bounces have occurred, the ball can be either volleyed or played off the bounce (Figure 18-16).

5. *Fault*
   a. Hitting the ball out of bounds
   b. Not clearing the net
   c. Stepping into the nonvolley zone and volleying the ball
   d. Volleying the ball before it has bounced once on each side of the net, as outlined in rule 4

6. *Scoring.* A team scores a point only when serving. A player who is serving continues to do so until a fault is made by his team. The game is played to 11 points; however, a team must win by 2 points.

POSITION OF PLAYERS FOR DOUBLES AT START OF GAME

Determining Serving Team. Players may toss a coin or rally the ball until a fault is made. Winner of the toss or rally has the option of serving first.

Doubles Play. Two alternative positions for players are shown in Figures 18-17 and 18-18.

1. Player 1 in the right-hand court (see Figure 18-18A) serves diagonally across court to receiver (3) in opposite right-hand court. The ball must clear the nonvolley zone and land in the right-hand serving court. The receiver (3) must let the ball bounce before returning the serve. Serving team must *also* let the return bounce before playing it (see rule 4, the double-bounce rule). After the two bounces have occurred, the ball may then be either volleyed or played off the bounce until a fault is made.

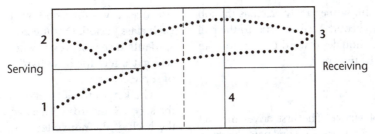

Figure 18-16 Illustration of double-bounce rule.
Courtesy of Pickleball, Inc., Seattle, WA.

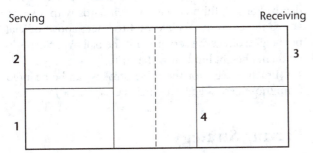

Figure 18-17 Position of players for doubles at start of game.
Courtesy of Pickleball, Inc., Seattle, WA.

2. If the fault is made by the receiving team, a point is scored by the serving team. When the serving team wins a point, its players switch courts, and the *same* player continues to serve. When the serving team makes its first fault, players stay in the same court, and the second partner then serves (see Figure 18-18B). When they make their second fault, they stay in the same courts and turn the ball over to the other team. Players switch courts only after scoring. A ball landing on any line is considered good.

Singles Play. All rules apply, with the following exception: When serving in singles, each player serves from the right-hand court when her score is 0 or an even number, and from the left-hand court when her score is an odd number.

Suggested Learning Sequence

A. Nature and purpose of pickleball.

B. Acquainting players with equipment and court.

C. Skills and techniques. Relate skills to tennis techniques; use drills to develop forehand and backhand drives, lobs, service, and volleys. Use practice drills using rebound volleying against a wall; play mini-games using only the forehand or backhand. Combine gamelike drills while introducing rules of the game.
   1. Grip, stance, and footwork
   2. Forehand and backhand drives
   3. Service—lob, drive
   4. Volley—forehand and backhand
   5. Lob

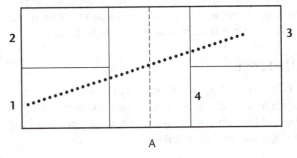

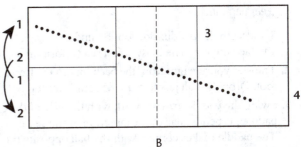

Figure 18-18 Doubles play: (A) serve by player 1; (B) serve by player 2.
Courtesy of Pickleball, Inc., Seattle, WA.

D. Rules of the game. Introduce the rules when appropriate; introduce the nonvolley zone and rules governing net play as soon as possible.

E. Strategy. Strategy can be introduced with a skill as soon as appropriate levels of skill are attained. Gamelike drills that combine elements of strategy are introduced early to help the player learn more quickly.

F. Game play.

Skills and Techniques

The techniques and skills required to play pickleball are identical, for the most part, with those used in tennis. (Refer to Chapter 25 for the skill breakdowns for the eastern grip, the stance or ready position, forehand and backhand drives, the forehand and backhand volleys, and the lob.) Good footwork is also essential in pickleball. For movement to the ball requiring two steps or less, feet slide into position. Use drills in which the player is placed in a ready position and slides the feet from side to side in that position. For balls hit farther away, such as the lob over the head to the backcourt, turn and run to the ball while looking over the shoulder toward the net to note where opponents may be moving.

SERVICE

There are two types of service. The first drives the ball over the net in a flat arc, whereas the second type of service results in an arc best described as a lob. When initiating the serve, there are three important rules to remember: (1) The paddle must pass below the waist in the serving motion; (2) the ball must be dropped and hit out of the air; and (3) one foot must remain behind the back line.

LOB SERVE

The lob serve (Figure 18-19) is used as a defensive technique to keep the opponents in the backcourt area. This high-arcing serve will tend to bounce higher and keep the opponent in a defensive mode.

▶ Learning Hints

1. Stand with the paddle-side foot behind the other, and face the net. The body is in a ready position.
2. Transfer your weight from the back foot to the front foot. Drop the ball just forward of your front foot.
3. Swing the paddle arm forward, with the face of the paddle perpendicular to the direction of the serve. The paddle makes contact with the ball opposite the front foot.
4. The arm continues forward and upward, giving the ball the necessary lift for a high-arcing serve.

DRIVE SERVE

The drive serve (Figure 18-20) is an effective defensive serve when executed correctly. This low, flat arcing serve will land deep in the opponent's backcourt, forcing the player away from the volley zone.

▶ Learning Hints

1. Stand with the paddle-side foot behind the other and face the net. Assume a ready position (knees flexed, bent at waist).
2. Transfer your weight from the back foot to the forward foot, and drop the ball opposite the forward foot.
3. Swing the paddle arm forward; cock your wrist.
4. At contact opposite the front foot, snap your wrist through and pronate your forearm as you execute the follow-through.

▶ Practice/Organizational Suggestions

The serve must be in play for points to be scored; therefore, consistent serving is essential to the game.

Practice serves for 5 to 7 minutes at the beginning of each class period. Outline zones on the floor and have students direct serves toward specific zones. Players will get a feel for how hard it is to hit the two types of serves.

The key to the lob serve is the height and depth of the serve. Standards with a badminton net placed across the back of the nonvolley zone at a height of 10 to 15 feet force the server to practice hitting the ball high enough to carry to the backcourt.

The key to the drive serve is also the height and depth. For helpful practice, use standards with a string across the court at a height of 4 to 5 feet above official net height; direct the server to hit the ball over the regulation net height but below the string.

(Practice drills for the other strokes can be adapted from those described for tennis in Chapter 25.)

Playing Strategy

1. Serves are most effective when they hit into the far backcourt and into the corners. It is best to vary the serve to keep your opponent off balance.
2. To receive the serve, place yourself in a ready position behind the back line; this enables you to return either a drive serve or a lob serve. Return the service in the backcourt and corners. Vary the placement of the shot so your opponent is forced to hit a backhand or a forehand.
3. On ground strokes, attempt to position yourself near the baseline and play the ball on the rise at waist height.
4. Positioning in midcourt is not desired because the bounce is often near the feet, which results in a defensive off-balance stroke.
5. Force your opponent to move from side to side and up and back.
6. In doubles, try to take control of the net by forcing your opponents to hit shots from the backline.
7. In doubles, hit the ball down the center of the court occasionally; this shot forces opponents to make choices that sometimes put them out of position to hit the return.
8. Use a lob shot occasionally when you have drawn your opponent to the net. If you and your opponent are near the net, however, use a lob as a defensive technique to allow you to get back into position.

Safety Considerations

1. Always wear the strap around your wrist so that if the paddle slips from your hands, it stays with you.

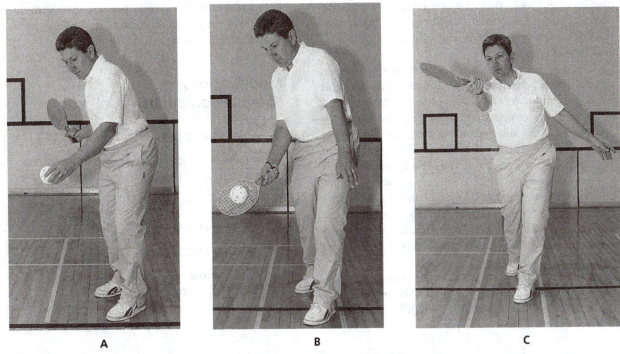

A   **B**   **C**

Figure 18-19   The lob serve. Note that the racquet contacts the ball below the waist.

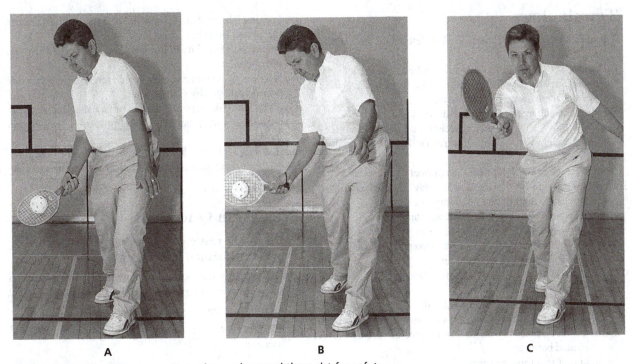

A   **B**   **C**

Figure 18-20   The drive serve. Note the cord around the wrist for safety.

2. Warm up properly before starting the game. Stretching exercises for the shoulder girdle, hamstrings, and abductors of the legs are recommended.

3. Get used to calling for the ball so that you avoid running into your doubles partner.

Skill Assessment

The most important skill is the ability to keep the rebounding ball in play using either the forehand or backhand stroke.

Rebound Test. The testing area is a flat surface 10 feet wide and 10 feet high marked off on a wall. Most gyms have enough wall space for several testing stations. There should be at least 10 feet between stations. On the floor, mark a restraining line 10 feet from the wall and parallel with it.

Three or four students test at each station. One is the participant, another is the counter/recorder, and the remaining student assistants provide extra balls and retrieve errant ones. Students rotate responsibilities.

From behind the restraining line, the participant drops a whiffle ball to the floor and plays it to the 10-feet-by-10-feet wall space. The rebounding ball, with at least one bounce to the floor before each hit, is repeatedly played (forehand or backhand) to the target space. The participant may not cross the restraining line to hit the ball. If another ball is needed, an assistant provides one and the participant again drops it to the floor to continue the assessment.

An assessment consists of as many trials as the participant can complete in 30 seconds. The final score is the total number of times the ball legally contacts the wall. A ball hit totally outside the target or without a bounce does not count. The count continues after an errant ball and does not start at one again.

Modifications for Special Populations

ORTHOPEDICALLY IMPAIRED

See modifications discussed in the chapters that cover Tennis and Handball/Racquetball.

COGNITIVELY IMPAIRED

Minimal modifications are needed.

SENSORY IMPAIRED

See modifications discussed in the Tennis and Handball/Racquetball chapters.

Terminology

approach shot A shot hit inside the baseline while the player approaches the net.
backcourt The area near the nonvolley zone and baseline.
backhand Stroke hit with the back of the hand holding the paddle facing away from the body.
baseline The end line of the pickleball court.
down-the-line A shot hit near a sideline that travels close to, and parallel with, the same line from where it was initially hit.
drive A low shot that is hit near the opponent's backcourt.
drop shot A ground stroke hit in such a way that the ball drops just over the net into the nonvolley zone.
error A mistake made by a player during competition.
fault A serve that lands out-of-bounds or out of court area.
foot fault Failure on the server's part to keep at least one foot behind the baseline during the serve.
forehand The shot hit on the right side of a right-handed player.
game A game is determined in pickleball when one side has reached 11 points; however, a team must win by 2 points.
half-volley A ball hit only inches from the court surface after the initial bounce.
let Any point that must be replayed.
let serve A serve that touches the top of the net and falls in the proper service court; it must be replayed.
lob A ball that is hit sufficiently high to pass over the reach of an opponent but falls within the court.
nonvolley zone The 7-foot area on either side of the net. A player may not step into the nonvolley zone to play a ball before it bounces or on the follow-through of a stroke.
pace The speed of the ball.

passing shot The shot that passes beyond the reach of the net player and lands in-bounds.
placement A shot hit in-bounds and untouched by an opponent.
poach To cross over into your partner's territory to play a ball normally played by your partner.
serve The lob or drive stroke used to put a ball into play at the beginning of the point. The serve must use an underhand motion.
smash A shot hit forcefully from above the player's head.
volley To hit the ball in the air before it bounces on the court.

Discussion Questions

1. Discuss the reasons for including pickleball in the physical education curriculum.
2. Discuss why the nonvolley zone and double-bounce rules are good adaptations to the sport.
3. Identify the tennis skills that are used in pickleball.
4. Discuss playing strategy in pickleball that leads to success.

Web Sites

www.pickleball.com—offers information about the court and history; also offers products and instructional materials.
www.usapa.org United States of America Pickleball Association (USAPA)—offers an explanation of pickleball, information about the USAPA, message board, and a source of products.

SHUFFLEBOARD

Nature and Purpose

Shuffleboard may be played by two people (*singles*) or by four (*doubles*). The game is played by propelling round wooden discs by means of a cue stick with a curved end over a hard, smooth surface on which the outlines of the court have been drawn.

History

The founding date of the game of shuffleboard is not known, but it has been established that a similar game was played in England during the 15th century under the reign of King Henry IV. In the original game, called *shovel board* or *shoveboard*, discs or "shovel-pennies" were shoved by hand or with an implement on a board or on a floor. The game became so popular that King Henry IV banned it because archers were spending too much time playing shuffleboard rather than practicing their archery.[1]

Played on a table, the game became a favorite of the American colonists and was played in the great homes of the period and even in salons.[2] Played on a cement or deck surface, the game became a favorite of passengers on ocean-going liners.

Shuffleboard, as it has evolved today, was introduced to the United States in 1913 in Daytona Beach, Florida. Its popularity spread throughout the country but most notably in retirement communities. The modern game of shuffleboard came into being with more standardized rules in St. Petersburg, Florida, in 1924. In 1931, the National Shuffleboard Association was formed, which adopted a list of standardized rules. These rules covered the description of discs, the length of the cues, the order of play, and the scoring system.[3]

Whether played on the floor or courts, shuffleboard is a good recreational activity that people of all ages can enjoy. Several junior high schools and high schools have lines painted on their gymnasium floors so that students can enjoy the game as part of a recreational unit or as an intramural activity.

The Court and Equipment

THE COURT

The court is 52 feet long and 6 feet wide, with a triangular target and scoring diagram at each end (Figure 18-21). One end of the court is designated as the head of court, and the other as the foot of court.

EQUIPMENT

Each player is provided with a cue stick measuring 6 feet 3 inches maximum; it must have no metal parts touching the playing surface. There are two sets of discs, four in each set—one set painted red, and the other black. The discs must be 6 inches in diameter, weigh not less than 11½ ounces nor more than 15 ounces, with thickness ranging from ¾ inch to 1 inch. Shuffleboard can be easily adapted to many types of surfaces; shuffleboard courts can be painted on the floors of classrooms, gymnasiums, hallways, sidewalks, or other concrete surfaces found at schools. Shuffleboard sets are available from most suppliers of physical education and recreation equipment at a reasonable price. The discs are usually

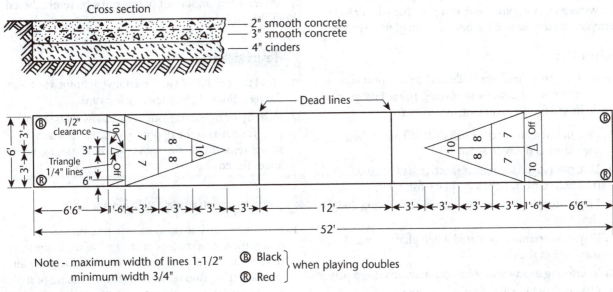

Figure 18-21 Shuffleboard court.

made of a durable composition material that can be used both indoors and outdoors.

Disc color is chosen by playing one disc to the farthest deadline; the player of the disc closest to the deadline receives his choice of colors. In starting a game, the owner of red discs shoots first, followed by black, then by red, alternating until all discs are shot. In singles play, after all discs are shot from head of court, the players walk to foot of court and, after tallying the score, continue play toward head of court with the owner of black discs shooting first.

In doubles, with two players at each end of the court, a game starts when the owners of red discs shoot all discs first from the head of court, followed by owners of black discs. Owners of red discs again shoot first from the foot of court, followed by black. On the second round, owners of black discs shoot first at each end of the court, followed by owners of red discs. Playing of all discs from one end of the court and back constitutes a round. So, in doubles play, the lead in starting to shoot changes after each round, whereas in singles play, the lead changes after each half round.

Basic Rules

SCORING

The scoring area contains one 10-point area, two 8-point areas, two 7-point areas, and one 10-off area. To count, a disc must lie entirely within one of the scoring areas, with no part of the disc touching any sideline; the separation line in the 10-off area is not considered. A game may end at 50, 75, or 100 points. Play continues until all discs have been shot, even if game point has been reached during the early part of a half round. In doubles, if a tie score results at game point or over, two additional rounds are played. If the score is still tied, play continues as outlined. In singles, one additional round is played to determine the winner in a tie game. In match play, the winner is determined on the basis of the best two out of three games.

PENALTIES

From 5 to 10 points are deducted from the player's score for some infractions of playing rules. Five points are deducted for the following infractions:

1. Disc not in its respective half of 10-off area when the player is ready to shoot
2. Disc not played from its respective half of 10-off (red played from right side, black from left)
3. Player stepping on or over baseline in making their shot
4. Player not remaining seated when play is toward their end of the court
5. Interfering in any way with opponent making a play
6. Players touching live discs at any time

Ten points are deducted for the following infractions:

1. Player making hesitation or hook shot
2. Player making remarks to disconcert opponent
3. Making any remarks that may be construed as coaching a partner making a play
4. Player shooting before opponent's disc has come to rest

PLAYING RULES

A disc returning or remaining on the court after having struck any object other than a live disc is called a *dead disc* and will be removed from the court before the play is resumed. If a dead disc strikes a live disc, that half round will be replayed. A disc that stops in the area between the farthest deadline and starting point will be considered dead and be removed from the court. Any disc that stops just beyond the farthest baseline will be moved a distance of at least 8 inches from baseline. Any disc stopping more than halfway over sidelines, or that rests or leans on the edge, will be removed from the court.

Skills and Techniques

The skills involved in playing shuffleboard are few; however, it is a game requiring the development of touch—to know just how hard to push the disc. It is extremely important for the shuffleboard player to "read" the surface on which the game is being played because the disc will react with different speeds on different surfaces. When the player executes the push or forward thrust of the cue, it is important that the cue be placed against the disc before beginning the pushing action. Do not jab at the disc because this motion will result in a loss of power. A few important points must be remembered about the push.

▶ Learning Hints

1. Hold the cue handle at the end, weight forward on the feet, body slightly leaning forward.
2. Push by straightening out your elbow while stepping forward on the opposite foot. As your arm straightens, follow through toward the target, with knees flexed.

▶ Practice/Organizational Suggestions

1. Have students line up in squads, one behind the other. Place one student at the end of the court to retrieve discs and push them back to students awaiting their turn. Rotate students from pushing position to retrieving position.

2. Place discs in different scoring areas and allow the students to practice pushing the discs out of the area with their own disc.

3. Practice shooting for position. Develop a "feel" for the push by attempting to push the disc to various boxes. Begin with no competition, and then add competition.

Skill Assessment

Shuffleboard is another target activity that is assessed by aiming at a marked area. A group of three students (participant, scorer, recorder) takes separate turns pushing four discs in succession for score. The participant pushes discs, the scorer tabulates points, and the recorder writes down the score. Students rotate responsibilities. Each student takes three trials; the final score is the sum total of all three.

The points acquired are those on the target (10, 8, 7 or 10 off). To count, a disc must lie entirely within one of the scoring areas and not touch any lines.

Modifications for Special Populations

ORTHOPEDICALLY IMPAIRED

See modifications discussed in the Field Hockey chapter.

COGNITIVELY IMPAIRED

Minimal modifications are needed.

SENSORY IMPAIRED

See modifications discussed in the Field Hockey chapter.

Terminology

cue A stick used to propel discs toward the target.

dead disc A disc that returns to or remains on the court after having struck an object other than another "live disc." A disc is also dead that stops between farthest dead line and starting line.

foot of court That end of the court opposite the head.

head of court That end of the court from which play starts to begin a match.

hesitation shot Stopping and restarting during forward motion of the disc.

live disc A disc that is in play; that is, it has gone past the farthest foul line and has not gone beyond the farthest baseline.

round The playing of all discs from one end of court and back.

Discussion Questions

1. Discuss the historic evolution of shuffleboard.

2. Identify the reasons why a disc is removed from the court.

3. Tell what happens when the score is tied at the conclusion of play.

Web Sites

www.shuffleboard.eu—offers explanation of the game, equipment, history, rules, information about tournaments, and more.

TABLE TENNIS

Nature and Purpose

Table tennis (popularly called *ping-pong*) may be played by two or four people. Equipment consists of a table with a smooth playing surface, a net, balls, and rackets (also called paddles). The game may be played by both old and young and seems destined to remain one of our most popular recreational activities.

At the competitive level, the game requires fast reflexes, remarkable hand-eye coordination, and strong, flexible leg strength. In just an instant, the participant responds with quick reactions and moves a short distance to hit a ball traveling up to 100 MPH.[1]

History

Table tennis originated in the 19th century when lawn tennis players, because of inclement weather, sought to practice indoors. They used cigar box lids for racquets and stacked up a row of books for the net. The ball was a rounded champagne cork. One early name for table tennis was whiff-whaff.[2] As the game evolved, it has been called by several names, including *indoor tennis, gossima* (a name given to it by the British Manufacturing Company), *ping-pong* (a name derived from the sound of the ball striking paddle and table), and *table tennis*. The name Ping-Pong was trademarked by the Parker Brothers, manufacturers of indoor play equipment in the United States.

The game enjoyed some popularity in the United States when it was introduced under the name ping-pong in 1900 and continued to spread in popularity until 1902. Considered to be a newfangled fad or craze, the game lost favor, and it did not become popular again until the late 1920s.

A dispute over the use of the term *ping-pong* was instrumental in the adoption of the name *table tennis* in the 1930s. The English Table Tennis Association was formed in 1923, and in 1926 an International Table Tennis Federation (ITTF) was organized. The ITTF controlled all rules and standards, and changes were not made unless approved by a majority of members. The American Ping Pong Association was formed in 1930, followed by other organizations. Since that time, the organizations have merged, and now the U.S. Table Tennis Association governs play in the United States.

On a worldwide level, table tennis continues to flourish. Once dominated by the Europeans, Asian countries now dominate the world championship scene. The skills and techniques developed by Asian players have been copied by many throughout the world. Table tennis became an Olympic sport in 1988.[3]

Equipment

The equipment necessary to play table tennis is of simple construction and relatively inexpensive. School physical education programs can have rackets and tables made by the industrial arts department at a nominal cost. Many physical education and recreation supply companies sell table tennis sets and balls for a reasonable price. Obviously, as their competitive level and skill increases, players may want more expensive rackets.

TABLE

The table is 9 feet long and 5 feet wide, with a height of 30 inches from floor to top surface (Figure 18-22). Most tables are made of ¾-inch pressed wood or good-quality plywood, but other materials can be used. Tables that come in halves and have a collapsible undercarriage are easy to store. Some are constructed so that one half can be folded up into a backdrop and used for a rebound wall in practicing various strokes.

NET

The playing surface is divided by a net secured in the center and parallel with the end lines. The top edge of the net is 6 inches above the playing surface.

BALLS

The balls are spherical, with a diameter of 40 mm, and weigh 2.7 g. The ball is made of celluloid plastic or a similar plastic material and is white or orange, with a matte finish. A good ball should be perfectly round and without wobble when spinning. The U.S. Table Tennis Association seal of approval on a ball is a good indication of quality.

RACKET

A variety of rackets (paddles) can be purchased at most sporting goods stores. Some have grips that fit a player's hand size. All have a rubber or sponge covering of some type that covers the playing surface. A covering of inverted sponge is most often used and is recommended for all levels of players.

Basic Rules

SINGLES GAME

Scoring. The winner of a game is the player who first scores 11 points, unless both players have 10 points, in which case the winner must gain a 2-point lead to win. The choice of ends and service at the start of the game is decided by toss. A match consists of the best of any odd number of games.

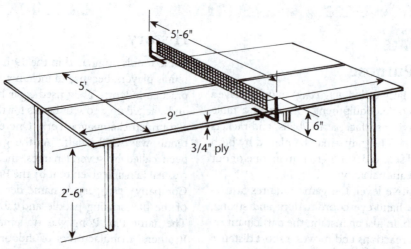

Figure 18-22 Table tennis table.

Change of Ends and Service. When one player or pair has chosen to serve or to receive first or to start at a particular end, the other player or pair has the other choice. After each 2 points have been scored, the receiving player or pair becomes the serving player or pair, and so on until the end of the game, unless both players or pairs score 10 points or the expedite system is in operation. In such cases, the sequences of serving and receiving are the same, but each player serves for only one turn. Players or teams change ends at the end of every game. In the final game, sides change ends when the first side scores 5 points. At this point in a doubles match, the receiving team switches receiving order. The player or pair who served first in the preceding game receives first in the next game.[4]

The Service. The server delivers the service by releasing the ball, without imparting any spin on release, and striking it with the paddle outside the boundary of the court near the server's end. Finger spins and rubbing the ball against the racket face are illegal. Any spin imparted to the ball must come from action of the racket on impact with the ball. The ball must be struck so that it first drops into the server's court and then into the receiver's court by passing directly over or around the net.

A Good Return. A ball having been served or returned in play is struck by the player so that it passes directly over or around the net and lands in the opponent's court; if the ball, during play, returns of its own impetus over or around the net, it may be played the same as a returned ball.

Let Ball. The served ball is a *let* if it touches the net or its supports and later lands in the receiver's court. A let is declared when a serve is made before the receiver is ready, unless the receiver makes an effort to strike the ball. It is a let if either player, because of conditions not under the player's control, is prevented from making a serve or a return.

Points are lost

1. If the server fails to make a good service, unless a let is declared.
2. If a good service or a good return is made by an opponent and the player fails to make a good return.
3. If the racket, or any part of a player or clothing, touches the net or its supports while the ball is in play.
4. If the player moves the table in any way while playing the ball.
5. If a player's free hand touches the table while the ball is in play.
6. If, at any time, a player volleys the ball. (A volley consists of hitting the ball before it has bounced.)

DOUBLES GAME

The rules for singles games apply to doubles except as indicated below.

Service Line. A $\frac{1}{8}$-inch white line drawn down the center of the table parallel with the sidelines is called the service line.

A Good Service. The ball must touch first the server's right half-court or the center line on the server's side of the net and then, passing directly over or around the net, touch the receiver's right half-court or the center line on the receiver's side of the net.

Choice of Order of Play. The pair who has the right to serve the first two services in any game decides which partner will do so, and the opposing pair then decides similarly which will first be the receiver.

Order of Service. Each server serves for 2 points. At the end of each term of service, the one who was receiving becomes the server, and the partner of the previous server becomes the receiver. This sequence, in which the receiver becomes the server and the partner of the previous server becomes the receiver, continues until the end of the game or the score of 10-all. At the score of 10-all, the sequence of serving and receiving continues uninterrupted, except that each player serves only 1 point in turn, and the serve alternates after each point until the end of the game.

Order of Play. After the server makes a good service, a good return is made by the receiver, then by the partner of the server, then by the partner of the receiver, and then by the server, and thereafter each player, in that sequence, will make a good return.

The Expedite System. Except where both players or pairs have scored at least 9 points, the expedite system comes into operation if a game is unfinished after 10 minutes' play or at any time at the request of both players or pairs. In this system, each player serves for 1 point in turn until the end of the game, and if the receiving player or pairs makes 13 good returns, the receiver scores 1 point. Once introduced, the expedite system remains in effect until the end of the match, with sides alternating serves after every point.

Skills and Techniques

Table tennis requires much concentration and excellent reactions. Because of the close similarity to tennis, the basic fundamentals regarding stroking the ball may be applied in some instances. The beginning skills needed to get the player started will be discussed in this section.

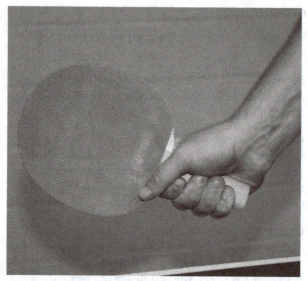

Figure 18-23   Standard "shake hands" grip.

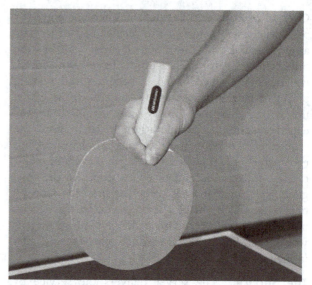

Figure 18-24   Penholder grip.

GRIP

The most common grip used by players is the "shake hands" grip used in tennis (Figure 18-23). The great Chinese players use a grip known as the penholder grip (Figure 18-24); however, this style of grip is usually best only for an attacking type of game.

 Learning Hints

1. With the racket perpendicular to the floor, grasp the racket as you would shake hands.
2. Wrap the last three fingers around the handle, and place your forefinger close to the lower edge of the racket face.

STROKES

The beginner should master the forehand and backhand push shot before playing the game. A right-handed player should use the forehand stroke when the ball approaches from the right, and the backhand when the ball approaches from the left. Preparatory to any stroke, the player should assume a good athletic stance in a ready position. The knees are bent, weight is evenly distributed on the forward half of the foot, arms are in front of the body, elbows are bent, and the racket is held parallel with the ground.

When executing both shots, remember that the ball is directed over the net by a pushing action, not a hitting action. Variations in arm movement and wrist movement will allow spin to be imparted to the ball.

Learning Hints: Backhand Push

(Figures 18-25, 18-26)

1. Play the ball in front of your body at the point of highest contact.

2. As the ball approaches, draw your right arm back by pivoting at the elbow and draw your right shoulder back by pivoting past the elbow; turn your right shoulder and point it toward the table.
3. Push the racket forward toward the ball, extending your arm in a horizontal plane.
4. Transfer your body weight from your back foot to your forward foot throughout the stroke.

Learning Hints: Forehand Push

(Figure 18-27)

1. As the ball approaches, draw back the racket; turn your shoulders so that your left shoulder points toward the table.
2. Push the racket forward toward the ball, extending your arm in a horizontal plane; turn your shoulders back.
3. Transfer your body weight from the back foot to the forward foot throughout the stroke.

SERVES

It is important for the beginner to remember that the ball must be stationary, resting freely in the palm of the server's free hand. The ball is then projected upward at least an inch without imparting spin and then falls without hitting anything before being struck. As the ball is falling, it is struck with the paddle. The ball must make contact with the server's side of the table first.

Learning Hints: Topspin Serve (Forehand Side)

(Figure 18-28)

1. The body assumes a stance three quarters sideways to the table, the ball rests on the fingers of the left

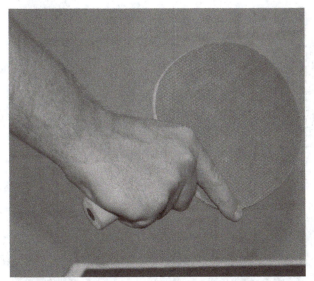

Figure 18-25   Position of the hand in a backhand push.

hand, and the racket assumes the position of a fore-hand push shot.

2. Toss the ball upward; bring the racket face (slightly closed) forward and continue pushing forward after making contact with the ball.

3. As the racket face follows through, it rolls over the top of the ball, thus imparting topspin to the ball.

The mechanics for a backhand topspin serve are essentially the same, except that the serve is initiated from the left side for the right-handed player.

▶ Practice/Organizational Suggestions

1. If a folding table is available, fold up one side perpendicularly so that it can be used as a rebound wall to practice strokes and serves.

2. Practice the toss (6 to 8 inches high) needed for the serve, concentrating on a smooth, rhythmic toss.

3. Practice against a wall, either letting the ball bounce once or volleying the ball as long as possible. As a variation, mark a target (circle or square) on the wall and try to hit the ball into the target.

4. To develop a feel for the racket and ball, continuously tap the ball upward off the face of the racket, then downward, while walking. Note the importance of concentration as you execute this drill.

5. When practicing the strokes and the serve, give equal time to developing skills on the backhand side as well as the forehand side.

Figure 18-26   Position during a backhand push shot.

Skill Assessment

The most important skill in table tennis is the ability to keep the rebounding ball in play using either the forehand or backhand stroke.

Rebound Test. Some tables are constructed so that one half can be folded up into a backdrop and used as a rebound wall. Such a setup facilitates skill testing.

A group of three students (participant, scorer/recorder, ball assistant) per table alternates taking as many 30-second trials as time allows. The participant hits the ball, the scorer/recorder counts and writes down points scored, and the ball assistant gives balls to the participant and retrieves errant balls. Students rotate responsibilities.

The participant drops the ball on the table and plays it (forehand or backhand) to the rebound wall. The ball must hit above the net and not higher than a line on the rebound surface marked 3 feet above the horizontal table surface. The rebounding ball must bounce on the table before being played off the wall. Each time the ball legally hits the wall, it counts as 1 point. The count continues after a lost ball and does not start at one again. The final score is the sum total of all trials.

Figure 18-27 Position of the body during a forehand push shot. Note that the left shoulder points toward the table.

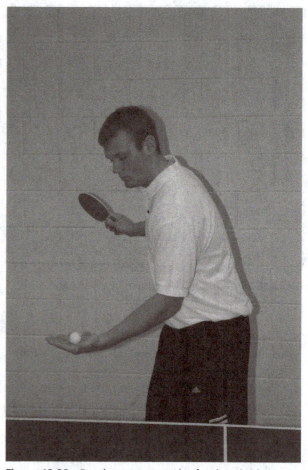

Figure 18-28 Ready to serve on the forehand side.

Modifications for Special Populations

ORTHOPEDICALLY IMPAIRED

1. See modifications discussed in the Tennis and Handball/Racquetball chapters.
2. Set up a modified table-top tetherball game. Tether a small whiffle-ball with a string to a 12- to 16-inch vertical dowel rod. Instead of a regulation paddle, use a large square piece of cardboard strapped to the student's hand.

COGNITIVELY IMPAIRED

Minimal modifications are needed.

SENSORY IMPAIRED

Tape cardboard railing to the sides of the table to create a bumper board. Students who have a visual impairment or are blind can rally an auditory ball on the table top without a net. Also see modifications discussed in the Tennis and Handball/Racquetball chapters.

Terminology

ace A service that completely eludes the receiver.

advantage (ad) Next point made after a deuce score. It is "advantage out" if the receiver wins it and "advantage in" if the server wins. The player wins the match who first wins a point after gaining "advantage."

all Term used to denote an equal score; for example, 20-all.

backhand Stroke frequently used by right-handed player when returning a ball hit to the left. The paddle is held so that the back of the hand faces the ball; the ball is usually hit with side of paddle opposite the side used in the forehand.

backspin A ball hit so that the top of the ball rotates toward the stroker, the bottom moving away.

block shot A quick, fast return immediately as the ball contacts the table (half-volley).

dead ball A ball is dead if a let is called, if the ball bounces twice on the table, and at the conclusion of a point or rally.

deuce When the score is even at 20-all. To win, a player must score 2 consecutive points.

drop shot A shot played so softly that it dies before the opponent can reach it, or places her at a disadvantage if she does play it.

finger spin An illegal procedure whereby fingers impart spin to the ball in serving.

forehand A stroke or volley made in such a fashion that the palm is the leading part of the movement. Usually hit with the opposite face of the paddle from that used in the backhand. In this stroke, the left foot of a right-handed player is toward the table.

let Means "play the point over" and occurs when the ball strikes the top of the net and falls into the correct service court; also if a ball breaks or if a player is interfered with by an official or spectator.

mixed doubles Doubles game in which each team has one man and one woman player.

push shot A ball struck with a pushing motion of the paddle near the top of the bounce so that no spin is placed on the ball.

service court In singles, the entire table area on the receiver's side, 5 feet by 4½ feet. In doubles, the table is divided by a center line so each service court is 4½ feet by 2½ feet.

slice A stroke in which the ball is stroked late so that it tends to spin in a direction away from the paddle.

topspin A ball stroked so that the top spins forward in the direction of flight; the opposite of backspin or underspin.

volley Illegal stroking of ball while it is in the air and before it has touched the table.

Discussion Questions

1. Trace the development of the game and its evolution from ping-pong to table tennis.
2. Compare the basic rules for singles and doubles.
3. Discuss the techniques used for imparting spin on the ball.
4. Discuss the "expedite system" in doubles.

Web Sites

http://tabletennis.about.com—offers useful coaching tips, rules, articles of interest, equipment, and what's happening in table tennis around the world. Also includes information about disability competition (wheelchairs rules).

www.tabletennis.gr—offers information about tactics, coaching tips, basics of table tennis, rules, video and movie clips, and much more.

www.teamusa.org/USA-Table-Tennis USA Table Tennis—contains an instructional guide, rules, information about equipment, tips of the week, and more.

www.pongworld.com—provides rules, tips, history, equipment reviews, and facts.

| # Skating: Inline

This chapter will enable you to

- Understand the history of inline skating
- Select and fit a first pair of inline skates
- Select and fit protective gear and a helmet
- Demonstrate safety position, ready position, A-frame stance, rotary motion, nose-knees-toes alignment, full foot recoveries, edgings, scissor positions, toe rolls, and how to get to the skating surface and a safe fall using protective gear
- Skate, stop, and turn confidently using duck walk, stride 1 and 2, swizzles, sculling, heel stop, A-frame, and parallel turns
- Understand and effectively use the "rules of the road"

Nature and Purpose

Inline skating is a graceful mode of self-transportation that can be accomplished with an economy of effort. It is an excellent nonimpact exercise. Inline skaters range from 3 years old to adults well into their 70s. The sport has gained national exposure as an aggressive discipline, the X Games being one example.

Other forms of skating are also popular. Speed skating and roller hockey are growing sports, both indoors and out. Dancers and trick skaters are in the rinks and at the parks everywhere. Fans of traditional sports have put on skates to play roller soccer and basketball.

However, most skaters are amateurs, skating for recreation, and, for this reason, inline skating has become most popular in its recreational form. In addition to being fun, it also has a fitness factor. Inline skaters have exhibited many health benefits, including improved cardiovascular health, increased muscular strength and endurance, improved flexibility, reduced stress, and weight control. Because inline skating is a low-impact activity, it is easy on a person's joints. It is an activity that almost anyone can enjoy, which is one of its greatest attractions.

Parks and trails are the usual venue, but inline skaters can also be found on the streets with or without traffic in major cities all over the world. Many skaters also use paved trails that are part of the United States' greenway systems, as a venue for their recreation and fitness pursuits. *Street skates* are sponsored and scheduled by skate clubs. They offer, sometimes with police escort, a wonderful way to see a city. These events can occur during day or night. In recent years, Paris, France, has hosted the largest street skate, drawing as many as 30,000 skaters. Atlanta, Georgia, has the oldest organized street skate, dating back to 1979.

This chapter introduces the fundamentals of beginning and intermediate inline skating skills. These fundamentals can become the foundation for a lifetime of skating. For those who master these basics, there are always more advanced techniques to learn and different disciplines to explore.

History

People have skated on ice for centuries. The earliest skaters were probably the *Skrid Finnai*, or the Sliding Finns, ancient inhabitants of Scandinavian lands, who skated on blades of wood or bone. Metal blades on skates first appeared about A.D. 200 during the Iron Age.[1]

The first skates with wheels were invented by Joseph Merlin. He created the first rolling skates circa 1760, made with wooden spools arranged in a row, following the pattern of an ice blade. In 1819, a Frenchman named Monsieur Petitbled obtained the first patent on a similar skate made of copper, wood, and ivory. In 1849, another Frenchman, Louis Legrange, made skates to simulate ice skating for the opera *La Prophete*. These early examples of roller skates were all constructed as inline skates and were difficult to control.

ROLLER SKATING

In 1863, New Yorker James Leonard Plimpton created the "rocking" skate, which had two wheels side by side in the front and the back. These skates anchored the wheel assembly with a rubber cushion that compressed as the skater leaned, allowing the wheels to turn slightly with weight shift. This skate was the precursor to the modern quad roller skate.

Roller skating was made even easier after the invention of ball bearings in 1884, which precipitated its popularity as a national pastime in the 20th century. The true modernization of roller skates occurred in the 1970s with the introduction of polyurethane wheels.

INLINE SKATING

Although primitive inline skates have been recorded as early as 1760, it was not until the beginning of the 1980s that a truly functional and durable inline skate was developed and mass produced. Scott and Brennan Olsen, two hockey players from Minnesota, were looking for a way to cross-train. When they stumbled on an old inline design, they reinvented it, and Rollerblade was born. Rollerblade is a registered trademark and, therefore, does not refer to all inline skates. Some of the other major manufacturers are K2, Salomon, and Roces.

In the 1980s, there were only two types of skates: high boots and low boots. High boots rose above the ankle and were constructed of a hard plastic exterior boot with a vinyl and fabric boot insert. A three- or four-wheel frame, depending on foot length, was attached. Low boots originally intended for ice or roller speed skating were fitted with metal five-wheel frames. The technology of all types of inline skates has developed exponentially in the past 25 years. Boot construction materials today have become stronger and lighter. Design has dramatically increased foot comfort and skate performance for the many types of inline skates that exist now.

Since the mass marketing of inline skates for consumers in the 1980s, the activity has become significantly more popular. Now, millions of people participate in some form of skating throughout the world. Inline skating appeals to children; to athletes who use it to cross-train; to adults who wish to incorporate inline skating as part of their physical fitness routine; to others who like the social pleasure of recreational skating; and to some who participate in inline skating as a sport.

Equipment

Before you begin skating, you need the proper equipment: inline skates and protective gear. Skates come in many different types, including recreational, fitness, aggressive, freestyle, hockey, and speed skates. Protective gear, at a minimum, consists of a helmet, wrist guards, elbow pads, and knee pads. Padded shorts as well as specific gear for hockey or aggressive skating are also available.

SKATES

The basic features that are common to nearly all skates include a boot with exterior bracing and cuff, laces and buckle(s) or strap(s), frames with hardware (axles and bearing spacers), wheels, and bearings (see Figure 19-1). These features are explained in the following paragraphs.

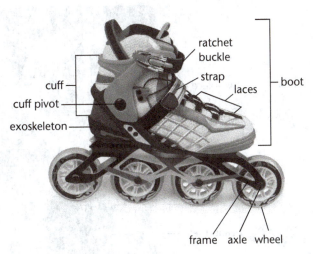

Figure 19-1 Parts of a skate.
Photo courtesy of Shutterstock.

Speed and hockey boots are the exceptions, having no cuff. Aggressive, hockey, and the majority of speed skates have no heel brake.

Boots.   The boot is the upper part of the skate that attaches to the frame. The boot is made of soft materials that encase the foot and is attached to a hard exterior platform and bracings. A cuff is mounted to the hard exterior bracing to restrict the lateral movement of the ankle and to allow it to flex. The heel, ankle, and calf muscle differ for men and women; therefore, most skate manufacturers now create gender-specific boots and skates. Boots with a higher cuff have greater lateral stability, helping to prevent sideways falls. Speed skates are low and have no cuff. This design gives the ankle flexibility, allowing more pressure to be applied downward during longer strokes. Hockey boots are high with no cuff to protect ankles during games with considerable contact. Speed and hockey boots are notoriously hard to break in. Aggressive skates have a tougher construction to withstand abuse.

Laces, Buckles, Straps.   The laces, buckles, and straps allow adjustments to secure the boot to your foot. There should be laces and at least one ratchet buckle on the cuff. There can be additional straps. Avoid skates that have only buckles, because laces are more versatile and are usually more comfortable.

Frames.   The skate frame attaches the wheels to the boot of the skate. Frames can accommodate three, four, or five wheels. Most inline skates have four wheels; speed skates have five wheels or four large wheels. Frames hold wheels, bearings, and bearing spacers in place with axles. The frame may be permanently attached to the boot or movable. Frame construction can be of composite material, extruded metal, or cast metal. Frame length on a recreational skate usually extends

Figure 19-2   Inline skating wheels, bearings, and bearing spacers are attached to the frame of a skate by axles.

slightly beyond the toe and heel. Speed skate frames are much longer. Short frames are more maneuverable and easier to propel, even with bad form. Longer frames are more stable at speed and require better technique to achieve speed.

Wheels.   Urethane wheels are permanently attached to a core or hub and come in a variety of diameters, degrees of hardness, and profiles. See Figure 19-2 for a view of wheels and the components that attach the wheels to a skate frame. Wheels wear in relation to use and technique. Heavy use will wear down wheels and make them smaller; individual technique determines how the profile of the wheel changes as it is worn down (e.g., wearing more on one side of the wheel than the other). Aggressive skates use the smallest wheels; speed skates, the largest. Some properties of wheels include the following:

- *Diameter* is measured in millimeters (mm). Wheels range from small, 50 mm, to large, 110 mm. The normal range for recreational skates is 76 to 80 mm in diameter. Smaller wheels are slower and generally more stable for a beginning skater. Larger wheels are easier to keep at speed, but balance and technique are even more critical.

- *Hardness* is measured in durometers (A). Urethane wheels range from a soft 74A to a hard 101A. The symbol *A* on a wheel denotes its durometer; 78A to 82A are normal durometers for recreational wheels. A low durometer wheel grips the surface better, has more cushion, and will wear faster than a higher durometer wheel. A soft wheel is slower than a hard wheel. The skater's weight can be a factor in choosing wheels with an appropriate durometer.

- *Profile* is the shape of the wheel as it contacts the surface. A wide profile has more wheel in contact with the skating surface and thus is more maneuverable for dancing and tricks. A narrow profile is used for speed, having a low coefficient of friction. The recreational wheel's profile lies between the two: narrow enough so pushing is not difficult, but round enough to be stable in turns.

Axles.   Wheels are attached to the frame by hardware called *axles*. Two-piece axles come as a shaft and screw that attach to each other through the frame and wheel. A one-piece axle passes through the frame and wheel, attaching directly to the frame.

Bearing Spacers.   Bearing spacers support the wheels and bearings within the frame and are determined by the diameter of the axle passing through it.

Bearings.   Ball bearings make wheels spin more smoothly and reduce unwanted friction. Two bearings are seated within each wheel's core or hub, one on each side, with a spacer connecting them within the wheel. Each bearing contains individual ball bearings, which are evenly distributed between an inner and outer casing. The size of a bearing is determined by the openings on each side of a wheel's core. Precision and materials vary greatly. Some bearings are permanently sealed and disposable; others are designed to be taken apart and maintained. Bearing rating systems can be confusing, but the common belief is that the higher the number following a series of letters, the better the bearing. More important than the rating is the maintenance of the bearings. Clean bearings that are free of water, sand, grit, and other substances result in a better performance. Lubricants, which vary from greases and creams to light oils and sprays, can also increase performance.

Heel Brake. Using the heel brake is the most effective way to control speed and stop. There are two types of brake assemblies: standard and active. A replaceable brake pad is secured to the standard brake assembly, which is rigidly attached to the frame behind the rear wheel. Right-handed people usually brake with it mounted on the right skate; left-handers, the left skate. Active brake assemblies engage the skating surface when the skate with brake is pushed forward and its cuff pivots back. These assemblies are attached to the rear of the frame and boot cuff with moving parts. If you are left-handed, make sure you purchase skates with a heel brake assembly that can be transferred to the left skate.

BUYING INLINE SKATES

A recreational or fitness skate is the usual first purchase for a beginner. For more advanced skaters, the skate discipline will determine all other considerations. When buying inline skates, beginners should make comfort their prime consideration. Wheels and bearings should not be major factors in determining a beginner's initial skate purchase. Expert advice is helpful; therefore, a skate shop will often be a better resource than a sporting goods store.

To judge a pair of skates in a store, wear socks that you will wear when skating. These socks should be made of a moisture-wicking material that rises above the cuff of the boot. Stand, do not sit, for at least 15 minutes in the skates to determine how comfortable the skates are.

An expensive inline skate is not an ideal first purchase. As a rough rule of thumb, a retail list price of $150 is the approximate demarcation between lower-quality toy skates and more serious sporting equipment. Skates usually last 1 to 3 years, depending on amount and type of use (bad technique can hasten wear).

PROTECTIVE GEAR

Protective gear must always be worn; it allows a skater to fall to the ground without injury. Falls are inevitable for all skaters. Protective gear can minimize or eliminate injury. Falls then become a skill rather than an accident to be avoided at all costs.

A helmet, wrist guards, elbow pads, and knee pads are essential. Padded shorts can protect hips, thighs, and tailbones. Protective gear varies greatly in construction, material, and degrees of protection. Consider all factors, or ask for expert advice when buying protective gear.

Helmet. The helmet should fit securely to the head and fasten closely to the jaw. Bike helmets, most often worn by skaters, usually offer better ventilation to allow heat to escape. Skate helmets cover the entire occipital lobe and are favored by aggressive skaters and those seeking maximum protection. The primary considerations should be fit and impact certification (American National Standards Institute, American Society for Testing and Materials, and Snell Memorial Foundation).

Wrist Guards. Wrist guards are modeled after wrist splints. They allow flexion but not hyperextension. A hard protruding splint cups the heel of the palm to protect against abrasions. Wrist guards vary in materials, quality, and style. Fit and quality are the most important factors to consider when purchasing wrist guards.

Elbow Pads. Elbow pads should be comfortable, secure, and sized correctly. They are constructed of a stretchy material with closures, with padding and a plastic protective plate.

Knee Pads. Fit, comfort, and security are especially important to consider when you shop for knee pads. Cushion will minimize impact. A knee pad should not be able to slip down the leg or hinder knee movement. Knee pads are constructed of a stretchy material with closures, padding, and a protective sliding plate.

Rules of the Road

Students should be familiar with the "rules of the road." Following these rules will enable skaters to coexist with pedestrians, cyclists, other skaters, and vehicles and have a fun, safe skating experience.

SKATE SMART

1. Always wear your protective gear, including helmet, wrist guards, knee pads, and elbow pads.
2. Master the basics: striding, stopping, and turning.
3. Maintain your equipment in proper working condition.
4. Check the heel brake for wear, and replace it when necessary.
5. Carry a skate tool, your identification, and insurance card.

SKATE LEGALLY

1. Obey all traffic regulations. When on skates, you have the same obligations as any wheeled vehicle.
2. Wear a helmet. In most states, there are laws requiring use of helmets. See www.helmets.org/mandator .htm.

SKATE ALERTLY

1. Skate under control at all times.
2. Watch out for road hazards. Differences in the color of the road surface can indicate gradient changes.
3. Avoid water, oil, and sand.
4. Avoid heavy traffic.

SKATE POLITELY

1. Skate on the right; pass on the left.
2. Announce your intentions by saying, "Passing on your left."
3. Always yield to pedestrians.

Suggested Learning Sequence

A. Equipment, safety, and rules of the road
B. Skills and techniques
  1. Introduction on grass or carpet
      a. Gear up
      b. Basic standing position: safety position
      c. Edging
          i. Inside edges
          ii. Outside edges
          iii. Center edges
          iv. Corresponding edges
      d. Rotary motion
      e. Basic moving positions
          i. Ready position
          ii. A-frame stance
          iii. Nose-knees-toes alignment
          iv. Full foot recovery
          v. Scissor position
      f. Falling on grass
      g. Duck walk on grass
  2. Introduction on pavement
      a. Getting to the pavement
      b. Falling on pavement
  3. Skating skills
      a. Duck walk
      b. Stride 1
      c. Rolling ready position
      d. A-frame turns
      e. Swizzles
      f. Sculling
      g. Stride 2
      h. Toe rolls
      i. Heel stop
      j. Parallel turns

Skills and Techniques

Before even strapping on a pair of inline skates, beginners must be instructed in the issues of equipment, safety, and rules of the road. Once informed in these issues, the first skating lesson for beginners should begin on dry grass or carpet.

INTRODUCTION ON GRASS OR CARPET

The dry, high-friction surface of grass or carpet will allow the students to feel at ease while practicing the basic stances and movements. Following the suggested learning sequence without rolling should allow the student to have some confidence and body memory before attempting the movements on pavement. When the student feels confident with the following basics, move on to the Introduction on Pavement.

Gear Up.   The first step in skating is getting into your skates. Sit low to the surface, adjacent to grass or carpet. It is sometimes necessary to put on knee pads before skates. Disengage or loosen all buckles, straps, and laces, and slip your foot into the skate, making sure the tongue is pulled up. The straps and laces should be secure but not too tight. The ankle buckle on the cuff should be the tightest closure, restricting the ankle's lateral movement. Avoid cutting off circulation. Tap the skate's rear wheel or brake to seat the heel back into the skate. Finish gearing up by donning all protective gear, making sure that helmet, wrist guards, and elbow and knee pads are fitted properly. Crawl on the grass or carpet to a position of safety away from the skating surface. Readjust the equipment for comfort, if necessary, after you stand on the skates.

Basic Standing Position.   The basic standing position is the safety position, shown in Figure 19-3. This

Figure 19-3 Safety position.

position is used to stand on skates and prevent unintended motion. Begin from a kneeling position.

1. Raise a knee so that all wheels of one skate are in contact with the ground.
2. Lean forward, chest to that knee, with both hands touching the ground in front and on either side of that leg.
3. Straighten the knee. Your bottom will rise.
4. Drag or roll the other skate to contact so that the skates form a T, with all wheels touching the ground.
5. Rise slowly, keeping your arms close and pressure equal on both feet.

▶ Learning Hints

1. Position the skate heel without the brake into the arch of the skate with the brake.
2. Reposition your hands so that you can rise easily.
3. To help maintain safety position, clench your rear muscles lightly.

Edging. *Edging* is the angle of the wheel to the surface. Inside, outside, center, and corresponding edges are produced by ankle movement or by body position. A slight edge is better than a severe edge for maintaining traction. Some form of edging is always applied whenever wheels are on the ground; it is the varying of edging that enables the skater to perform all types of skate maneuvers. Practice the following while standing to get a feel for each type of edging.

1. *Inside edges.* Collapse ankles *inward* until you feel a little pressure on the top *outside* of the skate boot. An inside edge while you glide on one skate produces inward skate movement toward the center of the body. Inside edges allow you to slow down while turning and give you power when pushing.
2. *Outside edges.* Collapse ankles *outward* until you feel a little pressure on the top *inside* of the skate boot. Outside edges are rarely used simultaneously with both feet. An outside edge while you glide on one skate produces a turning motion in the direction of the outside edge and away from the center of the body. With practice, you can combine the force of gravity with outside edges on advanced stroke or push techniques to achieve faster turns and increased power.
3. *Center edges.* Find center edges by rocking ankles laterally from inside edges to outside edges. Be aware of the pressure you feel at the top of your skates to gauge the location without looking down. Pressure should be equal, and wheels should be exactly perpendicular to the surface. Center edges allow the greatest balance and speed. It is the optimal wheel

position for the ready position and nose-knees-toes alignment, which will be discussed later in this chapter.

4. *Corresponding edges.* Corresponding edges involves using inside edging on one skate and outside edging with the other. Allow your knees to lean comfortably in the direction of the skate with outside edging. Corresponding edges used with differing weight transfers can produce either fast turns or speed-controlling turns.

Rotary Motion. Rotary motion defines the upper body action that results in change of direction. Imagine a vertical axis passing straight down the center of the body from the top of the head to the ground at the midpoint between the legs. Rotary motion is the clockwise or counterclockwise motion around that axis. Look left with your eyes and head first. Keep your hips level and rotate your upper body to the left. Feel the resulting pressure on the right heel (and vice versa). Always let your head and eyes lead rotary motion. Hip movement is much more effective than shoulder movement.

Basic Moving Positions. Basic moving positions are used to maintain balance and to facilitate coasting, turning, stroking (pushing), gliding (coasting on one skate), and striding (stroking and gliding in a continuous motion). These are not intuitive, but they can be learned first in steps and then incorporated into body memory with experience. For these basic movement positions, more weight should be on the heel than on the balls of the feet.

READY POSITION. The balance and coasting position for inline skating is called the *ready position* (Figure 19-4). Stand on grass with feet shoulder-width apart and pointing directly forward. Bend knees slightly, with shoulders stacked above hips and over heels.

▶ Learning Hints

1. Keeping your back slightly slouched or slumped will make balancing on the back half of each foot easier.
2. Toes should be easily wiggled without directing pressure through the balls of the feet.
3. Knees should be flexible to allow downward movement.
4. Quad muscles should have some tension.
5. Elbows should be in, and shoulders and arms should be relaxed to the fingers.
6. Hands should stay low and in front of the body.
7. Head should be upright and positioned midway between skates.
8. It is helpful to try a poorly balanced ready position for purposes of contrast. Lean the upper body forward, transferring weight to the balls of feet, and

Figure 19-4 Ready position.

Figure 19-5 To regain balance, remember the mantra "Oh no, get low" to assume a lower ready position.

feel the heels lift from the insoles. A heel-balanced ready position should be relaxed enough to hold for many minutes.

9. The usual reaction to losing balance is to straighten knees and throw arms up or out. On skates, this will result in a backward fall. To regain balance easily, use the mantra: *"Oh no, get low"* (see Figure 19-5). Assume a lower ready position with more knee bend, extending your arms and hands in front of your body, leaning as little as possible, and keeping eyes forward to look for danger.

A-FRAME STANCE. The A-frame stance, shown in Figure 19-6, facilitates easy and controlled turns using rotary motion. Step in the grass to a stance more than shoulder-width apart, allowing your ankles to drop inward. Weight should be equal on your heels, with knees bent. Hands should be low and in front of your body, and elbows relaxed and close to your side. While you are in the A-frame stance, add rotary motion, either clockwise or counterclockwise, and feel the resulting pressure on your leg and skate of the opposite side. Concentrate on keeping weight on your heels.

Maintaining the A-frame stance, inside edges, as you look in the direction of the turn and add rotary motion, will result in an A-frame turn on pavement.

NOSE-KNEES-TOES (NKT) ALIGNMENT. NKT alignment (Figure 19-7) is the secret to one-foot balance and allows advanced strides and turns, as well as the heel brake to be used safely. Assuming this alignment results in a *support leg*, that is, one leg supports a greater amount of the skater's weight, while the other leg, the *action leg*, supports less weight and is free to move into other positions to perform other skills.

To implement a support leg, first assume the ready position. Without changing eye level, shift body to one side in a nose-over-knees-above-toes vertical alignment, with weight on the supporting heel. The support leg skate should be on a center edge; the other skate, because of the body shift, will be on an inside edge. Moving too far in that direction beyond NKT can result in a sideways fall. Stopping short of NKT alignment can inhibit a glide (coasting on one skate), hastening the process of placing the other skate down on the ground, resulting in a shortened stride. Shifting balance to the other side results in a new NKT alignment. An *action leg* (the leg creating an action), when used in conjunction with the *support leg* in NKT

Figure 19-6 A-frame stance.

Figure 19-7 NKT alignment.

alignment, will create turns, movement, or speed control. NKT alignment allows stability and safety as each skate touches the ground. A support leg will have more knee bend than an action leg.

FULL FOOT RECOVERY. Full foot recovery (Figure 19-8) is the balanced position of the lifted skate that extends the glide. Foot recovery is the movement that begins with the lifting of a skate off the surface and ends in full foot recovery. The NKT alignment of the skate that is set down is coupled with the movement of the recovering skate swinging to a close and trailing full foot recovery position. Knees should also be close together because separated knees will shorten a glide. Full foot recovery is the position necessary for a support leg to become an action leg.

SCISSOR POSITIONS. In the scissor positions, one skate travels forward of the other without allowing the legs to spread. Skates should track closely. The most common scissor position is scissor forward, which involves balancing on the trailing skate's heel. This position is used for coasting on less than ideal skating surfaces and for the heel stop. Scissor back position, which involves balancing on the leading skate's heel, is used for parallel turns and toe rolls (to be discussed later). Center edges are used on both action and support legs. The action leg is the scissoring leg.

Figure 19-8 Full foot recovery.

Figure 19-9 Scissor forward position.

Figure 19-10   Scissor back position.

To assume the scissor forward position, shown in Figure 19-9, follow these steps:

1. Begin in the ready position with skates closer together, about 1 to 4 inches apart, and toes pointing forward.

2. Create NKT alignment on the support leg. The majority of balance and weight remains on the back skate's heel. The less weight you have on the front skate, the easier it will be to maneuver.

3. Roll the action skate forward until that heel wheel is even or slightly forward of the support leg's toe wheel. All wheels maintain contact with ground.

To assume scissor back position, as shown in Figure 19-10, follow these steps:

1. Begin in the ready position with skates closer together, about 1 to 4 inches apart, and toes pointing forward.

2. Create NKT alignment on the support leg. The majority of balance and weight remains on the front skate's heel.

3. Roll the action skate back until the toe wheel is even or slightly back of the support leg's heel wheel. All wheels maintain contact with ground.

▶ Learning Hints

1. Keep slight inner thigh contact to prevent skates from drifting apart width-wise.

2. Keep the lateral distance between your feet of 2 to 4 inches during steps 1–3.

Falling on Grass.   Falling can be less stressful and injurious if practiced often. Trying to avoid falling at all costs can result in greater loss of balance and more injury. Remembering *"Oh no, get low"* as a response to loss of balance will many times prevent falling. Even if falling results, getting low will lessen the distance to the ground.

1. Start from the *"Oh no, get low"* position (refer back to Figure 19-5).

2. Pick a support leg and assume NKT alignment on it, bringing arms in on each side. Do not reach down. Keep your eyes up, looking forward for danger.

3. Lower the knee pad of the action leg to the ground next to the support leg's skate (see Figure 19-11).

▶ Learning Hints

1. The action leg's skate should pivot on the toe wheel's center edge and travel slightly back.

2. Do not drag wheels. The knee of the action leg should bend naturally.

3. Keep all weight on the support leg even after the knee has touched down.

4. Practice the ability to get to the ground safely and then slowly expand the comfort zone.

Figure 19-11 Falling.

Duck Walk on Grass. The duck walk is a beginning forward movement that mimics the walk of a duck. With toes pointed in a 90-degree angle from each other, the duck walk provides a stable base for traversing short distances at a controlled speed. To help place your foot, imagine a line starting from under you and extending to the destination point.

1. Begin in the safety position.
2. Move your right skate forward, setting down the heel wheel on the imaginary line with toes pointing toward 2 o'clock. (Left-handed skaters may feel more comfortable starting with their left foot; reverse steps 2 and 3.)
3. Move left skate forward, setting down the heel wheel on that imaginary line with toes pointing toward 10 o'clock.
4. Repeat, alternating feet.

▶ Learning Hints

1. Draw a line with chalk instead of using an imaginary line.
2. All four wheels on each skate alternately leave and touch the ground simultaneously. Do not toe off, letting the toe wheel be the last to leave the skating surface. It is better to let the heel wheel be the last to leave the ground. Always balance forward movement on the heels.

3. The upper body should move forward in space without leaning and balance briefly above each heel as it lands.
4. Keep your head upright with your eyes watching the terrain ahead as well as below. Keep your arms relaxed and near the body.

INTRODUCTION ON PAVEMENT

Once students have mastered the basic moving positions on grass, they will be ready to start skating on pavement. Monitor skate traffic and class size carefully to prevent incidents. It is important to have a skate site that is relatively flat and free of debris. A site that forms a shallow bowl, with inclines on opposing sides, can make coasting easier without the necessity of braking. A certain amount of speed tolerance or ability to coast without fear increases the comfort zone and will allow enough time to perform some of these maneuvers.

Getting to the Pavement. Sidle up to the curb or edge of the pavement, keeping skates parallel to the edge of the pavement. Start in a low ready position on the grass next to the pavement. Head level should remain the same throughout this maneuver.

1. Assume NKT alignment on the skate farthest from the pavement, and lower the action leg skate to the pavement. Pull the lowered skate's heel back to the edge of the curb.
2. Bring your hands and arms near the action leg. Transfer balance and weight to the lowered skate with a new NKT alignment. The lowered leg is now the support leg.
3. Take a deep breath to release tension and, without straightening the support leg's knee, lift and move the new action leg to safety position next to the support leg on the pavement.
4. Assume a higher safety position once balanced on the pavement.
5. If you are stepping off of a curb, continue to step away from it so that each step ends in a safety position until you are at least one body length's distance from the curb in case of a fall.

▶ Learning Hints

1. You can roll on grass with enough downslope, so do *not* point your skates down the slope when approaching the pavement.
2. Pavement is rarely level. If any incline is present on the pavement, orient toward the incline. Gravity will help you hold a safety position better when you face up an incline.

Falling on Pavement

Prerequisite: Falling on grass

The eventual goal of falling on pavement is to be able to safely lower a knee pad to the surface while moving; slide on the knee pad while maintaining balance on the support leg; and then to rise on the support leg, lifting the knee pad off the pavement to resume skating. This skill will be difficult on pavement. Note that falling onto both knees is not necessary to learn to fall correctly.

1. Without rolling, repeat steps 1–3 of falling on grass.

2. After falling, get up into the safety position. This action should be deliberate and smooth. Throwing the body up can result in a backward fall.

3. *While* you are rolling, repeat steps 1–3 of falling in grass.

4. After falling, get up into the safety position.

5. Readjust protective gear, if necessary, after falling.

▶ Learning Hints

1. To gain confidence, practice falling and getting up with progressively more movement.

2. Keep eyes forward, watching for danger.

3. Do not reach down with your hands and throw balance away. Wrist guards will offer protection from slapping the pavement in uncontrolled falls to the side and will protect your hands while you fall forward. Keep fingers extended, never curled, during a fall, to protect knuckles from the pavement. The farther the action leg's knee pad lands away from the support leg's skate, the harder the fall will be.

4. If your balance transfers to the action leg, your legs may split and stretch your groin.

5. Bend the knee of the action leg, pivoting on the toe wheel only. Do not drag wheels on their inside edges as you try to lower the knee of the action leg.

SKATING SKILLS

These skills and drills will allow the skater to propel, turn, and control speed. The following are beginner to early intermediate skills:

- Duck walk
- Stride 1
- Rolling ready position
- A-frame turns
- Swizzles
- Sculling
- Stride 2
- Toe rolls
- Heel stop
- Parallel turns

Duck Walk. This beginner skill introduces forward inline movement on pavement and is imperative for learning balance and control. The objective is to maintain balance without rolling. Staying on center edges will make this maneuver much easier.

Prerequisite: Duck walk on grass

1. Begin in the safety position. Heel wheels will remain on an imaginary line, with toes pointing at 10 o'clock and 2 o'clock.

2. Transfer your balance to the heel wheel of your forward foot, lifting your rear foot and bringing it forward to set down the heel wheel on the imaginary line.

3. Transfer your balance to the new forward foot, lifting the new rear foot and bringing it forward to set down the heel wheel on the imaginary line.

▶ Learning Hints

1. Keep your head upright and look forward as well as down.

2. If the skate touching the ground moves forward on contact, pressure is on the heel. If the skate travels backward, pressure is on the toe. No movement indicates an evenly balanced skate front and back.

3. If the skate is difficult to lift, your weight is not fully transferred to the support leg. The action leg and support leg change with each step.

4. The knee angle will change little, and your upper body should be relaxed and comfortably slouched.

Stride 1

Prerequisite: Duck walk and ready position

Stride 1 is more fluid than a duck walk, producing forward movement with a stroke (a push accomplished by straightening the knee and keeping pressure on the heel) and glide (a one-foot coast facilitated by a knee bend). The linking of a *glide* and *stroke* creates a *stride*.

1. Begin in the safety position, with the left skate in front of the right, assuming NKT alignment on the left skate.

2. Lift the right skate briefly and place the right heel in front of the left skate on an imaginary line pointing toward your destination in NKT alignment.

3. Straighten the left knee and lift the left foot, which creates a left stroke and initiates a glide on the right foot. Be sure to always have one knee bent.

4. Place the left heel in front of the right skate on an imaginary line in NKT alignment.

5. Straighten the right knee and lift the right foot, which creates a right stroke and initiates a glide on the left foot.

6. Repeat the sequence until you can glide easily and are comfortable with the movement.

Learning Hints

1. Stride 1 will often develop naturally from a duck walk with the use of heel pressure.

2. Shorter strides are better at first, using a slight inside edge. Center edges produce longer glides with NKT alignment. Outside edges can result in a sideways fall.

3. Keep your head upright to avoid leaning and falling forward, as well as to see easily.

4. Slightly slouch your shoulders and back to avoid falling backward and to relieve back strain.

5. Do not twist or use rotary motion. Do not throw your arms to induce movement.

6. If you move faster than desired, use the ready position while rolling for stabilization and *"Oh no, get low"* for any balance lost.

Rolling Ready Position. Rolling ready position (Figure 19-12) is coasting while you remain equally balanced on both skates. The objective is to find balance while moving and to increase tolerance of speed. This position is used to build confidence, save energy, and achieve an effortless ride on two feet. Skaters use either rolling ready position or the scissor forward position whenever coasting.

FINDING BALANCE

1. Execute stride 1 on a flat surface to build the desired momentum.

2. Point both skates directly forward, bending your knees to increase heel pressure.

3. Coast until you stop.

Learning Hints

1. Both skates will roll side by side when heel pressure is equal. Too much toe pressure may result in tripping, the inability to change toe direction, and even backward skate movement.

2. At slow speeds, try a little toe pressure to feel how balance is lost; then resume heel pressure.

Building the Comfort Zone. Find a skating surface shaped like a shallow bowl, with a gradual incline in opposing directions, or an incline with a long flat runoff. From the lowest point, skate a short distance up the incline, and stop skating by adopting a safety position as forward motion ends. Turn to look behind you, down the incline.

1. Stand in safety position, facing up the incline, with heel and arch in constant contact. Turn your upper body to look down the incline. Then gradually move one skate's toe around, pivoting your body until the one skate is pointed downhill.

Figure 19-12 Rolling ready position.

2. Breathe, sink slightly, and release the contact of safety position, allowing the other skate to point down the hill, relaxing into the ready position. Coast, breathe, and feel the speed.

3. Coast until you stop, using *"Oh no, get low"* only if needed. Remember, after the downhill comes an uphill or a long flat runoff. Gravity and friction will stop momentum.

Learning Hints

1. Practice stride 1 and rolling ready position from point to point until you achieve a comfortable rolling ready position. As your comfort zone increases, try a lower, and thus faster, position.

2. Practice coasting with skates closer or farther apart than in ready position. Make these transitions slowly and easily, returning to a normal ready position for confidence and using *"Oh no, get low"* when balance or confidence is compromised.

3. It is important to be able to relax into the ready position; body movements should be subtle.

4. Use *"Oh no, get low"* only when needed. Learn to balance with a knee angle that is comfortable. Knees must remain flexible and able to bend or straighten at will.

A-Frame Turns. Now that you have gotten comfortable taking strides and coasting, the next step is to control the direction of movement by turning. A-frame turns will allow you to turn in any direction desired and use the terrain (such as traversing or turning up a hill) to control speed. This turn is composed of an A-frame stance with inside edges and rotary motion. Speed is lost when you make this turn; thus, some speed is necessary to complete this skill.

1. Start from an A-frame stance with inside edges on both skates. You should feel equal pressure on the top outsides of both boots. Do not force knees inward.
2. Look in the direction of the desired turn with your eyes and head to make sure the turn can be safely made (refer back to Figure 19-6).
3. Still looking, slowly orient your hips toward the goal. You should feel pressure on the heel opposite the direction of the turn (Figure 19-13).
4. As the goal of the turn is achieved, return to ready position.

▶ Learning Hints

1. Do not allow your outside arm to fly away.
2. Always lead the turn with your eyes to be safe and aware of the surroundings, rather than watching only the ground.
3. If either skate tracks straight ahead while the other turns, the skate straight ahead has too much weight or pressure on its toe.
4. Leaning in the direction of the turn will reduce control.
5. Maintain heel pressure throughout the turn. If toes are weighted, the feet will not turn in the desired direction.
6. A right heel feels pressure in a left turn, and the left heel feels pressure in a right turn. A body shift to the outside will make the turn faster and increase centrifugal force.
7. Control is best learned by keeping your back straight at first.

Swizzles. A swizzle is a method of propulsion where both feet maintain contact with the skating surface at all times, simultaneously pushing, recovering, and coasting. When two or more are linked together, they are called swizzles, and the action is called swizzling. When teaching young children, instructors often call swizzles balloons, lemons, or footballs. The goal of swizzles is to propel forward with both skates, always touching the ground and mirroring all movements and pressure applications. Body position will be lower when feet are apart and higher when feet are closer together.

Figure 19-13 A-frame turn.

Swizzling uses gravity to initiate movement by quickly lowering the body's weight. This technique will only work with weight on the heels.

1. Start with your heels together and toes pointing to 10 o'clock and 2 o'clock. Use your body weight to initiate a downward sitting movement, simultaneously swinging your hips forward and bending your knees. Be sure to maintain your weight on your heels throughout. This position will allow the skates to move apart quickly. Be sure to keep your hands and arms low and close to your body so that you do not fall over backward (Figure 19-14A).
2. When you achieve an A-frame stance, straighten both knees with equal intensity, keeping weight on the heels and thus generating pushes from both skates. If heel weight is maintained, both toes will immediately point inward (Figure 19-14B).
3. Finish the swizzle by coasting into a close rolling ready position (skates 2–4 inches apart). You do not need to use inner thigh strength to pull skates together; the momentum from the pushes in step 2 should be sufficient to roll skates into a close ready position. Your head will rise as the skates come close together (Figure 19-14C).

A　　　　　　　　**B**　　　　　　　　**C**

Figure 19-14　Swizzling.

4. Repeat the sequence, initiating the next swizzle with a slight lean forward from the hips as the head and body begin new forward movement. If skates left tracks on the ground, the pattern traced would resemble a series of hourglasses. If you were observed from the side, you would resemble a pendulum swinging, the skates being the bottom of the pendulum.

▶ **Learning Hints**

1. Using an inside edge will make it easier to start, but slower.
2. Gravity feeds the push, but don't let the skates get too far apart before pointing them together again.
3. The faster your legs extend, the greater your speed.
4. It is easier to learn the rhythm of swizzles on a slight decline, but proficiency comes with the ability to swizzle uphill.

Sculling

Prerequisite: Swizzles
Sculling is a method of propulsion that keeps both skates on the ground at all times, with each skate alternating pushes. Sculling looks like a stride without lifting a skate up. Sculling divides swizzling in half. Body position will be lower than a swizzle position, without the rise-and-sink

motion. One leg supports with a knee bend as the action leg pushes by straightening the knee. This sequence is followed by recovery and a coast. Weight and pressure must be on the heels. The goal is to use NKT alignment and direction of foot placement for a better coast, heel pressure for more power, and timing for efficiency.

1. Start with the support leg on a center edge, pointing straight ahead with NKT alignment. The action leg should start in its appropriate 10 o'clock or 2 o'clock toe point, with a slight inside edge. If you are rolling, start in a close ready position, then assume the appropriate foot position.
2. Bend the support leg quickly, simulating a fall. While bending the support leg, push down through the heel on the action leg. The action leg should move at least laterally and, ideally, a little forward of the support leg. When the knee straightens on the action leg, that toe should point inward if pressure has remained on the heel (see Figure 19-15).
3. Rise on the support leg and allow the action skate to recover, coming closer to the support leg's skate in a close ready position.
4. Coast, regrouping in the ready position, feeling equal heel pressure on center edges.
5. Repeat the sequence on the other side, using the opposite foot as the action leg.

Figure 19-15   Sculling.

▶ Learning Hints

1. The sculling path should be straight if you maintain a center edge on the support skate. Weaving indicates edging on the support leg's skate.

2. This maneuver generates more power if your head does not bob.

3. The more pressure on the heels, the more fluid this skill will feel. Heel pressure is as important for the support skate as it is for the action leg's push.

4. Practice sculling on a flat surface until you are comfortable with the rhythm; then move to a gentle incline to practice.

Stride 2

Prerequisite: Stride 1

Stride 2 uses a more powerful stroke than stride 1, introduces the *fall* (different from falling), and extends the glide by the full foot recovery. During stride 2, only one skate at a time will be in contact with the skating surface. A quicker knee straightening creates a greater push or stroke and will initiate the *fall* to the other skate. The fall begins as the action leg's push occurs and ends on a new support leg's NKT landing. Knee bend is used as shock absorption to counter the fall. Full foot recovery is used for balance during the one-foot *glide* (coast), which results from the fall. Recovery of the skate begins when it is lifted off the ground after a push. It finishes when the skate swings in behind the gliding skate with knees close, the foot not yet touching the ground in a full recovery position.

1. Begin with stride 1, adding a deeper bend on the support leg, with the other leg in full foot recovery position.

2. Straighten the support knee to create push and initiate fall to the side, not forward. This movement changes the support leg to the action leg.

3. Lift the action skate immediately and move to full foot recovery position as the newly bent support leg lands on a center edge in NKT alignment. This sequence will produce a glide. The knee bend to absorb the fall will be greater than in stride 1 because the push is greater.

4. Straighten the support knee to create a new stride and initiate a fall to the other side.

▶ Learning Hints

1. The fall will initiate a longer glide by landing on a center edge; inside or outside edging shortens the glide.

2. Pointing toes forward in the direction of travel, not out, will also allow for a longer glide. At first, you may feel pigeon-toed when landing on your feet with toes pointing forward.

3. If you trip, your weight is on your toes rather than your heels.

4. The fall is more evident if the skater delays putting down the landing skate and uses a little sideways hip swing.

5. *"Oh no, get low"* works even when you are on only one skate.

Toe Rolls.   A toe roll is almost the same position as full foot recovery. The difference is the trailing skate's toe wheel is rolling on the ground rather than being completely off the surface. The skill of toe rolls (Figure 19-16) is used to find better foot balance for a full foot recovery and a longer one-foot glide. This skill is helpful when you are practicing stride 2 and learning parallel turns (covered later in the chapter).

1. Begin rolling in a close ready position, skates 1 to 4 inches apart.

2. Use NKT alignment on a support leg. Then bend the support knee, keeping your weight on your heel.

3. Touch the action leg's knee to the support leg's calf muscle for extra balance. Point the action leg's toe back to pivot onto the toe wheel only. The toe wheel should roll one skate length behind the support foot.

▶ Learning Hints

1. Allow only slight pressure on the toe wheel.

2. A wobbling action indicates too much toe pressure.

3. More knee bend will allow better balance.

Figure 19-16   Toe roll.

Heel Stop

Prerequisite: Scissor forward position

If you have practiced the skills in this chapter, you have already experienced stopping with methods such as the A-frame turn, skating up an incline, or just allowing friction to do its work. You need to be able to tolerate a small amount of speed before it is really possible to practice stopping, so it is not practical to learn stopping skills until you are comfortable with basic strides and coasting. Stopping or controlling speed can be accomplished by many methods: heel stops, T-stops or snowplows, hockey stops, or power slides. The safest and most readily learned is the heel stop. The other methods are more advanced and are not covered in this chapter. The goal of the heel stop is to use the heel brake to control speed and to stop when necessary.

Heel brakes are either standard (connected to the frame with no moving parts) or active (attached to the cuff of the boot and the frame). The procedures for both are nearly the same. The heel brake should be on the same foot you would use to kick a ball.

Use a site that allows for some coasting without building speed. It is important when first learning to have confidence that even if you fail at the heel stop, you will still be able to stop. Heel stops use the ready position, a scissor position, and knee bend.

1. Assume a close ready position by allowing skates to roll within 1 to 4 inches of each other, with pressure equal on both heels. Let elbows hang next to ribs, and allow the tips of your thumbs to touch as your forearms extend in front, no higher than parallel to the surface (Figure 19-17A).

   - Leaning or twisting will be obvious with this upper body posture. Keep orientation directly ahead.
   - Practice rolling from the regular ready position to step 1 and back to ready. Then practice with lesser and greater knee bend.
   - Pressure is always equal on both heels.

2. Adopt NKT alignment on your support leg. The support leg is the skate without a braking mechanism. Scissor the action foot forward until the heel wheel is even or slightly forward of the toe wheel of the support leg (Figure 19-17B).

   - About 75 percent of your weight should be on the support leg's heel. If the support skate stays in place, heel pressure was maintained. If the support skate travels backward, toe pressure was used.
   - Keep slight inner thigh pressure to prevent skates from drifting apart in width. The distance between your feet should remain 1 to 4 inches.
   - Practice ready position to step 1, to step 2, and then back to step 1 and ready position while rolling. When you are comfortable making one- and two-foot balance changes, proceed with step 3.
   - For skates with active braking assemblies, step 2 will initiate friction and some speed control without moving to step 3. Standard brakes will still roll freely at this point. (Skip step 3 if you are using active braking assemblies).

3. Lift the toe of the action skate slowly, pivoting on the heel wheel and engaging the heel brake lightly, as in Figure 19-17C.

   - Balance and speed control are the goals initially, not stopping. Listen for the steady, light sound of the brake engaging.
   - Practice dropping the toe to roll on all wheels in the step 2 position and returning to step 3.
   - Try to take pressure off the heel brake by finding a better NKT alignment on the support leg.
   - Avoid putting weight on any part of the support leg's toes when you are rolling in step 3.
   - Steering is accomplished during step 3 when the action toe tilts, causing the rear wheel to initiate an outside or inside edge. Stopping or slowing straight ahead will always be on center edges.
   - Always maintain your weight on the support foot's heel.

4. To stop quickly, bend the support leg further. Back position is upright but slouched, and eyes are forward. Keeping your knee bent and maintaining steady pressure (still at least 75 percent on the support leg) through the heel will allow for balance and

A

B

C

D

Figure 19-17 Heel stop.

A   B   C

Figure 19-18 Parallel turn.

stability even in a fast stop. Extend hands and arms slightly forward to counterbalance as the knee bend increases (see Figure 19-17D).

▶ Learning Hints

1. Experiment with different degrees of knee bend. Feel how straightening the knee allows speed to return.
2. Pick a specific spot to stop as a goal.
3. Be comfortable before climbing farther up the incline.
4. Try skating faster and stopping shorter using the same starting positions on the inclines.
5. As your comfort and skill build, pick a slightly higher point on the incline and begin heel brake skills anew.

Parallel Turns

Prerequisite: Scissor back position

A more advanced turning technique than the A-frame turn is the parallel turn, which allows you to turn quickly without losing speed. This skill uses a scissor back position, corresponding edges, and rotary motion to maintain speed. Some speed is necessary. Look around first to determine whether it is safe to turn. The following instructions are for a right turn:

1. Assume a scissor back position, balanced on the right foot. Maintain your weight on the heel of the forward (right) skate. The lead leg will be bent and balanced in NKT alignment. The back leg will be straighter than the support leg (Figure 19-18A).
2. Shift your body slightly to the right so that corresponding edges are achieved (Figure 19-18B).

Direction of travel is still forward at this point. An immediate turn indicates you are leaning too far to the right.

3. Still looking, twist your hips clockwise with rotary motion, without twisting your shoulders or arms toward the turn (Figure 19-18C).
4. Orient your hips, then your arms and shoulders, toward the goal as you complete the turn, ending in a ready position.

▶ Learning Hints

1. Using a toe roll for step 1 will reinforce the balance of a parallel turn.
2. During the entire sequence, following a path at eye level toward the goal direction is more important than directly watching the skating surface.
3. Learn to control the direction of the turn, even in the midst of the turn, using degrees of rotary motion.
4. Left turn: Opposite of the preceding steps.

Skill Assessment

The skating skills identified in this chapter for beginner to intermediate levels provide targets for assessing. Evaluating and judging the performance is based on *how* it is performed. The Skill Assessment section in the Gymnastic and Tumbling chapter provides guidance in constructing a checklist that requires either a Yes or No response identifying necessary mechanical capabilities for quality skill attainment.

This same approach can be used for assessing any of the ten inline skating skills listed by developing a checklist for each.

Modifications for Special Populations

Safety issues are a concern when teaching inline skating because skates are difficult to control and the potential for falling, skating out of control, or skating into obstacles is great. Choose a safe setting and activities that are appropriate and can be controlled. Protective gear should be of the highest quality, with maximum padding for safety. Individual circumstances must be considered to determine the appropriateness of inline skating as an activity for students with impairments. For all students, lessons on grass to experiment with balance are the best starting point, and any further lessons will depend on the student's capabilities with regard for safety.

ORTHOPEDICALLY IMPAIRED

1. Inline skating is not recommended for students with orthopedic impairment.
2. For students with balance impairment, consider the use of quad rollerskates on grass or walkers within a safe, controlled site.

COGNITIVELY IMPAIRED

1. Safety issues are a concern. Consider lessons on grass within a controlled site.
2. Use peer teachers or paraprofessionals to provide manual assistance until the student completely understands the activity.
3. Make sure all students with Down syndrome are screened for ATLANTO-AXIAL syndrome. This can be completed with an x-ray study of the C_1 and C_2 vertebrae.

SENSORY IMPAIRED

1. Inline skating is not recommended for students who are blind or have a visual impairment. If appropriate, partner visually impaired students with two peer teachers or paraprofessionals. The student can wear skates; the teachers should not wear skates. The teachers can take the student by each arm to support and pull the student, allowing the student to experiment with edging and other skating movements.
2. For students who are deaf or have a hearing impairment, provide lessons within a safe, controlled site, and make sure that visual cues are provided for starting and stopping skating.

Terminology

action leg The leg, usually opposite of the support leg, that does the "action" portion of the skill.

axle Axles attach wheels to frames. They come as a two-piece shaft and screw that attach to each other through the frame and wheel assembly or one piece passing through the frame and wheel assembly, attaching directly to the frame.

balance The state of the body when its center of gravity is above the base of support.

bearings Skate wheels use a rolling-element bearing, which carries a load by placing round elements between the two casings. The relative motion of the pieces causes the round elements to roll (tumble) with little sliding. Ball bearings make wheels spin more smoothly and reduce unwanted friction. There are two sets of bearings per wheel, one on each side. Each bearing contains individual ball bearings, which are evenly distributed around the inner casing and held together by an outer casing. Construction materials can vary.

brake The brake consists of a brake assembly and a brake pad. The brake assembly attaches either to the frame or the frame and the cuff of the skate. The brake pad should be replaced when worn.

center The middle of the wheel edge when it is perpendicular to the pavement.

center of mass An imaginary point around which the mass of the body is balanced. It is located just below the navel in most people.

coast Forward or backward movement without propulsion, rolling on two feet in either ready position or scissor position.

comfort zone The speed, conditions, and terrain with which the skater feels relaxed and confident.

corresponding edges The position in which both skates are angled in the same direction, with one skate on an outside edge and the other on an inside edge.

durometer Measurement for hardness of the wheel. A smaller number indicates a soft wheel. A larger number indicates a harder wheel. The symbol A on a urethane wheel denotes its durometer. A durometer is also an instrument that measures hardness on a scale from 0 to 100. There are many scales for different materials identified by different letters.

edging The angle of the wheel relative to the skating surface.

fall As part of a skating motion (as opposed to falling to the ground), the gravity-fed action that happens during the transfer of balance from one skate to the other. The fall begins as the action leg's push occurs and ends on a new support leg's NKT landing.

frame A skate frame attaches the wheels to the boot of the skate. Frames can accommodate three, four, or five wheels. Shorter frames offer better response for turns. Longer frames offer better stability for speed down hills.

glide Coasting on one skate.

inside edge The side of the wheel that is closest to the center line of the body.

nose-knees-toes (NKT) alignment A plumb position in which the skater stacks nose over knee over toes on the support leg.

outside edge The side of the wheel that is farthest from the center line of the body.

profile The shape of the wheel as it contacts the surface. A wide profile has more wheel in contact with the skating surface. A narrow profile is used for speed, having a low coefficient of friction.

protective gear Equipment designed to protect the body in case of a fall or collision. Basic protective gear includes a helmet, wrist guards, knee pads, elbow pads, and padded shorts.

rotary motion Turning around a central axis of the body.

spacer Plastic or aluminum hub that separates the bearing casings and allows the axle to pass through.

speed tolerance The ability to coast without fear.

striding The combination of gliding and stroking in a continuous, fluid motion.

stroke A skate push generated by straightening a knee and directing pressure down through the heel.

support leg The leg on which a greater amount of the skater's weight is balanced.

Discussion Questions

1. Discuss the physical benefits and advantages of inline skating.

2. Identify and discuss the progressive invention and development of the inline skate.

3. Discuss the basic skate features and the effect they have on the skating process.

4. Identify the "rules of the road" that enable skaters to coexist with pedestrians, cyclists, and other skaters.

5. Compare and contrast the various edging techniques and the effect they have on skating outcome.

6. Discuss how the NKT alignment affects success in skating.

7. Protective gear varies greatly in construction, material, and degree of protection. Discuss these factors as they relate to helmets, wrist guards, knee pads, elbow pads, and padded shorts.

Web Sites

http://inlineskating.about.com—provides information on history, health and fitness benefits tips, and physical needs.

www.inlineplanet.com—is an online magazine with skating articles, tutorials, and news.

www.skatecity.com—provides general information; has New York City affiliations.

www.rollerskatingmuseum.com—National Museum of Roller Skating provides the history of roller skating; based in Lincoln, Nebraska.

www.skatecentral.com—world-renowned inline speed skater Eddy Matzger's Web site features a wealth of information and images.

www.skatelog.com—includes articles and news about all types of skating, a frequently updated calendar of events, biographies and photos of skaters and events, and information about skating.

ORGANIZATIONS

Aggressive Skaters Association (ASA) **www.asaskate.com** The aggressive skaters organization for the inline skate industry.

USA Roller Sports (USARS) Roller Derby Guide **http://usars .info/misc/2012_Roller_Derby_Guide.pdf** Information on how to join USA Roller Sports and requirements for roller derby clubs.

Fédération Internationale de Roller Sports (FIRS) **www.rollersports.org/** The international governing body of roller skating.

Roller Skating Association International (RSA) **www.rollerskating.org** Trade association representing skating center owners and operators; teachers, coaches, and judges of roller skating; and manufacturers and suppliers of roller skating equipment.

CHAPTER 20 | Soccer

This chapter will enable you to

- Understand the origins and evolution of the game of soccer
- Identify and put into practice the rules governing the game
- Practice and then execute the basic skills, including kicking, passing, trapping, heading, tackling, the throw-in, and goalkeeping
- Discuss and employ basic offensive and defensive strategy and tactics
- Identify and discuss the nature of the game, including player responsibilities, field markings, and player positioning
- Identify and use basic terminology associated with the game

Nature and Purpose

Soccer is played with 11 players on each team. The game starts at midfield with a free kick called the kickoff as each team is in its own half of the field. The offensive objectives are to maintain possession of the ball, keep the ball wide until near the goal, and then get the ball in front of the opponent's goal where a player can propel it between the uprights, beneath the crossbar, and completely across the goal line for a score. The ball may be propelled with any part of the body except the hands and arms; however, the foot, body, and head are the main parts of the body used.

The defense's main objectives are to contain the opponents and the ball, forcing excessive passes; mark (guard) opponents in scoring position; tackle the opponent, taking the ball away whenever possible; funnel the ball to the middle of the field toward their own goal; and concentrate in front of their goal when the ball is in scoring position. The goalkeeper provides great assistance to the defense by being allowed to use the hands to contact the ball, and he also attempts to clear the ball away from the scoring area by throwing, punting, or drop-kicking it.

Systems of play are comprised of attackers (strikers/wings/forwards), midfielders (linemen/halfbacks), and defenders (stoppers/sweepers/fullbacks). The attacker's primary contribution to the system is scoring. The midfielders support the offense and are the first line of defense. The defenders support the midfielders and are the last line of defense. The defender's primary objective is defending against the opponent's attack. Systems are numbered from the defenders forward (e.g., 4–2–4), depending on the number of players comprising each of the three lines, excluding the goalkeeper.

The game is continuous, with no time-outs allowed, and time is stopped only for an injury, a temporary suspension of play by the official, the end of a period, or a score.

The players use basic skills of kicking, trapping, dribbling, heading, tackling, and throwing (where allowable) to propel or control the ball. The game is low scoring as a result of the difficulty of executing the skills, plus the nature of some rules.

The game requires constant adjustments by all players and calls for short sprinting plus slower jogging. Good physical conditioning is necessary. The constant activity, use of the big muscle groups, large numbers competing, and low equipment expense make the game highly suitable for competitors of all ages and sexes.

History

Although the modern game of soccer is popularly thought to have originated in England, there is considerable evidence to indicate that a game involving kicking a ball into a net was played around the 2nd or 3rd century in China. Other sources point to a similar activity played by the ancient Greeks and Romans.[1]

Early British folklore and literature cite activities that point toward the evolution of modern soccer. Ultimately, two different games developed: rugby—which allowed players to use both their hands and feet, and soccer*—which allowed only the use of feet.

*Note: The sport known as *soccer* in the United States is called *football* in Europe and South America. To avoid confusion with the U.S. game of football—also discussed in this section—this text uses soccer.

In 1846, a group of Cambridge University students who supported the kicking game—soccer—attempted to draw up a set of rules. These "Cambridge Rules" did not gain favor, but they did lead to a meeting in 1863 at Freemason's Tavern in London where the two camps attempted to resolve the rule differences. This meeting is recognized as the birth of "The Football [Soccer] Association" and separated the rugby supporters from the soccer proponents.

Historians agree that a form of the game appeared in the Americas as early as 1609. As in England, early participation resembled mob violence, resulting in a ban of the sport. However, by the early 1800s, versions of the game were being played on college campuses in the eastern United States. And as with the English games, there were two variations, one in which players ran with the ball in their hands, and another in which the ball was kicked and the use of hands was not allowed.

Some colleges attempted to adopt rules similar to "Association Football [Soccer]," which disallowed throwing or carrying the ball. Harvard's strong dissent from these rules and its participation in games with McGill University in Montreal in 1894 are considered the birth of what is now called football in the United States. After the formation of the Intercollegiate Football Association in 1876, the throwing and running game became the favorite among universities in the United States. Thereafter soccer's popularity diminished dramatically; there is no record of intercollegiate soccer in the United States from 1877 to 1902, during which U.S. football gained favor.

The kicking game, however, gained increasing acceptance overseas, and the Federation Internationale de Football Association (FIFA) was formed in 1904. The sport became an official Olympic event by 1908, with teams consisting of amateurs. Professional teams also formed in Europe and South America, and in 1903 FIFA held the first World Cup competition in Uruguay.

The United States Soccer Federation (USSF), originally known as the United States Soccer Football Association (USSFA), was founded in 1913 and is the governing body for most of soccer in the United States. The U.S. collegiate soccer community did not crown a national champion until 1959, when the National Collegiate Athletic Association and the National Association of Intercollegiate Athletics held tournaments. Soccer's popularity among younger players grew primarily as a result of the formation of local clubs, with the United States Youth Soccer Association (founded in 1974) leading the way. Most state high school associations now host championships for boys and girls.

Professional soccer in the United States started in 1933 with the founding of the American Soccer League. Several groups have come and gone. Currently, the Major League Soccer organization, founded in 1996, governs the professional game.[2] The sport is extremely popular worldwide, with FIFA estimating there are approximately 265 million men and women participating. This total, with the estimated 3 million officials involved, represents approximately 4 percent of the population in the world.[3]

Field of Play

A regulation field measures 100 to 120 yards in length and 65 to 75 yards in width (Figure 20-1). The dimensions and areas can easily be modified to suit the number, age, and sex of the participants. The field can be made longer or shorter and various grids can be applied (as discussed later) to provide practice areas for modified games.

In the list here, the numbers correspond to the numbers in the diagram of Figure 20-1.

1. *End line.* When the ball goes out of play over this line, it is put in play with either a (a) goal kick (offense last touched the ball) or (b) corner kick (defense last touched the ball).

2. *Goal area.* The area where the ball is placed for the defending team to take a goal kick. It is placed on the front line of the area in that half field in which the ball went out of play.

3. *Penalty area.* Restriction area where (a) the goalie is allowed to play the ball with the hands; (b) the offensive team has to stay out of when the defending team is taking a goal kick; (c) on the goal kick, the ball must be kicked out of this area for the ball to be legally in play; (d) if a foul committed in this area by the defending team results in a *direct free kick*, then a *penalty kick* is awarded to the team fouled; (e) players from both teams must stay outside on a penalty kick with the exception of the goalie and the person taking the penalty kick.

4. *Side or touch line.* A ball going out of bounds over this line is put in play with a throw-in by the opposite team of the one that last touched the ball.

5. *Penalty kick mark.* The spot where the ball is placed when a penalty kick results.

6. *Penalty kick arc.* This arc is a 10-yard radius from the ball, and players from both teams must stay behind it. On a penalty kick, both teams (except one offensive player and the goalie) must be out of the penalty area and at least 10 yards from the ball.

7. *Center, mid, or halfway line.* This line (a) ensures that both teams are in their own half of the field on the kickoff, and (b) is used to help regulate the offside rule.

8. *Center circle.* A 10-yard radius circle to restrict players of the defending team on the kickoff. They must stay out of the circle until the ball is contacted.

9. *Corner arc.* One yard from each corner there is a corner arc. The ball is placed on this arc when the offensive team is taking a corner kick.

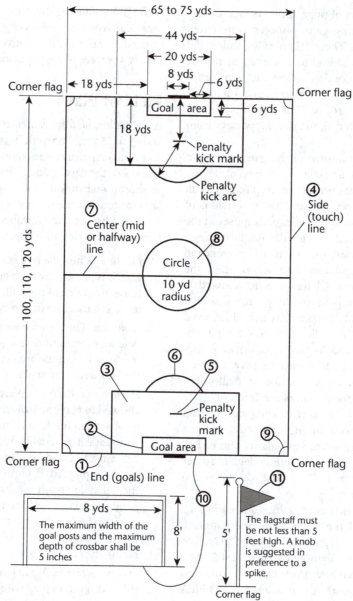

Figure 20-1 Regulation soccer field markings. (For further explanation of numbers, see text.)

10. *Goal line.* The line between the uprights of the goal. When the whole ball crosses it below the crossbar, either on the ground or in the air, a goal results.

11. *Corner flag.* The flag is at least 5 feet high and located in each of the four corners to assist in locating the boundary lines.

Basic Rules

Kickoff. At the beginning of the game, choice of ends and the kickoff are decided by the toss of a coin. The ball is placed in the center of the field on the halfway line, and the team kicking off plays the ball forward from the line. The player usually kicks the stationary ball legally (one circumference of the ball) forward to her teammate, attempting to maintain control of the ball. All players from both teams are in their own half of the field, with the defending team at least 10 yards from the ball. A goal cannot be scored from the kickoff.

Fouls. Fouls and misconduct committed during the course of play result in a free kick to the offended team. The severe infractions, which are most often injurious, result in a direct free kick, meaning a goal can be scored directly from that kick. A direct free kick foul occurring in the penalty area and against the defending team results in a penalty kick, the most severe infraction. Less severe infractions result in an indirect free kick, meaning someone else must contact the ball following the kick before a goal can be scored. When making a free kick, the opponents must be 10 yards from the ball, unless standing on their own goal line between the uprights, until the ball is kicked. The ball must be stationary on the free kick, must travel the circumference of the ball to be in play, and may not be recontacted by the kicker until someone else touches it.

Direct Free Kick Offenses. A direct free kick is awarded for any of the following offenses:

1. Handling the ball: intentionally contacting the ball with the hands or arms. This offense also applies to goalies outside the penalty area.

2. Holding an opponent with the hands or arms.

3. Pushing an opponent; includes the hands or arms.

4. Striking or attempting to strike an opponent; the goalie also is not allowed to use the ball to strike a player.

5. Jumping at an opponent.

6. Kicking or attempting to kick an opponent.

7. Tripping or attempting to trip an opponent.

8. Using the knee on an opponent.

9. Charging an opponent violently or dangerously; includes the goalie in the penalty area or from the rear unless being obstructed.

All direct kicks awarded to the attacking team in the penalty area are penalty kicks.

Indirect Free Kick Offenses.   An indirect free kick is awarded for any of the following offenses:

1. A player playing the ball a second time before it is played by another player at the kickoff, on a throw-in, on a free kick, on a corner kick, or on a goal kick (if the ball has passed outside the penalty area).

2. A goalkeeper holding the ball longer than 6 seconds without releasing it or punting. Running with the ball is permissible, but if it is dropped to the ground, the goalkeeper cannot touch it again with hands until an opponent touches it.

3. Making a substitution or resubstitution without reporting to the referee, or having a substitute replace the goalie without informing the referee and then handling the ball in the penalty area.

4. Persons other than the players entering the field of play without the referee's permission.

5. Dissenting by word or action with a referee's decision.

6. Discourteous behavior. For persistent infringement of the rules, a warning or expulsion may follow.

7. Dangerous play by raising the foot too high or head too low while attempting to play the ball, thus endangering a player.

8. Resuming play after a player has been ordered off the field.

9. Offside.

Figure 20-2 Legal charge.

10. Charging illegally (not violently or dangerously).

11. Interfering with or impeding the goalkeeper in any manner until the goalkeeper releases the ball, or kicking or attempting to kick the ball when it is in the goalkeeper's possession.

12. Obstruction other than holding.

13. Player leaving the field of play during the progress of the game without the consent of the referee.

Physical Contact.   Body contact is allowed provided it is legal. A legal charge consists of a gentle nudge (not violently or dangerously), shoulder to shoulder, in an upright position, at least one foot contacting the ground, the arms close to the sides of the body, and playing the ball at the exact moment (Figure 20-2). The body may not be used as an obstacle to shield an opponent from getting to the ball unless actually playing the ball at that moment. This obstruction (Figure 20-3) allows for an opponent legally to charge the person obstructing, provided the contact is not violent or dangerous.

Penalty Kick.   The penalty kick (Figure 20-4) is taken from any spot on the penalty mark; all players except the kicker and the goalkeeper must be outside the penalty area. The goalkeeper must stand, without moving the feet, on the goal line between the goal posts until the ball is kicked. For any infringement by the defending team, the kick is retaken if a goal does not result. On an infringement by the attacking team, other than the player making the kick, the kick is retaken if a goal results. An infringement by the player making the kick results in an indirect free kick by the opposing team at the spot where the violation occurred.

Figure 20-3   Legal obstruction. Note use of body to protect the ball while playing it.

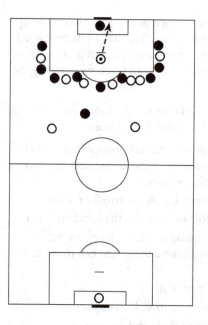

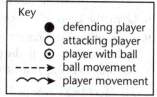

Key

- ● defending player
- ○ attacking player
- ◉ player with ball
- - - -> ball movement
- ∿∿∿> player movement

Figure 20-4   Penalty kick.

Goal Kick.   The ball is in play as long as it is not totally across the boundary lines (goal line or sideline), either on the ground or in the air. When it goes out of bounds over the goal line, the ball is put in play either with a goal kick (last touched by the attacking team) or a corner kick (last touched by the defending team). A ball put out-of-bounds over the sideline by a player is put in play with a throw-in by the opponents.

On the goal kick, the ball is placed on the front line of the goal area in that half of the field nearest to where it crossed the goal line (Figure 20-5). Any player on the team may take the kick. It is kicked from the ground. The opposing players remain outside the penalty area until the ball is kicked, and the ball must travel beyond the penalty area for it to be in play. The kick is retaken for any infringement.

Corner Kick.   The corner kick is taken by the offense from the arc in that half of the field nearest to where the ball crossed the goal line. A goal may be scored directly from the corner kick (Figure 20-6).

Throw-in.   The throw-in is taken from where the ball went out of play. It is thrown equally with both hands on the sides of the ball from a point behind the head and delivered directly over the head. Both feet must remain on the ground during the throw and be either in contact with the sideline or outside the field of play.

Offside.   The players must be concerned with their position in reference to the ball as play progresses. An offside infraction is called if a player is nearer the

opponent's goal line than the ball at the moment the ball is played, with limited exceptions. The offside rule is for assisting the defending team so that the offense will not be able to have players continually lurking in front of the goal. Lurking can lead to an unskilled game with team strategy consisting of no more than long, uncontrolled kicks from one end of the field to the other, and back again.

A player nearer the opponent's goal line than the ball at the moment the ball is played is considered *offside* (Figure 20-7B) unless (1) he is in his own half of the field of play (Figure 20-8); or (2) there are two opponents nearer their own goal line than he (Figure 20-7A); or (3) the ball was last touched by an opponent; or (4) he received the ball directly from a dropped ball by the referee, a goal kick, a corner kick, or a throw-in; or (5) he is behind the ball. A player in an offside position does not have to be penalized except if he is gaining an advantage by his position, seeking to gain an advantage, or interfering with an opponent. Once offside, the only way for a player to put himself onside again is if (1) an opponent next contacts the ball; (2) he is behind the ball when it is next contacted by his teammates; or (3) there are two opponents near their goal when he is in an advanced position of the ball and the ball is played to him by his teammates. The key factor for offside is always the position of the player in relation to the ball at the moment the ball is contacted.

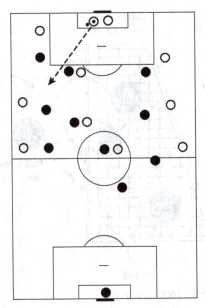

Figure 20-5 Goal kick.

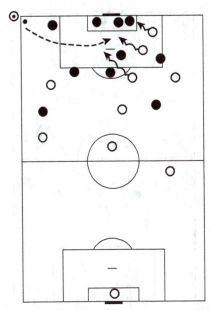

Figure 20-6 Corner kick.

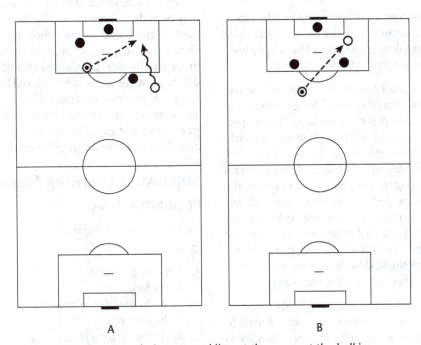

Figure 20-7 (A) Two opponents are nearer their own goal line at the moment the ball is played, *plus* the receiver is behind the ball at that moment—*not offside*. (B) Two opponents are *not* nearer their goal line—*offside*.

Dropped Ball. Temporary stopping of play while the ball is still playable results in the game restarting with a dropped ball. Two opponents face each other and the referee standing between them drops the ball to the ground for either to contact. It is dropped where the ball was when play stopped unless in the penalty area. Then it is brought to the nearest point outside the penalty area and dropped. Common reasons for a dropped ball occurring are (1) simultaneous contact by opponents, causing the ball to go out of bounds; (2) temporary stopping for injury; (3) the ball becoming deflated; or (4) simultaneous fouls by both teams.

Goalkeeper. When the ball nears the scoring area, the goalkeeper enjoys certain privileges not granted to other players while in the penalty area. The goalkeeper may use hands and arms to stop a ball from scoring; catch and hold it; punt, throw, or drop-kick the ball;

Figure 20-8   Player is in own half of field—*not offside*.

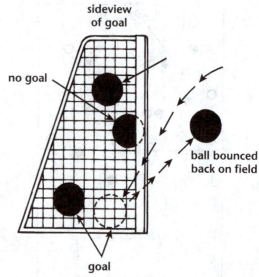

Figure 20-9   Scoring a goal.

and is free from interference by opponents while in possession of the ball (see item 2 under Indirect Free Kick Offenses for the complete goalie rule). The keeper loses these privileges when outside the penalty area.

Scoring.   A goal is scored when the whole of the ball passes over the goal line, between the goalposts, and under the crossbar, provided it has not been thrown, propelled by hand or arm, or carried by a player of the attacking side (Figure 20-9). If a member of the defending team, other than the goalie, deliberately deflects the ball with his hand or arm attempting to stop a goal, it should be scored a goal if it crosses the goal line between the uprights. Goals also may be scored on direct free kicks, penalty kicks, and corner kicks. A goal counts one point for the team scoring the goal. After a goal is scored, a kickoff is made at the center of the field by the team scored against. Teams change ends after each regular and extra period.

Time and Players.   How long the game lasts, number of substitutes allowed, and when substitutes are allowed to enter the game vary according to the age and ability levels of the players. The organizations governing competition provide rule guides; however, there are only minor differences in them. Men and women are playing by basically the same rules regardless of the organization, and quite often girls and boys play together at an early age (6 to 11).

Equipment

The only equipment absolutely necessary for playing soccer are a ball and two goals. There are many makes and price ranges of soccer balls. The molded ball with a rubber bladder, nylon wound carcass, and compressed weatherproof leather or synthetic panels is recommended. Goals can be purchased or may be constructed of two-by-fours

or pipe. Soccer shoes, shin guards, and nets for the goals may be added when progressing from physical education class to intramural to interscholastic competition levels. Gym shoes may be substituted for soccer shoes, thick magazines for shin guards, and chainlink fencing for nets. The fact that the game can be played by a large number of players at minimal expense makes it particularly appealing. Competition apparel is not a major factor. Colored jersey vests and game jerseys are inexpensive. For pants, gym shorts, sweatsuits, or game trunks may be worn.

Suggested Learning Sequence

BEGINNING LEVEL

A. Stretching and running

B. Basic rules

C. Fundamental skills
1. Kicking
   a. Inside of foot push pass
   b. Instep
2. Trapping (receiving)
   a. Sole of the foot
   b. Inside of the foot
   c. Chest
3. Dribbling
   a. Inside of the foot
   b. Outside of the foot
4. Heading; power standing
5. Tackling: front
6. Throw-in: standing
7. Goalkeeping
   a. Catch—roll or bounce
   b. Catch—waist or chest
   c. Catch—head or above
   d. Punt

D. Strategies
  1. Tactics
     a. Possession
     b. Space—receiving ball
  2. Group
     a. Superiority around ball
  3. Team
     a. Communication
     b. Functional training combining two or more positional lines

E. Principles
  1. Attacking
     a. Depth/support
     b. Width
     c. Penetration
  2. Defending
     a. Delay
     b. Depth/support
     c. Width
     d. Balance

F. Systems
  1. W formation
  2. M-W formation
  3. Defensive style—zone
  4. Offensive style—static positioning, long pass, and short pass

G. Restarts
  1. Corner kick
  2. Goal kick
  3. Throw-in
  4. Kickoff

INTERMEDIATE LEVEL

A. Partner stretching and interval training

B. Review beginning unit

C. Fundamental skills
  1. Kicking
     a. Outside of foot
     b. Lofting the ball
  2. Trapping (receiving)
     a. Outside of foot
  3. Dribbling
     a. Screening
     b. Sole of the foot
  4. Heading: power jumping
  5. Tackling: side
  6. Throw-in: running
  7. Goalkeeping
     a. Tip
     b. Throw—overhand

D. Strategies
  1. Review beginning unit
  2. Tactics
     a. Space-creating

  3. Group
     a. Space-restricting
     b. Tempo
  4. Team
     a. Rhythm
     b. Functional training involving tactical passing restrictions

E. Principles
  1. Attacking
     a. Mobility
     b. Improvisation
  2. Defending
     a. Concentration
     b. Control

F. Systems
  1. 4–2–4
  2. 3–3–4
  3. Defensive style—diagonal and player to player
  4. Offensive style—dribbling and fast/slow

G. Restarts
  1. Indirect free kicks
  2. Direct free kicks
  3. Defensive wall

Skills and Techniques

The fundamentals of soccer are dribbling, heading, trapping, kicking (shoot or pass), tackling, throwing, and goalkeeping. Because the game of soccer is primarily a kicking and trapping game, it is essential that players master the technique of controlling the ball without use of the hands or arms. In observing good soccer players, one sees that they control the ball and keep it reasonably close to their bodies when passing or advancing it down the field. The ball is kept close to the ground and not kicked into the air where it is difficult for the player to keep possession and control.

When learning or teaching each of the skills, keep in mind that the following factors are important for understanding common problems, both their causes and corrections:

1. Alignment to ball
   a. Position the body early in preparation to contact the ball.
   b. Position at the best spot in the line of flight for making initial contact.
   c. Prepare the contact surface at the proper angle required for optimum execution.
   d. Be as stable as possible.

2. Base
   a. Position the feet for optimum stability.
   b. Position the feet so that the contact surface can be at the proper angle for execution.
   c. Position the grounded foot in the direction the ball is to be propelled or received.

3. Whole body position
   a. Position specifically the feet, knees, hips, shoulders, arms, and head before, during, and after ball contact.

4. Power/absorption

Power
   a. Ball contact surface—speed of ball
   b. Joints providing force—range of motion and speed of motion
   c. Proper line of force (see #5)
   d. Total body parts alignment as they relate to the desired trajectory
   e. Follow-through (see #7)

Absorption
   a. Ball contact surface—speed of ball
   b. Joints involved in receiving force
   c. Proper line of receiving force (see #5)
   d. Total body parts alignment as they relate to receiving the trajectory and force of the ball
   e. Direction (away from ball) of body parts used for absorbing the ball

5. Line of giving/receiving force
   a. Correct direction of all body parts related to the desired trajectory, rotation (spin), and final destination of the ball

6. Ball contact
   a. Surface and angle of body part used to make contact
   b. Exact spot on the ball to contact for accomplishing the desired end result
   c. Alignment to ball (see #1)
   d. Base (see #2)
   e. Whole body (see #3)
   f. Power/absorption (see #4)
   g. Line of giving/receiving force (see #5)

7. Follow-through
   a. Full range of motion (arc) of the primary power joints used and the exact point at which to stop to provide the desired power plus trajectory to the ball
   b. When receiving the impetus (trapping) of the ball, the primary joints used in recoiling, giving, or absorbing that lead to cushioning the impact—follow-through away from the line of flight of the ball.

Each of these factors will be considered as we discuss the learning hints for performing each specific skill or technique. Either a *B* (Beginning) or *I* (Intermediate) is indicated with each skill or technique to designate the appropriate ability level for presenting that skill. Where suitable, verbal learning hints are given in capital letters.

KICKING (PASS OR SHOT)

Kicking is primarily used for passing, shooting, and clearing. The rotation (spin) on the ball denotes proper

Figure 20-10 Inside of foot push pass.

or improper contact. Different parts of the foot can be used to contact the ball.

▶ Learning Hints: Inside of Foot Push Pass (B)

1. *Alignment to ball.* Quickly position as near the direct flight (180 degrees) of the ball as possible—ALIGNMENT.

2. *Base.* Place grounded foot toward target and position it to the side of the ball approximately 6 to 12 inches and either even with or slightly behind the ball (Figure 20-10A), depending on desired flight (on the ground or in the air)—GROUNDED FOOT. Knee slightly flexed.

3. *Whole body position.* Contact foot raised with toe pointed out—TOE OUT; knee pointed out—KNEE OUT; and ankle joint locked at 90-degree angle—ANKLE LOCKED. Draw leg backward from the hip in a straight line. Raise the contact leg to the rear, bending the knee until the lower leg is close to parallel with the ground with the inside of the foot facing the ground—COCKED POSITION (Figure 20-10B). Position head directly above ball (to keep ball on ground) or slightly behind the ball (to loft off ground)—HEAD. Hips and shoulders near 90 degrees to approaching ball, with slight pivot out as the contact leg is drawn back. Arms comfortable, away from body for balance (Figure 20-10).

4. *Power.* Power results from the height that the contact foot is raised off the ground (Figure 20-10B), the speed that the contact leg is snapped forward

Figure 20-11 Inside of foot push pass. Note leg, ankle, and knee of contact foot.

Figure 20-12 Instep kick. Note toe, ankle, and knee of contact foot.

to meet the ball, the speed of the approaching ball, correct ball-foot contact (hard surface), and the amount of follow-through.

5. *Line of giving force.* The foregoing power items applied in the correct line depend on the approaching flight of the ball and the desired final destination. The correct line involves the body alignment to the ball (as near 180 degrees as possible), the direction the grounded foot is pointed (Figure 20-11A), straight linear (180 degrees) cocking of the contact leg, and the straight linear snap down plus follow-through of that leg—LINE OF FORCE.

6. *Ball contact.* The correct contact surface is the hard area near the heel of the foot and ankle area (Figure 20-11B) with the inside of the foot facing the approaching ball. The ball is contacted near its midline and either high, middle, or low depending on the desired speed and trajectory.

7. *Follow-through.* The height the contact foot and leg are allowed to lift after contact depends on the desired trajectory or force.

▶ Learning Hints: Instep Kick (B)

1. *Alignment to ball.* Approach the path of the ball from a 45-degree angle—ALIGNMENT.

2. *Base.* Same as inside of foot push pass except the grounded foot is approximately 10 to 18 inches to the side of the ball—GROUNDED FOOT. Knee flexed.

3. *Whole body position.* Contact foot lifted with toe pointed down—TOE DOWN; knee rotated in—KNEE IN; and ankle joint locked as near 180 degrees with the lower leg as possible—ANKLE LOCKED (Figure 20-12). Lift heel upward toward the buttocks—COCKED POSITION. Hip extends and rotates

slightly. Position head directly above the ball (to keep ball on ground) or slightly behind the ball (to loft off ground)—HEAD. Hips and shoulders should be near 90 degrees to approaching ball with slight pivot out as contact leg is drawn back. Arms should be comfortably away from the body for balance.

4. *Power.* Power results from the height that the contact foot is raised—HEEL RAISED, the speed that the contact leg is snapped forward to meet the ball—SPEED, the speed of the approaching ball, correct ball-foot contact, and the amount of follow-through.

5. *Line of giving force.* The foregoing power items applied in the correct line depend on the approaching flight of the ball and the desired final destination. The approach angle of the body to the flight of the ball approximates 45 degrees. The grounded foot is pointed toward the intended destination (Figure 20-12A) as the remainder of the power joints naturally correct to a direct alignment with the desired line of flight.

6. *Ball contact.* The correct contact surface is the hard area on the top of the arch (Figure 20-12B). The ball is contacted near the midline and either high, middle, or low depending on the desired speed and trajectory.

7. *Follow-through.* The height the foot and leg are allowed to lift is dependent on desired trajectory or force.

▶ Learning Hints: Lofting the Ball (I)

1. *Alignment to ball.* Same as for instep kick.

2. *Base.* The grounded foot is approximately 10 to 18 inches to the side of the ball and slightly behind it. Knee flexed.

3. *Whole body position.* Same as for instep kick, except that the head is positioned slightly behind the vertical plane of the ball—HEAD BACK.

Figure 20-13 Outside of the foot kick. Note toe, ankle, and knee of contact foot.

Figure 20-14 Outside of the foot kick and dribble. Note toe, knee of contact leg, and contact surface.

4–7. *Power, line of giving force, ball contact, follow-through.* All same as for instep kick.

▶ Learning Hints: Outside of Foot Kick (I)

1. *Alignment to ball.* Same as inside of foot push pass.

2. *Base.* Same as for inside of foot push pass.

3. *Whole body position.* Contact foot lifted with the toe extended down and rotated inward—TOE DOWN AND IN; knee rotated in—KNEE IN; and ankle joint locked—LOCKED ANKLE. Lift heel backward and upward toward the buttocks—COCKED POSITION (Figure 20-13).

4–5. *Power* and *line of giving force.* Same as for inside of foot push pass.

6. *Ball contact.* The correct contact area is the hard area on the top outside surface of the foot (Figure 20-14). The ball is contacted near the midline and either high, middle, or low depending on the desired trajectory and speed.

7. *Follow-through.* Same as for instep kick.

TRAPPING

Many surfaces of the body can be used to trap (catch) the ball. Trapping means controlling a ball that is received by a player. There is "immediate" or "deflect" trapping. The first denotes control of the ball right where the player receives it, while the second means redirecting the ball close to the receiver (3 to 4 feet) to avoid an on-rushing opponent. When a body trap is used, a foot trap usually follows to "settle" the ball to the ground.

▶ Learning Hints: Sole of Foot Trap (B)

1. *Alignment to ball.* Quickly position as near to a direct line (180 degrees) with the path of the ball as possible—ALIGNMENT.

2. *Base.* Body weight is totally supported by the grounded foot as the contact leg is raised with the sole facing the approaching ball.

3. *Whole body position.* Ankle of contact foot is flexed (90 degrees) with toe higher than heel, toe up, providing a wedge-like surface for ball contact. The contact leg and foot are extended in front of the body and reach out as the grounded leg provides support with a slight flexion of the knee. Hips and shoulders should be near 90 degrees to the approaching ball. Arms should be slightly away from body to provide balance and stability.

4. *Absorption.* The ball at contact is cushioned by slightly flexing the knee of the contact leg and slightly flexing the knee of the support leg with a slight pike at the waist, which moves the head forward toward the ball—GIVE.

5. *Line of receiving force.* The foregoing absorption factors are applied as near a direct line with the path of the ball as possible.

6. *Ball contact.* The ball is contacted on the top and slightly to the rear by the sole of the foot. The contact foot approximates a 45-degree angle with the ground, providing a wedge between the sole of the foot and the ground.

7. *Follow-through.* There is negative follow-through as the contact leg and foot at impact gives in the same direction that the ball is traveling to stop the ball.

▶ Learning Hints: Inside of Foot Trap (B)

1–3. *Alignment to ball, base,* and *whole body position.* Same as for inside of foot push pass (Figure 20-15).

Figure 20-15   Inside of the foot trap. Note alignment to ball, base, and whole body position.

Figure 20-16   Chest trap.

4. *Absorption.* The force of the ball is cushioned by the soft, relaxed contact surface, the wedging of the ball against the ground by the contact foot—WEDGE, and the movement of the contact leg away from the path of the ball at about the same speed of the approaching ball—GIVE.

5. *Line of receiving force.* The foregoing absorption factors applied in the correct line depend on the path of the ball and the desired final destination for the ball. The correct line involves the body alignment to the ball (as near 180 degrees as possible), direction the grounded foot is pointed, angle of the contact foot, and direction the contact leg is moved on impact.

6. *Ball contact.* The correct contact surface is the soft area on the inside of the foot near the arch. The ball is contacted on the top and back, wedging it to the ground to the rear of the grounded foot for "immediate" control. It is contacted nearer the bottom and back (imparting back spin) in advance of the grounded foot for "deflecting" the ball away from but close to the body.

7. *Follow-through.* The contact leg lowers the foot on the ball, wedging it (immediate control), or the leg and foot make a relaxed, sweeping action, "deflecting" the ball away from but close to the body.

▶ Learning Hints: Chest Trap (B)

1. *Alignment to ball.* Quickly position as near to a direct line (180 degrees) with the path of the ball as possible.

2. *Base.* The feet are in a staggered stance, with the body weight evenly distributed—STANCE.

3. *Whole body position.* The knees are flexed, hips thrust forward bending backward, shoulders back farther than the hips, placing the upper chest near parallel with the ground, the head away from the body for balance—BACKBEND (Figure 20-16).

4. *Absorption.* On ball contact, the knees flex deeper, allowing the chest to "give" quickly, absorbing the impact.

5. *Line of receiving force.* Same as item 4. The ball rebounds off the chest in a low upward trajectory, falling to the ground near the feet. Turning the shoulders at impact causes the ball to rebound to the side of the body, if desired.

6. *Ball contact.* The contact surface is the high, flat part of the chest just below the throat.

7. *Follow-through.* Following contact and rebound, quickly stand straight and prepare to "settle" the ball to the ground by using one of the foot traps—SETTLE.

▶ Learning Hints: Outside of Foot Trap (I)

1. *Alignment to ball.* Same as for sole of the foot trap. The path of the ball is to the outside of the grounded foot—approximately 6 to 12 inches.

2. *Base.* Body weight is totally supported by the grounded leg while the contact leg is off the ground.

3. *Whole body position.* The contact leg reaches across and in front of the grounded leg—REACH ACROSS, with the ankle rotated inward and down, preparing the outside of the foot for contact. The upper body leans—LEAN, at an angle in the direction the ball is to be deflected. The arms are away from the body for balance.

4–5. *Absorption* and *line of receiving force.* The sweeping action of the contact leg from one side of the body to the other—SWEEP, absorbs force and controllably deflects the ball in the desired direction (approximately 90 degrees) away from the approaching flight of the ball. The ankle rotates out with a flicking action—ANKLE FLICK.

Figure 20-17 Outside of the foot trap.

Figure 20-18 Inside of the foot dribble.

6. *Ball contact.* The contact surface is the outside of the foot, and the contact is high on the ball. The ankle that is rotated inward and downward before contact makes a forceful outward rotation at impact—ANKLE FLICK, flicking the ball to the side of the body as the whole contact leg sweeps across the body (Figure 20-17).

7. *Follow-through.* The contact leg sweeps across and in front of the body in the direction that the body is leaning, providing controlled redirection to the ball.

DRIBBLING

The skill of dribbling involves controllably propelling the ball with the feet in an effort to move the ball to another area without relinquishing possession to another player. Different surfaces of the foot can be used to dribble.

▶ Learning Hints: Inside of Foot Dribble (B)

1. *Alignment to ball.* The body is directly behind the ball prior to contact.

2. *Base.* The grounded foot is behind and to the inside of the ball while the other foot is slightly off the ground for contact.

3. *Whole body position.* The body is in a continuous running action, with the ball making repetitive contacts with either foot (Figure 20-18).

4. *Power/absorption.* The contact surface (inside of the foot) can provide either force or absorption, depending on how close to the body one wants to keep the ball.

5. *Line of giving/receiving force.* The speed of the running action provides force at contact. Contacting

high on the ball takes away force and keeps the ball close, contacting near the middle applies force forward, and contacting low on the ball lifts the ball, which is not desired.

6. *Ball contact.* The toe of the contact foot is pointed out; knee out, foot slightly off the ground, and sole parallel to the ground. The angle of the contact surface depends on the path desired for the ball after impact.

7. *Follow-through.* There is a continuous running action, with repetitive contacts with the ball by either foot, TAP-TAP, propelling it along the ground in a controlled action.

▶ Learning Hints: Outside of Foot Dribble (B)

1–3. *Alignment to ball, base,* and *whole body position.* All same as for inside of the foot dribble.

4. *Power/absorption.* The contact surface (outside of the foot) can provide either force or absorption, depending on how close to the body one wants to keep the ball.

5. *Line of giving/receiving force.* Same as for inside of the foot dribble.

6. *Ball contact.* The toe of the contact foot is pointed in and extended, down, with the knee inwardly turned. The contact surface is high on the outside of the foot near the ankle joint. The angle of the contact surface depends on the path desired for the ball after contact (Figure 20-19).

7. *Follow-through.* Same as for inside of the foot dribble.

Figure 20-19　Outside of the foot dribble.

Figure 20-20　Screening. Note leaning body contact.

▶ Learning Hints: Screening (I)

1–2. *Alignment to ball* and *base*. Same as for inside of the foot dribble.

3. *Whole body position*. The body and ball are under definite control as the body is used to screen the opponent from the ball. Slight leaning contact against the opponent aids in protecting the ball plus determining the path the opponent desires to take to reach the ball (Figure 20-20).

4. *Power/absorption*. None.

5. *Line of giving/receiving force*. Light leaning force against the opponent.

6–7. *Ball contact* and *follow-through*. Which dribbling technique (inside, outside, or sole of the foot) the player decides to use depends on how the player wants to keep the ball away from the opponent. These techniques are often used in combination to feint the opponent prior to breaking away.

HEADING

The head is used to play the ball when shooting, passing, or clearing the ball. Beginners use the *standing* approach; intermediates use the *jumping* play.

▶ Learning Hints: Power Heading, Standing (B)

1. *Alignment to ball*. Quickly position as near as possible to a direct line (180 degrees) with the path of the ball.

2–3. *Base* and *whole body position*. Same as for chest trap (see Figure 20-16).

4–5. *Power* and *line of force*. From the foregoing position the whole body snaps forward—SNAP (Figure 20-21). The upper body starts forward as the arms are vigorously thrust backward—ARMS; the weight transfers more to the front foot and the neck snaps—NECK SNAP, thrusting the head toward the ball. All are directed in a straight line toward the approaching ball.

6. *Ball contact*. The contact surface is near the hair line on the forehead. The contact on the ball is dependent on the desired trajectory and target. Low ball contact propels the ball upward, middle contact propels the ball straight forward parallel with the ground, while high ball contact propels the ball downward to the ground.

7. *Follow-through*. All power components continue forward following contact, providing continued force and direction.

▶ Learning Hints: Power Heading, Jumping (I)

1. *Alignment to ball*. Same as for power heading, standing. Position in the arc of the trajectory where the ball can be contacted with a maximum height jump.

2. *Base*. A two-foot takeoff provides stability while suspended in air. A running one-foot takeoff provides height in jumping. Use both where desirable.

3. *Whole body position*. The arms are close to the sides, the back arches, and the neck cocks in preparation for contact.

4. *Power*. The proper contact surface, back, neck, and proper jump timing assist with power as the upper

Figure 20-21 Power heading: Standing position.

Figure 20-22 Front tackling.

body snaps forward to meet the ball while suspended in mid-air.

5–6. *Line of giving force* and *ball contact*. Same as for power heading, standing.

7. *Follow-through.* Same as for power heading, standing. A two-feet landing after execution of the skill is necessary for stability.

TACKLING

The tackle is a skill used for taking the ball away from an opponent and maintaining control of the ball following that confrontation. Beginners use the frontal approach; for intermediates, tackling may be from the side.

▶ Learning Hints: Front Tackle (B)

1. *Alignment of ball.* Quickly position as near as possible to a direct line (180 degrees) with the path of the approaching player and ball (Figure 20-22).

2. *Base.* From a running approach, position the grounded foot near and to the side of the ball as that foot supports the full body weight.

3. *Whole body position.* The head is above or slightly in front of the ball, grounded foot, and flexed knee. The arms are down and close to the body, and the hips are behind the ball. All are in a forward-leaning position. The contact foot is slightly raised backward, with the toe and knee out.

4. *Power.* The knee of the contact leg snaps forward as the contact foot blocks the ball—BLOCK, at the same instant that the opponent makes contact. Do not kick the ball but block it, attempting to simultaneously tie up the ball.

5. *Line of giving force.* At that instant of contact, the near shoulder contacts the opponent with a gentle nudge. The straight contact leg is pushed/pulled forward from the groin—DRAG, as the whole body leans into the opponent, attempting to knock her off balance.

6. *Ball contact.* The ball is contacted exactly in the middle with the inside of the foot at the exact time the opponent makes contact, blocking the ball.

7. *Follow-through.* The whole body leans into the opponent as the contact foot lightly rolls over the top of the ball, causing it to roll over the opponent's foot and propelling it behind the opponent.

▶ Learning Hints: Side Tackle (I)

1. *Alignment to ball.* The approach angle is from the side at approximately 90 degrees to the path of the player.

2. *Base.* Same as for front tackle. The grounded foot is firmly planted in a direct line (180 degrees) with the path of the player and ball.

3. *Whole body position.* The firm plant of the grounded foot and transfer of total body weight to that foot allow the body to correct itself, facing the oncoming player as in the front tackle. (Refer to Front Tackle.)

4–7. *Power, line of giving force, ball contact, follow-through.* Same as for front tackle.

Figure 20-23 Throw-in: Standing or running.

THROW-IN

The throw-in is the only time that players, other than the goalkeeper, can use their hands to propel the ball. This move is allowable only when the ball goes out of bounds over the touch line.

▶ Learning Hints: Standing Throw-in (B)

1. *Alignment to field.* Face in the direction that you intend to deliver the ball.
2. *Base.* Either a parallel or staggered stance can be used. The staggered stance (Figure 20-23) provides the best stability for a forceful throw.
3. *Whole body position.* From the stance, the back arches and arms raise the ball directly over and to a position behind the head.
4. *Power.* The snap forward of the arms, wrists, and upper body provides power.
5. *Line of giving force.* All power factors are delivered in a straight line as the body weight transfers to the front foot. The back foot must stay in contact with the ground throughout the throw.
6. *Ball contact.* The hands must be on the side of the ball and the ball delivered equally with both hands.
7. *Follow-through.* See #5.

▶ Learning Hints: Running Throw-in (I)

1. *Alignment to field.* Same as standing throw-in.
2. *Base.* A run prior to delivery, with a skip step followed by a stride (staggered), stance is used.
3–7. Same as for standing throw-in.

GOALKEEPING

The goalkeeper uses skills for fielding and for clearing the ball. The hands may be used while in the penalty area. Catches are made in different positions, depending

Figure 20-24 Kneeling catch: Roll or bounce ball.

on how the ball arrives. Clearing involves either throwing or kicking skills.

▶ Learning Hints: Kneeling Catch—Roll or Bounce (B)

1. *Alignment to ball.* Quickly position in a direct line (180 degrees) with the path of the ball.
2. *Base.* Kneeling (Figure 20-24), the knee of one leg and foot of the other are placed on the ground on opposite sides of the path of the ball for stability and blocking purposes. Standing (Figure 20-25), the feet are placed together in a direct path with the flight of the ball.
3. *Whole body position.* Kneeling, the hands and arms are extended downward in front of the body to receive the ball. The lower leg of the kneeling limb is placed at an angle (45 degrees or greater) directly behind the path of the ball to block it if it gets past the hands. The head is directly above the ball, and the shoulders are 90 degrees to the path of the ball. Standing, the upper body bends over at the waist with both legs straight. The hands and arms are extended downward in front of the legs to receive the ball. The head is directly over the ball, and the shoulders are 90 degrees to the path of the ball.
4. *Absorption.* The soft contact surface (hands) makes initial contact as the ball is curled to the forearms, biceps, and chest.
5. *Line of receiving force.* The movement of the contact surface and absorption factors away from the line

Figure 20-25 Standing catch: Roll or bounce ball (front view).

Figure 20-26 Catch: Ball head high or above.

of flight at about the same speed as the ball assist in receiving the force.

6. *Ball contact.* The little fingers of both hands are close together, all fingers are spread, and the palms are facing the approaching ball. This surface contacts the ball below its center, bringing it to the forearms, biceps, and chest in one smooth curling action.

7. *Follow-through.* Immediately stand up for balance and stability.

► Learning Hints: Catch—Waist or Chest High Ball (B)

1. *Alignment to ball.* Same as for catching a rolling or bouncing ball.

2. *Base.* The feet are even in a parallel stance.

3. *Whole body position.* The hips and shoulders are parallel with the goal line. The hands and arms are extended together in front of the body, reaching forward for the ball.

4. *Absorption.* A ball traveling at a slower speed is cushioned the same way as when catching a rolling or bouncing ball, by first contacting the hands, forearms, biceps, and finally chest. A fast-approaching ball is cushioned by taking some of the impact immediately on the body while simultaneously curling the hands and arms around the ball as in catching a rolling ball. A slight jump in the air at contact also aids in absorption.

5–6. *Receiving force* and *ball contact.* Same as for catching a rolling or bouncing ball.

7. *Follow-through.* Bring the knee forward for protection against approaching players, if necessary.

► Learning Hints: Catch—Ball Head High or Above (B)

1. *Alignment to ball.* Same as for catching a rolling or bouncing ball (Figure 20-26).

2. *Base.* From a parallel stance, raise the knee of one leg forward, while the weight is supported on the other (exactly the same if a jump is required).

3. *Whole body position.* The hips and shoulders are parallel with the goal line, while the arms extend upward and forward to the desired height for fielding the ball.

4. *Absorption.* The soft contact surface (hands) makes initial contact as the ball is quickly brought to the chest area for protection.

5. *Line of receiving force.* Movement by the contact surface and arms is away from the line of flight at the same speed as the approaching ball.

6. *Ball contact.* The thumbs of both hands are close together, all fingers are spread apart, and the palms are facing the approaching ball. This surface contacts the ball near its center and brings the ball to the chest area in one smooth action.

7. *Follow-through.* Land with both feet in a wide stance and lower the hips to a medium standing position for balance and stability.

► Learning Hints: Tip (I)

1. *Alignment to ball.* Same as for catching a rolling or bouncing ball.

2–3. *Base* and *whole body position.* Same as for catching a ball above the head.

4–5. *Power* and *line of giving force*. The contact surface (one or two hands) thrusts upward and backward, deflecting the ball over the crossbar.

4. *Ball contact*. The ball is contacted on its bottom area with the heel of the palm(s) as the wrist(s) is flexed for deflecting the ball upward and backward.

5. *Follow-through*. The knee is brought forward for protection, and the landing is on two feet for stability.

▶ Learning Hints: Punt (B)

1. *Alignment to ball*. Hold the ball with both hands in front of the body.

2. *Base*. From a walking or running motion, transfer the body weight to one foot while the other prepares to kick the ball.

3. *Whole body position*. Bring the kicking leg behind the body with a high heel raise as you extend arms in front with the ball in the hands preparing to drop it.

4. *Power*. The proper contact surface, the height that the contact foot is raised behind the body, the speed that the contact leg is snapped forward to meet the ball as it is dropped, and the amount of follow-through all provide power.

5. *Line of giving force*. The foregoing power factors applied as near as possible to a 180-degree angle with the intended flight provide the line and amount of force.

6. *Ball contact*. The ball is contacted in the back/bottom area. The closer to the ground that the ball falls prior to contact, the lower its trajectory. The contact surface is the top hard area of the foot (instep).

7. *Follow-through*. As it continues to lift following contact, the contact leg provides both height and force as the grounded foot supports the body weight.

▶ Learning Hints: Overhand Throw (I)

1. *Alignment to ball*. The thrower holds the ball near the shoulder at the side.

2. *Base*. A medium stance is used.

3. *Whole body position*. Hold the ball in one hand and bring it behind the body about head high, with the arm flexed. Extend the nonthrowing arm in front of the body for balance. Keep the knees slightly flexed. Rotate the hips and shoulders slightly toward the throwing arm.

4. *Power*. The distance that the ball is brought behind the body, the speed that the throwing arm is brought forward and the nonthrowing arm is brought back, and the follow-through of the throwing arm plus the upper body all provide power.

5. *Line of giving force*. The foregoing power factors applied in a straight line provide maximum force and the desired direction.

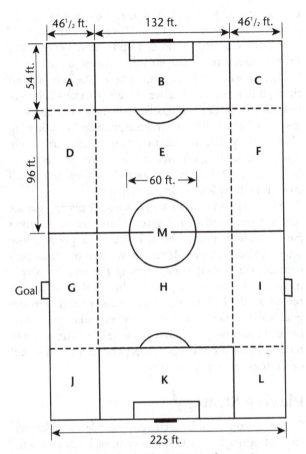

Figure 20-27 Grid for setting up practice areas.

6. *Ball contact*. Hold the ball in the palm of the throwing hand and at the back/bottom of the ball.

7. *Follow-through*. As it releases the ball overhand, the throwing arm continues forward and the body bends forward, providing force and direction.

Suggestions for Modified Practice Games and Areas

Figure 20-27 is a model grid showing various ways of modifying a regulation field to provide areas of different sizes. The larger the area, the more competitors possible. Examples are 2 on 1, 3 on 1, 2 on 2, 3 on 2, 3 on 3, 4 on 2, 4 on 3, 4 on 4, 5 on 3, 5 on 4, 5 on 5, and so on. A modified goal, objective, or soccer strategy and tactic are used in the games. Cones, flags, or other players are used as two-sided goals. These may be placed opposite each other on the end line of the area, slightly on the field with space behind them or in the middle of the area. One, two, or more goals may be used.

Combining grids allows for actual games with modified field sizes. An example is using grids D, E, and F together, placing a goal on the sideline of the field and centered in the middle of the area. The size of the field is now 96 feet by 225 feet, where an actual game might consist of 6 on 6, 7 on 7, or 8 or 8. Two games may be played at once if grids G, H, and I are used similarly.

Combining areas A through F provides an even wider field, whereby more players can compete in an across-field game, as in the foregoing example. The same area (A through F) is used to practice offense (attackers and midfielders) versus defense (goalie, defenders, and midfielders) playing half field as on the regulation field. Scoring objectives are that the offense gets one point for scoring a goal, hitting the goalposts, or causing the goalkeeper to field the ball. Defense scores one point if they get the ball past the halfway line under their control.

Here are some other suggestions for playing games within a restricted area: A given number of consecutive passes without losing the ball receives a point; allow only one contact per player; allow no more than two contacts per player; after receiving the ball the player must out-dribble an opponent; the receiver of a pass must take the ball (pass or dribble) away from her own goal before it next goes forward; every other pass must be in the air; no pass above knee height. The possible modifications are endless and dependent on what skill or strategy one wants to stress.

Playing Strategy

Skilled execution of the techniques blended with knowledge of principles, tactics, and systems leads to a winning combination in soccer. *Principles* are factors that lead to skillful, organized, controlled play. *Tactics* denotes the execution of techniques and application of principles in a competitive situation. These fall into categories of individual, group, and team. *Systems* refers to the formational placement of players on the field where they apply techniques, principles, and tactics.

PRINCIPLES

The basic principles are possession and space. Possession can be by one's own team (attack) or by the opponents (defend). The knowledgeable use of space when attacking or defending is the basis for successful play. The field size (space), understanding of the importance of each third of the field, attack principles, and defense principles provide the initial foundation for team play.

Space.   The position of players on the large field area (75 × 120 yds.) presents a variety of available spaces. When in possession of the ball, the objectives are to attack the space behind, between, or in front of the opponents or to create new spaces by forcing them to move. The defensive objective is to deny the use of these spaces. The larger the space, the more time a player has to maintain possession, leading to more controlled play.

Strategic Field Areas.   The field is divided into thirds (Figure 20-28). The following factors, when applied in each area, lead to systematic team coordination.

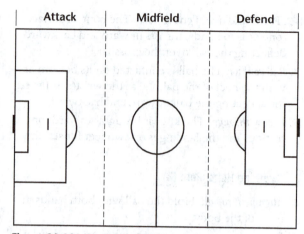

Figure 20-28   Strategic field areas.

DEFEND

1. Distribute the ball wide immediately upon possession.
2. Always provide support behind the teammate with ball.
3. Do not pass the ball across the goal mouth.
4. Do not give the ball away.
5. Control pass to midfield area as quickly as possible.
6. When in trouble, clear the ball (a) to midfield, (b) out of bounds over the sideline, (c) to goalie, or (d) over the end line (as a last resort).

MIDFIELD

1. Slow down the tempo of the ball and the players.
2. Maintain control.
3. Initiate diagonal cross-field flow of the ball.
4. Back pass to supporting players—reverse field to opposite side.
5. Penetrate to the attack zone.
6. Keep the ball wide.
7. Overlap extra players for numerical superiority.

ATTACK

1. Wide passes for control plus spread defense.
2. Penetrate with the ball when possible.
3. Center or cross the ball in front of the goal mouth, preferably in the air.
4. Short passes, one- or two-touch contact.
5. Back pass to maintain possession.
6. Shoot whenever possible.
7. Pressure the ball when it is lost.

Offensive Principles.   As illustrated in the diagrams (Figure 20-29), the following principles aid the attacking team:

1. *Width*—distributing the ball wide spreads out the defense, opening larger areas for penetrating by either the ball or another player.

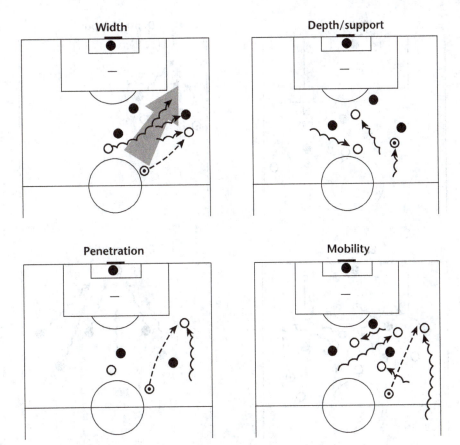

Figure 20-29 Offensive principles.

2. *Depth/support*—10- to 15-yard positioning ahead or behind the ball provides additional possible passing angles and enhances possession.

3. *Penetration*—the ball that goes past an opponent toward the end line is the most threatening pass. The deeper the controlled penetration, the better.

4. *Mobility*—the movement by players without the ball to different positions can provide superiority around the ball, create surprise, and create new situations to which the opponents must adjust.

5. *Improvisation*—the ability to adjust to ever-changing situations during the course of the play.

Defensive Principles. As illustrated in the diagrams (Figure 20-30), the following principles aid the defending team:

1. *Delay*—positioning in front of the player with the ball so that the ball cannot make immediate penetration, thus gaining the important defensive ingredient: time.

2. *Depth/support*—positioning beside and behind teammates, restricting the space that the ball/opponent might move.

3. *Balance*—the spread of players across the field, protecting all areas.

4. *Concentration*—all defensive players funneling toward the goal scoring area, causing congestion.

5. *Pressure*—forcing mistakes through aggressive play.

6. *Control/restraint*—applying all other principles of defense, awaiting the best opportunity for winning the ball; also not committing and being beaten by either the ball or the player.

TACTICS AND PRACTICE SUGGESTIONS

The execution of techniques and application of principles in a competitive situation is called tactics. These may be either individual, group, or team.

Individual. A player with the ball has the opportunity to dribble, pass, or shoot, and has possession of the ball for only about 2 minutes of a 90-minute game. Developing technique and proficiency in the foregoing skills is important; however, it is more important to learn what to do for the other 88 minutes when one does not have the ball. A player must learn how to use the available space for receiving the ball, how to create new space for either the ball or a teammate, and how to apply the principles of attacking or defending.

Group. The basic soccer objective of superiority around the ball initiates group tactics. When superiority is gained, the factors of using space, creating space, restricting space, and controlling tempo (time) are applied in small side games. Small side games (2 on 1, 2 on 2, 3

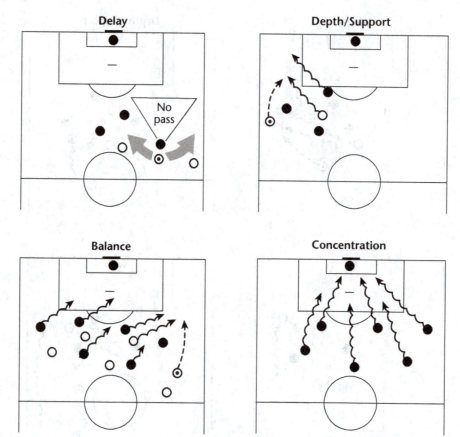

Figure 20-30 Defensive principles.

on 1, 3 on 2, 3 on 3, etc.) in restricted areas provide excellent opportunities for learning individual and group tactics.

Team. The grouping of a larger number of players leads to team tactics. Organized restrictive games, often with two lines of players (e.g., four attackers and three midfielders versus two midfielders, four defenders, and the goalkeeper), requires additional continuity.

Playing within the boundaries of the suggested one-third field areas (see Figure 20-28), the players can concentrate on the factors governing systematic team coordination. Communication becomes critical because more players are involved. Short one-word cues aid in communication. Using cue words such as *square, back, through, lead, leave, touch, carry, turn, settle,* and so on lets teammates know what to do with the ball.

Special rules in such competitions help reinforce specific tactics. Examples of special rules are as follows: Allow only one or two touches per player; a back pass must be used before a penetrating pass; no passes over 15 yards; after receiving a pass, the player must dribble past an opponent; all passes must be longer than 15 yards; no passes above knee high; all passes above the head.

The next step in developing playing strategy is the application of principles and tactics within a specific system.

SYSTEMS

The formational placement of players on the field is called a system (Figure 20-31). The players are numbered, starting with the defenders (fullbacks), midfielders (half-backs), and then attackers (forwards). The goalkeeper is not included in the numbering. The first attempt to develop new systems occurred when the five forwards of the 2–3–5 system changed their relative positions, thus forming either a W or M because of their alignment with each other on the field. Since that first change, many new systems have evolved, and all systems have strengths and weaknesses. Each evolved as a result of the specific abilities and knowledge of the players involved. The choice of which system to use should always depend on those two factors—abilities and knowledge.

Style. Within a system, there are varying styles of play. Offensive styles are long pass, short pass, fast, slow, static positioning, improvisational movement, and dribbling. Defensive styles are zone, player to player, switching player to player, rotational, and diagonal.

Many current coaching books discuss principles, tactics, and systems in more detail. The Further References section lists several books that provide additional information.

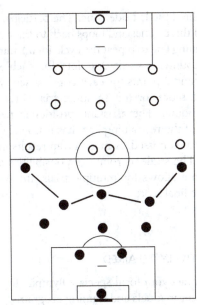

Figure 20-31 A systems alignment at kickoff. Numbers 2–3–5 (W) versus 3–3–4.

DEAD BALL SITUATIONS

When the ball goes out of play or there is an infraction of the rules, the game restarts from a dead ball situation. This situation allows a team the opportunity to initiate set plays. Goal kick, corner kick, kickoff, throw-in, or indirect and direct free kicks provide such an opportunity. The defending team also has time to prepare. There are many such plays and plans.

References in coaching books can provide a variety of set plays for dead ball restart situations.

PLAYER POSITIONAL RESPONSIBILITIES

Traditionally, the player positions have been called forwards, halfbacks, fullbacks, and goalkeeper. In recent years, the three basic lines are referred to more commonly as attackers, midfielders, and defenders. Each line has specific responsibilities related to that particular position. Listed here are the basic responsibilities for each line. Differing systems of play demand varying responsibilities, and the Further References section can provide more information.

Attackers. Attackers are the forward line players, who include wings, insides (strikers), center forward, or other teammates who overlap into the attacking area.

1. Scoring by shooting (head or foot)
2. Setting up scoring opportunities by dribbling to commit an opponent; center or crossing the ball in the air into the penalty area; running to create a new space for the ball or a teammate and to receive the ball; distributing the ball strategically and quickly wide, backward, or forward
3. Performing offensive restarts such as direct, indirect, and corner kicks in scoring area

4. Pressuring the opponents immediately on their gaining control
5. Positioning for counterattacks on regaining possession of the ball

Midfielders

1. Supporting the attackers on offense
2. Redistributing the ball wide, forward, or backward on gaining possession for sustaining offense
3. Shooting outside the penalty area
4. Overlapping into the attack area for additional strength or surprise
5. Retreating, delaying the opponents on their gaining definite control of the ball
6. Challenging for a loose ball when there is a 50/50 chance of gaining possession
7. Receiving goal kicks, both offensive and defensive
8. Taking a majority of the throw-ins
9. Defending against opponent's corner kicks
10. Positioning for counterattacks on regaining control of the ball by one's own defenders or goalkeeper

Defenders

1. Supporting midfielders when attacking
2. Challenging for ball at midfield when there is a 60/40 chance of gaining possession
3. Retreating, delaying the opponents on their gaining definite control of the ball in the midfield area
4. Funneling toward the goal and concentrating in the scoring area
5. Supporting each other when challenging for the ball
6. Clearing (kick or head) the ball out of the scoring area and when possible out of the defensive one-third
7. Keeping balance across the field; not allowing weakened areas
8. Positioning wide for counterattacking
9. Protecting the goal when the goalkeeper leaves the goal mouth
10. Forming walls for protecting against free kicks
11. Assisting or taking goal kicks
12. Overlapping occasionally for added superiority or surprise
13. Defending against corner kicks
14. Taking free kicks in the defensive one-third
15. Sprinting to the goal when beaten by both the ball and the player

Skill Assessment

Pass, trap, and dribble are the most important individual skills for success at the beginning to intermediate levels of soccer. All three skills are incorporated in this suggested test. A space 25-feet wide and 40-feet deep is necessary for one station. A smooth flat wall (25-feet wide) is required. The test involves three individuals—a participant, a counter, and an assistant.

Pass/Trap/Dribble Test. Position with three cones equidistant on a restraining line 10 feet from the wall and across the 25-foot course. The participant faces the wall behind the right half of the restraining line. The participant passes and traps the ball three times in succession. On the third trap, the participant dribbles the ball around the left-side cone, which is part of a three-cone diagonal zigzag course. The second cone is located 15 feet directly behind the middle cone on the restraining line. The third cone is 30 feet behind the left-side cone. The participant dribbles around all three cones and loops back to the right side of the restraining line to repeat the cycle for a 1-minute trial.

The counter awards 2 points for each successful pass/trap and 2 points for each cone passed while dribbling. The score for the 1-minute trial is the accumulation of points. The assistant, positioned next to the right half of the restraining line, has extra balls available when a trap is missed. A missed trap results in 0 points awarded. The students rotate responsibilities after each trial. If time allows for multiple trials, the best trial is used as the final score.

Modifications for Special Populations

ORTHOPEDICALLY IMPAIRED

1. Access the National Disability Sports Alliance (NDSA) Web site at http://nation aldisabilitysportsalliance.webs.com/ for rules and information on indoor wheelchair soccer.

2. Allow students using crutches, canes, or walkers for ambulation to move the ball up and down the field or court with their assistive devices.

3. Use a commercial product called the Omnikin Ball, which is a large ball the size of a traditional cage ball. The Omnikin Ball is extremely lightweight and floats when tossed into the air—a great modification for students using wheelchairs. The Omnikin Company's Web address is www.omnikin.com.

COGNITIVELY IMPAIRED

1. Contact your local Special Olympics for their soccer manuals and training programs.

2. Keep playing sessions short, allowing for frequent rest periods. Fitness levels are generally low in the student who is cognitively impaired.

SENSORY IMPAIRED

1. Individual considerations must be taken into account to determine the appropriateness of soccer for students who are visually impaired or blind. An appropriate alternative might be to tether a sighted student at the wrist to the student who is blind or has a visual impairment.

2. Minimal modifications are needed for students who are deaf or have a hearing impairment.

3. Review suggestions from the Orthopedically Impaired section for soccer.

Terminology

center A pass from the outside of the field near the sideline into the center.

charge The body contact between opponents that may be either illegal or legal.

chip The lofting of the ball into the air using the instep kick technique; contacting the ball low, causing it to loft quickly with back spin.

clear Playing (kick or head) the ball a great distance, attempting to move it out of a danger area.

corner kick A direct free kick awarded to the attacking player on the corner arc when the defending team last played the ball over their own end line.

cross A pass from the outside of the field near the end line to a position in front of the goal.

dead ball situation The organized restarting of the game following the stopping of play.

direct free kick A free kick from which the kicker may immediately score from that initial contact.

dribble The technique of the player self-propelling the ball with the foot so that the player maintains control of the ball while moving from one spot to another.

drop ball The method used for restarting the game after temporary suspension of play when the ball is still playable.

goal area The rectangular area in front of the goal where the ball is placed for a goal kick.

half-volley Contacting the ball just as it hits the ground after being airborne.

head The technique of playing the ball with the head.

indirect free kick A free kick from which a player other than the kicker must contact the ball before a score can result.

kickoff The free kick that starts play at the beginning of the game, after each period, or after a score.

obstruction The illegal use of the body to shield an opponent from reaching the ball.

one-touch receiving Immediately passing a ball being received without stopping it.

penalty area The large rectangular area in front of the goal where the goalkeeper is allowed to use the hands to play the ball.

penalty kick A free kick awarded for a direct free kick foul in the penalty area against the defending team.

settle The act of taking a ball that is off the ground and getting it settled on the ground so that it is rolling and no longer bouncing.

square pass A pass that is directed toward the side of a player.

tackle A technique for taking the ball away from the opponent.

through pass A pass that penetrates between and past the defenders.

throw-in The technique used for restarting the game when the ball goes out of play over the sideline.

touchline The sideline of the field.

trap The technique used for receiving the ball, bringing it under control.

two-touch receiving Trapping a ball and immediately repassing it.

Discussion Questions

1. Discuss the main objectives of offense.
2. Discuss the main objectives of defense.
3. Explain when physical contact is legal or not.
4. Identify the types of infractions that result in a direct free kick.

5. Discuss the factors that lead to systematic team coordination when defending, attacking, and playing midfield.
6. Present and discuss the offensive and defensive principles.
7. Compare the various dead ball situations.
8. Discuss the factors involved in determining an offside infraction.
9. Attackers, midfielders, and defenders have different responsibilities related to their positions. Identify and discuss these differences.
10. Compare and contrast the application of individual, group, and team principles within a competitive situation.

Web Sites

www.socceramerica.com *Soccer America* magazine—provides unlimited access to any soccer topic.

www.usyouthsoccer.org U.S. Youth Soccer—lists numerous instructional tips under "Coaches Corner." The information ranges from skills, strategies, rules, and development to fitness training for youth.

www.finesoccer.com—helps participants and coaches increase their knowledge of soccer; the search function allows for unlimited access to information.

www.nscaa.com National Soccer Coaches Association of America—addresses skill and strategy development in detail.

www.soccercoachinginternational.com—presents skills and tactics each day of the week with a steady addition of new articles.

www.soccerwebsite.org—provides extensive information on books, rules, history, skills, small side games, sites, and much more.

CHAPTER 21 | Softball

This chapter will enable you to

- Identify the necessary basic equipment of softball
- Understand the rules of slow-pitch and fast-pitch games
- Demonstrate the skills of batting, baserunning, sliding, fielding, throwing, pitching, and catching, and of playing the infield and outfield positions
- Identify drills and lead-up games for the teaching of skills
- Identify the terminology necessary to understand the game
- Observe the procedures to make the game safe for participants

Nature and Purpose

In 1887, George W. Hancock of Chicago, Illinois, developed an indoor version of the game of baseball. He used smaller playing dimensions and a larger and softer ball. The game became extremely popular and was moved outdoors. Today, this game, softball, is played throughout the world. Almost 5 million youths are estimated to participate in youth softball programs, making softball the most popular youth sport. Participation in softball games range from informal games at picnics, in parks, in backyards, and on the streets to formal leagues sponsored by schools, playgrounds, recreation departments, churches, and industrial organizations. The traditional forms of softball games included in league play are fast-pitch, 12-inch slow-pitch, and 16-inch slow-pitch games. With the variety of types and modifications of the basic game of softball, men and women of all ages can enjoy the game. Softball is considered to be one of the safest sports for all ages.

History

Softball had its beginnings in the late 1800s and early 1900s, when professional baseball players felt it would be helpful to play indoors in winter. The ball was constructed with large raised seams and was 16 inches in circumference to restrict the flight. By 1895, Lewis Rober, a Minnesota fireman, created the outdoor game to stay in shape. He developed a 12-inch slick-cover ball. The original game had a variety of names—indoor baseball, recreation baseball, playground ball, kitten ball, ladies' baseball, mush ball, soft baseball, and sissy ball—before arriving at the name softball.

The sport was developed in the Midwest, and the first league formed in 1900 in Minnesota. The first

rule book appeared in 1906. The National Amateur Playground Association in 1908 published its first rule book in Chicago. The National Recreation Congress in 1923 met in Springfield, Illinois, to form the Playground Baseball Committee. Ten years later it expanded to the Joint Rules Committee of Softball, which still governs the rules.

The first national tournaments were established by the National Diamond Ball Association in 1931 and 1933 and were hosted by Minneapolis and Milwaukee, respectively. Leo H. Fischer and M. J. Pauley at the 1933 World's Fair in Chicago conducted a championship event. Because of a conflict in the rules of the various teams, Fischer formed the Amateur Softball Association of America. Establishment of the association led to the formation of the International Softball Association, which has regulated the sport since 1952 and has more than 120 member countries.[2]

The Depression Era fostered the growth of softball. Recreation was prevalent, and the sport was inexpensive to play. The slow-pitch version with the 16-inch ball needed little equipment. The sport has grown, especially as a recreational activity, and an estimated 40 million U.S. residents currently play slow-pitch.[3]

Fast-pitch is one of the National Collegiate Athletic Association's major women's team sports. This high-level competition led to the acceptance of softball, another U.S.-originated team sport, to the Olympic program in 2000.

Basic Rules

The rules of softball are patterned after those of baseball. Pitching, rules concerning field dimensions, and equipment are different. A summary of the rules is given here, but players should study a copy of the Official Rules to become familiar with all regulations governing the game.

The games of slow-pitch softball and fast-pitch softball have many similarities: The ball must be pitched underhand, the game is 7 innings long, and the purpose is to get on base and score runs. The major difference, as the names imply, is in the speed of the pitched ball. In slow-pitch softball, the ball must be thrown underhand with a specific arc (6 to 12 feet), whereas in fast-pitch softball, the ball is thrown underhand with great velocity in a straight line—much like a baseball. Other differences are noted here.

Slow-Pitch	Fast-Pitch
No bunting	Bunting
No stealing bases	Stealing bases
Runners may leave the base after the ball crosses home plate	Runners leave base after the pitcher releases the ball
10 players per team	9 players per team
65-foot base paths (men)	60-foot base paths
60-foot base paths (women)	
A mask and chest protector for the catcher recommended	A mask and chest protector for the catcher required

GAME REGULATIONS

The purpose of the game is to score more runs than the opponent. A regulation game consists of 7 innings, or 6½ innings if the team second at bat has scored more runs than its opponent. The umpire may call (terminate) a game if five or more complete innings have been played or the team second at bat has scored more runs than the other team has scored in five or more innings. The score of a forfeited game shall be 7–0 in favor of the team not at fault.

PLAYERS AND SUBSTITUTES

A team consists of 9 players in fast-pitch, 10 players in fast-pitch with a designated player (DP), and 10 players in slow-pitch. A team must have the required number of players to start or continue a game. A substitute may take the place of a player whose name is on the team's batting order. Any of the starting players, including a DP, may be withdrawn and re-enter once, provided such a player occupies the same batting position whenever he is in the line-up. A player, other than one in the starting line-up, removed from the game may not participate in the game again except as a coach. The DP may be used for any player, provided it is made known prior to the start of the game and his name is indicated on the line-up sheet. The DP must remain in the same position in the batting order, may enter the game on defense, and may be substituted at any time by a player who has not yet been in the game.

PITCHING REGULATIONS

Fast-Pitch. In fast-pitch, the pitcher must take a position with both feet firmly on the ground and in contact with, but not off the side of, the pitcher's plate. Before pitching, the pitcher must come to a full and complete stop for a least one second and not more than 10 seconds, facing the batter, with both shoulders in line with first and third base and with the ball held in both hands in front of the body. The pitcher may not take the pitching position without the ball. The pitcher may wind up in the delivery, provided there is no stop in the forward motion or reverse in the direction of the arm swing. The release of the ball and the follow-through of the hand and wrist must be forward past the straight line of the body, and, when the arm passes the body in the forward swing, the hand must be below the hip and the wrist not farther from the body than the elbow. The pitcher cannot take more than one step, which must be forward toward the batter (within the length of the pitcher's plate), simultaneous with the delivery of the ball, and the pivot foot must remain in contact with the pitcher's plate until the stepping foot has touched the ground.

Slow-Pitch. In slow-pitch, the pitcher can take the pitching position with one or both feet touching the pitcher's plate, but both the pivot and nonpivot foot must be within the length of the pitcher's plate. A full stop must be made for 1 second and not more than 10 seconds, with one or both hands holding the ball in front of the body and the shoulders in line with first and third base, preliminary to pitching. The pivot foot must remain in contact with the pitcher's plate until the pitched ball leaves the hands. It is not necessary to step, but if a step is taken, it must be forward toward the batter within the length of the pitcher's plate. The pitch must be released at a moderate speed (umpire's decision—if warned about excessive speed and the act is repeated, the pitcher will be removed from the pitcher's position for the remainder of the game), and at a perceptible arc of at least 6 feet and no higher than 12 feet from the ground.

BATTING REGULATIONS

The batter takes a position within the lines of the batter's box and may be called out for stepping on home plate or having the entire foot touching the ground completely outside the lines of the batter's box when the ball is hit. A batter is removed from further participation in the game if an illegal bat is used. Players must bat in regular order, as indicated in the starting line-up. Batting out of order is an appeal play, and if the error is discovered while the incorrect batter is at the plate, the correct batter must replace the incorrect batter and assume the ball and strike count. If the error is discovered after the incorrect batter has completed the turn at bat and before there has been a pitch to another batter, the player who should have batted is out, and the next batter is the player whose name follows that of the player declared out. Any runs scored are cancelled, and base runners must return to bases held when the incorrect batter came to the plate. If the error is not discovered until after a pitch is made to the next batter, no one is declared out and all play is legal.

A strike (fast-pitch) occurs when the ball passes over any part of home plate and is between the batter's armpits and the top of the knees when in a natural batting stance. In slow-pitch, the strike zone is over any part of home plate between the batter's higher shoulder and the knees when in a natural batting stance.

A foul tip is a foul ball that goes directly from the bat, not higher than the batter's head, to the catcher's hands and is legally caught. In fast-pitch, the ball is in play and baserunners may advance at their own risk. In slow-pitch, the ball is dead.

The batter is declared out when an infield fly is hit with baserunners on first and second or on first, second, and third with less than two out (infield fly rule). The batter is also called out in slow-pitch when the ball is bunted, is hit with a downward chopping motion, or is hit foul after the second strike.

BASERUNNING RULES

Base runners must touch the bases in regular order and if forced to return while the ball is in play, the bases must be touched in reverse order. Two base runners may not occupy the same base simultaneously. The runner who first legally occupied the base must be entitled to it, and the other base runner must return or be put out. A base runner is out when she (1) runs more than 3 feet from a direct line between bases in regular or reverse order to avoid being touched by the ball in the hand of a fielder; (2) passes a preceding base runner before that runner has been put out; (3) leaves a base to advance before a caught fly ball has been touched, provided the ball is returned to a fielder who touches that base while holding the ball, or a fielder with the ball touches the base runner before returning to the base; (4) fails to keep contact with the base until a legally pitched ball has been released by the pitcher in fast-pitch (whether on a steal or batted ball); or (5) fails to keep contact with the base until a legally pitched ball has reached home plate in slow-pitch (batted ball only). A pitcher in slow-pitch who desires to walk a batter intentionally may do so by notifying the plate umpire, who then awards the batter first base.

DEAD BALL RULES

The ball is dead and not in play under the following circumstances: (1) on an illegally batted ball; (2) when the batter steps from one box to another as the pitcher is ready to pitch; (3) on an illegal pitch; (4) when a pitched ball touches any part of the batter's person or clothing; (5) when a foul ball is not caught; (6) when a base runner is called out for leaving a base too soon; (7) when any part of the batter's person is hit with a batted ball while in the batter's box; (8) when a blocked ball is declared; (9) when a wild pitch or passed ball in fast-pitch goes under, over, or through the backstop; and (10) in slow-pitch after each strike or ball.

SCORING REGULATIONS

A base hit results when a batted ball permits the hitter to reach first base safely when no fielding error is involved. A base hit is not recorded when a base runner is forced out by a batted ball, or would have been forced out, except for a fielding error.

Sacrifices are scored when, with less than two out, the batter advances one or more base runners with a bunt and is retired at first base, or when a run is scored by advancing runners after a fly ball is caught.

Assists are scored to each player who handles the ball in any play or series of plays that result in a put-out, but only one assist is credited to a player in any one put-out.

Put-outs are credited to players who catch a batted fly ball, catch a thrown ball that retires a base runner, or touch a base runner with the ball while the runner is off the base.

Errors are recorded for the player who commits a misplay that prolongs the turn at bat of the batter or the life of the base runner.

A run batted in (RBI) is a run scored because of (1) a safe hit; (2) a sacrifice bunt or fly; (3) an infield put-out or fielder's choice; (4) a base runner forced home because of interference, or in fast-pitch, the batter being hit with a pitched ball, or the batter being given a base on balls; and (5) a home run and all runs scored as a result.

WINNING AND LOSING PITCHER

A pitcher is credited with a win if he starts and pitches at least 4 innings and the team is not only in the lead when the replacement occurs but remains in the lead the remainder of the game. When a game is ended after 5 innings of play and the starting pitcher has pitched at least 3 innings and the team scores more runs than the other team when the game is terminated, the pitcher will be declared the winner. A pitcher will be charged with a loss regardless of the number of innings pitched if replaced when the team is behind the score and the team thereafter fails to tie the score or gain the lead.

Playing Field

The regulation playing field is 60 × 60 feet square (Figure 21-1). The accompanying indications of the required distances for fast-pitch and slow-pitch are used in the majority of age groups. For official distances for specific age groups, consult a current Amateur Softball Association (ASA) rule book. Ground or special rules

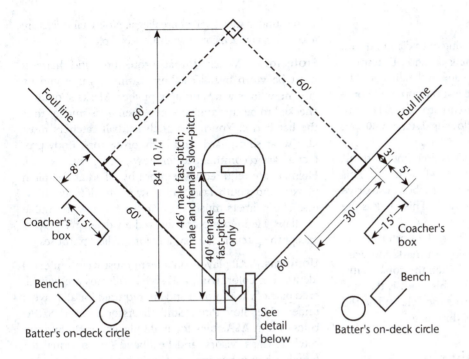

	Distances	
	Fast-pitch	**Slow-pitch**
Bases		
Male	60 feet	65 feet
Female	60 feet	60 feet
Pitching		
Male	46 feet	46 feet
Female	40 feet	46 feet
Fences		
Male	225 feet	275 feet
Female	200 feet	250 feet

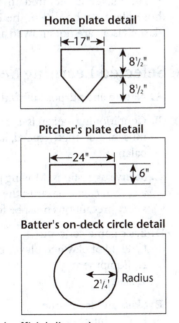

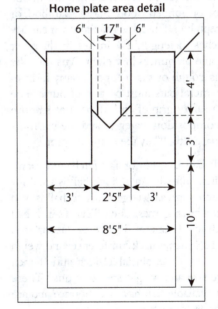

Figure 21-1 Softball field, official dimensions.

establishing the limits of the playing field may be agreed on by leagues or opposing teams whenever backstops, fences, stands, vehicles, or other obstructions are within the prescribed area.

The home plate is generally made of rubber and is a five-sided figure, 17 inches wide across the side facing the pitcher, 8½ inches long on the sides parallel with the inside lines of the batter's box, and 12 inches long on the sides of the point facing the catcher.

The pitcher's plate is made of wood or rubber and measures 24 inches long and 6 inches wide. The top of the plate must be level with the ground; the front line of the plate measures the following distances from the outside corner of home plate: men's fast-pitch and slow-pitch and women's slow-pitch—46 feet; men's fast-pitch—40 feet.

The bases other than home plate must be 15 inches square and made of canvas or other suitable material and not be more than 5 inches thick. The bases should be securely fastened in position. A double base may be used at first base. This base is 15 by 30 inches. The half of the base in fair territory is white and the half of the base in foul territory is orange.

LAYING OUT A DIAMOND

The following directions are for laying out a diamond with 60-foot bases and a 40-foot pitching distance. Determine home plate position by running a line in the direction desired for the diamond. Place a stake at the corner of home plate nearest the catcher. Tie a cord to the stake with knots or other markings at the following distances: 40 feet, 60 feet, 84 feet 10¼ inches, and at 120 feet.

Place the cord along the direction line without stretching it. Place a stake at the 40-foot mark. This mark is the front edge of the pitching rubber. Also drive a stake at the 84 feet 10¼ inches mark. This mark is the center of second base.

Now place the 120-foot mark on the center of second base. Hold the cord at the 60-foot mark and walk to the right of the direction line. When the cord is taut, drive a stake at the 60-foot mark. This mark is the outside corner of first base. Walk across the field and do the same thing to mark the corner of third base.

Equipment and Clothing

Bats. The official softball bat is round and made of one piece of hardwood or bonded wood. Plastic, bamboo, or metal is also acceptable. The bat's maximum measurements are 34 inches in length, 2¼ inches in diameter at its barrel end, and 38 ounces in weight. Bats must be free of rivets, pins, rough or sharp edges, or any form of exterior fastener; metal bats must be free of burrs. The handle requires a safety grip of cork, tape (not smooth plastic tape), or composition material, and the bat must be marked "Official Softball" by the manufacturer.

Balls. A 12-inch ball is used for fast-pitch and men's and coed slow-pitch softball. An 11-inch ball is used for women's slow-pitch games. A larger 16-inch ball is also used for some slow-pitch games. The official 12-inch ball must be a smooth-seam concealed-stitch or flat-surfaced ball from 11⅞ to 12⅛ inches in circumference, and weigh from 6¼ to 7 ounces. (The official 11-inch and 16-inch balls have relative size and weight specifications.) There are softballs now available that have less bounce and are suitable for indoor use during inclement weather.

Gloves. Gloves (which have fingers) may be worn by any player, but mitts (which have no fingers) may be used only by the first baseman and catcher. The pitcher's glove must be a solid color other than white or gray. Multicolor gloves are acceptable for all other players, but gloves with white or gray circles on the outside resembling a ball are illegal.

Shoes. Shoes may have canvas or leather uppers or similar materials. The soles either may be smooth or have soft or hard rubber cleats. Ordinary metal sole and heel cleats may be used if the spikes on the plates do not extend more than ¾ inch from the sole or heel of the shoe. Shoes with rounded metal spikes are illegal. No metal spikes are allowed in any division of youth or coed play.

Protectors. Masks, throat protectors, and helmets must be worn by all catchers during a game and by anyone who is warming up a pitcher. Masks should be checked to be sure the wire eye opening is smaller than the bat barrel. Youth fast-pitch softball catchers must also wear shin guards and body protectors. Body protectors are recommended for slow-pitch games as well. Helmets are required to be worn by all adult fast-pitch players and youth fast- and slow-pitch offensive players. The helmets must be of similar color with double ear flaps. Helmets are not allowed for defensive players except the pitcher, catcher, and for medical purposes.

Uniforms. All players on a team must wear uniforms identical in color, trim, and style. Ball caps are considered part of the uniform and are required for all players under U.S. Slow-Pitch Softball Association (USSSA) rules and in ASA rules for male players, including the catcher. Caps, visors, and headbands are optional for female players but may not be mixed on a team. No female player is required to wear headwear, but for those players who do so, the headwear must be alike. Plastic visors are not allowed as headwear.

Selected Learning Sequence

A. Nature and purpose of softball

B. Conditioning—exercises and drills for developing muscular strength, speed, agility, coordination, and balance

C. Safety suggestions. Moving people and moving objects can create hazards; therefore, from the first day, safety precautions must be followed without fail.

D. Basic game concepts
   1. Field of play and player positions
   2. Equipment
   3. Safety

E. Skills and techniques
   1. Catching
   2. Throwing
      a. Grip on ball
      b. Arm motion
      c. Body movement
   3. Fielding the ball
      a. Ground balls
      b. Fly balls
   4. Batting
      a. Grip on bat
      b. Stance
      c. Stride
      d. Rotation of body and arms
      e. Follow-through

5. Bunting
   a. Grip on bat
   b. Stance
   c. Direction of bunt
6. Baserunning
7. Sliding
8. Pitching and catching

F. Rules—start with those essential to play the game and expand in depth and comprehensiveness as playing ability increases.
   1. Terminology
   2. Playing field
   3. Equipment
   4. Players and substitutes
   5. The game
   6. Pitching regulations—fast- or slow-pitch, for whichever game is being taught
   7. Batting
   8. Baserunning
   9. Dead ball—ball in play

G. Playing strategy. The fast-pitch game uses many strategies of baseball, whereas the slow-pitch game is the adaptation of field positions to batting strengths or weaknesses.

Skills and Techniques

Although adaptable for general recreational use, softball is a game that demands a good performance of certain fundamental skills and techniques. Enjoyment from participation in the game intensifies as skills improve. Skill techniques are described, followed by short hints to use in teaching each of the skills. Practice suggestions include drills and lead-up games to enhance skill development.

CATCHING

Catching is a fundamental skill that must be mastered before other skills are attempted.

▶ Learning Hints

1. Watch the ball into the hands or glove.
2. Position fingers up and thumbs together for balls chest high or higher. Position fingers down and little fingers together for balls waist high and lower.
3. Relax the fingers and arms.
4. On contact with the ball, absorb the force by bringing the ball close to the body—"Give with the ball."

▶ Practice/Organizational Suggestions

1. Provide each student with a ball. The students toss the ball up in the air and catch it, trying to toss the ball higher and higher and still be able to catch it.

2. A student tosses the ball up in the air and everyone claps and counts until the ball comes down and is caught. Take turns to see who can get the most claps.

3. Catch balls thrown by a partner from short range. Initially use foam balls or whiffle balls to eliminate fear of being hurt. Gradually increase the distance.

4. Catch balls a partner throws high, low, and to each side.

THROWING

Throws should be made quickly, accurately, and to the correct base or fielder. Players should be able to throw using an overhand, sidearm, or underhand motion. But spend more time on the overhand throw because with it one can attain the greatest accuracy. The sidearm throw imparts a side spin on the ball that causes it to curve.

▶ Learning Hints

1. Grip the ball across a seam with index and second fingers (all four fingers if hand is small), thumb underneath, and third and fourth fingers to the side (Figures 21-2 and 21-3).
2. Point the elbow away from the body as the arm moves backward (Figure 21-4).
3. Move body weight to the foot on the same side (rear foot) and rotate the trunk in that direction.
4. Keep the wrist extended until just before release.
5. Push off with the rear foot and step with the other foot in the direction of the intended throw.
6. Rotate hips, trunk, and shoulders as the arm comes forward.
7. Lead with the elbow and snap the wrist as the ball is released opposite the peak of the cap.

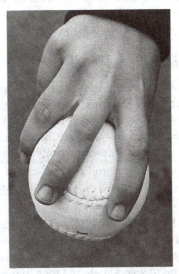

Figure 21-2 Two-finger grip for adult.

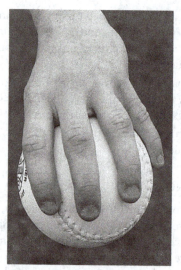

Figure 21-3   Four-finger grip for children.

Figure 21-4   Overhead throw. As the arm moves backward, point the elbow away from the body.

8. The throwing arm continues across the body for the follow-through.
9. Use a natural, rhythmical movement.

▶ Practice/Organizational Suggestions

1. Throw to a partner. Start with a short distance and then increase that distance. Throw to a specified target on the partner, such as the chest. Vary the target and the speed of the throw. Stay at a distance until accurate for four out of five throws (preferably all five).
2. Throw at a target from various distances.
3. Throw to different bases from different field positions.
4. Play "Beatball." A runner stands at home plate and a catcher has a ball, preferably a softball. On a signal, the runner begins running the bases. The catcher throws the ball to third base. The ball is relayed from third to second base and then to first base and home plate. The runner scores one point for each

base touched before the ball returns to home plate. *Variation:* Allow the runner to continue around the bases until the ball reaches home plate prior to the runner on the same trip around the bases. Place a maximum of three trips around the bases.

FIELDING GROUND BALLS

The ability to field ground balls is crucial to the success of any defense. With proper guidance, most players can learn to field routine ground balls successfully and improve their ability to field cleanly hard-hit balls and bad bounces.

▶ Learning Hints

1. Prior to the pitch, assume a ready position with the feet parallel and wider than shoulder-width apart. Flex the knees and hips and place the hands close to the ground.
2. When possible, move forward ("charge") toward the ball when it is hit.
3. Stay in front or get in front of ground balls. This enables you to handle them if they take bad bounces to the left or right.
4. Field ground balls with the feet in a parallel wide, stride position, knees slightly bent, and the body crouched: *wide stance.* On hard-hit balls, it may be advisable to close the feet or drop to one knee to block the ball.
5. Catch a ground ball just as it leaves the ground on a bounce or after it has reached the peak of its bounce.
6. Keep the body and glove low on ground balls and move upward to make the catch. One can move more quickly upward, and because the body is already low, more bad bounces may be blocked by the body or glove.
7. Keep the glove open and watch the ball into the glove. (Figure 21-5)

▶ Practice/Organizational Suggestions

1. Slowly roll ground balls between partners.
2. Increase the speed of the rolls and then increase the distance between partners.
3. Toss ground balls to the right and to the left of the partner.
4. Field ground balls with a partner tossing balls at varying speeds and in different directions.
5. Field ground balls hit by a partner at varying speeds and directions. Throws can be made to a catcher next to the hitter or to a base.
6. Play "Pegging First." One team is at bat and the other is in the field. Using a fungo bat, each batter hits the ball on the ground and runs to first base. If the batter reaches first before the ball, one point is scored. All members of the batting team bat before teams change positions.

Figure 21-5 Fielding ground ball position.

FIELDING FLY BALLS

Catching fly balls can be a difficult skill for beginners to learn. Once the basic catching skill is mastered, judging the ball's speed and distance must be learned to field fly balls.

▶ Learning Hints

1. Get under the ball as quickly as possible. Use two hands.
2. To catch a ball hit over the head and to the right or left, pivot on the foot on the ball side, turn and run diagonally backward, and watch the ball over the shoulder opposite the ball side.
3. Relax the fingers slightly and have the hands and arms give with the ball as it is caught to reduce the force of impact.
4. Catch the ball, when possible, close to the throwing side so that the throwing arm can move into position for the throw as soon as possible.
5. Watch the ball into the glove.
6. Know where to throw the ball before you catch it, and then move quickly to accomplish the throw after the catch.

▶ Practice/Organizational Suggestions

1. Catch fly balls thrown by a partner. Gradually increase the distance.
2. Catch fly balls hit by a partner. Throw to a relay person, directly to a catcher next to the hitter, or to a player at a base.

3. Play "Five Hundred." Using a fungo bat, one player hits to a group of fielders. Fielders score successful catches. A fly ball is worth 100 points; a ground ball, 50 points; and a catch on a first bounce, 50 points. If a catch is tried and missed, the respective number of points is deducted. A player scoring 500 points exchanges with the batter.

BATTING

The key to offensive softball lies in effective batting—a complex motor task—coupled with baserunning.

▶ Learning Hints

1. The basic position has the batter standing in the batter's box with feet slightly more than hip-width apart, knees relaxed and flexed slightly, and with the body bent slightly forward at the hips.
2. The bat is gripped by the handle in such a manner that the second joints of each finger on each hand are in alignment (Figure 21-6). This unlocks the wrists for greater bat speed.
3. Before hitting, the bat is held in a position over the rear shoulder with the forearm (closer to pitcher) fairly straight and raised so that the elbow is chest-high. The back arm is bent slightly with the elbow away from the body (Figure 21-7A).
4. The forward leg should step forward toward the pitcher, and during the swing the weight should shift over to the front leg, which should be straight.
5. In executing the swing, the body, arms, and bat first rotate slightly away from the pitcher. This gives the

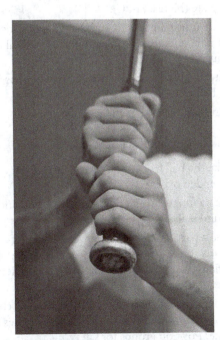

Figure 21-6 Batting grip.

A   B   C

Figure 21-7 Batting: (A) stance; (B) bat, arms, hips, and body start the rotation; (C) follow-through.

bat more distance over which to gain momentum and enables the body to exert more torque in hitting (Figure 21-7B).

6. Rotate the hips as the bat comes forward. The arms should straighten, and the wrists should straighten forcefully just before the ball is hit and should continue to straighten forcefully as the ball is hit.

7. The trunk and hips rotate until the batter almost faces the pitcher and the ball is struck about half an arm's length in front of the shoulder that is closer to the plate (Figure 21-7C).

8. The rear foot initiates a push forward but should maintain contact with the ground as the ball is hit (Figure 21-7C).

9. Watch the ball from the time the pitcher has it until just before hitting it.

10. Swing only at pitches in the strike zone.

▶ Practice/Organizational Suggestions

1. Strike the ball from a stationary tee or from a rope suspended overhead.

2. Using a fungo bat, hit fly balls, line drives, and ground balls.

3. Have a partner toss balls from a distance of 2 to 3 yards to the side (about a 45-degree angle). Students can hit the balls into the playing field or into a fence.

4. Get in groups of four or five with batter, pitcher, and two or three fielders. Hit 10 or 15 pitches and rotate. Position groups for safety.

BUNTING

Bunting is an effective offensive weapon in the fast-pitch game but is illegal in slow-pitch softball. Although the fielders are closer to the batter in softball than in baseball, it takes just as much time to field and throw a softball as a baseball. Therefore, the batter in softball should have a slight advantage over the baseball player in using the bunt as a means to reach first base safely.

▶ Learning Hints

1. The initial stance is the same as for hitting because bunting is most effective as a surprise maneuver and its declaration must be withheld as long as possible.

2. Just before the pitcher releases the ball, the batter should pivot on the front foot and bring the back foot forward parallel with the front foot so that the batter is facing the pitcher and is near the front of the batter's box.

3. The knees should be bent and the body should crouch low, especially on low balls. Move the body up and down and maintain the bunting stance rather than moving the arms for high and low pitches.

4. The arms bring the bat downward to a position parallel with the ground in front of home plate and perpendicular to the ball's line of flight. As the bat comes down, slide the top hand up the bat to a position beyond the center of the bat, where the thumb and index finger grasp the bat on the rear side to avoid having the fingers hit. Arms should be half flexed (Figure 21-8).

Figure 21-8   Bunting position.

Figure 21-9   Sprinter's stance.

5. By flexing one arm a little more while extending the other arm, the ball may be guided down either the first or third base lines.

6. The ball should contact the bat slightly above the top hand.

7. The arms should give slightly as the ball hits the bat to keep the ball from rebounding too far into the playing field.

8. Keep the bat higher than the ball and hit the top half of the ball so that the ball is more likely to be hit downward.

▶ **Practice/Organizational Suggestions**

1. In front of a mirror, practice turning from batting stance to bunting stance.

2. Bunt balls that a partner tosses slowly.

3. Bunt to a glove placed on the ground at various positions.

BASERUNNING

In running the bases, the batter follows the base lines and avoids making wide turns when rounding a base. The proper method is to pull out about 3 feet from the base line a couple of strides before reaching the base, and then by timing steps, hit the inside corner of the base with the left foot. As the left foot hits the base, the body twists slightly to the left so that the right foot lands just beyond the next base line. The runner comes back to the base line and continues.

When advancing from first to second, watch the third-base coach for directions. The coach is usually in a better position to see the entire field of play and tell the runner whether to stop at second or continue on to third base. Because the runner must remain on base until the ball leaves the pitcher's hand (fast-pitch) or reaches home plate (slow-pitch), a sprinter's stance (Figure 21-9) should be taken with one foot on the base in readiness for a quick departure (whether on a steal or a batted ball).

▶ **Practice/Organizational Suggestions**

1. Run the bases after hitting in batting practice.

2. Practice hitting the ball and starting for first base.

3. Practice starting from a base with the sprinter's stance.

SLIDING

To avoid injury, no one should attempt sliding without prior instruction and practice in the technique. Knowing how to slide correctly will also prevent overrunning a base.

The *hook slide*, which is the most popular, is performed by sliding on a thigh and hip with the body leaning away from the base. When sliding on the right hip and thigh, the base is hooked with the left toe, and the right leg is either bent under the left leg with the right toe pointing backward (to keep from getting caught in the ground) or is extended forward in the air (to prevent the spikes from catching in the ground and injuring ankles and knees). The left leg is raised slightly off the ground, and as the body, which is slightly to the right of the base line, approaches the base, the toe hooks onto

Figure 21-10 Hook slide.

the base (Figure 21-10). It is important to start the slide soon enough so that by the time the toe hooks the base, the body's momentum is slow enough to avoid pulling the toe off the base.

The *bent-leg slide* is used by players who wish to get to their feet quickly to advance to another base on an overthrow or misplay. In this slide, the player slides on the bent underneath leg, with the upper leg making contact with the base. The forward momentum of the slide is used to raise the body to an upright position after making contact with the base.

The *head-first slide* is often used when it becomes necessary to return to a base. The use of a head-first slide in any other situation should be strongly discouraged.

▶ Practice/Organizational Suggestions

1. Practice in a gym, on wet grass, or in a sliding pit. Wear long pants and socks, no shoes.
2. Judge one another on technique.
3. Slide for a square marked on the grass.
4. Slide into a base opposite a catch made by a partner who receives the toss from another player. Rotate.

PITCHING

The success of a winning team depends largely on the consistency of its pitching. A good pitcher must have control and command a variety of pitches that can be used whether playing slow-pitch or fast-pitch softball. Special movement requirements are outlined under "Pitching Regulations" in the Basic Rules section.

Slow Pitching. Place the foot on the throwing-arm side on the front of the pitching rubber. The opposite foot is behind the throwing-arm-side foot. The throwing arm is brought behind the body in an underhand, pendulum motion. The opposite foot steps toward home plate. The arm is swung forward, with the fingers under the ball. The ball should be released about shoulder high, which helps to attain the 12-foot arc and to drop the ball over the plate (Figure 21-11). Lower releases tend to flatten the pitch and give it more velocity. Varied spins as well as different speeds on the ball should be developed to keep the batter mixed up in the timing of the swing.

Fast Pitching. Several different types of deliveries are possible, including a sling shot or half windmill and a windmill. The beginning stance for each delivery is the same as for slow pitching except that the back foot must be in contact with the pitching rubber. The half windmill is the same motion as slow pitching but faster, and the release is by the hip with a snap of the wrist. A windmill involves moving the pitching arm through a full circle. The body is twisted away from the batter at the top of the swing. As the arm begins the downward swing, the hips are rotated to a position facing the batter. The leg on the throwing side pushes forcefully against the pitching rubber as the ball is released at the hip with a strong wrist snap (Figure 21-12).

▶ Practice/Organizational Suggestions

1. Throw to a partner who moves the target around the strike zone.
2. Throw to a target—such as an old mat tacked on a wall, fence, or backstop. In slow-pitch, place an empty bucket, milk crate, or circle on the ground as a target.
3. Play "Pitcher vs. Pitcher." Two players work together. One pitches and the other catches. The pitcher pitches to an imaginary batter. The catcher calls balls and strikes. The "batter" is either struck out or walks. "Runners" advance as additional "batters" become "runners." One player continues to pitch until three "batters" are out, then the players exchange positions. The winner is the pitcher with the fewest "runners" scoring.

PLAYING CATCHER

The catcher is frequently called the "defensive center of the infield" because the catcher handles all the pitched balls and is in a position to see all the infield proceedings. The catcher should call the player's name on

A

B

C

D

Figure 21-11 Pitching delivery: slow-pitch.

infield flies, tell the fielder of a bunt where to throw, and keep all players informed of the number of outs. The catcher gives the pitcher the signal for the type of pitch to be thrown, gives a target to throw to, makes every effort to block wild pitches with runners on base, and makes plays at home plate. The catcher assumes a squat position as close to the batter as possible without interfering with the swing and with the weight forward on the balls of the feet so that quick movements in any direction can be made. In making a throw, the catcher brings the ball up to a position behind the ear, steps forward with the left foot, and throws by bringing the arm forward quickly and with a strong wrist snap just prior to release.

PLAYING FIRST BASE

The first-base player in fast-pitch softball must always be alert for fielding a bunt, which is used frequently. The first-base field position in fast-pitch is in toward home plate 10 to 20 feet; a greater distance is used with no one on base, and a shorter distance is used with a runner on first and a double-play possibility. In slow-pitch, the playing position is approximately 10 feet behind the base but varies in depth and distance from the foul line according to the strength or weakness of the batter. To be in a position to receive a throw from another fielder, run quickly to the base when the ball is hit and assume a position facing the fielder, with the heels touching the

Figure 21-12 Windmill pitch.

inside edge of the bag. The first-base player should shift the body according to the direction of the throw. When the throw is to the left (toward home plate), bring the toe of the right foot to the edge of the bag by the left heel and then step toward the ball with the left foot. Reverse the procedure for a throw on the right (toward the outfield).

▶ Practice/Organizational Suggestions

1. Do the footwork without catching until it is an automatic response.
2. Have a partner toss balls to both sides of the base.

3. Have fielders throw balls to the base.
4. Have the coach hit ground balls to fielders and let them throw to first base.
5. Field bunts and ground balls hit to various spots in the first-base area.
6. Practice catching fly balls in the vicinity of first base.

PLAYING SECOND BASE AND SHORTSTOP

The fielding position for the second-base player is approximately 15 feet from second base toward first base and about 12 feet behind the base line. The position varies with the strength and weakness of the batter. The second-base player should attempt to field all batted balls to the first-base side of second base. On a double-play situation from the third-base side, the fielder should move quickly toward the base in a path that puts second base between the person fielding the ball and the second-base player. The fielder should time the move so that the ball is caught as the right foot hits the bag, and then finish fielding by stepping forward with the left foot toward the infield and first base to avoid the baserunner and, with a pivot, throwing to first base.

The shortstop takes a field position similar to the second-base player's position but closer to third base; the position varies with the strength and weakness of the batter. The shortstop should attempt to field all batted balls to the third-base side of second base. In a double-play situation, the shortstop moves quickly to the base in a direct line with second base and the player fielding the ball. The shortstop should time the move to catch the ball just before reaching the bag, and then finish fielding by stepping to the outfield side with the left foot, dragging the right foot across the bag, and pivoting and throwing to first base. Both the shortstop and second-base player can stop just before they reach second base, catch the ball and touch second base with the left foot, push back with that foot, landing on the right foot, and then pivot and throw to first base.

▶ Practice/Organizational Suggestions

1. Field ground balls hit to various positions and with varying speeds.
2. Move across the bag and throw to first base.
3. Make the step-back-and-throw maneuver.
4. Complete the double-play situation after fielding ground balls.
5. Make the double play with a runner moving with the hit ball.
6. Tag runners stealing second base.
7. Catch infield fly balls.

PLAYING THIRD BASE

The position of the third-base player in fast-pitch is similar to that of the first-base player—in a position to field bunted balls by playing in toward home plate 10 to 20 feet, depending on the game situation. The third-base player should attempt to field all batted balls hit down the third-base line and as many as can be reached that are hit to the second-base side. The momentum developed by moving toward second base should aid the throw to first base.

▶ Practice/Organizational Suggestions

1. Field bunted balls and throw to first base and second base.

2. Field batted balls hit to various positions at varying speeds. Throw to first base and to second base.
3. Field batted balls and practice the double-play situation.
4. Catch pop-ups in the vicinity of third base.
5. Tag runners stealing third base.

PLAYING THE OUTFIELD

The position of the outfielders should enable them to cover their area from the infield to the fence, and it should vary according to the strength and weakness of the batter. The overhand throw is used when throwing to the infield because it is usually more accurate due to the fact that side spin is not put on the ball, which causes it to curve. Use the techniques for fielding ground balls and fly balls.

▶ Practice/Organizational Suggestions

1. Catch fly balls hit to various positions, including over one's head.
2. Field ground balls hit to various positions.
3. Make throws to second base, third base, home plate, and to a relay player. Do the same with players running the bases.
4. Throw to targets at the various bases.

Playing Strategy

Fast-pitch softball permits most of the team strategies used in baseball. It is varied according to game situation and the philosophical beliefs of the coach. One difference is that the second-base player covers first base on bunts rather than the pitcher. The winning team will be the one that not only masters individual fundamentals but also functions as a unit in the execution of team plays. In slow-pitch softball, there are no offensive plays because a base runner cannot leave the base until the pitched ball reaches home plate and cannot advance until the ball is hit or the batter is walked.

Safety Procedures

The following procedures should be observed to minimize the possibility of accidents and injuries.

1. Organize throwing and catching warm-up drills in parallel lines. Adjacent players should be a safe distance apart. When a ball is missed, it should be retrieved and the student should return to the line before making a throw to the partner.
2. The receiver should indicate the target before any ball is thrown.
3. Players should wear proper protection (helmets, masks, gloves, etc.) at all times.

4. Perfect sliding techniques before using them. Always avoid unnecessary slides.

5. Anchor bases firmly to the ground.

6. Students should swing bats only in designated areas, and no one other than the batter should be allowed to enter batting areas.

7. Have batting practice organized so that one group does not hit toward another group.

8. Grip the bat tightly so it will not slip from the hands. Keep the hands dry and only use bats with the proper safety grip. After batting, *drop* the bat, do not throw it.

9. Players of teams waiting to bat should be in a specific safe area.

10. Keep equipment organized and in the dugout. Do not leave it scattered around or in the playing area.

11. Keep the playing area clear of rocks, depressions, obstructions, or any foreign objects.

12. To avoid collisions, learn the correct procedure for calling for fly balls and for covering bases.

13. Organize drills so that students are facing away from the sun.

Skill Assessment

Throwing (accuracy and power) and fielding (ground and fly balls) are important skills at the beginning to intermediate levels. They are incorporated in the suggested skills tests. A wall space at least 20 feet high and 10 feet wide is necessary for one station. The tests involve three students—a participant, a counter, and an assistant.

Throwing and Fielding Ground Balls. Mark a restraining line on the floor 12 feet from the wall and another 8 feet high on the wall. The participant faces the wall and throws the ball overhand from behind the restraining line on the floor to below the restraining line on the wall. The participant fields the ball behind the 12-feet restraining line after it rebounds from the wall and bounces at least twice, then quickly throws the ball against the wall again, repeating the total process. The trial is performed for 30 seconds. The counter records the total number of successful ground balls fielded in 30 seconds. A dropped ball or one not bouncing at least two times does not count. The assistant has extra balls in case the participant loses one. The students rotate responsibilities.

Throwing and Fielding Fly Balls. In this test the participant must catch the ball in the air. Mark a floor restraining line 5 feet from the wall and another 12 feet high on the wall. The ball must be thrown hard above the wall line and caught on the fly by the participant behind the floor restraining line. The trial is for 30 seconds. Each catch counts as long as the ball is not dropped and the participant remains behind the restraining line.

It is suggested that a student's final score be a combination of the ground ball and fly ball tests.

Modifications for Special Populations

ORTHOPEDICALLY IMPAIRED

1. Access the National Wheelchair Softball Association Web site at www.wheelchairsoftball.org for suggestions.

2. Allow students using crutches, canes, or walkers to strike the ball from a stationary position (e.g., batting tee or traffic cone).

3. Use plastic bats and balls (e.g., whiffle ball).

COGNITIVELY IMPAIRED

1. Contact your local Special Olympics to obtain a copy of their softball manual.

2. Plan "one-base" softball in which the batter runs only to first base and not the entire diamond. Add additional bases as skills and concepts of the game improve.

3. Do not play "three out"; allow all players from one team to hit before exchanging offensive and defensive positions.

SENSORY IMPAIRED

1. Access the National Beep Baseball Association at www.nbba.org for the rules of "Beep Baseball."

2. For students who are blind or have a visual impairment, construct modified baselines with jump ropes from home plate to first base.

3. Strike the ball from a stationary position (e.g., batting tee), and instruct the runners to move to an auditory cue (e.g., bell or buzzer at first base).

4. Minimal modifications are needed for students who are deaf or have a hearing impairment.

Terminology

appeal play A play in which an umpire cannot make a decision until requested by a player or a coach.

assist Fielding credit for a player who throws or deflects a batted or thrown ball in which a put-out results or would have resulted except for a subsequent error.

battery The pitcher and the catcher.

batting average The number of hits divided by the times at bat.

blocked ball A batted or thrown ball that is touched or stopped by a person not engaged in the game or that touches any object that is not part of the official equipment or official playing area.

blooper A batted fly ball that goes just over the head of the infielders and just in front of the outfielders.

cleanup hitter The number four batter in the batting order, a position usually occupied by the team's power hitter.

control The ability of a pitcher to throw the ball to a desired area when pitching.

count The number of balls and strikes on the batter.

cut-off A throw from the outfield that is intercepted by an infielder for the purpose of throwing out a runner other than the intended runner.

double play Two consecutive put-outs occurring between the time the ball leaves the pitcher's hand and its return to the pitcher.

error A misplay or mistake by the defensive team that results in prolonging the turn at bat of the batter or the time on base of the base runner.

fielder's choice The batter is safe because the defensive player elected to retire a preceding base runner.

force out An out as a result of a defensive player with the ball tagging a runner or the base to which the base runner must go because the batter became a base runner.

fungo bat A lightweight bat used in hitting balls to fielders during practice.

grand slam The batter hits a home run with the bases loaded.

hit A ball hit in such a way that the batter or preceding base runners are not retired by good defensive play.

hot corner The third-base area.

infield fly A fair fly ball that can be caught by an infielder with runners on first and second, or first, second, and third, before two are out. The batter is declared out by the umpire.

keystone sack The second-base area.

on deck The player in line to follow the batter at the plate. The place for waiting is the on-deck circle.

overthrow A thrown ball that goes into foul territory beyond the boundary lines of the playing field on an attempt to retire a runner who has not reached or is off a base.

passed ball A legally delivered pitch that should have been held or controlled by the catcher, which allows a base runner to advance. A dropped third strike that permits the batter to reach first base in fast-pitch is an error, not a passed ball.

put-out An out credited to the fielder who last handles the ball on a play that retires the batter or a base runner.

running squeeze A play in which the runner on third base starts for home with the pitch because the runner knows the batter is going to bunt the ball.

sacrifice bunt A play in which the batter bunts for the ball to advance a base runner and is thrown out at first base or would have been if the ball were played properly.

sacrifice fly A fly ball that is caught and after which a base runner crosses home plate to score a run.

safety squeeze A play in which the base runner on third base starts for home after the batter bunts the ball.

switch hitter A batter who bats both right- and left-handed.

Texas leaguer Same as a *blooper*.

wild pitch A legally delivered pitch so wide or low or high that the catcher cannot stop or control the ball, which allows a base runner to advance.

Discussion Questions

1. Discuss the evolution of softball from its recreational origin to the competitive game it is today.
2. Compare the rule differences between the slow-pitch and fast-pitch games.
3. Discuss the rules affecting base runners.
4. Identify scoring regulations that determine hits, sacrifices, assists, put-outs, errors, runs-batted-in (RBI), and winning/losing pitcher.
5. Identify batting regulations that affect the batter.
6. List circumstances that determine when a ball is a "dead ball."
7. Discuss the various responsibilities of the catcher.
8. Discuss the positional play of the infielders and their collective responsibilities.

Web Sites

www.usasoftball.com USA Softball—includes information about the USA National Teams.

www.asasoftball.com Amateur Softball Association (ASA)—includes information about rule books, umpire programs, Hall of Fame, videos and books for players, and more. ASA is the national governing body of softball.

www.serioussoftball.com—includes photos of softball players in action as well as team pictures. It is possible to post pictures to this site.

www.champonline.com/softball.html—lists many outstanding softball books and videos that can be ordered directly from the site. Information on Coaching Essentials, Injury Management, and Mental Training & Motivation is offered as well.

www.pitchsoftball.com—provides pitching instruction, training aids, books, and videos.

CHAPTER 22

Speedball

This chapter will enable you to

- Understand the historical origins of speedball
- Identify and put into practice the rules governing the game
- Practice and execute the basic skills, including kicking, passing, catching, trapping, dribbling, and aerial ball conversions
- Identify differences and similarities of skills, rules, and strategies found in other sports
- Discuss and employ basic offensive and defensive strategies and tactics
- Identify and use basic terminology associated with the game

Nature and Purpose

The game of speedball is a combination of the skills, rules, and strategies of soccer, basketball, and football. It is a vigorous, continuous-motion activity involving running (sprinting and jogging) and changes of direction (dodging, cutting, stopping, restarting). It is played outdoors on a football- or soccer-sized field by teams of 11 players, yet with limited modifications it can be played indoors in smaller areas and with fewer players.

Originally a men's activity, the game was modified for women's participation and has evolved into a sport that both can play by the same set of rules. Speedball is an adaptable game, and the leader can alter the rules to meet individual preferences.

The object of the game is to propel a ball to the opponent's end of the field and score points. The ball is propelled either as a ground ball (soccer skills) or an aerial ball (basketball and football). The skills involved are kicking, passing (hands or feet), catching, trapping, and dribbling.

In advancing the ball, the offense attempts to score either by a field goal, touchdown, drop kick, penalty kick, or end goal. The defenders attempt to impede the attack by guarding. Players on both teams are organized into forwards, halfbacks, fullbacks, and a goalkeeper, as in soccer.

History

The game of speedball was developed by E. D. Mitchell at the University of Michigan in the early 1920s. Mitchell had identified the need for a vigorous team game that could be played outdoors in the fall and combined many of the elements found in other well-known sports. Many of the boys and girls who had gone to high school in the

Midwest had been introduced to basketball in public schools and did not like soccer much because of its restrictions on using the hands during play. Touch football, although a popular game, allows only some players on the team to handle the ball regularly. Speedball eliminated many of these objections; the game Mitchell invented permitted all players to participate in all aspects of the game.

The game evolved into a separate activity for men and women with separate rules. Both sets of rules were presented in previous editions of this book. However, because boys and girls often play the game together, this chapter combines the rules into one set with recommended modifications.

Field of Play

A football, soccer, or field hockey field can be used. The regulation field is shown in Figure 22-1. The field consists of a middle/halfway line, restraining lines, end zone/penalty area, penalty kick mark, end lines, goal lines, and sidelines.

MIDDLE/HALFWAY LINE

The middle/halfway line is used on the kickoffs to ensure that the team taking the kick is in its own half of the field.

RESTRAINING LINE

The opponents of the team taking the kickoff must stay behind the restraining line until the ball is contacted. The ball must travel beyond (10 yards) the restraining line on kickoff, or be touched by an opponent, before those taking the kickoff can replay the ball.

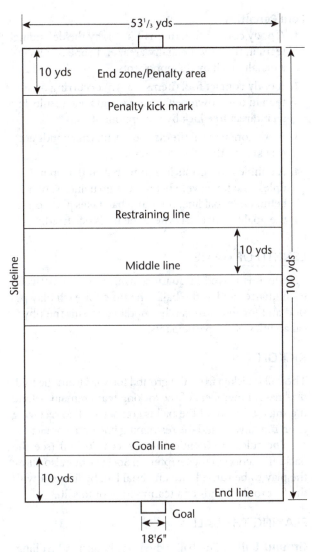

Figure 22-1 Speedball field.

END ZONE/PENALTY AREA

The size of the end zone/penalty area may vary if using football field markings. The area has four purposes: (1) A ball thrown from the field of play, across the goal line, and caught in the end zone by the team attacking that end results in a score (touchdown as in football). (2) Any "contact foul" or "personal foul" committed in this area and against the team defending that end results in a penalty kick. (3) On a penalty kick, no player from the defending team except the goalie can be in this zone. (4) A legal attempt to score on a ground ball within this area by the offense results in an end goal if it crosses the end line but not in the goal.

PENALTY KICK MARK

The penalty kick mark is the spot to place the ball for taking a penalty kick.

END LINE

The end line serves as a boundary, and when the ball goes out of bounds without scoring, it is put back in play by the opposing team from that spot. The end line also determines an end goal in men's rules (see End Zone/Penalty Area, purpose 4). On a penalty kick, the defensive players stand behind this line.

GOAL LINE

The goal line separates the field of play from the end zone/penalty area. On a penalty kick, players stand behind the goal line so that they are not in the penalty area.

SIDELINE

The sideline is a boundary line, and when the ball goes out of bounds it is put back in play with a throw by the opposing team from that spot.

Basic Rules

Although there are two sets of official rules for men's and women's competition, separate rules are no longer necessary. The following is a combined and simplified set of rules.

SCORING

The regulation methods for scoring are listed in Table 22-1 and described here. The points can be adjusted to meet the needs of varying age groups or for emphasizing specific skill usage. From experience, most players elect to overuse the "touchdown" method of scoring. Adding a higher point value than the one listed for a "field goal" leads to players using their kicking skills more often, thus de-emphasizing throwing and catching. Another suggestion is to eliminate the "end goal" method of scoring.

Field goal: propelling the ball with the feet or body (no hands or arms) into the goal—identical to a legal soccer score.

Touchdown: throwing the ball across the goal line to a teammate who catches it in the end zone/penalty area—similar to a football touchdown.

Drop kick: drop-kicking the ball over the goal crossbar and between the uprights from outside the end zone/penalty area.

Penalty kick: free kicking the ball as a result of a personal contact foul against the defending team when in their own penalty area. The ball is kicked from the penalty kick mark into the goal. Suggested modification: Place the ball on the ground (men's rules), as with a soccer penalty kick, rather than drop-kicking the ball (women's rules).

Table 22-1 **Speedball scoring: Official and recommended**

	Official	Recommended
Field goal	3	3
Drop kick	2	2
Touchdown	1	1
Penalty kick	1	1
End goal	1	X

End goal: the offense kicking the ball over the end line from within the end zone/penalty area without the ball going into the goal. Suggested modification: Do not use this method of scoring; instead, allow the opponents to receive a pass or kick-in from the spot where the ball went over the end line.

VIOLATIONS, FOULS, AND PENALTIES

The penalties for infractions vary according to the severity of the infraction. The following list combines the infractions and classifies them as either fouls (severe) or violations (less severe).

Violations

1. Touching a ground ball with the hands or arms
2. Taking too many steps with the ball—two steps if received while running and one step while standing
3. More than one aerial dribble per possession
4. Holding the ball more than 3 seconds
5. Kicking or kneeing a fly ball before catching it
6. The offense drop-kicking the ball in the defense's penalty area
7. The offense throwing the ball to a teammate when both are in the defense's penalty area

Violation Penalties

1. A violation outside the penalty area results in an indirect free kick at the spot of the infraction. See chapter on Soccer—Indirect Free Kick Offenses.
2. A violation inside the opponents' end zone/penalty area gives the opponents a penalty kick.
3. A violation inside one's own end zone/penalty area results in an indirect free kick by the opponents at the spot of the infraction.

Fouls

1. Illegal contact with opponents
   a. Kicking
   b. Pushing
   c. Tripping
   d. Holding
   e. Blocking
   f. Charging—see chapter on Soccer, Physical Contact, for legality
   g. Hacking
   h. Obstruction—see chapter on Soccer, Physical Contact, for legality
   i. Unnecessary roughness
2. Illegal substitution
3. Unnecessary delay of game
4. Taking more than three time-outs
5. Having more than 11 players on the field
6. Unsportsmanlike conduct

Foul Penalties

1. A body contact foul (items 1.a–1.i) by the defending team in their own penalty area/end zone results in a penalty kick by the opponents.
2. A body contact foul (items 1.a–1.i) occurring other than in one's own penalty area/end zone results in an indirect free kick by the opponents.
3. A noncontact foul (items 2–6) results in an indirect free kick to the offended team.
4. A double foul results in a jump ball at that spot unless the fouls were behind the goal line. When behind the goal line, the jump ball takes place on the goal line nearest where the fouls occurred.

LENGTH OF GAME

Speedball is played in quarters, with intervals between each quarter and at the half. The time for each play period and for intervals can be modified to suit the physical abilities of the participants.

KICKOFF

The ball is kicked from the ground forward from the middle line. All members of the kicking team remain behind the middle line until the ball is contacted. The receiving team remains behind the restraining line until contact.

The rules are identical to a soccer kickoff (see the 'kickoff' section in the chapter on Soccer), but also allow the play to be turned into an aerial ball by lifting it with the feet to the hands of a teammate (not to self).

PLAYING THE BALL

Ground Ball. The ball, when on the ground (rolling, bouncing, or stationary), is played as in soccer, with skills of dribbling, kicking, heading, or trapping. For the ball to be thrown, it must first be brought from the feet immediately into the hands.

Aerial Ball. The legal conversion of a ground ball using the feet to lift or kick it into the hands is called an aerial ball. When in the hands, it can be thrown, passed, and caught as in football and basketball. The ball can be air dribbled to oneself only one time each new possession. The air dribble consists of throwing the ball in the air and relocating to regain possession by catching it. On the air dribble, steps do not count while the ball is in the air. A player is legally allowed one step with the ball when holding it if obtained while standing, or two steps if running prior to receiving it. Additional steps are illegal and are called traveling. Holding the ball with the hands for more than three seconds without giving up possession is illegal. This speeds up the game and is a rule that can be modified.

Physical Contact. Rules allow for the same body contact as in soccer (see Soccer, Physical Contact) when the ball is on the ground. With the ball in the hands, guarding as in basketball (see Basketball, Individual Defense) is appropriate. Other personal contact fouls were identified in the foregoing listing of speedball fouls.

Jump Ball (Toss-up, Tie-ball).   Two opponents simultaneously holding the ball results in a jump ball. Likewise, a jump ball results if it is not possible to decide which team put the ball out of bounds. The jump ball method is the same as in basketball. Two opponents face each other and jump to tip the ball, which is tossed between them. All other opponents must be at least 5 yards away on the toss-up. The ball remains an aerial ball off the tip provided it does not contact the ground, in which case it is considered a ground ball.

Out of Bounds.   A ball going off the field of play over the sideline is put back in play with a throw (overhand, underhand, two hands, one hand, etc.). A ball over the end line is either thrown or kicked into play.

Free Kick.   Certain identified infractions result in a free kick as in soccer (see Soccer, Basic Rules), except that the opponents only need to be 5 yards from the ball. The kick is taken at the spot of infraction. It can be turned into an aerial ball. Indirect free kick means that someone must touch the ball prior to a score.

Penalty Kick.   Certain foul situations previously identified result in a penalty kick, which is a free kick. The ball is placed on the penalty kick mark (line), and one of the offended team members is allowed a free kick to score a field goal against the opposing team goalie. The offensive team members position outside the defenders' penalty area. The defensive players, aside from the goalie, position either behind the end line or outside the penalty area.

Goalkeeper.   The goalie primarily defends the goal against field goal attempts. The goalkeeper is bound by the same rules as all other players, with no special privileges or rules.

Equipment

The only necessary equipment is a ball and two goals. The regulation speedball is slightly larger than a soccer ball, but a soccer ball, which is more readily available, is most often used. Other similar size balls, which are softer or have less bounce, may be desirable for better control or for safety. Figures 22-2 B and C show such a ball being used. Any type of goal (soccer, football, field hockey, team handball, etc.) can be used, but the soccer and football goals (uprights extending from the ground up) are most often available. The regulation goal is 18 feet wide for women and 18 feet 6 inches for men.

Suggested Learning Sequence

A. Stretching and running

B. Basic rules

C. Fundamental skills
1. Passing
   a. Soccer—inside of foot, instep kick, lofting the ball, and punt
   b. Basketball—chest, overhead, and baseball
   c. Football—forward
   d. Speedball—drop kick
2. Catching/trapping
   a. Soccer—sole of foot, inside of foot, outside of foot, and chest
   b. Basketball—two hands above and below the waist, pivoting
   c. Football—over the shoulder
3. Heading
   a. Soccer—standing and jumping
4. Dribbling
   a. Soccer—inside and outside of foot
   b. Speedball—aerial
5. Individual defense
   a. Soccer—tackling from the front and side
   b. Basketball—guarding and denial of ball
   c. Football—pass defense
6. Personal conversion to aerial
   a. Speedball—roll up, two-foot lift, and one-foot lift
7. Goalie
   a. Soccer—catch at waist, chest, and above head; tip; throw and punt

D. Strategies
1. Offense
   a. Soccer—possession, superiority around the ball, creating space, tempo, communication, depth/support, width, penetration, mobility, and improvisation
   b. Basketball—cutting, fakes/feints, attacking a player to player and zone defense, fast break
   c. Football—dodging, faking, and change of pace
2. Defense
   a. Soccer—pressure, depth/support, width, balance, delay, concentration, and control
   b. Basketball—player to player, fast break, and zone
   c. Football—pass defense

E. Systems
1. Style—long or short pass, static positioning, aerial or ground ball, player to player or zone
2. Formations—(M or W as in soccer), V or inverted V

F. Restarts
1. Kickoff
2. Throw-in
3. Free kick
4. Penalty kick

Skills and Techniques

Only a few skills are specific to speedball. Most of the skills needed are described in the basketball, soccer, and football chapters. The skills from these sports are identified, and a review of these sections will prepare the speedball player for skilled participation.

Basketball skills: pivoting; chest pass; overhead pass—one-hand overhead pass (baseball); two-hand catch and holding the ball; cutting; individual defense against a player with the ball, player without the ball and denial defense.

Soccer skills: inside of foot pass; instep kick; lofting the ball; sole of foot trap, inside and outside of foot trap; chest trap; inside and outside of foot dribble, heading, standing, and jumping; tackling from front and side; goalkeeping—catching ball at waist, chest, and above head plus falling to side, tip, punt, and overhand throw.

Football skills: forward pass and over-the-shoulder catch.

AERIAL CONVERSIONS

Ball control and scoring opportunities are enhanced by having the ball in the hands. The ball must go from the feet directly into the hands for it to be a legal aerial ball. This conversion may happen as a result of punts, soccer-style kicks, and drop kicks to other players. An individual can personally convert a ground ball to an aerial ball by using either a roll-up, two-foot lift, or one-foot lift.

▶ Learning Hints—Roll-Up

1. Stand erect with the ball wedged evenly between the feet (Figure 22-2A).
2. Bend at the waist so the back is parallel with the ground.
3. Extend the arms downward and perpendicular to the ground.
4. Place pressure on the bottom half of the ball with the inside of one foot, rotate the knee outward, and roll the ball up the inside ankle and calf of the opposite leg (Figure 22-2B).
5. Grab the ball off the foot and leg with the hand, converting it to an aerial ball (Figure 22-2C).

▶ Practice/Organizational Suggestions

Wedge the ball with the inside of both feet and roll the ball up and down one leg by applying more pressure with the foot opposite that leg. Do not attempt to pick up the ball at this point, but repeatedly roll it up and down the leg to get the feeling so that control is not lost. Progress next to bending over to grab the ball off the foot and leg with the hands. Gradually attempt to speed up the whole process.

A   B   C

Figure 22-2 Roll-up: (A) wedge ball; (B) rolling ball up leg; (C) converting to an aerial ball by grabbing it with hands.

Figure 22-3 Two-foot lift: (A) lifting the ball to convert to an aerial; (B) catching the ball from lift.

▶ Learning Hints—Two-Foot Lift

1. Stand erect with the ball wedged evenly between the feet as in Figure 22-2A.

2. Hop up, keeping the ball wedged evenly between the feet and lifting it higher toward the hands.

3. In the air, lean forward, extending the arms and hands downward to grab the ball from the feet (Figure 22-3A).

4. Catch the ball and land on two feet with the converted aerial ball, ready to pass it (Figure 22-3B).

▶ Practice/Organizational Suggestions

Wedge the ball with the inside of both feet and hop in the air, attempting to lift the ball as high as possible. Keep the body erect and do not yet attempt to lean over to grab the ball. Continue this exercise, attempting to bring the ball higher each time. Progress next to leaning over to grab the ball with the hands before it drops to the ground.

▶ Learning Hints—One-Foot Lift

1. Stand erect with one foot extended in front of the body and the sole of that foot applying light pressure on the top of the ball (Figure 22-4A).

2. Apply more pressure on the top of the ball with the sole of the foot and roll the ball quickly toward the body.

3. Place the toe of the foot rolling the ball under the rotating ball to lift it upward.

4. Bend forward at the waist, extend the arms and hands downward, and lift the ball with the toe toward the hand (Figure 22-4B).

5. Catch the ball with two hands as it is lifted waist-high into the air (Figure 22-4C), converting it to an aerial ball.

▶ Practice/Organizational Suggestions

In an erect position, reach forward with an extended leg and apply pressure on the ball with the sole of the foot. Roll the ball backward and forward, keeping foot pressure on it, to get the feeling of rolling. Gradually, on the backward roll, apply more pressure, causing rapid rotation on the ball as that foot releases from the ball. Next, attempt to place the toe of that foot quickly under the ball and lift the ball as high as possible into the air without catching it. Try to lift it at least waist-high. Finally, repeat all of the foregoing and lean forward to catch the ball. Once consistency is obtained, attempt to use the one-foot lift on an approaching ball that is already rolling toward you.

DROP KICK

The drop kick is used as one method of scoring. It also can be used to kick the ball a great distance, similar to punting, except that a drop kick tends to have a lower trajectory, which adds distance to the kick.

Figure 22-4 One-foot lift: (A) rolling ball backward; (B) lifting backward rolling ball with toe; and (C) catching ball from the toe lift.

▶ Learning Hints

Refer to the Soccer chapter's Learning Hints on punting. Hints 1–5 apply to speedball. The following techniques differ for drop-kicking.

1. *Ball contact.* The ball is contacted with the instep (hard top surface) of the foot immediately upon the ball's touching the ground (bounce). The contact is in the back/bottom surface of the ball. The higher the contact surface on the ball, the lower the trajectory of the ball, and vice-versa.

2. *Follow-through.* A short follow-through by the contact leg results in a low trajectory, and a long one results in a higher trajectory.

▶ Practice/Organizational Suggestions

Face a wall 10 yards away and drop the ball, attempting to drop kick it with a low trajectory (no higher than the head). Allowing the ball to bounce too high from the ground results in a high trajectory, so attempt to contact the ball the instant it contacts the ground. Gradually attempt to kick the ball higher without sacrificing accuracy. Alternate between high and low trajectories to reinforce the timing of ball/ground/foot contact.

Playing Strategies

The placement of players on the field assists continuity in offense and defense. Speedball players consist of forwards, halfbacks, fullbacks, and a goalkeeper, and their responsibilities are the same as in soccer. The basic strategies are for the players to position systematically on the field, maintain possession of the ball, propel the ball toward the opponent's goal line, and score points.

OFFENSE

A quick reference to the Soccer chapter will prepare participants for offensive play. Note especially the information on space; strategic field areas; offensive principles; individual, group, and team tactics; and styles of play.

One difference in speedball offense is that there are several methods of scoring. One method (touchdown) can be accomplished any place along the entire width of the field, while others (field goal and drop kick) can only be accomplished at the goal on the end line in the center. Converting an aerial ball to a ground ball for a field goal attempt provides an opportunity to score more points. Because of this, the ball in the middle of the field near the goal is a good offensive strategy specific to speedball.

Because ball control and possession are easier in speedball than in soccer, and there is no offside rule, it is an advantage to have many players in front of the ball to increase penetration and scoring opportunities. Passers should immediately attempt to locate in advance of the ball upon relinquishing possession.

Varying the ways the team attempts to score makes it more difficult for the opponents to defend against the offense.

DEFENSE

The Soccer chapter identifies defensive principles that apply to speedball. The player-to-player defense is imperative in speedball because the offense can use the aerial ball, which leads to ball control. Defenders must be close to their assigned individual to disrupt the offensive advantage. Quick transition from offense to defense is extremely important. The defenders need to know where their opponents are at all times and be close enough to protect against a pass.

The aerial ball rules in speedball make it important that the defender position far enough away from the player with the ball so that the player cannot air dribble quickly, getting behind the defender. The offensive player cannot move very far on one air dribble and has only 3 seconds to get rid of the ball. If the aerial ball is converted to a ground ball by the offense, the defender should immediately pressure the opponent and get closer so as to destroy control and reduce the chances of making a long kick or shot on goal.

SYSTEMS

The placement of players on the field and their responsibilities reflect systematic cohesion among teammates. The team systems in soccer are appropriate for speedball. Field balance is important for either offensive or defensive success, and a system provides this. The system used is dependent on what the opponents use or the strengths and weaknesses of one's own team.

Skill Assessment

The major skills necessary to play speedball are the same as those in football and soccer. The skills tests for those activities can be used. The three skill techniques for converting a ground ball to an aerial ball might be tested utilizing the following skills test.

Aerial Conversion Test. The test involves three students—a participant, a counter, and an assistant. The participant sequentially performs the roll-up, two-foot lift, and one-foot lift to convert a stationary ball into an aerial. Following each try, the ball is dropped to the ground where it is trapped stationary (soccer style) for the next aerial conversion. This sequence is repeated for 30 seconds. One point is awarded for each successful aerial conversion; a dropped ball during the conversion try earns zero points. The score is the total number of conversions within the time trial. The counter determines the score and the assistant has a ball ready for an errant trial by the participant. The students rotate responsibilities. Additional trials are suggested for reliability.

Modifications for Special Populations

See modifications listed in the Soccer and Team Handball chapters.

Terminology

aerial ball A ball that has been thrown or propelled into the air by the feet and that can legally be played with the hands.

air dribble A ball tossed to oneself in an attempt to relocate.

double foul Two opponents simultaneously committing a foul, which results in a jump ball (toss-up).

dribble Propelling the ball with the feet (soccer) so that the individual maintains control while moving.

drop kick The skill of dropping the ball from the hands to the ground and kicking it upon ground contact; also a method of scoring.

end goal A score resulting from the offense kicking the ball across the opponent's end line while in the penalty area (men's rules).

field goal A score resulting from the offense propelling the ball, as in soccer (no hands or arms), into the opponent's goal.

foul An infraction of the rules that is penalized severely.

free kick An unguarded kick from the ground, such as penalty kick, kickoff, or indirect free kick.

goalkeeper The player responsible for protecting the goal against the field goal.

ground ball A ball that cannot be touched by the hands but must be propelled as in soccer by dribble, kicking, heading, and so forth.

guard The act of defending against an opponent.

indirect free kick A free kick in which someone other than the individual making that kick must touch the ball before it can go into the goal.

infraction A breach of the rules.

jump ball (toss-up) Tossing the ball upward between two players who jump to tip the ball, restarting play.

kickoff A free kick at the middle line at the start of the game, following a score, and following suspension of play each period.

kick-up The conversion of a ground ball to an aerial ball.

one-foot lift The skill of converting a ground ball to an aerial ball by rolling and lifting it with the foot.

pass Propelling the ball, with either the hands or feet, to another player.

penalty kick A free kick to attempt a field goal as a result of a foul.

punt The skill of immediately kicking the ball after dropping it from the hands.

roll-up The skill of converting a ground ball into an aerial ball by rolling it up the leg with the foot and grabbing it with the hands.

throw-in Putting the ball back in play after it has gone out of bounds over the sideline.

touchdown A score made when a teammate throws the ball to a partner who catches it in the opponent's end zone/penalty area.

trapping The skill of receiving (catching) the ball with the foot or body to bring it under control.

traveling Taking too many steps with the ball in the hands: one step if received while standing and two if while running.

two-foot lift The skill of converting a ground ball to an aerial ball by hopping to lift the ball to oneself.

violation An infraction of the rules that is not severely penalized.

Discussion Questions

1. Compare the skills required for speedball to those needed for other sports.

2. Discuss the origin of speedball as an activity.

3. Identify the variety of scoring methods and discuss the reasons for assigning different point values.

4. Discuss the techniques for converting a ground ball into an aerial ball.

5. Compare the offensive strategies that are common to other sports.

6. Compare the defensive strategies that are common to other sports.

CHAPTER 23

Swimming, Diving, Water Exercise, and Fitness Swimming

This chapter will enable you to

- Identify important historical events in the evolution of swimming
- Understand and apply the principles of safety involved in aquatic-related activities
- Understand the fundamental skills, biomechanics of swimming, and progressions used in the beginning through intermediate levels of swimming and diving
- Identify and correct common errors of beginning swimmers and divers
- Understand and participate in the benefits of water exercise
- Participate in and contribute to aquatic games and contests

SWIMMING AND DIVING

Nature and Purpose

Aquatic activities are among the leading forms of recreation in the United States. More than 75 million Americans enter the water in some form of recreational aquatic activity each year. An estimated 5,000 drownings occur annually in the United States. Many of these result from the inability to swim or from preventable accidents. These statistics indicate that a knowledge of basic swimming skills may be life saving. The goal of physical educators who teach swimming and diving is to provide sound information to students using our nation's recreational aquatic facilities.

In addition to increased safety in the water, swimming improves cardiorespiratory fitness levels. Also, people who are otherwise restricted from land activities as a result of physical handicaps may benefit from swimming because the body's natural buoyancy in water reduces strain in the knee and hip region. Regular participation in water activities can improve flexibility, agility, balance, and strength.

History

It is difficult to determine when swimming was first used as a means of locomotion through the water. Wall carvings of swimmers have been found dating back to 9000 B.C. The first written account of the teaching of swimming was found in records from the Middle Kingdom in Egypt (2160–1780 B.C.). One of the earliest references to swimming in the United States is an account of Benjamin Franklin teaching swimming to children on a visit to England.

Competition has always been the means of accelerating the development of sports, and swimming is no exception. The first records of competition date from the 1880s, and from that date forward the development of water skills was very marked. Much of the development was because of the expansion of, and resulting interest in, competitive swimming.

There are several notable highlights concerning the development of swimming:[1]

- The lifebelt was invented in 1804 by W. H. Mallison. However, the U.S. Navy, concerned that the lifebelt would encourage seamen to jump ship and desert, did not initially accept the invention.
- By the mid-19th century, the breaststroke was British swimmers' stroke of choice. In 1844, however, a group of American Indians participated in a competition in London using a variation of the crawl stroke, which was much faster and enabled them to win. Their British hosts considered it a barbaric stroke and continued to use the breaststroke in competitions well into the early 1870s.
- The Trudgen stroke, another variation of the front crawl, was introduced into England in 1873 by John Trudgen. Because it was a faster stroke, it became popular throughout the world.
- Mathew Webb, an Englishman, was the first person to swim the English Channel, a distance of more than 21 miles.
- Synchronized swimming was introduced in the late 19th century and was initially a men-only event.
- Swimming appeared as a sport in the 1896 Olympics in Athens as a men's competition.

- Australian swimmer and teacher Richard Cavill modified the Trudgen stroke with a flutter kick and soon broke swimming records. This new stroke became the Australian crawl and later the front crawl.
- In 1908, the world swimming association, Federation Internationale de Natation de Amateur (FINA), was formed.
- Women were allowed to compete in the Olympic swimming events in the 1912 Stockholm games. It was at the Stockholm games that Hawaii native Duke Kahanamoku, using the six-beat flutter kick for the front crawl, won the 100-meter crawl.
- Johnny Weismuller burst on the swimming scene in 1922, winning five Olympic medals and many national championships. Weismuller went on to become Tarzan in the famous movie series of the 1930s and 1940s.
- In 1935, David Armbruster and Jack Sieg modified the breaststroke into a variation that was to become the butterfly stroke, in which the swimmer's legs kick like a dolphin.
- Aldoph Kiefer modified the backstroke and developed the technique of bending the arms beneath the water during the pull phase. This improvement made the stroke more efficient and faster.
- The Olympic games from 1936 to 1956 introduced several developments: topless swimsuits for men, which decreased drag in the water; two-piece swimsuits; swimming underwater longer distances after the start and turn in some events, which enabled the swimmer to go faster; and new techniques for turns, including the body roll. Later, a turn that resembles a forward tumble was developed for the backstroke.
- In 1972, U.S. swimmer Mark Spitz won seven gold medals at the Munich games. Michael Phelps in the 2004 Athens games won a total of eight medals, six of them gold.

In 2008 U.S. swimmer Michael Phelps won eight gold medals at the Beijing games, a new record. In 2012 he became the most decorated Olympian of all time with a total of 22 medals (18 gold). Recently, both men and women have made their mark in the Olympic games. Missy Franklin, Allison Schmitt, Ryan Lochte, Janet Evans, Amy Van Dyken, Natalie Coughlin, Amanda Beard, Jenny Thompson, Dara Torres, Mark Spitz, Rowdy Gaines, and Aaron Piersol have added to U.S. swimming lore.

Today, swimming records are being broken faster than ever before because of several factors: age-group swimming, which allows for more intensive development of skills; better training methods; and recognition that strength is necessary for speed swimming, which has led to the development of weight-training programs that contribute to the conditioning of swimmers. In addition, there are more competitive events than ever before, and any swimmer who has a desire to master fundamentals and develop maximum endurance has a chance to succeed in top-flight competition.

The American Red Cross has done much to advance safety in swimming and to popularize swimming as a recreational activity. Swimming has become a major means of rehabilitation after certain types of surgery, and old and young alike use many basic strokes in water aerobics, programs designed to increase fitness. Moreover, newer athletic activities, such as triathlons and iron man competitions, incorporate swimming as a major component.

Equipment

Most of the equipment needed for instruction, activities, and aquatic games is generally found in and around aquatic facilities. A well-equipped aquatic program would include but is not limited to the following: kickboards, pull buoys, float belts, personal flotation devices (PFDs), instructional flotation devices (IFDs), masks, fins, snorkels, water volleyballs (rubber) and net, water polo equipment (balls, hats, flag, goals), inner tubes, rescue equipment (reaching pole, ring buoys, throw bag, backboard, head-immobilizing device, cervical collars, pocket masks, first-aid kit, rescue tubes, rescue board, shepherd's crook, whistles), water basketball and goals, various types of floatable toys, hula hoops, rubber diving bricks and rings, resolite mats, and net bags for equipment storage.

A hose or water source, other than the pool's, should be available to rinse all equipment at the end of each session, and a preventive maintenance program should be developed to help keep all equipment in good working order. A planned equipment replacement and expansion budget should be instituted.

Suggested Learning Sequence

BEGINNING SWIMMING

A. Water orientation

B. Holding positions
  1. Entry
  2. Front
  3. Back
  4. Drafting
  5. Streamlining on the front
  6. Streamlining on the back

C. Skills
  1. Bubble bobs
  2. Safety bobbing
  3. Front float
  4. Back float
  5. Front glide

6. Back glide
7. Front glide with kick
8. Back glide with kick
9. Front beginner stroke
10. Back beginner stroke
11. Jump from the wall (shallow water)

INTERMEDIATE SWIMMING

A. Strokes
   1. Front crawl
   2. Elementary backstroke
   3. Back crawl
   4. Breaststroke
   5. Sidestroke

DIVING

A. Types of dives (in order of difficulty)
   1. Slide-in dive
   2. Sitting dive
   3. Kneeling dive
   4. Scale or tip-in dive
   5. Shallow push dive
   6. Deep push dive
   7. Forward standing dive (1 meter)
   8. Standing back dive (1 meter)

Beginning Swimming

WATER ORIENTATION

Beginning students may approach their first swimming session with great anxiety. It is important that the instructor create an atmosphere conducive to learning under these circumstances. The following gradual steps should be taken with beginning swimmers. Teachers should demonstrate all skills prior to students' attempt.

1. Sit on pool side with feet and lower legs in the water.
2. Use hands to splash water on themselves.
3. Slide into shallow water and remain holding the wall. Teacher may need to assist students into the pool.
4. Sink into the water until water covers the shoulders.
5. Teacher—demonstrate bubble blowing with chin and lips in the water. Student's turn!
6. Blow bubbles from mouth and nose.
7. Immerse face completely and blow bubbles.
8. Put head under water.

Note: The student should be asked to do these skills, never forced. Remember that fear levels may be high. The peer pressure of classmates doing the skill should be ample external motivation. Student readiness will determine the level of accomplishment.

HOLDING POSITIONS

Entry. The beginning swimmer may need assistance entering the water, particularly if the student cannot touch the bottom. The teacher reaches under the armpits of the student and lowers the student from a sitting position on the deck into the water. Students should be reminded to hold onto the wall.

Front. The front holding position, to be used when instructing the front float, front glide, and so on, is best accomplished by having the student cross one hand over the other and place both hands in one of the teacher's hands. The teacher's other hand supports the student's hip. The student's arms are then extended at the elbow, as the student stretches to the glide position (Figure 23-1).

Back. The back holding position provides the student with security when learning the back float, back glide, and so on. The student places both hands on the wall, pushes the abdomen toward the wall, and places the head back toward the teacher. The teacher cradles the student's head in one hand while reaching to the small of the back with the other. The student is instructed to straighten the elbows and to keep an arch in the back (Figure 23-2).

Drafting. Drafting helps students gain confidence in their ability to float. The student is held in either the front or back holding position directly perpendicular to the teacher. The teacher begins to move backward while pulling the student along. Once the student is moving, the teacher intermittently reduces support or, depending on the student's confidence level, lets go. The student's body will be pulled by inertia toward the teacher and follow her wake (Figure 23-3).

Streamlining on the Front. Streamlining helps reduce water resistance. The most important part of this skill is the clasp of the hands. Have students place both hands over their heads while standing. Without clasping their hands, they should try to squeeze their ears with their arms. Then, have students place one hand over the other and lock the thumb of the top hand over the bottom hand. Now, when students squeeze their ears again, they should note that they are much stronger with hands locked into position. Finally have students sink into the water and push off into a front or prone glide, keeping arms straight, hands locked, finger tips pointed, and body in line.

Streamlining on the Back. Streamlining on the back can be accomplished in the same manner as the frontal streamlining, just turned over. However, when floating on the back, most beginning students find it easier to leave hands and arms straight down at the sides. This position is acceptable at the beginning level.

BEGINNER SKILLS

Bubble Bobs. The student holds the wall with both hands approximately shoulder-width apart, then submerges and blows bubbles toward the wall. This exercise should be done systematically at the beginning

Figure 23-1 Holding position for front/prone glide.

Figure 23-2 Holding position for back/supine glide.

A
B

Figure 23-3 The transition from back glide holding position to drafting.

of each class, and students should build to about two sets of 10 rhythmic bubble bobs. Emphasis is placed on blowing out under water, taking a breath above water, keeping eyes open during both phases, and not wiping face with hands.

Safety Bobbing. Once the student is comfortable with bobbing, safety bobbing can be taught. The teacher takes students one at a time into water slightly over their heads. Practice at 5 feet from the wall and have students bob to the wall systematically and rhythmically, bouncing from the bottom and pushing toward the wall. The teacher should assist as much as needed.

Front Float. Students can achieve a front float once they are comfortable putting their faces in the water. With minimal support from the teacher, a student allows legs and arms to dangle in the water with the face in. Breath should be exhaled slowly from mouth and nose.

Back Float. With minimal support from the teacher, the student lays his head back in the water while pushing his hips and abdomen toward the surface gently; arms are extended laterally and knees are bent.

Front Glide. From the front holding position, have the student push gently away from the wall. Once moving, remove the support hand from the hip and then from the hands. If the student is comfortable and can push from the wall in the streamline position and maintain a glide for 5 to 10 seconds, the student is ready to move on to the front glide with kick.

Back Glide. Generally, students are less comfortable in the supine position. The teacher needs to assess student readiness before attempting any removal of support from the back holding position. To start, have the student ease off the wall in the back holding position; request that the student make eye contact with the teacher and keep the belly up. Drafting can be used to increase the student's confidence.

Front Glide with Kick. The flutter kick (freestyle) should be first practiced on the wall, using the wall holding technique shown in Figure 23-4. Simultaneous practice of the kick and head position for breathing can be done as shown. Once a satisfactory kick is established, the student may push off the wall in the streamline position, glide (5 feet), and begin kicking. The kick should generate from the hip area, with knees

Figure 23-4 Flutter kicking with head in breathing position.

flexing slightly and toes pointed on the downbeat; the kick is finished with a straight leg. The foot then moves upward until the heel breaks the water surface. Legs are alternated. The kick should not splash water. Proper head position is accomplished with the water line at the middle of the forehead.

Back Glide with Kick. The backstroke kick (flutter) is accomplished by allowing the foot to first sink in the water about 12 inches by bending the knees. The up-beat, which is the propulsive phase, is done by straightening the leg. The foot should not come out of the water, but the leg and toes do come near the surface. This technique maintains proper body position. The student eases off the wall on the back, glides (5 feet), and begins a gentle backstroke kick; arms should remain at side. Proper head alignment is indicated by the chin being slightly up and the water line just over the ears.

Front Beginner Stroke. This stroke is taught when the front glide with kick can be done for 10 seconds. The stroke consists of the front glide with kick and an armstroke. The armstroke is accomplished by alternating arms from the streamlined position to the thigh. The arms are moved in perfect alternation with an underwater recovery and pull, push, slice, reach action. The pull phase is initiated by pulling down and back on the water with the hand from the overhead position. Then, keeping the elbow high and beginning a bend at the elbow, the hand passes down the centerline of the body. Once the hand passes mid-chest, a pushing action is made toward the feet. The hand should be angled so that the palm is facing and pushing toward the feet. Breathing can be accomplished by turning the chin to either shoulder. The breathing is timed so that when the hand of the desired breathing side is in the push phase, the chin is turned to the shoulder of the breathing side. The breath pattern should be such that the student blows bubbles into the water with the face in, completes the exhaling phase when the mouth exits

Figure 23-5 Teacher-assisted jump from wall.

the water, and inhales with the mouth out of the water. Immediately after taking the breath, the student turns the head so that the face is in the water and begins to exhale. The breath is not held.

Back Beginner Stroke. The student who can streamline from the wall in the back streamline position (arms down), glide (5 feet), and begin the backstroke kick is ready for the back beginner stroke. Simultaneous arm movement is started by running the thumbs up the sides of the body to the shoulders and then extending arms laterally. Palms should face the wall the body came from. Using straight arms, the student pushes the water toward the feet and hands to the hips, the start position. Arm cycle is repeated after a short glide. ARM CUE: Up, Out, Together, Glide.

Jump from the Wall (Shallow Water). This activity can be exciting for the beginner. Although the skill is relatively easy, safety precautions must be given. Advise students not to turn around toward the wall when jumping into the pool. It is a good idea to assist the swimmer for the first few jumps. The teacher stands facing the student, holds hands with the student, either right to left or left to right, then turns so that the student does not jump on top of the teacher (Figure 23-5). Students should look at the area where they are going to enter the water. The teacher can enhance this aspect by placing the free hand in this area so that the student may spot it.

Intermediate Swimming

Before moving on to the intermediate level, students must thoroughly understand and be able to demonstrate the beginner skills in the previous section and be able to swim approximately two widths of the pool. The intermediate skills described in this section will enable students to be more proficient in the water.

STROKES

This section reviews the biomechanics of swimming and applies the principles to the teaching of the strokes. Similarities will be found among the strokes in propulsive force, pull patterns, rhythmic breathing patterns, and high elbow positions.

Front Crawl.   The fastest of the strokes and most preferred for fitness swimming activities is the front crawl (freestyle). This stroke is characterized by the crawling motion of the arms.

1. The *arm cycle* is similar to that described in the beginner stroke, except that the arm recovery is above the water. The hand enters the water in front of the head, extending straight up from the shoulder and entering with the thumb and forefinger side first (30- to 40-degree pitch). Upon entry, the arm should be extended fully forward and slightly downward. The catch of the stroke begins with the fingers pointing downward toward the bottom as the wrist and elbow begin to flex. Keeping the elbow above the hand, the swimmer begins to pull the body forward across the hand. The palm of the hand should face the wall the swimmer came from, the hand should move down the centerline of the body, and the elbow should bend to approximately 90 degrees to provide maximum leverage. The push phase is the final underwater stage and is accomplished by extending the elbow and pressing the hand to the thigh.

2. The *recovery* begins with the hand turning to the little finger side, by the thigh, and slipping out of the water. The elbow is lifted to a 90-degree angle at the elbow joint above the water, and the fingertips are carried close to the water surface to the entry point. ARMSTROKE CUE: Slice, Down the Hill, Up the Hill, Push to Thigh, High Elbow, Slice.

3. The *freestyle kick* is identical to the front kick in the beginner section, with a six-beat rhythmical pattern to stroke cycle.

4. Breathing is accomplished to either side, with the head beginning the turn during the push phase of the armstroke to that side. The breath should not be held during any part of the stroke cycle.

Elementary Backstroke.   The elementary backstroke is a resting stroke that provides the swimmer with an opportunity to relax and breathe continuously.

1. The *arm cycle* is identical to that described for the beginner backstroke. The kick now becomes an inverted breaststroke kick instead of a flutter kick.

2. The inverted *breaststroke kick* is learned by sitting on the pool edge with legs together and extended over the water. Drop the heels to the pool wall by bending the knees. Keeping the knees close together (less than 6 inches), curl ankles away from each other and toes toward surface of the water. The propulsive phase is accomplished by straightening the legs and pushing water with the insoles of the feet. KICK CUES: Drop, Curl, Together.

3. Overall coordination begins with the thumbs up the side of the body to shoulder level while the heels drop at the knee (Up); the arms reach laterally while the ankles and toes curl up and out (Out); the pull begins slightly ahead of the extension of the legs; and hands touch thighs as toes come together (Together). CUE: Up, Out, Together, Glide.

Note: Hips, knees, and chest should remain in alignment throughout the entire stroke.

Back Crawl.   The back crawl is the second fastest competitive stroke and is characterized by the crawling motion in the supine position.

1. The *armstroke* of the back crawl begins with a straight arm entry of the little finger side of the hand, at arm's length, above the head (karate chop). The fingertips turn toward the bottom and sweep downward. The catch of the water takes place by an upward rotation of the hand and a bend of the elbow. The pull is an elliptical pattern and can be described as arm wrestling the water. The final underwater phase is a push downward and toward the feet. Arms alternate simultaneously.

2. The recovery begins by letting go of the water and bringing the hand out of the water with thumbs up. The arms remain straight during the above water phase, and the shoulder shrugs past the cheek. CUE: Karate Chop, Fingertips Down, Catch, Arm Wrestle, Push, Let Go, Thumb Up, Straight Arm, Shrug, Little Finger.

3. The kick is a six-beat flutter on the back similar to the beginner backstroke.

Breaststroke.   The breaststroke can be used as a resting stroke although it is one of the four competitive swimming strokes.

1. The armstroke of the breaststroke differs from the front and back crawl in that the arms do not alternate and the recovery is underwater. The armstroke begins with the body in the streamlined position. The hands separate and press outward in a sculling motion. The hands rotate as the elbows bend slightly and move to an inward sweep. This phase ends as the hands come together beneath the chin. The hands then move upward and forward to the streamlined

position with forearms close together. This movement can be described as drawing a heart on the pool bottom with the fingertips and then cutting the heart in half as the arms recover and extend forward.

2. Breathing takes place during the pull phase of the armstroke and is done simply by lifting the chin to water level. The breath should not be held during any phase of the stroke.

3. The kick is accomplished by taking the inverted breaststroke kick that was learned for the elementary backstroke and turning it over. A slight difference to be noted is that the heels should be pulled to the buttocks and the knees should not be pulled toward the abdomen.

4. The stroke starts with the streamline, followed by arm pull, breathe, extend arms and recover heels to buttocks simultaneously, kick and glide into the streamlined position. *Hint:* Students may have trouble getting back to the streamlined position and holding it for the glide. Have students grab the thumb on the extension phase of the arms and hold the thumb until their toes touch from the kick, then glide, then separate and angle hands for pull. CUE: Hold Thumb, Pull, Breathe, Grab Thumb, Extend Arms, Kick, Toes Touch, Glide, Pull.

Sidestroke. The sidestroke is the stroke of choice used in lifeguard rescues. The sidestroke uniquely allows a rescuer to carry a victim comfortably and efficiently.

1. The arm cycle begins with the body on a preferred side with the top arm (trailing arm) extended over the hip and the bottom arm (leading arm) extended forward. The ear in the water (bottom ear) lies on the shoulder of the leading arm, and the water line runs down the cheek, with the mouth out of the water. Arms move simultaneously, with the leading arm sweeping downward and inward (Pull) in line with the body, while the trailing arm slices to position under the chin. With the hands near each other, the leading arm begins to slice forward as the trailing hand sweeps downward, backward, and upward (Push) in close proximity to the abdomen and finishing at the thigh.

2. The kick used in the sidestroke is the scissors kick, characterized by the scissor motion. The standard scissors kick begins with top leg resting on the lower, with knees straight and toes together and pointed. This is the start and end position. Legs are bent at the knees and drawn in line to the hips, with heels toward buttocks. The top leg and bottom leg separate simultaneously, with top leg forward, bottom leg backward, knees slightly flexed, and toes pointed, to the stride position. Legs can then be straightened to the glide position, producing propulsion with the back of the top leg and the front of the bottom leg.

3. The overall timing begins in the glide position on the side; as the pull takes place, the heels are drawn up, and as the hands meet, the legs separate to stride, then the push and kick occur together, and the stroke finishes with a glide. CUE: Pull and Draw, Push and Kick, Glide.

Diving

Diving from the pool deck, dock, springboard, or platform can be exciting and exhilarating. Unfortunately, diving can also be dangerous if not taught and executed properly. It is estimated that 95 percent of all the diving injuries each year involve an untrained diver and less than 5 feet of water. This fact should make students and teachers follow proper progressions and ensure proper water depth when diving. The recommended depth for teaching diving from deck level is 9 feet or greater. The recommended depth for teaching from a 1-meter springboard is 12 feet or greater, with the board extending 6 feet over the water, and a landing area of the 12-foot depth extending forward 20 feet from the end of the board.

The following dives should be taught in sequence to ensure diving safety among participants. Dives must be taught in appropriate-depth water.

TYPES OF DIVES

Slide-in Dive (9 feet deep). The slide-in dive is the most basic of all dives. The teacher has the student lie face down on a smooth resolite mat (preferred) or on the side of the deck, with arms extended overhead and body slightly arched (Figure 23-6). The teacher then holds the student's ankles, lifts the legs, and slides the student into the water. The student holds the body rigid and adjusts angle of entry by raising or lowering the arms and hands. If the student points the fingertips to the bottom, a deep dive will result; if the student raises fingertips and points to the other side of the pool, a shallow distance dive will result.

Sitting Dive (9 feet deep). The sitting dive is the next in the sequence shown in Figure 23-6. Head position and arm position are essential. The early learning phase should consist of the chin being on the chest, arms over ears, and the student should remain in this position throughout the dive. This position will minimize the probability of smacking the chest and abdominal area. As the student becomes more accomplished, she will be able to adjust head and arm position to achieve desired depth or distance of dive. The teacher may assist from the water by holding the student's fingertips and leading her down into the water.

Kneeling Dive (9 feet deep). The student kneels on one knee, with toes of foot on opposite leg over the pool edge (see Figure 23-6). Arms are extended overhead in the streamlined position, and the chin is on the

Figure 23-6 Sequence illustrating (right to left) slide-in dive, sitting dive, kneeling dive, and shallow push dive.

chest. Initially, the student simply pivots over the knee and enters the water. As skill and readiness increase, the student can push with the foot of the nonkneeling leg. The teacher can assist in the same manner as for the sitting dive.

Scale Dive or Tip-in Dive (9 feet deep).   The scale dive begins from the standing position, with arms overhead and in the streamline position. The diver then performs a gymnastic-type scale and balances with one leg vertical and one leg horizontal. The teacher may assist the student by lifting the horizontal leg. The student pivots around on the foot of the vertical leg and, while keeping knees straight, brings legs together with toes pointed as he enters the water fingertips first. Emphasis should be placed on keeping the chin on chest and keeping the vertical pivot leg straight.

Shallow Push Dive (9 feet deep).   The shallow push dive starts with hands together in front of the body. The toes of both feet are over the pool edge and knees are bent (see Figure 23-6). The student begins the dive motion by extending the arms over the water surface, extending legs straight, and pushing with the ankles. Emphasis should be placed on getting the heels higher than the head to achieve a fingertip head-first entry.

Deep Push Dive (9 feet deep).   The deep push dive is used for reaching the bottom of the pool rapidly. As in all dives, emphasis should be placed on keeping the arms overhead when entering the water to prevent the head from striking the bottom or another object in the water. Additionally, the diver should always check the area for swimmers or other obstacles before diving.

The diver begins in a more vertical position than in the previous dive. Arms are overhead in the streamline position, knees and hips are flexed, and toes are over the edge of the pool. The emphasis is on springing or jumping the hips up as the head and arms move downward toward the water. Once the diver is in the air, she must extend the body into a straight position to enter the water vertically and be projected to the pool bottom. It is helpful if the diver maintains a slight pike at the hips upon entry so that the legs are not flopped over and the back arched.

Forward Standing Dive from the 1-Meter Springboard (12 feet deep).   The forward standing dive is performed in a similar manner as the deep push dive from the deck. The only notable difference is instead of jumping forcefully, the diver should use the spring of the board by extending the legs and riding the board to achieve maximum height. Body position upon entry should be stretched and rigid as shown in Figure 23-7.

Standing Back Dive from the 1-Meter Springboard (12 feet deep).   The back dive may cause some anxiety among students and teachers, but if proper safety precautions and instructional techniques are followed carefully, attempts will be more successful and less subject to trial and error or injury. The diving board must extend 6 feet over the water, and the depth from the end of the board back to the wall must be at least 12 feet, the distance of the diver's underwater path. Backward and inward dives should not be attempted from the pool side or from backyard pool diving boards because the diver may hit the pool wall.

The diver needs to understand that he will pivot around the tip of the board at the heels and that it is essential to keep straight legs. Also, the diver must realize that the body will follow the head and that the head must stay back, with eyes looking for the water. The diver then places the arms above the head, arches the lower back slightly, looks up at the hands, and falls head and shoulders first while keeping legs straight.

The teacher assists the diver by placing the student in proper body alignment. The teacher places one knee against one of the student's knees, to keep him from bending the leg, and assists him in clearing the board. To maintain balance, the teacher must stand in the stride position. The teacher's hands are placed on the student's sides level with the small of the back. The student is cued with *fall*, and the teacher manages rate of fall by extending the arms. The teacher then moves hand positions to spot the diver by going to the back of the calf and adjusting the diver for a vertical entry (Figure 23-8).

Learning/Helpful Hints

The teaching of aquatic-related skills in schools since the advent of the YMCA and American Red Cross programs traditionally has been one of assembly-line-like instruction. A recent contrast to this approach comes in contemporary prescriptive aquatic instruction, or a developmental approach. This approach is based on the principles common to movement education. Both of these approaches should be given consideration and aligned with the goals of the particular instruction program offered at the institution.

Figure 23-7 Standing dive from 1-meter board; water depth is 12 feet.

This section outlines basic knowledge involved in many swimming/aquatic skills and includes methods of instruction, biomechanical/hydrodynamic principles related to swimming, effective pool use, water entry and exit, water orientation, bobbing and safety bobbing, buoyancy and floating, gliding, kicking, strokes, basic diving mechanics, and basic dives.

TEACHING METHODOLOGY

Teaching swimming skills successfully depends on the teacher's knowledge of biomechanics of strokes, student readiness, the student's desire to practice, and the teacher's ability to communicate constructive observations. The method used to teach swimming is dependent on two factors: (1) the complexity of the skill to be learned and (2) the motor ability of the learner. For simple skills involving average to above-average ability, the whole method of teaching is used (verbal description, demonstration, and swimming of the whole stroke). For complex skills, the part method (breakdown of skill into body position, kick, arm-stroke, breathing, coordination) should be used. For assessment of a swimmer's ability, a whole method is recommended because it allows the teacher to establish the overall ability of the class and ascertain levels of student fear. Where fear is not evident and swimmers are of average ability, swimming skills would be

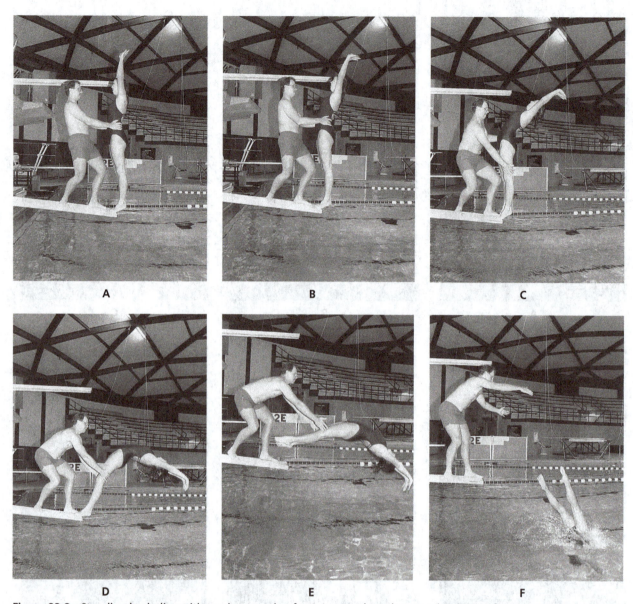

Figure 23-8 Standing back dive with teacher spotting from 1-meter board; water depth is 12 feet.

classified as simple and the whole method of instruction should be used.

BIOMECHANICAL PRINCIPLES OF SWIMMING

It is essential that the teacher understand how the biomechanics of the stroke affect swimming efficiency. A swimmer's forward progress through the water is affected by many factors—in particular, propulsion, resistance, and buoyancy.

Propulsion. The propulsive force is created by the different hand positions, pulls, and kicks used by the swimmer. Regardless of the stroke used, the hand should be held firm, slightly cupped, and the fingers relaxed but close together. The hands follow an elliptical pattern as opposed to a straight line. In the underwater phase of all strokes, the pull arm(s) come to a bent arm position,

minimizing up and down movements in the water. Propulsion in all strokes must be optimized to overcome the laws of inertia. Other important laws of movement include the law of acceleration, whereby the swimmer must apply an equal force (even stroke) in the direction in which the force acts. A variation in application of force will be required in strokes other than the front and back crawl strokes. The law of action/reaction, which states that every action has an equal and opposite reaction, is also critical to the swimmer. For example, if a swimmer's armstroke in the front or back crawl is wide and sweeping, then the swimmer's legs and trunk will move in the opposite direction, thereby creating more resistance.

Resistance. Often referred to as drag resistance is the combination of forces that slows a swimmer's forward progress. Frontal resistance is created by the water directly in front of the body: the more vertical the body is in the water, the greater the frontal resistance. Skin function resistance is created by the water that is flowing immediately next to the body. Tail suction, or "eddy" resistance, is caused by poorly streamlined body parts creating a momentary void in the water, making the body pull or suck water with it. All three of these resistance factors can be reduced by streamlining the body during all phases of strokes and turns.

Buoyancy. Various physical factors affect an individual's ability to float, among them bone size, fat tissue, muscular development, weight distribution, and lung capacity. A swimmer with dense bone structure and heavy muscle tissue will tend to sink lower in the water than a person with a higher body fat percentage. This explains why some swimmers float better than others.

The center of buoyancy is that point of the body around which it rotates in the water. The center of buoyancy is located higher in the body than the center of gravity. In general, on land a female's center of gravity is in the hip region and a male's is in the lower rib area. In the water, however, the center of buoyancy is generally located much higher in males than in females, likely because of the more dense leg structure of the male. This information is important when teaching floating and gliding skills and explains why men find it more difficult to float and glide horizontally than do women. Another reason is that men float lower in the water, which requires them to overcome greater frontal resistance and skin friction due to the greater submerged body surface.

▶ Practice/Organizational Suggestions

Efficiency of pool use is necessary when classes are large. Beginner classes offer more restraints than advanced classes because only shallow water is used. The teacher will need to be in the water when teaching beginning-level classes, but in teaching more advanced swimmers, the teacher may wish to be on the deck. In both situations, it is recommended that the teacher use the width of the pool for teaching and making corrections. When the teacher performs demonstrations in the water, the swimmers should stand on the deck. If the pool has windows, the students watching the demonstration should have their backs to the windows. These two recommendations allow students to get a better view of the demonstration by reducing glare.

Students need to be reminded that most accidents in the pool area occur on the pool deck and during water entry and exit. Teachers should remind students at the beginning and throughout each pool session that they should enter by sitting on the pool side and slipping into the water or jumping in feet first and facing the center of the pool. Students should exit the pool by using the ladders.

In classes with swimming students of many different skill levels, the teacher should test students along the shallow end of the pool and divide them into groups according to their skill level: beginner, intermediate, or advanced. Advanced students can then assist the teacher. Advanced students will gain valuable insight into their own swimming by assisting in the instructional process. This experience also may entice these students into moving toward obtaining their water safety teacher certification in the future. The teacher should set aside time at the end of the class period to work with the advanced students on advanced skills, while beginners and intermediates practice basic skills unassisted, yet supervised. This strategy works well with the middle school ages and up. However, for elementary school students, the divide-and-conquer strategy, which groups swimmers by skill levels, using the more advanced to work with the less skilled to assist the teacher, will differ and should not be used.

The swimming teacher should request that students be grouped by skill level beforehand so that beginners are taught in one class period, intermediates in another class period, and so forth. Also, the teacher should indicate what the appropriate student/teacher ratios are for the different skill levels. Recommendation:

Beginners: 10:1 maximum
Advanced beginners: 15:1 maximum
Intermediate: 20:1 maximum

If classes cannot be set up this way, the teacher must go to the divide-and-conquer method within the class period. Because many students of elementary school age may not be able to even stand in the shallow end, it is imperative to have assistance in the pool classroom. A rule to which there can be no exception is to work with students one-on-one. Stress that the students may not leave the wall, and maintain constant vigilance with the students on the wall. If the school is combined with older grade levels, use older volunteer students from study hall or activity periods to assist with instruction.

WATER EXERCISE

Nature and Purpose

Water exercise is one of the nation's fastest growing fitness activities. There are many advantages to this exercise venue. It is only in water that three-dimensional resistance to movement is possible. This resistance provides improved muscle tone and joint stability. Water also provides smooth resistance that is accommodating over the full range of motion. The participant in water exercise is buoyed up by the water, which provides protection from injuries often associated with land exercise. This factor allows almost complete elimination of injurious ballistic stress on joints, connective tissues, and muscles. Water training allows the participant to simulate almost any sport movement, and if a proper program is adhered to for 20 to 30 minutes, three times a week, there can be an aerobic training effect for the heart and circulatory system. Clearly, therefore, water activity holds great value for rehabilitation, and in fact many individuals who cannot walk, run, or make ballistic movements on land can do so in the water.

Although it is recommended that participants know how to swim, it is not necessary that they have deep-water swimming ability because water exercise can be taught completely in the shallow water. However, if water exercise classes wish to use deep water for conditioning, it is recommended that the teacher screen participants for deep-water swimming ability.

Equipment

Necessary equipment includes a music player, battery-operated microphone, and amplification equipment.

Suggested Learning Sequence for Water Exercise

A. The teacher
1. The teacher should teach from the pool deck. This position allows students to see the teacher demonstrating techniques and allows the teacher to see students' performance. Additionally, being on deck enables the teacher to access any audio equipment that may be in use.
2. The teacher's demonstration on deck must be slowed to allow the students who are in the water to keep pace with the teacher.
3. The teacher should select music with lyrics appropriate for the students' age group.
4. Music tempo should correspond to the students' ability to keep pace and the desired physiological response, for example, warm-up, aerobic, and so on.

B. The participant
1. Appropriate swimwear should be worn (bathing suits). Cut-offs, gym shorts, and T-shirts should not be allowed.
2. Participants may wish to wear aqua sock–type footwear to support the arches and protect the balls of the feet.
3. Participants should take a soap shower and discard any chewing gum, candy, and so forth before entering pool.

C. Teaching techniques
1. Water should be approximately chest level for most exercises (3½ to 5 feet deep).
2. Some participants may prefer to remain in the shallower water and squat down to chest level; this will increase their stability. Others may wish to reduce stability by standing in deeper water.

Each participant should find a comfortable depth in which to achieve the maximum desired results.
3. When exercising, the body weight should move in the same direction as the motion of desired area being exercised; that is, if arms are moving forward, body weight should be moving forward.
4. Leg position is the key to stability. Depending on the exercise goal, the feet should position either shoulder-width apart (straddle) or one foot in front, one foot in back (stride).

D. Exercises

Table 23-1 lists a number of common exercises that can be done in the water to work out various muscle groups. Many other variations are, of course, possible. Water exercises are limited only by one's imagination and creativity. Teachers can readily select or design exercises to meet specific needs.

FITNESS SWIMMING

Nature and Purpose

Fitness swimming as an avenue for exercise has been popularized in recent years as a result of cross-training and the increase in the number of triathalons. This section discusses the principles involved with fitness training and workout construction for swimming.

The three most common factors that must be adhered to in an effort to derive a benefit physiologically from any exercise program are frequency, intensity, and time (FIT). *Frequency* refers to the number of days per week that one should or can work out. Obviously, time constraints, schedules, and pool availability affect this factor. One should understand that swimming once per week is better than not swimming at all, but to obtain the greatest benefits, four to five times per week would be best.

Intensity is an indication of how difficult the training is physically. The principle of overload must be applied to improve physiological systems. The body, when trained at more intense rates than normal daily activity, will adapt accordingly with improved strength, endurance, and flexibility, as well as benefit the cardiovascular system. When overloading the systems, one must rely on proper progression and specificity, so as to avoid injury. Therefore, it is important to measure the intensity of workouts through one or a combination of four indicators: heart rate, time of swim, breathing rate, and perceived effort.

In terms of an aerobic training zone for adults, heart rate is best if between 120 and 170 beats per minute (bpm). To obtain the heart rate, one should take the pulse rate for 10 seconds at the carotid artery and multiply this number by 6. Note: Individuals who cross-train will generally find lower heart rates of 8 to 10 bpm in swimming as compared with land activities of equal perceived exertion. The physiological basis for this 8- to 10-bpm

Table 23-1 **Water exercises for various muscles**

Name	Muscle group	Body position	Foot position
Upper body			
Push/pull	Chest/back/arms	Standing/wall	Straddle
Push-down/pull-up	Shoulders/upper arm	Squat	Straddle
Lateral pull/press	Shoulders/upper chest and back	Squat	Straddle
Horizontal fly	Shoulders/upper chest and back	Standing	Stride
Front raise/press back	Shoulders/upper chest and back	Standing	Stride
Water punch	Upper arms	Squat	Stride
Arm circle	Shoulders/trunk	Squat	Straddle
Arm rowing	Upper back/trunk	Squat	Stride
Single-arm circle	Shoulders	Standing/wall	Straddle
Trunk			
Trunk rock	Abdomen/lower back	Standing	Straddle
Waist circle	Abdomen/lower back	Standing	Stride
Grapevine/cross-kick	Abdomen/lower back	Standing/wall	Straddle
Legs			
Walking/running	Buttocks	Standing/wall	Stride
Alternating leg kick—straight	Buttocks/thigh	Standing/wall	Stride
Alternating leg kick—bent	Buttocks/thigh	Standing/wall	Stride
Lateral leg kick—straight	Inner/outer thigh	Standing/wall	Straddle
Lateral leg kick—bent	Inner/outer thigh	Standing/wall	Straddle
Squat-tuck jump	Abdomen/thigh	Squat	Straddle
Knee lift	Abdomen/thigh	Squat/wall	Straddle
Roundhouse horizontal kick	Buttocks/abdomen/lower back	Standing/wall	Straddle
Leg circles front/back	Buttocks/thigh	Standing/wall	Straddle
Hamstring/quadricep curl	Thigh	Standing/wall	Straddle

lowering stems from facial bradycardia, which is a result of the mammalian diving reflex. Simply, when a mammal places the face in the water, the heart rate is slowed.

The *time* of the overall training session should last 30 to 60 minutes to improve aerobic levels. Once again, proper progression should be used to avoid injury.

Breathing rate as an indicator of intensity is less exact than heart rate. Breathing rate can be assessed by counting the number of breaths taken in a 5-second interval. When training at an appropriate level, one should take three to four breaths in the 5-second interval.

Perceived effort can be determined through swimming speed. One can develop workouts by developing a baseline maximal-effort swim time and then use percentages of this swim time to determine effort. For example, the swimmer swims and times an all-out maximal-effort 100-yard swim. The target, then, is to train at 75 to 90 percent of the maximal-effort time and identify the feeling of effort that accompanies the times. The aerobic range of perceived effort should fall in the 7 to 8 range on a 10 scale, with 10 being equal to the maximal-effort swim. This baseline may have to be adjusted as training levels and physiological conditioning improve.

Interval Training

There are several methods of training that can be applied to fitness swimming. Examples are straight long slow distance, fartlek, interval, speed-assisted, and speed-resisted. The most popular method is interval training because of the diversity of workouts that can be developed. The workouts are more interesting for the swimmer, therefore increasing motivation.

Interval training workout construction is best accomplished by using four factors: distance, interval, repetition, and time (DIRT). *Distance* is the yardage of each repeat within a set of repeats. The distance per repeat for aerobic training generally ranges between 50 and 1,000 yards. *Interval* refers to the amount of rest between each repeat. The rest should be less than half the time required to swim the distance of the repeat, a 2:1 work-to-rest ratio. Short rest periods between repeats improve aerobic fitness because of the maintenance of the heart rate above 120 bpm. If longer rest periods were allowed, the heart rate would recover, thus limiting the aerobic benefit.

The number of *repetitions* per set should allow for aerobic overload. This overload can be accomplished by establishing a number of repetitions and rest intervals that take a minimum of 10 minutes to complete. Therefore, if the training period for a particular day is to last 30 minutes, three sets of 10 minutes will constitute the workout. The *time* for each repeat must be developed in accordance with the swimmer's ability, the goal of the workout (aerobic vs. anaerobic), and the desired intensity of the workout. Refer to the aforementioned information concerning intensity in the FIT principle.

The fitness swimmer may wish to use the following plan when constructing workouts:

1. Warm-up   2–5 minutes
2. Main sets   Aerobic 20–30 minutes
3. Kick   5 minutes
4. Pull   5 minutes
5. Sprints   Optional
6. Warm-down   2–5 minutes

The development of workouts in this manner will not only accomplish fitness goals, but also decrease boredom.

Safety Considerations

All swimming activities require a lifeguard on duty.

A. For progressive swimming levels
  1. Encouraged behavior:
    Soap shower
    Proper swimwear
    Care for others' safety
    Cooperation with lifeguards
  2. Discouraged behavior:
    Diving from starting blocks
    Diving from poolside into less than 9 feet of water
    Running, pushing, or other unsafe acts
    Swimming in springboard diving area
    Food, gum, or drinks in pool area

B. For springboard diving
  1. Divers must pass deep-water swim test.
  2. Check area in front of diving board.
  3. Allow only one person on diving board at a time.
  4. Probibit excessive bouncing.
  5. Exit diving area promptly to nearest ladder.
  6. Difficult dives must be supervised.
  7. Reserve 3-meter diving boards for competitive use only.

C. For water exercise
  1. Permanently attach the pool safety lifeline, which separates the shallow and deep water sections.
  2. Before embarking on any physical fitness program, participants should consult a physician.
  3. Minimal teacher certification includes water safety instruction, first aid, and cardiopulmonary resuscitation.
  4. Teacher must understand physiological concepts of conditioning as they pertain to the aquatic environment, which differ considerably from those for land aerobic activity.

D. For fitness swimming
  1. A physical examination by a physician is recommended before starting any exercise program.

Failure to comply with the aforementioned safety considerations may result in serious or fatal injury!

Aquatic Safety Standards and Accident Prevention

INSTRUCTOR CERTIFICATION

In most states, the Board of Education requires that the public school teacher teaching in the pool be currently certified as an American Red Cross Water Safety Instructor (WSI) or equivalent. An acceptable equivalent is the YMCA's progressive swimming instructor certification.

LIFEGUARDS

A trained lifeguard certified through the American Red Cross or YMCA lifeguarding program must be on duty at water side for the duration of the activity and may not be assigned any other duties than guarding the participants during the time they are in the water. If the school budget does not provide for a lifeguard, the teacher or coach may not also act as a lifeguard, which requires a specific certification.

RISK ASSESSMENT

The Aquatic Council to the American Association of Health, Physical Education, Recreation and Dance (AAHPERD) established risk assessment procedures for aquatics in the AAHPERD publication *Principles of Safety in Physical Education and Sport.* Some of the topics to be considered include design safety, hazard identification, maintenance, state regulations, pool checklists, remedial maintenance protocols, supervision/instruction, record keeping, insurance, and emergency accident management procedures.

POOL SAFETY CHECKLIST

Pool safety is achieved only through a continuous program of quality supervision, maintenance, and inspection by trained and knowledgeable aquatic professionals. A pool safety checklist should be developed for the facility and should be used on a regular basis. Different areas of responsibilities may be assigned to different individuals according to their daily duties.

EMERGENCY ACCIDENT PLAN AND EQUIPMENT

1. The pool must have a telephone accessible to the lifeguard and teacher with emergency numbers posted, a first-aid kit, towels, blankets, and an easily accessible emergency entrance/exit able to accommodate ambulance personnel and equipment.
2. A written emergency plan should be posted and records of staff rehearsals kept on file. The local emergency medical services system should be consulted and used in the development of the emergency plan and subsequent rehearsals.

ATTENTION

The teacher should have all equipment for the lesson moved to the pool edge prior to the participants' entry into the water. The lifeguard or teacher should not handle phone calls or other interruptions until the exit of all students from the water. It only takes 20 to 60 seconds for a swimmer to drown.

Skill Assessment

Three types of skill tests can be used to assess swimming. One test can assess stroke form, or *how* the stroke is performed. This test uses a checklist similar to the Skill Assessment found in the Gymnastics chapter. Refer to that chapter for assistance in developing a checklist for assessing form. This same assessment technique is easily applied to diving since it is also judged for aesthetics.

Another type of test evaluates the student by speed, distance, and type of stroke. How fast can the student swim 50 meters using the breaststroke? The test assessment is the time accomplished. This type of test is best suited for intermediate to advanced swimmers. The third type test measures cardiorespiratory fitness. The length of time it takes to swim a preestablished distance is the test result. The distance and norms depend on the ages of the students. This test is similar to a 1½ mile run test for fitness.

Modifications for Special Populations

ORTHOPEDICALLY IMPAIRED

1. Use flotation devices such as inner tubes to play water games in shallow depths.
2. Use kickboards for stability in vertical positions.
3. Provide assistive stability, with peer teachers or paraprofessionals positioned behind student, stabilizing the trunk at the waist.
4. For striking games, use hand paddles attached with elastic.

COGNITIVELY IMPAIRED

1. Keep all activities in the shallow end until the student completely understands the rules of the game or task.
2. Keep your instructions short and to the point, avoiding excessive directions.
3. Use peer teachers or paraprofessionals to provide manual assistance until the student completely understands the rules of the game or task.
4. Make sure all students with Down syndrome have been screened for ATLANTO-AXIAL syndrome. This screening can be completed with an x-ray study of the C_1–C_2 vertebrae.

SENSORY IMPAIRED

1. Use peer teachers or paraprofessionals until the student completely understands the rules of the game or test.
2. Allow students who are blind or have a visual impairment additional practice prior to initiating the game or task.
3. Use cue cards (symbols) to change direction for students who are deaf or have a hearing impairment.
4. Use cue cards (color codes) to represent a change in sequence and/or directions for the game or task.

Discussion Questions

1. Discuss the advantages of learning to swim.
2. Present the steps for water orientation for beginning swimmers.
3. Identify the various skills that the beginning swimmer should attain before moving to stroke skills.
4. Compare and contrast the kick and arm actions of the basic strokes.
5. Identify the sequence of skills in diving that need to be taught to ensure safety.
6. Discuss the biomechanical principles that affect stroke efficiency.
7. Present and apply the FIT formula as it affects a fitness swimming workout.
8. Identify the various methods of training that can be applied to fitness swimming.
9. Discuss why interval training is the most popular method and apply the DIRT formula for developing a workout.
10. Identify safety considerations that the teacher should implement when teaching swimming.

Web Sites

www.usadiving.org United States Diving—includes information on diving safety, education, and resources.

www.usms.org United States Masters Swimming—includes drills, resources, and a club finder.

www.aeawave.com Aquatic Exercise Association—includes resources, links, training ideas, and product information.

www.redcross.org American Red Cross—includes information on first aid, CPR, water safety, and lifeguard training programs.

www.funandgames.org/games/GameSwim.htm—offers a list of games with instructions from a variety of sources.

http://swimming.about.com—offers information and articles covering a wide range of topics, including swimming workouts, lessons, safety, and history. Also provides recommendations on videos, books, and much more.

www.usaswimming.org USA Swimming—provides official information on competitive swimming in the United States.

www.swimnews.com *Swimnews* magazine—includes news, events, rankings, links, and more.

CHAPTER 24

Team Handball

This chapter will enable you to

- Understand how the sport of team handball evolved
- Identify and demonstrate the basic skills associated with team handball
- Develop at least one practice formation for each of the basic skills: pass, catch, throw, and dribble
- Understand and demonstrate simple rules and regulations
- Understand and demonstrate free throw, penalty throw, corner throw, throw-in, and throw-off
- Identify and name the positions of players

Nature and Purpose

Team handball may be played indoors or outdoors by children or adults of both sexes. Team handball employs fundamental motor skills such as running, throwing, catching, jumping, and defensive and offensive strategies similar to the motor skills used in basketball, soccer, and hockey.

The object of the game is to pass or dribble the ball toward the opponent's goal and then shoot the ball into the goal. The ball is played primarily with the hands; however, any portion of the body above the knee can be used to play the ball.

History

The modern game of team handball grew out of three sports, independently, in three separate European countries: Germany, Denmark, and Czechoslovakia. It was based on soccer, but the hands were used instead of the feet to propel the ball. The Germans, Danish, and Czechs each developed their own rules around the end of the 19th century.

In 1919, Carl Schelenz of Germany combined the elements of two of the games to create the new sport called *handball*. This game flourished in Europe, and in 1928 the International Amateur Handball Federation (IAHF) was formed. Handball was designed to be played outdoors with 11 players. The Danish game was played in a smaller indoor venue and consisted of seven players.[1]

The popularity of the sport spread to other countries when it was added to the official Olympic program in 1936. The first world championship for the seven-player game was sponsored by the IAHF in 1938. Following World War II, the seven-player game prevailed, and the sport was restored to the Olympics in 1972. Women's

Olympic competition began in 1976. Team handball is now guided by the International Handball Federation.[2]

The United States began playing a version of the sport in the 1930s. It was promoted by the YMCA and played almost exclusively by women. This early version was called fieldball or field handball. The name *team handball* was later attached to the seven-player game. The game's popularity in the United States grew slowly, but in 1959 the U.S. Team Handball Federation was formed. This organization still governs the sport.[3]

Court, Equipment, and Players

THE PLAYING AREA

1. The playing area (indoors or outdoors) should be a rectangular surface with dimensions of 126 to 147 feet in length and 60 to 73 feet in width (Figure 24-1). For a physical education class, a basketball court can easily be adapted to an indoor playing court by taping the goal-area line and the free-throw line.

2. The goal area is a semicircular space marked off by the goal-area line, which is drawn in front of the goal at a distance of 20 feet, with a radius of 20 feet from the back inside edges of the goal posts.

3. The free-throw line is drawn as a broken line parallel with and 10 feet beyond the goal-area line.

4. The penalty-throw line is 3 feet 3 inches long and is drawn at a distance of 23 feet from the goal.

5. The goal is in the middle of each goal line and measures 6 feet 7 inches in height and 10 feet in width. If possible, a loose net, measuring 2 feet 8 inches at the top and 3 feet 3 inches at the bottom, should be attached behind the goal post. For a physical education class, two poles, such as volleyball or

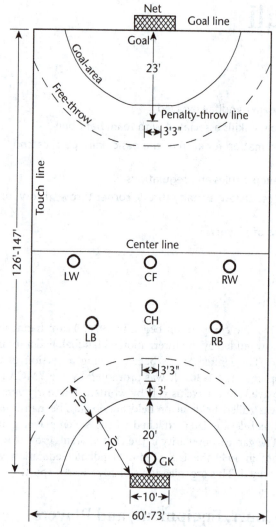

Figure 24-1 Team handball court and players' positions.

badminton poles, with a rope tied across them will serve as a goal.

THE BALL

A round ball is used that will vary in weight and circumference according to the age and sex of the players. For males over age 15, the ball should weigh 15 to 19 ounces and be 23 to 24 inches in circumference; for females and boys under age 15, the ball should weigh 11½ to 14 ounces and measure 21 to 22 inches around. For physical education classes, a playground ball or volleyball will serve the purpose of the game. However, basketballs and soccer balls should not be used.

PLAYERS

Each team consists of seven players (six court players and one goalkeeper) with five additional players for substitution. The positions of players are designated as goalkeeper, center half, right and left backs, center forward, and right and left wingers (see Figure 24-1).

Basic Rules

DURATION OF THE GAME

1. Playing times for a regulation game will vary depending on the age and sex of the players: for men—two periods of 30 minutes, with an interval of 10 minutes; for women and junior males—two periods of 25 minutes, with an interval of 10 minutes; and for all other players—two periods of 20 minutes, with a 10-minute interval.

2. The winning team from the referee's coin toss has the choice of either the end or defense, or offense.

3. By referee's whistle, the game must start at the center of the court only by passing the ball to another teammate. All players must be within their own half of the court at the beginning.

4. After each goal is scored, the other team will always start the game at the center of the court.

5. A goal cannot be scored directly from the throw-on.

PLAYING THE BALL

1. The ball can be played in any manner with any part of the body except below the knee. (For violation of this rule, a free throw is awarded to the opposition.)

2. The ball cannot be held for more than 3 seconds if the player is not moving. (Otherwise, a free throw is awarded to the opposition.)

3. The ball can be bounced once or repeatedly with either hand while moving or standing—like a dribble in basketball.

4. Once the ball has been seized with one or both hands, it must be played off within 3 seconds or after three steps have been taken. (Otherwise, a free throw is awarded to the opposition.)

5. Any ball that touches a referee or goal post is still playable.

6. Players cannot dive for rolling balls that are on the ground.

7. The ball may be continuously rolled on the ground with one hand.

8. When the ball has passed the touch line, the ball can be put into play by the other team, as in basketball, and the throw-in should take place from the point where the ball crossed the touch line.

9. If the ball is touched by a defensive player, except the goalkeeper, and travels across the goal line outside the goal, a corner throw is awarded to the attacking team. The ball is put back in play by the goalkeeper with a throw-off if the goalkeeper last touched it.

APPROACH TO OPPONENT

Players are not permitted to

1. Block an opponent with arms, hands, or legs (free throw awarded to opposition).

2. Hold, hit, push, run into, or jump at the opponent or throw oneself in front of or endanger an opponent in any other way (free throw awarded to opposition).

3. Throw the ball intentionally at an opponent or execute a dangerous feint by moving the ball toward the opponent (free throw awarded to opposition).

THE GOAL AREA

1. No player except the goalkeeper may enter the goal area.

2. Entry of a player from the defending team, provided the entry is intentional and for the clear purpose of defense, results in a penalty throw (23 feet) awarded to the attacking team.

3. There shall be no penalty if a player enters the goal area after playing the ball.

4. Inside the goal-area line, the ball belongs to the goalkeeper. No other player can touch a ball that is lying, rolling, or being held by the goalkeeper inside this area.

5. The ball can neither be thrown into one's own goal area nor to the goalkeeper. (A penalty throw is awarded to the opposition team.)

6. A ball in the air is not considered to be in the goal area.

THE GOALKEEPER

1. As long as the goalkeeper remains inside the goal area, he is allowed to defend the goal in every possible way, including kicking the ball with the feet while the ball is moving toward the goal or is inside the goal area.

2. The goalkeeper is allowed to leave the goal area without the ball. When he does, the same rules apply to the goalie as to the rest of the team.

3. The goalie may not touch a ball that is lying or rolling outside the goal area.

SCORING

1. A goal is made when the ball has passed the goal line inside the goal with its *entire* circumference.

2. A goal made by the defending team is also scored as a goal.

3. After every goal, the team that did not score restarts the game from the center of the court.

PENALTY THROW

1. When the offensive player has lost a clear chance of scoring by the defensive player's foul, the offensive player is awarded a penalty throw from the 23-foot line.

2. During a penalty throw, no other player except the goalkeeper is allowed between the goal-area line and the free-throw line.

3. The penalty throw must be aimed directly at the goal.

FREE THROW

1. All violations of the rules, except the penalty throw, will result in a free throw awarded to the opposing team.

2. All free throws are taken from the point where the violation occurred, except a violation between the free-throw line and the goal-area line, in which case the free throw is taken at the free-throw line.

3. During a free throw, players of the defending team must stand 10 feet away from the player having the free throw.

4. A goal may be scored directly from a free throw.

Suggested Learning Sequence

Team handball is an activity that can be learned very quickly. A basic game can be played at an early stage of the physical education class; offensive and defensive formations and styles of play may be added as the level of skill increases. It is important to discuss terminology, rules, skills, and strategies at a time when appropriate and meaningful to the discussion of a particular concept.

A. Purpose of the game

B. Skills and techniques. The skills of passing, shooting, and dribbling are best taught in combination with each other.
   1. Short-distance passes
      a. Bounce
      b. Close hand-off
      c. Hook
      d. Chest
      e. Shovel
      f. Overhead
   2. Medium-distance passes
      a. Ground
      b. Jump
      c. Shoulder (baseball)
      d. Side arm
   3. Catching
   4. Dribble
   5. Shooting
      a. Jump shot
      b. Dive shot
      c. Underhand shot

    d. Reverse shot

    e. Side throw

    f. Lob shot

    g. Penalty throw

  6. Goalkeeping. Goalkeeping should be started early in the sequence. A few minutes' practice each day will add to the quality of the game.

C. Playing strategies

  1. Defensive formations

  2. Offensive formations

D. Rules. Discuss the rule when applicable to a given situation or skill.

E. Terminology. Terms should be discussed as they arise in the normal progression.

It is recommended that scrimmage time be included in early lessons. The length of scrimmage time will increase as the unit progresses.

Skills and Techniques

PASSING

Passing is the most important element of team handball. It allows a player to move the ball quickly and accurately to advance the ball and set up scoring opportunities. Team handball passing fundamentals are quite similar to those used in basketball.

▶ Learning Hints

1. The speed of the receiver as well as the distance between the receiver and the passer will determine how hard the ball should be thrown and the type of pass to be used.

2. For practice purposes, point the nonthrowing arm in the direction of the throw. (In actual game situations, more deception must be used to avoid "telegraphing" the pass.)

3. Use fingertip control to ensure a more consistently accurate pass.

4. Maintain proper balance and distribution of body weight to ensure a more accurate pass. Shift your weight from the back to front foot, maintaining momentum behind the ball for a crisp pass. (Do *not* throw a pass when you are off balance except in improvised or emergency situations.)

5. Step forward with the leg opposite to the throwing arm.

6. Snap your wrist on release.

7. Select a pass that is appropriate for a specific situation.

8. After you pass, always be ready to penetrate the defense and await a return pass.

9. A properly thrown pass will usually enable your teammates to catch the ball more easily.

10. When passing the ball, always make a threatening motion (feint) to score before passing to a teammate.

Passes can be divided into three categories characterizing the distance, trajectory, and type (arm form) of the throw.

Short-Distance Passes. Passes that are normally used in short distances include the following:

1. *Bounce.* The ball should be thrown so that it bounces approximately 3 feet in front of the receiver. The receiver should move toward the ball and try to catch it on the short hop (as in baseball) in such a manner that she is immediately prepared to throw the ball.

2. *Close hand-off (front and back).* In this pass (which usually occurs in close quarters around the goal area), the player merely hands the ball to a teammate in a manner similar to an "end-around" (reverse) play in football. Deception is of utmost importance in this pass. It should be used only after considerable practice and by players who are familiar with each other because the chance for error is much greater than with other passes.

3. *Hook.* This pass is useful when a player is closely guarded by two or more players. It can also be used when a player is in the air for a jump shot. The player simply releases the ball at the top of his jump to a teammate who might be penetrating toward the goal. This pass is the same as the "hook shot" in basketball.

4. *Chest (push).* This pass should be one of the most frequently used in short distances. It is one of the most accurate passes and relatively simple to learn. The same fundamentals can be applied as for the two-hand chest pass.

5. *Shovel (scoop).* This pass is less frequently used than the other passes. The player picks a low ball upon the short hop and remains in a crouched position while quickly tossing the ball (underhand) to a teammate.

6. *Overhead (two hands).* One of the methods of putting the ball back into play after it has crossed one of the sidelines, this throw is taken by a player of the team that did not cause the ball to go out. The player making the throw must have both feet touching the surface outside the sideline and throw in to the playing area with one or two hands in any manner.

Medium-Distance Passes. Passes that are normally used in medium distances include the following:

1. *Ground ("roller").* When all other passing lanes are blocked it may, on occasion, be appropriate to roll the ball between a defender's legs. Also, when there is a scramble for a loose ball on the court and a player cannot control the ball completely, she can roll it to a nearby teammate.

Figure 24-2 The jump shot.

2. *Jump.* When normal passing lanes are impeded, a player can use this pass by jumping into the air and releasing the ball in a manner similar to the shoulder throw (Figure 24-2).

3. *Shoulder (baseball).* When throwing, the player should not attempt to grip the ball as if it were a baseball. Rather, allow the ball to rest in the hand with a flexed wrist and fingers spread wide enough to cover as much of the ball surface as is comfortably possible.

4. *Side arm.* This pass is the same as the shoulder pass, except the positioning and action of the throwing arm may be likened to a three-quarters or "submarine" pitching motion, as in baseball. The length of stride for the lead leg should correspond (approximately) to the length of the pass. For a right-handed throw, the right foot can remain in place (with weight back), and the left foot can stride forward simultaneously with the arm-throwing motion.

CATCHING

An accurate throw will result in an accurate catch.

▶ Learning Hints

1. Whenever possible, players are to catch the ball with two hands to ensure best control.

2. The player should always attempt to catch the ball with the fingertips spread. Whenever possible, the ball should not be allowed to make contact with the palms.

3. The elbows should be flexed and the body relaxed to absorb the impact of a hand-thrown ball.

4. Whenever possible, the player should move forward to meet the ball, maintaining eye contact with the ball as it comes into the hands.

5. On receiving a pass, a player should be immediately prepared to shoot, dribble, or pass the ball again.

DRIBBLE

In team handball, the dribble is used to advance the ball up the court when a player is not closely guarded and to gain "rhythm" when attempting to move the ball for purposes of attacking the goal or setting up a possible scoring play. Because of their strong basketball orientation, most Americans have a tendency to dribble too much in team handball.

The dribble is similar to that used in basketball except that the player may take three steps when the ball is seized by either one or both hands. When the ball is seized, it must be played off within three steps or 3 seconds.

SHOOTING

The primary objective of attacking the goal in team handball is to score. Shooting will not occur in team handball as frequently as in basketball. Players must learn to be patient and work for a good opportunity to score a goal. However, players should not be overcautious, as team handball is an aggressive game in which the offense must continuously attack the goal and generate its own scoring opportunities.

▶ Learning Hints: Basic Shooting Principles

1. The shooter must have a definite throwing direction in mind prior to releasing the ball. Shots blocked and easily caught by the goalie often result in fast-break two-on-one situations for the opposing team. The most vulnerable shooting lanes are the high and low corners of the goal mouth. It is generally agreed that shots directed to the lower corners of the goal have greater scoring percentages.

2. The momentum of the shooter should always be toward or perpendicular to the goal.

3. The use of deception is of utmost importance. The shooter should attempt to draw the goalkeeper toward one corner of the goal and, depending on the commitment of the goalkeeper, the player should aim his shot for the opposite corner.

Figure 24-3 Setting up for the reverse shot: fake to one side.

4. The shoulder pass is the most frequently used in team handball shooting.

   a. The ball is held behind the head, with the arm cocked to hide the ball from the goalie and make it more difficult for defensive players to take the ball away.

   b. The nonshooting arm remains forward to ward off defenders and assist in maintaining balance.

   c. The shot should be released with a snap of the wrist and follow-through (as in throwing a football or baseball).

5. Many foot-movement patterns can be used in team handball shots, including hop steps, crossover steps, and running steps. New players are encouraged to experiment with different step and dribble combinations that fit their individual abilities.

SPECIFIC SHOTS AND THEIR USES

Jump Shot. This shot simply involves the use of the shoulder throw (pass) in which the ball is released at the height of the jump, with the momentum of the body directed toward the goal rather than falling away. By jumping high in the air, the player is able to see the goal more clearly and determine the direction of his shots (Figure 24-2).

Dive Shot. This shot also uses the shoulder throw. The shooter stretches his body out and directs his momentum toward the goal. The ball is released at the last possible moment and as close to the goal mouth as possible.

▶ Learning Hints

1. The weight is evenly distributed on both feet as the shot is initiated.
2. The body is leaning, moving in a position parallel with the floor.

3. The upper body is thrust upward in a diving action toward the goal.
4. Snap the wrist and release the ball quickly.
5. Break the fall with your chest and both hands positioned at your sides about chest level.

Underhand Shot. The side-arm or three-quarter pitching motion is used in this shot. The right-handed thrower turns (twists) the left side toward the goal. To generate increased power, a crossover step is used with the push-off coming from the rear foot. This shot is used when upper scoring lanes are cut off by the defense. The shot is on a low trajectory with a continuous follow-through.

Reverse Shot (Circle). This shot is used around the goal area when the defender is playing behind or over-playing to the shooting side (Figure 24-3). When you are unable to execute a normal shot, lower your center of gravity (bend knees), fake to the strong (normal shooting) side, turn, and quickly pivot away from the strong side on your right foot (if you are right-handed), releasing the ball in a side-arm motion (Figure 24-4). This side-arm motion is similar to the initial backward motion in the discus throw. As the ball is released, body momentum should be directed toward the goal.

Side Throw (Twister). This throw is a relatively weak shot, but with the proper element of surprise, it can be successful. Most frequently, it is used in close to the goal area when an attempted shot with a regular shoulder throw is stopped by a defender. If you are right-handed, drop your left shoulder, step across your body with your right foot, then execute the same arm motion described for the reverse shot with body momentum directed toward the goal.

Lob Shot. This shot is often used in a one-on-one fast-break situation and also in certain two-on-one situations. When the goalie comes out to challenge, the offensive player lobs the ball over his head into the goal or to his teammate if this is a two-on-one situation. Timing is of utmost importance in the execution of this shot.

Penalty Throw. This throw is taken at the 23-foot penalty-throw line. It is a one-on-one situation with the goalie as the only defender. The goalie may move about and come within 10 feet of the penalty line. The player who is awarded the penalty throw cannot move her foot or touch the penalty line until the ball is released. The offensive player has 3 seconds in which to shoot from the time the referee blows the whistle to begin the throw. The type of shot normally used in this situation is the shoulder or side throw. The other players must remain outside the free-throw line area until the shot is taken. They should strategically position themselves around the goal to be ready for a blocked shot, which might possibly rebound out into the area of play.

Figure 24-4   Reverse shot: release with side-arm motion.

▶ Practice/Organizational Suggestions—Basic Skills

Drills for team handball basic skills—passing, catching, and dribbling the ball—are similar to those used in basketball. Therefore, basketball drills should be used to practice the basic skills, particularly passing, catching, and dribbling the ball, with the following points in mind:

1. The ball is much smaller than the ball used in basketball. Therefore, the ball can be easily handled by either one or both hands.

2. It is permissible to take a maximum of three steps or 3 seconds with the ball in either one or both hands. For example, after catching the ball from another player, you may take three steps and start dribbling. When you stop dribbling, you must either pass or shoot after taking no more than three steps or 3 seconds.

GOALKEEPING

The goalkeeper is the most important defensive player in team handball. The goalie should have quick hands and feet, be fearless of the ball, and be able to throw the ball well in initiating fast-break plays. The main task of goalkeeping is to stop the ball by any manner possible. The goalie can use any part of the body to deflect shots. Within the goal area there is no restriction on how many steps the goalie may take or the time the ball may be held. Without the ball, the goalie may become a court player at any time; in that case, all rules applying to court players apply to the goalie.

▶ Learning Hints: Goalkeeping Fundamentals

1. The goalie should know the position of the ball on the court at all times.

2. The goalie should maintain a low center of gravity, with weight evenly distributed on the balls of the feet.

3. In blocking shots, the goalkeeper's palms should always face out toward the field of play. The hands should be relaxed enough to give with a shot to keep it under control in the area and not allow the ball to rebound back out onto the field of play.

4. Low shots in close to the goalie's legs should be fielded (blocked) in a manner similar to an infielder fielding a ground ball.

5. On shots that are low and to the side, the goalie should stride to the side with hands and outside foot stretching simultaneously to block the ball.

6. Similar to the goalkeeping used in hockey or soccer, the goalie should move out away from the goal mouth in an attempt to cut down the best shooting angles.

7. On high hard shots, the goalie should not try to catch the ball, rather she should deflect the ball over the top of the goal.

8. In defending against the penalty shot, the goalie should move out toward the 23-foot penalty line to cut down the shooter's angle.

9. The goalie should always play one foot out from the goal line to avoid a self-scored goal.

10. When the goalie recovers a blocked or missed shot, she returns the ball to play by means of a "throw-out." In this instance, the ball is free, and the defense can try and intercept the throw-out and score directly.

11. It is recommended that the goalie wear a protective supporter, long pants, and a long-sleeved shirt to cut down on the sting of blocked shots.

Playing Strategies

Various defensive and offensive strategies are described below. These can be understood better and developed further with reference to similar team sports such as soccer, basketball, field hockey, and football.

DEFENSIVE FORMATIONS

When the ball is lost, all players of the team become defensive players with certain defensive responsibilities according to the defensive strategies employed. Generally, defensive strategies are divided into (1) player-to-player defense, (2) zone defense, and (3) a combination of the two. In defensive play, a player should always attempt to keep the opponent in front of him, or else the opponent should be slightly overplayed to the shooting-arm side. ("Stay between your opponent and the goal" is a general rule to follow.)

Player-to-Player Defense. Each defensive player must cover one designated player of the attacking team regardless of whether she has the ball. The offensive player is continually blocked off and hindered in attacking actions.

Zone Defense. Each defensive player is responsible for protecting a particular area against the attacker. Zone defense may require less running, but it requires more teamwork to be effective.

COMBINATIONS

6–0 Defense (Figure 24-5). Six court players stand alongside and in front of the goal-area line, each having the specific responsibility to protect a certain area. The players must coordinate to cover any space that may be left uncovered when a defensive player attempts to attack an opponent with the ball. Taller players should be placed in the center of the defensive zone and shorter players on the outside.

5–1 Defense (Figure 24-6). The 5–1 concept is similar to that of a box and 1 defense used in basketball.

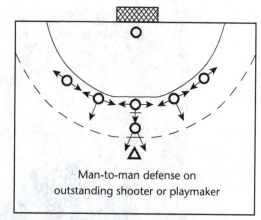

Man-to-man defense on outstanding shooter or playmaker

Figure 24-6 The 5–1 defensive formation.

Five players stand in front of the goal-area line. One player, pulled out to the free-throw line, has the two assignments of covering the opponent with the ball or covering a good shooter. This player, who frequently originates the fast break, must be an all-around athlete.

4–2 Defense (Figure 24-7). Four defensive players are positioned on the goal-area line and shift as a unit. Two defensive players move out to the free-throw line to concentrate on intercepting passes and harassing the ball handlers to prevent their taking the most advantageous routes toward the goal area. These two players not only have to protect the central axis but also are responsible for filling in gaps between defensive players behind them.

3–3 Defense (Figure 24-8). Three defensive players stand on the middle of the goal-area line and the other three players stand in front of the free-throw line. The three players on the free-throw line have to shift together toward the attacking point of the offensive team to protect against long-distance shootings. This formation is vulnerable against the team having shots from angles and requires a capable goalkeeper.

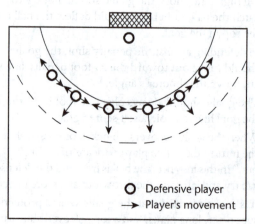

○ Defensive player
→ Player's movement

Figure 24-5 The 6–0 defensive formation.

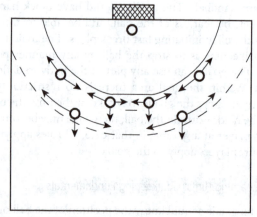

Figure 24-7 The 4–2 defensive formation.

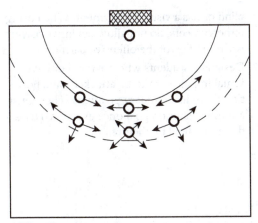

Figure 24-8 The 3–3 defensive formation.

OFFENSIVE FORMATIONS

In the deployment of any offensive alignment, every effort should be made to use the entire offensive floor area. Fast, continuous movement must be maintained at all times. On receiving a pass, every player should make a motion of threatening to score whenever in scoring range. To spread out the defense as much as possible, it is important that players maintain good spacing and that most plays be initiated from approximately 40 feet. Dribbling should be avoided if possible, and the ball should be passed quickly between players. Effective screening (similar to that used in basketball) is a key to the success of most offensive patterns. Screens and double screens can be improvised from any of the offensive formations presented. The following represent some common offensive formations.

2–4 Offense.   The 2–4 is the most frequently used offensive formation in team handball. In this formation, the two backcourt players are situated at around 40 feet. The wing players are spread out wide for the best possible shooting angles. The circle runners are strategically positioned between the two wing players at 20 feet. A variety of offensive maneuvers can be initiated from this basic offensive pattern. This offense will spread out most zone defenses and allow opportunities for scoring between the defensive players.

3–3 Offense.   This offense is also effective in spreading out the coverage of a zone defense. If a team possesses three strong shooters, this is an excellent offensive formation to employ. Constant movement of the ball is essential, and each player must threaten to score each time she receives a pass.

1–5 Offense.   This offensive formation can best be employed by a team that has some strong inside players who are physical. Effective inside screening is the key to a successful 1–5 offense. It is of utmost importance that

one player always stay back to guard against a possible fast break.

Skill Assessment

Similar to basketball, the most important skills in team handball are the pass, catch, dribble, and shot. The passing (chest)–catching (two-hand) skills test in basketball is applicable to team handball as is the passing (forward pass)–catching (two-hand) test in football.

An additional test for consideration is a shooting test. A wall space 7 feet high by 10 feet wide is necessary for one station's goal area. Four targets 2 feet by 2 feet are marked in each corner of the 7 feet by 10 feet goal area. A throwing restraining line 23 feet from the target is marked on the ground and is parallel with the wall.

Each station has a participant, scorer, and assistant. The participant attempts 10 overhand throws for score. The scorer records the results, and the assistant provides or retrieves balls for the participant. The two low corner targets are worth 3 points, the two high corner targets are worth 2 points, and any ball in the goal area (but not in the corner targets) receives 1 point. Any ball completely out of the 7 feet by 10 feet target area earns 0 points. A ball contacting the target line is awarded the higher score. The final score is the sum of the 10 attempts. Students then rotate responsibilities within their group.

Modifications for Special Populations

ORTHOPEDICALLY IMPAIRED

1. Access the National Disability Sports Alliance (NDSA) Web site at www.ndsaonline.org for rules and information on indoor wheelchair soccer. The game of indoor wheelchair soccer is a hybrid of soccer and team handball.

2. Set up stationary positions using desk chairs placed on the goal perimeter arch and have students without and with disabilities try to score.

3. Allow students with limited grip to use smaller objects (e.g., bean bags) instead of regulation team handballs.

4. For students using wheelchairs, consider playing the game on a flat, hard-top surface.

COGNITIVELY IMPAIRED

1. Create smaller groups and lead-up games.

2. Allow students to move the ball up the field in any manner possible.

3. Spend considerable time teaching concepts of the game, such as offense, defense, goal area, and penalties. Use visual prompts to help with your instructions.

SENSORY IMPAIRED

1. One appropriate option may be to tether a sighted student to the wrist of a student who is blind or has a visual impairment. When using tethered peers, do not allow defensive players within 10 feet of the offensive partners.

2. Designate students who are blind or have a visual impairment to be attackers, and position them in stationary positions. They must attempt a shot on goal once every two trips down the field by their team.

Terminology

corner throw When a defending player (except the goalkeeper) plays the ball over his own goal line on either side of the goal, the game is restarted by means of a throw from the corner of the court by one of the attacking players. The player must place one foot on the corner and throw the ball in, using either hand.

court player Member of the handball team actually playing on the court, except for the goalie.

dive shot A means of trying to score a goal by launching the entire body into the air toward the goal in an attempt to gain more distance.

free throw A throw awarded to the opposing team when the other team is in violation of certain rules of the game.

free-throw line The broken line parallel with the goal-area line at an extra distance of 10 feet; from this line, free throws awarded near the goal area are taken.

goal A goal is considered scored when the ball has passed wholly over the goal line between the uprights and underneath the crossbar of the goal.

goal area The area of the playing court inside and including the goal-area line.

goal-area line The semicircular line drawn in front of and on either side of the goal.

goalkeeper (goalie) The player who is allowed to play freely inside the goal area to defend the goal.

goal line The line forming the end of the court that runs between the uprights of the goal and meets the sidelines at the corners of the court.

penalty throw A shot attempted by any offensive player when an offensive player is prevented from making a clear goal-scoring chance by foul means. The player attempting the penalty throw is required to make a direct attempt to score a goal from the penalty-throw line.

referee's throw A ball bounced by the referee to restart the game after an interruption of play caused by players of both teams committing simultaneous infractions of the rules or if the game has been interrupted for some other reason.

throw-in The method of putting the ball back into play after it has crossed one of the sidelines. The throw is taken by a player of the team that did not cause the ball to go out. The player making the throw must have both feet touching the surface outside the sideline and throw the ball into the playing area with one or two hands in any manner.

throw-off The means the goalkeeper takes of throwing the ball onto the court after obtaining possession of the ball in his goal area.

throw-on The method of putting the ball in play at the start of the game and after a goal is scored. The throw is made from the center of the court.

throw-out Same as a throw-off except that defensive players may place themselves at the goal-area line.

Discussion Questions

1. Discuss the development of team handball including skills and countries of origin.

2. Compare the rules of team handball with similar sports.

3. Compare the strategies and skills of team handball with similar sports.

4. Discuss why the 2–4 offensive formation is most frequently used.

5. Discuss the strengths of the four defensive formations listed in the chapter.

6. Present the suggested learning hints for the goalkeeper and discuss the reasoning for each.

Web Sites

www.hickoksports.com/history/teamhand.shtml—provides an explanation of how the sport is played and its history.

http://en.wikipedia.org/wiki/Team_handball—presents the history and simplified rules of the game.

www.coachinghandball.com—offers more than 1,000 animated drills and video exercises suitable for various age groups.

CHAPTER 25

Tennis

This chapter will enable you to

- Identify key historical events contributing to the evolution of tennis
- Select tennis equipment that is appropriate for the player
- Demonstrate the proper grips and techniques for the following strokes: serve, return of serve, approach shot, forehand, backhand, volley, lob, and overhead
- Understand the scoring procedures and the basic rules of play
- Identify the playing courtesies, safety considerations, and basic terminology associated with tennis

Nature and Purpose

Tennis has always appealed to both sexes, young and old. Many consider it to be one of the best forms of recreational sports. The pace can be adjusted to the players' abilities, ranging from a mild form of exercise to a strenuous test of strength and endurance. Speed, agility, coordination, and endurance can be developed, and indeed are needed, to play even a recreational game of tennis.

Tennis can be played as either singles or doubles. The singles game has two participants, one individual opposing the other. The doubles game has four participants, two individuals teaming up to compete against another team of two. The doubles court is 9 feet wider than the singles court, having a 4½ foot alley on each side of the singles court (Figure 25-1). The basic rules are the same for men's and women's tennis.

History

Tennis is most widely thought to have been derived from handball, which originated in Ireland as early as the 10th century. However, some authorities believe that tennis dates back 20 to 30 centuries, when early Irish royal families were great sport devotees. Handball moved from Ireland to England and Scotland, but it did not take hold in either of these countries.

The French adopted a game of handball but soon discovered, as did others, that it was hard on the hands, so they began to devise methods to protect their hands by wrapping them with cords, wearing gloves, and eventually using a paddle. The game of *jeu de paume* (game of the palm) became popular with the royalty. But with the paddle, the forerunner to the modern game was born. The name tennis was derived from the French word *tenez*, meaning "take it" or "play." The English coined the term *tennis*; thus, *jeu de paume* became tennis.

During the 1500s, the paddle was replaced by a racket with a head that was strung with sheep gut. However, tennis's popularity decreased because of the wars in England and the French Revolution. Tennis reappeared in the mid-19th century. Major Walter Wingfield reintroduced the game in England in 1873, and it became known officially as *lawn tennis*.

The game was first intended to be played on a lawn, but eventually the use of hard surfaces grew in popularity. Today tennis is played on a variety of hard synthetic surfaces, cement, and clay. However, the annual Wimbledon Lawn Tennis Championships are played on grass. The terms *grass*, *hard*, *clay*, and *indoor* are used to designate all tournaments sanctioned by the United States Tennis Association (USTA).

The popularity of the game spread rapidly. A British officer who had observed the game introduced it in Bermuda. Mary Outerbridge, who was vacationing in Bermuda from her home in Staten Island, New York, was attracted to the game. She bought some equipment, learned the rules, and is credited with introducing tennis to the United States. The game spread quickly in the United States, and by 1879 it had crossed the continent to California. In 1881, E. H. Outerbridge, the older brother of Mary Outerbridge, called a meeting of the tennis leaders of that time, who organized themselves into the United States Lawn Tennis Association, now known as the USTA. The first National Lawn Tennis Tournament Championship was played in 1881.

Tennis has become a worldwide sport. The Grand Slam of tennis consists of the Australian Open, the French

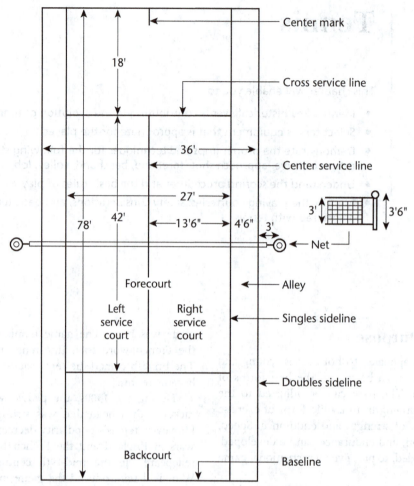

Figure 25-1 Lawn tennis court, singles and doubles.

Open, Wimbledon, and the U.S. Open, which is played at the National Tennis Center in Flushing Meadows, New York. Few men or women have won all four tournaments over their lifetime. Other important tournaments include the Davis Cup, for which men's teams from all over the world compete; the Wrightman Cup, for which women representing the United States and England compete; and the Federation Cup, for which women representing teams from around the world compete.

Tennis is once again an Olympic sport. Removed after the 1924 Olympics, tennis reappeared at the 1996 Atlanta games. Singles and doubles matches took place featuring men and women from countries participating in the games. Noted players such as Andre Agassi, Lindsay Davenport, Jennifer Capriati, Roger Federer, and Venus and Serena Williams have all represented their countries in the Olympic games.

Besides the USTA, the International Lawn Tennis Federation (ILTF) determines and enforces uniform rules that are in effect in many countries. At the professional level, men's play is governed by the Association of Tennis Professionals (ATP) and women's play by the Women's Tennis Association (WTA).

Selection of Equipment

The selection of proper equipment is of utmost importance to the beginning tennis player as well as to the professional player. With good equipment, the beginning player can eliminate many handicaps and get more enjoyment from mastering the fundamental skills.

TENNIS RACKETS

In selecting the racket, consider the weight, balance, grip size, stringing, and quality of the frame (Figure 25-2). Rackets are manufactured in three different weights: light, medium, and heavy; they range from 11 to 15 ounces. Women tend to prefer light rackets whereas men usually select medium or heavy racket frames. The feel of the racket as you swing it should be the most important consideration. When shopping, you should make this comparison test and take into account differences in materials and manufacture.

Most rackets are 27 inches long and measure 9 inches across the racket face. Currently, tennis rackets are being manufactured in different lengths, with oversized racket heads, and use various combinations of wood,

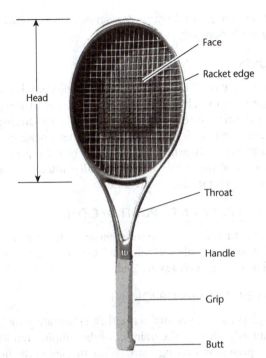

Figure 25-2   Parts of a tennis racket.

aluminum alloy, steel, magnesium, fiberglass, and graphite. Choose a racket of good quality, with a frame sturdy enough to withstand at least four or five restringings. Cheap rackets soon lose their shape and are usually not a good long-term investment.

There are two types of strings: gut and nylon. Gut strings are more expensive but also more resilient and pliable. This type is preferred by most tournament players. Gut requires more care than nylon and is vulnerable to humidity and wetness. Nylon strings do not have the elasticity of gut but are still comparable in play. Also, nylon strings are more durable, impervious to dampness, and less expensive. Nylon is adequate for the beginning player.

When you are purchasing a racket, the retailer will usually want to know your preference for string tension. The greater the tension (or tightness), the less control the player tends to have. Also, the racket frame cannot withstand as many restringings when it is strung tightly. The recommended string tension for beginning and intermediate players is between 55 and 57 pounds. Most rackets come with recommended tensions.

Rackets are manufactured to be evenly balanced, head-heavy, or handle-heavy. Head-heavy rackets are preferred by players inclined to be ground strokers or baseline players. Handle-heavy rackets are used by individuals who are predominantly net players. It is suggested that beginners select an evenly balanced racket.

Another important factor in choosing an appropriate racket is the size of the grip. Grips usually range in circumference from 4 to 5 inches. The proper grip size depends on the user's hand size, and selection may require professional assistance. If the individual grips the racket in an

Eastern forehand grip (described later), the thumb should come just past the first knuckle of the middle finger.

TENNIS BALLS

Most tennis balls are pressure-packed with compressed air and marked with numbers for identification. Manufactured according to USTA specifications, a ball must weigh two ounces, measure 2½ inches in diameter, and have a wool-felt covering.

Tennis balls are also produced to be court specific. Some are made especially for hard courts (asphalt or cement) by having more felt on the ball's cover. Others are made for soft-court play on such surfaces as clay or grass.

Basic Rules

To start the game, the server stands just behind the baseline to the *right* of his center service line and puts the ball into play by striking it in the air in such a manner that it lands in the opponent's right service court. The server has two chances to put the ball into play. The ball that does not land in the proper service court is called a *fault* and is not played. A served ball that touches the net during flight and lands in the proper service court is called a *let*; a let is not counted as a fault, nor is it played, but is served again.

The receiver must return the serve to the server's court on its first bounce. The rally continues until one of the players fails to return the ball within the boundaries of his court.

When the point has been completed, the server stands just behind her baseline and to the *left* of the center service line and serves to the opponent's left service court, continuing to alternate left and right after each point until the game is completed. On completion of the game, the server becomes the receiver. Players change sides at the completion of each odd-numbered game.

In doubles, each player serves a game in turn—first a member of one team, then a member of the other team, and so on. The same order of serving is kept throughout the set.

SCORING

Points in tennis are called Love, 15, 30, 40, Deuce, Advantage, and Game.

Zero, or nothing, is called Love.
First point won by a player is called 15.
Second point won by a player is called 30.
Third point won by a player is called 40.
Fourth point won by a player is Game, provided the opponent does not have more than 30 (2 points).

If each player has won three points (40-all), the score is deuce. The next point won by a player gives that player advantage. However, if the next point is lost, the score is again deuce. When either player wins two *consecutive* points following the score of deuce, the game is won by that player. The server's score is always given first. The score should be called loudly and clearly after every point.

In scoring, the player who first wins six games wins a *set* unless both players have won five games; then it takes an advantage of two games to win, so the score could be 7–5, or 8–6, or 9–7, and so on.

In scoring the *match*, the player first winning two sets is generally declared the winner. In professional tennis, the winner of three sets is declared the winner of the men's match, whereas in the women's game, the winner of two sets is declared the winner. For example, match scores could be 6–0, 6–3, 6–2; 9–7, 4–6, 10–8; 2–6, 6–4, 6–4; 6–1, 6–1, 6–3; 4–6, 6–4, 6–4, 6–4; 6–0, 5–7, 7–5, 2–6, 8–6.

TIE-BREAKER PROCEDURES

A tie-breaker game has been put into effect in an attempt to reduce the length of a match when the score is tied at six games all. The 12-point tie-breaker is most commonly used today. To win the tie-breaker, a player must win at least 7 points and establish a margin of 2 points. Score is kept numerically. When the score of the set reaches six games all, the server whose turn it is begins serving in the tie-breaker. The first server serves only 1 point from the right service court. The second server begins from the left court and serves 2 points. From this point on, the server always serves 2 points in a row. The players change ends of the court after a total of 6 points have been played, with a continuation of the rotation. The first player to win 7 points with a 2-point margin is declared the winner of the set. The score of the set is then recorded 7–6, with the score of the tie-breaker in parentheses: 7–6 (7–5).

SERVER AND RECEIVER

Players stand on opposite sides of the net; the player who delivers the ball is called the server, and the other the receiver.

DELIVERY OF SERVICE

The service is delivered in the following manner. Immediately before commencing to serve, the server stands with both feet at rest behind the baseline and within the imaginary continuations of the center mark and sideline. The server then tosses the ball by hand into the air and before it hits the ground, strikes it with her racket. The server is not permitted to touch the court inside the baseline until after the racket has made contact with the ball.

FROM ALTERNATE COURTS

In delivering the service, the server stands alternately behind the right and left courts, beginning from the right in every game. The ball served passes over the net and hits the ground within the service court, which is diagonally opposite.

FAULTS

The service is a fault if the server commits any breach of the rules of delivery of service or delivery of service from alternative courts; if he misses the ball in attempting to strike it; or if the ball served touches a permanent fixture (other than the net) before it hits the ground. However, if the server tosses the ball without making an effort to hit it, there is no fault.

BALL IN PLAY UNTIL POINT DECIDED

A ball is in play from the moment at which it is delivered in service. Unless a fault or a let is called, it remains in play until the point is decided.

PLAYER HINDERS OPPONENT

If a player commits any act, either deliberately or involuntarily, that, in the opinion of the umpire, hinders the opponent in making a stroke, the umpire in the first case awards the point to the opponent, and in the second case orders the point to be replayed.

BALL FALLING ON LINE

A ball falling on a line is regarded as falling in the court bounded by that line and is therefore a good ball.

GOOD RETURN

The return is good if

1. The ball touches the net, posts, cord or metal cable, strap, or band, provided that it passes over any of them and hits the ground within the court.
2. A player's racket passes over the net after the player has returned the ball, provided the ball passes the net before being played and is properly returned.
3. A player succeeds in returning a ball, served or in play, that strikes another ball lying in the court.

WHEN PLAYERS CHANGE SIDES

The players change sides at the end of the first, third, and every subsequent alternate game of each set, and at the end of each set unless the total number of games in such set is even, in which case the change is not made until the end of the first game of the next set.

DOUBLES, ORDER OF SERVICE

The order of service is decided at the beginning of each set. The pair who serve in the first game of each set decide which partner will do so, and the opposing pair decide similarly for the second game. The partner of the player who served in the first game serves in the third; the partner of the player who served in the second game serves in the fourth. The order of serving may be changed following the completion of any set.

A complete staff of officials for a tennis match includes a referee, an umpire, a net-court judge, and at least seven linespersons. However, most dual matches are played with only a referee or, at most, a referee and an umpire.

DOUBLES, ORDER OF RECEIVING

The order of receiving is decided at the beginning of each set. The pair who receive the first game decide which partner will continue to receive the first service in every odd game throughout that set. The opposing pair likewise decide which partner will receive the first service in the second game, and that partner continues to receive the first service in every even game throughout that set. The order of receiving may be changed following the completion of any set.

Suggested Learning Sequence

In the beginning stages, it is important to stress that the learner acquire the ability to hit the ball consistently across the net. Early drills and skill development should focus on gaining familiarity with the basic stroke mechanics and racket skills. Students should be introduced to all strokes as quickly as possible; much time will be spent developing consistency in both the stroke and return of the tennis ball.

The following outline includes everything one would need to cover; the sequence might vary from teacher to teacher.

A. Introduction
   1. Scoring
   2. Tie-breaker procedures

B. Equipment

C. Rules and etiquette (best to introduce when directly related to skill or strategy being taught)

D. Skills and techniques
   1. Grips—Eastern, Eastern backhand, two-handed backhand
   2. Strokes
   3. The serve—serve motion and serve and volley
   4. One-handed backhand
   5. Two-handed backhand
   6. Forehand
   7. Lob
   8. Overhead smash
   9. Backhand volley
   10. Forehand volley
   11. Backhand return of serve
   12. Forehand return of serve

E. Playing Strategy
   1. Singles game—focus on consistently returning the ball into the court
   2. Doubles game—regular and mixed

Skills and Techniques

THE GRIP

The importance of a proper grip cannot be stressed enough. Adjustments may be made in a player's swing, but a proper grip will last a player for a lifetime.

Special names have been given to the forehand grips, based on the position of the palm against the racket handle:

When the palm sits upon the top right side, the grip is called the *Continental* (Figure 25-3). This grip requires a strong wrist and is used by some professionals for both forehand and backhand strokes.

When the palm sits on the back side of the handle, it is called an *Eastern* grip (Figure 25-4). The palm and the racket face are on the same plane, which gives the sensation of hitting the ball with the palm of your hand.

A　　　　　　　　B

Figure 25-3　Continental grip (front and back views).

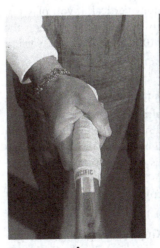

A　　　　　　　　B

Figure 25-4　Eastern grip (front and back views).

A   B

Figure 25-5 Western grip (front and back views).

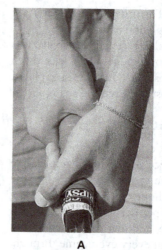

A   B

Figure 25-6 Two-handed backhand grip: (A) front view, (B) top view.

This is the most common grip and the one strongly recommended in this chapter.

When the palm rests on the bottom of the handle, so that the palm points at the sky, it is called a *Western grip* (Figure 25-5). This is the least common grip, although some players use it to great advantage.

Eastern Grip. The Eastern grip is recommended for the forehand and is the only grip described in detail. A teacher without an extensive tennis background cannot go wrong by suggesting this grip.

If you are right-handed, start by holding the throat of your racket with your left hand so that the racket face is vertical to the ground. Then hold the racket at waist level with the right palm vertical and your fingers pointing slightly downward at approximately a 45-degree angle. The thumb should overlap and lie next to the middle finger, with the index finger spread. Now hold the racket out away from you and look at the top edge of your racket and the top edge of your right palm to see if they are both absolutely vertical. If you play this game correctly, you'll rarely hit a shot that requires the racket to vary more than 10 degrees from the vertical position.

Eastern Backhand Grip. The backhand grip advocated in this chapter is the Eastern backhand grip. It is attained by putting the palm on the top of the racket, with the knuckle of the index finger riding the top right ridge; the thumb can be placed either behind the racket or underneath. This grip position provides the most stability and requires the least amount of wrist adjustment in order to provide a vertical racket head at impact.

Two-Handed Backhand Grip. This grip uses a regular backhand grip with the dominant hand, which is at the base of the racket. The nondominant hand should be placed comfortably above the other hand, similar to gripping a baseball or softball bat (Figure 25-6).

STROKES

Strokes are described in terms of a right-handed player's actions. Some general principles that the player must be aware of:

1. The direction in which the ball spins is determined by the trajectory taken by the racket before and after contact with the ball. If the racket comes from below the ball, is vertical at impact, and finishes above the ball, topspin (low to high) will be attained. If the racket starts above the ball and sweeps down to the ball, underspin (high to low) will be attained.

2. Nearly every successful hit is accomplished with a vertical racket head. A player does *not* come over the ball for topspin or under the ball for underspin!

3. With the exception of the serve and overhead, all strokes in this chapter are to be hit with a locked wrist. The swing will come from the shoulder and not the wrist.

THE SERVE

The serve is the first ball hit in every point. The motion is similar to that of a baseball pitcher's throwing motion. A good way to start teaching the serve is to have students throw the ball over the net while pretending the ball is the racket. Watch their throws until you are satisfied the perfect motion is attained.

Many beginners prefer to use the regular forehand grip to hit a basic "flat" serve, but intermediate and advanced players should use the Continental grip, halfway between the Eastern forehand and Eastern backhand, to facilitate greater ball rotation with less stress on the wrist.

To attain a good service motion, it is necessary to coordinate two movements simultaneously—the ball toss and the action of the racket. The toss is made by holding the ball with the fingertips, the palm up, and then releasing the ball upward with all fingers letting go at the same time.

Achieving spin on the ball is an important aspect of serving. Three kinds of serves are recommended.

1. *Flat.* A totally flat serve is a myth because every ball has some amount of spin. This serve has the least amount of spin and is attained by snapping the wrist up and forward through the middle of the ball.

2. *Slice.* Much like a curveball in baseball, this serve results when the racket face moves across the back side of the ball on an almost horizontal plane, thus producing sidespin. Using the face of a clock as a reference, the right-hander would hit the ball from nine o'clock to three o'clock.

3. *Topspin.* The principle of applying topspin on a serve is basically the same as on a forehand or backhand. Swing the racket from low to high and brush the back side of the ball at about a 45-degree angle. On the imaginary clock, hit the ball from eight o'clock to two o'clock.

The Serve Motion. Figure 25-7 shows the sequence of motions involved in the service (refer to views A–D):

A. *Ready position.* It is important to be totally relaxed before attempting to serve. The feet are shoulder-width apart, and the front shoulder is pointing in the direction the ball will be served.

B. To start the motion, the player's arms go down together and then start up together. The player also begins to lean forward slightly.

C. Position C is crucial. At this point the ball is released and shoulder rotation must begin. The racket is slightly above the shoulder, and the tossing arm is pointing toward the right net post, so the toss will be 10 to 12 inches to the player's right. The height of the toss is 18 inches out of the out-stretched tossing arm. The object of the shoulder rotation is to let the right shoulder replace the position of the left shoulder. The weight at this point is mainly over the front foot, with both feet still in contact with the ground.

The racket is forming a loop behind the player's back. The racket does *not* scratch the back but forms a loop. This loop is accomplished by maintaining a loose arm and rotating the shoulders at the proper time. If the racket is hitting or touching the student's back at any time, the motion is out of sync.

D. *Point of contact.* At impact, the arm should be extended but not necessarily at the peak of one's reach (depending on spin desired). The chin is held upward, and for optimal power both feet should be in contact with the ground, though the weight should

have transferred forward. Notice that contact is made to the right of the player's head and in line with the hitting shoulder.

E. *Follow-through.* The right shoulder has replaced the position of the left shoulder, and the player's momentum following impact has brought the back foot a step into the court. If the player wishes to serve and volley, this will naturally become the first step toward the net. If not, the participant may step back and rally off of the baseline.

Serve and Volley. The footwork recommended for serve and volley is to step with the right foot, left foot, right foot, and then bring both feet into alignment (see Figure 25-8). This is called a "split step." The closer the player can get to the service line, the better.

▶ Learning Hints

1. No fancy movements. Just relax and take your time.
2. To toss the ball, hold the ball with the fingertips and not the palm.
3. The toss must fit into the motion.
4. Chin up and hit up and out. This sequence is true for all serves.
5. Think positive. Picture in your mind a successful serve before starting the motion.
6. Shoulder rotation, *not* the strength of the arm, is the main source of power.
7. Hit the second serve with the same motion as the first—just with more topspin.

▶ Practice/Organizational Suggestions

1. Hit buckets of balls at specific targets to each service court.
2. Before serving, determine the spin to be desired (flat, slice, topspin) and then evaluate your success accordingly.

ONE-HANDED BACKHAND

Figure 25-9 illustrates the sequence of motions involved in executing the one-handed backhand (refer to views A–F):

A. *Ready position.* In a good ready position, the player's feet are shoulder-width apart and knees are slightly bent. Elbows are winged out, and the racket position is at a 45-degree angle to the ground. Note that the player is holding the racket with an Eastern forehand grip.

B. *Backswing.* The first move, once determining the ball is coming to the backhand side, is to turn the shoulder and change the grip simultaneously. The grip recommended is the Eastern backhand. The body should be turned enough so that the back of the shoulder is pointing at the oncoming ball.

Figure 25-7 The service sequence.

C. *Position viewed from behind.* Notice how low the racket is and also that the racket face is slightly tilted downward. The arm is a radius, and if the racket is to be horizontal at impact and the wrist locked throughout the swing, the racket face must be tilted downward at this point. The left hand may be used to help push the racket downward, but this is optional.

D. *Three movements happen simultaneously in this photo.* The right foot steps into the ball, the racket drops

to the bottom of the loop, and the knees bend to a crouch position. The racket must be below the level of the oncoming ball if topspin is to be achieved.

E. *Impact with the ball.* The racket face is vertical and the arm is extended well in front of the body (8 to 10 inches in front of the right foot). Eyes are focused right on the point of contact. The knees have lifted upward so as to help lift the ball up (topspin), and the hips have rotated toward the net. Body weight has transferred forward slightly before impact.

A   B   C   D

Figure 25-8 Footwork for serve and volley.

F. *Follow-through.* Following impact, let the racket face and knuckles follow the flight of the ball until the arm is fully extended. Freeze at this point and check that your weight is forward and over your front foot and that the racket forms an archway. If one were to drop the shoulder straight down, the racket should still form a perfect hitting position.

TWO-HANDED BACKHAND

If you lack strength, the two-handed backhand may be the stroke for you. With it you can hit a heavy ball that penetrates the court and you can disguise it easier than the one-handed backhand. Figure 25-10 illustrates the sequence of motions involved in executing the two-handed backhand (refer to views A–E):

A. *The grip.* Use a regular backhand grip with the dominant hand at the base of the racket. The nondominant hand should be placed comfortably above the other hand, similar to gripping a baseball or softball bat.

Ready position. Use the same position as the one used for one-handed backhand except hold the racket with two hands on the grip in front of the body.

B., C. *Backswing.* Turn your shoulders away from the ball, with the racket arms extended off the hip. Be sure the racket is pointed directly behind you toward the fence. The body should be perpendicular to the ball, with the majority of the weight on the back foot.

D. *Contact.* Weight is transferred from the back foot to the front foot. At the same time, the racket is

brought around the body from slightly below the ball to make contact with it in front of the hip.

E. *Follow-through.* The racket should continue to move through the ball and diagonally across your body and wrap around your shoulders. The hips have rotated with the ball, but the feet remain in contact with the ground.

▶ Learning Hints

1. Change the grip and pivot the body as early as possible.
2. Concentrate on bending the knees and getting low. The legs are a tremendous source of power.
3. Work hard to swing easy.
4. Reach forward and out away from the body for contact.
5. Let the knuckles of the hitting hand be the guide for direction. As the knuckles go, so goes the racket head.
6. Reach out and upward for the follow-through.
7. Always check the follow-through at the completion of a swing.
8. While the body is lifting, the head must remain stationary. Leave head and eyes glued on the point of impact.

▶ Practice/Organizational Suggestions

1. Hit backhands toward a specific target area either from a ball machine or from someone feeding from across the net.
2. Hit off of a backboard.

Figure 25-9 One-handed backhand sequence.

FOREHAND

Figure 25-11 shows the forehand sequence (refer to views A–D):

A. *Ready position.* The feet are shoulder-width apart and knees are slightly bent. Elbows are winged out, and the racket is at a 45-degree angle to the ground. The player is holding the racket with an Eastern forehand grip.

B. *Backswing.* Turn the shoulders so that the back of the left shoulder is pointing toward the oncoming ball. It is important that this movement happens well before the ball crosses the net. The left hand is held in front of the body for balance and may also be an aid on the follow-through.

C. *Bottom of the loop.* Three movements happen simultaneously in this photo. The left foot steps forward and the racket and knees drop down together. Notice that the racket face is turned slightly downward. The arm is a radius, and if the wrist is to remain locked and the racket face be vertical at impact, then the racket face must be tilted slightly downward at this point.

A

B

C

D

Figure 25-10 Two-handed backhand sequence.

Impact with the ball. The racket face is vertical, and the player's eyes are focused on the point of contact. Legs are lifting upward and hips are turning forward. Body weight has been transferred forward to the left foot.

D. *Follow-through.* There are two important points on the follow-through. One, the palm of the hitting hand should be pointing toward the intended target. Two, the hitting arm should be extended until the shoulder and chin touch, as shown in Figure 25-11D.

Also, the legs are totally extended, and the majority of weight is on the left foot.

▶ Learning Hints

1. Rotate both shoulders together when turning the body.

2. Keep the wrist firm and let the palm be the guide for direction.

3. Synchronize the movement of the racket and body.

A   B

C   D

Figure 25-11 Forehand sequence.

4. Keep the swing short. Do not let the racket get lost behind the body.

5. Power is generated from the leg lift and hip rotation—not just the arm.

6. On completion of the follow-through, the palm should face the intended target and the player's chin and hitting shoulder should touch.

7. Always check the follow-through at the completion of the swing.

8. While the body is lifting, the head must remain stationary. Leave head and eyes glued on the point of impact.

▶ Practice/Organizational Suggestions

1. Hit forehands toward a specific target area either from a ball machine or from someone feeding from across the net.

2. Hit off of a backboard.

LOB

With some practice, the lob stroke should resemble the forehand and backhand ground strokes as much as possible. To conceal the lob, remember to turn the front shoulder and have a loop swing identical with the forehand and backhand ground strokes. Run to the ball with the racket head up and already back, but instead of turning the racket face down as the racket drops, work on a bevel (slight backward tilt of the racket face) and lift the ball high into the air, using the opponent's baseline as a target.

OVERHEAD SMASH

Figure 25-12 shows the ready position for the overhead smash. The motion from this point is exactly like that of a flat serve. When teaching, stress keeping the chin up through contact and also reaching up for the ball.

BACKHAND VOLLEY

The sequence of motions recommended for the backhand volley is illustrated in Figure 25-13 (refer to views A–C):

A. *Ready position.* The player is waiting to determine the direction of the ball; he is holding the racket with an Eastern forehand grip.

B. *Backswing.* The player pivots the body and changes his grip (Continental grip). There is little or no backswing. The racket should always remain in front of the body. Notice how the left elbow is held high to keep the racket face on line with the ball.

Figure 25-12 Ready position for overhead smash.

C. *Contact and follow-through.* The key points are:
1. The racket head must remain above the wrist.
2. The ball is contacted well in front of the body—8 to 10 inches.
3. The arm and racket form a V.
4. The player's head, racket head, and ball should all be on the same plane. During the follow-through, the racket head should remain above the wrist, and ideally the racket face should follow the flight of the ball to gain depth on the volley. The follow-through is short. From an instructional standpoint, it is good technique to try to have the student freeze the racket right at the point of impact to assure that the wrist isn't breaking.

FOREHAND VOLLEY

The sequence of motions recommended for the forehand volley is shown in Figure 25-14 (refer to views A–C):

A. *Ready position.* The player assumes a ready position, holding the racket with a Continental grip.

B. *Backswing.* The player pivots the body, striving to get the shoulders sideways to the net. The racket should go back as far as the body turn takes it, yet never be out of the player's peripheral vision—the less backswing, the better.

C. *Contact and follow-through.* As the player reaches forward to the ball, impact should take place slightly in front of the left shoulder. The nature of the swing will give the ball natural underspin. The player should not break the wrist or chop at the ball. The arm and the racket form a V, and the player's head, racket head, and the tennis ball should be the same height at contact. During the follow-through, the wrist is kept firm and the racket face in line with the ball. The player should not let the racket head drop.

▶ Learning Hints for Volleys

1. Always step forward and attack the volley. Also, change the grip when necessary.
2. Use little or no backswing.
3. Contact well in front of the body, especially on backhands.
4. Keep the wrist locked.
5. Finish with the racket head above the wrist.
6. Use the knuckles for direction guidance on the backhand and the palm on the forehand.

▶ Practice/Organizational Suggestions

1. Hit off a ball machine or a feeder with a specific target in mind.

A **B** **C**

Figure 25-13 Motion recommended for backhand volley.

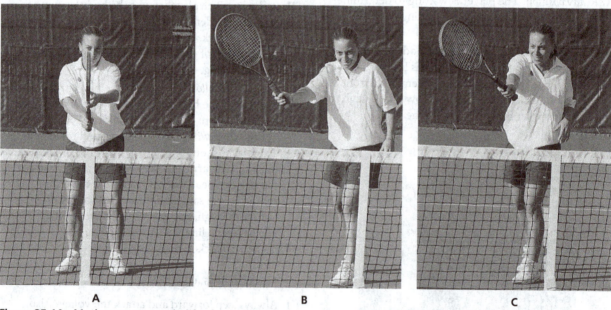

A **B** **C**

Figure 25-14 Motion recommended for forehand volley.

2. Alternate hitting a forehand and then a backhand to get used to the shoulder rotation.

3. Hit off of a backboard.

BACKHAND RETURN OF SERVE

The suggested technique for backhand return of serve is analyzed in Figure 25-15 (refer to views A–C):

A. *Ready position.* The player should be up on his toes, slightly leaning forward and holding an Eastern forehand grip.

B. The player pivots the body sideways while changing the grip to an Eastern backhand. The backswing is short, the emphasis being on a blocking motion similar to the volley.

C. *Contact and follow-through.* At this point, it is crucial that the returner has stepped forward and is reaching out to contact the ball 8 to 10 inches in front of the body. This shot is hit with underspin. The player should concentrate on putting the ball back in play rather than on hitting a winner. The follow-through is the same archway as described for the backhand ground stroke.

A   B   C

Figure 25-15 Suggested technique for backhand return of serve.

FOREHAND RETURN OF SERVE

The suggested technique for forehand return of serve is illustrated in Figure 25-16 (refer to views A–D):

A. *Ready position.* The player keeps the elbows raised and is ready to move forward.

B. The player rotates both shoulders sideways while limiting the length of the backswing. The player holds the racket face on level with the ball and remembers that a blocking motion similar to a volley is desired.

C. *Contact.* The ball is met just in front of the player's left shoulder. A step forward as well as body weight transfer is important. The shot is hit with slight underspin, with emphasis on putting the ball back in play.

D. *Follow-through.* This position is the same as described for the forehand ground stroke.

▶ Learning Hints

1. Start with a forehand grip rather than in between the two grips.

2. Use a short backswing and a long follow-through.

3. Keep the wrist locked.

4. Always try to have the weight forward on the feet, never back on the heels.

5. Contact the ball in front of the body, especially on the backhand.

6. Follow-throughs are the same as for ground strokes.

▶ Practice/Organizational Suggestions

Have a fellow participant practice serves while you hit returns to a specific target area. Alternate between both service courts.

Playing Strategy

SINGLES STRATEGY

You win the game of tennis usually by forcing your opponent into making errors. Your second option is to place the ball where the opponent cannot reach it. Both of these strategies are good, whether you are a beginner or an advanced player.

Another option is to play a patient ground stroke game from the baseline. The object is to move your opponent around the court and keep the ball in play. This strategy requires a great deal of patience because the rallies are usually long. A serve and volley style of game produces shorter points, but the individual is also taking a greater risk of making an error. Finally, your fourth option is an all-court game, which uses the baseline and the net play for an assortment of shots.

As an individual, you should choose which type of play best suits your personality and your skill level. Whichever style you choose, have fun with it!

DOUBLES STRATEGY

The game of doubles is entirely different from the game of singles, with the exception of which strokes are used. Besides the obvious difference of having two players on each side, doubles is an attacking game. Most doubles play is located at the net, and you will find that points are generally attained much quicker (usually three to five hits).

The beginner does not always experience the full challenge of the game because of its attacking nature, but usually enjoys working with someone for a common cause. For most, doubles will be the individual's

Figure 25-16   Suggested technique for forehand return of serve.

first experience on the court, especially if being taught in a large group setting.

One-up and one-back strategy occurs when one partner plays the net position and the other plays the baseline position. If you are not confident with your transition game (moving from the baseline to the net), this is a good style of play for you. In the two players-back strategy, both players stay at the baseline for the majority of their points. This style of doubles is definitely for those who want to play a more defensive game. Two-up is the most assertive style of doubles. Both players, whether returning or serving, are always trying to get to the net. This is an exciting style of play.

Most players will find themselves in the situation of playing more doubles than singles. Find the style of play that works best for you and your partner.

Safety Considerations

1. Warm up sufficiently before starting strenuous play.
2. If injured, stop and report the injury to the instructor.
3. Remove rings, bracelets, watches, and other objects that may cause bruises and cuts.
4. Check the playing surface for glass, nails, stones, slippery spots, and so forth.
5. Stay in line, on mark, or in your own area when swinging or hitting.
6. Control your emotions; do not throw the racket or hit a ball in anger.
7. Shout a warning when there is danger of a ball hitting someone.
8. Avoid showing off and horseplay.
9. Be aware of the distances between the baselines and walls, fences, screens, and so on.
10. When playing in excessive heat, make sure to drink plenty of fluids.

Helpful Reminders

1. Keep your eye on the ball at all times.
2. Strive for accurate placement rather than speed.
3. Always play the game to win, but if you go down in defeat, give your opponent due credit.
4. Play to your opponent's weaknesses.
5. When calling the score, always call the server's score first.
6. Keep your weight on the balls of both feet so you can move in any direction with ease and speed.
7. Acquire an understanding of the fundamentals of stroking, and practice faithfully to master them.
8. Notice how your opponent strokes the ball so when he uses the chop or slice stroke you can play the bounce accordingly.
9. Turn your body sideways to the net on all ground strokes.
10. When stroking the ball, avoid stiff leg action by keeping the knees loose and relaxed.
11. On ground strokes, return the ball deep into the opponent's backcourt near the baseline.
12. On ground strokes, attempt to hit the ball at waist level and on the rise.
13. Hit the ball squarely on the strings of the racket face by hitting "through" the ball instead of chopping under it.
14. The follow-through of the racket is in the direction of the intended flight of the ball.
15. After completing each stroke, return to a ready position, facing the net and loosely grasping the throat of the racket with the left hand to facilitate change of grip if necessary.
16. Well-placed lobs out of reach of the net rusher will help keep her away from the net.
17. When serving, attempt to get the first serve in the proper court as often as possible. Stress control and accuracy if a second serve is necessary, and concentrate on getting the ball into the proper service area.
18. The server should always have two balls in his possession before starting the service.
19. The receiver should not retrieve or return the ball if the opponent's first serve is a fault. Rather, the receiver should remain in receiving position so the server can immediately follow with a second attempt.
20. Devote periodic practice sessions to correcting specific weaknesses.

Etiquette and Playing Courtesies

To make the game more enjoyable for yourself and others, you should follow certain court courtesies or rules of etiquette. If one of your tennis balls rolls into another court, wait until the players on the court have finished their rally before asking for your ball. When you return someone's ball that has rolled into your court, roll the ball back to the player asking for it instead of trying to gain some stroking practice. If they are engaged in playing a point, roll the ball back against the screen out of their field of play. If your opponent is interfered with in any way during the play for a point, stop the play, call a let, and then play the point over. You call lines on your side of the net, and let your opponent call lines on her side. When leaving or entering the courts, do not walk behind a player playing a point. Wait until the rally is over, then quickly cross the rear of the court close to the back screen.

Skill Assessment

The most important skills in tennis are the ability to keep the ball consistently in play and the ability to consistently serve the ball. The suggested skills test is a rebound test almost identical to the one described in the Handball and Racquetball chapter. The only suggested changes are that a line on the rebound surface be marked at 3 feet 6 inches (net height) above the surface; to legally count, a ball must be returned on or above the line; and forehand, backhand, or volley strokes are allowed.

Modifications for Special Populations

ORTHOPEDICALLY IMPAIRED

1. Access the United States Tennis Association Web site at www.usta.com for the rules on wheelchair tennis.

2. Allow students using wheelchairs two bounces before returning a shot.

3. Students using assistive devices (e.g., canes, walkers, crutches) might play from a seated position with another student in a seated position. For the nonimpaired student, you might be able to borrow a wheelchair from a local hospital's rehabilitation unit.

4. For students with limited grip, use Velcro straps to secure the racket to the student's hand.

5. Allow students with limited grip to use flat paddle boards instead of rackets. Secure the boards with strapping.

6. See modifications for handball and racquetball.

7. Use larger balls or ones made from different material (e.g., Nerf or beach ball).

COGNITIVELY IMPAIRED

1. Have students throw the ball back and forth across the net to help them understand the concepts of the game.

2. Have students practice in a smaller area (e.g., a smaller court) or rebound ball off of a wall.

3. Reduce the tension in the stringing of the racket to allow a slower moving ball.

SENSORY IMPAIRED

1. Individual considerations must be taken into account to determine the appropriateness of tennis for students who are visually impaired or blind.

2. You might consider playing lead-up games, such as goalball, for the visually impaired. You can obtain rules from the United States Association of Blind Athletes at www.usaba.org.

3. Place small bells inside whiffleballs and use as an audio ball for rebounding against a gym wall.

4. Minimal modifications are needed for students who are deaf or hearing impaired. Consider using visual stop-and-start signals for these students.

Terminology

ace A ball served and untouched by the opponent's racket.

advantage (ad) scoring term The next point won after the score is "deuce."

alley The 4½ foot strip on either side of the singles court, used to enlarge the court for doubles.

approach shot A shot hit inside the baseline while approaching the net.

backcourt The area between the service line and the baseline.

backhand Strokes hit on the left side of a right-handed player.

backspin Spin acquired on a ball dropping from a vertical position, which forces the ball to bounce back toward the hitter.

backswing The beginning of all ground strokes and service motion requiring a backswing to gather energy for the forward swing.

baseline The end line of a tennis court, located 39 feet from the net.

break Relates to the act of winning a game in which the opponent serves.

center mark Short mark that bisects the baseline.

center service line The line perpendicular to the net, which divides the two service courts.

center strap A strap placed at the center of the net and anchored to the court to facilitate a constant 3-foot height for the net at the center.

center stripe Same as the center service line, which divides the two service courts into halves.

chip Refers to the short chopping motion of the racket against the back and bottom side of the ball.

chop Used in the same manner as "chip" by many. Refers to the placement of backspin on the ball with a short high to low forward swing.

cross-court A shot hit diagonally from one corner of the court over the net into the opposite corner of the court.

cut off the angle To move forward quickly against an opponent's cross-court shot, so the ball can be hit near the center of the court rather than near the sidelines.

deep (depth) A shot that bounces near the baseline on ground strokes and near the service line on serves.

default A forfeit in a tournament through failure to play a scheduled match.

deuce Scoring term used when the game score is 40–40.

dink A ball normally hit softly and relatively high to ensure its safe landing.

double fault When the server has served two serves out of bounds on the same point.

doubles line The outside sideline on a court—used in doubles only.

down-the-line A shot hit near a sideline that travels close to and parallel with the same line from which the shot was initially hit.

drive An offensive shot hit with extra force.

drop shot A ground stroke hit in such a manner as to drop just over the net with little or no forward bounce.

drop volley A volley hit in such a manner as to drop just over the net with little or no forward bounce.

error A mistake made by a player during competition.

face The hitting surface of the racket.

fault A serve that lands out of bounds or is not hit properly.

flat shot A ball hit in such a manner as not to rotate when traveling through the air.

foot fault Illegal foot movement before service, penalized by the loss of that particular serve. Common foot faults are stepping on or ahead of the baseline before the ball has been contacted and running along the baseline before serving.

forecourt The area between the net and the service line.

forehand The stroke hit on the right side of a right-handed player.

frame The rim of the racket head plus the handle of the racket.

game Scoring term when a player wins 4 points before his opponent and holds a minimum 2-point lead.

grip That portion of the racket that is grasped in the player's hand.

ground stroke Any ball hit after it has bounced.

half-volley A ball hit only inches away from the court's surface after the ball has bounced.

hold serve To win your own serve. If you lose your own serve, your serve has been "broken."

let (ball) A point that is played over because of some kind of interference.

let serve A serve that touches the net tape and falls into the proper square and is played over.

linesperson A match official who calls balls in or out.

lob A ball hit sufficiently high to pass over the outstretched arm position of the net player.

lob volley A shot hit high into the air from a volleying position.

love Scoring term: zero points or games.

match A contest between two or four opponents.

match point The point immediately preceding the final point of a match. The player who holds this point is said to be serving for match point.

midcourt The area in front or in back of the service line of the playing court.

net ball A ball that hits the net and falls back on the same side as the hitter.

net player The player who has gained position at the net and is prepared to volley.

no player's land A general area within the baseline and proper net position area; when caught in that area, the player must volley or hit ground strokes near his feet.

offensive lob A ball hit just above the racket reach of an opposing net player.

open face racket A racket whose face is moving under the ball. A wide open racket face is parallel with the court surface.

overhead A shot hit from a position higher than the player's head.

overhead smash A shot hit extremely hard from a position higher than the player's head.

overhitting Putting too much force into each shot.

pace The speed of the ball.

passing shot A shot that passes beyond the reach of the net player and lands inbounds.

placement A shot hit inbounds and untouched by the opponent.

poach To cross over into your partner's territory.

racket face The hitting surface of the racket.

racket head Top portion of the racket frame that houses the strings.

rally The act of hitting balls back and forth across the net. A rally includes all shots other than the serve.

receiver The player about to return the opponent's serve.

retrieve Normally refers to a fine defensive shot in response to an opponent's well-placed offensive shot.

server The player initiating play.

service line The end line of the service courts, running parallel with the net.

set Scoring term: The first player to win six games with a minimum two-game lead has won a set.

set point The point that, if won, will give the player the set.

sidespin A ball hit and rotating on a horizontal plane.

signals in doubles Signaling your partner that you are going to poach at the net.

singles line The first sideline closer to the center mark and running the entire length of the court.

slice Motion of the racket head going around the side of the ball, producing a horizontal spin on the ball.

tape The band of cloth or plastic running across the top of the net.

telegraphing the play To indicate the direction of one's intended target before actually hitting the ball.

topspin The clockwise rotation of the ball at a 90-degree angle.

touch The ability to make delicate soft shots from several positions on the court.

twist A special rotation imparted to the ball during the serve, causing the ball to jump to the left (of right-handed server).

umpire The official used in tournament play to call lines.

underspin A counterclockwise spin placed on the ball by catching the ball's backside and bottomside with the racket head.

volley To hit the ball in the air before it has bounced on the court.

Discussion Questions

1. Trace the origin of tennis and the evolution of its name.

2. Discuss the tie-breaker procedures.

3. Compare the Continental and Eastern grips.

4. Discuss the theory for providing backspin or overspin on the ball on strokes.

5. Describe and discuss the sequence of motions involved in the serve.

6. Compare the mechanics between the one-handed and two-handed backstrokes.

7. Discuss the learning hints for the volley which lead to playing success.

8. Compare the singles and doubles strategies.

9. Identify the etiquette and playing courtesies that lead to more enjoyable play for yourself and others.

10. Discuss the safety considerations that apply to tennis.

Web Sites

www.tennis.com *Tennis* magazine's Web site—offers instruction elements, including 101 tips, with drills, rules, history, tip of the week, grip guide, and frequently asked questions.

www.tennisserver.com—provides references, including rules, code of ethics, book and video listings, and much more.

www.tennisone.com—includes instructional tennis hints, a lesson library, professional strokes, grips, rules, and much more.

www.littletennis.com—has content devoted to youth instruction.

www.usta.com United States Tennis Association—contains information about USTA organizations, library resources, instructional tips, and more.

http://tennis.about.com—offers instructional tips, information about rackets, articles and resources for the beginner, history, rules, and much more.

www.itftennis.com/wheelchair International Tennis Federation—features information about wheelchair tennis, including tips for getting started, rules and regulations, and publications.

CHAPTER 26

Track and Field

This chapter will enable you to

- Understand the origins and evolution of track and field
- Understand the learning sequence for the hurdling, jumping, and throwing events
- Demonstrate and perform basic skills and techniques of various running, hurdling, jumping, and throwing events
- Set up a training program for a participant in various running and hurdling events
- Identify the basic terminology used in the sport of track and field
- Identify the basic rules of the sport

Nature and Purpose

The more than 30 different track and field events in the Olympic games involve walking, running, jumping, and throwing. Each requires different combinations of sports fitness (endurance, strength, speed, and flexibility) and motor skills to be successful. Yet the great variety of events requiring these different combinations of natural and acquired abilities gives practically every individual, no matter the body size, shape, or form, the opportunity to participate successfully. Often young boys and girls do not realize they have the natural ability to become successful in track and field until they give it a try. Many track and field stars "discovered themselves" in a physical education class or intramural sport. In fact, participants can easily assess their natural abilities of strength, speed, endurance, and power by performing specific tests. These talent tests could include a 30-meter timed sprint, standing long jump for distance, vertical jump for height, five alternate leg bounds for distance, 5-kg shot tossed backward overhead for distance, or an 800-meter timed run.

History

Most track and field events are as old as human history. People around the world have devised and participated in competitive forms of running, jumping, and throwing. Primitive forms of these activities appeared in Egypt more than 4000 years ago. Cretans were the first to engage systematically in these events around 1500 B.C.[1] It was the Greeks during their Golden Age, however, who developed the pattern for the modern events.

Track and field participation was originally referred to as *athletics*. *Athlete* comes from the Greek word *athlos*, which means "competition." The Greeks held many athletic competitions, but the most famous were the Olympic Festivals, which began in 776 B.C. These competitions were held every 4 years until A.D. 394, when they were discontinued.[2]

Modern track and field competitions evolved in England around the 18th century. The original sport consisted primarily of running and walking events. Universities in England became involved, and the first British championships were held in 1866. The sport spread throughout Europe and the United States, and track and field events were included in the first modern Olympic games in 1896.[3]

Track and field events were included in the earliest interscholastic and intercollegiate programs in the United States. The Amateur Athletic Union (AAU) governed early open competitions and Olympic participation. In 1992, USA Track and Field (USATF) became the national governing body.

Equipment

The equipment required in track and field varies with events. Proper equipment is important and can affect the learning of skills and technique as well as help reduce injuries. Lighter-weight throwing implements for shot or discus should be used for smaller and younger athletes. For the beginning hurdler, modified hurdles using light-weight wooden rods placed on small cones or bricks and easily displaced should be used instead of heavy solid hurdles. In the high jump, a soft foam pit made from gymnastic mats or high jump mats is essential. The crossbar should be of soft plastic rather than solid metal. Also, a bungee cord can be used as the crossbar for safety.

Spiked shoes must be worn not only for safety but also for optimal performance, particularly in the jumping events. For the elite performer, shoes designed specifically for various events may be purchased.

Track and field shorts, shirts, and warm-up suits vary in price depending on the quality of the material. These can be purchased from catalog suppliers or sporting goods or department stores.

Basic Rules

SPRINTING

1. For most elementary to college events, one false start disqualifies a runner.
2. For many youth, club, and international events, disqualification results on the second individual false start.
3. A false start is the result of the athlete moving or leaving his mark before the gun is fired.
4. A starter may not touch on or over the line before the firing of the gun.
5. Some part of each foot must be in contact with the track in the blocks.
6. Runners must stay in their own lanes without stepping on a lane line.
7. The athlete is timed and places are determined when the torso crosses the finish line, which does not include the hand, arms, or legs.

RELAY RACES

1. The baton must be passed inside the 20-meter passing zone.
2. The baton must be carried in the hand throughout the race.
3. After passing the baton, the runner may not interfere with an opponent.
4. A baton dropped outside the zone must be retrieved by the runner who dropped it.
5. A baton dropped inside the zone may be retrieved by either runner.
6. For relay legs that are 200 meters or less, the outgoing runner may line up 10 meters in front of the exchange zone, but the pass must occur within the 20-meter zone.

HURDLING

1. The entire body must pass over the hurdle.
2. A hurdler may not interfere with a hurdler in another lane.
3. A hurdler may not intentionally knock over the hurdles with the hand or foot.

HIGH JUMP

1. The jumper must make a jump from one foot.
2. Three trials are allowed at each height.
3. Displacing a bar, passing under it, or crossing the line of the bar extended on leaving the ground counts as a foul and trial.
4. The jumper goes out of the competition when he has three consecutive misses at any height. The participant is credited with the best mark that was successfully cleared.
5. Leaving the ground is not considered an attempt unless the plane of the crossbar is broken.

LONG JUMP

1. Touching the ground at any point past the foul line (the front edge of the takeoff board) as the participant jumps is considered a foul and not measured.
2. The jump is measured at right angles to the board and at the point of landing closest to the takeoff.
3. If the jumper leaves the pit to the side and moves backward to a point that is closer to the takeoff board than the mark made in the pit, it is considered a foul.

TRIPLE JUMP

1. The legal measurement of a jump is the same as described in the long jump.
2. A foul jump is the same as described in the long jump.

SHOT PUT

1. Touching on the top or outside of the circle or toeboard with any part of the body constitutes a foul.
2. The thrower must leave by the back half of the circle.
3. The shot must be thrown within a 60-degree sector (in high school competition and below) and within a 40-degree sector in college and international competition.

DISCUS THROW

1. The discus must be thrown within a 60-degree sector (40-degree in college). As in the shot put, after entering the ring, the thrower must pause before starting.
2. The thrower may not touch any part of a painted line, or the top of a band used to outline part of the ground outside the circle.

Suggested Learning Sequence

The running and field events described in this chapter may be taught in any order, taking into account particular student needs, the time available, and the type of facilities available. It is, however, important to follow a simple-to-complex progression leading up to the completion of a skill. Other important keys to successful learning include positive reinforcement through feedback and using good learning hints.

In all instances, rules, hints, cues, and terminology should be introduced only when significant to the learning progression and when dealing with the particular event. Safety considerations are of prime importance during the initial stages of learning.

A. Orientation
  1. Safety considerations
  2. Discussion of equipment
  3. Importance of warm-up and cool-down
  4. Warm-up
     a. Raise body temperature with a cardio session, elevating the heart rate.
     b. Use dynamic and static stretches as needed.
     c. Apply specific event technique drills.
     d. Increase intensity of each for final preparation of workout.
  5. Cool-down
     a. Gradually reduce body temperature and heart rate.
     b. Use static stretches of major muscles used to relax muscles to alleviate soreness.

B. Rules, skill development, terminology, and specific safety instructions are given in connection with the particular event.

C. Running events
  1. Sprinting
  2. Middle- and long-distance running
  3. Relays
  4. Hurdling

D. Field events
  1. High jump (flop style)
  2. Long jump
  3. Triple jump

  4. Shot put
  5. Discus throw

Skills and Techniques

SPRINTING

Although speed or sprinting ability is largely determined by inherited traits—the white muscle fiber composition of the body—a sprinter's innate speed can be greatly improved through technique work and training. Technique work involves improving a sprinter's start, ability to lift ("change gears"), and ability to relax, thereby sustaining speed.

The Start.   The placement of the starting blocks is essential to a good start. Most sprinters favor the medium start. In this start, the front block is set in approximately two foot lengths from the starting line, and the back block three to four foot lengths. These distances may vary according to the sprinter's body structure, height, and length of limbs.

The starting commands are "on your marks" and "set" and the firing of the gun.

In the on-the-mark position, the hands are parallel with the starting line, the arms are shoulder-width apart, the dominant leg is forward in the blocks with the opposite knee resting on the track, and the head is relaxed. After assuming this position, the sprinter will then slide or roll forward until the shoulders are over or in front of the starting line, with the pressure being on the knee and fingertips.

On "set," the sprinter raises the hips until slightly higher than the shoulders. In this position, the knees are parallel or at a slight angle to the track. The sprinter feels good power in both legs in this position if the blocks are spaced properly. The head is relaxed with no tension on the neck (Figure 26-1).

At the gun, the sprinter concentrates on good sprint form: opposite arm/opposite leg action while keeping the driving angle low and forward (Figure 26-2). It is important that the sprinter's movement be forward, not

Figure 26-1   An excellent "set" position is demonstrated by the two sprinters.

Figure 26-2   At the gun, these two sprinters demonstrate good sprint form and drive forward out of the blocks.

upward. Forward movement is the result of the proper "set" position.

Lifting. After coming out of the blocks, the sprinter concentrates on lifting, or "shifting gears," by driving the knees high, which will continue acceleration. This action continues until the sprinter has reached maximum speed, somewhere between 30 to 40 meters, at which time an upright running position and full running stride length will have been achieved.

Free-Wheeling. In this phase, which is also referred to as floating, the sprinter works to sustain speed through total body relaxation. Total relaxation is achieved by running tall while keeping the hands, arms, and jaw loose and the shoulders down to reduce tension in the antagonistic muscle groups of the neck (Figure 26-3).

The Finish. The sprinter drives or runs through the tape at the finish in regular sprint form and does not attempt to jump or lunge.

▶ Practice/Organizational Suggestions—Training Workout

In training for the sprinting events, quality work is important over quantity work. Basic sprint training should include *long sprints* consisting of 200 to 250 meters for the 100 meters, 250 to 300 meters for the 200 meters, and 500 to 600 meters for the 400 meters; *medium sprints* consisting of 50 to 75 meters for the 100 meters, 100 to 150 meters (around turn) for the 200 meters, and 300 to 350 meters for the 400 meters; and *short sprints* using a

Figure 26-3 Free-wheeling. A 400-meter sprinter displays total relaxation, which is important in sustaining speed.

starting gun, consisting of 20 to 30 meters for the 100 meters, 50 to 75 meters for the 200 meters, and 100 to 150 meters for the 400 meters. A weekly competitive season training program is given in Table 26-1. Each workout should be preceded by a good warm-up, which includes stretching and flexibility exercises, easy running, and sprint drills, and should be followed by a good cool-down of easy running and stretching.

▶ Practice/Organizational Suggestions—Sprinting Skills

1. *High knee drill.* Running 20 to 30 meters with knees lifted so that the thighs are at least parallel with the ground. Emphasize quality lifting; the drill should not be hurried. The vertical action is fast, but the horizontal movement forward is slow.

2. *Block drill.* Sprinter A gets into the blocks in the on-the-mark position. Sprinter B stands facing him with hands on the shoulders of sprinter A. Upon continued hand pressure, sprinter A comes to set position. On the command "go" from sprinter B, sprinter A drives out of the blocks, concentrating on driving the arms and lifting the knees while sprinter B continues to offer resistance.

3. *Figure 4 drill.* Running 20 to 30 meters, the sprinter concentrates on the heel coming up under the buttocks as the foot comes off the track; this will elevate the knee parallel with the track.

4. *Sprint-float-sprint drill.* The sprinter runs 150 meters, running the first 50 working hard, the next 50 meters floated (relaxed running), and the last 50 meters working hard. The sprinter runs the floated 50 meters within 1 second of the hard 50 meters by concentrating on good sprint form and relaxation, so as not to decelerate.

MIDDLE- AND LONG-DISTANCE RUNNING

Middle-distance races include the 800-meter, 1,500-meter, and mile races. Long-distance races include the 3,000-meter steeplechase, 5,000-meter, 10,000-meter, and marathon races. Running form in these events is not significantly different from the sprinting events except that as the speed of a runner is reduced, the stride length becomes shorter, the body is more erect, and the foot strikes the ground mid- to forefoot for efficient running.

In training for these events, it is important to train both energy systems of the body—the aerobic and anaerobic.

Aerobic Training. Aerobic training, which improves a runner's endurance or stamina by increasing the ability to take in and use oxygen, is accomplished through runs of 3 to 10 miles or longer at different tempos (speeds). An easy tempo involves relaxed recovery running; a brisk tempo involves running at steady state or

Table 26-1 **A weekly training program for sprinting events**

	100 Meters	200 Meters	400 Meters
Monday	4 × 250 m at 95% effort; walk 8 min.	3 × 300 m at 95% effort; walk 10 min	2 × 600 m at 90% effort; walk 15 min
Tuesday	Baton work; 8–10 × 30–40 m gun starts	Baton work; 8–10 × 75 m gun starts (around turn)	8–10 × 150 m gun starts (around turn)
Wednesday	5–6 × 75 m at all-out; walk back for recovery	6 × 150 m at all-out; walk back for recovery	2–3 × 300 m at race pace
Thursday	Baton work; 5–6 × 20–30 m gun starts	Baton work; 6–8 × 50 m gun starts	5–6 × 100 m at 95% effort
Friday	Meet	Meet	Meet
Saturday	1–2 miles easy distance golf course	1–2 miles easy distance golf course	2–4 miles easy distance golf course
Sunday	Rest	Rest	Rest

oxygen balance; and a hard tempo involves running beyond steady state but not all-out. Using all three tempos in a run produces a type of training called *Fartlek* (Swedish for "speed play") or playing with speed. Early training should include only easy and brisk tempo runs for several weeks; later, hard tempo and hard Fartlek runs with hills may be alternated with easier runs. An example of this pattern of training is given in Table 26-2.

Anaerobic Training. Anaerobic training, which improves the body's ability to run while under oxygen debt, is best developed through intermittent or interval-type training. Interval training consists of running a number of short distances at a given pace, interspersed by 1 to 5 minutes of rest or jogging fixed distances. For example: 8 × 200 meters at 30 seconds; jog 200 meters. Interval training is used basically to develop race rhythm and for sharpening speed.

▶ **Training Workout Suggestions**

A weekly competitive-season aerobic/anaerobic training program for high school and college is outlined in Table 26-3. These distances would be reduced for elementary or middle school runners.

RELAYS

There are two types of relays: *sprint relays* (400; 800; 1,600 meters), which include sprint medley (200; 400; 800 meters), and *distance relays* (3,200; 6,000 meters), which include distance medley (400; 800; 1,200; 1,600 meters). Four runners compete for a team, each running an equal distance (except in medley relays), and pass a baton to the next runner. The baton must be exchanged within a 20-meter exchange zone. There are two general methods of exchanging the baton, the *blind pass* and the *visual pass*.

Blind Pass. The blind pass is used in sprint relays. In this exchange, the outgoing runner stands in a good sprint position at the back of the 10-meter fly zone located beyond

Table 26-2 **An aerobic training program**

Sunday	3–5 times race distance or longer if mature enough (easy tempo)
Monday	2–5 times race distance (hard tempo)
Tuesday	3–4 times race distance (brisk tempo)
Wednesday	4–7 miles of Fartlek
Thursday	3–4 times race distance (brisk tempo)
Friday	2–5 times race distance (hard tempo)
Saturday	2–4 times race distance (brisk to easy tempo)

the 20-meter zone (Figure 26-4). The runner stands on the left side of the lane if the baton is to be received in the right hand and the right side of the lane when the baton is to be received in the left hand. When the incoming runner hits a predetermined mark on the track, called the "go mark," the outgoing runner leaves, concentrating on good sprinting action. This go mark may vary by 5 to 8 meters and is established by a trial-and-error method. The baton is exchanged at a given point in the zone, preferably in the last 10 meters of the 20-meter passing zone, without the receiver looking back. The exchange is made by the incoming runner extending the baton forward as far as possible and placing the baton downward into the receiver's opposite hand, which has been extended backward, palm up (Figure 26-5). In the 400-meter relay, it is best to hand off the first exchange right to left, the second exchange left to right, and the third exchange right to left to make it possible for curve runners to be on the inside of the running lane.

Visual Pass. The visual pass is used in all distance relays. It enables the outgoing runner to judge the speed and fatigue of the incoming runner. In this exchange, the outgoing runner, who is turned toward the inside of the track facing the pole lane, stands on the right side of the lane and receives the baton in the left hand, palm up, from the incoming runner's right hand. On receiving the baton, the outgoing runner should always immediately transfer the baton to the right hand.

Table 26-3 **A weekly competitive-season aerobic-anaerobic training program**

	800 Meters	1,500 Meters	5,000 Meters
Sunday	6 miles (easy tempo)	8 miles (easy tempo)	10 miles (easy tempo)
Monday	1 mile (easy tempo)	2 miles (easy tempo)	3 miles (easy tempo)
	2 × 600 m	5 × 800 m	4 × 1,200 m at race pace; jog 600 m;
	at race pace; walk 5 min;	at slower than race pace; jog 400 m; 20	25 min (easy tempo)
	15 min (easy tempo)	min (easy tempo)	
Tuesday	40 min (brisk tempo)	50 min (brisk tempo)	60 min (brisk tempo)
Wednesday	2 miles (brisk tempo)	3 miles (brisk tempo)	4 miles (brisk tempo)
	4 × 400 m	8 × 400 m at race pace; jog 200 m;	12 × 400 m
	at faster than race pace; walk	25 min (easy tempo)	at faster than race pace; jog 200 m;
	4 min; 15 min (easy tempo)		35 min (easy tempo)
Thursday	20 min (brisk tempo)	30 min (brisk tempo)	50 min (brisk tempo) 8 × 200 m at
	4 × 200 m at 90% effort; jog 200 m	6 × 200 m at 90% effort; jog 200 m	90% effort
Friday	20 min (easy tempo)	30 min (easy tempo)	40 min (easy tempo)
Saturday	Meet	Meet	Meet

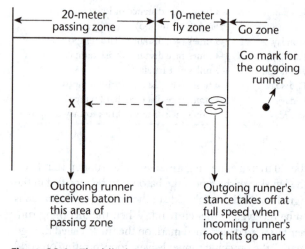

Figure 26-4   The blind pass, used for all sprint relays.

Figure 26-5   These two relay runners demonstrate excellent hand-off technique in the 400-meter sprint relay.

▶ Practice/Organizational Suggestions—Sprint Relay Drills

1. *Standing hand-touch.* Two relay runners standing in their hand-off positions and moving their arms in a running motion touch hands on the command "reach" or "hand."

2. *Running hand-touch.* This drill is the same as for the standing hand-touch, but with the two relay runners now running at a slow pace.

3. *One-on-one drill.* Two relay runners first start at 2 to 5 meters apart and, running at 75-percent speed, pass the baton. The runner in front takes off when the back runner yells "go." This drill progresses, with the incoming runner moving back 20 to 25 meters and hitting a mark set up 7 to 10 meters from the outgoing runner.

4. *Four-runner baton drills.* After mastering the first two drills, progress to using all four relay runners

and a baton. First standing still and then running, the runners gradually increase their pace as they practice handing off the baton. The relay runners should be staggered to the right or left, according to the receiving hand. Care must be taken to keep the proper spacing between runners to allow good extension of the passing and receiving arms.

HURDLING

Hurdling is rhythmical sprinting and should be done with as little deviation from sprinting as possible. Clearing a hurdle is a *run over* action, not a jumping movement, and all hurdling is taught with this concept in mind (Figure 26-6).

The physical attributes of height, good leg split, speed, flexibility, and coordination along with the mental qualities of courage, patience, and concentration are important for success in hurdling.

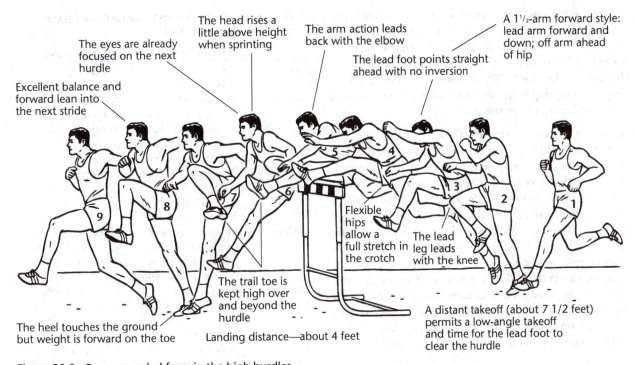

The eyes are already focused on the next hurdle

The head rises a little above height when sprinting

The arm action leads back with the elbow

A 1½-arm forward style: lead arm forward and down; off arm ahead of hip

The lead foot points straight ahead with no inversion

Excellent balance and forward lean into the next stride

Flexible hips allow a full stretch in the crotch

The lead leg leads with the knee

The trail toe is kept high over and beyond the hurdle

The heel touches the ground but weight is forward on the toe

Landing distance—about 4 feet

A distant takeoff (about 7 1/2 feet) permits a low-angle takeoff and time for the lead foot to clear the hurdle

Figure 26-6 Recommended form in the high hurdles.
From J. Kenneth Doherty, *Modern Track and Field.* Englewood Cliffs, NJ: Prentice-Hall, Inc., 1953.

▶ Learning Sequence

One of the best ways to teach hurdling is to use dowel rods and different-height cones or sticks and bricks so the hurdles may gradually be raised. The hurdler progresses through the following steps:

1. Set the first hurdle at 15 meters from the starting line and three other hurdles at 7 or 9 meters apart, depending on the ability of the hurdler and her stride length.

2. Have the hurdler sprint over the hurdles at full speed. Begin with the sticks or dowel rods flat on the track so that the hurdler can experiment with the proper lead leg and steps to the first hurdle and practice taking three steps between the hurdles.

3. Have the hurdler run over the hurdles, gradually increasing the height while working on the correct stride pattern to the first hurdle and the three-stride pattern between the hurdles.

4. When the stick reaches 24 inches above the ground, introduce specific hurdling techniques—proper lead leg, trail leg, and arm action—by means of a wall drill.

5. *Wall drill—first part.* Work on the proper lead leg and arm action. The hurdler, standing a few feet from a wall, starts by lifting the lead knee and leg toward the wall, letting the weight fall forward. The leg is planted on the wall at hurdle height, the chest drops down toward the knee, and the opposite arm is driven toward the opposite leg.

6. *Wall drill—second part.* Work on the trail leg. Standing facing the wall, the hurdler leans forward with both hands against the wall. The trail leg is brought up under the armpit and reaches out for a long step forward.

7. The next step is to walk over a 30-inch hurdle and then gradually increase the speed running over this hurdle height. As the speed of the hurdler increases, the distance between the barriers can be increased until regulation hurdle spacing is reached. However, never increase the distance between the hurdles if it causes the hurdler to stretch their stride because it will lead to poor hurdle form. Also, do not raise the hurdle height if doing so causes the hurdler to jump rather than sprint over the hurdle.

8. The last step is to gradually increase the height of the hurdles as technique improves; however, the participant will learn correct form more readily if the hurdles are fitted to the participant rather than trying to fit the participant to the hurdles.

Hurdle Start. The hurdle start differs from the regular sprint start in that the hurdler must come up to the running position sooner. A high hurdler will take 7 or 8 steps to the first hurdle; an intermediate hurdler 21,

22, 23, or 24 steps. The hurdler who takes an odd number of steps to the first hurdle will have the same leg forward in the blocks as leads over the hurdle. With an even number of steps, the lead leg over the hurdle is the back leg in the blocks. The hurdler determines the lead leg by attempting to hurdle with each leg. The one most comfortable should be the lead leg.

Running Between the Hurdles. In the highs, an experienced hurdler takes three steps between the hurdles. The beginner may take four or five steps depending on their development and training age. Factors such as hurdle height, stride length, and speed affect the number of steps. The intermediates take 13, 15, or 17 steps. The intermediate hurdler can use a 14-stride pattern if the lead leg is alternated. The hurdler must concentrate on good sprint action between the hurdles, running up on the balls of the feet, with knees high and arms driving hard with relaxation. Good sprint rhythm between the hurdles is important. The hurdler should never gallop or overstride, which often is caused by not getting a good step off the hurdle with the trail leg.

▶ Learning Hints

1. In the lead leg action, lead with the knee, not the foot.
2. Keep the trail leg flat, toe out and up, and bring it up high under the armpit and out.
3. The opposite arm or opposite leg action is used over the hurdle.
4. Sprint through the hurdle, rather than jumping over the hurdle.

▶ Practice/Organizational Suggestions—Hurdling Drills

1. *Wall drill.* (See Learning Sequence 7 and 8, preceding.)
2. *Lead leg over hurdles.* Performed with the lead leg over the side of four to six hurdles spaced 7 to 9 meters apart for the three-stride rhythm, or 9 to 13 meters apart for a five-stride rhythm. The hurdle height varies between 12 and 36 inches.
3. *Trail leg over hurdles.* Same as the preceding lead leg drill, except the trail leg passes over the hurdle.

Table 26-4 presents a weekly competitive-season training program for hurdling. Each of these workouts is preceded by a good warm-up consisting of specific hurdling flexibility and stretching exercises, easy running, and sprint work and is followed by a good cool-down of easy running and stretching.

HIGH JUMP (FLOP STYLE)

The flop or back layout style of jumping, originated by 1968 Olympic champion Dick Fosbury, is currently used by the majority of high jumpers. The technique can be

Table 26-4 **Hurdling—A weekly competitive-season training program**

	110 m Hurdles	400 m Hurdles
Sunday	2 miles (easy tempo)	3–4 miles (easy tempo)
Monday	Go over flights of 7, 6, 5, 4, and 3 hurdles 3 times at full effort; walk back for recovery 1 × 400 m at full effort	Go over flights of 8, 6, 4, and 2 hurdles, from blocks, working on stride pattern at race pace
Tuesday	"Five-step" 5 hurdles, 2–3 times, 3–4 × 150 m at 90% effort; walk back for recovery	2 × 300 m at full effort
Wednesday	Go over 5 flights of hurdles (70 meters) 5 times at full effort 1 × 300 m at full effort	Go over flights of 5, 4, 3, 2, and 1 hurdles at race pace
Thursday	5–6 gun starts over 2 hurdles, 3–4 × 100 m 90% effort; walk back for recovery	4 × 200 m at 90% effort
Friday	Easy stretching and jogging, "five-step" 3 hurdles, 2–3 times	3–4 gun starts over 1st hurdle, working on stride pattern
Saturday	Meet	Meet

broken down into three phases: approach, plant/takeoff, and bar clearance.

1. *Approach.* The recommended approach is a curve "J" consisting of 10 steps (Figure 26-7). The first five steps are the straight portion of the "J" gaining forward acceleration. The final five steps—or curve portion—involve the turn and plant, with the inside foot initiating the inward move from the straight line. The body leans inward and maintains the accelerated speed, generating centripetal force for the plant and take-off at the nearside standard.

   A suggested method for determining the "depth" (curve portion) of the "J" is to stand at the jumping-side standard and take 15 heel-to-toe steps straight out to the side of the pit. Mark this spot and use it to determine how wide the start of the approach should be. Shortening this width increases velocity.

2. *Plant/takeoff.* The next-to-last stride (ninth, called the "penultimate") is longer to enable the jumper to lower the center of gravity for gathering for the jump. The last stride (takeoff) is from the outside foot farthest from the bar and is shorter so the body is in a lean-back position. The free-knee leg is kicked upward and coordinated with an upward swing of the arms (arm/knee drive). The kick, combined with the curved approach and the takeoff foot planted toward the left standard, causes the jumper's back to rotate toward the bar at takeoff. As the

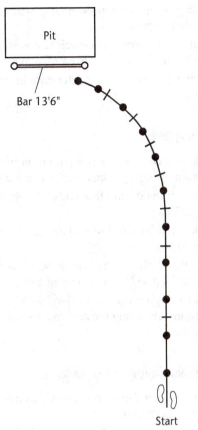

Pit

Bar 13'6"

Start

Figure 26-7 The "J" approach used in the back layout (flop style) high jump.

5. Running three strides over bar with back jump

6. Running three- to five-stride approach jumps away from pit on curve

7. Running five-stride approach jump

8. Running seven to nine strides with "J" or curved approach jumps

Learning Hints

1. Approach the bar fast but relaxed with good sprint technique.

2. Use the same speed for all heights.

3. Quicken the last two strides and lower the hips.

4. Plant the foot farthest from the crossbar, heel first, and at an approximate 15-degree angle to the bar.

5. Drive the lead knee upward at takeoff.

6. At clearance, keep the legs apart—"frog" position—and squeeze the buttocks muscles together.

7. Drop the chin to the chest after the hips pass over the bar.

Practice/Organizational Suggestions—Drills

1. *Plant/takeoff drill.* (Based on flop style description.)

2. *Approach drill.* (Based on flop style description).

3. *Clearance drill.* Stand on a small box at the edge of the pit with your back to the pit. Jump up and backward, working on the clearance technique.

LONG JUMP

The long jumper must possess good sprinting speed, a rhythmic, consistent stride pattern, and powerful jumping ability. The basic technique of the long jump can be broken into four phases: the run-up, plant/takeoff, flight, and landing.

1. *The run-up or approach.* During the approach, the jumper must get to the takeoff board with maximum controlled speed and be in a position to lift. Therefore, relaxation and consistency of stride length are important during the approach. To ensure that the jumper hits the takeoff board with consistency, checkmarks are established in the following manner:

a. The jumper, one step from the takeoff board, runs 10 to 19 strides in the opposite direction of the jumping pit until the same foot that is to hit the takeoff board lands on the track. Start at the foul line of the takeoff board, run 10 to 19 strides in the opposite direction of the jumping pit until the same foot that is to contact the takeoff board lands on the runway (beginner 10–12, intermediate 13–15, and experienced 13–19 strides). The varying length depends on the strength, skill, and ability of the athlete.

takeoff is being executed, the jumper should look over the inside shoulder.

3. *Bar clearance* (layout position). During bar clearance, the lead knee remains up with the plant by catching up to it. The legs are spread, with the knees out in a "frog" position and the feet together. The hands are placed alongside the body. There is a laying back of the head and an arching of the back until the bar passes along the back and hips. At this point, the chin is tucked down to the chest so that the body folds up in an "L" position.

Learning Sequence

1. Arm/knee drive while standing still.

2. Running two to four strides with the arm/knee drive.

3. *Arch drill.* Lie flat on your back, heels against buttocks, with heels shoulder-width apart and shoulders on the floor. Grab your ankles with your hands and arch your back.

4. *Back jump drill.* The crossbar is below hip height. With your back to the bar and feet shoulder-width apart, execute a two-foot takeoff in front of bar, driving your body up and arching over the bar to land on the mat.

b. The jumper continues with four to five run-throughs in this direction until the takeoff foot hits consistently at the same point.

c. The jumper then places a checkmark at that point and, standing one stride away, hits the mark with the takeoff foot.

d. Now running toward the jumping pit, the jumper makes four to five run-throughs until hitting the board consistently.

e. The checkmark may be moved forward or backward depending on whether the jumper is over or under the takeoff board.

2. *Plant/takeoff.* Like in the high jump, the next-to-last stride is a longer, settling stride preparing for the lift. The last stride is shorter, and the takeoff hits in a heel-toe action. The free leg comes through as in a normal running stride.

3. *The flight.* After leaving the board, the jumper can use one of three types of techniques in the air: the hitch kick, hang, or sail. The *hitch kick* is done with a run-in-the-air action (see Figure 26-8). The *hang* is performed by letting the legs hang down, with the hips forward and the upper body back. In the *sail*, the legs are tucked up under the body. The purpose of these flight positions is to prevent forward rotation and to get good leg extension in landing.

4. *The landing.* Getting good leg extension is important in landing. This extension can only be achieved when the flight positions are done correctly. On landing, the jumper must work through the jump so as not to sit back by dropping the chin to the chest and driving the arms back forcefully behind the body.

▶ Learning Sequence

1. *Arm/knee drive.* While standing, drive arm and knee upward. Take off as in plant/takeoff (see Figure 26-8).

2. *Arm/knee drive*, landing on two feet (emphasize vertical lift).

3. Running three- to five-stride approach with split landing on opposite foot from takeoff.

4. Running five-stride approach jump with switching legs (hitch kick).

5. Running seven-stride approach jumps off of an 8- to 10-inch box placed at the front of high jump mats.

6. Running nine-stride approach jumps into the long jump pit.

▶ Learning Hints

1. Work for a consistent stride pattern in the approach, using a gradual, uniform acceleration.

2. Run up off the takeoff foot with 1-2-3 rhythm last three strides.

3. At takeoff, drive the free-leg knee up and push the hips forward.

4. After takeoff, the hips remain forward, and the arms are used for good balance (Figure 26-9).

5. Work through the jump and land with good leg extensions, sweeping the arms backward to prevent falling back.

▶ Practice/Organizational Suggestions

1. *Pop-ups.* Repeat three- to five-stride jumps, working on the 1-2-3 rhythm.

2. *Flight pop-ups.* Repeat three- to five-stride jumps from a box, working on the flight-in-the-air technique, the sail, hang, and hitch kick.

3. *Landing and extension pop-ups.* Repeat three- to five-stride jumps from a box, concentrating on correct landing procedures as to leg extension, collapsing of the knees, and driving the arms back forcefully.

TRIPLE JUMP

Formerly called the "hop, step, and jump," the triple jump is an event requiring good speed, great leg strength, and excellent coordination. Proper knee action, with thighs parallel with the ground, and equal rhythm are the keys to good performance.

Figure 26-8 Recommended form in long jump, using a modified hitch kick.

Figure 26-9 This NCAA all-American long jumper uses excellent in-flight technique after leaving the takeoff board.

Figure 26-10 Excellent technique in the second phase of the triple jump. The "step" is demonstrated by this triple jumper.

The technique in the triple jump can be broken down into the approach, plant/takeoff, flight, and landing.

1. *Approach.* To ensure hitting the takeoff board with consistency, check marks are established using the same method as in the long jump. However, the approach is slower and more controlled than in the long jump.

2. *Plant/takeoff.* Because the movement at takeoff is more forward than upward as compared with the long jump, the jumper does not need to settle or gather at takeoff. The takeoff foot is planted flat, with the center of gravity directly over the foot.

3. *Flight.* The first phase of the flight is the hop. The *hop*, or first jump, is performed by bringing the take-off leg forward after it has fully extended from the takeoff board. The thigh of the hopping leg is held parallel with the ground; the hopping foot lands flat in preparation for the next phase. The *step*, or second jump, is performed by bringing the free leg forward and parallel with the ground, riding it forward until there is a good thigh split (Figure 26-10). The third phase, or *jump*, uses the same technique as described in the long jump. However, the hang or sail should be used rather than the hitch kick because there is less time to perform the action.

4. *Landing.* The landing techniques are the same as those used in the long jump, except that some jumpers sit out in landing rather than falling forward, as in the long jump.

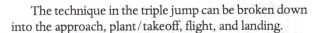

▶ Learning Sequence

1. Standing on one foot, the jumper performs a standing triple jump, saying out loud "same, other, both," which refers to the landing leg or legs.

2. The jumper progresses to three-stride and then five-stride short approach-run jumps. Cones are placed at equal distances for each phase of the jumps so that the jumper keeps a rhythmical pattern and equal distances.

3. Once proper technique is mastered, these short run jumps are transferred to the runway and jumping pit.

▶ Learning Hints

1. Run off the board, jumping out not up and keeping the legs low.

2. The body remains upright throughout the jump.

3. Work through each phase of the jumps with active heel first or midfoot landings.

4. Coordinate the arms with the leg action to maintain speed throughout the jumps.

5. Keep the rhythm even during all three phases of the jump.

1. *Rhythm drills.* Use short 5- to 7-stride approach runs, working on the equal length of each phase and overall rhythm.
2. *Power-bounding drills.* Short 25- to 50-run intervals, on soft surfaces, hopping on one leg.
3. *Box drills.* Box drills are done jumping on or over various sizes of boxes. As technique improves, the boxes can be moved farther apart.

SHOT PUT

The world record for shot put distance has been increased through improved techniques and greater emphasis on speed, strength, and explosive power training. Today, putters use one of two styles of throwing: the glide (O'Brien) and the spin (discus-turn).

Glide Style. With the putter facing opposite the direction of the throw, he glides (shifts) across the circle, lifts the shot with the back, hips, and legs, and then explodes with the arm. It is important to keep the legs and hips ahead of the upper body and throwing arm, thus using the stronger, larger muscle groups of the lower body.

In learning this shot technique, it is helpful to think of the circle as the face of a clock with the 12 o'clock position at the back, and two lines dividing the circle in four equal parts: one a line of direction, the other, a cross-line. The following descriptions are for a right-handed putter.

1. *Grip.* The weight of the shot is placed where the fingers meet the palm of the hand. The thumb and little finger support and guide the shot. The three middle fingers are used for power.
2. *Shot placement.* The shot is held against the neck under the jaw bone underneath the ear.
3. *Starting position.* The putter stands at the back of the circle with the right foot in the 11 o'clock position on the line of direction. The putter keeps the eyes focused on a focal point in the back of the circle, with the nonthrowing arm and shoulder kept square and held back.
4. *Glide.* From the starting position, the body weight drops down over the right leg, raising the left leg. The left leg makes an easy swinging motion toward the throwing direction. At the same time, the right leg begins its pushing action across the circle. This ball-to-heel motion causes a stretching action, not a hopping or jumping movement. As the body weight moves toward the front of the circle, the right leg snaps underneath the thrower to the middle of the circle in the 9 o'clock position. The left leg lands at the same instant in the 5 o'clock position just to the left of the line of direction.

5. *Throwing (power) position.* This position at the front of the circle is called the power position; it is the key to a successful throw. Hitting this position correctly for a right-handed thrower means the feet and hips are turned to the left side of the circle, the head faces the back of the circle, body weight is over the right leg, and the right and left legs are bent. The left (nonthrowing) elbow is thrust back toward the middle of the ring; the hips lead the shoulder area and right arm; the throwing arm vigorously extends; and the wrist snaps forward flicking the shot off of the fingers or hand.

1. Because 80 percent of the distance in the throw comes from the leg and the trunk, begin with standing power position throws, emphasizing the rotation of the right foot-knee-hip.
2. Next, the glide across the ring is developed, with concentration on getting the bent right leg up under the body and keeping the shoulders square to the back of the circle, which ensures a leg or trunk throw.
3. The finish of the throw emphasizes an explosive right-leg drive over a braced left leg.

1. Keep the shot against the neck during the movement across the circle.
2. Leg and hips lead and shoulders remain square to the back of the circle during the glide across the circle.
3. The right leg is snatched up under the body quickly during the glide across the circle and must remain bent.
4. Use concentration and explosive action from the power position—with the force coming from the ground up, through legs, hips to shoulders, and then the arm.

1. *Standing throw drill.* Execute standing throws from the power position, concentrating on perfect technique and leg or trunk force.
2. *T-drill.* From a standing position, the thrower drops down in a T-position as if starting the throw.
3. *A-drill.* From the standing T-position, the thrower drops down and kicks the left leg until his body is in the A-position.
4. *Crossbar drill (right leg).* With arms draped over a crossbar, the putter snaps the right leg under; the crossbar prevents the shoulders from turning.

5. *Crossbar drill (left leg).* With arms draped over a crossbar, the putter concentrates on driving the left leg low and to the toe-board without turning the upper body.

Spin Style. In the spin (discus-turn) style, the thrower makes a 1¾ spin as in the discus throw. The thrower must accelerate across the circle gradually to hit the power position. As in the glide style, the legs and hips lead the throw, and the shot is held against the neck at the jaw.

DISCUS THROW

As in the shot put, world distance records for the discus have increased with improvement in techniques and greater emphasis on speed, strength, and explosive power training. The following descriptions are for right-handed throwers.

1. *Grip.* The thrower holds the discus on the last crease of the fingers with the fingers spread or the first two fingers placed together.

2. *Preliminary swings.* The thrower begins by standing at the back of the circle with the back opposite to the direction of the throw. With the legs bent slightly and the weight on the balls of the feet, the thrower initiates several preliminary swings, shifting the weight from the right foot to the left as the discus is swung back and forth in a horizontal plane.

3. *Turn.* At the end of the final swing to the right, with the discus as far back as the thrower can reach, the thrower prepares to enter the turn, pivoting over the left leg. The right leg is picked up and moves in an arc toward the front of the circle as the left leg drives forward. The legs and hips are kept ahead of the shoulders as the turn is performed.

4. *Power position.* After the right foot lands in the middle of the circle, the thrower keeps pivoting until the left leg lands slightly bent. The thrower is now in a power position with the legs bent and the shoulders and the throwing arm back in a torqued position.

5. *Follow-through.* The right hip drives through as the bent legs drive upward and the weight shifts to the left leg. The throwing arm is whipped through by this powerful leg or trunk action and the discus is released.

▶ Learning Sequence

1. The grip and release are taught first. The thrower, with legs bent, flips the discus in the air or bowls it on the ground, making sure the discus comes off the index finger in a clockwise rotation (for a right-handed thrower).

2. The standing throw is taught next. In the power position, with the bent right leg at the 9 o'clock position and the left leg at the 6 o'clock position, the thrower, shoulders torqued and throwing arm back, performs a series of standing throws. Concentration is on a right foot or right hip action beginning the initial movement of the throws.

3. The step back throw is now introduced. The thrower, standing in the center of the circle with the feet together, steps back with the left leg while sinking on the right, which achieves a power position. From this power position, the thrower performs a series of throws.

4. The thrower is now ready for the 1¼-turn throw. Standing at the rear of the circle sideways to the direction of the throw, the thrower transfers weight to the left foot, pivots, and using a running sprint across the circle, lands in a good power position. From this position, the thrower performs the throw.

5. After mastering this progression, the thrower can learn the 1 ¾-turn discus throw.

▶ Learning Hints

1. Keep the throwing arm up at shoulder level throughout the turns.

2. Before starting the turns, the shoulders and throwing arm are torqued back as far as possible.

3. The shoulders remain level during the turns and the legs are bent.

4. Legs and hips always lead, which creates a "leg throw."

▶ Practice/Organizational Suggestions

1. *Flip and bowling drills.* Used to teach the release, these drills are best learned with partners.

2. *Swing drill.* With discus taped to the hand, practice the weight shift for the preliminary swings and getting the discus all the way back.

3. *Line-turn drill.* Facing the direction of the throw, the thrower pivots or turns on the right foot, ending up for a power position throw. To simulate the discus throw, cones may be used in this drill.

4. *Standing throw drills.* With a traffic cone or any other soft, weighted object, the thrower, with feet together and back facing opposite to the throw, steps with the right foot into the power position, practicing leg or hip pop throws.

Safety Considerations

SPRINTING

1. Warm up thoroughly before starting.

2. Do *not* jump or lunge at the finish tape.

3. Do *not* take starts after a hard training session.

RELAY RACES

1. After passing the baton, remain in your lane until all others have passed.
2. Pass the baton to opposite hands, right to left or left to right, to avoid a collision.

HURDLING

1. Warm up and stretch well before hurdling.
2. Never attempt to go over a hurdle from the wrong direction.

HIGH JUMP

1. Make certain the pit is positioned correctly.
2. If using gymnastics mats, they should have a depth of 24 inches.

LONG JUMP

1. Keep the landing pit area soft and smooth.
2. Wear jumping shoes with heel cups or rubber pads in the takeoff heel.

TRIPLE JUMP

1. Wear heel cups or rubber pads in both jumping shoes.
2. Keep the landing pit area soft and smooth.

SHOT PUT/DISCUS

1. Roll or carry implements back to the circle rather than throw them.
2. Practice in a protected area.
3. When retrieving implements, never turn your back to the throwing circle.

Skill Assessment

Track and field units are comprised of running, hurdling, jumping, and throwing skills. Skill assessment essentially consists of testing an individual's accomplishment in the chosen events. The teacher must determine the number and types of events to test, the length of time necessary for assessing each individual, and the equipment available for mass testing.

It is suggested that class of 30 students be divided into thirds to assess their skill in the 400-meter run, long jump, and shot put. The 400-meter run result is recorded to the nearest second as the individual crosses the finish line. The long jump is measured—with a tape measure—immediately following a student's jump. Each shot put throw is marked by a wood stick with the student's name written on it stuck in the ground. Distances are measured after everyone has thrown. The total number of jump and throw trials depends on the time allocated for assessing. The three event groups rotate following the time allocated for each.

Modifications for Special Populations

ORTHOPEDICALLY IMPAIRED

1. Contact the National Wheelchair Athletic Association (NWAA), the United States Cerebral Palsy Athletic Association (USCPAA), or the United States Les Autres Sports Association (USLASA) for their information on track and field.
2. Hold mock track and field meets in the gymnasium using modified equipment (for example, toss bean bags instead of shot puts; suspend a rope between two standards and throw Nerf balls over the rope to simulate the high jump; vary the height of the rope).

COGNITIVELY IMPAIRED

1. Contact the local Special Olympics for their track and field manuals.

SENSORY IMPAIRED

1. Contact the American Athletic Association of the Deaf (AAAD) or the United States Association of Blind Athletes (USABA) for their track and field manuals.

Terminology

aerobic running Running done at low-intensity speeds so that oxygen intake and oxygen output are the same; therefore, this type of running can be sustained for a long period.

anaerobic running Running done at great-intensity speeds so that oxygen intake is less than oxygen output; therefore, this type of running can be sustained only for a short period.

anchor leg The last leg for a runner on a relay team.

baton The stick that is passed from one relay runner to another.

blind pass A nonvisual baton exchange used in sprint relays.

crossbar The bar that a high jumper or pole vaulter must clear.

discus One of the field events in track and field in which a circular object is thrown. The weight and size of the discus may vary according to the age of the participants.

false start Moving or jumping before the gun is fired.

Fartlek Swedish term for *speed play*, a type of training in which a runner varies running speeds over a long distance, usually in a forest, on a golf course, or some other nontrack area.

flight The in-the-air techniques for the long jump and triple jump.

flop style The style of high jumping in which the jumper's back passes over the bar.

fly zone The 10-meter zone outside the passing zone used by the outgoing runner to get a flying start.

gather In jumping events, the settling or lowering of the hips during the last few strides prior to takeoff or penultimate step.

heat Preliminary race whose winners qualify for the semifinals or finals.

hitch kick A running-in-the-air action during flight in the long jump, used to prevent forward rotation.

interval training A type of running training containing four variables: the number of repetitions, distance, tempo of run, and rest interval.

passing zone The 20-meter zone in which the baton in a relay must be exchanged (passed).

penultimate step The next to last step on an approach, which is slightly longer than the others and allows the jumper to lower the hips and "gather" to a lower, more powerful jumping position.

relay leg The distance each runner travels in a relay.

takeoff board The board from which the long jumper takes off.

throwing sector The specified arc in which a thrown implement must land.

toe-board A board, in the form of an arc, on which or over which the shot putter must not step.

trial An attempt in a field event.

visual pass The pass used in the distance relays in which the outgoing runner visually watches the incoming runner during baton exchange.

Discussion Questions

1. Discuss the evolution of track and field from the Golden Age of Greece to the modern Olympics.
2. Discuss the basic rules of each event.
3. Identify the steps involved in setting the starting blocks correctly and the technique for obtaining a good start.
4. Discuss the safety considerations for each event.
5. Identify the major differences when preparing an aerobic and anaerobic workout.
6. Discuss the strengths and weaknesses of the blind and visual passes for the relay events.
7. Compare the three types of leg techniques used in the air following takeoff in the long jump.
8. Compare the glide and spin styles for the shot put.

Web Sites

www.american-trackandfield.com *American Track and Field*—publishes content dedicated to the improvement of both the image and the performance of American athletes in the sport of track and field.

www.everythingtrackandfield.com— includes training zone section with resources for technique training for various events, plus numerous articles.

www.trackandfieldnews.com/technique Web site for *Track and Field News* magazine—provides access to a compilation of articles dealing with performance enhancement.

CHAPTER 27

Volleyball

This chapter will enable you to

- Describe the nature and adaptability of volleyball
- Identify important historical events that contributed to the evolution of volleyball
- Apply basic skills in modified practice games
- Describe and execute in game play the skills of overhand pass, forearm pass, serve, spike, and blocking
- Describe, discuss, and put into practice the rules of power volleyball during a game or match
- Describe play in power volleyball using the correct terminology associated with the sport

Nature and Purpose

Volleyball is an adaptable team sport that may be played by various numbers of players (from two-on-two to six-on-six); by all-male, all-female, or mixed teams; with net height adjustments for men, women, coed, or age-group differences; and using a variety of playing surfaces (wood, rubberized material, sand, or grass).

Volleyball is a net game and a rebound sport in which, following the initiation of play (serve), the ball may not visibly come to rest. Each team is allowed a maximum of three contacts before the ball is returned across the net. A player may not play the ball twice in succession.

The basic objective of the game is to keep the ball, which is served over the net, from contacting the floor on your side and to return it so that it contacts the floor on the opponents' side before they can return it. Skillful, organized play involves using the three allowable contacts to pass, set, and attack the ball (offense). The opponents attempt to block the ball at the net before it crosses, dig it if the ball evades the block, or pass a nonforcefully returned ball, skillfully making the transition back onto offense. The continuous cycle repeats until the rally is terminated; hence, a point is scored or a side-out is awarded, with the opponents earning the right then to serve. The sequence is repeated until one team reaches the designated points for a set with at least a 2-point advantage. To shorten the length of time it takes to play a set or match, new scoring rules are used by various levels of play (club, high school, college, international), whereby a point is scored on every serve. A team wins on reaching 15, 25, or 30 points, with a 2-point advantage.

Because all players on the team must rotate one position clockwise each time they earn a side-out, this assures that one-half of the time individual players have restrictions concerning net play. This controls domination of the net by taller players and requires that each individual become a more complete player, possessing a variety of skills and techniques.

There are five basic skills, each having a variety of techniques. The air skills of attack and block are normally performed in the attack area near the net, whereas the ground skills of forearm pass, overhand pass, and serve are used while in contact with the playing surface.

Teams involving six players use organized systems for serve reception, attack coverage, defense, and offense. The organized game involves specialization, using the individual talents and skills of players such as setters, attackers, passers, and so on.

The flexibility in number of players, sexes, equipment adjustments, variety of rules, and playing surfaces allows for individual preference and for selecting a variety of competition levels. Because of its adaptability, volleyball may be played on any level—from recreational to national, international, and professional.

History

Volleyball was invented in 1895 by William P. Morgan at a YMCA in Holyoke, Massachusetts. The game was initially called *mintonette* and borrowed characteristics and rules from the sports of badminton, tennis, basketball, baseball, and handball. At a public exhibition of the activity in 1896, Dr. A. T. Halstead suggested it be called "volley ball," and that name was adopted. The sport's name remained as two words for more than 50 years until 1951, when it first appeared as one word on the cover of a United States Volleyball Association (USVBA) publication.[1]

Initially the sport was developed as an indoor activity for middle-aged men who found the new game of basketball too vigorous. For many years, this initial purpose inhibited volleyball's growth as a competitive sport. As early as 1912, a YMCA rules publication suggested that volleyball be promoted as a national recreational game. Additionally, in 1916, when the National Collegiate Athletic Association (NCAA) was invited to work with the YMCA in adopting the rules, the NCAA recognized volleyball's potential as a new intramural (recreational) activity. Competitive advocates at various times (1920s and 1950s through 1970s) attempted to differentiate the two versions by referring to the game as "intensive volley ball"[2] and "power volleyball."

National competition started in 1922, when the YMCA conducted its first National Championship Tournament in Brooklyn, New York. In 1928, Dr. George J. Fisher, called the "Father of Volleyball," founded the USVBA in an effort to offer a national open championship, thus expanding competition to any organization or team. The USVBA throughout the years established a variety of national championships, such as the YMCA Men's Open, Women's Open, Collegiate, Armed Forces, Masters, and others, which promoted the competitive nature of the sport.

The dichotomy between the recreational and the competitive aspects of volleyball in the United States most clearly appears when its growth pattern is compared to that of its older sibling, basketball. The two games were invented just 6 years apart at the same organization (YMCA), yet they took different competitive paths at the collegiate level. The USVBA, not a collegiate governing body, first offered a national collegiate championship in 1949, 54 years after the game's birth, whereas basketball was accepted immediately by college athletic organizations. It took another 20 years for a national collegiate governing body, the National Association for Intercollegiate Athletics (NAIA), in 1969, to sponsor a national volleyball championship. The following year, the NCAA held a men's championship and, in 1981, it held a women's championship. This recognition, plus national legislation of Title IX in 1973, provided a grassroots growth explosion for the women's sport, which continues today.

The popularity of volleyball throughout the world is attributed to the YMCA and soldiers in World War I and World War II. Internationally, volleyball was popularized immediately as a competitive indoor sport, unlike in the United States. In 1947 the Federation Internationale de Volleyball (FIVB) was formed by 14 countries and is the international governing body for the sport. The first world championships were held in 1959; however, it was not until 1964 that volleyball was added to the Olympics. In 1996, the Olympic program added men's and women's two-player beach competition.[3]

It took 80 years for volleyball to become a professional sport. In the United States, the International Volleyball Association (IVA) was formed and established six-player teams made up of men and women. The IVA lasted until 1980. It was followed by the Association of Volleyball Professionals (AVP) in 1983, which organized a tour of the two-player beach game. FIVB first recognized the professional beach game in 1987 and today has a championship series for men and women. The six-player indoor game is played on a professional basis internationally but currently not in the United States.[4]

Volleyball is recognized as one of the world's most popular sports; an estimated 800 million people play at least once a week. According to the FIVB, approximately 1.1 billion people watched or played volleyball in 2006.[5]

Equipment

Volleyball is an inexpensive activity. The player's equipment is minimal, requiring only rubber-soled shoes and possibly knee pads (individual preference) for hard playing surfaces or for safety. A ball, net, and net supports are the only other equipment necessary. Volleyballs are available in different sizes, weights, and coverings. The recommended covering is either synthetic leather or leather with a molded carcass. Care should be taken in selecting a ball that is not too hard and that meets the abilities of the players.

The Court

The court (Figure 27-1) is divided into equal halves separated by a center line and net. Each half has a front court attack area, which restricts back-row players from attacking or blocking in that area. The boundary lines are considered a part of the court; thus, a ball landing on these lines is considered inbounds.

Nets should extend at least 1 foot on each side of the court (32 feet), have 4-inch-square mesh openings, and have a flexible cord or cable running through a 2-inch-wide white band at the top. The net supports should be located at least 19½ inches outside the sideline and anchored securely enough to allow the net to be safely stretched tight without any sag below the required height. Supports with easily adjustable settings assist in quickly varying net height.

The net height is adaptable for differences in player size, sex, and team composition. Men's regulation height is 7 feet 11⅝ inches, and women's is 7 feet 4⅛ inches. A ball contacting the net within the boundaries of the court is considered playable. In regulation play, antennas extend upward from the net directly above the sideline to assist in determining whether the ball crossed the net within the court. A ball contacting the antenna is out of play.

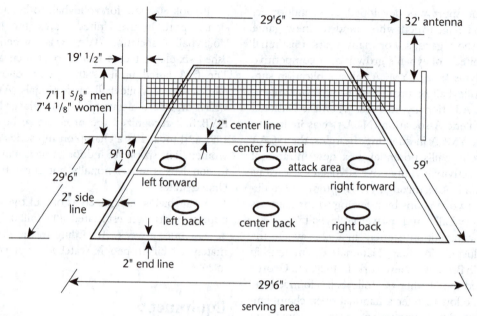

Figure 27-1 The official volleyball court markings and dimensions.

Basic Rules

Players and Rotation. When the ball is not in play, the players must remain in the proper rotation order, which establishes the sequential service order. Proper rotation order (six-on-six) establishes three front-row and three back-row players (Figure 27-2). The back-row players may not legally enter the front court attack area to block or attack the ball over the net. When the ball is dead, players may not overlap with a player who is in an adjacent position. "Adjacent" refers to the player in the corresponding position on the opposite row (example: center back with center front), plus the teammate(s) next to that player on the same row (example: center back with *both* left back and right back). The players all rotate one position clockwise following a rally in which they win the right to serve.

The libero is a backcourt specialist who has an unlimited number of entries that do not count against the team's substitution limit. Some rules now allow this player to serve. In addition to the rules already cited for a back-row player, the libero may not set the ball for an attacker.

Serve. The player who rotates to the right back position serves or, if at the start of the set, is the first server. The serve is initiated from within the serving area (see Figure 27-1) behind the end line. The objective is to serve the ball across the net into the opponent's court. However, some levels of play now allow a "net serve" to be playable without ruling it a fault. It is a fault (illegal) if the ball contacts the net, contacts the antenna, or does not land in the court.

Playing the Ball. Each team is entitled to a maximum of three contacts each time the ball crosses into their court. A ball contacting the block does not count as one of the three allowable contacts. No player may play the ball twice in succession, except if they contacted the ball as a blocker.

The ball may not visibly come to rest; if it does, it is considered a held ball (fault). A held ball frequently results when a player uses the hands in executing an overhand pass. The ball may not be guided, lifted, or pushed in an effort to redirect it.

Net Play. A player may not contact any part of the net, or it is a fault. A ball contacting the net is considered playable. A player may reach across the net to contact the ball on the opponent's side, provided it was attacked by the opponent. Likewise, a player may

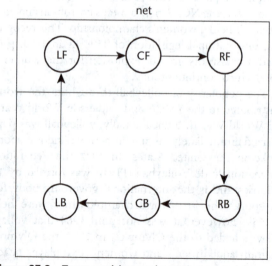

Figure 27-2 Team position and rotation.

cross the net when attacking the ball, provided part of it was on the attacker's side when it was contacted. Opponents simultaneously blocking the ball may result in a held ball, which is then replayed with no point scored (play-over).

A player may contact the ball on the opponent's side *underneath* the net while attempting to save the ball. The boundary line below the net separating the court restricts players from stepping into the opponent's area. Standing on the line is legal; having any other part of the body on the floor and across the line is illegal.

Scoring.   The serve starts play, and the objective is to keep the ball from contacting one's own floor and, without violating the rules, rally until the opponents fail. When the team serving wins the rally, a point is scored. If the rally is won by the nonserving team, that team receives a point, earns a side-out, rotates, and serves next. In rally scoring, a point is awarded to whoever wins each rally. The first team to score 15 points and be ahead by at least 2 points wins the set. Some levels of play go to 25 or 30 points. A match consists of either winning two out of three or three out of five sets.

Suggested Learning Sequence

BEGINNING LEVEL

A. Running, stretching, and explosive sprinting/jumping

B. Introduction—nature and purpose

C. Basic rules

D. Fundamental skills
  1. Movement skills
     a. Low position
        1. Shuffle step
        2. Forward/backward
     b. Medium position
        1. Shuffle step
        2. Run lateral/forward
        3. Backpedal
  2. Forearm pass
     a. Serve reception
     b. Free-ball pass
     c. Side to target
     d. Back to target
  3. Overhand pass
     a. Set forward
     b. Free-ball pass
  4. Serve
     a. Underhand
     b. Overhand floater
  5. Attack
     a. Spike roll
     b. Spike

E. Play modified games (instant winner)
  1. one on one, two on two, three on three
  2. Small court—½ wide front court
  3. Toss on serve
  4. Vary type of contact required

F. Strategies
  1. Use three contacts
     a. Pass to center front—8 feet × 8 feet
     b. Set to left front
     c. Spike roll/spike
  2. Make opponents play the ball
  3. Serve in court 80–90 percent of the time

G. Systems
  1. Five-person, "W" serve reception pattern
  2. Free-ball defense
  3. 6–6 or 4–2 offense

INTERMEDIATE LEVEL

A. Running, partner stretching, and explosive sprinting or jumping

B. Review beginning unit

C. Fundamental skills
  1. Serve
     a. Overhead floater
        1. Deep
        2. Short
  2. Forearm
     a. Dig
        1. Stride and slide
  3. Overhand pass
     a. Set backward
  4. Attack
     a. Spike
        1. Power angle
     b. Lob
        1. Dink
        2. Roll
  5. Block
     a. One blocker
     b. Two blockers

D. Strategies
  1. Serve—weak opponent or deep corners
  2. Dig to middle of court 15 × 15 feet
  3. Set forward and backward—12- to 15-feet high to 3 × 3-feet target
  4. Spike crosscourt and lob over block short
  5. Block
     a. Take away crosscourt
     b. No hole between blockers

E. Systems
  1. Repeat beginning unit
  2. Spiker coverage

3. 2–1–3 defense

4. 4–2 or 5–1 offense

F. Play modified games and six-on-six
   1. Modifications (point on each serve—5 points winner stays)
      a. Court ½ wide, full length three-on-three— must use three contacts
      b. Full court four-on-four (three back, one at net)—no block
   2. Full game—six-on-six with no modifications

Skills and Techniques

Volleyball comprises five basic skills: forearm pass, overhand pass, serve, attack, and block. Each skill uses techniques that players need as they progress from beginning to advanced levels of competition.

The ball-handling skills—*forearm pass* and *overhand pass*—and their associated techniques constitute at least two-thirds of the ball contacts during play. The *serve* often dominates play both positively and negatively at the beginning to intermediate levels and is a crucial skill. The *attack* adds offense and power to the game but can only be used when the ball-handling skills become accurate and consistent. The *block* is used only when the opposing team consistently attacks the ball from a point near or above the net, forcefully driving it downward into one's court.

FOREARM PASS

The forearm pass (also called pass, bump, or dig), with its associated techniques, is the most frequently used ball-handling skill. It is used to pass the serve, play balls below the waist, play hard-driven balls, and contact balls located far from the player. Employing this skill avoids official ball-handling violations.

▶ Learning Hints

1. Feet are shoulder-width apart, in a stagger stance (heel-toe relationship), and the body weight is forward on the inside front half of each foot with the heels slightly off the ground.

2. Knees are flexed approximately 90 degrees, inside the feet and in front of the toes.

3. The upper body is in a front-leaning position with waist flexed approximately 90 degrees and the shoulders in front of the knees (Figure 27-3).

4. Hands are connected by pressing the pads of both thumbs together with the base of the thumbs even and level (Figure 27-4A). The grip is relaxed, with the hands extended downward. Two methods for clasping the hands together are shown: the back of one hand across the palm of the other (Figure 27-4B), and the closed fist of one hand conjoined and supported

Figure 27-3   Body position for the forearm pass.

in the grasp of the cupped fingers of the other hand (Figure 27-4C). These methods are acceptable as long as the thumbs stay next to each other.

5. Arms reach out in front of the body and elbows rotate inward together and are locked, exposing the fleshy part of the forearm. The arms are parallel with the thigh of the leading leg (refer to Figure 27-3). Attempt to align with the approaching ball as near as possible to the midline of the body.

6. Ball contact is on the fleshy part of the forearm, approximately 2 to 6 inches above the wrist. The trajectory angle of the rebound is dependent on the angle of the forearms. The eyes focus on the ball until contact and following rebound.

7. Force is provided to the ball when needed by a slight bunting action of the arms, extension of the legs, and body lean toward the intended target. A hard-driven ball from the opponents might require absorption of the force at contact by dropping of the forearms upon contact as a cushioning effect.

▶ Practice/Organizational Suggestions

Use the part method for learning to isolate and reinforce correct contact of the forearm pass. Have students start on one knee, leaning forward, and bunt a controlled tossed ball back to a partner standing 10 feet away. Establish accuracy standards to check progress and to motivate students. Next, students repeat the drill from

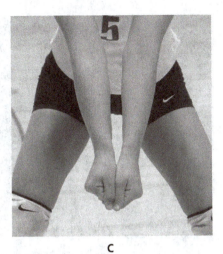

Figure 27-4 Hand position and forearm surface.

the correct whole-body position before adding lateral shuffle steps prior to the toss. Finally, have students attempt to pass the ball repeatedly back and forth between partners who are 15 feet apart. When control is achieved, move students to a small court to play modified small-side competitive games (see Modified Games).

OVERHAND PASS

The overhand pass is the most controllable of the ball-handling skills. It is used for accurately passing any ball above the head to a teammate and for the setting technique of passing the ball to an attacker with specific height, trajectory, and placement. Ball-hand contact and precise alignment with the ball make the skill more susceptible to official ball-handling violations.

▶ Learning Hints

1. Feet, knees, and upper body are in same position as for forearm pass (items 1, 2, and 3).
2. Ball is aligned with the forehead hairline (see Figure 27-5).
3. Arms are raised, elbows are flexed (90 degrees) at approximately chin height, and the hands are equally positioned 6 inches above the forehead, with the wrist flexed back (Figure 27-6).
4. Fingers and hands are spread into the shape of the approaching ball, thumbs pointing toward the nose and wrists flexed back (Figure 27-7). The thumbs are approximately 3 inches apart and the index fingers about twice as far apart.
5. Ball contact is on the inside edge of the first digital areas of the thumbs, index, middle, and ring fingers, and the ball is allowed to almost slide through, with the hands on the sides.

6. Force is initiated by the thighs, ball-hand contact is made, and finally the arms are extended fully. The synchronized action is THRUST (thighs)—CONTACT

Figure 27-5 Body position and alignment to ball on overhand pass.

Figure 27-6   Arms, hand shaping, wrist flex, and finger-thumb position prior to overhand contact.

Figure 27-7   Whole-body ready position prior to overhand contact.

(hands)—EXTEND (arms) for the correct, smooth, and sequential action. Weight finishes forward on the front (right for right-handers) foot, with all body action directed toward target.

▶ Practice/Organizational Suggestions

The part method aids in the development of the many aspects for skillful execution of the overhand pass. Start on the left knee with the right foot forward in a kneeling position. Place the arms and hands in the correct position for receiving the ball (see Learning Hints, items 3 and 4). The ball is tossed accurately and gently into the hands by a partner who is just 3 feet away. Play the ball 6 feet straight up so it drops on the tosser's head. Use the force sequence of CONTACT-EXTEND to play the ball (see Learning Hints, items 5 and 6). Next, assume a full squat position and duplicate the foregoing, playing it 10 feet high. The force sequence now entails THRUST-CONTACT-EXTEND to play the ball.

When accuracy and synchronization are established, stand in a ready position (refer to Figure 27-7) to receive a ball tossed from a partner 10 feet away. Adjust to the tossed ball and play it 10 feet high, returning it to the tosser. Finally, attempt to volley the ball repeatedly with a partner and move to modified small-side competitive games (see Modified Games) when control and accuracy is achieved.

SERVE

A consistent serve is important because the serving team can score instantly. The serve has an expected success rate that is 80 to 90 percent higher than the other skills because the server tosses the ball to himself rather than receiving the ball from another player. Equally important is the fact that the serve is the first opportunity

a team has to put the opponent at a disadvantage. The overhand floater serve provides both power and consistency (Figure 27-8A–C).

▶ Learning Hints

1. Stand or step and stride with the foot opposite the striking arm (left foot for right-handed person). That lead foot is positioned 2 feet in front of the back foot and is pointed directly toward the intended target. The stride starts as the ball is tossed into the air.

2. The toss is made in front of the striking shoulder and at contact is in front of the striding body parallel with the front foot. The ball is tossed low (1 to 2 feet above head height) for controlled accuracy. A two-handed spin-free toss aids accuracy.

3. The striking arm action on the toss resembles an overhand throwing motion (Figure 27-9). As the ball is released (approximately shoulder level) on the toss, the arm flexes, the elbow draws back at

A   B   C

Figure 27-8 The overhand floater serve.

shoulder height, and the upper body rotates so that the nonstriking shoulder is in a leading position and the alignment of both shoulders is approximately 45 degrees with the back line of the court (Figure 27-8A). The elbow snaps forward ahead of the wrist, and the forearm accelerates in preparation for ball-hand contact.

4. The wrist of the striking arm is tense and locked, the hand is open wide, presenting a flat contact surface, and the ball is aggressively contacted with the bottom half (heel) of the hand at a point slightly higher than head level.

5. Velocity is generated by the elbow snap throwing the forearm forward, and the ball accelerates rapidly as it is contacted with the hard surface (heel) of the hand.

6. Body weight transfers to the front foot, and the forearm of the striking arm is immediately stopped at contact, producing a recoil action (Figure 27-8B).

7. Body balance is maintained as both feet remain in contact with the floor and all movement is directly at the target on the follow-through (Figure 27-8C).

▶ Practice/Organizational Suggestions

Practice the toss and stride (Learning Hints, items 1 and 2), letting the ball drop to the floor. The ball should land to the side of the body, in front of the striking shoulder, and parallel with the front foot.

Progress to the whole skill with a partner. Students stand 10 feet from the net on opposite sides. The ball

is tossed and served at the net (1 to 3 feet above) on a straight line, using the upstretched arms and hands of the partner to check accuracy. Observe the served ball to make sure it is not rotating in flight but floating spin-free.

Gradually move back from the net, maintaining (1) a straight line trajectory, (2) spin-free (floater) flight, and (3) accuracy. The greater the distance, the more force needs to be applied to ball contact (Learning Hints, items 3–6). Continue moving back until the serve can be initiated legally from behind the back line.

ATTACK

The attack is used in aggressive play to keep opponents from returning the ball or making a transition to return it aggressively. The types of attack are the spike, lob, and drive. These techniques should be performed from as high a position off the floor as possible.

The *spike* is contacted above the midline and at the back of the ball, in an attempt to impart top spin and drive the ball downward into the opponent's court. The *lob* is contacted below the midline and at the back of the ball, in an attempt to play it up over the block. The *drive* is contacted in the middle back of the ball, in an attempt to propel it off the blocker's hands.

In beginning to intermediate levels of play, a player does not consistently receive a ball from teammates in a manner that allows time to jump and attack the ball. The technique of the *spike roll* provides an intermediate step between returning the ball easily (free ball) to the opponents and jumping to spike the ball downward

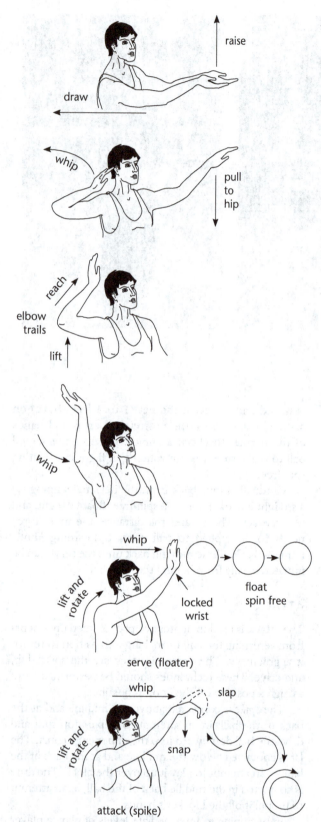

Figure 27-9 The striking arm action for the overhand serve and the attack (ball-hand contact and wrist action are different).

into the opponent's court. It also gives a short player an opportunity to attack the opponents, even though that player may be unable to contact the ball above the net.

▶ Learning Hints

SPIKE ROLL

1. Align with the ball so that it is dropping directly above the striking arm's shoulder.

2. The feet are in a stagger stance (see the first sentence in Serve, Learning Hints, item 1).

3. Both arms lift above the head. The shoulders rotate approximately 45 degrees with the nonstriking arm in a leading position (Figure 27-10A). The nonstriking arm fully extends and points at the descending ball. The striking arm, in a motion resembling an overhand throw, flexes at the elbow as it draws back at shoulder height.

4. The nonstriking arm starts the hitting action by pulling toward the hip on that side as the striking arm's elbow snaps forward, simultaneously lifting higher. The hand and forearm of the striking arm move from a lead position of the elbow to a position trailing it. The hand is open, fingers spread, and wrist flexed back fully (Figure 27-10B).

5. The firm, open hand is thrown at the ball, with initial contact made on the bottom back quarter of the ball, with the palm simultaneously snapping the wrist forward (SLAP and SNAP). The hand goes from a below-ball initial contact to one at follow-through, which is over the top. This imparts the essential topspin on the ball (Figure 27-10C).

6. Body weight transfers to the front foot, and the striking arm finishes in an extended high position, with the wrist fully snapped forward, fingers pointing toward the ground on completion (Figure 27-10D).

7. Body balance (see Serve, Learning Hints, item 7).

SPIKE

1. The approach to jump is started from a point approximately 12 feet from the net, depending on the length of the attacker's stride. The attacker runs at an angle directly to where the ball is descending; the angle depends on the approach position (left, center, or right front) and the handedness of the attacker. A right-handed person's approach is 45 degrees toward the net from the left front (LF) position and increases moving to the remaining positions (CF and RF). A left-handed player also makes a 45-degree angle in approaching from the opposite side (RF), the angle increasing when in CF and LF positions. Figure 27-11 shows the approach to jump sequence.

Figure 27-10   Spike roll: (A) both arms positioned to strike; (B) nonstriking arm pulls down and striking arm elbow snaps forward; (C) open hand contacts the bottom back quarter of the ball; (D) SLAP ball, SNAP wrist, and finish in high position.

Figure 27-11   Spike: approach footwork and arm positions prior to jump in attack (right-handed).

2. The footwork consists of four final steps: a short step with the same side foot as the striking arm (Figure 27-11A), followed by an elongated running stride with the opposite foot, followed by an almost simultaneous step, step or close gathering for a maximum vertical jump (Figure 27-11B). The length of the second step depends on the desired distance and speed. The next step, step or close, is a breaking heel plant, rocking to the balls of the feet for a two-footed takeoff in the jump. The feet are 8 to 10 inches apart on the step or close, with the foot opposite the striking hand ahead of the other foot

(Figure 27-11C). The legs flex approximately 90 degrees for maximum jumping thrust.

3. The arms assist in providing force for jumping. They function identically during the approach and are extended straight, behind, and nearly parallel with the floor at the two-footed takeoff (Figure 27-11C). The arms thrust vigorously forward and upward for lifting force as the legs thrust for the vertical jump (Figure 27-12A).

4. The takeoff point aligns the body with the ball so that it can be contacted 6 to 18 inches in front of the body and in front of the striking shoulder.

Figure 27-12   Attack: (A) arm lift and heel lift; (B) striking action of arms and legs snap down; (C) leg flex landing.

5. The arm action for striking starts as the body leaves the floor (see Spike Roll, Learning Hints, items 3 and 4 and Figure 27-12A).

6. The firm open hand is thrown at the ball, with initial contact made on the top back quarter of the ball, with the palm simultaneously snapping the wrist forward (SLAP and SNAP) (see Figure 27-9). This imparts topspin on the ball and drives it downward toward the opponent's court.

7. The simultaneous coordination of the arm and leg action while suspended in air provides force and body control. The arm action is performed as the legs are flexed and then vigorously snapped down (Figure 27-12B), providing a piking action by the upper and lower body.

8. The legs are flexed upon contacting the floor to prevent injury and to regain stability (Figure 27-12C).

LOB

1. The approach, footwork, arm action, alignment to ball, upper and lower body coordination, and landing are identical to the spike (see Spike, Learning Hints, items 1–5 and 7). The only difference is the ball-hand contact.

2. Ball-hand contact is made in the lower back quarter of the ball, causing it to take an upward trajectory over the block. As the hand comes forward on the striking action, the fingers and thumb make contact

with the surface of the ball with the first digital area of each. The contact is referred to as a dink, which is the most common type of lob used at the beginning to intermediate level of play.

DRIVE

1. As with the lob, the only difference between the drive and the spike is the ball-hand contact.

2. The ball is contacted in the middle back, causing it to take a trajectory parallel with the floor and deflecting off the blocker's fingers. The hand contact, as in the spike, is with the firm open surface of the palm but driving the ball straight ahead instead of downward.

▶ Practice/Organizational Suggestions

The ball-hand contact (SLAP) is developed by holding the bottom of the ball firmly with the nonstriking hand. Position the ball at arm's length in front of the striking shoulder and at head height. With the striking arm hanging straight down at the side, initiate the correct arm action by lifting it straight forward and upward until it is beside the ball. Use the throwing action (see Spike Roll, Learning Hints, items 3 and 4) and ball-hand contact (see Spike, Learning Hints, item 6) to aggressively slap the back top quarter area of the ball, developing the feeling of the palm contact. Repeat the foregoing, but hit the ball downward out of the holding hand to the floor. Stand 6 feet from a wall so that the ball hits the floor and then rebounds off the wall. Emphasize the ball-hand contact and power component (wrist snap) for force—SLAP and SNAP. Finish with the striking arm high and fully extended, with the palm facing the floor and fingers pointing down.

Next, toss the ball in front of the striking shoulder, using both hands to toss it precisely 4 feet high. Both arms extend up as if jumping (see Spike Roll, Learning Hints, item 3) and duplicate the complete arm action (Learning Hints, items 3 and 4), contacting the ball (see Spike, Learning Hints, item 6) and driving it to the floor as in the previous practice suggestion.

Next toss the ball and then jump off both feet, repeating the arm lift, striking action (both arms), and ball-hand contact.

Practice the approach footwork (see Spike, Learning Hints, items 1, 2, and 3) toward the net and mimic the correct striking arm actions previously described without using a ball. Next, place a tennis ball in the striking hand and repeat the approach, footwork, jump, and arm action, throwing the tennis ball over the net with an aggressive wrist snap. Emphasize the SNAP and a high straight arm finish of the throwing arm.

Proceed to hitting a volleyball over the net. A partner, with side to net and 3 feet from the net, tosses the ball 12 feet straight up so the attacker can approach, jump, and attack the ball. The tosser stands on the attacker's hitting-arm side and is careful to use a two-handed underhand toss such that the ball goes straight up and down directly in alignment with the attacker's striking arm. The tosser gradually moves laterally away from the attacker, tossing higher (15 to 18 feet) with a trajectory that drops in alignment with the approach path of the attacker.

BLOCK

The block is used to counter a forceful attack defensively. This technique is accomplished by jumping and positioning the hands above and over the net, thus decreasing the area available for the attacker to drive the ball downward forcefully into the blocker's court. The use of two blockers on one attacker increases the area of the block, conversely decreasing the court area available for a downward attack. Defensive systems are developed around the block.

The objective of the block, aside from reducing the area an opponent can attack, is to render the ball nonreturnable while it is in the opponents' court. The success rate for effective blocking is low and negative outcomes are possible. Therefore, the decision on whether to block is governed by the attacker's ability to drive the ball downward into the court from a position near or above the net.

▶ **Learning Hints**

READY POSITION (FIGURE 27-13A)

1. The feet are in a parallel stance, shoulders parallel with the net. Stand 6 to 12 inches from the net, with knees slightly flexed for quick movement.
2. The hands are positioned between the net and the body at shoulder height, with fingers spread and palms facing the net.
3. The elbows are flexed and touching the rib cage, with the forearms perpendicular to the floor.
4. The back is straight.

JUMP

1. The knees flex to a near 100-degree angle for a quick and maximum jump (Figure 27-13B).
2. Thrust off from the floor equally with both legs, and thrust the arms straight upward parallel with the net.
3. As the hands clear net height, gently push them across as far as possible, being careful not to touch the net (Figure 27-13C). Position the outside hand slightly toward the court to deflect the ball inward.
4. Pike slightly at the waist for balance and power (Figure 27-13C).
5. While descending, gently withdraw the hands, returning them in front of the shoulders.
6. On floor contact, bend the knees to absorb shock and for balance. Pivot away from the net, following the direction of the ball.

MOVEMENT FOOTWORK

1. To adjust 3 to 6 feet laterally, use one to two shuffle steps, keeping hands up, feet parallel, and shoulders parallel with the net prior to jumping.
2. A longer adjustment requires a step, run, and plant footwork:
   a. *Step.* Take a step with the foot nearest the ball, pointing the foot toward the sideline.
   b. *Run.* The shoulders rotate from a parallel position to perpendicular as the trail leg takes a running stride for distance and speed toward the sideline.
   c. *Plant.* Both feet hop into a plant, with both returning to a perpendicular position of toes toward the net. The hop breaks momentum as the knees flex for a vertical jump.
3. The hands remain in the ready position throughout all footwork prior to jumping.

▶ **Practice/Organizational Suggestions**

A blocker stands facing a partner who is 3 feet away and holding a volleyball firmly with arms fully extended upward. In a standing ready position, the blocker thrusts

A   B   C

Figure 27-13 Block: (A) ready position, (B) knee flex, (C) net penetration and piking action.

the arms upward, surrounding the held ball to assume ball-hand contact. Next, have both players squat to jump prior to arm action and ball-hand contact. Movement footwork can be added, plus a net between partners. The blocker assumes the ready position directly in front of the partner who is standing 3 feet away from net on the other side. The partner self-tosses the ball and jumps to spike (see Spike, Practice / Organizational Suggestions) the ball into the hands of the blocker, who has jumped to intercept it on the spiker's side of the net. Later add two blockers to this drill.

Modified Games

It is not necessary to master a skill or that all skills be taught before playing on the court. When players can adjust to a moving ball and perform the whole skill, it is time to play modified games on the court.

Modifications can be made for a variety of criteria: court size, height of net, number and alignment of players, number of contacts allowed, type and combinations of skills, special rules for desired outcomes, and so on. The games should have an immediate winner or loser so that everyone is participating quickly without waiting.

Games provide motivation, enjoyment, teamwork, communication skills, strategy, and most of all,

immediate feedback on performance. Following is an example:

Court: ½ court wide and 10 ft front (10 × 15)
Players: two-on-two
Rules:

1. Immediate winner of the rally; winner moves to winner's side of the net; losers move to end of waiting line; two new players challenge winners.

2. Play starts with an easy toss (serve) from the challengers to the winners.

3. Each side must make *two* contacts only.

4. First contact *must* be a forearm and second contact *must* be an overhand.

5. On each contact, that player *must* call "mine" (communication) prior to contact.

6. The rally continues until play terminates—rules are broken or ball is not returned.

7. A point is scored if the players on the winner's side of net win. If challengers win the rally, they change to the winner's side of net to have an opportunity to score a point, and their opponents rotate out to the end of the waiting line (Note: Have no more than eight persons per half-court—two volleyball courts equal 32 players).

8. Losers chase the ball. Each waiting couple has a ball.

9. The first to accumulate five points wins the game.

10. Option: Change partners each time the losers go to the end of the line. Each player would then carry the individual score forward instead of a team score.

Playing Strategies

OFFENSIVE PLAY

Offenses in volleyball have developed widely in the past several years. Although the techniques of passing and spiking have changed relatively little, the methods by which the spike is obtained vary greatly.

In most beginning programs or physical education classes, the 6–6 offense would be the simplest to administer. In this offense, all six players spike when rotating to the spiking positions and set when rotating into a setting position. The 4–2 offense is similar, except that four members of the team are basically spikers and four members are used essentially as setters. For the alignment of the 4–2 offense, see Figure 27-14A.

The 4–2 offense can be used in physical education classes. It allows smaller players to develop skills as setters and become an integral part of the volleyball team. Although relatively simple, the 4–2 offense includes some of the concepts used in the more complex 5–1 and 6–0 offenses.

In preparing to receive a serve (Figure 27-14B), players face the server in a semi-crouched position, prepared to return the ball with a forearm pass. Every attempt is made to direct the first pass to the center front position (setter, either with or without switching) with an arc of 12 to 16 feet. This high pass gives the setter ample time to get to the ball. The setter positions under the ball and faces the direction she plans to set the ball for the spiker.

The setter attempts to pass or set the ball 6 to 10 feet above the net, 2 to 3 feet from the net, and near the sideline. This sideline set gives the spiker three advantages: (1) the center blocker has a greater distance to travel; (2) the spiked ball may rebound back out of bounds; and (3) a ball spiked diagonally across court has a greater area in which to land for a point.

Team coverages on the spike for the 4–2 offense are shown in Figure 27-15.

It is necessary for the spiking team to form a cup around the spiker to protect against a blocked spike that returns immediately back into their court. The players not in the cup follow the ball, looking for a ball that is blocked high and deep.

When the offensive team is serving, the frontline players are close to the net in preparation for the blocking of a spike (Figure 27-16).

DEFENSIVE PLAY

Defenses in power volleyball may vary as widely as the offenses, but the primary job of the defense is to offset the spiking action of the opponents. Defensive players can block and reject the ball or control it on their own side of the court using a passing-setting-spiking combination.

Players move to base defensive positions when the ball goes into the opponent's court (see Figure 27-17A). Switching positions between players is usually done to capitalize on any specialization skills. For example, at the beginning level the setter might switch to the center front position to set.

PLAYER-BACK DEFENSE

The player-back or 2–4 defense provides good deep coverage, with four players stationed near the court's perimeter and two blocking. The starting positions

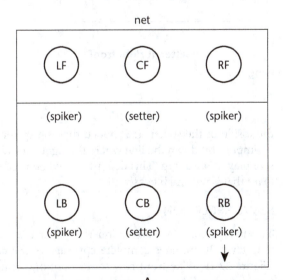

A

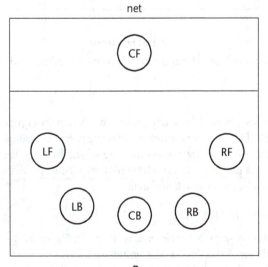

B

Figure 27-14 The 4–2 offense: (A) serving, (B) receiving in the "U" formation. The "W" formation is demonstrated in Figure 27-19.

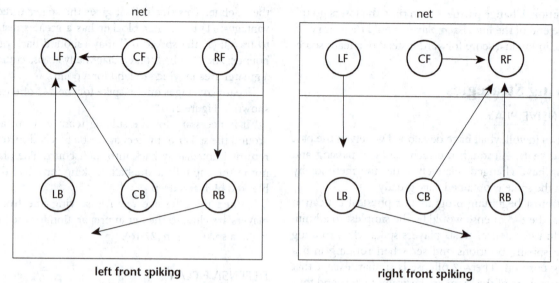

Figure 27-15 Coverage for the spiker in the 4–2 offense when serving.

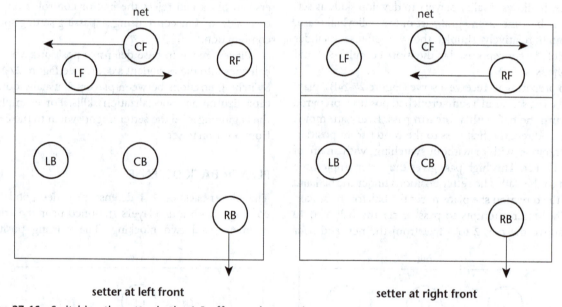

Figure 27-16 Switching the setter in the 4–2 offense when serving.

and areas covered by each player are shown in Figure 27-17B. The blockers attempt to protect more against the sideline spike by the positioning of the block. This defense is used by a team whose players are not particularly tall but very quick and agile.

PLAYER-UP DEFENSE

The player-up or 2–1–3 defense is shown in Figure 27-18. The player that is "up" is the center back, who moves to a position behind the block and covers all dinks, or deflections, that fall short. The blockers attempt to protect against a crosscourt spike by establishing their block to

the inside of the spiker. It is hoped that the spiker will attempt to hit down the line where the right back defensive player is waiting. This defense would be used by a team that is tall and blocks well.

SERVE RECEPTION

The five-person "W" formation is used at the beginning level. It provides complete coverage of the court (Figure 27-19). The front-row setter positions near the net in each of the three rotation positions to set the second contact. The setter is careful not to be out of position by overlapping with a teammate who is in an

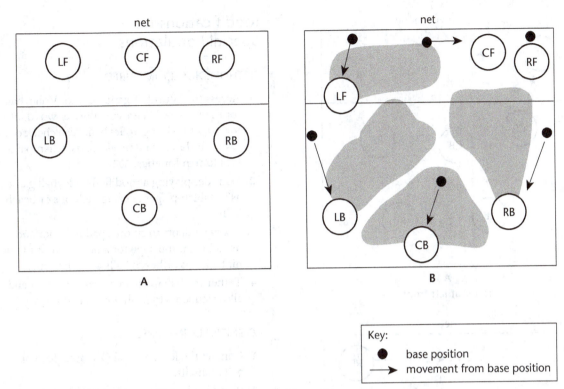

Figure 27-17   The player-back or 2–4 defense: (A) base positions, (B) area responsibilities.

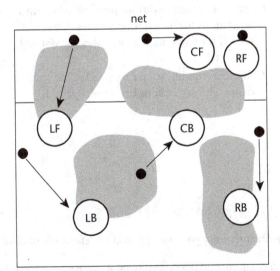

Figure 27-18   The player-up or 2–1–3 defense and area responsibilities.

adjacent position until contact is made on the serve. On contact, the setter quickly positions with the right side to the net approximately 12 feet from the right sideline, keeping the middle of the court in front where the passed ball descends.

Skill Assessment

Ball-handling (forearm and overhand pass) skills are the most important and most used in successful volleyball play. The suggested skills test is a repeated alternating forearm or overhand pass for a 30-second trial.

Each testing station has a participant, a counter, and an assistant. The participant self-tosses the ball up and alternates playing it with the forearm and overhand pass at a height of at least 10 feet for 30 seconds. The score is the total number of successful passes during the trial. If the ball is lost during the trial, the assistant provides another one immediately and retrieves the errant ball. The participant again self-tosses the ball and continues the alternating process. The count continues with the next pass accomplished and does not start at one again. The counter stays approximately 15 feet away from the participant and records balls that successfully go at least 10 feet high as indicated by a line marked on the wall. A ball played below the 10-foot line does not count.

The group rotates responsibilities after each trial. At least five trials are suggested. Throw out the highest and lowest scores and average the remaining three for the final score.

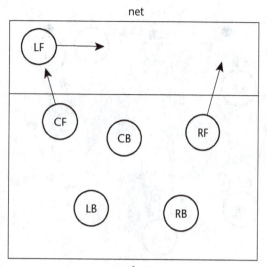

A
setter at left front

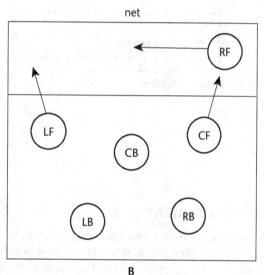

B
setter at right front

Figure 27-19 Five-person "W" formation serve reception: (A) setter at left front, (B) setter at right front.

Modifications for Special Populations

ORTHOPEDICALLY IMPAIRED

1. Access the World Organization of Volleyball for the Disabled Web site at www.wovd.info for rules for sitting volleyball. Also check out Davis, R. *Inclusion through Sports*. Champaign, IL: Human Kinetics, 2002.
2. Consider playing a modified volleyball game as a "tabletop" game using balloons or beach balls.
3. Allow students to sit on a padded floor and use a long jump rope for a net. Have students hit balloons or beach balls over the rope.
4. Tether the ball from an overhead height and allow students to push it back and forth.

COGNITIVELY IMPAIRED

1. Contact the local Special Olympics for volleyball manuals.
2. Play a lead-up game of Newcomb to develop a concept of the game. Newcomb is played like volleyball, except that the players are allowed to throw and catch the ball.
3. See suggested modifications for tennis.

SENSORY IMPAIRED

1. Individual considerations must be taken into account as to the appropriateness of volleyball for students who are blind or visually impaired.
2. Minimal modifications are needed for students who are deaf or hearing-impaired.

Terminology

attack Any method used to return the ball across the net in an attempt to put the opponents at a disadvantage.

ball handling Execution of any passing fundamental.

block The process of intercepting the ball just before or as it crosses the net. A block may be executed by any front-row player.

bump (See forearm pass.)

court coverage The court assignment of each player on defense.

dig An emergency pass, usually used to defend a hard-driven attack.

dink A soft shot off the fingertips, used to lob the ball over the block.

double foul Infraction of rules by both teams during the same play.

drive An attack contacted in the center that attempts to hit the ball off the blocker's hands.

fault An infraction of the rules.

forearm pass A pass made off the forearms. Used to play served balls, hard-driven spikes, or any low ball.

free ball A return of a ball by the opponent that may easily be handled.

front court The playing area in which it is legal to block or attack.

held ball A ball that is simultaneously contacted above the net by opponents and momentarily held on contact.

kill An attack that cannot be returned directly as a result of that attack.

libero A player who specializes in backcourt skills and has unlimited back-row entries into the game.

lob A soft attack that is contacted in the back bottom quarter of the ball, causing it to take an upward trajectory.

overhand pass A pass made by contacting the ball above the head with the finger pads.

overlap An illegal foot position, when the ball is dead, with an adjacent player putting one out of position.

play-over The replay of a rally because of a held ball or the official prematurely suspending play. The server re-serves with no point awarded.

point A point is scored when the receiving team fails to return the ball legally to the opponents' court.

rally scoring In rally scoring, a point is awarded to whoever wins each rally.

rotation Shifting of the players clockwise upon gaining the ball from the opponents.

serve The method of putting the ball in play over the net by striking it with the hand.

set The placement of the ball near the net to facilitate attacking.

set Term used to identify the playing of a single "game," which has culminated when a designated number of points (15, 25, or 30) are reached.

setter Player assigned to set the ball.

side-out Side is out when the serving team fails to win a point or plays the ball illegally.

spike A ball hit with topspin and a strong downward force into the opponents' court.

spiker Player assigned to attack the ball.

spike roll An attack that first takes an upward trajectory using the spiking actions (with or without jumping).

topspin (overspin) Imparting of a forward spin to the ball during the serve, spike, or spike roll.

Discussion Questions

1. Identify the factors that make volleyball a truly adaptable sport.

2. Discuss the reasons why volleyball in the United States remained a recreational sport for so long.

3. Discuss the basic rules that dictate that most players must develop *all* of the basic skills.

4. Discuss and defend the amount of practice time that should be devoted to each of the five basic skills at the beginning to intermediate levels of play.

5. Compare the overhand and forearm passing techniques.

6. Compare ball contact techniques when executing the spike, lob, or drive.

7. Discuss the strengths and weaknesses of the three offensive systems identified.

8. Discuss the strengths and weaknesses of the two defensive systems identified.

9. Present the three positions of the front-row setter before the serve when using the five-person "W" serve reception pattern.

10. Discuss the term "adjacent" position as it pertains to players' legal positioning when the ball is dead.

Web Sites

www.teamusa.org/USA-Volleyball.aspx USA volleyball—provides information on volleyball education, officiating, modifications for the disabled, tips on high performance, national teams, merchandise, and more than 30 links to other volleyball sites.

www.volleyball.com/drill.aspx—lists 74 drills in 15 different categories.

http://volleyball.org—includes a beginner's section on volleyball's characteristics, history, rules, basic skills, glossary, and books.

http://volleyball.about.com—covers a large variety of subjects and gives descriptive explanations of how to perform basic skills and drills, with accompanying pictures and diagrams.

www.wovd.info World Organization of Volleyball for the Disabled—provides rules for sitting volleyball.

www.volleyball.com—a wide variety of skill practice drills.

www.volleyballtoolbox.com—the toolbox features information and videos of all the skills and techniques.

CHAPTER 28

Weight Training

This chapter will enable you to

- Identify key historical events that contributed to the evolution of weight training
- Identify and compare the key points associated with Olympic lifting, power lifting, athletic weight training, and bodybuilding
- Identify the differences and similarities among weight-lifting equipment
- After practice, demonstrate the various skills and techniques necessary to execute the various weight-training lifts
- Identify and discuss facts and myths related to female weight lifting
- Identify the necessary safety concerns of weight training
- Become familiar with basic terminology required to carry out a successful weight-training program

Nature and Purpose

During the past two decades, the effectiveness of carefully planned weight training as a method of improving body development and sports performance has been accepted on the basis of well-controlled studies. Although being muscle-bound, having reduced localized muscle endurance, and loss of speed and agility were once thought to result from weight training, such claims have no physiological basis.

Much may be gained from the systematic and intelligent application of modern weight-training principles. The principle of overload (taxing the muscles beyond their normal daily activities), coupled with progressive resistance through a full range of motion, appears to be the most effective means of acquiring dynamic strength. The closer the weight-lifting movement simulates the actions in sports, the greater the transfer of strength to motor performance. Weight lifting is also an excellent way to develop flexibility, provided the exercise is executed through the entire range of motion. Muscle enlargement does not reduce muscle endurance because an increase in capillarization usually accompanies the cross-sectional increase of muscle fibers, which helps to delay the onset of fatigue. Weight training does not necessarily affect cardiorespiratory endurance unless movements are executed for this specific purpose. Increasing cardiorespiratory endurance requires specific training. To achieve this, heart and respiratory rates must be intensely increased and maintained at higher than normal resting values for a duration of time. Systematic weight training that applies the principles of resistance, overload, and specificity will have positive effects on motor performance parameters and contribute to successful participation in sports.

Many individuals become involved in weight training as a means of gaining or losing weight. The use of weight training is of greater benefit to gaining body weight than to losing it. This is because of the activities' physiological effect on the body. The overload principle causes proteins to be readily incorporated into the muscle, thus increasing muscular mass (hypertrophy), while on the other hand, the energy expenditure of weight lifting is too low to be of much benefit in body weight reduction. However, the overweight person may want to include weight training as part of a weight-reduction program to increase body tone while reducing weight with diet and an aerobic program.

Many centers of rehabilitation find the use of weights valuable in developing weak or injured muscles, strengthening underdeveloped muscles, or rebuilding muscles affected by atrophy following casting or hospitalization.

History

Weight lifting was created out of the human drive for continued existence. Primitive peoples, to improve their chances of survival, were forced to push, lift, and throw heavy objects. Weight lifting took on sporting aspects in 776 B.C., when by will of Ayrominus, young men who desired to compete in the Olympics were required to lift a rough ball of iron before being permitted to participate in the games.

The first attempts to organize weight lifting as a formal sport occurred almost concurrently in France, Germany, and Austria, around 1870. With elementary rules to govern and provide standards, the activity thrived, and soon professional competition emerged.

In France, Hyppolyte Trait (1813–1881), the "Apostle of Physical Education," always maintained that weight-lifting exercises were the most useful for preparation of athletes. As a result of his effort and enthusiasm, weight lifting found an especially fertile ground in France.

Germany, early in the 19th century, contributed immensely to the development of weight lifting as a sport through the Turnverein movement. Dr. Friedrich Jahn, who founded the Turnverein, advocated special clubs within its organization that emphasized specific activities. One of these special clubs was for weight lifting. In the middle of the 19th century, a period of large German immigration, Turnverein clubs were established in the United States.

Dr. Winship, an early pioneer of weight lifting, toured the United States and Canada from 1859 to 1872, giving exhibitions of weight lifting. By the end of the 19th century, weight lifting began to find its way into athletic clubs and YMCAs. At this time, weight lifting also became a theatrical attraction, and many "strong men" were headliners in theaters with their weight-lifting exhibitions.

In 1885, a Frenchman, Edmond Desbonnet, established the first series of records and was able to formulate regulations, which are still in use today, such as the two-phase, two-hand clean and jerk, and press.

In 1894, the first international championship was held at Mouseron, France. French, Belgian, and Dutch athletes participated. In 1902, the first world championship was held in London, and in the following year the international championship for professionals and amateurs was organized in Paris. It was also in Paris (in 1914) that the Fédération Française des Poids et Halteres was founded and later recognized by the Comité National des Sports.

Weight lifting was a part of the modern Olympic program as early as 1896 but was omitted after 1906. However, in 1920, it made a triumphant return to remain and gain rightful recognition as one of the "great sports." Competitive weight lifting in the United States began in 1929 under the jurisdiction of the Amateur Athletic Union. The first national championsips were held in 1929.

Weight lifting has changed since the early years. Today some people participate in bodybuilding, others in weight lifting, and others in power lifting. Bodybuilding uses weight to sculpt the body, and competition is based on the lifter's physical appearance. Weight lifting and power lifting are more closely related to each other: Power lifting judges the squat, the bench press, and the deadlift, whereas weight lifting is judged by two movements, the snatch and the clean and jerk. Weight lifting is the Olympic sport.[1]

Weight lifting has also become popular because of the benefits involved in developing strength. The San Diego Chargers and Nebraska Cornhuskers credited their initial success as football teams to lifting programs.

Today many schools and sports incorporate lifting programs. In addition, as the medical field became aware of the benefits, weight lifting has become an essential component of rehabilitation and muscle rebuilding after muscle injuries and surgery. Popular reports such as 1990's *Physical Activity and Health: A Report of the Surgeon General* specified that weight-training programs can contribute to increased muscular strength, endurance, flexibility, and lean body mass.[2]

As a result, weight lifting has become a popular activity for the athlete and the fitness enthusiast alike. Schools have well-equipped weight-training rooms, YMCAs and YWCAs offer extensive programs, and individual consumers now have weight equipment or resistance-training machines in their homes. In a country that has a high incidence of obesity and a plethora of devices that take the effort out of life, weight training offers one way to obtain much-needed vigorous, large-muscle exercise.

Equipment

VARIABLE RESISTANCE MACHINES

Variable resistance weight-training machines are manufactured by many companies under a variety of trade names. The most widely used are Cybex (Eagle) (Figure 28-1) and Paramount (Figure 28-2). These units consist of weight stacks connected by pulleys or cams to levers of lifting bars. The levers and pulleys allow a variable resistance through a fixed and oftentimes limited range of motion. This type of equipment is available in separate units and may also be found in a jungle gym arrangement on which several athletes can work out at one time. Weight-training machines offer a number of conveniences and time-saving features that appeal to the coach and the lifter. These machines may be placed within restricted space and offer the safety of confined weight stacks, which are not features of traditional free weights. Because the amount of resistance can be changed rapidly by a pull of a pin in the stack, the amount of time required to complete a training session is also greatly reduced over free weights. One disadvantage to all machines is in the transfer of strength gains to performance. Although the machines offer great safety, they also remove the interaction between the weights and the lifters needed to balance or coordinate movements while lifting. This interaction is of greatest importance for maximum benefit to performance. When time is a restricting factor, training on machines is an excellent way to maintain strength.

ISOKINETIC EQUIPMENT

Isokinetic devices are probably the most talked about and misunderstood equipment available today. The term *isokinetic* means "moving at a constant speed."

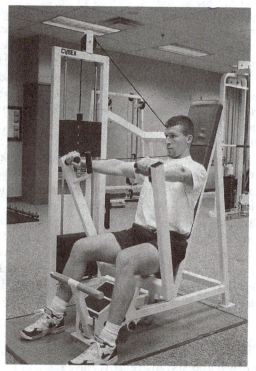

Figure 28-1 The Cybex chest press.

Figure 28-2 The Paramount machine.

These machines require no weights because the resistance felt from this equipment is self-generated. The machines can set at a variety of training velocities. If the athlete is capable of moving through a range of motion that approaches this velocity, then resistance is felt through that range. If the velocity is not reached, resistance is not felt. For this reason, to train on these devices requires a highly motivated athlete with constant supervision. The significance of training at a variety of velocities is found in the physiology of the muscle fibers. Because muscle fibers are of a fast or slow nature, it is felt that training at fast and slow speeds will increase recruitment of these fibers.

The value of isokinetic devices in rehabilitation is well founded. The Orthotron and Cybex 340 (Lumex, Inc., see Figure 28-3) are most commonly used for rehabilitation, whereas the Mini Gym is used for sports training. One problem with isokinetic devices is that they do not relate well with other forms of strength training. There is also doubt as to their effectiveness in building muscular bulk.

FREE WEIGHTS

The oldest forms of weight training have been done with free weights. There are two types: the Olympic form and the standard 1-inch barbell. A well-equipped training room will have both types of bars. The Olympic bar offers more balance, is more durable, is 2 inches in diameter to fit Olympic weight plates, and is a must for power and Olympic lifts. If properly used with

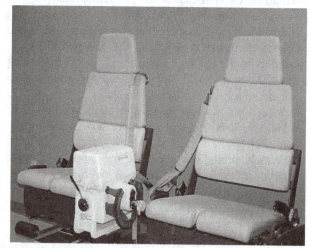

Figure 28-3 The Cybex 340 isokinetic testing unit.

supervision from an experienced lifter, free weights offer the most substantial strength program available. The cost of equipment is low, but the risk may be high with improper accessory equipment or lack of supervision.

OTHER EQUIPMENT

The following items may become necessary to the lifter of free weights as the training becomes more intense.

Lifting Belt. The lifting belt is made of thick leather and is used to give physical support to the lower back and moral support to the mind. There are two types of belts: training and competition. The training belt is 5 inches wide and gives a wide support to the lower back. The competition belt is 4 inches wide and may not exceed this width in Olympic and power lifting competitions. The belt is generally worn when doing free-weight squats and cleans.

Lifting Straps. Lifting straps are loops of leather or canvas belting about 1-inch wide. The straps are placed around the hands and then under and around the bar. With an overhand grip, the lifter secures the strap, and the bar is held tightly to the hand. Straps are used with dead lifts and cleans for training only. Lifting straps may not be used in competition.

Knee Wraps (Super Wraps). Wraps are long, 3-inch-wide strips of tough elastic material. They are worn extremely tight around the knee to add spring to the rebound phase of the squat and clean. They are needed only with heavy weights and may be worn in competition.

Super Suits. Super suits are made of tough elastic material and look like wrestling gear. The suit gives support and spring to the body during heavy squats and cleans. They are generally not worn in training but are almost always worn in competition.

The Female Weight Lifter

The fundamentals, techniques, and training programs described in this chapter are directed at both sexes. Female athletes need strength training every bit as much as their male counterparts. Competitive power lifting and bodybuilding are becoming popular among women. Coeducational weight-training classes are an effective way of destroying weight-lifting myths concerning females.

Myth: Women are not as strong as men.
Fact: Through elementary school, middle school, and well into high school, girls are as strong as if not stronger than boys, although with age and training men will surpass women pound for pound.
Myth: Women should execute lifts differently because they are built differently.
Fact: Anatomical differences in bone and muscle are so slight that they have no bearing on lifting technique.
Myth: Women will become extremely muscular if they lift heavy weights.
Fact: Women can increase strength up to 70 percent with little change in physical appearance. It is the male hormone (testosterone) that causes the noticeable hypertrophy in men. Most women have such small amounts of this hormone that bulk muscularity is next to impossible. Women bodybuilders who show extreme hypertrophy have (1) low body fat, (2) unusually high levels of testosterone, or (3) may take anabolic steroids (a testosterone-like drug).

Myth: Women (as well as men) are concerned that their muscles will turn into fat if they stop working out.
Fact: Just as lead cannot turn into gold, muscle cannot turn into fat. Muscle generally atrophies (becomes smaller) when training ceases. People who appear to have gained weight after they stopped training may not have changed their eating habits and consequently may be gaining weight.
Myth: Women should not train during various stages of the menstrual cycle.
Fact: The overwhelming majority of female athletes report no adverse effects on performance as a result of this physiological process.

Most women who train with weights find they have gained the following benefits:

1. Increased physical strength that improved performance in sporting events.
2. Overall body fat decreased while muscular tone increased.
3. An improvement in self-image and a feeling of well-being.

Suggested Learning Sequence

Weight training as part of a physical education program should be approached as a skill-oriented class and not merely as an activity. Weight training requires an overall philosophy, the development of techniques, and the ability to execute the skills of each lift.

A 4-day-a-week lifting program that splits the various lifts into two groups is recommended. Monday and Thursday lifts emphasize legs and back whereas Tuesday and Friday lifts emphasize upper body. If time restricts the number of lifts that can be accomplished, then some leg and back lifts may be done on Monday and some may be done on Thursday. The same arrangement can be used with the upper body lifts. A practical approach for use of equipment would be to split the class into two groups containing subgroups of three students (matched for strength, if possible). By doing this, one group can do Monday/Thursday lifts on Tuesday and Friday, thus allowing the amount of time needed to execute a proper program. The subgroups of three students lift as a team and are responsible for spotting each other when this is required. Each member of the subgroup should complete a set before any member repeats a set.

The following instructional approach is recommended:

1. Students should be informed of the various forms of strength training and how they differ.
2. Each lift should be demonstrated to the student, with emphasis placed on key points as well as safety factors. Students should also understand the

purpose of each lift. (Olympic lifts may be omitted from the demonstration because they are not part of the training program.)

3. If the course meets five times a week, the nonlifting day should be devoted to instruction about related areas (stretching techniques, aerobic exercises, guest speakers or lifters).

4. Begin the lifting schedule as soon as techniques have been demonstrated and safety tips have been emphasized.

Outlined below is a basic plan that may be adopted as is or with modifications. This program may be done almost entirely on variable resistance machines (Universal Gym or Cybex and Paramount), totally with free weights, or in combination. Students should begin with an amount of weight that can be handled through the recommended number of repetitions (reps). The first set should be lighter than the second or third set. The student may increase the weight in a set when there is no longer difficulty in completing the last few reps of the second or third set.

FW = free weights; VRM = variable resistance machines.

Monday and Thursday Lifts:

Exercise	Sets	Reps
Back		
Dead lifts (FW)	2	5
Bent-over rows (FW)	2	10
Lat pullovers (FW)	2	10
Lat pulldowns (VRM)	2	10
Biceps and Forearms		
Barbell curl (FW or VRM)	2	8
Reverse curl (FW or VRM)	2	8
Legs		
Squats (FW)	1	10
Leg lunge (FW)	2	10
Leg press (VRM)	2	10
Leg extensions (VRM)	2	10
Leg curls (VRM)	2	10
Calf		
Donkey calf raise	2	15
Dorsal flexion	2	15
Abdominals		
Sit-ups	2	15 (may vary)

Tuesday and Friday Lifts:

Exercise	Sets	Reps
Power cleans (FW)	3	5
Shoulders		
Military press front (FW or VRM)	2	10
Military press back (FW or VRM)	2	10
Dumbbell shrugs (FW)	2	10
Chest		
Bench press (FW or VRM)	3	5
Incline bench press (FW)	3	5

Tuesday and Friday Lifts:

Exercise	Sets	Reps
Triceps		
Lying triceps extensions (FW)	2	10
Calf		
Same as Mon/Thur		
Abdominals		
Same as Mon/Thur		

Skills and Techniques

The correct lifting form is essential for obtaining quick results and for safety.

THE GRIP

The overhand, palms-down grip is used in practically all exercises (Figure 28-4). The thumbs may be hooked underneath the bar or in some instances, as in the bench press, may remain on the same side of the bar as the other fingers. The latter grip requires more balance and is not recommended to the novice lifter.

The underhand grip is the exact opposite of the overhand grip, with palms placed upward under the bar. This grip is used in executing the curl maneuver (Figure 28-5).

The alternating grip, with one hand palm down and the other hand palm up, is favored for dead lifts. Regardless of style, the hands must be spaced evenly on the bar to execute the lift properly as well as provide safety (Figure 28-6).

When involved in Olympic or power lifting, the use of chalk on the hands is recommended. The chalk will increase the bar or hand friction, facilitating a better grip.

THE FEET

When the bar is being lifted from the floor, as in cleans or dead lifts, place the toes approximately under the bar, with the feet spread about 1 foot apart. The feet should always be in the same line, although the distance between them may vary. Many beginners make the mistake of not starting close enough to the bar; consequently, when they start the lift, the bar swings toward the feet instead of going straight up. Many experienced lifters find that a slight angling outward of the feet, not more than 15 degrees, is a more comfortable and efficient lifting style. This is a technique that should be developed as the lifter improves.

BREATHING

Breathing should come naturally during the course of the exercise, letting the body regulate the demand. Forced gasping and hyperventilating (rapid puffs of breath) only

Figure 28-4   The overhand grip.

Figure 28-5   The underhand grip.

Figure 28-6   The alternating grip.

interfere with proper breathing and may even lead to lightheadedness. The best pattern of breathing is to inhale during the lifting phase and exhale with the return movement. As the weight increases, many lifters find it more effective to take one deep breath and hold it through the repetition of the lift. The lifter should never hold a breath for more than one repetition. Not breathing puts undue pressure on the body cavities as well as the blood vessels of the head. Getting a purple face in the weight room will not improve your lifting ability.

THE BAR AND BODY PLACEMENT

A technique of utmost importance in a weight room is lifting a bar from a power rack or squat stands. Injuries that occur during this phase of lifting with free weights can usually be traced back to carelessness on the part of the lifter. To properly place your body under the bar to execute a lift, check the following items:

1. The bar should be no higher than the shoulder nor more than 3 to 4 inches below the shoulder.
2. Grip the bar evenly and space your hands wider than your shoulders.
3. Move under the bar in such a way that the midpoint of the bar is in line with your backbone.
4. The bar should rest on the base of the neck and the shoulders.
5. If the muscles of the neck and shoulders lack mass to cushion the bar, foam pads or towels should be wrapped around the bar so as to protect the bony parts of the back. Cushioning is extremely important for young lifters and, as a rule, is a good policy for women to follow.
6. By bending at the knees, align your body as vertically as possible under the bar.
7. With the head up, lift straight up with hip and leg power to a vertical position.
8. Step backward out of the rack no more than 2½ feet.
9. With spotters on both ends of the bar, execute the lift.
10. Rerack the weights by stepping back into the rack, with alignment by spotters, and set the bar down.

Training Programs

As weight training has come of age and specificity has become a recognized factor in a successful program, it has become difficult to recommend training programs without knowing what equipment is available and what purpose the program will serve. There are publications that speak to many specific programs in weight training. For this reason, specific programs will not be proposed, but rather comments concerning programs will be presented. For training manuals, refer to the references at the end of the chapter.

LIGHT CONDITIONING PROGRAMS

Light conditioning programs for weight trainers range from in-season athletic programs to the programs typically offered at health clubs. The programs generally consist of a 3-day-a-week lifting routine. All of the basic lifts are done at every session, beginning with brief stretching and a warm-up followed by one set of 10 to 15 reps of the various lifts. This "circuit" or "circus" training approach is also known as the "get them in—get them out" routine. This approach is a lifelong battle that yields nondramatic results.

HEAVY CONDITIONING PROGRAMS

Heavy conditioning programs are practiced by a smaller group of lifters, including preseason athletes, power lifters, Olympic lifters, and bodybuilders. The programs run from 4 to 7 days per week. On a given day, muscle groups, rather than the entire body, are worked. The average workout lasts around 2 hours; however, bodybuilders, prior to a contest, may actually train on a split-day routine, thus doubling the workout time. This routine is an effective program for those who can afford the time. The general rule followed in heavy training is to thoroughly overload and exhaust the muscle each time it is trained, with at least 1 day between training of that muscle group again. Overtraining in heavy programs is a real problem, and it affects different people at different times. Constant muscular pain with a loss in strength are the warning signs. The large muscle groups are the first to be affected, especially the lower back.

A heavy training program, although there is much variation, may consist of a 5 × 5 approach of 5 sets with 5 reps, not including a warm-up or stretch. A current variation of the 5 × 5 approach is to include 1 day of extremely high rep work at 50 to 60 percent of maximum.

An important point concerning heavy training for sport is that the movements of the sport should also be done before or after the lifting. Performing the sport movement will allow new motor skills to develop with the new strength gains.

Description of Training Groups

OLYMPIC LIFTING

Olympic lifting requires strength, power, and quickness. In competition, there are two lifts: the two-hand snatch and the two-hand clean and jerk. Training for competition requires explosive lifts such as power cleans as well as bench press, military press, and parallel squats for strength development. Olympic lifters are also concerned with muscular endurance and often include running in a training regimen. Although Olympic lifting is an Olympic sport, its popularity in this country has dropped off dramatically in past years. This drop-off is because of several reasons:

1. The reluctancy of lifters to adopt modern training techniques
2. The lack of experienced strength coaches
3. A new emphasis on power lifting
4. The acceptance of bodybuilders in society

In competition, the competitor attempts to lift the heaviest weight he can in each lift, and the individual with the highest total is declared the winner in his body weight class as established by the Amateur Athletic Union.

TWO-HAND SNATCH

1. Place the bar on the floor horizontally in front of you.
2. Grip the bar with both hands, palms down, at least shoulder-width apart.
3. With the legs bent, drive with the legs and pull with the arms until the bar is supported vertically above the head with straight arms.
4. You may split the legs or squat with the weight to achieve the vertical arm position. You must stand erect on completion of the lift.
5. You must stand motionless with feet in the same line for the snatch to be judged a good lift.

TWO-HAND CLEAN AND JERK

1. Place the bar horizontally on the floor in front of you.
2. Grip the bar with both hands, palms down, at least shoulder-width apart.
3. The bar is brought to the shoulder from the floor in one continuous motion with bent or split legs.
4. The bar may rest on the chest while the feet must return to an even alignment with straight legs before continuing with the jerk.
5. By bending the legs and then extending them and the arms vertically, bring the bar to a vertical extension above the head.
6. The lift is complete when you are motionless with the weight vertical above the head and with feet evenly aligned.

POWER LIFTING

While flexibility and explosive power are of utmost importance in Olympic lifting, power lifting relies mainly on sheer strength. Although technique is important, the power lifts are easier to master than the Olympic lifts. The power lifts are the bench press, the parallel squat, and the dead lift. As in Olympic lifting, the competitor attempts to lift the greatest amount of weight in each lift. The largest total lifted wins the individual weight class. The competition begins with the parallel squat, and the lifter must have one of three attempts judged good to continue into the other lifts. Although power lifting is not an Olympic sport, it is popular in the United States with women and men.

BENCH PRESS (Figures 28-7 and 28-8)

1. Lie horizontally with head, trunk, and buttocks on the bench.
2. The palms are placed up against the bar, with the thumb placed on the same side as the other fingers or hooked on the opposite side. The hands may

Figure 28-7 Starting position for proper execution of the bench press.

Figure 28-8 The bar is lowered to the chest region with the back flat on the bench.

Figure 28-9 Starting position for the parallel squat.

Figure 28-10 With the back flat, the weight is lowered to a position where the thighs are parallel with the floor.

not be placed with more than 32 inches between forefingers.

3. The bar is pressed vertically to straight arm length and held for 2 seconds.

4. The bar is lowered to the region of the chest but may not sink into the chest.

5. The bar is then raised evenly to a vertical position without moving the trunk, buttocks, or feet. Movement is grounds for disqualification.

PARALLEL SQUAT (Figures 28-9 and 28-10)

1. Begin in an upright position with the bar resting across the shoulders.

2. Keep the head up.

3. Keep the back flat, arching the small of the back.

4. Keep the feet aligned 12 to 16 inches apart.

5. Keeping the back straight, squat slowly with the weight until the tops of the thighs are parallel with the floor.

6. From the squat position, drive with the legs and hips to an upright position. The small of the back should remain arched slightly so as to prevent leaning, which may lead to injury.

DEAD LIFT (Figures 28-11 and 28-12)

1. Place the bar on the floor horizontally in front of you.

2. Begin in the squat position, thighs parallel with the floor, head up, feet 12 to 14 inches apart, and back flat.

3. Place the palms on the bar approximately shoulder-width apart, using a palms-down grip or an alternating palms-up, palms-down grip.

4. The lift also may be done with the "sumo" style: the feet spread widely apart, 36 to 40 inches, with the hands placed about 14 inches apart.

Figure 28-11 Begin the dead lift close to the bar, back flat and head up.

Figure 28-12 End the dead lift by standing erect.

5. With the arms straight and the back flat, drive upward with leg and hip strength.

6. Pull with the back once the bar is past the knees.

7. The lift is complete when an upright body position is attained.

Training includes a few other lifts that strengthen secondary muscle groups involved in the power lifts. These lifts will be discussed in the next section. For information concerning training schedules for Olympic and power lifting, consult the Further References at the end of the chapter.

BODYBUILDING

Bodybuilding for men and women is a rapidly growing activity. Increased media coverage and the popularity of self-improvement are the main contributors to its popularity. Bodybuilding is as much an art form as it is a sport and may well be called a form of kinetic sculpture. Bodybuilders are not concerned with muscular strength, although all maintain a strength that matches their muscular size. They do not train with the specificity needed for a particular sport activity, yet all are athletic. Bodybuilders train with weights to achieve muscularity with symmetry. They perform a multitude of lifts that are variations of the lifts described in the weight-training conditioning section.

WEIGHT-TRAINING CONDITIONING

Weight training in the preseason and during the season is important for every athletic team or conditioning class. The key to a successful weight-training program is specificity and supervision. Specificity means that the program is designed to fit the needs and movements of the athlete. Supervision by a strength coach or a member of the teaching or coaching staff is important for safety as well

as building morale. This section will describe a number of the lifts commonly used in building a strength program.

Behind-the-Neck Press. The behind-the-neck is an excellent exercise for the development of the shoulders, especially the deltoid group. The exercise may be done with a barbell or with a machine (Figure 28-13).

1. With the barbell resting behind the head on the shoulders, inhale and press the weight to a vertical position above the head (Figure 28-14).

2. Lower the weight until it nearly touches the shoulders behind the head and exhale.

3. The exercise may be done standing or seated.

The Military Press. The military press is another excellent lift for shoulder development and may be done with free weights or on a machine (Figure 28-15).

1. With the barbell resting on the chest, inhale and press the bar to a vertical position above the head (Figure 28-16).

2. Lower the weight until it nearly touches the chest and exhale.

3. The exercise may be done standing or seated.

Bent-over Rowing. Rowing has long been used as an overall back developer. It will add thickness and width to the "lats" while developing strength very quickly. This exercise must be done with a barbell.

1. Place the barbell horizontally on the floor in front of you (Figure 28-17).

2. Bend at the hips and grip the bar palms down, shoulder-width apart. Bend the knees slightly to remove hamstring tension.

3. With the back stationary and flat, pull the bar to the chest (Figure 28-18).

Figure 28-13 Begin the behind-the-neck press with the barbell resting on the shoulders.

Figure 28-14 Raise the bar to a vertical position above the head.

Figure 28-15 Starting position for the military press.

Figure 28-16 Raise the bar to a vertical position above the head.

Figure 28-17 Starting position for bent-over rowing.

Figure 28-18 Raise the bar to this height to complete the lift.

4. Slowly lower the bar to near the starting position (bar need not touch the floor).

The Bench Press. Much controversy continues as to which muscle gains the principal benefit from the bench press. Most biomechanic experts would agree it primarily exercises the anterior deltoid and triceps, with the pectoralis major a secondary mover. To put more emphasis on the "pecs," the incline bench press may be incorporated in advanced training programs.

The correct procedure for the bench press has been outlined in the Power Lifting section. It should be emphasized that athletes, trainers, and coaches who recommend benching by bouncing the weight off of the chest or arching the back and pushing with the legs to achieve the lift are toying with injury. The athlete will gain more physiologically and mentally if taught the proper technique in this exercise. The lift should be done with free weights and spotters, but also may be done on a machine.

Upright Rowing. Upright rowing is often done to supplement training for Olympic lifting. The front deltoids and the trapezius musculature are thoroughly exercised. The lift must be executed with a barbell and may be done explosively or at a slower speed.

1. Grip the bar palms down, about shoulder-width apart.
2. Begin by standing with the bar held at the level of the thighs.
3. Pull the bar straight up the front of the body to the area of the chin (speed may vary).
4. Slowly return the bar to the front of the thighs.

Dumbbell Lat Pullover. The dumbbell lat pullover is a lift for all sports from tennis to the shotput. The exercise is designed to work the musculature of the back and rib cage. For this reason, it should be included in all training regimes for track events. The pullover should be done with a dumbbell but may be done with a light barbell. Traditional lat work is done on some form of lat pulldown machine and will not be described in this text.

1. Lie on a flat bench, with only the upper shoulder region supported by the bench (Figure 28-19).
2. The knees should be bent, with the feet flat on the floor.
3. The buttocks should dip slightly to keep an arch in the small of the back.
4. Grip the weight by cupping the hands in such manner that the palms are against the weight plates. This grip will cause the weighted ends to be in an up-and-down position.
5. Extend the arms vertically so that the weight is over the face (Figure 28-20).
6. Lower the weight slowly in an arc so as to miss the head, until the weight is nearly touching the floor behind the bench.
7. Return the weight to the vertical position slowly by contraction of the lats, keeping the arms nearly locked out.

The Barbell Curl. The curl is well known to anyone who has ever touched a weight. The exercise builds the biceps and is tremendously overused, especially by teenage boys. It is most often used to increase the size of the arms for visual rather than functional reasons, and therefore should be considered a bodybuilding exercise. Coaches will generally have little trouble getting males to do an arm workout. The lift may be done with a straight barbell, a bent (E-Z curl) barbell, dumbbells, or machines. All provide slightly different results in terms of appearance.

1. Grip the bar palms up, about shoulder-width apart (Figure 28-21).
2. Begin with the bar in front of the thighs and the elbows kept at the sides.

Figure 28-19 Start the dumbbell lat pullover with the thighs low and the shoulders flat on the bench.

Figure 28-20 Keeping the hips low, raise the arms to a vertical position above the head.

Figure 28-21 Begin the barbell curl with the bar in front of the thighs and the elbows at the sides.

Figure 28-22 Contract the biceps and raise the bar in an arc toward the shoulders.

Figure 28-23 Begin the reverse curls with palms down.

Figure 28-24 Contract the biceps and raise the bar in an arc toward the shoulders.

3. Contract the biceps so that the bar moves in an arc toward the shoulders (Figure 28-22).
4. Slowly lower the bar against gravity to ensure a good stretch to the starting position and repeat.

The Reverse Curl. The reverse curl is done to strengthen the forearm and biceps. The lift is most effective when done with a barbell.

1. Grip the bar with palms down, about shoulder-width apart (Figure 28-23).
2. Start with the elbows at the sides and the bar in front of the thighs.
3. Move the bar in an arc toward the shoulders (Figure 28-24).
4. Lower the bar to starting position and repeat.

Donkey Calf Raise. When traditional calf machines are not available, the donkey calf raise will give the best all-around calf development. This exercise is done with a partner and does not involve weights. The partners should be approximately the same weight.

1. Place the feet on a large disk, with the balls of the feet on and the heels off the disk (Figure 28-25).
2. Bend at the waist until the back is flat while supporting the body weight on a chair or bench.
3. The partner should sit on the exerciser's back, on the hips if possible.
4. The lifter should then lift up as far as possible onto the toes (Figure 28-26).
5. Once the toes are locked out, lower the heels until they are below the elevated toes, and then repeat.

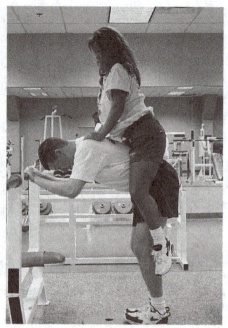

Figure 28-25 Begin the donkey calf raise with the heels lower than the toes.

Figure 28-26 Complete the lift by raising up on the toes.

Figure 28-27 Begin the leg lunge in this position.

Figure 28-28 Lunge forward with a straight back until opposite knee touches the floor.

The Parallel Squat. The parallel squat, described in the power lifting section, is the ultimate exercise for leg development. It has long been used to develop strength and size in the leg. Done properly, the parallel squat will give quick results. The current belief held by many coaches that the parallel squat will damage the knees is both biomechanically and medically unfounded. The use of a bench for the athletes to squat on is popular but not necessary. In fact, bouncing up and down on the bench may lead to more serious injuries because of aggravation of the spine. If safety is the reason for bench use, the problem can be eliminated by using spotters at both ends of the bar or by the use of safety squat racks.

Leg Lunge. The lunge is done to strengthen the thighs and is an exercise that might be used as a means of stretching prior to doing squats. The motion of the lunge should be mastered without weights before actual weighted lifts.

1. Begin the lift with the bar resting across the back (Figure 28-27).
2. Take a lunging step forward, about 3 to 4 feet, so that the rear knee dips and touches the floor (Figure 28-28).

3. Return then to an upright, starting position.

4. Balance is of utmost importance with this lift, and any amount of weight should be worked up to gradually.

Dumbbell Shrugs.   The shrug is probably the best exercise for development of the trapezius and neck muscles. It is a must for additional training in the power lifts. The lift may be done with a straight bar, but the best results are obtained with the dumbbell.

1. Begin the exercise with dumbbells in both hands and arms at the sides (Figure 28-29).

2. Raise the shoulders as far as they will go toward the ears (Figure 28-30).

3. Hold that position for a 3-count and relax.

4. The lifter may also roll the shoulders while executing the lift.

Lying Triceps Extensions.   The triceps extensions work to strengthen the posterior portion of the arm. This exercise should be done as a secondary lift with the bench press. The exercise may be done with a bar or a machine.

1. Lie on your back on a flat bench.

2. Grip the dumbbell, which should be behind your head on the floor, with a palms-up position.

3. Raise the dumbbell such that it is positioned vertically over the face, with the arms locked out (Figure 28-31).

4. Lower the dumbbell from the elbows while keeping the upper arm in a near-vertical position. The dumbbell should be lowered to the forehead (Figure 28-32).

5. Extend the forearm back to the vertical position.

Leg Extensions.   The leg extension works directly on the quadriceps muscle group. The exercise can be done with a weight boot, but most workout areas are now

Figure 28-29   Begin the shrugs with dumbbells at the sides.

Figure 28-30   Keeping the arms straight, shrug the shoulders upward.

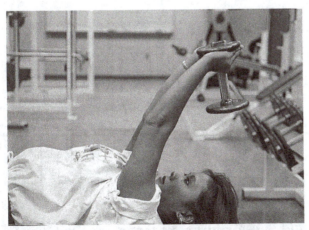

Figure 28-31   Triceps extensions begin with dumbbell held vertically over the face, arms locked out.

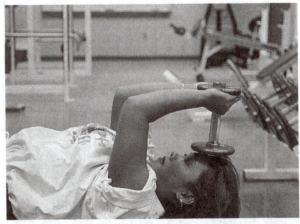

Figure 28-32   Dumbbell is lowered to forehead and then raised to a vertical position.

equipped with extension machines. The leg extension is generally part of a rehabilitation program for people who have weak knees or who have recently undergone surgery.

1. Sit on the bench of the extension machine and put your feet behind the lower pad so that your toes point out. You should sit so that you are leaning slightly back (Figure 28-33). This position will put the quadriceps at the optimal angle for maximum extension.

2. Hold on to the sides of the bench and raise the lower weighted bar so that your legs are parallel with the floor (Figure 28-34).

3. If you cannot achieve full extension, there is too much weight on the machine.

4. Slowly lower the weight to the starting position.

The Leg Curl. The leg curl is a most effective way of strengthening the hamstring muscles of the upper leg. Unless the athlete is on a good parallel squat program, there is a tendency for the "quads" to become too strong in relationship to total quad or hamstring strength. Although the exercise may be done with weighted boots, most workout areas are equipped with leg curl machines.

1. Begin by lying stomach down on the machine and position the heels behind the heel pad (Figure 28-35).

2. Prop yourself up slightly with your elbow so as to keep the hamstrings as prime movers of the lift.

3. Contract the hamstrings and attempt to touch the heels on the buttocks (Figure 28-36).

4. Slowly return to the starting position and repeat.

Figure 28-33 Begin the leg extension in this position.

Figure 28-34 Extend legs so they are parallel with the floor.

Figure 28-35 Begin the leg curl in this position.

Figure 28-36 Flex the legs so they are vertical to the floor.

Dorsal Flexion of the Foot. A group of muscles on the front of the lower leg are generally forgotten about in training, except by bodybuilders. It is this musculature that causes many athletes a great deal of trouble in the form of shin splints. Although the exact cause of all shin splints is not known, it generally results from an overdeveloped calf muscle and an underdeveloped anterior tibial muscle (front of the lower leg). This condition is found in many runners and may result from prolonged wearing of high heels. The exercise is simple and really requires no equipment other than what may already be found around the home.

1. Begin in a seated position with the feet hanging freely above the floor.
2. A weighted device is hung from the toes so that resistance is felt. The weight may be as simple as a

Figure 28-37 Contract the foot and point the toes upward.

Figure 28-38 Relax the foot and let the toes point downward.

bucket filled with water or sand, which allows the amount of resistance to be altered easily.

3. Contract the foot so as to bring the toes up (Figure 28-37) and point to the knee (active dorsal flexion).
4. Relax the foot and repeat (Figure 28-38). Repetition is the key to this exercise.

The Power Clean. The power clean is probably the most total body lift that can be successfully executed short of the clean and jerk. More than any other single lift, the power clean will significantly improve the vertical jump with greater total body strength. All training programs should include the clean to some intensity. The lift must be done with free weights, preferably Olympic weights. The sequence is shown in Figures 28-39 through 28-43.

1. Begin with the bar horizontally at the feet.
2. Grip the bar, palms down, about shoulder-width apart.
3. The feet should be placed inside the hands so as to provide a firm base of support.

Figure 28-39 The power clean starting position.

Figure 28-40 Initial pull phase should not be rapid.

Figure 28-41   Rapid acceleration phase. Note extension onto the toes.

Figure 28-42   The bar has lost momentum—time to move under it.

Figure 28-43   The catch phase—knees are bent.

4. Squat low, as in the beginning dead lift position.
5. The head should be up, with gaze fixed toward the ceiling.
6. Drive with the hips and legs to lift the bar from the floor.
7. Continue to drive with the legs as the bar gains acceleration, and as the bar passes the knees, pull with the back and shoulders.

8. As the bar reaches the chest region, it will begin to lose momentum.
9. At this point, the body needs to move slightly under the bar as the elbows drive forward under the bar to catch the weights on the chest. This arm movement should be somewhat passive because this is not a reverse curl. If the lifter must reverse curl the weight, the weight is too heavy or there was insufficient momentum in the drive phase.
10. You will find it necessary to bend at the knees to achieve the correct catch position. When bending occurs, stand erect with the weights before lowering them to repeat.

▶ Learning Hints

To ensure a successful training lift in the clean, be sure to follow these instructions:

1. The bar should move almost vertically up the front of the body.
2. This is an explosive lift; therefore, rapid acceleration of the bar is important.
3. Do not jerk the weight from the floor with the arms, rather drive it up with the legs.
4. Extend up on the toes when possible to increase leg-drive force.
5. Do not actively reverse curl the bar back to the chest.

Safety in the Weight Room

1. Stretching exercises and a warm-up should precede the training program.

2. Until you are familiar with the movements involved with the lift, do not attempt a great amount of weight on the bar.

3. Collars should always be used on the bars, and they should be secure.

4. Keep adequate distance between the lifters and the equipment in the training room.

5. Always use spotters on the squats and the bench press.

6. Avoid dropping weights any place other than on a lifting platform. Also, avoid banging the weight stacks up and down on machines.

7. It is always best to unload both sides of a weight bar partially before removing the final batch of weights.

8. When weight plate racks are available, replace all weights after use.

Drug Education

ANABOLIC STEROIDS AND WEIGHT TRAINING

Anabolic steroids are protein-building drugs that are used by some weight-training individuals for effects that are believed to enhance performance. These drugs may be legally prescribed by physicians and veterinarians. Anabolic steroids are used in conjunction with weight training because they increase weight and because there is evidence that they help induce muscle hypertrophy (enlargement of individual muscle fibers, which results in increased muscle mass). They also are credited with enhancing endurance, improving recovery time, and increasing aggressiveness, but none of these claims has been objectively proven. Many of the drugs come from black market sources. Because there is no regulation of these sources, counterfeit and deliberately misidentified anabolic steroids have become a widespread problem. The health risks of anabolic steroid use are not well known. There is little medical information on the effects of anabolic steroids at the doses used by weight-training individuals. However, their link with the development of liver tumors and a consistent decrease in high-density lipoprotein (HDL) cholesterol with increased low-density lipoprotein (LDL) cholesterol is well documented. The change in cholesterol fractions has been identified as a significant risk factor for heart disease. The health risks associated with anabolic steroid use are likely to increase with larger doses and longer use.

Skill Assessment

The typical light weight conditioning program for physical education classes consists of a circuit program. The students rotate from station to station performing pre-established lifts at available equipment and machines. The skill assessment is determined by each individual's improvement progress throughout the unit.

Modifications for Special Populations

ORTHOPEDICALLY IMPAIRED

1. Follow the same guidelines used for students without movement difficulties, with the following adaptations:
   a. Do not allow students with cerebral palsy to move the resistance too ballistically. Ballistic movements will increase flexor tone for students dominated by spasticity; therefore, concentrate on less resistance and more range of motion.
   b. Before a student in a wheelchair begins to lift weights, make sure the brakes on all wheels are locked.
   c. For students with spinal cord injuries, be sure to identify the level of injury and consult with an adapted physical educator or physical therapist prior to initiating a program.
2. Consult your local fitness clubs for commercial equipment modified for individuals with orthopedic impairments.
3. Wrist weights, weighted sandbags, and other homemade equipment make great modified equipment for fitness training.

COGNITIVELY IMPAIRED

1. Fitness levels for individuals who have cognitive impairments are generally low; therefore, it is important to start a weight-training program slowly. Take time to build in a solid base, and increase resistance slowly in the early stages of the program.
2. Minimal modifications are needed; however, the use of peer teachers and paraprofessionals, improvement charts, T-shirt clubs, and the like are excellent incentives for the student.

SENSORY IMPAIRED

1. During a lifting program, maintain close supervision of students who are blind or have a visual impairment.
2. Use weight machines to increase safety precautions.
3. Students who are deaf or have a hearing impairment require minimal adaptations. Visual cues need to be established for starting and stopping a lifting session when the student with a hearing impairment works out with a large number of students in a small area.

Terminology

barbell A steel bar 5- to 7-feet long on which circular iron plates of known weight may be placed.

cheating A lift that is executed with the addition of muscle groups other than the prime movers involved in the lift.

clean The power clean or beginning phase of the clean and jerk.

dumbbell A short barbell, 12 to 16 inches, with fixed or removable weight plates.

"lats" The latissimus dorsi muscles of the back.

overload principle Progressively increasing the intensity of the workouts over the course of the training program.

"quads" The four quadriceps muscles of the thigh front.

"pecs" The pectoralis major muscles of the chest.

rep Repetition or the continuation of identical motions.

set The completion of a predetermined number of repetitions.

specificity The development of a training program aimed at increasing one's ability to succeed in a particular skill.

spotter An individual responsible for the safety of the lifter. Generally, two spotters are used, one at each end of the bar, in lifts such as the squat and the bench press. They are not used in Olympic lifts.

Discussion Questions

1. Discuss weight training misconceptions and their effect on sports performance.

2. Discuss why weight training has greater benefits for gaining body weight than losing it.

3. Trace the historical events that contributed to the evolution of weight training.

4. Compare the use of variable resistance machines, isokinetic equipment, and free weights for weightlifting.

5. Identify the principles applied to weight training that have a positive effect on motor performance parameters.

6. Compare the principles followed in light conditioning and heavy conditioning programs.

7. Discuss the similarities and differences between Olympic lifting, power lifting, bodybuilding, and weight-training conditioning programs.

8. Discuss the negative effects that anabolic steroids have on an individual's health.

9. Discuss the safety considerations that lead to safe training procedures.

10. Identify and discuss facts and myths related to female weight training.

Web Sites

www.nsca-lift.org National Strength and Conditioning Association—offers information about the organization, publications, and memberships.

www.acsm.org American College of Sports Medicine—offers information about health and fitness, publications, and membership programs.

www.yorkbarbell.com York Barbell Company—provides a free online journal, information about equipment, and more.

www.WebMD.com—features user-friendly information on health, fitness, and medical issues.

CHAPTER 29

Yoga and Pilates

This chapter will enable you to

- Identify historical events adding to the evolution of yoga
- Provide an introduction to yoga and the ways in which it differs from other physical activities
- Present some of the benefits that follow the practice of hatha yoga
- Explore some principles of movement that underlie many forms of yoga
- Discuss practice and safety considerations
- Provide in-class activities as the physical education teacher
- Find yoga classes, practice manuals, yoga videos, and music that embody the spirit of yoga
- Understand the growth of Pilates and the basic principles, benefits, equipment, learning sequence, skills and techniques, session development, safety considerations, and assessment for initiating a beginning mat program

YOGA

Nature and Purpose

Yoga is one of the hottest fitness practices of the 2000s. As celebrities and athletes have praised its ability to strengthen, stretch, and tone the body, as well as to nourish the spirit and calm the mind, more and more not-so-famous people have felt encouraged to investigate the power of yoga to help them shape up and release stress, all in one practice session. Yoga has grown in popularity because it delivers on its promises. This chapter presents some critical hatha yoga (pronounced "hah-tah") concepts useful to public or private school professionals incorporating health and fitness yoga into their curriculum. These practices are, as Feuerstein notes, "technological" rather than philosophical in nature and can comfortably be used to the benefit of anyone who chooses to explore them.[1]

In its broadest sense, yoga is a holistic discipline that is approximately 5,000 years old. In its original forms, yoga has something to say not only about movement but also about personal behavior, diet, breathing, relaxation, and the meditative practices that open our spirits to joy as they discover their true identity. The word *yoga* can mean "union" or "integration" or "discipline" and is frequently literally defined as meaning "to yoke" or "to join" the small personal self to some much larger self. Much of yoga's enduring attraction lies in its non-denominational spiritual power.

As yoga has surged in popularity in the United States, hatha yoga practices have been adopted by those who have little interest in yoga philosophy but who have much interest in yoga's stress-relieving and health-promoting aspects. Yoga expert Maria Carrico has called this approach "health and fitness yoga."[2] Hatha yoga—the yoga of health and the body—is the most popular form of yoga practiced in the United States today. Usually, a hatha yoga class designed for the fitness setting will consist of selected yoga postures (*asanas*) and a period of deep relaxation. It may or may not include some observation of or manipulation of the breath (*pranayama*). In the health-and-fitness setting, the yoga practice usually does not include chanting and other reminders of non-Western approaches to spirituality. It may or may not retain a spiritual flavor.

History

Yoga first appeared in the United States in the 1880s. It was through the writings of the transcendentalist authors Ralph Waldo Emerson and Henry David Thoreau that yoga had its first impact on life in the U.S. For almost 100 years thereafter, however, the 5,000-year-old discipline was of limited interest, isolated to a select group of philosophers, students of religion, and, later, to the health conscious.

It could be said that the United States was truly introduced to yoga in 1893, when a 29-year-old yogi named Vivekananda drew passionate attention at the Parliament of World Religions, held on the shores of Lake Michigan as part of the Columbian Exposition. In his heartfelt address he spoke about the universality of consciousness and the path of yoga as a tool to world harmony, tolerance, and acceptance.[3] From that time until the 1930s, most yoga practitioners in the United States focused on self-realization through meditation.

The gradual integration of yoga into mainstream America can be attributed to four students of the great yoga master Krishnamacharya (1888–1989): Indra Devi, B. K. S. Iyengar, Patthabhi Jois, and T. K. V. Desikachar. In the late 1930s, the first of these four students of Krishnamacharya arrived in the United States. Russian-born Indra Devi (1899–2002), the first Western woman ever permitted to train in yoga, opened a studio in Hollywood, California, that attracted film greats of the time, such as Gloria Swanson.

From the 1930s through the 1960s, this form of yoga, called hatha yoga, existed in a strange neverland. It appeared too passive to be of interest to physical culturalists and too acrobatically strange to be of interest to any but an unusual fringe minority, or the "Hollywood types." During the 1960s and 1970s, however, public perception of yoga began to change. Respectability was conferred by teachers such as the charmingly wholesome Lilias Folan, who brought yoga classes to public television. Multitudes of educated viewers were exposed to the practice of yoga and discovered its benefit right in their own living rooms. Yoga began to lose its strangeness. It also became more physical.

Krishnamacharya's second student, B. K. S. Iyengar (Krishnamacharya's brother-in-law), arrived just as the 1970s were dawning. He first appeared in the United States at the Ann Arbor, Michigan, YMCA. This location in itself illustrates the profound shift that had occurred in the American perception of yoga. Iyengar yoga is generally accepted as the first rigorously physical hatha yoga style to emerge in the United States and the first hatha yoga practice to attract a popular following.

Patthabhi Jois soon followed Iyengar, first traveling to the states in the 1980s at the request of students he had trained in India. Jois is the source of astanga yoga, the "parent" of today's power yoga and the most athletically demanding of the physical practices. Now gaining in influence is viniyoga, the name given by T. K. V. Desikachar, Krishnamacharya's fourth influential student and son, which emphasizes individual needs and the building up of each person.

Many other yogis have traveled to the West. Some of the most influential teachers and the style of yoga attributed to them are Maharishi Mahesh Yogi, transcendental meditation; Amrit Desai, kripalu yoga; Yogi Bhajan, kundalini yoga; Swami Muktananda, siddha yoga; Paramahansa Yogananda, self-realization; and Swami Rama, Himalayan yoga. Forms of Tibetan yoga have also appeared in the second half of the 20th century. The yoga styles mentioned are by no means a complete list.[4]

Many of these notable swamis (or teachers) established teaching institutions throughout the United States during the 1970s. As the swamis arrived, they attracted the attention of scientific researchers, who were eager to discover the truth about the amazing powers that these advanced yogis were said to possess. The yogis were eager participants.

Those studies led to major advances in medical science, including the development of biofeedback, the development of the science of stress reduction, the use of meditation to alleviate chronic pain, and the demonstration by Dean Ornish, MD, that coronary artery disease caused by arterial plaque could be reversed.[5]

The scientific study of yoga helped make it mainstream by demystifying the practice and simultaneously demonstrating it to be a powerful means of accessing strength, flexibility, and control. The other major contributor to the popularity of yoga was its adoption as both a physical and mental aid to winning athletic competitions. A key moment seems to have been the coining of the term *power yoga* by Yogini Beryl Bender Birch, fitness director of the New York Road Runners Club, who made Patthabhi Jois's astanga sequences easier and then taught them to Western athletes. Another was Phil Jackson's phenomenal coaching success with the Chicago Bulls. Shortly after, the Miami Dolphins were doing team yoga practice. And then there was the glamor conferred by the practices of numerous Hollywood stars.

Yoga has truly taken on an American identity and has become a favorite national form of lifetime fitness. And it continues to fascinate scientists and physicians who remain intrigued by the healing claims that have accompanied yoga since the beginning.

Basic Principles

POSTURES

The postures are the most accessible part of yoga. In the classic *Light on Yoga*, Iyengar includes instructions for 216 postures, but only about 50 to 60 of these postures are commonly practiced.[6] Postures can be classified as standing, sitting, forward or lateral bending, balancing, backward bending or twisting, inversions, and the relaxation pose. Most forms of yoga include poses of each type in every class. Poses are sequenced in a way that balances the whole body. The physical practice of hatha yoga is extraordinarily adaptable. Postures can be modified to provide nourishing movement for those with limitations in mobility, balance, or strength; they can be linked together to provide challenging workouts for conditioned athletes; and they can be practiced by the young, the old, and all of us in between, as our own strength, flexibility, and desire dictate.

The usual yoga practice will move the spine in all six of its directions and will also take the joints through their full range of motion. Yoga postures lengthen, strengthen, and balance the musculature of the body, creating greater flexibility, strength, and stamina, and both the movements and the breath massage the internal organs. Gentle approaches emphasize relaxation and range of motion, whereas more athletic styles, such as power yoga–based and Iyengar-based practices, both demand and create strength, flexibility, and endurance. Yogis have long claimed that either type of practice can profoundly impact physiological and psychological states.

BREATHING

The attention to the breath may simply teach students how to relax and breathe more fully, or it may involve breathing exercises, called *pranayama*. Some forms of yoga ask students to move with the breath—performing opening and stretching movements on inhalation, and forward bending and work on exhalation. Power yoga students learn a specific yogic breathing technique called *ujjayi* (pronounced "ooo-jai"), which creates heat and strength, as well as an audible rhythm with which to move. (Think of *Star Wars*' Darth Vader, but turn down the volume.) Breathing practices improve vital capacity and bring peace and clarity to the mind.[7] The ancient yogis claimed that pranayama practices can extend life and youthful vitality.

RELAXATION

Relaxation at the end of the yoga practice period brings much-needed balance to our typically overactive lives. Although there are different ways of approaching the relaxation period, generally students lie on their backs in a formal relaxation pose. The body is consciously relaxed in a systematic way for anywhere from 5 to 15 minutes (and in some practices, even more). Attention or awareness is brought to a part of the body, and it is encouraged to soften and to let go of all tension. Sometimes the scan moves down the body from the head to the toes and then back up again; sometimes it moves from the toes up. Sometimes, the technique is more complex and may include imagery or visualization.

Students are usually and accurately told that the relaxation pose Savasana (pronounced "sha-vas-an-ah") is the hardest pose to do correctly. For most of us, it is the one we are most eager to practice over and over again because it is so revitalizing. The usual goal of the relaxation period is to release all mental and physical tension. The student is encouraged to broaden his or her awareness, to let thoughts pass like clouds, and to keep a light, clear awareness of the coming and going of the breath, relaxing the body a little more with each exhalation. Sleepiness is almost inevitable, and the challenge is to learn to remain in the pose in a tranquil yet alert state.

BENEFITS THAT CAN EMERGE FROM THE PRACTICE OF HATHA YOGA

- Less reactivity to stressors
- More energy
- Better sleep
- Better digestion
- Improved aliveness, vitality, and inner peace
- Greater appreciation for the complexity of the union of body, mind, and spirit

- More ability to identify with others
- More interest in the health of the environment
- Interest in healthier diet and lessening or cessation in the use of mood-altering drugs, including tobacco and alcohol
- Ability to breathe diaphragmatically, thus improving vital respiratory capacity and heart health
- Ability to turn attention toward (rather than away from) sensations within the body, thus becoming more able to respond appropriately to stress, ill health, etc.
- Ability to "watch the mind" at work and to simply choose to turn away from distraction to one's chosen object of attention
- Strength and length in the musculature of the body, which results in greater agility and fewer injuries among athletes
- Improved posture
- Appreciation for similarities as human beings
- Appreciation for noncompetitive physical practices, as well as for the competitive spirit
- Improved coordination
- More centered energy
- Greater awareness of the need to rest and a willingness to balance rest and activity through more careful lifestyle choices

It is important to remember that these benefits come as the result of consistent, systematic practice. Some benefits may come quickly, some quite slowly. As George Leonard notes, it is the willingness to practice for the pleasure of practicing, rather than for the results, that characterizes the path of mastery.[8]

Equipment

The basic equipment required for yoga practice is a human body and a few square feet of space. However, having a warm, clean practice space with natural light and fresh air enhances yoga practice. Outdoor practice, when the sun is not hot and high, is delightful. Indoors, a yoga mat placed on a clean wood floor or firm carpet is the ideal underfoot surface. It can be helpful to have a mirror available so that students can check their alignment, but constantly facing a mirrored surface detracts from the inner sensing that is vitally important. Some teachers never use music; others use it all the time. Music is particularly useful in a classroom setting where noises from corridors or other rooms invade the yoga class, or when the teacher wants to create an atmosphere that says, "This isn't your usual gym class." In addition, yoga props can be valuable in adding comfort and stability to otherwise difficult poses. Yoga props include the following:

1. Mats
2. Straps

3. Chairs

4. Foam and wood blocks

5. Eye pillows

6. Blankets and bolsters

7. Balls

8. Headstanders and back benches

Mats. Mats are probably the most necessary piece of yoga equipment. Many yoga studios and programs ask their students to supply their own mats, a more sanitary practice than sharing mats. It is helpful to specify the type of mat the student will need because mats come in a variety of types and tend not to be interchangeable among types of yoga practices. For extremely gentle yoga, thick, padded mats are desirable. For more athletic yoga, in which standing poses are a central feature of the practice, the "tapas" mat or "sticky" mat is the mat of choice. Within this general category are mats of several different types.

Straps. Yoga straps are used to extend the reach, to provide guidance and support for either a limb or a whole body, and to improve comfort in postures. The best straps for yoga are made of woven cotton, with either D-ring or quick-release buckles. Although it is possible to improvise straps from bathrobe belts and old neckties—and these can be great for personal use—it is safer to use an official yoga strap that is designed not to break under force and weight. A strong strap is especially important if you are going to support a whole body posture, as in downward-facing dog pose. Adjustable rings or buckles on the straps also provide more utility.

Chairs. Chairs are excellent yoga props. Many yoga studios use a special yoga chair, which looks much like a basic metal folding chair with the back support cut away, but the basic metal folding chair on which they are based also works quite well. Chairs can be used to facilitate standing stretches, as a training ground for "office yoga" postures, and as supports for those who need assistance with balance, who have muscular weakness, or inflexibility.

Foam and Wood Blocks. Foam and wood blocks can be used to raise the level of the floor for standing postures—an invaluable help for those who have limited flexibility in their hip flexors, legs, and back—and as supports for a variety of other asanas. Foam blocks have the advantage (and disadvantage) of having some give to them, and they are more comfortable than wood to drop on your foot. Blocks come in a variety of sizes. Having at least one per student is highly desirable.

Eye Pillows. Eye pillows are frequently the first yoga prop that the new yoga student acquires. They create total darkness for the relaxation period, and their weight gently reduces eye movement and encourages relaxation of the eye muscles. Covers are generally silk. Contents range from scented flaxseed to unscented plastic beads.

Blankets and Bolsters. Blankets and yoga bolsters are helpful in many postures. Both can be positioned under the knees to flatten the lower back during relaxation—a definite help to most people with lower back problems. Yoga blankets tend to be either cotton or wool. Cotton blankets can be used as covers in cool rooms, rolled to create breathing bolsters, and used to create special support for the neck and head that will allow the spine to lengthen comfortably. Official yoga bolsters come in several sizes and shapes and reduce the time required to provide support for many poses. These props tend to be used by people trained in the system of yoga developed by Iyengar.

Balls. Physio balls (also called "fit balls" and "proprio balls") make great yoga props. They are inexpensive and facilitate a variety of movements, from back bends and side stretches to strength poses. They promote balance and even opening of muscles on both sides of the body.

Headstanders and Back Benches. As yoga grows in popularity, so do the number of props available to aid in its practice. Two are worth mentioning. The headstander is designed to take weight off the neck while allowing the student to become inverted, as in a headstand. The back bench allows the student to gradually increase the extent of a backward bending posture. It prevents overarching of the lower back and provides support to those who are not strong enough to push up into a back-bending posture from the floor. Neither is an essential piece of equipment. Before acquiring any special props, try to use them in a yoga studio to assess their value in meeting your needs.

Suggested Learning Sequence

1. Appreciating the difference between yoga and other forms of exercise

2. Recognizing the "edge" of a pose

3. Underlying movement principles

4. Relaxation pose (Savasana)

5. Breath observation

6. Diaphragmatic breathing

7. Pelvic rock (cat and dog tilts and pelvis-neutral position)

8. Fundamental standing pose (mountain pose)

9. Shoulders back and down

10. Safe forward bending

11. Making waves

12. Extension through extended child's pose

13. Moving on into "the dog"

14. Floor sequence for the whole body

15. Surya Namaskara, the sun salutation

16. A yoga game

17. Lee's chair suite

Skills and Techniques

APPRECIATING THE DIFFERENCE BETWEEN YOGA AND OTHER FORMS OF EXERCISE

One of the key differences between yoga and other forms of movement is a responsive, nonjudgmental attention to internal sensations. The student is always engaged in a dance of balancing movements and opening lines of energy with awareness of the breath and with regard to joining comfort and muscular effort. Because most of us are unfamiliar with this type of observation, just learning how to start paying attention is part of the yoga effort. Some styles of yoga seek to open access to a sensation of internal energy streams by insistence on a precise external form. Other styles emphasize allowing the physical body to open gradually as internal sensations direct the movement. Consciously feeling the internal sensations is important in both styles. This tuning in, as well as out, is one of the qualities that distinguishes yoga. A second hallmark that makes yoga distinct is the attention paid to the breath and breathing.

RECOGNIZING THE "EDGE" OF A POSE

The "edges" of the pose have been described by Kramer[9] and by Schiffmann.[10] By "playing the edge," one can keep the body in a state where both it and the mind are in a state of pleasure. The edge of greatest importance is the boundary beyond which pain is felt. The delight of hatha yoga occurs in the exploration of the territory at the edge of a pose, where there is intensity and opening, but no pain—and this demands awareness of sensation and an ability to concentrate the attention inside the body. The edge is a flexible boundary that relaxes and moves with gentle attention, conscious movement of the breath into the area being opened, and relaxation. When the body knows that its limits will be honored, it will enter poses with much less background tension.

UNDERLYING MOVEMENT PRINCIPLES

Donna Farhi, international expert on yoga, discusses seven movement principles that underlie the practice of yoga.[11] She believes that these principles work with all the various styles of hatha yoga now practiced. When followed, these principles give rise to an expressive and satisfying external form as well as a stable and comfortable pose. Yoga asks that the student (1) develop a sense of being moved by the breath; (2) find the central balance (which Farhi calls "yielding") between collapsing toward the earth and hardening and lifting the body away from it; (3) have an awareness of the power center of the body and an ability to radiate energy from that core; (4) develop an awareness of the central axis of the body (the spine), its natural curves, and how to both extend and revolve around this central axis; (5) embody the importance of the foundation of the pose; (6) create

alignment by following the lines of energy suggested by the bones; and (7) engage the whole body in the practice—muscles, organs, bones, and more.

Through focus on these principles of grounding, extending, and balancing, the student begins to improve her posture and vitality of movement, which can also be thought of as a fundamental expression of how one is in the world. All movement is affected by basic postural habits, and it is through changing this fundamental orientation of the body and its stereotypic response patterns that athletic performances improve, personal confidence changes, and a different sense of the self emerges. Because our habits blind us to what we are actually doing with our bodies, to move beyond the habitual usually requires observation by and feedback from an experienced teacher. However, yoga has a vast tradition of self-study, self-observation, and self-reliance. So it is possible to begin this exploration on your own or with friends, using some of the excellent yoga manuals and videotapes that now exist.

RELAXATION POSE (SAVASANA)

> ▶ Learning/Helpful Hints

1. Sit on your yoga mat with your knees bent.
2. Thread your spine onto the mat, maintaining both length and normal curves. When you are on your back, the line formed by the top of the head, nose, and chin should extend through the center of the body. The position should be comfortable for the lower back. If it is not, and the pose is going to be held, use a chair or a bolster to lengthen the lumbar curve (Figure 29-1).
3. Both feet and both hands should be equidistant from this midline and a comfortable distance apart. Usually the feet are about 18 to 24 inches apart. The hands are 8 to 12 inches away from the hips. Rotate the arms at the shoulders so that the palms of the hands face the ceiling.

Figure 29-1 Relaxation pose.

4. To check your positioning, use your awareness to compare the places in contact with the floor on the right and left sides of the body. They should feel more or less the same in terms of size and shape. Make tiny adjustments until you feel you are well aligned in the pose.

5. Try to limit your consciously created movement in this pose to the first minute or so. You may well need to readjust as your body relaxes and lengthens, but the essence of the pose is mental and physical stillness while the mind remains tranquil and alert.

BREATH OBSERVATION

Most of us have never spent any time noticing our breath, yet our breath is more important to our survival than our diet, which is often a focus of obsessive attention. While lying in relaxation pose, ask yourself some or all of the questions listed here. You may want to ask only one or two questions per relaxation, and you may want to observe your breath frequently over time.

▶ Learning/Helpful Hints

1. What does my breath feel like as it enters and leaves my nostrils?

2. Is one stream of breath freer and bigger than the other?

3. Where does the breath go? Where in my body can I feel evidence of my breathing?

4. Do I feel more movement on the right or the left side of my torso? On the top or bottom of my body?

5. What moves when I breathe?

6. Do I feel sparkles, waves, or a sense of current anywhere in the body?

7. Does my breath "hit a wall" or feel like it wants to have more room than it has?

8. If I place my left hand on my breastbone and my right hand on my abdomen, which hand seems to move up and down the most? (As diaphragmatic breathing is learned, the left hand will barely move.)

DIAPHRAGMATIC BREATHING

Most of us have learned to tighten our abdominal muscles, and often the side ribs and chest, drawing them in and up. This chronic, often unnoticed tension inhibits our breathing. It may take a while to fully relax the musculature of the abdomen, chest, and side ribs, which is necessary for the downward movement of the diaphragm that comes with a full inhalation.

▶ Learning/Helpful Hints

1. Lie on your back with your knees bent. Place both hands on the lower abdomen, little fingers near the legs and thumbs above the navel. Feel the warmth of your hands melting any tightness in your abdominal muscles. Sense this warmth penetrating to the inner core of the body.

2. Begin to ask the breath if it is willing to come deep enough into the body to meet the warmth radiating from your hands.

3. Release any tension you feel with each exhalation.

4. Continue to practice as long as it is both an interesting and gentle inquiry. If you become frustrated or think that you should be achieving more than you are, it is time to stop. Come back at another time and begin again.

PELVIC ROCK

Most styles of yoga ask the student to become aware of the normal curves of the vertebral column and to maintain an awareness of the position of the spine in each of the postures performed. Both Jean Couch[12] and master teacher Erich Schiffmann[13] describe the basic orientations of the pelvis that impact the entire length of the spine (and hence the posture) as (a) cat tilt, where the back is rounded and the tailbone moved forward; (b) dog tilt, where the back is swayed, the buttock bones (or sit bones) and tailbone are lifted; and (c) pelvis neutral, where the tip of the tailbone is at its furthest extent from the crown of the head. These three positions are easily explored through pelvic rocking, performed on the back with the knees bent (Figure 29-2), or from the table posture described in Making Waves. It is useful to perform these explorations before attempting mountain pose (basic standing pose) because mountain pose requires a sensitivity to bringing the pelvis into the neutral position.

▶ Learning/Helpful Hints

1. Lie on your back with your knees bent. Synchronize your movements and your breathing.

2. As you exhale fully, press the lower back into the mat. Use the muscles of the torso, rather than pushing

Figure 29-2 Pelvic rock.

into the feet to accomplish this movement. Note that the tip of the tailbone rocks up toward the ceiling.

3. As you inhale fully, arch your back, moving the tip of the tailbone toward the floor.

4. Repeat, noting the place in the middle where the back is neither arched nor flattened.

5. Come to rest in the pelvis neutral position. Take a mental snapshot of the sensation you feel in this position.

FUNDAMENTAL STANDING POSE (MOUNTAIN POSE)

In yoga, the aligned body is the body characterized by the sense of lightness that comes when right and left and front and back are in harmony and balance. In this fundamental standing posture, the normal S-curvature of the spine is reinforced. Body weight is balanced front to back and side to side in both feet, and the musculature of the body balanced so that a plumb line would fall through the following points on the side body: ear lobe, shoulder, hip, knee, and the front edge of the ankle bone. The head is balanced and light over the shoulders. The toes point straight ahead. Arches are lifted into the feet, and the kneecaps are lifted and the knees pointed straight ahead over the center of the feet. There is both a sense of pressing down in the feet and lifting up through the crown of the head. The eyes are level and the chin parallel to the floor. This position is maintained without hardness; it permits springy, fluid movement when the body comes into motion. All the standing poses begin and end with mountain pose (Figure 29-3). When we think of mountains, we think of majestic, enduring bodies that are undisturbed by all the things that happen on their surface. When they move, the movement comes from deep inside.

SHOULDERS BACK AND DOWN

Keeping the shoulders back and down is performed successfully when the pelvis is also maintained or moved into neutral position. It is a counter to all our

Figure 29-3   Mountain pose.

head-forward, body-slumped activities, working at the computer and the TV slouch chief among them. There are different ways to achieve this posture. Here's a suggested sequence performed from standing.

▶ Learning/Helpful Hints

1. Begin by squeezing the shoulders up and in toward the ears.

2. Roll the shoulders back and down, broadening across the collarbones, feeling the shoulder blades slide, like hands, down the body toward the waist.

3. When accompanied by a slight firming of the abdominal muscles to maintain the neutral pelvic position and a resolution to avoid military hardness, this movement does much to bring the upper body into alignment.

SAFE FORWARD BENDING

Many students come to yoga looking for greater flexibility. Athletes tend to be most aware of the benefits they gain from increasing their flexibility. Many are also convinced that they are "just not flexible" people. This misconception is often based on long-term poor "stretching" practices that maintain tight hamstrings and tight shoulders. Persuading athletes to give the following stretch a sincere effort can be a challenge in itself. However, when performed exactly as described, the stretch is safe for the lower back, and it actually does isolate a controllable stretch in the belly of the hamstring muscle. According to Jean Couch, athletes need to consciously learn and use effective stretches for the legs and for the back. This movement accomplishes both a lengthening of the spine and a healthy stretch to the muscles in the backs of the legs.[14]

▶ Learning/Helpful Hints

1. Keeping the back extended so that it retains its normal curves, begin to sit down, as though you were going to sit in a chair.

2. Roll the abdomen and the ribs into contact with the thighs.

3. Relax the shoulders, neck, and jaw.

4. Begin straightening the legs; do *not* lose the contact between the thighs and the ribs.

5. Straighten the legs slowly, find the first "edge" of the pose, stop and breathe, allowing the backs of the legs to soften (Figure 29-4). Stay in the territory between the first and second edge of the pose, allowing the lengthening to occur.

MAKING WAVES

Most of us have learned to alternate from a back-rounded (cat tilt) position to a scooped-back (dog tilt) position by hinging in the lower back. It is also possible to move

Figure 29-4 Safe forward bending.

Figure 29-6 Making waves, tailbone up.

Figure 29-5 Making waves, back arched.

between these positions by making waves that travel up from the pelvis one segment of the back at a time. This amazingly satisfying and (for most people) healthy back movement lengthens all the muscles of the back and provides some toning of the abdominal musculature. It also often opens the window of internal awareness a little wider. As its name suggests, this movement helps maintain a sense of the fluidity of the body and teaches coordination of the breath and movement. This pose goes by other names, including the cat, cat-cow, and cat-dog tilt.

▶ Learning/Helpful Hints

1. Begin in the table posture, hands directly underneath the shoulders, fingers spread and pointing straight ahead. The knees are directly underneath the hips. On each side, all the bones of the leg and foot are in the same plane as the hip socket. When you peek down between your knees, you see only the inner soles of the feet.

2. As you exhale, curl the tailbone down, hollow the belly below the navel, then move this arch up through the rib cage and neck. Move one vertebra at a time. The head will move down as a natural result of the arching of the full extent of the back (Figure 29-5).

3. As you inhale, pull the tailbone back and up, focusing this time on lengthening the entire front of the body. As the wave travels from the seat toward the head, the breastbone also moves forward and up, and the neck and chin rise as a natural extension of this forward movement from the core of the body (Figure 29-6).

4. Each movement phase lasts only as long as the phase of the breath with which it is paired.

5. The following tip will help you get the most from this movement: Stay wide across your collar bones, keeping the shoulders well away from the ears. It is fairly common for students to make a tunnel around the neck with their shoulders pulled close to the ears. Many times when this occurs, the student tries to compensate for the lack of movement in the core of the body by an extreme lift of the chin. Remember that you want to extend the entire length of the spine in an organic way—each segment of movement grows out of the last opening out, much like a tree grows in the spring.

EXTENSION THROUGH EXTENDED CHILD'S POSE

The extended child's pose broadens both the chest and the shoulders, evenly lengthens the muscles of the upper arms, helps correctly position the shoulders, and lengthens the lower back muscles. It is a wonderful resting pose that naturally follows the making waves movement (Figure 29-7).

▶ Learning/Helpful Hints

1. From the table position, let the seat come as close to the heels as possible. Keep the shoulders back, down, and wide.

2. The arms will lengthen and, by pushing, help bring the seat closer to the heels. The back lengthens, and, as the shoulders rotate into an arms-extended position, the head will naturally come between the

Figure 29-7 Extended child's pose.

Figure 29-8 Using props to increase comfort and ease in executing downward-facing dog pose.

upper arms. Instead of moving the forehead toward the floor, keep the neck extended and the ears directly between the upper arms. The neck should retain its normal curve and the throat feel open—just as though you were standing up.

MOVING ON INTO "THE DOG"

An excellent posture for lengthening the entire back of the body is the downward-facing dog pose. All the principles explored in basic standing posture and the two postures above come into play in an open and extended dog pose.

▶ Learning/Helpful Hints

1. From the extended child's pose, curl the toes under; bring the weight onto the hands and the knees.
2. Rotate the pelvis into dog tilt, and push the body back and up—tailbone aiming toward the intersection of the wall and ceiling behind you. In dog pose, as in fundamental standing posture, the normal curves of the spine are maintained. As in fundamental standing posture and shoulders back and down, the collarbones are wide and the shoulder blades moved toward the waist. The body forms an inverted V; the space between the toes and the hands is about the same distance as the length of the legs. Generally this is the distance between the hands and the feet that occurs in extended child's pose. If the backs of the legs are tight, discomfort can usually be alleviated by bending the knees and by letting the heels come away from the floor. If the back of the body is tight, raising the level of the floor through the use of yoga props under either the hands or the feet can make an immense difference in the comfort and ease of this pose (Figure 29-8). Typically, if the legs are tight, props under the feet help, whereas if the shoulders are tight, props under the hands help.
3. From dog pose, return the knees to the floor and then move the body back into extended child's pose.

FLOOR SEQUENCE FOR THE WHOLE BODY

Doing a sequence on the floor eliminates the problem of maintaining balance, which for beginners can be an occasion of tightening and concern about alignment, rather than a pleasurable exploration of movement principles. Although standing poses are critical to a beginning yoga practice, and in some systems are the heart of the practice for beginning students, it can be helpful to work with the principles of extension, grounding, and breathing before bringing the exploration to standing. This sequence moves the entire body, encourages the spine to move in all six of its directions, and is usually acclaimed by students for the wonderful feeling it leaves.

▶ Learning/Helpful Hints

Have a strap handy.

1. Stretch out on the front of the body. Place your right hand on top of your left, rest your right cheek on your right hand, and breathe deeply for about 1 minute, changing the hand on top and the resting cheek about halfway through. Focus on coming into the body, feeling the breath moving the ribs and feeling the lower back flex and the head move on inhalation and exhalation.
2. Bring your hands under your shoulders, fingers pointed straight ahead, and push back into extended child's pose on an exhalation. Keep your shoulders wide and away from the ears.
3. As you inhale, come up onto the hands and knees into cat tilt. Keep the head down (see Figure 29-5).
4. Still inhaling, move into dog tilt, swaying the back, lengthening by moving both the breastbone forward and up and the tailbone back and up (see Figure 29-6).
5. Push back into extended child's pose.
6. Repeat steps 3, 4, and 5 a total of four times.

Figure 29-9 Part of whole body sequence; note position of head, arms, and extended hand.

Figure 29-10 Part of whole body sequence, left cheek and shoulder to floor.

Figure 29-11 Part of whole body sequence, "wagging;" note position of head and shortened left side.

7. From extended child's pose, come onto the hands and knees. Hands are directly under the shoulders, knees under the hips.

8. Lengthen through the body and, on an inhalation, raise the right hand directly up toward the ceiling, looking at the fingers (Figure 29-9). Stay for one full breath.

9. As you exhale, rotate the extended arm down, then bend the elbow and slide the right hand straight out from the shoulder, back of the hand toward the floor. At the end of the extension, bring the right cheek and shoulder to the floor (Figure 29-10).

10. Repeat steps 7, 8, and 9 on the right three more times, then repeat steps 7, 8, and 9 on the left four times.

11. Level off in the table pose, looking straight down, lifted to the top of the range of motion in the shoulders.

12. Push back to extended child's pose. Lengthen the spine and breathe deeply. Balance your inhalations and exhalations.

13. Come forward into the table posture. Make sure the fingers are spread and the middle fingers point straight ahead. Leave the arms fully extended. Curl the toes under, move the pelvis into dog tilt, and lift the sit bones toward the intersection of the wall and ceiling, coming into downward-facing dog pose. Lengthen the arms. Press firmly down into the index finger and thumb as you continue to lengthen through the sides and the back. The ears are between the upper arms. The arms form a straight line that extends through the hips.

14. Lift the buttock bones as much as the back and backs of the legs will allow. If the stretch is too intense, bend the knees.

15. Remember to breathe and to be pliable in the pose. Stay for two or three deep, smooth breaths, then come down to the hands and knees and exhale into extended child's pose.

16. Come again into the table pose. Turn the head from eyes down to eyes to the right, and shorten the right side of the body, as though wagging to the right. This pose is called "wag the tail of the dog."

17. Turn eyes down and then to the left. Shorten the left side of the body, as though wagging to the left (Figure 29-11).

18. Repeat steps 16 and 17, wagging either two or four times to each side.

19. Level off in the middle, eyes down.

20. Push back into extended child's pose.

21. Roll up into thunderbolt pose, head coming up last, and sit with seat to heels, spine with all its normal curves, and the weight of the body over the heels (Figure 29-12). Do this only if you are able to sit back on the heels without pain in the knees or ankles. If this pose is painful, sit in simple cross-legged position. Sit for several breaths. Then roll onto your back for relaxation pose.

SURYA NAMASKARA, THE SUN SALUTATION

There are many versions of the sun salutation. This one is usually relatively easy for beginners to do. It warms and awakens the entire body.

Figure 29-12 Thunderbolt pose.

Figure 29-14 Sun salutation, lunge position.

Figure 29-13 Sun salutation, arms overhead.

▶ Learning/Helpful Hints

1. Come into mountain pose (see Figure 29-3). Sense the balance and stillness of the body and the movement of the breath before going on to the next pose.

2. As you inhale turn the palms forward. As you exhale, bring the hands together at the center of the chest in Namaste position.

3. As you inhale, circle the arms out and up overhead, palms facing the midline of the body (Figure 29-13). Have the palms face the ceiling when the arms are at shoulder height and fingertips when arms are fully extended.

4. As you exhale, come into safe forward bend.

5. As you inhale, keep the fingers on the floor (or low on the legs) and lift the body parallel to the floor, lengthening the spine.

6. As you exhale, come into safe forward bend.

7. As you inhale, spread the arms wide, and come all the way up to arms overhead.

8. As you exhale, return to the Namaste position.

9. Repeat steps 3 through 7 to make this movement sequence a total of four times.

10. Inhale and circle the arms overhead.

11. Exhale into safe forward bend, and step back with the right foot. In this version, the right knee comes to the floor (Figure 29-14).

12. Inhale and look up, lengthening the back, keeping the hips even and the shoulders away from the ears.

13. Move into plank position with the breath held. In plank, the hands and toes support the weight, and the body forms a straight line from the back of the head to the heels. The hands are underneath the shoulders, fingers spread and pointing forward (Figure 29-15).

14. Exhale both knees to the ground, and stretch into extended child's pose.

15. Inhale and flow forward into low cobra pose. In this version of the cobra, the toes point, the legs are either touching or no more than hip-width apart, the tailbone presses down to engage the abdominal muscles (which prevents overarching the lower back), and the hands are under the shoulders with the fingers spread and pointing forward. The lift is

Figure 29-15 Sun salutation, plank position.

Figure 29-16 Sun salutation, low cobra pose.

both forward and slightly up. The back of the neck remains lengthened (Figure 29-16).

16. On an exhalation, push back into downward-facing dog pose.

17. On an inhalation, step the right foot forward into the lunge position, taking care to get the right knee directly over the right ankle and foot (see Figure 29-14). Many people will find this the most difficult move in the sun salutation and will want to leave the foot well behind the knee. It is much healthier for the knees if the foot comes directly under the knee. The leg can be picked up and placed if necessary.

18. On an exhalation, step the left foot forward, coming into safe forward bend.

19. On an inhalation, circle the arms overhead, remembering to turn the palms toward each other and to look up at the thumbs.

20. On an exhalation, return the hands to the Namaste position.

21. Repeat from steps 10 to 20, using the left foot to step into and out of the lunge positions. After the lunge in step 17, step the right foot forward into the forward bend.

A YOGA GAME

The following game is a great deal of fun and can be used to encourage students to reflect on the values of cooperation, not taking mistakes too seriously, helping those less skilled, and more. This game, which is essentially group juggling, was taught at a mindfulness meditation retreat for health care professionals led by Jon Kabat-Zinn and Saki Santorelli.

EQUIPMENT   Beanbags in a variety of colors or patterns—having five to six different covers is helpful.

▶ Learning/Helpful Hints

Every student will need a beanbag. Students count off to form groups of five to seven players. This number can vary, but when groups are too small the game is boring. When they are too large the fun of getting all the bags in play at one time is lost.

Each group forms a circle. All but one person places their beanbags by their feet. The person holding a beanbag starts by tossing the bag to another person in the circle; this one beanbag makes the rounds of every person in the group, without repetition, before returning to the starter. Players are asked to remember to whom they tossed the bag. The same pattern is repeated four or five more times, and then another bag is added. Players are reminded to follow the original pattern. If the group is too cautious and decides just to pass the bag around the circle, the teacher may want to invoke the "you can't just pass it around the circle" rule, unless the teacher wants to make the point that being too safe is pretty boring. Players *always* throw to the same person. Bags are added until all are in play (or until the teacher decides to end the game). It is possible to debrief the game by asking a question such as, "If this were the game of life, and you were going to play life just like you played this game, what would the rules be?" It is also possible just to let students have the fun of it without the analysis.

LEE'S CHAIR SUITE

Lee's chair suite is pleasant, safe for most people, and can easily be performed by those who have desk jobs. Many people in wheelchairs can perform the first 11 steps. It is refreshing, relaxes shoulder and neck tension, and lengthens the lower back and the deep muscles along the length of the spine.

EQUIPMENT   A folding chair with a straight seat or other armless chair with a firm bottom cushion.

▶ Learning/Helpful Hints

1. Sit away from the back of the chair. Sit tall in a way that is both relaxed and erect. Have the normal curves in the spine. Place your feet at least as wide apart as the chair legs. Inhale and stretch your arms overhead. As you stretch your arms up, also keep your shoulders wide and away from your ears, so that your neck remains long. You may want to arch back slightly as you stretch up. At a minimum, have your arms in line with the sides of your body, and tilt the head back enough to see your thumbs (Figure 29-17).

2. As you exhale, bend forward with the back extended. When your ribs meet your thighs, round your back so that your head and arms relax and extend between your legs (Figure 29-18).

3. Place your hands on your thighs, just above your knees, and slowly roll your body back to a sitting

Figure 29-17   Tilt head back enough to see thumbs.

Figure 29-19   Lee's chair suite, using hands to bring knee into chest.

Figure 29-18   Arms should be relaxed.

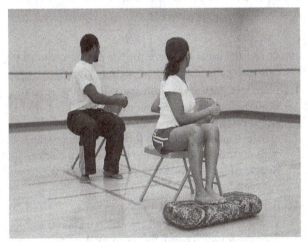

Figure 29-20   Lee's chair suite, twisting to left.

position. The movement is like the unfurling of a fern, with the head the last part of the body to roll into place.

4. Repeat steps 1 through 3 four times.

5. Move the feet closer together; thigh bones can come straight out from the hips, so that some space remains between the legs, but not as much as in step 1. Bring the right knee into the chest, assisting with the hands either interlaced over the shin or behind the thigh. Give a good squeeze on exhalation, and then replace the right foot on the floor. Follow the same sequence on the left (Figure 29-19).

6. Turn sideways to the left, then place the left hand on the right edge of the chair back and the right hand on the left edge. Inhale, sit straight, and as you exhale, twist to the right (Figure 29-20). Start the

twist deep in the belly behind the navel, and spiral up. Turn to the right side of the chair, and perform this same twist to the left.

7. Slide to the back of the seat, reach over the chair back and interlace the fingers, roll the shoulders back and down, straighten the arms as much as you can, and lift the center of the chest up toward the ceiling. (Do *not* leave the core of the body stationary and just lift from the chin.) Feel the elongation of the entire front of the body as well as the pleasant stretch in the neck and shoulders.

8. Slide forward again. Raise the arms to shoulder height (remember, normal curves in the spine, shoulders away from the ears!), then bend gently to the right on an exhalation; come up. Keep the arms up; bend gently to the left (Figure 29-21).

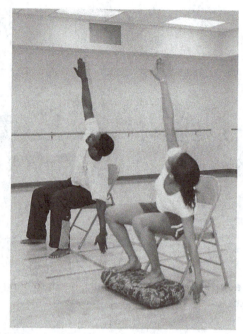

Figure 29-21   Lee's chair suite, arms at shoulder height and body bent gently to left.

9. Lower the arms. Squeeze the shoulders toward the ears, then drop them three or four times.

10. Place feet chair legs-width apart. Raise the arms to shoulder height (remember to elongate the back and drop the shoulders), then bend forward as you exhale, touching your left foot (or ankle, or shin) with your right hand. Come up on an inhalation. Repeat, this time touching your right foot with your left hand.

11. Repeat steps 1 through 3 again.

    You can end here, or you can stand up and do a hip-opening forward bend, followed by the "chair dog," and chair relaxation.

12. Place the chair against a wall or piece of heavy furniture so that it cannot slide away from you as you push on the chair seat.

13. Stand to the left edge of the chair, and place your right foot on the chair seat toward the side edge closest to your right side. On inhalation, bring the arms up, and then fold forward on an exhalation, letting the arms come toward the floor in front of your body. You can assist yourself up by placing your right hand on the chair seat, or you can roll up as in step 3. Do this movement two or four times. Then move to the right side of the chair and repeat the sequence with the left foot up.

14. To lengthen and balance the back, move on to the "chair dog." Facing the chair, place your hand on the outer edges of the seat. Walk back, until your feet are 3 or 4 feet away from the chair; then, pressing your weight onto your hands, lengthen your back until your hips are squarely over your feet. Keep your shoulders away from your ears, your ears between your upper arms. Stay wide across your collarbones. Lengthen your back until it has all its normal curves again. Try to avoid (1) overarching the lower back, (2) hunching the shoulders, and (3) tucking the tailbone. If the stretch is too intense in the backs of your legs, bend your knees slightly.

15. If you can, end with the following relaxing posture. Lie down on the floor, put your lower legs on the chair seat, let your arms relax by the sides of your body, palms up, and let go! As you lie on the floor, let your lower back relax and lengthen, relax your lower belly, and watch the gentle rise and fall of your belly as you breathe diaphragmatically. Stay as long as you are comfortable.

Safety Considerations

The phrase "not every pose is for every body" is true. Most of us have been schooled into the "no pain, no gain" and "just do it" mentality; these adages are about as far from yogic thinking as you can get. In yoga, you

- Listen to your body
- Look for the edge (or edges) of the pose
- Stay within your comfortable capacity
- Avoid strain (but not work)
- Stay with your breath
- Wait at least 2 and preferably 4 hours after eating to practice

Most poses can be adapted to avoid causing or aggravating injury, and there is an evolutionary path to even the most difficult poses. However, actually practicing these principles is as great a mental challenge as practicing some of the more difficult poses is a physical challenge. We are so used to our habitual ways that we employ them even when they are not helpful.

Listening to your body means that you *evaluate* uncomfortable sensations. These can be out-and-out pain in the muscles, joints, or mind, or just a sense that something is not quite right. For muscular pain, you ask if it hurts "so good" or if it hurts "so bad." If the answer is the former, and the stretch seems to alleviate an existing discomfort, the feeling is fundamentally a positive one, which means that it really is not pain. If the answer is the latter, it is probably advisable to back off until the pain returns to the "hurts good" category.

Joint pain is usually a sign of misalignment and a signal to stop whatever you are doing immediately. After you stop, the next step is to see how you can rearrange the pose to eliminate the discomfort. Rearranging may involve rotating a limb, shifting the body weight, lengthening the spine or lessening the arch of the back, shifting the weight from foot to foot, or something else. What is important is to be aware of discomfort and act creatively to alleviate it. It is suggested that this rearranging begin with an evaluation of the position of the feet (if the pose is a standing pose) or with the buttock bones and the pelvis (if the pose is a seated pose). Poses, like buildings, are best built from the ground up. Breathing more deeply and relaxing can also be powerful steps in the right direction. If discomfort persists, it is best to not do the pose and to seek some advice from an experienced teacher.

Schiffmann[15] notes that it is difficult for novices to distinguish between intensity and pain. Any time there is a fear about the experience of intensity or worry about getting hurt, a state of resistance is created, and resisted intensity is experienced as pain. Progress comes from recognizing that one is either at a mental or physical edge, accepting it, and being willing to play at the edge.

Avoiding strain is *not* avoiding work. Yoga teachers frequently say "Keep breathing." Breathing is especially important if the pose is difficult. It does not matter why the pose is hard; any difficulty tends to cause us to hold the breath. Holding the breath causes the body to become tighter. If you have to hold your breath to do whatever it is you are doing, or if your body shakes and the breath is ragged and uneven, you have exceeded your comfortable capacity and it is time to back off.

Learning Strategies

Practice. Find a good yoga class or a good manual or video and make a commitment to regular practice. Look at your schedule and pick a realistic time to practice. Start with short sessions and increase your time as your pleasure grows. Practice at least 2 hours after eating a light meal and 4 after a larger meal. Make sure you have an empty bladder and bowels before you start.

Setting. Practice in a warm room (or outdoors) on an even surface. Use a yoga mat suited for your type of practice. Avoid direct sun. Try to have fresh, but not cold, air. Be sure that your cell phone, pager, and small children are not going to distract you. Yoga has its roots in observation of natural movement and conditions (both internal and external) and is, according to internationally acclaimed teacher Angela Farmer, deeply organic. So, try to have a view of the natural world.

Bare Feet and Comfortable Clothes. Yoga is traditionally practiced in bare feet. The feet appreciate the opportunity to strengthen, breathe, and be liberated from the prison of their shoes. Bare feet also allow you to have a sense of the ground on which you stand (literally and figuratively). Your clothing should not restrict your movement *or* distract you with the need to make adjustments every few seconds, such as having to tuck your T-shirt in.

Movement. Your movements need to be slow enough to allow you to maintain awareness. Be sensitive. If you use a video or manual, carefully look at the alignment of the pose *before* you attempt it. You want to be comfortable, able to breathe, aware of the edge, and consciously relaxing as much tension as you can while still maintaining the pose. Yoga asks you to eliminate all extra effort. So check your eyes, jaw, neck, throat, shoulders, lower back, belly, and seat to see whether you have tightened any body part you don't need to use to hold the pose.

Pain. If you feel pain or discomfort, you may begin to tighten both around the pain and in other areas of the body, such as the eyes and the jaw. When you observe this happening, instead of quitting, try softening as much as you can and begin to find out about the pain and tightness by observation and dialogue. If the tightness or pain is persistent, you might want to explore Phoenix Rising Yoga Therapy as a technique to bring greater understanding. Phoenix Rising Yoga promotes the integration of mind/body states. For more information, visit the Phoenix Rising Yoga Web site at www.pryt.com.

Turn Your Awareness In. As you hold the pose, stay present! Be aware of the constant stream of communication that comes from your body. Does the pose cause fatigue? Is the pose alive (can you feel the movement of your breath?) or cast in concrete? What do the emotions have to say? It is so important to be willing to hear what the body has to say in practicing yoga, and it can be a difficult process as well as a liberating and joyful one.

Injuries. Jean Couch[16] recommends that following an injury to muscles, tendons, or ligaments that you *not* do poses that stretch the area for at least 3 weeks. As you resume, start with the easiest pose for that area and add only one pose at a time. Observe for a week before adding a second pose. Impatience and a "macho" attitude (and this can exist in women as well as in men) are enemies of full recovery, so be patient and observant as you resume.

Skill Assessment

The targets for success in yoga are for the student, through yoga poses, to develop an internal relaxation. Differing from other forms of movement, yoga assessment is a responsive, nonjudgmental attention to internal sensations. Tuning in and attention paid to breath and breathing are the hallmarks of yoga. Assessment then is based on an internal feeling for which there is no traditional tool for establishing success levels.

PILATES

Nature and Purpose

Pilates has grown in popularity and has become one of the most popular fitness methods in the United States. The Pilates method embraces the development of the whole being—body, mind, and spirit, or a holistic approach. It is a path to total health. It in many ways is closely associated with the advantages of hatha yoga exercises and philosophies. Several yoga poses and postures are similar to Pilates exercises. In addition, the benefits that can emerge from the practice of each discipline are similar. A review of the yoga material in this chapter might serve as a foundation for similar understandings when proceeding into a Pilates unit of instruction.[17]

Both activities aim to improve strength, flexibility, balance, and aspects of mind and body fitness. They value technique and body positioning with correct form. However, in Pilates the exercises are performed at a different tempo, moving more quickly in a dynamic fashion without holding a pose while melding moves from one to the other. Basic moves have variations making them progressively more difficult or easier.[18]

The Pilates method works to strengthen the center (centering), build muscle tone, lengthen the spine, and increase flexibility and body awareness. The method also serves as a vehicle for rehabilitation of the back, hip, knee, shoulder, and injuries caused by repetitive stress. It attempts to return the body into balance by correcting the body's asymmetries and chronic weaknesses.[19]

The exercise program is practiced either on a mat or on apparatus specifically designed for Pilates. The exercises are performed in a specific order for designated levels of difficulty—beginning, intermediate, and advanced. At times when advancing to another level, a more difficult version of the same exercise is performed. One needs to learn the form, function, and intent of the exercises; gain knowledge of human science; recognize the abilities of the individual; and plan the workouts.

Because of the complexity and variety of exercises and apparatus, the information provided here is limited to the beginning fundamental level on the mat. Mat work is the foundation of the system. The References and Further References found at the end of the *Handbook* as well as the Web Sites section at the end of the chapter provide excellent resources for those wishing to explore more progressive levels and other apparatus possibilities.

History

The founder, Joseph Pilates (1880-1967), was born in Dusseldorf, Germany. In his youth, he was sick with a variety of serious ailments. His attempt to overcome these physical setbacks drove him to seek physical activities for remediation. He became an accomplished circus performer, notable boxer, and gymnast. His youthful ailments plus injuries from his physical pursuits lead to the development of a series of mat exercises to overcome each.[20] The exercises (Greek and Roman) and philosophies (Eastern and Western) he studied greatly influenced the system that he continued to develop throughout his life.

Living in England during WWI, Joseph was detained as a German citizen in a British internment camp. While in camp he continued to develop his physical fitness exercise series program. He used his carpentry background to build innovative apparatus for rehabilitation of the injured and sick.[21] He used the dilapidated hospital beds of wood and metal piping; attached straps, pulleys, and springs; and constructed rehabilitation apparatus for the bedridden. The Pilates bed called the "reformer" along with more than 100 exercises grew to become the basis for the Pilates method.[22]

He moved to the United States following the war and married. In 1926, he and his wife, a school teacher, opened a studio in New York. It appealed to a variety of groups such as gymnasts, circus performers, and athletes, as well as to the social elite who were intrigued by the new movements' benefits. The dance community became believers in the system as they recognized the performance and rehabilitation benefits.

All activities evolve throughout time, resulting in various methods. Today there are those who elect to follow the program exactly as Pilates did. Some practitioners elect to emphasize the holistic aspect without addressing the original method, thus having a loose identity with the source. Others seek out specific groups to serve, such as athletes and dancers, and adjust the method for these various populations while foregoing the original philosophy. Still others stress and target the rehabilitation aspect of the method.

One thing is certain. Pilates forged the way in providing exercise with an early connection between mind and body while maintaining a methodology that has appeal and options for diverse populations. However, not until 2000 did the method start to become popular with the masses as people became aware of the diverse benefits.[23]

Basic Principles

The key to Pilates lies in its principles of targeting the full potential of body, mind, and spirit in an attempt to attain balance in each. The system focuses on the aspects of one's movement such as endurance, strength, and range of motion while additionally addressing one's balance, control, awareness, function, and harmony. The goal of a good conditioning program is thus attained through improved mechanics of movement, refined posture, improved stabilization, reeducated muscle recruitment patterns, and reinforced well-being and function.

The philosophy of the system is the integration and balance of body, mind, and spirit into all exercises; the attainment of automatic or subconscious motor movement actions through practice; and the efficient graceful movements and muscular development reflected by animals (which Joseph Pilates greatly admired). All of these serve as a basis for his system.[24] Understanding this focus and the following principles provide a deeper understanding of the philosophy underlying the Pilates method. The method requires mental focus, and if one does not understand the Pilates concepts, the exercise program just becomes a series of stretches and exercises. The use of the mind for imagery and visualization is another important concept because it assists in correct body alignment. Movement cues of similar actions, feelings, or visual pictures lead to a quicker and better understanding of the correct movement. Sometimes these are offered by the instructor and other times are developed through the individual's experiences. These are developed over time and are a great assistance for mind focus.

The following movement principles provide the key concepts to keep in mind and to integrate into every exercise during practice.

AWARENESS

The mind and body need to be present—aware of the body alignment and how it moves for the process of correct realignment. Awareness is the starting point, and little can be accomplished without it. The environment needs to be void of outside distractions.

CONCENTRATION

Develop a list of important data before starting the exercise. Know the desired breathing pattern, muscles needed, and body alignment. Concentration helps good breathing rhythm; recruitment of the proper muscles required for alignment; and the accurate and intense firing of the selected muscles.

Concentration and awareness are similar. However, concentration is a process of understanding the movement, whereas awareness is a state of mind and feeling it. Together they provide a deep meditative focus.

BREATHING

Breathing is essential to Pilates because it is considered a link between body, mind, and spirit. It distinguishes Pilates from most other forms of exercise. Yoga and Pilates have specific breathing patterns for every exercise. It is essential to the movement flow and proper muscle balance. Deep breathing (inhale and exhale) increases and exercises the lungs, which provides relaxation as a pleasing side effect. Optimal body control also is gained by focusing on breathing, which maximizes the body's ability to stretch and release tension.

BALANCE

Balance has a variety of targets when applied to Pilates. Proportionate muscle development is important and needs to be addressed. The balance of body, mind, and spirit is another target. Body symmetry is another. The

fitness components like strength and flexibility require balance. The program design balancing muscle groups is of concern. Participants have different needs resulting from the foregoing and must identify any imbalances. It is an initial step on the road to attaining balance.

CENTERING

Centering refers to the importance of locating the center of gravity and to uniting the body, mind, and spirit. In physical terms, the center of gravity, which varies because of individual differences and is located in the abdominal area, is the *powerhouse* because all movement emanates from this core.

Eastern practices refer to the life source being physical and metaphysical. The Pilates method, when referring to centering one's self, means more than locating the center of gravity; it also means uniting the body, mind, and spirit.

CONTROL

Control is a blending of all the previous principles. One of Pilates's fundamental rules is to control the body's every movement. It includes the control of the specific exercises, the transitions between the exercises, how one mounts and dismounts apparatus, and the attention devoted to detail in the workout.

Control comes into play when performing mat exercises at the beginning and ending of each movement. When ending the movement, it is important to place the muscles on hold in a lengthening manner with smooth and even movements. This aids in the development of long and strong muscles. Additionally, it assists in the recruitment of smaller "helper" muscles, which results in greater coordination and balance.

EFFICIENCY AND STABILITY

The focus of this principle—striving to conserve energy—is centered where the work is needed. Exertion is relaxed and calm, concentrating on only the energy necessary for the task. The movement is focused, directed, and specifically honed-in.

Mat exercises target the stability of the torso. The focus is specifically directed and honed-in on by not moving a part of the body while another part is being challenged yet remaining calm and relaxed. Many of the exercises address stabilization of the spine, thus using the abdominal muscles. The strength of these muscles is responsible for torso stability and is one of the most important concepts of the Pilates method. Learning to direct the focus and stabilize parts of the body assists in injury prevention and rehabilitation.

FLOW

Flow is continuous motion that connects one movement to the next seamlessly and effortlessly. It is physical as well as mental. The specific muscles are recruited and fire effortlessly with precise timing. The essence of the Pilates movement is to move freely, effortlessly, and continuously through exercises with precision and control. Also, Pilates sessions should flow with continuous motion, connecting one exercise to the next in a continuum without pause.

PRECISE

Precision is a goal of Pilates, where one focuses on the exact muscles that should be used and relaxes those that want to help but should not. The participant knows exactly where the movement starts and ends. Precision requires total muscle integration followed by the isolation of specific muscles or muscle groups. It is a mindful process, which draws upon previous principles of awareness, concentration, and control. Pilates requires much precision in both the performance of each movement and the activation of each muscle and specific muscle fiber.

HARMONY

Pilates is more than just addressing the physiological components of exercises such as flexibility and muscle strength. The philosophy and principles presented are what contributes to its uniqueness. Using the mind to direct exercise throughout each of the principles taps into one's potential. It provides a path for harmony with one's self by being focused, aware, centered, and controlled, with efficient movement involving flow and precision. It is a holistic approach of body, mind, and spirit directed at well-being.[25]

Human Movement

The basic principles previously cited addressed the mind-body system, and these make the Pilates method unique. This section only briefly addresses the science of human movement concepts and their relationship to the Pilates method. The Further References section at the end of the *Handbook* provides a resource for more complete details and understandings.

MUSCULOSKELETAL STRUCTURE

The skeletal and muscular systems both are important to achieve effective and efficient movement. They are the basis for all movement analysis. If the frame (skeletal structure) is out of alignment, the entire structure is affected, resulting in inefficient muscle action fatigue and ailments. The first step in the attainment of a positive outcome and success for achieving the desired goals for Pilates is correct alignment.

Spine. The lower spine and pelvis are important because they contain the powerhouse, or core, where all movement emanates. The spine serves as a solid platform to support movement of the limbs, yet it is extremely mobile, allowing multidirectional movement of the trunk.

Pelvic Bowl. The muscles of the pelvic floor should be integrated into a comprehensive program. The pelvis serves as a bridge to the upper and lower body. Correct alignment is of paramount importance. If the pelvis is misaligned, it adversely affects the function of body segments up and down the kinetic chain. The result is muscle imbalance, inefficient movement, and stress on the body structure. When the pelvis is out of alignment, the body is out of alignment. Working with precision when exercising the pelvic-lumbar is imperative.

Muscles of the Powerhouse. The first step in the achievement of good alignment and correct movement mechanics is a well-balanced musculoskeletal system. Certain deep muscles of the pelvis and trunk play a crucial role. The back extensors and abdominal muscles are key because they provide stability and support to the spine. The back, abdominal, gluteus (butt), and, at times, inner thigh muscles when working together constitute the powerhouse. This is where many of the Pilates movements can be initiated for the specific area that is being challenged in various exercises.

ALIGNMENT AND POSTURE PRINCIPLES

Correct alignment is a process of neuromuscular reeducation, requiring significant patience, commitment, and guidance by a trained eye. Posture is observed through the alignment of joints and bony identification points and understood in terms of function and muscle balance. Ideal posture is a guideline and a reference for detecting deviations and gauging changes. Posture affects every exercise, movement, and decision in the exercise program.

Spine Alignment. Correct spine alignment leads to less stress on the spine and more economical muscular activity. The body works in harmony, is balanced, and is not overworked. Maintaining the natural curve serves to absorb shock, protecting the body. Thus, always strive to attain ideal alignment and to develop the musculature to support it. Ideal alignment also serves to facilitate efficient functioning of the internal organs.

Head Alignment. The positioning of the head is one of the most common and important factors for correct alignment and posture. The head should follow the line of the spine. Because of its weight, head movement away from the base of support significantly affects the musculature, and this is an effect that exponentially grows as the head moves further away from the midline of the body.

Neutral Pelvis and Neutral Spine. Neutral pelvis is defined as when the pubic bone and hip bones are on the same plane when upright. Neutral spine is when the natural curves of the spine are evident. Together, they are considered "good posture" where the muscles do not have to work hard to keep one upright and moving. When both are in a neutral position, it helps align the body during Pilates exercise. However, there are times in mat work that the pelvis is neutral and the spine is not because of the requirements of the movements involving abdominal exercises.

Foot Alignment. Misalignment of the feet results in deviations and compensations up the kinetic chain. When the Achilles tendon is perpendicular to the floor, the foot is considered to be in correct neutral alignment.[26]

BENEFITS

- More body awareness
- Better posture—sit, stand, bend, lift, and move
- Provides an avenue for better focus and concentration
- Relieves stress
- Promotes relaxation
- Better body control
- Longer or leaner musculature
- Promotes proper muscle activation
- Better balance
- Focuses on breathing as a link between body, mind, and spirit
- Promotes all aspects of physical fitness (strength, agility, flexibility, coordination, endurance, and speed)
- Promotes strong abdominals, positively affecting back problems[27]

It is important to remember that these benefits come as a result of consistent, systematic practice. Some come quickly and some come quite slowly.

Equipment

The attire for Pilates is similar to that worn in yoga, aerobics, dance, or stretch classes. Something form-fitting is desirable because it allows for observation of the stomach area for breathing and body landmarks for correctness. Attire that is too loose inhibits movement. Nothing should be binding, such as waistbands or clothing with buttons, both of which restrict free movement. Bare feet are recommended because socks tend to slip, and gripping the floor with bare feet is beneficial. The hair pulled back allows for noninterference in sight and movement.

The equipment is classified as either mat or apparatus. The focus of this section is restricted to mat work at the novice level. It is a good place to start with the Pilates method because the target participants are usually beginning students or future teachers. This method serves as a jumping-off point before advancing to other levels and the use of apparatus. The variety of apparatus and cost might prove prohibitive for mass programs, and are therefore used only in studios.

Mat. The surface should be firm enough to support the back when rolling on the floor and not too spongy. The area or mat needs to be as long as the spine and as wide as the body. There are mats specifically designed and sold for Pilates, but they are not required. Existing mats such as gymnastic and wrestling are viable, as well as fold-up tumbling mats.

Apparatus. Pilates was a man ahead of his time when it comes to developing machines and apparatus for exercise. Some of the following apparatus are an example of his genius.

- Exercise Balls—Some practitioners incorporate balls with the exercises. The ball is either small or large, consisting of medium softness with elasticity constituted of either rubber or plastic.

  The small ball is at times used as a replacement for the magic circle, which is a classic piece of Pilates equipment. The ball is cheaper, thus conducive for large class sizes such as physical education. The ball is used mostly in ankle, knee, and inner thigh exercises. It can be held between the hands for pushing and working the chest muscles. Many Pilates exercises are appropriate for ball work.

  The big balls are different sizes dependent on the height of the participant. One should be able to sit on the ball with both feet on the ground and with the hips and knees at right angles. The fitness ball, which is big and bouncy, was developed by physical therapists in Europe for aerobic conditioning of injured patients. When using this ball with Pilates exercises, it helps core stability, balance, control, and strength. The use of the ball makes the simplest movement a challenge while adding variety to the workout.[28]

- Universal Reformer—It is the most popular, recognizable, and versatile apparatus of Pilates's inventions. The bench movements "range from fundamental to extremely advanced, and are performed in every conceivable position and for every possible purpose."[29] Each piece of Pilates apparatus has unique features and specific advantages. The "reformer" is uniquely suited to footwork, placing the body in a non weight-bearing supine position, which is comfortable, while recruiting muscles in a balanced manner. Likewise, the apparatus uniquely stretches the hamstring, hip flexor, and adductor muscles. The variety of movements for the upper body, the jumping series, and the full range of motion accommodations are unique.

- Cadillac—The apparatus resembles a hospital bed, which originated when Pilates was interned during WWI. It is unique, versatile, and has unending uses. It provides a constant stable base of support because it does not move. It is easy to mount and dismount because it is high off the ground. The structure provides hanging exercises serving both the upper and lower body. It aids in range of motion, even more so than the reformer.

- Wunda Chair—The chair is another early creative invention of Pilates. It is shaped like a box with four spring settings. The exercise possibilities are unlimited and for every fitness level and part of the body. It is difficult to use because it identifies imbalance and weaknesses. It is suited for development in these areas and for the improvement of general fitness and athletic performance. Limitations are that movements are of short range, affecting full range of motion, and there are fewer opportunities for flexion of the limbs.

- Barrels—There are high barrel stands with an attached ladder and low step barrels (half-barrel and baby arc) that sit on the ground. They provide active and passive back extensions for all ability levels. Unique stretches, hip and body work, and full-body integration exercises can be performed. Because the barrels use gravity, hand and ankle weights aid in strength development. Barrels can be integrated into the workout sessions as opposed to comprising a full session of barrel work.

- Ped-A-Pull—This apparatus is another of Pilates's early inventions. It is not used as commonly as other apparatus but has unique possibilities. The Ped-A-Pul is used in a standing position and complements balance and alignment. It targets the arms and shoulder area with exercises from beginning to advanced levels. The apparatus is either self-standing or attached to the wall. Additionally, it may be adjustable for weight resistance.

- Arm Chair—The chair provides support, offers resistance, and is good for learning correct shoulder mechanics and trunk stabilization during arm work.

- Magic Circle—The metal circle with two cushions on opposite sides for gripping is used in mat work for variety and challenge. It can be used for arm or leg work. The variety of uses are for encouraging continuous activation of identified groups of muscles, to facilitate alignment of the body or particular body parts, and for added resistance to movements.[30]

Suggested Learning Sequence

A. Recognize the basic nature and purposes of Pilates.

B. Identify the historical evolution of the activity.

C. Identify the basic principles and how they affect the program.

D. Discuss the implications and relationship of basic movement principles regarding Pilates exercises.

E. Recognize the benefits of participation.

F. Identify the various equipment needs.

G. Recognize the progress levels for programs.

H. Identify considerations for the development of a Pilates workout session.

I. Present the safety considerations involved in participation.

J. Perform the exercises of the sample session provided and research additional experts' exercise session programs.

Skills and Techniques

MAT WORK

Mat work is the foundation of the Pilates method. It is the basis from which all movement, difficulty levels, and apparatus exercises flow. It consists of a series of focused movements performed in a specific order each session. The work embodies continuous flow with transitions and movement without pause. Because of this continuity of motion, cardiovascular endurance is promoted. The session usually starts with a little relaxation and inner focus followed by a series of exercises that warm up the spine and concludes with a relaxation period for the mind and body.

The work progresses with the adding of more difficult exercises as the participant becomes more experienced. The order and types of exercises included in the fundamental, intermediate, and advanced levels often are at the instructor's discretion and expertise. The following series of exercises[31] is designed for the novice and can be performed with continuous movement and flow from one exercise to another. More progressive exercises and sessions rely on mastery of the previous movements. A review of the listed references provides their suggested workouts.

NEUTRAL SPINE BREATHING

> Learning Hints

Focus—breathe deeply, recruiting air into the deepest parts of the lungs. *Position*—lie down on the back (supine), knees bent, and feet flat on the floor; hands placed on either side of the ribcage just above the waist; thumbs toward the back and fingers toward the breastbone. *Exercise*—(1) Inhale: breathe in deeply as ribs expand into the hands—fill lungs to capacity without arching back. (2) Exhale: allow air to escape and pull navel in toward spine. *Repetition*—continue until relaxed and grounded mentally and physically.

SHOULDER SHRUGS

> Learning Hints

Focus—relax muscles in the back of neck and shoulders. *Position*—lie down on back (supine), knees bent and feet flat on floor (hip distance apart); arms straight down at side; and relax into Neutral Spine. *Exercise*—(1) Inhale: bringing shoulders up by ears contracting the upper trapezius muscles. (2) Exhale: relaxing and releasing shoulders, let them drop down quickly away from ears. *Repetition*—four repetitions and on last repetition, slow down, and on the exhale, let shoulder blades melt slowly down the back.

SHOULDER SLAPS

▶ Learning Hints

Focus—relax and release shoulder muscles. *Position*—(same as Shoulder Shrugs) lift arms straight up, pointing fingers at the ceiling. *Exercise*—(1) Inhale: reach arms toward the ceiling, allowing shoulder blades to come off the mat. (2) Exhale: keep arms straight (no bend); reach up as you relax; and release the shoulder muscles, letting the shoulder blades slap back to the mat. *Repetition*—four repetitions and, on the final one, allow shoulder blades to return slowly, pushing the blades into the mat.

ARM REACH AND CIRCLES

▶ Learning Hints

Focus—open the chest muscles if they are tight and do *not* let the upper back arch up off the mat. *Position*—(same as Shoulder Shrugs). *Exercise*—(1) Inhale: reach arms straight up to the ceiling with 90-degree angle to the floor, keeping the arms shoulder distance apart. (2) Exhale: reach arms straight back toward the ears; drop the ribcage; and, use the upper abdominals to keep the back flat with no arch. (3) Inhale: circle the extended arms (keep on the floor) out away from the head, down to the sides, and return them to starting position pointing toward the ceiling. *Repetitions*—complete three repetitions slowly and reverse direction three times.

PELVIC CURLS

(Figure 29-22)

▶ Learning Hints

Focus—maintain shoulder relaxation while keeping them on the ground to bridge for development of the abdominals and hamstring control. *Position*—(same as Shoulder Shrugs). *Exercise*—(1) Inhale: breathe in deeply. (2) Exhale: pull the navel in toward the spine (Abdominal Scoop); gently squeeze the gluteus maximus (butt) muscles; and flatten the lower back onto the mat. (3) Inhale: release and go back to a comfortable Neutral Spine. (4) Exhale: again, pull the navel in toward the spine; gently squeeze the gluteus maximus (butt) muscles; then keep rolling the tailbone slowly up off the mat to the count of 5; roll up to the bridge position making a straight line, from the shoulders to the knees, with the body. (5) Inhale: hold the bridge position. (6) roll down one vertebra at a time by pulling the belly in and return to Neutral Spine at the end. *Repetition*—three repetitions and each time make the movement smaller and smaller until, on the last one, the body is not leaving Neutral Spine, but the abdominals are pulling in.

TINY STEPS

(Figure 29-23)

▶ Learning Hints

Focus—keep Neutral Spine position, pull the navel in toward the spine (Abdominal Scoop) and do not

A

Figure 29-22 Pelvic Curl.

B

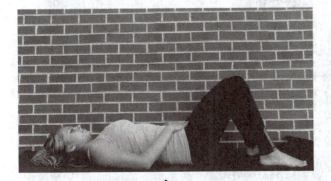

A

Figure 29-23 Tiny Steps.

B

move the hips or lower the back while moving the legs up and down. Use the lower abdominals to provide stability. *Position*—(same as Shoulder Shrugs) relax the back into Neutral Spine and place the hand on the hip bone so as to feel whether there is moving or rocking from side to side. *Exercise*—(1) Exhale: pull the navel in toward the spine and lift the right knee up to the chest. (2) Inhale: hold the position. (3) Exhale: hold the navel in toward the spine and return the right leg back down to the mat, controlling the movement from the center. Return to the starting position. *Repetition*—alternate legs and complete eight repetitions each.

CHEST LIFT

(Figure 29-24)

▶ Learning Hints

Focus—strengthen abdominal muscles and develop pelvic stability and control. *Position*—lie down on the back, knees bent and feet flat on the floor at hip distance apart; with the back in Neutral Spine, put the hands behind the head with interlaced fingers; and take a deep breath. *Exercise*—(1) Exhale: pull the navel in toward the

spine, lift the head, pull the chin toward the chest, and roll up so that the shoulders blades are barely off the mat. (2) Inhale: hold the position. (3) Exhale: control the movement slowly back down to the mat. *Repetition*—eight slow repetitions.

HIP RAISE

(Figure 29-25)

▶ Learning Hints

Focus—strengthen abdominal muscles and develop pelvic and lumbar stabilization. *Position*—lie on back, legs extended up toward ceiling, legs bent, and feet crossed at ankles. *Exercise*—(1) Inhale: pull navel in toward spine, rock back, and raise hips off the mat; push against mat with arms to aid lift; use legs to assist rocking action. (2) Exhale: pull in the abdominals, control hip lowering, and use arms if necessary. *Repetition*—nine repetitions, raising the hips higher with each rock. Avoid rolling onto the neck.

"C" CURVE ROLL DOWN PREP

(Figure 29-26)

Figure 29-24 Chest Lift.

Figure 29-25 Hip Raise.

Figure 29-26 "C" Curve Roll Down prep.

▶ Learning Hints

Focus—stretch vertical spine, strengthen abdominals, and increase awareness of lower back curve. *Position*—sit up erect and tall; bend the knees and extend the feet in front placing them flat on floor; wrap arms around outside of thighs using hands to grasp the thighs underneath knee juncture. *Exercise*—(1) Inhale: sit tall and breathe in deeply. (2) Exhale: pull navel in to spine; round the back to a "C" curve; roll backward down the spine, tucking the tailbone underneath; slide hands and arms deliberately down thighs; roll until the back bones are felt pressing on the mat; head, shoulders, and back resemble a "C." (3) Inhale: pause and take a breath. (4) Exhale: pull navel

in toward spine; focus on pressing lower back into mat using abdominal muscles; roll back up deliberately using hands and arms to slide up thigh for assistance; continue the roll with tucked tummy until the head touches the knees; arms slide under knees and back is still rounded in a tucked "C" position. (5) Inhale: return to tall, vertically erect sitting position with head relaxed until fully erect. (6) Exhale: in erect sitting position in proper starting place, relax and drop the shoulders, feeling the upper back muscles control the shoulders. *Repetitions*—six repetitions.

BALANCE POINT/TEASER PREP

(Figure 29-27)

A

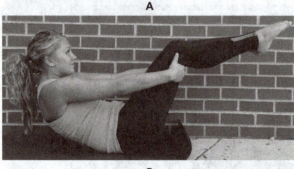

B

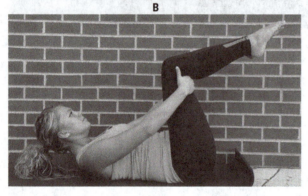

C

Figure 29-27 Balance Point.

▶ Learning Hints

Focus—balance, deep abdominal strengthening, and articulation of the spine moving one vertebrae at a time for stability and muscle strengthening. *Position*—sit up with bent knees and feet off the floor; hands grasp under each thigh; body balance immediately behind tailbone with navel pulled toward spine and lower back rounded. *Exercise*—(1) Exhale: roll down spine pushing thighs away from body for counterbalance; pull navel in; control movement from center; limit backward roll distance for control and stability. (2) Inhale: hold in controlled balanced position. (3) Exhale: press legs away and use abdominal muscles to assist in returning to starting balanced position. *Repetitions*—six repetitions, attempting to go lower with each one.

ROLLING LIKE A BALL—MODIFIED

(Figure 29-28)

▶ Learning Hints

Focus—articulation of the spine, abdominal control, center and balance. *Position*—sit up (See Balance Point/Teaser Prep Figure 29-27). *Exercise*—(1) Inhale: roll back onto upper back; raise hips using abdominals to aid in lift; squeeze gluteus maximus (butt) for extra lift. (2) Exhale: roll forward returning to starting balanced position and pull navel in toward spine to stop forward momentum. *Repetitions*—six reps.

Summary of Exercises

Mastering this sample lead-up series of exercises serves as a foundation for moving to beginning, intermediate, and advanced sessions. Several of the foregoing exercises are precursors for similar movements for other levels of mat work.

Strategies for Session Development

Mat exercise sessions, as previously mentioned, should be continuous movement from the start, during each exercise, from one exercise to the next until the end. Preparing mentally and physically in a warm-up is important. The same is true for a relaxing "coming-down" in a cool-down. The length of a session varies; but regardless of the length, the same movement philosophy applies. The benefits of the continuous movement are:

* Motivation and organization
* Elevation of body temperature
* Cardiovascular development
* Development of muscle endurance
* Requires focus and concentration
* Releases tension
* Uses allotment of time

SESSION GUIDELINES

1. Progressive exercise demands from easy to harder
2. Early in session perform large muscle group exercises
3. Perform lower-risk abdominal exercises early
4. Use as many muscle groups as possible
5. Practice each function of the muscles
6. Use all types of muscle contractions
7. Address all ranges of motion
8. Balance exercise functions to primary joints (i.e., flexion and extension, abduction and adduction, rotation)
9. Address individual specificities, yet consider overall balance
10. Following adequate warm-up, provide challenging and appropriate exercises
11. Stress the harmony of mind and body
12. Stress progressive program using range of motion, resistance, complexity, and speed

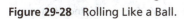

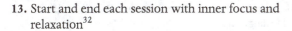

Figure 29-28   Rolling Like a Ball.

13. Start and end each session with inner focus and relaxation[32]

Safety Considerations

Apparatus presents many more obstacles than mat work. These are not addressed here because the concentration is on Pilates mat work. Following are some considerations for safety:

1. Warm up and cool down adequately (physical and mental)
2. Monitor the heart rate
3. Listen to the body
4. Evaluate uncomfortable sensations—misalignment
5. Stay within your capabilities
6. Avoid strain
7. Stay within your breath—relaxed and rhythmic—do *not* hold

Safety Considerations

A review of the "Skill Test Concerns" and "Skill Test Suggestions" in the 'Considerations for Effective Skill Learning' chapter (Chapter 1) of the *Handbook* identifies the difficulties involved in assessing. Pilates, like many physical activities, has suggested assessing methods, available upon review of the references section.

Modifications for Special Populations

ORTHOPEDICALLY IMPAIRED

1. Students who use wheelchairs or have mobility problems can perform poses while sitting in a chair or wheelchair, or from a mat.
2. Use bolsters and wedge mats to assist in positioning students into poses.
3. Use peer tutors or paraprofessionals to manually guide students through yoga and pilates.

Special Note: Consult with a physical educator or physical therapist for procedures to use in removing students from wheelchairs, ways to use bolsters and wedge mats for positioning, and range-of-motion limitations.

COGNITIVELY IMPAIRED

1. Use peer teachers and paraprofessionals to guide students through the yoga and pilates poses.
2. Keep instructions short and to the point, avoiding excessive directions.

SENSORY IMPAIRED

1. Use adaptive physical educators or paraprofessionals to manually guide students who are blind or have visual impairments through the yoga and pilates poses. Their assistance can be gradually withdrawn as students learn the feel of the poses.

2. Minimal modifications are needed for students who are deaf or have hearing impairments. Instructional considerations include the use of sign language, videos, and pictures.

Terminology

adho mukha svanasana Downward-facing dog pose.

asana Pose or posture.

hatha Sun and moon; active and receptive life forces.

hatha yoga The yoga of health and physical discipline.

namaste Term meaning "The center of spirit and love in me recognizes and salutes the center of spirit and love in you."

prana Life force, energy.

pranayama The studied practice of controlled breathing to increase vital life-force energy.

raja yoga The royal path: includes eight rungs, or limbs, of practices that lead the practitioner to a state of complete absorption in universal consciousness or bliss. The path of kings: holds union with the supreme universal spirit; the eight-fold path of Patanjali, first codifier of yoga practice between 800 and 200 B.C.

savasana The relaxation pose.

surya namaskara The sun salutation.

ujjayi breathing "Victorious breathing": a controlled form of nose-only breathing used to help focus the mind and pace the movements during yoga practice.

yoga Union or to yoke.

Discussion Questions (Yoga)

1. Discuss the "health and fitness yoga" approach.
2. Trace the evolution of yoga in the United States.
3. Discuss what is meant by the term "power yoga."
4. Discuss the three basic principles of yoga.
5. Discuss the benefits that can emerge from the practice of hatha yoga.
6. List the various types of equipment that might be used in an exercise session and identify the contribution of each to the workout.
7. Discuss the difference between yoga and other forms of physical activity movement.
8. Identify the seven movement principles that underlie the practice of yoga.
9. Discuss what is meant by recognizing the "edge" of a pose.
10. Discuss safety considerations as they relate to yoga.

Discussion Questions (Pilates)

1. Compare the similar and different benefits derived from Pilates and yoga.
2. Trace the evolution of Pilates.
3. Discuss the movement principles that provide the key concepts for integration into every exercise during practice.
4. Discuss the importance of the skeletal and muscular systems, along with alignment and posture principles, as they relate to the Pilates method.
5. List the various types of equipment and apparatus that might be used in Pilates and identify the contribution of each to a workout.
6. Discuss the session guidelines identified for mat exercise workouts.
7. Identify safety considerations when performing a mat workout.

CDs

Adagio—Music for Relaxation. Peter Davidson, Livingarts.

The Mask and Mirror. Loreena McKennitt, Warner Brothers.

Music for Zen Meditation. Tony Scott, Verve.

Nada Yoga: The Ancient Science of Sound. Russill Paul, Healingmusic.

Web Sites

YOGA

www.yogafinder.com—offers a yoga directory with information on yoga events, music, and products.

www.yogajournal.com *Yoga Journal*—features contents of the current issue, book and audio resources, articles on yoga and health, teacher directory, and more.

www.himalayaninstitute.org/yoga-international-magazine—features contents of the current issue, study online, workshops and retreats, teacher certification, and more.

www.traditionalyogastudies.com Georg Feuerstein's yoga Web site—features information on Green Yoga, a glossary of yoga terms, articles, and FAQs for beginning yoga students.

PILATES

www.pilates.com—features comprehensive information on history, books, videos, equipment, training, and more.

www.kcpilates.com—introduces benefits; terms; basic exercises; beginning, intermediate, and mat exercises; plus a few apparatus exercises.

www.pilatesmethodalliance.org—explains Pilates, presents youth program, teacher training, and much more.

CHAPTER 30 | Lifetime Activities

This chapter will enable you to understand and take part in

- Canoeing and Kayaking
- Cross-Country Skiing
- Indoor Climbing
- Scuba Diving
- Skin Diving
- Skateboarding
- Snowboarding
- Snowshoeing

Introduction

Several activities that are popular today are not typically included in most school physical education curricula. The activities have become popular as recreational pursuits and are enjoyed by thousands of participants throughout the world. Space does not permit a full discussion or skill breakdown of each activity. However, this chapter provides an overview of each activity, including basic equipment requirements and a list of the important skills and concepts the learner would be expected to master.

In addition, each activity is accompanied by a number of references that provide a description of the skills and a more thorough discussion of the specific activity. An extensive list of Web sites with many links provides further valuable information.

Some of the activities are deemed high risk, and it is recommended that if they are included in a curriculum, the teacher be proficient in teaching the skill or call on an expert to provide instruction.

CANOEING AND KAYAKING

Nature and Purpose

Canoeing and kayaking are outdoor recreational activities that offer broad appeal to people of all ages. Both can be done individually or with groups or families; in still or moving water; on lakes, rivers, or the ocean; and they can be incorporated with camping and extend over a period of several days or weeks. On the one hand, these small crafts may be used in a leisurely fashion, allowing a person without a high degree of fitness to enjoy the freedom of the outdoors. On the other hand, use of canoes and kayaks in fast-moving water that includes rapids and other obstacles can also satisfy the most ardent extreme sport enthusiast.

Canoeing and kayaking can provide a satisfying experience for people of all levels of ability. Both are skill-based activities that require some skill and safety instruction before beginning. First and foremost, any novice paddler should be able to swim a distance of 200 yards unassisted. Beginning instruction should be completed in a relatively sheltered open water area in calm, still water. Preferably, instruction will take place in a small craft in a swimming pool before the student advances to open water. Prior to entering water in any small craft, boaters should first have a pool orientation. Orientation should include a swim test, basic paddling skills, self-rescue skills, and buddy rescue skills.

For the beginner, slow-moving rivers and relatively calm seas and lakes are essential for enjoying a positive first experience.

Equipment

Canoeing and kayaking require relatively little equipment— a craft, paddle, and personal flotation device. As the student becomes more skilled, equipment requirements may change. Beginners, however, should rent a canoe or kayak from a knowledgeable outfitter that can place them into a craft that meets their needs.

CANOEING

Canoes are commonly constructed of aluminum, fiberglass, kevlar, or wood and come in different lengths, widths, and hull shapes. Generally, the average canoe is 16 feet long; however, canoes can be longer. A shorter canoe is more maneuverable but is generally not a type that would be taken on a long trip or tour. A longer canoe can hold supplies for long trips and tracks better in the water. The width of a canoe at the waterline determines the canoe's stability. Wider canoes are more stable but are slower. Canoes have a variety of hull shapes—straight, flat bottom, round bottom, and a shallow V-hull. Each shape has an impact on performance. For the recreational canoeist, the shallow V-hull is the preferred shape because it is more stable and easier for the beginner to handle.

Other equipment needed by the canoeist includes a personal flotation device (PFD). This life-protecting device is required by many states. U.S. Coast Guard approved PFDs are rated by the wearer's weight and are designed to keep the wearer in a vertical to slightly backward position in the water. Size and weight information is contained on a label affixed to the jacket. Preferably, the PFD should be orange, yellow, or red so that it can be easily spotted by rescuers. Other safety equipment includes an extra paddle and a throwable seat cushion or throwbag to assist with a rescue.

Paddles enable the canoeist to maneuver the craft. Paddles used for canoeing are made of wood, fiberglass, or aluminum and come in different lengths, shaft shapes (straight or bent), and blade sizes (narrow to wide). The type of paddle is determined by the performance the canoeist wants, the type of conditions, and the canoeist's ability and strength. Generally, the paddle should be long enough for the grip to reach eye level while the tip rests on the ground.

KAYAKING

Kayaks are made of plastic, fiberglass, kevlar, carbon fiber, or wood. They are either rigid, folding, or inflatable. Most beginners use kayaks made of plastic. They are rigid, durable, and can take more abuse. Folding or collapsible kayaks consist of a wood or aluminum frame with a fabric skin stretched over it. Inflatable kayaks are easily portable and can be folded up and easily stored.

There are two major types of kayaks: river and sea. River kayaks are smaller, have rounded hulls, and are generally fast and nimble. Sea kayaks are larger, with V-shaped hulls. Sea kayaks may also include hand-operated bilge pumps for bailing water and sealed compartments for storing camping equipment. Sea kayaks are more stable than river kayaks but tend to be slower and have a much larger turning radius because of their size.

River kayaks, by the nature of their rounded hulls, are unstable. They are highly susceptible to rolling. The kayaker should be able to re-right from a roll, but this requires a great deal of practice. It is essential that those who wish to pursue this type of kayaking learn how to exit their craft while underwater.

The type of craft selected depends on where the boater will be kayaking (river, open lake, sea),

experience in the craft (beginner to expert), the portability and weight of the craft (how much the kayak will be used, whether it will be stored), and the capacity needed (single-person or two-person kayak, storage for camping and long tours). An additional factor is the fit of the kayak. For high performance, a snug cockpit is necessary, whereas for long tours, a looser fit enables the kayaker to move around and stretch his legs.

In addition to the kayak itself, a two-bladed paddle is required. The blades are feathered, or set at opposite angles, to provide a better angle of effectiveness for the paddler. Although there are some kayaks, called sit-on-top kayaks, that have no enclosed cockpit (the boater sits in a depression), most kayaks require the boater to sit in a cockpit that encloses the legs and lower torso.

Other equipment found in a kayak includes a sprayskirt, which is a neoprene device that the kayaker wears around the waist and fastens to the edge of the cockpit. The sprayskirt helps keep water out of the enclosed kayak hull, which preserves the boat's integrity and helps keep the kayaker warm. Other personal equipment worn by the kayaker may include a neoprene wet suit, with gloves and boots for warmth.

The PFD used by the kayaker is slightly different from the canoeist's. It is designed to provide more freedom of movement. In cases of river kayaking in swift water, the boater may also wear a lightweight helmet to prevent head injuries and other injuries sustained from making contact with the bottom.

Basic Skills

CANOEING

Although one experienced boater may canoe alone, two boaters can enjoy an activity called *soloing*. The bowman is stationed at the front of the boat and normally paddles and looks out for obstacles and hazards. The sternman sits in the rear of the boat and paddles as well as steers the canoe. The more experienced boater should normally act as the sternman. The direction of a canoe is controlled by a series of strokes, many initiated by the sternman, but sometimes in conjunction with the bowman. When paddling, the canoeist should submerge at least three-quarters of the blade in water. A person should expect to learn the following basic skills:

- Safety skills—swimming, self-rescue, buddy rescue techniques
- Selecting a canoe
- Selecting a paddle
- Choosing a PFD
- Carrying a canoe
- Boarding a canoe
- Reentering a capsized and upright canoe

- Rocking a canoe dry
- Strokes—forward stroke, C-stroke, J-stroke, sweep stroke, draw stroke, pry stroke

KAYAKING

Unlike canoeing, kayaking is generally a solo sport performed by a boater using a double-bladed paddle. The paddle is gripped with both hands, approximately shoulder-width apart, and is alternately dipped on both sides of the kayak to move the kayak forward. The beginner should be cautioned not to try to kayak without proper instruction. The beginner should learn the following basic skills:

- Safety skills—swimming, self-rescue, buddy rescue techniques
- Selecting a kayak
- Selecting a double-bladed paddle
- Choosing a PFD
- Entering the kayak
- Falling out of a kayak
- Eskimo roll (righting the kayak)
- Strokes—forward stroke, reverse stroke, sweep stroke, draw stroke
- Reverse sweep
- Bracing
- Tracking

Web Sites

www.canoekayak.com *Canoe and Kayak* magazine—offers tips, product information, articles, and trip advice.

www.clubkayak.com—offers links to paddling sites, online classified section for buying and selling equipment, and news for the world of kayaking.

www.kayakonline.com—includes kayak buying tips, information on manufacturers of kayaks and kayaking gear, and links to sea and whitewater kayaking clubs and events.

www.americanwhitewater.org *American Whitewater* —provides information on conservation and restoration of U.S. rivers, safety information for all paddlers, and a database with maps and information on all U.S. waterways.

CROSS-COUNTRY SKIING

Nature and Purpose

Cross-country skiing, also known as *Nordic skiing*, is an activity that people of all ages, skills, and abilities can enjoy. Although there are various forms of Nordic skiing, including touring, backcountry touring, skating, telemarking, and randonee, most people engage in recreational touring and backcountry touring. Skiing is a popular winter activity because it can be easily learned; a person can engage in cross-country skiing almost anywhere there is no traffic—on unplowed roads, groomed trails that have prepared tracks to follow, fields, woods, and hills. Both able-bodied people and people with disabilities can participate. In addition, Nordic skiing, whether you are touring or skiing in a competitive event, is an excellent physical fitness activity because it contributes to cardiovascular endurance, muscular endurance and strength, and flexibility; for those who wish to compete, there are extensive racing programs offered in many snow states. Moreover, cross-country skiing is relatively inexpensive; a total ski package (skis, boots, bindings, and poles) can be purchased for $200 to $300.

Cross-country skiing can be offered as part of a physical education program in high school or college. Many state parks and ski shops offer rental programs at moderate prices, and basic skills can be taught and learned in 2–3 sessions so that the student can begin to participate on flat and slightly rolling terrain. Obviously, greater skills and advanced techniques take more time and instruction.

Classical cross-country skiing, or general touring, involves a skill set in which the arms and legs move in a smooth, rhythmic movement. For the more advanced skier, skiing is best described as ice skating but on skis; it involves vigorous activity using angled gliding strides and powerful pole thrusts across a smooth, well-groomed surface. For people who seek adventure, backcountry skiing, which involves basic techniques and some advanced skill executed in the woods and on steep inclines and descents, is the way to go. Telemarking, developed many years ago by the Swedes, involves a form of gliding with a specific technique for carving turns on uneven terrain and mountainsides. And for the most adventuresome, randonee is a form of cross-country skiing that combines touring and ski mountaineering and uses a binding that allows the skier to either be free-heeled for touring or fixed-heeled for alpine skiing.[1] No matter what the choice, there is something for everyone of all ability levels in cross-country skiing.

Equipment

Thirty years ago, the individual interested in ski touring would have found a limited selection of equipment from which to choose. Today, almost every Alpine ski manufacturer has added a line of cross-country ski equipment. For the beginning skier, the process for selecting equipment can be mystifying, so it's best to go to a store that has knowledgeable salespeople. The most important consideration for the beginner is that the equipment function properly and serve the skier through and after the initial stages of learning and participation. Basic equipment for cross-county skiing includes skis, bindings, boots that match the binding width (norm-fitted), ski poles, and proper clothing.

SKIS

Cross-country skis come in a variety of sizes, both in length and width. Often they are categorized according to their use. Skis used for racing are narrower (35–44 mm), are shorter than recreational touring skis, and have a rounded, shorter tip for skating. Mid-touring skis are heavier and slightly wider (40–50 mm). Beginners, novices, and recreational skiers frequently learn on this type of ski because it's heavier, provides greater stability, and can withstand greater abuse. Many learn-to-ski programs rent this type of ski to the beginner. The touring ski is still wider (45–60 mm) and heavier than the others. The touring ski can also be used by the expert for deep-powder skiing and backcountry skiing because the extra width helps keep the ski above the surface rather than sinking into the snow.

Skis come in assorted lengths, and the choice depends on a number of factors such as use (racing, touring, telemarking, and so on); the size and weight of the skier (generally the heavier a skier, the longer the ski; the more lightweight the person, the shorter the ski); and the flex of the ski (the stiffer the ski, the harder it is to make contact with the surface; heavier skiers would probably want a stiffer ski than would lightweight skiers). A good salesperson can inform you about the squeeze test in determining flex of a ski.

Another important factor in selecting a ski is whether to choose a waxless or waxable ski. Cross-country skis are designed to grip the snow's surface to obtain a good forward motion (kick and glide). Their ability to do so depends on the type of wax used on the bottom of the ski (the points of the snowflakes actually penetrate the wax to allow it to grip when pressure is applied to the kick zone) or, on waxless skis, the design of the bottom surface (indentation pattern).

Waxless skis are easier to maintain, and for this reason would best serve the occasional skier. However, there are some disadvantages to this type of surface; the waxless ski is not as adaptable to changing snow conditions as are waxable skis. Applying different waxes in the kick zone is generally not possible or effective, so the ski cannot provide maximum gripping performance. Additionally, the waxless ski sacrifices high-level performance and speed. However, most beginners and recreational skiers find waxless skis to be satisfactory for their purposes.

Waxable skis are for the ski purist who wants maximum performance and enjoys waxing skis. Obviously, different waxes enhance performance in changing snow conditions. Learning the different types and their advantages takes time and some basic knowledge of snow conditions and can be quite cumbersome to the occasional skier.

BINDINGS

Bindings enable the boot to be attached to the ski. There are several types of bindings. Some have cables that go around the bottom of the boot, and others have a clamp that attaches the toe of the boot to the binding. For the beginner and recreational skier, generally the three-pin binding is used; it consists of three pins that are projected or inserted into the sole at the toe. A metal clamp (bale) is then clamped down to secure the boot to the ski. Most boots are norm-fitted; that is, they will fit many bindings. However, newer boots now fall under the new Nordic norm classification. In this binding system, the toe clip is narrower, and the soles of the boot are made to fit into a track that is part of the binding. Other systems, such as Solomon, have their own specifications for a narrow toe clip. Generally, the wider the toe attachment, the more stability a skier will have. It is best for the beginner to consult with a ski expert before buying any of the more sophisticated bindings.

BOOTS

Properly fitting boots are perhaps the key to successful cross-country skiing and should be the most important piece of gear you own. Boots should be compatible to your bindings, tried on with the type of socks you will be wearing, and flexible enough across the crease so that they do not cut off circulation to the toes or cut across the toes. The heel of the boot should be snug, there should be little side-to-side flexibility, and there should be plenty of room for the toes.

Boots should be made of a leather upper (shoe part) and an injection-molded or bonded plastic sole. Some boots are higher than others; generally, a skier with weaker ankles should consider a heavier and perhaps higher boot that gives greater support. For the beginner, a light touring boot with a norm-sized toe would be best. If they are properly taken care of, boots will last for years.

POLES

Poles are used to aid in propelling the skier forward or as a means of balance and support. The pole consists of a grip, strap, basket, and metal point that is slightly bent or angled to facilitate extraction from the snow. The poles can be made of a carbon fiber material, fiberglass, or aluminum. Because poles tend to take a lot of abuse, most skiers prefer fiberglass or aluminum.

Three key factors to consider when selecting a pair of poles are the length, the type of strap, and the size of the basket. To check for the proper length, as you stand on the floor with your boots on, the pole should fit snugly under your armpit. A pole that is too long or short will hinder your performance. The strap should be adjustable to allow you to make adjustments to the size of the gloves or mittens you wear. Baskets, which are generally made of plastic, should be of medium size. Large baskets are used for deep powdery snow, whereas smaller baskets are used by competitive racers.

CLOTHING

Cross-country skiing is a vigorous activity done under varying weather conditions; therefore, choosing the proper clothing is extremely important to the well-being of the skier. The type of clothing depends on the temperature outside, the distance you plan to travel, and the type of skiing you have planned. Many beginners tend to wear too much clothing and, as a result, become overheated, which leads to discomfort, wet clothes, and even hypothermia.

Experts recommend dressing in layers of loosely fitting clothing. Layering allows you to add or take off articles of clothing according to prevailing weather conditions. Basic points to remember when selecting suitable ski wear include the following:

1. Wear a nonmoisture-absorbent layer (polypropylene materials) next to your skin (long underwear and a pair of liner socks). This layer transfers moisture and perspiration out to the next layer of clothing.

2. Avoid fabrics that do not breathe because they tend to hold in moisture and heat. Water-repellent fabrics are preferable.

3. Outer garments should be of a nonabsorbent material. Occasionally you will fall and you do *not* want outer clothing that will pass moisture inside to your other garments.

4. Because heat is lost through your head, neck, and wrists, wear enough clothing to cover these critical areas.

5. Wear loose-fitting pants or pants of a stretch material that allows freedom of movement.

6. Wool is preferable to cotton because cotton absorbs moisture.

7. Wear wool mittens with down fill or light wool lining with a leather outer shell. Many skiers prefer gloves because they allow for better control in handling the poles.

8. Wear sunglasses with UV protection and a thin layer of sunblock to prevent damage to your eyes and skin.

Other accessories to consider include gaiters to keep the lower leg dry, a fanny pack to carry emergency materials, a light backpack to carry additional clothes, and an insulated vest.

Basic Skills

Before venturing out on the slopes, beginners should take a class or two that covers an orientation to skiing, the equipment, clothing, safety tips, conditioning for skiing, and basic techniques that can be taught indoors. Once that is covered, it is best to begin outdoors on flat surfaces to learn basic strides, then try gentle inclines to teach uphill and downhill techniques. If you are beginning on a surface that does not have preg-roomed tracks, have an experienced skier make tracks, or use a snowmobile to pack down the snow and make a trail. It is best to master the skills listed here before trying to cross-country ski on larger hills or more rugged terrain.

- Indoors—selecting and fitting equipment, how to dress, and safety
  - Basic conditioning and flexibility exercises
  - How to hold a pole
  - Getting up from a fall
  - Gliding
- Outdoors—on flat terrain
  - Getting up from a fall
  - Kick turn
  - Diagonal stride
  - Double poling
  - Double poling or stride
- Outdoors—gentle hillside, uphill
  - Diagonal stride
  - Side step
  - Traversing
  - Herringbone
- Outdoors—downhill
  - Straight running
  - Snow plow turn
  - Step turn
  - Traversing

Once these skills are mastered, the skier is ready to move on to touring on many prepared trails. Beginners should ask about the conditions on the trail and the type of terrain that they will encounter. Many state parks, if they rent equipment, will have someone at the facility that has the necessary information about trails for the beginning skier.

Web Sites

www.xcskiworld.com—features training and conditioning information, instruction for beginners and more advanced skiers, waxing techniques, where to cross-country ski, and a variety of links.

www.cross-countryski.com—offers not only information on cross-country skiing but also on snowshoeing. Directs user to various links: providing information about best shopping sites; choosing skis, gear, poles, boots, and clothing; waxing and ski care; other organizations; and more.

www.trailsource.com Trail Source—identifies over 400 trails in the United States and around the world, provides up-to-date information about snow conditions, and is also a source for hiking and mountain biking.

www.crosscountryskier.com *Cross-Country Ski* magazine—features articles concerning instruction, equipment, ski reports, and more.

Nature and Purpose

Climbing is one of the fastest growing sports in America.[1] Indoor climbing attempts to mimic the outdoor experience through the use of artificial structures. It is safer, the holds are more accessible, and many outdoor features are difficult to duplicate.[2] This popular activity of climbing has grown to where there are over 3,000 facilities worldwide.[3] These facilities include schools, colleges, clubs, malls, and specialized climbing gyms. The concept of artificial wall climbing was originated in 1964 in England when Don Robinson, a lecturer of Physical Education, created an artificial climbing surface on a wall. The first commercial wall was developed in Sheffield, England.[4] The continued growth has led to organized competition over the years. However, the competitive aspect of climbing dates back to 1760 when rock climbing was officially recognized as a sport.[5]

Indoor climbing appeals to all age groups and offers challenges for novice beginners through competitive professional climbers. As an activity, it is "fun, exciting, physically beneficial, mentally challenging, and socially enjoyable."[6] The physical benefits include muscle strength, muscle endurance, coordination, balance, and cardiovascular development. Additional benefits include the development of positive risk-taking, self-confidence, personal trust, courage, willpower, and creative problem solving. Indoor climbing is a legitimate educational activity that provides physical, mental, social, and emotional development opportunities for all.[7]

Equipment

The type of indoor climbing desired—horizontal or vertical—requires different equipment needs. Walls that are popular for beginners in an educational setting where the students move more horizontally than vertically require very little equipment. These walls are usually low (8 - 10 ft high) with a variety of attached holds and often equipped with an attached mat. The mat folds up when not in use and has a locking device at the top for protection and safety. The holds are either screw-on or bolt-on, have changeable location patterns, and are various sizes, shapes, and colors. The participant traverses the wall, which has various panel widths that address individual facility requirements.

Vertical wall climbing requires additional equipment. Rope, belay device, harness, helmet, and crash pads are considerations since vertical height of the wall becomes a safety factor. The rope is anchored and a belay device allows the belayer (instructor or assistant) to keep the rope tight and secure for a safe climbing experience. The climber wears a harness around his/her bottom and thighs, and it is attached to the rope. The harness fits snuggly to the climber and the belayer controls the tension on the rope for safety as the climber ascends. The rope is equipped with a carabiner and a grigri. The carabiner is a safety device used to attach the climber to the rope, and the grigri is a metal device that allows the rope to move only in one direction, acting as a break if the climber slips. Helmets provide additional safety.

Walls commonly are constructed of plywood, multiplex board, aluminum, or manufactured steel.[8] The surface is often covered with some textured, granular product to simulate a rock surface. As mentioned earlier, hand and foot holds are of different shapes and are adjustable. Commercial climbing wall companies provide an excellent resource for meeting specific wants and needs.

Basic Skills

Horizontal and vertical climbing involves upper body strength. Strong fingers, forearms, and shoulders specifically are important for success. Stretching and muscle development of these areas benefit climbing skill. Exercise programs targeting these muscle groups prior to and during a climbing program are important regardless of participant ability levels or course difficulty.

The finger grip and forearm muscles are the first muscles to fatigue, and when they are exhausted, climbing cannot continue. The shoulders compliment climbing moves during sideward and upward movements. They can improve resting point muscle relaxation and provide a synchronized smoothness during these movements.

The development of these primary muscle groups provides a foundation for the performance of sound climbing techniques. These techniques include the proper use of the upper body for arm, finger grip, back, and shoulders; the balance factors of feet, legs, body positioning, and center of gravity; the movement factors of static and dynamic positioning, speed, synchronization, and resting points; and factors involved in falling.

Mental preparation prior to climbing, especially vertically, is a skill one develops. Reading the route technique of visualizing the sequence of hand, foot, and body positions, plus possible resting points, aid in a more skilled, relaxed climb.[9]

STRENGTH AND ENDURANCE DEVELOPMENT

- Grip—Fingers and forearms have similar functions in climbing. The fingers simultaneously move together as one action in forearm exercises.
  - Thumb strength provides a sideways position on holds or rocks, and it provides the function needed for holding.
  - Use of a rubber ball or rubber ring involving "squeezing actions" strengthens the thumb, fingers, and forearm. Squeezing the fingers to meet the thumb strengthens the fingers and pressing the thumb toward the finger tips strengthens the thumb. Both actions strengthen the forearm.

- Forearm exercises may be directed toward strength and endurance.

  - A bar for such as a chin-up bar is beneficial. Hang by both hands without movement until fatigue and then dismount shaking the arms, wrists, and fingers for a few minutes. Mount again, repeat until fatigue, and perform several sets. Execute the same action hanging by just one arm.

  - Perform chin-ups on the bar with the palms and fingers forward. Avoid sway and relax the upper body at the bottom of the exercise. Repeat with a smooth action.

  - Hang from the bar with one arm, grab the wrist with the other hand, and perform a one-arm chin-up. Add light weights to the body for additional resistance for building strength.

  - Hanging by two hands, lift the legs to the side and hold that position. This benefits stomach and upper body strength.

  - Traverse a vertical wall for a continuous extended time without a break. Occasionally, lower one arm at a time and shake, but stress the continuous low stress gripping for the extended time.

  - Grasp a dumbbell with the fingers pointing either down, up, or sideways, and do repeated curls to a maximum of 10. Do three sets and increase weight as wrist strength develops.

  - Grasp a dumbbell with the fingers pointing up, relax the grip allowing the bar to roll down the palm to the fingertips, and then roll it back into the palm. Gradually increase the amount of time for the exercise.

CLIMBING TECHNIQUE

Development of strength and endurance of the foregoing muscle groups provides the foundation for climbing. The techniques are dependent upon that foundation.

- Upper body (finger grip, arms, back, and shoulders)
  - Grip—Too much tension in the grip tires the forearms and affects the synchronized smoothness of the climb, thereby degrading the performance. The purpose of the grip is to lightly contact the hold for keeping the body in place with the least amount of energy and for maintaining balance.
  - Arms, back, and shoulder—The purpose of the arms are for balance and to assist in shifting weight and not for holding weight. They also provide strength for movement through sequences quickly.[10] The back and shoulders should remain relaxed.
- Balance factors
  - Arms and feet—As previously mentioned, the arms are for balance. The foot position varies from an even stance to narrow or wide. The position of the hands, arms, and feet determine the center of body mass or center of gravity.
  - Center of gravity—Maintain a balanced center of gravity (forward/backward and left/right directions) as often as possible for they are key for making moves smooth and effortless. It is important to keep close to the wall with the knees pointed out with low body posture for balance. Awareness of good body balance helps to plan sequential hand and foot movement.
- Movement factors
  - Static climbing movement—It is the movement when body position is controlled by muscle movement and not by momentum. Have both hands and feet stabilized before moving the body. Move the limbs, shift the body weight (not both at the same time), and repeat the process. Use arms for balance and the legs for supporting the weight of the body. Keep the body motionless, move the hand, move the foot exactly and quietly over the center of balance, and repeat.
  - Dynamic climbing movement—The "dead point" is useful for dynamic climbing technique. It is the point at which the body changes directions vertically. It helps to develop a smooth and graceful technique. The movement uses momentum for making a move that is further than can be reached by a static movement. At the "dead point," the hand should be on the hold at the top of the reach, the upward direction has stopped, and the next grip on a hold is initiated before the weight begins to settle.
  - Movement speed—Dynamic movement technique uses momentum to get through a move more quickly. This saves upper body stress that is associated with dynamic vertical climbing. Static movement is slower and more deliberate for well-balanced centering, carefully using the legs for weight support and arms for holding the body in place.
  - Synchronized movement—The smooth, fluid, coordinated movement defines well developed technique. A conscious effort to avoid unnecessary movement aids in sequential movement control.
  - Rest—The ability to anticipate and utilize rest spots is an important technique. Not managing rest spots results in fatigue and loss of body control, often causing a fall. Read the route in advance and plan rest spots approximately every 10 feet, especially in vertical climbing.
  - Fall technique—It is inevitable that a fall will occur. Practicing falling techniques improves climbing confidence. Vertical wall climbing surfaces present different techniques for falling than the lower horizontal traverse wall. On the vertical wall, practice by having the belayer "lock off" the rope and then push off away from the wall,

letting the rope come tight catching you in mid-air. Keep your feet down and in front of you as you swing in to catch the wall as the rope tightens. Always make sure that the rope is clear of your gear, feet, and arms, and that it is not looped around anything

On a horizontal traverse wall, mats are located at the base, the wall is low (8 – 10 ft. high), and a safety foot position line is often identified at a low level. The main techniques are pushing away from the wall and absorbing the landing with a wide and low knee flexion. Avoid using the hands and arms to brake any falling action.

Web Sites

http://www.mcofs.org.uk/walls-history.asp—provides an extensive history of indoor climbing, categories of climbing goals, what to expect at an indoor climbing wall, and much more.

http://www.abc-of-rockclimbing.com/info/indoor-climbing.asp—extensive information on history, basics, techniques, training, etc.

SCUBA DIVING

Nature and Purpose

From early times, many divers yearned for the ability to stay underwater longer than the period of time they could hold their breath. Early attempts at providing a continuous air supply included diving from diving bells. A diving bell was essentially a large container, weighted upside down and open at the bottom. Air was trapped inside, and the diver would travel to and from the bell, getting a breath of air when necessary. The Industrial Revolution brought machines that could actually pump air through a hose down to a diver underwater. Extended dives were possible, but they were still limited to the length of the hose or distance the diver could swim from the bell. Divers longed to carry their air supply with them and swim freely for an extended period of time.

SCUBA, an acronym that stands for *self-contained underwater breathing apparatus,* was first invented by Jacques Cousteau in the late 1940s. This invention finally allowed divers the freedom to remain underwater for longer periods of time. Many divers had experimented with self-contained units, but Cousteau was the first to succeed in designing a demand regulator that would give a breath of air when the diver desired. Previous regulators produced a constant flow, therefore wasting a lot of air and limiting underwater time. From Cousteau's early design, equipment has evolved to today's easy-breathing, comfortable items that are worn by thousands enjoying the sport all over the world.

Anyone 12 years old and older may participate. Basic swim skills and comfort in the water are essential. Because of the extended time spent underwater and the breathing of compressed air in a higher-pressure environment, formal training is required to dive safely. Scuba dive stores require a certification card as proof of training before selling scuba gear or taking individuals on dive excursions. Courses in beginning scuba generally require a minimum of 32 hours of instruction. The best courses begin with skin diving, then progress to scuba. The course includes lecture instruction, work in the pool, and supervised scuba dives in the open water prior to certification.

Once certified, divers have a wide variety of choices of dive sites. From the warm, clear waters of the tropics, to the many inland freshwater lakes, rivers, and quarries, to the cold waters under the polar icecaps—divers have explored them all. These explorations are safely limited to depths of 100 feet. Beyond those limits, different equipment and a higher level of training are required.

Equipment

Basic equipment needed by the scuba diver includes a mask, snorkel, wet suit, fins, and scuba apparatus. Well-fitted equipment is essential for the diver's safety and enjoyment. It is best to consult an expert at a dive shop or an experienced diver before obtaining new equipment. The scuba unit and wet suit are described here. A description of fins and mask is included in the Skin Diving section.

THE SCUBA UNIT

The scuba unit itself consists of multiple pieces of equipment assembled and worn by the diver. Tanks, or air cylinders made of steel or aluminum, hold the supply of compressed air. A single hose with a two-stage regulator attached to the tank transports air from the tank to the diver's mouthpiece. On a separate hose attached to the regulator is a gauge indicating the amount of air in the tank at all times. Additional gauges may be added to indicate depth and direction. The tank is strapped into the buoyancy compensator (flotation vest). The scuba unit is worn with the skin-diving equipment of mask, snorkel, fins, and any necessary thermal clothing.

Extensive instruction occurs in the classroom and pool concerning operation, selection, assembly, and use of this equipment underwater. The regulator and tank are the specific equipment items that can be purchased only with proof of certification. Use of this equipment without proper instruction and understanding can result in injury.

WET SUIT

A wet suit, made of neoprene, is thermal clothing worn in the water to slow heat loss from the body. Wet suits are available in a variety of thicknesses and designs. A full body suit keeps the scuba diver comfortably warm in cold water.

Basic Skills

Since Cousteau's invention of scuba, the sport has grown from relative obscurity to one that many people enjoy worldwide. Instruction is affordable, even in inland areas of the country far from the ocean. Proper instruction and regular practice reduce risk and eliminate most problems. Scuba allows the diver to enjoy another dimension of the world, one that most people will never see firsthand. When taking a scuba class, the prospective diver should learn the following skills:

- Identification, selection, and operation of scuba equipment
- Diving physics, physiology, and medical aspects of diving
- Environmental factors (diving procedures, safety considerations, ecological concerns, interaction with marine life)
- Diver first aid and rescue
- Entry-level swim test and fitness swims
- Use of mask, fins, snorkel, and flotation vest
- Assembly and use of scuba equipment underwater
- Safety techniques (buddy system, sharing air, rescue techniques)
- Required proficiency tests (in pool to demonstrate comfort and proficiency in use of skills and equipment)
- Open water dives (to test proficiency and skills)

SKIN DIVING

Nature and Purpose

Skin diving is an aquatic sport that people of all ages can enjoy. Skin diving, by definition, is primarily a combination of floating and swimming on the surface of the water while wearing a mask, snorkel, and fins. However, the skin diver also surface dives and swims under the water for a period of time that the breath can be comfortably held. By strict definition, the snorkeler wears the same equipment but stays on the surface of the water enjoying the sights below. Often the two terms are used interchangeably to mean the same sport.

The risk of injury is small in this sport. Because it is an activity involving water, the obvious precautions normally taken with any aquatic sport should be followed. Good swimming skills and comfort in the water are obvious prerequisites to participating in this sport. For optimal safety, skin divers should participate in small groups or, at a minimum, always with a buddy. Participants can take formal classes to learn techniques and procedures. However, the "water-oriented" person can easily learn to use the equipment and enjoy the sport with a little help from a friend or by reading one of the skin diving manuals on the market. Many of the swim strokes, kicks, and surface dives used in skin diving will have already been learned in the process of learning to swim. A little extra time is needed to learn to use the equipment that allows one to see, breathe, and swim easily while skin diving.

Skin diving has existed as long as people have been living around water. Skin divers collected food and other useful items from the sea. Written records have been discovered describing military and commercial salvage of sunken shipwrecks by skin divers as far back as 5,000 years. These activities usually occurred in coastal waters, in depths less than 100 feet. Divers with long breath-hold capability were prized by commercial salvage operations. Today, technology has provided better ways to explore, salvage, and conduct undersea operations. After World War II, Cousteau and his colleagues began to pursue skin diving for exploration and the hunting of fish with spear guns. It was Cousteau's love of this pursuit that led to his eventual development of scuba. Today, skin diving is primarily pursued for fun and recreation.

Vacationers to warmer climates and island resorts include skin diving on their list of leisure activities. Entire families can participate, enjoying the fish, colors, shapes, and other visual thrills of the coral reefs that surround many islands in tropical seas. In temperate climates, when the water becomes warm during the summer months, skin divers can learn about, explore, and enjoy the creatures and plants found in many inland freshwater lakes and quarries.

For those who wish to go on to the sport of scuba, skin diving is also an important first step. Scuba courses should always begin with lessons in skin diving.

Equipment

Skin diving is a relatively inexpensive activity. Initial outlay for a good mask, fins, and snorkel is necessary. A wet suit, which is optional for most people, is not really needed unless the diver is planning to dive in colder waters. Equipment can be purchased from a retail dive shop. For those who wish to try the sport, rentals are also available through dive shops. As with all activities, well-fitted equipment is a key to maximizing the enjoyment of the activity. It is best to consult an expert before buying equipment.

THE MASK

The mask used for skin diving is the same piece of equipment used in the sport of scuba. The first masks, or eye coverings, were goggles made of polished tortoise shell. These early goggles, like today's masks, restored the pocket of air in front of the eyes, thus enabling the skin diver to see clearly underwater. Early divers discovered, however, that although the tortoise shell goggles enabled them to see underwater, everything was out of focus.

Today's masks are made of long-lasting silicone. The faceplate should always be of tempered glass for optimal safety. The nose remains inside the mask. Exhaling air into the mask through the nose is important to prevent a malady called *mask squeeze*. Squeezes are injuries that result from the increased pressure exerted by the water on the diver's body as he swims to depth. Avoiding these problems is easy and covered in any text or course on skin diving.

Masks come in a variety of sizes, colors, and price ranges. The most important consideration in selecting a mask is the fit on the face. To check for proper fit, place the mask on the face, and then inhale through the nose. No air should leak in around the seal during the inhalation. A proper seal will ensure a minimum of water leakage when the mask is worn in the water.

THE SNORKEL

The snorkel is simply a breathing tube. It allows one to comfortably rest the face in the water while skin diving and eliminates the need to continually lift the head out of the water to take a breath. The J-shaped tube comes in a variety of designs, colors, and price ranges; however, the length is critical. Twelve to 15 inches is the maximum length for ease of breathing. Snorkels may be continuous tubes or have one-way drains called *purge valves* that allow for easier clearing of water. The snorkel is attached to the left side of the mask strap by a device called the *snorkel keeper*.

FINS AND OTHER EQUIPMENT

The fins increase the surface area of the foot for easier swimming. Fins come in two basic designs: full-foot, or bare-foot, fins; and open-heel fins. The full-foot fin is popular with skin divers. They are lightweight, cheaper in price, and easier to transport. Open-heel fins are designed to be worn with boots. The boots keep the feet warm and protect them when walking over rough or rocky shorelines. Open-heel fins are generally more costly and heavier, but they are more durable. They are popular among scuba divers but are certainly usable for both sports.

A properly fitting mask, snorkel, and fins are the minimum pieces of equipment needed to comfortably and safely enjoy skin diving. Additional equipment is sometimes used, depending on the circumstances. Flotation vests, also called buoyancy compensators, may be used by skin divers. Commercial boat charters taking skin divers on an excursion to open water usually require vests. The skilled and comfortable skin diver may elect not to wear a flotation vest but should put one on a friend who is skin diving for the first time. Consider the skill level and water comfort of others in determining the use of this item.

Basic Skills

Many YMCAs include skin-diving technique as part of the progressive swim lessons they teach. Any dive shop or organization that teaches scuba will also be able to train people to enjoy skin diving. The YMCA of the USA Scuba Program offers courses in skin diving for all ages. With minimal instruction and a reasonable level of water comfort, the entire family can enjoy skin diving. A prospective skin diver should expect to demonstrate proficiency in the following skills:

- Selection of properly fitting mask, snorkel, and fins
- Use of equipment in a pool or in shallow, open water
- Adjusting and sealing the mask
- Clearing water from the mask
- Clearing the snorkel—blast technique and displacement clearing
- Use of fins—the flutter kick, frog kick, and dolphin kick
- Water entries—standing and sitting
- Exit from water—on boat, on shore
- Surface dives (foot-first, head-first)
- Entry to surface—arm above head
- Safety considerations—buddy system, skin protection, temperature
- Equalizing pressure in ears
- Basic water physics
- Reacting to aquatic life, for example, fish, jellyfish

Web Sites

www.leaird-scuba.com—offers courses in skin and scuba diving, information on equipment sales, and skin and scuba diving sites in central Indiana.

www.padi.com Professional Association of Diving Instructors—offers information about courses to take, articles, environmental news, products, places to travel, and more.

www.naui.org National Association of Underwater Instructors—offers information about scuba and snorkeling, programs offered, articles and essays on all aspects of diving, and more.

SKATEBOARDING

Nature and Purpose

Skateboarding, enjoyed by more than 9 million participants, is a high-risk activity that is similar to surfing and snowboarding. For the participant using safety equipment and possessing good balance and body control, it provides a thrilling and exhilarating ongoing challenge.

Much has been said in recent years about the risk involved in skateboarding. However, a review of such other activities as inline skating, gymnastics, football, basketball, cycling, and roller skating shows that skateboarding is as safe, if not safer than, these other activities. The keys to minimizing the risk are proper instruction, body control, riding on smooth surfaces or approved areas, safety equipment, practice, and good judgment.

Skateboarding first appeared in the early 1900s, when children attached roller skate wheels to a board and played on the streets and sidewalks. The sport reached greater popularity in the 1950s, when surfers looked for a way to tie their love for surfing to the streets. As the years progressed, the sport went through many highs and lows because of the public's perception of the reckless nature of some participants, the liability involved, insurance issues, and the development of materials for wheels and the board that would be durable and safe. Skateboarding began on streets and sidewalks but made its way to pools, half pipes, and ramps. Skate parks were once popular, then lost popularity, but now appear to be making a comeback.[1]

California has long been a leading state in the development of skate parks. The International Association of Skateboard Companies has encouraged other states to follow California's example in constructing safe facilities.[2]

Equipment

THE SKATEBOARD

The skateboard consists of four primary parts: (1) the deck, on which the rider stands; (2) the trucks, which are the front and rear axle assemblies that are attached to the deck and hold the wheels; (3) the wheels, which are made of polyurethane; and (4) the bearings, which make the wheels go around.

The board is generally 28 to 34 inches long. The deck is concave, curved up at either end to perform specific tricks. Boards are made of thin layers of maple glued together to make a strong, durable surface. The deck is generally covered with a grip tape (with a sandpaper-like texture) that helps the rider grip the board with the feet.

The trucks should be made of metal. Anything less should be avoided. Good trucks are adjustable to allow the rider to steer and make quicker turns. The trucks are also the landing gear; the surface of the axle allows the rider to execute a skill called grinding.

The wheels, made of polyurethane, can be soft for a comfortable, smoother ride, or hard for a fast ride. The softer wheel tends to wear out faster but grips the surface better. The diameter of the wheels range from 39 to 66 millimeters.

Bearings make the board go faster or more slowly, depending on the bearing rating. A lower rating (slower ride) is best for a beginning rider.

SAFETY EQUIPMENT

Although the board is important for performance, there are other types of equipment that must be worn to minimize the risk of serious injury. The pieces of equipment that are essential for the beginning skateboarder include (1) a well-fitted helmet with a chinstrap to help prevent head injuries; (2) wrist guards, which help prevent broken bones; (3) knee-pads with a plastic cover, which slide over the surface and help disperse the impact when the skater falls; (4) elbow pads, which prevent broken bones, bruises, and scrapes; and (5) gloves, which also help prevent cuts and bruises.

Basic Skills

Experts concur that the first step to successfully negotiating the skateboard is to learn basic movements with the rider on the ground. Among the skills the beginner can expect to learn are the following:[3]

- Standing on the board—right foot or left foot forward
- Moving the board forward—pushing with one foot
- Stopping
- Turning
- Gliding—down a gradual hill
- Kickturn—frontside and backside
- Carving
- Ollies
- Dropping in
- Fakies

There are many other tricks that the rider can learn when he becomes more comfortable and in better control on the skateboard. Many of these are completed in the air and in combinations, as seen in some of the skateboard events on television. But even for beginners, a good board, well-fitting safety equipment, practice, and a safe place to skate with smooth surfaces can lead to a challenging and exciting activity.

Web Sites

http://skateboard.about.com—offers useful information for the beginner and beyond; also includes health and safety information, references, hints for maintenance, and much more.

www.skateboarddirectory.com—offers links to other skateboard sites, directs the reader to references, and contains information on snowboarding, BMX (bicycle motocross), and more.

www.skateboarding.com *Skateboarding* magazine—offers information on live skateboarding events, news, trick tips, skate parks, a chat room, and more.

www.spausa.org Skatepark Association of America—includes a downloadable guide on how to get a park in your community; also supports the skate park industry.

www.how2skate.com/tricktips.htm—provides a wide video assortment of tricks and how to build ramps.

SNOWBOARDING

Nature and Purpose

Snowboarding can be enjoyed not only by boys and girls but also by men and women of all ages. It requires a moderate degree of physical fitness, average coordination, and the ability to maintain balance while moving. Generally, skateboarders and skiers pick up snowboarding quite easily. The movements and some of the skills in the former two activities are also used in snowboarding. Snowboarding is easy to learn, provides good physical activity, and is relatively safe; moreover, the equipment is easy to use and less expensive than skiing equipment.[1]

The sport became popular in the late 1980s and since then has grown throughout the world. For many people, snowboarding either complements or provides a viable alternative to skiing. As late as the mid-1980s, most areas did not allow snowboarding; however, today virtually every ski area accommodates it. A good deal of its popularity has resulted from television exposure and its inclusion as an Olympic sport.[2]

Equipment

Snowboarding requires some basic equipment, including a snowboard, bindings, boots, waterproof and windproof apparel, goggles or sunglasses, padded gloves, kneepads, a leash to keep the board with you if you fall, and a hat or, preferably, a helmet. Wrist guards, similar to those used in skateboarding, can help prevent sprains or broken bones.

Beginners trying this sport should rent equipment first and then purchase from a shop that specializes in snowboard equipment. There are variations in the equipment. Selection depends on the person's sex, ability (beginner or advanced), and the intended use or type of snowboarding the person wishes to do. There are four styles of snowboarding: (1) freestyle, (2) free riding, (3) Alpine, and (4) racing. Each style generally requires a different board, boot, and binding. So it is important that beginners consult an expert and be fitted for the snowboard, boots, and bindings best suited to their ability.

THE SNOWBOARD

Snowboards come in different lengths, widths, flexes, and shapes. A snowboard consists of layers of laminated materials; the inner core is usually laminated wood or foam, and the outer layers are made of a variety of durable plastics. The anatomy of a snowboard can best be described as having the following parts: (1) a tip and a tail, whose curvature and height depends on the type of snowboarding the person wishes to do (freestyle, free riding, Alpine, racing); (2) a base surface made out of a durable polyethylene layer to withstand the ever-changing slope surface conditions; (3) the deck (top surface),

where the bindings are mounted; (4) a plastic or rubber stomp pad, mounted between the two bindings, where the back foot is placed when it is not in the binding; and (5) steel edges built into the board, which run along the bottom edges of the board and enable the skier to turn and carve. The cost of a snowboard ranges from $100 to $500. The size ranges from 130 to 175 centimeters.[3]

When selecting a board, the snowboarder can choose from among a variety of lengths and widths; some boards will be more flexible, some will have greater camber, some will be stiffer, and some will be designed specifically for women. Beginners should look for a board that is wider and has a softer flex.

BINDINGS

Bindings are mounted on the deck of the snowboard, generally at an angle. The angle depends on the type of snowboarding the person wishes to do. There are three kinds of bindings: (1) strap bindings (soft) have two straps that secure the boot, along with a high plastic back that extends up over the ankles and lower calves, which enables the snowboarder to control the board for turning and other maneuvers; (2) step-in bindings allow the snowboarder to step into the binding without worrying about straps; and (3) the plate binding, which secures the boot to the board through the use of bails and a snap-down lever. The plate binding is generally used for a hard boot, which is used by racers or Alpine boarders.[4]

BOOTS

As with skiing, one of the most important pieces of equipment is a boot that keeps the feet warm, dry, secure, and comfortable throughout the day. There are three types of boots: (1) Soft boots have an inner bladder that keeps the feet warm, dry, and comfortable. The soft outer boot allows flexibility and movement of the ankle. Soft boots are generally used by freestyle snowboarders and those who want comfort while snowboarding. (2) Hard boots have a sturdy inner boot but a stiff outer boot that increases edge control and allows the board to respond to the body as it leans into the heelside or toeside edges of the snowboard. Alpine racers use this type of boot. (3) Hybrid step-in boots generally have a hard sole and a flexible outer boot. A snowboarder wanting both flexibility and stiffness uses hybrid boots. Boots range in cost from $50 to $300.[5]

OTHER EQUIPMENT

Aside from water-repellent and windproof clothing, the snowboarder should have (1) a leash that attaches around the forward leg and to the binding and prevents a board from flying down the hill if the rider should come off; (2) sturdy, well-padded waterproof gloves, because the snowboarder tends to continually touch the ground; (3) a hat, preferably a helmet, to keep the head warm and protect against head injuries; (4) goggles or UV-protected sunglasses to protect the eyes; (5) kneepads to protect the knees (some pants have kneepads sewn in); and (6) wrist guards, much like those used by skateboarders to help prevent wrist injuries. Clothing should be comfortable. Avoid cotton clothing, such as jeans, because it retains moisture and can make for a long, cold day. Layering is a concept that the snowboarder should understand. For a discussion of layering, refer to Cross-Country Skiing.

Basic Skills

Many of the tricks used in freestyle snowboarding are similar in name and execution to those in skateboarding. This listing includes the basic skills needed to begin this exciting activity. Discussions of other, more advanced skills can be found in the sources listed in the References and Further References section and on the Web sites of interest.[6, 7]

- Etiquette
- Parts of the snowboard
- How to buckle up
- Balance
- Stance—regular or goofy
- Falling down and standing up
- Getting on and off ski lifts
- Walking
- Skating
- Edging
- Steering and pivoting
- Straight glide
- Toeside and heelside turns
- Skidded turns
- Traversing
- Linked skidded turns
- Carving

Snowboarding can provide fun-filled challenges for almost anyone. The skills that can be performed and the tricks executed are directly related to the amount of time spent practicing. Whether one wants the rush of speeding down a mountain, the peace and rhythm that comes with linking a series of turns together in deep-powder snow, or the daring of executing 360s or ollies, snowboarding can be a viable option.

Web Sites

http://snowboarding.about.com—offers useful information for the beginner; also includes articles of interest, tips, tricks, information about protective gear, and more.

www.usasa.org United States of America Snowboard Association (USASA)—offers many links, information for the snowboarder, events, history of the USASA, and more.

www.heckler.com *Heckler Magazine*—offers snowboarders and skateboarders articles, news, product reviews, ramp plans, and more.

SNOWSHOEING

Nature and Purpose

It's been said that if you can walk, then you can snowshoe. In some respects this is true because the learning curve for this activity is shorter than most similar activities. People have been snowshoeing for centuries. In North America, early origins can be traced to American Indians, who used snowshoes to travel from place to place and in some instances to hunt during the winter months. Although early snowshoeing was relegated to transportation purposes, the 1700s saw it introduced as a sport. The military, particularly in Canada, used snowshoeing as a form of training.[1] As snowshoeing became popular in Canada in the 1800s, many Canadian clubs were formed and competitions were held in a variety of activities, many of which tested competitors' physical fitness.[2] Today, snowshoeing is a popular activity in parts of the world that have snow. In North America, clubs sponsor races and other activities involving snowshoes.

Like many sporting activities, snowshoeing has evolved, and snowshoe technology has improved in the past 15 years. In contrast to other winter activities, snowshoeing is relatively inexpensive; it can be practiced on all types of snow and terrain; there is equipment to fit all ages; you do not need special clothing or in most instances special gear; and, most of all, it is easy to learn. As a physical education activity, it helps increase physical fitness, it can be integrated with a curriculum that might include camping and hiking during winter months, and it takes relatively little time to learn. In some respects, the beginner can attack steeper and more rugged terrain on snowshoes than on cross-country skis. It has the added benefit of being a good low-impact aerobic activity that can significantly add to a person's cardiovascular fitness throughout the winter months.

Equipment

THE SNOWSHOE

Originally, snowshoes were often cumbersome, wooden-framed devices that were strung with animal gut and came in a variety of shapes and types: Yukon, Ojibwa, Beavertail, Bearpaw, and Western. Although the showshoeing purist would like the natural look of these snowshoes, they require continual maintenance.[3] Newer models are made of aluminum frames with a synthetic decking designed to help you float across the snow. In addition, snowshoes have a binding to secure your boots to the snowshoe, a toe hole to allow your boots to move freely up and down, and some type of traction device that allows you to grip the snow or gain traction when conditions are hard packed or icy.

In selecting a snowshoe, ask yourself three questions: (1) What do you intend to do most of the time with the snowshoes (i.e., touring, hiking, competition, backcountry snowshoeing, walking on relatively flat terrain, fitness workout); (2) how much do you weigh; and (3) how much do you want to spend?[4]

For the recreational participant, most entry-level models are adequate. The bindings should be easy to adjust, and the traction system should be designed for moderate to rolling terrain. Most bindings consist of nylon straps that go around your boot, securing the snowshoe to your foot. Bindings may be attached by metal rods or to the deck by rivets or screws.

The frame should be made with aluminum tubing with a cold-resistant synthetic deck (perhaps of rubber or a plastic-like material). The bindings on most recreational models pivot at the point they are attached to the deck—under the balls of the feet. For people who wish to engage in a more rugged form of snowshoeing, the traction system (crampons or cleats) on the snowshoe will be attached beneath the front of the binding and beneath at the heel.

The size of the snowshoe is determined by your weight and the weight of the pack that you might be carrying most of the time. A heavier person generally requires larger snowshoes than a smaller person. Larger snowshoes are generally required in light, fluffy snow conditions, where an increased deck surface helps to increase the ability to float over the surface while walking. If you wish to use snowshoeing as a fitness activity, then smaller snowshoes would be easier to maneuver.

Certainly the cost of snowshoes is an important part of determining which snowshoes to buy. Snowshoes with aluminum frames cost more than snowshoes with wooden frames; however, they are stronger, are easier to maintain, are more efficient in fluffier snow (provide for increased flotation because of a solid deck), and will last longer. The important thing is to pick the pair that fits you best and is best suited to how you will be using them.

BOOTS

One advantage of snowshoeing is that you can wear boots that you use for hiking, backpacking, climbing, or walking. Boots should offer ample support, particularly if you intend to be out for longer periods of time. Generally snowshoes that are designed for workout purposes are best used with running shoes or cross-training shoes.

CLOTHING

See the section on cross-country skiing for suggestions about what to wear when snowshoeing. Layering is the best practice to employ; the innermost layer should be a material that can pass moisture and heat outward from the body to the next layer of clothing.

OTHER EQUIPMENT

Gaiters keep the lower leg warm and dry and also protect the ankles and feet from underbrush that might be encountered on a trail. Adjustable ski poles or regular ski poles with a smaller basket will aid in hiking, maintaining balance, and even during a workout. The smaller basket will be least likely to get caught in underbrush. Also consider adjustable poles; these can be helpful when you encounter hillsides because a standard pole may get bound up in the uphill side of a slope.

Basic Skills

Before going out to snowshoe, it is best to gain some basic knowledge in a classroom setting. Some skills, such as getting up from a fall, can be taught inside. In addition, begin a conditioning and stretching program. Among the skills the beginner can expect to learn are the following:

- Inside—classroom and gymnasium floor
  - Conditioning—aerobic activity and stretching
  - How to get up from a fall
  - Snowshoeing safety considerations
- Equipment
  - How to select a snowshoe
  - How to select boots and poles
  - Clothes for snowshoeing—layering concept
- Outdoors
  - Walking
  - Kick turn
  - Getting up from a fall
  - Using poles
  - Climbing up a hillside
  - Descending a hillside
  - Traversing a hillside
  - Breaking a trail
  - Stepping over objects in the snow

Web Sites

www.backpacking.net/winter—offers information about snowshoeing, including techniques, equipment, tips, fitness, and more.

www.tubbssnowshoes.com—is the definitive source for snowshoe trails around the world for all abilities.

www.snowshoeracing.com US Snowshoe Association—provides information on snowshoe racing, race events, general links, and links to worldwide snowshoe organizations.

www.rei.com REI—offers valuable information about selecting snowshoes, as well as snowboarding and cross-country skiing; also includes valuable tips on equipment and clothing for all winter activities.

REFERENCES AND FURTHER REFERENCES

Chapter 1

1. National Association for Sport and Physical Education (NASPE). *Moving into the Future: National Standards for Physical Education*, 2nd ed. Reston, VA: NASPE, 2004.

2. Ibid.

3. Cooper Institute for Aerobic Research. *FITNESSGRAM Test Administration Manual*, 2nd ed. Champaign, IL: Human Kinetics Press, 1999.

4. www.aahperd.org/publications.

5. Strand, B., and Wilson, P. *Assessing Sports Skills*. Champaign, IL: Human Kinetics, 1993.

6. NASPE. *Moving into the Future*.

7. http://www.iste.org/docs/pdfs/nets-s-standards.pdf?sfvrsn=2 (accessed September 26, 2012).

8. NASPE. *Moving into the Future*.

9. Buck, M., and McManama, J. Improving fitness and skill concurrently: Can it be done? Presentation at the 1995 ICHPERSD World Congress, Gainesville, FL, 1995.

10. www.ChooseMyPlate.gov (accessed July 21, 2012).

Further References
MECHANICAL ASPECTS

Adrian, M., and Cooper, J. *The Biomechanics of Human Movement*. Indianapolis: Benchmark Press, 1989.

Carr, G. *Mechanics of Sport*. Champaign, IL: Human Kinetics, 1997.

Enoka, R. *Neuromechanical Basis of Kinesiology*. Champaign, IL: Human Kinetics, 1988.

Gowitzke, B., and Milner, M. *Scientific Bases of Human Movement*, 3rd ed. Baltimore: Williams and Wilkins, 1984.

Hay, J. *The Biomechanics of Sports Techniques*, 3rd ed. Englewood Cliffs, NJ: Prentice Hall, 1985.

Hay, J., and Reid, J. *Anatomy, Mechanics and Human Motion*, 2nd ed. Englewood Cliffs, NJ: Prentice Hall, 1988.

Kreighbaum, E., and Barthels, K. *Biomechanics*, 4th ed. Needham Heights, MA: Allyn & Bacon, 1996.

Rasch, P. *Kinesiology and Applied Anatomy*, 7th ed. Philadelphia: Lea and Febiger, 1989.

PSYCHOLOGICAL ASPECTS

Anshel, M. *Sport Psychology: From Theory to Practice*. Scottsdale, AZ: Gorsuch Scarisbrick, 1990.

Cox, R. *Sport Psychology: Concepts and Applications*, 3rd ed. Madison: Brown & Benchmark, 1994.

Kremer, J., and Scully, D. *Psychology in Sport*. Bristol, PA: Taylor & Francis, 1994.

LeUnes, A., and Nation, J. *Sport Psychology: An Introduction*. Chicago: Nelson-Hall, 1989.

Murphy, S. (ed.). *Sport Psychology Interventions*. Champaign, IL: Human Kinetics, 1995.

Russell, G. *The Social Psychology of Sport*. New York: Springer-Verlag, 1993.

Suinn, R. *Seven Steps to Peak Performance*. Toronto: Hans Huber Publishers, 1986.

Williams, J. (ed.). *Applied Sport Psychology: Personal Growth to Peak Performance*. Mountain View: Mayfield, 1993.

The reader may want to consult any one of the many introductory psychology textbooks that address the basic psychological principles we have outlined.

PERIODICALS

Journals that particularly emphasize the relationship between psychology and physical activity include the following: *Journal of Sport and Exercise Psychology, Journal of Teaching in Physical Education, Journal of Applied Psychology, The Sport Psychologist, Research Quarterly*, and *Journal of Motor Behavior*. Instructors especially interested in working with students with disabilities or handicaps will want to look at *Adapted Physical Activity Quarterly* and *Palaestra*.

Chapter 2

1. American Alliance for Health, Physical Education, Recreation and Dance (AAHPERD). *AAHPERD Health-Related Physical Fitness Test Manual*. Washington, DC: AAHPERD, 1980.

2. American Alliance for Health, Physical Education, Recreation and Dance (AAHPERD). *AAHPERD Physical Best Manual*. Reston, VA: AAHPERD, 1988.

3. Ross, J. G., and Pate, R. R. The National Children and Youth Fitness Study II: A Summary of Findings. *Journal of Physical Education, Recreation and Dance*, Nov./Dec.: 66–70, 1987.

4. Gortmaker, S. L. et al. Increasing Pediatric Obesity in the United States. *American Journal of Disabled Children*, 141:535–540, 1987.

5. American College of Sports Medicine. Opinion Statement on Physical Fitness in Children and Youth. *Medicine and Science in Sports and Exercise*, 20:422–423, 1988.

6. American Heart Association. Statement on Exercise. *Circulation*, 86:340–344, 1992.

7. US Department of Health and Human Services. *Physical Activity and Health: A Report of the Surgeon General*. Atlanta: US Department of Health and Human Services, Centers for Disease Control and Prevention, National Center for Chronic Disease Prevention and Health Promotion, 2012.

8. www.healthypeople.gov/2020/topicsobjectives2020 (accessed July 24, 2012).

9. Centers for Disease Control and Prevention (CDC) and National Center for Health Statistics. Physical Inactivity. *Morbidity and Mortality Weekly Report*, 53, no. 55–2, 2004.

10. Center for Disease Control and Prevention (CDC) and National Center for Health Statistics. Physical Activity. 2012. http://www.healthypeople.gov/2020/topicsobjectives2020/objectiveslist.aspx?topicId=33 (accessed September 29, 2012).

11. National Center for Health Statistics. Prevalence of Overweight and Obesity Among Adults: United States, 1999–2002. www.cdc.gov/nchs/products/pubs/pupd/hestats/overwght99.htm.

12. Ogdin, C. L., Flegal, K. M., Carroll, M. D. and Johnson, C. L. Prevalence and Trends in Overweight Among U.S. Children and Adolescents, 1999–2000. *Journal of the American Medical Association*, 288:1728–1732, 2002.

13. Center for Disease Control and Prevention (CDC) and National Center for Health Statistics. Overweight and Obesity. www.cdc.gov/obesity/data/childhood.html (accessed September 29, 2012).

14. Miller, D. K., and Allen, T. E. *Fitness: A Lifetime Commitment*, 4th ed. New York: Macmillan Publishing Co., 1990, p. 3.

15. American Heart Association. Statement on Exercise. *Circulation*, 86:340–344, 1992.

16. www.cdc.gov/physicalactivity/everyone/health (accessed July 24, 2012).

17. Miller, A. J., Grais, I. M., Winslow, E., and Kaminsky, L. A. The Definition of Physical Fitness. *Journal of Sports Medicine and Physical Fitness*, 31:639–640, 1991.

18. Blair, S. N. et al. Physical Fitness and All-Cause Mortality: A Prospective Study of Healthy Men and Women. *Journal of the American Medical Association*, 262:2395–2401, 1989.

19. Blair, S. N. et al. Changes in Physical Fitness and All-Cause Mortality. *Journal of the American Medical Association*, 273:1093–1098, 1995.

20. US Department of Health and Human Services. *Physical Activity and Health: A Report of the Surgeon General.*

21. Kaminsky, L. A., Whaley, M. H., Miller, C. R., and Getchell, L. H. Vigorous Exercise Program Participation Associated with Reduced Cardiac Morbidity in Men. *Medicine and Science in Sports and Exercise,* 26:218, 1994.

22. Morris, J. N. et al. Exercise in Leisure-time: Coronary Attack and Death Rates. *British Heart Journal,* 63:325–334, 1990.

23. Lee, I. M., Hsieh, C. C. and Paffenbarger, R. S. Exercise Intensity and Longevity in Men. *Journal of the American Medical Association,* 273:1179–1184, 1995.

24. http://sportsillustrated.cnn.com/vault/article/magazine/MAG1134750/2/index.htm (accessed September 29, 2012).

25. American Heart Association and American College of Sports Medicine. Joint Position Statement: Recommendations for Cardiovascular Screening, Staffing, and Emergency Policies of Health/Fitness Facilities. *Medicine and Science in Sports and Exercise,* 30:1009–1018, 1998.

26. American College of Sports Medicine. *Guidelines for Exercise Testing and Prescription.* 7th ed. Baltimore: Lippincott, Williams & Wilkins, 2005.

27. American College of Sports Medicine. Position Stand: The Recommended Quantity and Quality of Exercise for Developing Cardiorespiratory and Muscular Fitness, and Flexibility in Healthy Adults. *Medicine and Science in Sports and Exercise,* 30:975–991, 1998.

28. Whaley, M. H., Kaminsky, L. A., Dwyer, G. B., Getchell, L. H. and Norton, J. A. Predictors of Over- and Under-achievement of Age-predicted Maximal Heart Rate. *Medicine and Science in Sports and Exercise,* 24:1173–1179, 1992.

29. American College of Sports Medicine. Position Stand: The Recommended Quantity and Quality of Exercise for Developing Cardiorespiratory and Muscular Fitness, and Flexibility in Healthy Adults. *Medicine and Science in Sports and Exercise.* 30:975–991, 1998.

30. Getchell, B. *The Fitness Book.* Indianapolis, IN: Benchmark Press, 1987.

31. For more information on designing interval training workouts, see E. L. Fox, *Sports Physiology.* New York: CBS College Publishing, 1984, pp. 378–380.

32. Wallace, A. G. Fitness, Health, and Longevity—A Question of Cause and Effect. *Inside Track,* 583, 1986.

33. Cooper Institute for Aerobic Research. *FITNESSGRAM Test Administration Manual,* 2nd ed. Champaign, IL: Human Kinetics, 1999.

34. Lacey, A., and Hastad, D. *Measurement and Evaluation in Physical Education and Exercise Science,* 4th ed. San Francisco: Benjamin Cummings, 2003.

35. Powers, S., and Dodd, S. *Total Fitness and Wellness,* 5th ed. San Francisco: Benjamin Cummings, 2009.

36. Robbins, G., Powers, D., and Burgess, S. *A Wellness Way of Life,* 4th ed. New York: McGraw-Hill, 1999.

Further References

Baechle, T., and Earl, R. (eds.). *Essentials of Strength Training and Conditioning: National Strength and Conditioning Assoc,* 2nd ed. Champaign, IL: Human Kinetics, 2000.

Brown, K., Thomas, D., and Kotecki, D. *Physical Activity and Health: An Interactive Approach.* Sudbury, MA: Jones and Bartlett, 2002.

Brubaker, P., Kaminsky, L., and Whaley, M. *Prevention and Rehabilitation of Coronary Artery Disease.* Champaign, IL: Human Kinetics, 2001.

Corbin, C., Welk, G., Corbin, W., and Welk, K. *Concepts of Physical Education: Active Lifestyles for Wellness,* 15th ed. New York: McGraw-Hill, 2008.

Davis, R. N. *Inclusion Through Sports.* Champaign, IL: Human Kinetics, 2002.

Fahey, T., Insel, P., and Roth, W. *Fit & Well: Core Concepts and Labs in Physical Fitness and Wellness,* 6th ed. New York: McGraw-Hill, 2004.

Friel, J. *Total Heart Rate Training.* Berkeley: Ulysses Press, 2006.

Hoeger, W., and Hoeger, S. *Lifetime Physical Fitness and Wellness,* 15th ed. Stamford, CT: Wadsworth/Thompson Learning, 2006.

Kominsky, L. (ed.) *ASCM's Resource Manual for Guidelines for Exercise Testing and Prescription.* Philadelphia: Lippincott, Williams and Wilkins, 2006.

Kravitz, L. *Anybody's Guide to Total Fitness,* 9th ed. Dubuque, IA: Kendall/Hunt, 2009.

Neiman, D. C. *Exercise Testing and Prescription,* 5th ed. New York: McGraw-Hill Higher Education, 2003.

Powers, S., and Dodd, S. *Total Fitness and Wellness,* 5th ed. San Francisco: Benjamin Cummings, 2009.

Powers, S., and Howely, E. *Exercise Physiology: Theory and Application to Fitness and Performance,* 6th ed. St. Louis: McGraw-Hill, 2007.

Schlosberg, S., and Neporent, L. *Fitness for Dummies,* 2nd ed. Hoboken, NJ: Wiley Publishing, 2005.

Wilmore, J. H., and Costill, D. L. *Physiology of Sport and Exercise,* 3rd ed. Champaign, IL: Human Kinetics, 2004.

Chapter 3

1. Cooper Institute for Aerobics Research. *FITNESSGRAM Test Administration Manual,* 2nd ed. Champaign, IL: Human Kinetics, 1999.

2. www.zumba.com/en-US/about (accessed July 21, 2012)

3. www.webmd.com/fitness-exercise/features/zumba-fun-is-secret-ingredient-of-latin-dance-workout (accessed July 21, 2012)

4. www.zumba.com/en-US/aboutop.cit.

5. www.zumba.com/en-US/aboutop.cit.

6. www.zumba.com/en-US/aboutop.cit.

7. www.webmd.com/fitness-exercise/features/zumba-fun-is-secret-ingredient-of-latin-dance-workoutop.cit.

8. www.zumba.com/en-US/trainings/overview (accessed July 28, 2012)

9. www.zumbawithhope.com/Home_Page.php (accessed July 22, 2012)

10. www.zumbawithhope.com/History_of_Zumba.html (accessed July 22, 2012)

11. www.zumba.com/en-US/aboutop.cit.

12. www.zumbawithhope.com/History_of_Zumba.htmlop.cit.

13. www.zumba.com/en-US/aboutop.cit.

Further References

American College of Sports Medicine. *ACSM Fitness Book.* Champaign, IL: Leisure Press, 1992.

American Council on Exercise. *Group Fitness Instructor Manual.* San Diego, 2000.

Baechle, T. R., and Groves, B. R. *Weight Training Steps to Success.* Champaign, IL: Leisure Press, 1992.

Bishop, J. G. *Fitness through Aerobics,* 6th ed. San Francisco: Benjamin Cummings, 2005.

Blahnik, J. *Full-Body Flexibility.* Champaign, IL: Human Kinetics, 2004.

Brick, L. *Fitness Aerobics.* Champaign, IL: Human Kinetics, 1996.

Cibrario, M. *A Complete Guide to Rubberized Resistance Exercises.* Buffalo Grove, IL: Spri Products, 1994.

Copeland, C. *Moves: The Fool Proof Formula for Creative Choreography.* Los Angeles: CompuThink, 1987.

Fernandez, A. *How to Zumba—Lessons for Beginners; Basics & Benefits.* Melbourne: Alan Rowley, 2012.

Franklin, E. *Conditioning for Dance.* Champaign, IL: Human Kinetics, 2004.

Greene, B. *Get with the Program.* New York: Simon and Schuster Paperbacks, 2002.

Kravitz, L. Circuits and Intervals. *IDEA Today for Fitness Professionals* (January): 33–43, 1996.

LeMay, M. *Essential Stretch,* New York: Penguin Groups, 2003.

Martin, S. *Stretching.* New York: DK Publishing, 2005.

Mazzeo, K. *Fitness through Aerobics and Step Training,* 4th ed. Stamford, CT: Wadsworth/Thomson Learning, 2007.

Perez, B., and Greenwood-Robinson, M. *Zumba—Ditch the Workout Join the Zumba Weight Loss Program.* New York: Hackett Book Group, 2009.

Robbins, G., Powers, D., and Burgess, S. *A Wellness Way of Life,* 4th ed. Dubuque, IA: WCB McGraw-Hill, 1999.

Schlosberg, S., and Neporent, L. *Fitness for Dummies,* 2nd ed. Hoboken, NJ: Wiley Publishing, 2005.

Stokes, R., and Trapp, D. *Aerobic Fitness Everyone,* 3rd ed. Winston-Salem: Hunter Textbooks, Inc., 2004.

VanGalen, P. *Exercising with Dyna-Band Total Body Toner.* Hudson, OH: Gilliam Enterprises, 1996.

Chapter 4

1. www.centenaryarchers.gil.com.au/history.htm (accessed August 23, 2012).

Further References

Axford, R. *Archery Anatomy: An Introduction to Techniques for Improved Performance.* London: Souvenir Press, 1996.

The Basic Guide to Archery. Torrance, CA: Griffin Publishing, 1997.

Boga, S. *Archery.* Mechanicsburg, PA: Stackpole Books, 1997.

Engh, D. *Archery Fundamentals.* Champaign, IL: Human Kinetics, 2005.

Falda, S. *Traditional Archery.* Mechanicsburg, PA: Stackpole Books, 1999.

Habeishi, B., and Mallory, S. *Basic Essentials of Archery.* Guilford, CT: Globe Pequot Press, 2004.

Haywood, K. and Lewis, C. *Archery Steps to Success,* 3rd ed. Champaign, IL: Human Kinetics, 2006.

Matthews, R. and Holden, J. *Archery in Earnest.* North Pomfret, VT: Trafalgar Square, 1998.

Reno, H. et al. *The Pocket Guide to Target and Field Archery.* Helena, MT: Greycliff Publishing, 1994.

Ruis, S., and Stevenson, C. (eds.) *Precision Archery.* Champaign, IL: Human Kinetics, 2004.

Wise, L., and Wert, L. *The Comprehensive Guide to Equipment, Technique, and Competition.* Mechanicsburg, PA: Stackpole Books, 1992.

Chapter 5

1. www.hickoksports.com/history/badmintn.shtml (accessed August 23, 2012).

Further References

Ballou, R. *Badminton for Beginners.* Englewood, CO: Morton Publishing, 1997.

Bloss, M. V., and Hale, R. S. *Badminton,* 8th ed. Dubuque, IA: William C. Brown, 2000.

Boga, S. *Badminton.* Mechanicsburg, PA: Stackpole Books, 1996.

Edwards, J. *Badminton: Technique-Tactics-Training.* North Pomfert, VT: Trafalgar Square, 1997.

Fernhall, B., and Paup, D. *Badminton.* Scottsdale, AZ: Holcomb Hathaway, 2000.

Grice, T. *Badminton Steps to Success,* 2nd ed. Champaign, IL: Human Kinetics, 2008.

Grice, T. *Badminton,* 6th ed. Boston: American Press, 2009.

Kim, S., and Walker, M. *Badminton Today,* 2nd ed. St. Paul: Wadsworth/Thompson Learning, 2002.

Johnson, D., Rong Rong, L., and Johnson, M. *Badminton.* Boston: American Press, 2000.

Metzler, M. *Badminton.* Needham Heights, MA: Allyn & Bacon, 2001.

Paup, D., and Fernhill, B. *Skills, Drills, and Strategies for Badminton.* Scottsdale, AZ: Holcomb Hathaway, 2000.

Roper, B. *The Skills of the Game of Badminton.* North Pomfert, VT: Trafalgar Square, 1995.

Shoope, D. *Badminton for Physical Education and Beyond.* Manhattan Beach, CA: HL Corp., 1997.

Sweeting, R., and Wilson, J. *Badminton: Basic Skills and Drills.* Mountain View, CA: Mayfield, 1992.

Chapter 6

1. Hares, J. *Ultimate Basketball: More Than 100 Years of the Sport's Evolution.* New York: DK Publishing, 2004.

Further References

American Sport Education Program. *Coaching Youth Basketball,* 4th ed. Champaign, IL: Human Kinetics, 2007.

Adkins, C., Bain, S., Dreyer, E., and Starkey, R. *Basketball Drills, Plays, and Strategies.* Cincinnati: Betterway Books, 2007.

Basketball Rule Book, published yearly by the National Federation of State High School Associations, P.O. Box 690, Indianapolis, IN 46206.

Brenton-Carroll, B. *The Confident Coach's Guide to Teaching Basketball.* Guilford, CT: Lyons Press, 2003.

Brown, B. *101 Youth Basketball Drills and Games.* Monterey, CA: Coaches Choice, 2002.

Brown, H. *Let's Talk Defense.* New York: McGraw-Hill, 2005.

Faucher, D. *The Baffled Parent's Guide to Coaching Youth Basketball.* Camden, ME: Ragged Mountain Press/McGraw-Hill, 2000.

Garfinkel, H., and Klein, W. *More Five-Star Basketball Drills.* New York: McGraw-Hill, 2004.

Gianni, J. *Court Sense: Winning Basketball's Mental Games.* Champaign, IL: Human Kinetics, 2009.

Goldstein, S. *The Basketball Coach's Bible.* Philadelphia: Golden Aura, 2002.

Head-Summitt, P., and Jennings, D. *Basketball: Fundamentals and Team Play,* 2nd ed. New York: McGraw-Hill, 1996.

Krause, J. *Basketball,* New York: McGraw-Hill, 1999.

Krause, J., Meyer, D., and Meyer, J. *Basketball Skills and Drills,* 3rd ed. Champaign, IL: Human Kinetics, 2008.

Mallozzi, V. *Hoop Drills: The Coach's Guide,* 2nd ed. Buffalo: Firefly Books, 2002.

McCarthy, J. *Coaching Youth Basketball,* 3rd ed. Cincinnati: Writer's Digest Books, 2006.

Miller, F., and Coffey, W. *Winning Basketball for Girls,* 3rd ed. New York: Checkmark Books, 2002.

Minisalco, K., and Kot, G. *Survival Guide for Coaching Youth Basketball.* Champaign, IL: Human Kinetics, 2009.

NCAA Men's and Women's Basketball Rules and Interpretations, published yearly by the National Collegiate Athletic Association, P.O. Box 6222, Indianapolis, IN 46206.

Oliver, J. *Basketball Fundamentals.* Champaign, IL: Human Kinetics, 2004.

Pim, R. *Winning Basketball Techniques and Drills for Playing Better Offensive Basketball,* 2nd ed. New York: McGraw-Hill, 2004.

Prusak, K. *Basketball Fun and Games.* Champaign, IL: Human Kinetics, 2005.

Scott, J. *The Basketball Book.* Needham Heights, MA: Allyn & Bacon, 2001.

Stier, W. *Coaching Modern Basketball: Hints, Strategies and Tactics.* Needham Heights, MA: Allyn & Bacon, 1997.

Wissel, H. *Basketball: Steps to Success,* 3rd ed. Champaign, IL: Human Kinetics, 2012.

Wootten, M. *Coaching Basketball Successfully,* 2nd ed. Champaign, IL: Human Kinetics, 2003.

Wright, F. *The Ultimate Basketball Book— A Complete Shooting Guide to Skills Needed to Be the Ultimate Player,* 2nd ed. Crystal Bay, NV: Sierra Vista, 2005.

Chapter 7

1. Hickok, R. *Bowling.* www.hickoksports.com/history/bowling.shtml#hist1 (accessed August 28, 2012).
2. Ibid.
3. Bellisimo, L., and Bennett, J. *The Bowler's Manual,* 4th ed. Englewood Cliffs, NJ: Prentice Hall, 1982, p. 10.

Further References

American Association for Health, Physical Education, Recreation, and Dance (AAHPERD): Division of Girls' and Women's Sport. *Official Bowling, Fencing and Golf Guide.* Washington, DC: AAHPERD.

American Bowling Congress. *ABC Bowling Guide* (current ed.). Milwaukee: American Bowling Congress.

Bohn, P., and Herbst, D. *Bowling: How to Master the Game.* Englewood, NJ: Universe Books, 2012.

Dregina, E. *Let's Go Bowling.* St. Paul, MN: MBI, 2005.

Durbin, M., and Herbst, D. *From Gutterballs to Strikes.* New York: McGraw-Hill/ Contemporary Books, 1998.

Forrest, A. J., and Iannucci, L. *Bowling for Dummies.* Hoboken, NJ: Wiley Publishing, Inc., 2010.

Grinfelds, V., and Hulstrand, B. *Right Down Your Alley: The Complete Book of Bowling.* 6th ed. Stamford, CT: Wadsworth/ Thomson Learning, 2007.

Herbst, D. *Bowl Like a Pro.* Lincolnwood, IL: NTC/Contemporary Publishing Group, 1992.

Hinitz, D. *Focused for Bowling.* Champaign, IL: Human Kinetics, 2003.

Jowdy, J. *Bowling Execution.* Champaign, IL: Human Kinetics, 2009.

Muellen, M. *Bowling Fundamentals.* Champaign, IL: Human Kinetics, 2004.

Weidman, D. *Bowling Steps to Success.* Champaign, IL: Human Kinetics, 2006.

Chapter 8

1. Hickok, R. Sports History—Cycling 1: Development of the Bicycle. http://www. hickoksports.com/history/cycling01. shtml (accessed August 28, 2012).

2. www.bikeleague.org/about/ (accessed September 20, 2012)

3. Ibid.

4. Hickok, R. Sports History—Cycling 1.

5. Harnish, C. *Bicycling in Sports and Recreational Activities,* 13th ed. New York: McGraw-Hill Higher Education Division, 2003, chapter 8.

6. www.pedalinghistory.com/PHhistory. html (accessed September 28, 2012)

Further References

Allwood, M. *The Complete Do-It-Yourself Bike Book.* New York: Carlton Books, 2006.

Allwood, M. *Mountain Bike Maintenance.* Buffalo: Firefly Books, 2004.

Barry, D., Barry, M., and Sovndal, S. *Fitness Cycling.* Champaign, IL: Human Kinetics, 2006.

Burke, E. *Serious Cycling.* Champaign, IL: Human Kinetics, 2002.

—— *Cycling Health and Physiology: Using Sports Science to Improve Your Riding and Racing.* Brattleboro, VT: Vitesse Press, 1992.

Burke, E., and Carmichael, C. *Fitness Cycling.* Champaign, IL: Human Kinetics, 1994.

Burke, E., and Pavelka, E. *The Complete Book of Long Distance Cycling: Build the Strength, Skills and Confidence to Ride as Far as You Want.* Emmaus, PA: Rodale Press, 2000.

Downs, T. *Bicycle Maintenance & Repair.* Emmaus, PA: Rodale, Inc., 2010.

Edwards, S. and Reed, S. *The Heart Rate Monitor Book for Outdoor and Indoor Cyclists: A Heart Zone Training Program.* Boulder: Velo Press, 2000.

Fehlau, G. *The Recumbent Bicycle (Tour Cover Edition).* Williamston, MI: Out Your Backdoor Press, 2004.

Friel, J. *The Cyclist's Training Bible,* 4th ed. Boulder: Velo Press, 2009.

Hewitt, B. *New Cyclist Handbook.* Emmaus, PA: Rodale Press, 2005.

—— *Training Techniques.* Emmaus, PA: Rodale Press, 2005.

Howard, J. *Mastering Cycling.* Champaign, IL: Human Kinetics, 2010.

Hunter, A. *Cutting-edge Cycling.* Champaign, IL: Human Kinetics, 2012.

League of American Bicyclists. *Smart Cycling.* Champaign, IL: Human Kinetics, 2011.

Lopes, B., and McCormack, L. *Mastering Mountain Bike Skills,* 2nd ed. Champaign, IL: Human Kinetics, 2010.

Panzera, R. *Cycling Fast.* Champaign, IL: Human Kinetics, 2010.

Pavelka, E. (ed.). Bicycling Magazine's *Cycling for Health and Fitness.* Emmaus, PA: Rodale Press, 2000.

Pavelka, E. (ed.). Bicyling Magazine's *Mountain Biking Skills, Tips, Techniques, to Master Terrain.* Emmaus, PA: Rodale Press, 2000.

Prehn, T., and Pelke, C. *Racing Tactics for Cyclists.* Boulder: Velo Press, 2004.

Pevelar, W. *The Complete Book of Road Cycling and Racing.* Camden, ME: McGraw-Hill, 2009.

Richardson, S. *Biking USA's Rail-Trails.* Cambridge, MN: Adventure Publications, 2004.

Ruth, K. *Bicycling a Reintroduction.* Minneapolis: Creative Publishing, Inc., 2011.

Sidwells, C. *7-Week Cycling for Fitness.* New York: DK Publishing, 2006.

Sidwells, C. *Bicycle Repair Manual.* New York: DK Publishing, 2005.

Sovndal, S. *Cycling Anatomy.* Champaign, IL: Human Kinetics, 2009.

Strassman, M. P. *Basic Essentials Mountain Biking.* Guilford, CT: Globe Pequot Press, 2000.

Wilson, D. *Bicycling Science,* 3rd ed. Cambridge, MA: MIT Press, 2004.

Zinn, L. *Zinn's Cycling Primer.* Boulder: Velo Press, 2004.

ORGANIZATIONS AND CLUBS

American Bicycle Association. 1645 W. Sunset Blvd., Gilbert, AZ 85223. www.ababmx. com (Off-road bicycle racing.)

International Mountain Biking Association (IMBA). P.O. Box 7578, Boulder, CO 80306. www.ibma.com

National Bicycle League (NBL). P.O. Box 718, Chandler, AZ 85244. www.usabmx.com

National Center for Bicycling & Walking (NCBW). 8120 Woodmont Ave., Ste. 520, Bethesda, MD 20814. www.bikewalk.org

National Off-Road Bicycling Association (NORBA). One Olympic Plaza, Colorado Springs, CO 80909.

Rails-to-Trails Conservancy. The Duke Ellington Building, 2121 Ward Ct., NW, 5th Fl., Washington, DC 20037. www. railtrails.org/index.html

Chapter 9

1. Pagett, M. *The Best Dance Moves in the World . . . Ever.* San Francisco: Chronicle Books, 2008.

Further References

GENERAL

Bennett, J. *Rhythmic Activities and Dance.* Champaign, IL: Human Kinetics, 2006.

Kassing, G. *History of Dance and Interactive Arts Approach.* Champaign, IL: Human Kinetics, 2007.

Meyer, F. *Implementing the National Dance Education Standards.* Champaign, IL: Human Kinetics, 2010.

Scheff, H., Sprague, M., and McGreevy-Nichols, S. *Exploring Dance Forms and Styles.* Champaign, IL: Human Kinetics, 2010.

COUNTRY WESTERN DANCE

Lane, C. *Chrisy Lane's Complete Book of Line Dancing,* 2nd ed. Champaign, IL: Human Kinetics, 2000.

Laufman, D., and Laufman, J. *Traditional Barn Dances with Calls and Fiddling.* Champaign, IL: Human Kinetics, 2009.

Trautman, S., and Trautman, J. *Picture Yourself Dancing.* Boston: Thompson Course Technology PTR, 2006.

Woodruff, N., and Nielsen, P. *The Big Book of Country Western Line Dancing.* Curtis, WA: NAP Productions Publishers, 1996.

SOCIAL (BALLROOM) DANCE

Allen, J. *The Complete Idiot's Guide to Ballroom Dancing.* New York: Penguin Group, 2002.

Bottomer, P. *Dance Class.* London: Hermes House, 2007.

Darnel, A., and Wals, P. *Beginners Only How to Dance Book: Learn Social, Ballroom, and Latin Dances.* Houston: Beginners Only Publishing, 1999.

Harris, J. A. et al. *Dance a While: A Handbook of Folk, Square, Contra, and Social Dance,* 9th ed. San Francisco: Benjamin Cummings, 2005.

Moore, A. *Ballroom Dancing*, 9th ed. London: A & C Black, 1986.

Schild, M. *Social Dance*. Dubuque, IA: Wm. C. Brown Publishers, 1985.

Smiley, P. *Ballroom Dance Guide: First Steps-Counting 5,6,7,8*. Dubuque, IA: Kendall/Hunt, 1998.

Smith, C. *Ballroom Dance*. Boston: American Press, 1995.

Stephenson, R., and Iaccarino, J. *Complete Book of Ballroom Dancing*. New York: Random House, 2001.

Trautman, S., and Trautman, J. *Picture Yourself Dancing*. Boston: Thompson Course Technology PTR, 2006.

Wals, P., and Wals, R. *Beginners Only How to Dance Book: Learn Social Level Dancing for Youth to Seniors*. Houston: Beginners Only Publishing, 1997.

Wright, J. *Social Dance: Steps to Success*, 2nd ed. Champaign, IL: Leisure Press, 2003.

SQUARE DANCE

Casey, B. *The Complete Book of Square Dancing and Round Dancing*. Denton, TX: University of North Texas Press, 2000.

Gunzenhauser, M. *The Square Dance and Contra Dance Handbook: Calls, Dance Movements, Music Glossary, Bibliography, Discography and Directories*. Jefferson, NC: McFarland and Company, 1996.

Harris, J. A. et al. *Dance a While: A Handbook for Folk, Square, Contra, and Social Dance*, 9th ed. San Francisco: Benjamin Cummings, 2005.

Laufman, D., and Laufman, J. *Traditional Barn Dances with Calls and Fiddling*. Champaign, IL: Human Kinetics, 2009.

Schild, M. *Square Dancing Everyone*. Winston-Salem, NC: Hunter Textbooks, 1987.

Trimmer, G. *Singing thru Mainstream*. Marlborough, NH: Supreme Audio, 1995.

HIP-HOP DANCE

Pagett, M. *The Best Dance Moves in the World... Ever*. San Francisco: Chronicle Books, 2008.

Sarig, R. *Third Coast—Outkast, Timbaland, and How Hip-Hop Became a Southern Thing*. Cambridge, MA: Da Capo Press, 2007.

Chapter 10

1. Fortin, F. *Sports: The Complete Visual Reference*. Buffalo: Firefly Books, 2000.

Further References*

Anders, B. *Fitness Training for Field Hockey*. Parkerford, PA: Longstreth, 1995.

——— *Lessons in Field Hockey*. Parkerford, PA: Longstreth, 1996.

——— *Field Hockey Steps to Success*. Champaign IL: Human Kinetics, 1999.

Davidson, J., and Steinbreder, J. *Hockey for Dummies*. 2nd ed. New York: Hungry Minds, Inc., 2000.

Mitchell-Taverner, C. *Field Hockey Techniques and Tactics*. Champaign, IL: Human Kinetics, 2005.

USA Futures 2001 Coaching Manual. The Official Manual of the United States Field Hockey Association's Futures Program. Published by the USFHA National Office, One Olympic Plaza, Colorado Springs, CO 80909.

van Asselt, B. *The Hockey Coaching Guide—Part 1*. Greenford, Middlesex England: Harrow Press, 1993.

——— *The Hockey Coaching Guide—Part 2*. Greenford, Middlesex England: Harrow, 1996.

——— *The Hockey Coaching Guide—Part 3*. Greenford, Middlesex England: Harrow, 1999.

Chapter 11

1. Langdon, T. *Brief History of Flag Football*. www.flagfootball.org/sitefootballhistory.htm (accessed September 6, 2012).

Further References

American Association for Health, Physical Education, Recreation, and Dance. *Rules for Coeducational Activities and Sports and Dance*, Revised ed. Washington, DC: AAHPERD Publications, 1980.

American Association for Health, Physical Education, and Recreation, and Dance, Division for Girls' and Women's Sports. *Soccer-Speedball-Flag Football Guide*, Current ed. Washington, DC: AAHPERD.

Chamness, D. *Coaching Kids Flag Football*. Lincoln, NE: Writers Club Press, 2002.

Cihon, M. *USFTL Rule Book & Officials Manual*. Cleveland: United States Touch and Flag Football League, 1988.

Little, M., Dowell, L., and Jeter, J. *Recreational Football: Flag and Touch for Class and Intramurals*. Minneapolis: Burgess, 1977.

Mood, D., Musker F. F., and Rink, J. E. *Sports and Recreational Activities*, 13th ed. St. Louis: Mosby, 2003.

National College Physical Education Association. *Touch Football—Official National Touch Football Rules*, Current ed. Chicago: Athletic Institute.

Reed, J. *Coaching Youth Flag Football*. Alamo, CA: J. T. Reed Publishers, 1999.

Stanbury, D., and DeSantis, F. *Touch Football*. New York: Sterling Publishing Co., 1979.

United States Flag and Touch Football League. *The United States Flag and Touch Football Rules*, Currented. Mentor, Ohio, United States Flag and Touch Football League.

YMCA of USA. *Coaching YMCA Rookies Flag Football*. Champaign, IL: Human Kinetics, 2001.

Chapter 12

1. Aultman, Dick. Golf Primer. *Golf Digest* (May): 113, 1979.

Further References

Borgatti, R. *A Swing You Can Trust*. New York: Simon and Schuster, 2007.

Bradley, N. *The 7 Laws of the Golf Swing*. New York: DK Publishing, 2005.

Casten, C. M. *Lesson Plans for Pangrazi and Darst: Dynamic Physical Education for Secondary School Students (Golf)*. Boston: Allyn & Bacon, 1997.

Clampett, B., and Brumer, A. *The Impact Zone, Mastering Golf's Moment of Truth*. New York: St. Martin's Press, 2007.

Clarke, G. *Golf Rules Illustrated*. New York: Callaway Editions, 2000.

Davies, C., and DiSaia, V. *Golf Anatomy*. Champaign, IL: Human Kinetics, 2010.

Dobereiner, P., and Elliot, B. *Golf Rules Explained*. London: David & Charles, 2000.

George, J. *Let's Golf: Driving Home Tips of the Game*. San Francisco: Benjamin Cummings, 2004.

Gilchrist, G., Hill, S., and Troesch, J. *Going for the Green*. New York: Sterling Publishing, 2009.

Hanney, H. *Essentials of the Swing*. Hoboken, NJ: John Wiley & Sons, Inc., 2009.

Humphries, S., and Townsend, B. *Two Steps to the Perfect Golf Swing*. New York: McGraw-Hill, 2004.

Jacobs, J., and Newell, S. *50 Greatest Golf Lessons of the Century: Private Lessons with Golf Greats*. Harper Resources, 2000.

Madonna, B. *Coaching Golf Successfully*. Champaign, IL: Human Kinetics, 2001.

McClean, J. *Golf Digest's Ultimate Drill Book: Over 120 Drills That Are Guaranteed to Improve Your Game and Lower Your Handicap*. New York: Gotham Books, 2004.

McCord, G. *Golf for Dummies*, 3rd ed. New York: Hungry Minds, 2006.

Metzler, M. *Golf: Mastering the Basics with the Personalized Sports Instruction Team*. Boston: Allyn & Bacon, 2001.

Monday, G. *Know Your Swing*. New York: McGraw-Hill, 2005.

Newell, S. *The Complete Golf Manual*. New York: DK Publishing, 2010.

Pepper, G. *The Secret of Golf*. New York: Workman Publishing, 2005.

*All sources are available from Longstreth Sporting Goods, P.O. Box 475, Old Schuylkill Rd., Parkerford, PA 19457.

Richardson, J. with Gearen, M. *Better Golf: A Skill Building Approach*. Palo Alto, CA: Wade Publishers, 2005.

Saunders, V. *Golf Handbook for Women: The Complete Guide to Improving Your Game*. New York: Three Rivers Press, 2000.

Saunders, V. *The Golf Handbook*, 3rd ed. New York: Three Rivers Press, 2006.

Schempp, P., and Mattsson, P. *Golf Steps to Success*. Champaign, IL: Human Kinetics, 2005.

Smith, S. *Breaking 100, 90, 80: Taking Your Game to the Next Level with the Best Teachers in Golf*. New York: Doubleday, 2004.

Stenzel, K. *The Women's Guide to Golf: A Handbook for Beginners*. New York: St. Martin's Press, 2002.

Suttie, J. *Your Perfect Swing*. Champaign, IL: Human Kinetics, 2006.

United States Golf Association: *Rules of Golf*. Current ed. Far Hills, NJ: United States Golf Association, 2004–2005.

Watson, T., and Hannigan, F. *The New Rules of Golf*, Current ed. New York: Random House.

Williams, S., and DeLacy, H. *Golf at the Top with Steve Williams*. Berkeley: Ulysses Press, 2006.

Winter, A. *The Little Book of Indoor Golf Games*. Naperville, IL: Sourcebooks, Inc., 2010.

Chapter 13

1. www.hickoksports.com/history/gymnastics01.shtml (accessed September 6, 2012).
2. Fortin, F. *Sports: The Complete Visual Reference*. Buffalo, NY: Firefly Books, 2000.
3. Ibid.

Further References

Cooper, P., and Trinka, M. *Teaching Basic Gymnastics: A Coeducational Approach*, 3rd ed. Boston: Allyn & Bacon, 1994.

Feigley, D. *Winning Gymnastics for Girls*. New York: Checkmark Books, 2004.

Ferralli, M. *A Guide to Beginning Tumbling*. Baltimore: American Literary Press, 2003.

Gruber, B. *Gymnastics for Fun*. Mankato, MN: Capstone Press, 2004.

Gula, D. *Dance Choreography for Competitive Gymnastics*. Champaign, IL: Human Kinetics, 1990.

Jones, J. *Gymnastic Skills: Beginning Tumbling*. Mankato, MN: Snap Books, 2007.

Lihs, H. *Teaching Gymnastics*. Boston: American Press, 1990.

Mitchell, D. *Teaching Fundamental Gymnastic Skills*. Champaign, IL: Human Kinetics, 2002.

Paciorek, M., and Jones, J. *Disability Sport and Recreation Resources*, 3rd ed. Traverse City, MI: Cooper Publishing Group, 2000.

Ryser, O. et al. *A Manual for Tumbling and Apparatus Stunts*, 8th ed. Dubuque, IA: Wm. C. Brown, 1990.

Turoff, F. *Artistic Gymnastics*. Dubuque, IA: Brown & Benchmark, 1991.

Ward, P. *Teaching Tumbling*. Champaign, IL: Human Kinetics, 1997.

Werner, P. *Teaching Children Gymnastics*, 2nd ed. Champaign, IL: Human Kinetics, 2004.

Chapter 14

1. The History of Racquetball, www.rbdepot.com/racquetball_history.asp (accessed September 29, 2012)
2. Summers, D. *The Sports Book—The Games, the Rules, the Tactics, the Techniques*. New York: DK Publishing, 2007.

Further References

Allsen, P., and Witbeck, A. R. *Racquetball*, 6th ed. Dubuque, IA: William C. Brown, 1988.

Amateur Athletic Union. *Official Handball Rules*. 231 West 58th Street, New York, NY 10019.

American Amateur Racquetball Association. *Official Rulebook*. 815 N. Weber, Suite 203, Colorado Springs, CO 80903.

Davis, F. *Championship Racquetball*. Champaign, IL: Human Kinetics, 2011.

Edwards, L. *Racquetball*, 2nd ed. Scottsdale, AZ: Gorsuch Scarisbrick, 1992.

Fisher, D. *Racquetball Steps to Success*. Champaign, IL: Human Kinetics, 2008.

Goldblum, E. et al. *Racquetball Today* (West Activity Series). Toronto: Thompson Publishing, 1999.

Hanlon, T. *The Sports Rules Book*, 2nd ed. Champaign, IL: Human Kinetics, 2004.

Hiser, J. *Racquetball: Winning Edge*. New York: McGraw-Hill, 1998.

Isaacs, L., Lumpkin, A., and Schroer, D. *Racquetball Everyone*, 3rd ed. Winston-Salem: Hunter Textbooks, 1992.

Kittleson, S. *Racquetball: Steps to Success*. Champaign, IL: Human Kinetics, 1992.

Lowy, C. *Handball Handbook: Strategies and Techniques*, 3rd ed. Boston: American Press, 1991.

Metzler, M. *Racquetball: Mastering the Basics with the Personalized Sports Instruction System: A Workbook Approach*. Boston: Allyn & Bacon, 2000.

Norton, C., and Bryant, J. *Beginning Racquetball*, 6th ed. (Wadsworth Activity Series). Stamford, CT: Brooks/Cole, 2004.

Roberts, T., and Dewitt, J. L. *Racquetball: Learning the Fundamentals*, 5th ed. Dubuque, IA: Kendall/Hunt, 2000.

Sauser, J., and Shay, A. *Beginning Racquetball Drills*. Chicago: Contemporary Books, 1981.

Turner, E., and Clouse, W. *Winning Racquetball: Skills, Drills and Strategies*. Champaign, IL: Human Kinetics, 1996.

Verner, B. *Racquetball: Basic Skills and Drills*. Mountain View, CA: Mayfield Publishing, 1991.

Walker, D. P. et al. *Skills, Drills, and Strategies for Racquetball*. Buena Park, CA: Hathaway Publishing, 1999.

Winterton, J. *Racquetball Fundamentals* (Sports Fundamental Series). Champaign, IL: Human Kinetics, 2004.

Chapter 15

1. Seaborg, E. and Dudley, E. *Hiking and Backpacking*. Champaign, IL: Human Kinetics, 1994.
2. http://en.wikipedia.org/wiki/Camping (accessed October 7, 2012).
3. Ibid.
4. Ibid.
5. www.acacamp.org/anniversary/timeline (accessed October 7, 2012).
6. Seaborg and Dudley, *Hiking and Backpacking*.
7. Ibid.
8. McManners, H. *101 Essential Tips: Hiking*. New York: DK Publishing, 1989.
9. Rutter, M. *Camping Made Easy*. Guilford, CT: Globe Pequot Press, 2001.
10. Ibid.
11. Hall, A. *The Essential Backpacker*. Camden, ME: Ragged Mountain Press, 2001.

Further References

Anderson, K., and Tavernier, A. *Wilderness Basics*. Seattle: Mountaineers Books, 2004.

Andrews, H., and Bowers, A. *The Pocket Disaster Survival Guide*. Accokeek, MD: Stoeger Publishing, 2007.

Bagshaw, C., *The Ultimate Hiking Skills Manual*. Cincinnati: A David and Charles Book, 2006.

Beatie, R. *The Campsite Companion*. Philadelphia: Running Press, 2007.

Beffort, B. *Joy of Backpacking*. Berkeley: Wilderness Press, 2007.

Berger, K. *Backpacking and Hiking*. New York: DK Publishing, 2005.

Berger, K. *Advanced Backpacking*, A Trailside Series. New York: W. W. Norton, 1998.

Berger, K. *Everyday Wisdom: 101 Expert Tips for Hikers*. Seattle: Mountaineers Books, 1997.

Berger, K. *Hiking and Backpacking: A Complete Guide*, A Trailside Series. New York: W. W. Norton, 1995.

Callan, K. *The Happy Camper—An Essential Guide to Life Outdoors*. Erin, ON: Boston Mills Press, 2005.

Curtis, R. *The Backpacker's Field Manual: A Comprehensive Guide to Mastering*

Backcountry Skills. Maynard, MA: Three Rivers Press, 2005.

Davenport, G. *Wilderness Survival.* Mechanicsburg, PA: Stackpole Books, 1998.

Elbroch, M., and Pewtherer, M. *Wilderness Survival.* Camden, ME: Ragged Mountain Press, 2006.

Forgey, W. *Wilderness First Aid.* Guilford, CT: Globe Pequot Press, 2007.

Gerke, R. *Outdoor Survival Guide.* Champaign, IL: Human Kinetics, 2010.

Goldenberg, M., and Martin, B. *Hiking and Backpacking.* Champaign, IL: Human Kinetics, 2008.

Gray, M., and Tilton, B. *Cooking the One-burner Way.* Guilford, CT: Globe Pequot Press, 2000.

Greenspan, R., and Kahn, H. *Camper's Companion—Your Guide to Planning Now and Playing Later.* Emeryville, CA: Avalon Travel Publishing, 2001.

Groene, J. *Camping Digest—The Complete Guide to Successful Camping.* Iola, WI: Krause Publications, 2002.

Haney, L. *Camping in Comfort.* Camden, ME: Ragged Mountain Press, 2008.

Hodgson, M. *Camping for Dummies.* Foster City, CA: IDG Books Worldwide, 2000.

Jacobson, C. *Camping,* 3rd ed. Guilford, CT: Globe Pequot Press, 2005.

Jacobson, C. *Canoeing and Camping: Beyond the Basics.* Guilford, CT: Globe Pequot Press, 2000.

Kestenbaum, R. *The Ultralight Backpacker—The Complete Guide to Simplicity and Comfort on the Trail.* Camden, ME: Ragged Mountain Press, 2001.

Logue, V. *Backpacking—Essential Skills to Advanced Techniques.* Birmingham: Menasha Ridge Press, 2002.

Randall, G. *The Outward Bound Backpacking Handbook.* New York: Lyons Press, 2000.

Roberts, H., and Hall, A. *Backpacking.* Guilford, CT: Globe Pequot Press, 1999.

Stevenson, J. *Backpacking and Hiking.* New York: Penguin Group Inc., 2010.

Tawrel, P. *Camping & Survival.* Lebanon, NH: EXXA, 2011.

Townsend, C. *The Advanced Backpacker: A Handbook of Year Round, Long-Range Hiking.* New York: McGraw-Hill, 2000.

Townsend, C. *The Backpacker's Handbook,* 4th ed. New York: McGraw-Hill, 2012.

Townsend, C. *Backpacker's Pocket Guide.* New York: McGraw-Hill, 2001.

Wiseman, J. *The Ultimate Survival Guide.* New York: HarperCollins Publishers, 2004.

Chapter 16

1. *Wikipedia.* http://en.wikipedia.org/wiki/Lacrosse. Accessed September 10, 2012.

2. US Lacrosse. www.uslacrosse.org. Accessed September 10, 2012.

3. Urick, D. *Lacrosse.* In Mood, D., Musker, F., and Rink, J. (eds.) *Sports and Recreational Activities.* Boston: McGraw Hill, 2003.

4. *Wikipedia.*

5. National Collegiate Athletic Association. *Lacrosse: 2008 Men's Rules and Interpretations.* Indianapolis: National Collegiate Athletic Association, 2008.

6. National Federation of State High School Associations. *Boy's Lacrosse Rules Book.* Indianapolis: National Federation of State High School Associations, 2008.

7. National Collegiate Athletic Association. *Lacrosse: 2008 Women's Rules and Interpretations.* Indianapolis: National Collegiate Athletic Association, 2008.

8. National Federation of State High School Associations. *Girl's Lacrosse Rules Book.* Indianapolis: National Federation of State High School Associations, 2008.

Further References

Amonte Hiller, K., Gersuk, A., and Elliott, A. *Winning Women's Lacrosse.* Champaign, IL: Human Kinetics, 2010.

Hanlon, T. *The Sports Rules Book.* Champaign, IL: Human Kinetics, 2003.

Maddox, J. *Lacrosse Attack.* Mankato, MN: Capstone Press, 2009.

Murrel, G., and Garland, G. *Coaching Boys' Lacrosse: A Baffled Parent's Guide.* Boston: McGraw-Hill/Ragged Mountain, 2002.

Perez-Mazzola, V., Brown, M., and Munro, J. *The Lacrosse Training Bible: The Complete Guide for Men and Women.* New York: Heatherleigh, 2007.

Piatramala, D., and Grauer, N. *Lacrosse: Technique and Tradition,* 2nd ed. Baltimore: The Johns Hopkins University Press, 2006.

Price, R. *Ultimate Guide to Weight Training for Lacrosse,* 2nd ed. Cleveland: Price World Enterprises, 2005.

Swissler, B. *Winning Lacrosse for Girls.* New York: Facts on File Publishers, 2009.

Tucker, J., and Yakutchick, M. *Coaching Girls' Lacrosse: A Baffled Parent's Guide.* Boston: McGraw-Hill/Ragged Mountain, 2003.

Urick, D. *Sports Illustrated Lacrosse: Fundamentals for Winning,* 2nd ed. Lanham, MD: Taylor Trade Publishing, 2008.

US Lacrosse/National Association for Sport and Physical Education. *U.S. Lacrosse Physical Education Curriculum.* Baltimore, MD/Reston, VA: US Lacrosse/National Association for Sport and Physical Education, 2006.

Chapter 17

1. Snell, M. Orienteering. In *Sports and Recreational Activities* (Chapter 13). 13th ed. New York: McGraw-Hill, 2003.

2. www.us.orienteering.org/history (accessed October 7, 2012).

Further References

Boga, S. *Orienteering: The Sport of Navigating with Map and Compass.* Mechanicsburg, PA: Stackpole Books, 1997.

Bratt, I. *Orienteering: The Essential Guide to Equipment and Techniques.* Mechanicsburg, PA: Stackpole Books, 2002.

Crouch, G. *Route Finding: Navigating with Map and Compass.* Helena, MT: Falcon Publishing, 1999.

Davenport, G. *Advanced Outdoor Navigation.* Guilford, CT: Falcon Press, 2006.

Geary, D. *Using a Map and Compass.* Mechanicsburg, PA: Stackpole Books, 1995.

Kals, W. *Land Navigation Handbook: The Sierra Club Guide to Maps and Compass.* San Francisco: Sierra Club Books, 1983.

Kjellstrom, B., Heisley, N. and Assoc. Staff of the U.S. Geological Survey Orienteering Services. *Be Expert with Map and Compass.* New York: Hungry Minds, 1994.

Mattern, J. *Orienteering.* Mankato, MN: Capstone Press, 2004.

McNeil, C., Renfrew, T. and Cory-Wright, J. *Teaching Orienteering.* Champaign, IL: Human Kinetics, 2010.

Palmer, P. *The Complete Orienteering Manual.* North Pomfret, VT: Trafalgar Square, 1998.

Randall, G. *The Outward Bound Map and Compass Handbook.* New York: Lyons Press, 1998.

Seidman, D. and Cleveland, P. *The Essential Wilderness Navigator.* 2nd ed. Camden, ME: Ragged Mountain Press, 2001.

Chapter 18
ANGLING

Further References

Ball, L. (ed.). *Fly Fishing Strategies and Tactics.* Chanhassen, MN: Creative Publishing International, 2006.

Baron, F. *What Fish Don't Want You to Know: An Insider's Guide to Freshwater Fishing.* International Marine/Ragged Mountain Press, 2003.

Bean, L. L. *Fly-Fishing Handbook,* 2nd ed. Guilford, CT: The Lyons Press, 2006.

Bean, L. L. *Ultimate Book of Fly Fishing.* Guilford, CT: The Lyons Press, 2005.

Borger, J. *Nature of Fly Casting: A Modular Approach.* Wausau, WI: Shadow Caster Press, 2001.

Deeter, K., and Meyers, C. *The Little Red Book of Fly Fishing.* New York: Skyhorse Publishing, 2010.

Gathercole, P. *Fly Fishing For Beginners.* Hauppauge, NY: Barrons' Educational Series, Inc., 2006.

Kamininsky, P. *Fly Fishing for Dummies*. New York: Hungry Minds, 1998.

Kreh, L. *Fishing Knots*. Mechanicsburg, PA: Stackpole Books, 2007.

Kreh, L. *Solving Fly Casting Problems*. New York: Lyons Press, 2000.

Kreh, L., and Walinchus, R. (illustrator). *Presenting the Fly*. New York: Lyons Press, 1999.

Lord, M., and Rowinski, J. *L. L. Bean Fly Fishing Handbook*. New York: Lyons Press, 2000.

Martin, D., and Leeson, T. *The Fly Fisher's Illustrated Dictionary*. New York: Lyons Press, 2000.

National Skish Board. *National Skish Guide*, Current ed. Washington, DC: NSB (Bond Building).

Pfeiffer, C. D. *The Field and Stream Tackle Care and Repair Handbook*. New York: Lyons Press, 1999.

Rosenbauer, T. *The Orvis Fly-Fishing Guide*. Guilford, CT: The Lyons Press, 2004.

Rosenbauer, T. *The Orvis Fly-Tying Manual: How to Tie Eight Popular Flies*, 2nd ed. Guiliford, CT: Lyons Press, 2006.

Rosenbauer, T. *The Orvis Ultimate Book of Fly Fishing*. Guiliford, CT: Lyons Press, 2004.

Rutter, M., and Card, D. *Fly Fishing Made Easy*, 4th ed. Old Saybrook, CT: Globe Pequot Press, 2007.

Ryan, W. *Smallmouth Strategies for the Fly Rod*. Guilford, CT: Lyons Press, 2004.

Schaupmeyer, C. *The Essential Guide to Fly-Fishing*. Renton, WA: Lone Pine Publishing, 1998.

Sosin, M. *The Complete Book of Light-Tackle Fishing*. New York: Lyons Press, 2000.

Sousa, R. *Learn to Fly Fish in 24 Hours*. Camden, CT: Ragged Mountain Press, 2007.

Talleur, D. *Fly-Tying Handbook*. Guilford, CT: Globe Pequot Press, 2006.

Toth, M. *The Complete Idiot's Guide to Fishing Basics*, 2nd ed. Indianapolis: Alpha Books, 2000.

FLOOR HOCKEY

1. http://metadot.vigoco.k12.in.us/metadot/index.pl?_id=15969&isa=Category&op=show (accessed September 12, 2012.

2. http://www2.milwaukee.k12.wi.us/riverside/Academics/phyed/PE%20Grade%2010/FLOOR%20HOCKEY.pdf (accessed October 7, 2012).

3. http://en.wikipedia.org/wiki/Floorball (accessed October 7, 2012)

Further References

Fronske, H., and Wilson, R. *Teaching Cues for Basic Sport Skills for Elementary and Middle School Students*. Boston: Benjamin Cummings, 2002.

Pangrazi, R. *Dynamic Physical Education for Elementary School Children*. San Francisco: Benjamin Cummings, 2004.

FLYING DISC

1. Gregory, S. *Disc Golf*. Duluth, MN: Trellis Publishing, 2003.

Further References

There are few books, periodicals, or videos devoted to disc activities. The Web sites listed provide the best references and most up-to-date information.

Baccarini, M., and Booth, T. *Essential Ultimate: Teaching, Coaching, Playing*. Champaign, IL: Human Kinetics, 2008.

Leonardo, P. *Ultimate: The Greatest Sport Ever Invented by Man*. Halcottsville, NY: Breakaway Books, 2007.

Parinella, J., and Zazlow, E. *Ultimate Techniques and Tactics*. Champaign, IL: Human Kinetics, 2004.

UPA Rules of Ultimate. Colorado Springs: Ultimate Players Association, Current ed.

HORSESHOES

1. Sullivan, D. *History of Horseshoe Pitching*. www.horseshoepitching.com/gameinfor/history.html (accessed September 12, 2012).

2. Ibid.

3. Ibid.

Further References

Boga, S. *Horseshoes (Backyard Games)*. Mechanicsburg, PA: Stackpole Books, 1996.

National Horseshoe Pitchers Association of America. *Official Rules for Horseshoe Pitching*, Current ed. Federation of 54 State Associations in the U.S. and Canada. (Contact local association for state address.)

The Horseshoe Pitchers' News Digest, published monthly, PO Box 1606, Aurora, IL 60507.

PICKLEBALL

1. History of Pickleball. www.pickleball.com/History.asp (accessed September 12, 2012).

2. http://usapa.org/aboutUSAPA/history.php (accessed October 7, 2012).

Further References

Clark, J. F. *Pickleball*. Dubuque, IA: Eddie Bowers Publishing, 1994.

Curtis, J. M. *Pickle-ball for Player and Teacher*, 3rd edition. San Francisco: Brooks/Cole, 1999.

Friedenberg, M. *The Official Pickle-ball Handbook*. Federal Way, WA: PB Masters, 1999.

Leach, G. *The Art of Pickelball: Techniques and Strategies for Everyone*. Bar Harbor, ME: Acadia Publishing, 2008.

Pickle-Ball, Inc. Rules and other publications, 3131 Western Ave., Seattle, WA 98121.

Squires, D. *The Other Racquet Sports*. New York: McGraw-Hill, 1978.

SHUFFLEBOARD

1. History and Rules of Shuffleboard. www.trigger.net/~sandy/history.htm (accessed September 12, 2012).

2. The History of Shuffleboard. www.shuffleboardfederation.com (accessed September 12, 2012).

3. History and Rules of Shuffleboard.

Further References

American Association for Health, Physical Education, Recreation and Dance. *Official N.A.G.W.S. Recreational Games and Volleyball Guide*. Current ed. Washington, DC: AAHPERD.

McKenzie, P. L. *How to Win at Shuffleboard*. New Smyrna Beach, FL: Luthers, 1989.

National Shuffleboard Association. *Official Rules*. Kissimmee, FL: NSA, 1997.

TABLE TENNIS

1. Summers, D. *The Sports Book—The Games, the Rules, the Tactics, the Techniques*. New York: DK Publishing, 2007.

2. Ibid.

3. Hickok, R. Table Tennis. www.hickok-sports.com/history/tabletenn/shtml (accessed September 12, 2012).

4. Hanlon, T. *The Sports Rules Book: Essential Rules for 47 Sports*, 2nd ed. Champaign, IL: Human Kinetics, 2004.

Further References

American Association for Health, Physical Education, Recreation, and Dance. *Official N.A.G.W.S. Individual Sports Guide*, Current ed. Washington, DC: AAHPERD.

Charyn, J. *Sizzling Chops and Devilish Spins: Ping Pong and the Art of Staying Alive*. New York: Four Walls Eight Windows, 2001.

English Table Tennis Association. *Know the Game: Table Tennis*. London: A&C Black Publishers, 2006.

Hodges, L. *Table Tennis: Steps to Success*. Steps to Success activity series. Champaign, IL: Human Kinetics, 1996.

McAfee, R. *Table Tennis: Steps to Success*. Champaign, IL: Human Kinetics, 2009.

Ryan, M. *How to Play Table Tennis: A Step by Step Guide*. Jarrold Sports. Norwich, UK: Jarrold Publishing, 1993.

Seemiller D., and Halowchali, M. *Winning Table Tennis: Skills, Drills, and Strategies*. Champaign, IL: Human Kinetics, 1996.

United States Table Tennis Association. *Table Tennis for You*, Current ed. Philadelphia: USTTA.

Chapter 19

1. Stevenson, S. *The BBC Book of Skating*. London: British Broadcasting Corporation, 1984.

Further References

Miller, L. *Advanced Inline Skating*. Camden, ME: Ragged Mountain Press, 2000.

Nottingham, S., and Fedel, F. *Fitness In-line Skating*. Champaign, IL: Human Kinetics, 1997.

Powell, M., and Svensson, J. *In-line Skating*, 2nd ed. Champaign, IL: Human Kinetics, 1998.

Chapter 20

1. www.worldsoccer.about.com/cs/historyand_stats/a/sochist.htm (accessed January 11, 2005).

2. Hollander, Z. *The Encyclopedia of Soccer*. New York: Everest House Publishers, 1980.

3. Summers, D. *The Sports Book—The Games, the Rules, the Tactics, the Techniques*. New York: DK Publishing, 2007.

Further References

Bangsbo, J., and Peitersen, B. *Soccer Systems and Strategies*. Champaign, IL: Human Kinetics, 2000.

Bangsbo, J., and Peitersen, B. *Defensive Soccer Tactics*, 2nd ed. Champaign, IL: Human Kinetics, 2002.

Bangsbo, J., and Peitersen, D. *Offensive Soccer Tactics*. Champaign, IL: Human Kinetics, 2004.

Bauer, G. *New Soccer Techniques, Tactics, and Teamwork*. New York: Sterling Publishing, 2002.

Brammer, R. *Soccer Skills and Drills*. Guilford, CT: Lyons Press, 2003.

Buxton, T., Jago, G., Leith, A., and Drewitt, J. *Soccer Skills for Young Players*. Willowdate, ON: Firefly Books, 2000.

Carpenter, M. *251 Essential Drills for Winning Soccer*. Paramus, NJ: Prentice Hall, 2001.

Coger, R. *101 Great Youth Soccer Drills*. New York: McGraw-Hill, 2005.

Crisfield, D., and Gola, M. *Winning Soccer for Girls*, 2nd ed. New York: Checkmark Books, 2002.

Fleck, T., and Quinn, R. *Guide to Great Soccer Drills*. Camden, ME: Ragged Mountain Press/McGraw-Hill, 2002.

Garland, J. *Youth Soccer Drills*, 2nd ed. Champaign, IL: Human Kinetics, 2003.

Getz, G. *Complete Conditioning for Soccer*. Champaign, IL: Human Kinetics, 2009.

Herbst, D. *Soccer, How to Play the Game: The Official Playing and Coaching Manual of the United States Soccer Federation*. North Hollywood: Universe Publishing, 1999.

LaPrath, D. *Coaching Girls' Soccer Successfully*. Champaign, IL: Human Kinetics, 2009.

Luxbacher, J. *The Soccer Goalkeeper*, 3rd ed. Champaign, IL: Human Kinetics, 2002.

Luxbacher, J. *Soccer Practice Games*, 2nd ed. Champaign, IL: Human Kinetics, 2003.

Luxbacher, J. *Soccer Steps to Success*, 3rd ed. Champaign, IL: Human Kinetics, 2005.

Mariman, H. *Build-up Play*. Spring City, PA: Reedswain Publishing, 2006.

Mariman, H. *Defending*. Spring City, PA: Reedswain Publishing, 2006.

McAvoy, N. *Teaching Soccer Fundamentals: A Progressive Guide to Maximize Player Development*. Champaign, IL: Human Kinetics, 1998.

McEntire, C. (ed.) *The Soccer Coaching Bible: National Soccer Coaches Association of America*. Champaign, IL: Human Kinetics, 2004.

McGill, S. *Soccer Skills and Drills*. Terre Haute, IN: Wish Publishing, 2005.

Mielke, D. *Soccer Fundamentals*. Champaign, IL: Human Kinetics, 2003.

Rees, R., and van der Meer, C. *Coaching Soccer Successfully*, 2nd ed. Champaign, IL: Human Kinetics, 2003.

Ward, A., and Lewin, T. *Junior Soccer*. Hauppauge, NY: Barons Educational Services, 2002.

Wein, H. *Developing Youth Soccer Players*. Champaign, IL: Human Kinetics, 2000.

Yakzan, R. *105 Practical Soccer Drills*. Orange, CA: Oceanprises Publications. 2000.

Yeagley, J. *Winning Soccer*. Indianapolis: Masters Press, 1994.

Chapter 21

1. Fortin, F. *Sports: The Complete Visual Reference*. Buffalo, NY: Books, 2000.

2. Summers, D. *The Sports Book—The Games, the Rules, the Tactics, the Techniques*. New York: DK Publishing, 2007.

3. Pagoni, M., and Robinson, G. *Softball Fast and Slow Pitch*. Lincolnwood, IL: Masters Press, 1995.

Further References

American Sport Education Program. *Coaching Youth Softball*. Champaign, IL: Human Kinetics, 2007. (Video also available.)

DeMichele, D., and Majeski, D. *Softball Everyone*, 3rd ed. Winston-Salem, NC: Hunter Textbooks, 2004.

Garman, J. *Softball Skills and Drills*. Champaign, IL: Human Kinetics, 2001. (Three videos also available.)

Joseph, J. *Defensive Softball Drills*. Champaign, IL: Human Kinetics, 1998.

Joseph, J. Project coordinator. *The Softball Coaching Bible/National Fastpitch Coaches Association*. Champaign, IL: Human Kinetics, 2000.

Kempf, C. *The Softball Pitching Edge*. Champaign, IL: Human Kinetics, 2002.

NAGWS Softball Guide Current ed. Reston, VA: AAHPERD.

National Fast Pitch Coaches Association. *The Softball Coaching Bible*. Champaign, IL: Human Kinetics, 2002.

Noren, R. *Softball Fundamentals*. Champaign, IL: Human Kinetics, 2005.

Official Softball Rules. Oklahoma City: International Joint Rules Committee on Softball, Current Ed.

Oster, D., and Hunter, J. *A Guide for Young Softball Pitchers*. Guilford, CT: Lyons Press, 2005.

Potter, D., and Johnson, L. *Softball: Steps to Success*, 3rd ed. Champaign, IL: Human Kinetics, 2007.

Sammons, B. *Fastpitch Softball: The Windmill Pitcher*. Lincolnwood, IL: Masters Press/McGraw-Hill, 1997.

Strahan, K. *Coaching Girls' Softball*. New York: Random House, 2001.

Veroni, K., and Brazlier, R. *Coaching Fastpitch Softball Successfully*, 2nd ed. Champaign, IL: Human Kinetics, 2006.

Walker, K. *The Softball Drill Book*. Champaign, IL: Human Kinetics, 2007.

Chapter 22 Further References

Fronske, H. *Teaching Cues for Sport Skills for Secondary School Students*, 3rd ed. San Francisco: Benjamin Cummings, 2005.

Griffin, L., Mitchell, S., and Oslin, J. *Teaching Sports Concepts and Skills: A Tactical Games Approach*. Champaign, IL: Human Kinetics, 1997.

Phillip, J., and Wilkerson, J. *Teaching Team Sports*. Champaign, IL: Human Kinetics, 1990.

White, J. *Sports Rules Encyclopedia*, 2nd ed. Englewood, CA: Prentice-Hall, 1990.

Chapter 23

1. History of Swimming. www. en.wikipedia.org/wiki/History_of_Swimming (accessed September 20, 2012).

Further References

American Red Cross. *Lifeguard Training*. Boston: Staywell, Current.

American Red Cross. *Water Safety Instructors Manual: Swimming and Diving: Teaching Aquatics*. Boston: Staywell, Current.

Berle, L. *Water Aerobics*, 2nd ed. Dubuque, IA: Kendall/Hunt Publishers, 1996.

Colwin, C. *Breakthrough Swimming*. Champaign, IL: Human Kinetics, 2002.

Cicciarella, C. *Water Polo*, 3rd ed. Boston: American Press, 2000.

Evans, J. *Total Swimming*. Champaign, IL: Human Kinetics, 2007.

Guzman, R. *The Swimming Drill Book.* Champaign, IL: Human Kinetics, 2007.

Guzman, R. J., and Guzman, R. *Swimming Skills for Every Stroke.* Champaign, IL: Human Kinetics, 1998.

Hannula, D. *Coaching Swimming Successfully*, 2nd ed. Champaign, IL: Human Kinetics, 2003.

Hannula, D., and Thornton, N. *The Swim Coaching Bible.* Champaign, IL: Human Kinetics, 2001.

Hines, E. *Fitness Swimming.* Champaign, IL: Human Kinetics, 1999.

Jendrick, M., and Jendrick, N. *Get Wet, Get Fit—The Complete Guide to Getting a Swimmer's Body.* New York: Simon and Schuster, 2008.

Katz, J. *Your Water Workout.* New York: Random House, 2003.

Kolwin, C. *Breakthrough Swimming.* Champaign, IL: Human Kinetics, 2002.

Laughlin, T., and Delves, J. *Total Immersion.* New York: Fireside Edition, 2004.

Maglischo, E. *Swimming Fastest.* Champaign, IL: Human Kinetics, 2003.

McLeod, I. *Swimming Anatomy.* Champaign, IL: Human Kinetics, 2010.

Montgomery, J., and Chambers, M. *Mastering Swimming.* Champaign, IL: Human Kinetics, 2009.

Pappas Baun, M. *Fantastic Water Workouts*, 2nd ed. Champaign, IL: Human Kinetics, 2008.

Salo, D., and Riewald, S. *Complete Conditioning for Swimming.* Champaign, IL: Human Kinetics, 2008.

Spitzer, T., and Hoeger, W. *Water Aerobics for Fitness and Wellness.*, 3rd ed. Stamford, CT: Wadsworth/Thomson Learning, 2003.

Thomas, D. *Swimming Steps to Success.*, 3rd ed. Champaign, IL: Human Kinetics, 2005.

United States Diving. *U.S. Diving Safety Manual.* Indianapolis: United States Diving, Current.

Chapter 24

1. Fortin, F. *Sports: The Complete Visual Reference.* Buffalo, NY: Firefly Books, 2000.

2. www.hickoksports.com/history/teamhand.shtml (accessed September 20, 2012).

3. Ibid.

Further References

Clanton, R., and Dwight, M. *Team Handball: Steps to Success.* Champaign, IL: Human Kinetics, 1997.

Frick, T. *Team Handball.* Kingston, ON, Canada: Rainbow Horizons Publishing, 2001.

Fronske, H. *Teaching Cues for Sports for Secondary Students*, 3rd ed. San Francisco: Benjamin Cummings, 2008.

Hamil, B., and LaPoint, J. *Team Handball: Skills, Strategies and Training.* Dubuque, IA: Eddie Bowers Publishing, 1994.

Neil, G. I. *Modern Team Handball: Beginner to Expert.* Montreal, PQ: McGill University, 1976.

Official U.S. Team Handball Rules. Waterford, CT: Jayfro Corp.

Chapter 25 Further References

Bryant, J. *Game-Set-Match*, 7th ed. Pacific Grove, CA: Brooks Cole, 2007.

Cayer, L. *Doubles Tennis Tactics.* Champaign, IL: Human Kinetics, 2004.

Chafin, M., Thornquist, R., and Daglis, T. *Tennis Everyone*, 6th ed. Winston-Salem, NC: Hunter Textbooks, 2007.

David, R. *Inclusion Through Sports.* Champaign, IL: Human Kinetics, 2001.

Dinoffer, J. *Tennis Practice Games.* Champaign, IL: Human Kinetics, 2003.

Douglas, P., and Brown, D. *101 Essential Tips on Tennis.* New York: DK Publishing, 1996.

Greenwald, J. *The Best Tennis of Your Life.* Cincinnati: F&W Publications, 2007.

Hoskins, T. *The Tennis Drill Book.* Champaign, IL: Human Kinetics, 2003.

Matsuzaki, C. *Tennis Fundamentals.* Champaign, IL: Human Kinetics, 2004.

Metzler, M. *Tennis: Mastering the Basics with the Personalized Sports Instruction System.* San Francisco: Benjamin Cummings, 2001.

Murray J., and Frey. R. *Smart Tennis: How to Win the Mental Game.* San Francisco: Jossey-Bass, 1999.

Rich, S. *The Tennis Handbook: A Complete Guide to Acing Your Game.* New York: Random House, Inc., 2006.

Rich, S. *The Tennis Handbook.* New York: Three Rivers Press, 2006.

Roetert, E., and Ellenbecker, T. *Complete Conditioning for Tennis.* Champaign, IL: Human Kinetics, 2007.

Sadzeck, T. *Tennis Skills—The Players Guide.* Buffalo, NY: Firefly Books, 2006.

Saviano, N. *Maximum Tennis.* Champaign, IL: Human Kinetics, 2003.

Smith, S. *Winning Doubles.* Champaign, IL: Human Kinetics, 2002.

United States Tennis Association (USTA). *Coaching Youth Tennis*, 3rd ed. Champaign, IL: Human Kinetics, 2002.

USTA. *Coaching Tennis Successfully*, 2nd ed. Champaign, IL: Human Kinetics, 2004.

USTA with Anderson, K. *Coaching Tennis Technical and Tactical Skills.* Champaign, IL: Human Kinetics, 2009.

Vasquez, R. *Kids Book of Tennis: Over 150 Tennis Games to Teach Children the Sport of a Lifetime.* Secaucus, NJ: Carol Publishing Group, 1997.

Chapter 26

1. Fortin, F. *Sports: The Complete Visual Reference.* Buffalo: Firefly Books, 2000.

2. Ibid.

3. Ibid.

Further References

American Sport Education Program. *Coaching Youth Track and Field.* Champaign, IL: Human Kinetics, 2008.

Bowerman, W., and Freeman, W. *High-Performance Training for Track and Field.* Champaign, IL: Human Kinetics, 1991.

Carr, G. *Fundamentals of Track and Field.*, 2nd ed. Champaign, IL: Human Kinetics, 1999.

Daniels, J. *Daniel's Running Formula.* Champaign, IL: Human Kinetics, 2005.

Green, L., and Pate, R. *Training for Young Distance Runners.*, 2nd ed. Champaign, IL: Human Kinetics, 2004.

Guthrie, M. *Coaching Track and Field Successfully.* Champaign, IL: Human Kinetics, 2003.

Houseright, E. *Winning Track and Field for Girls.* New York: Checkmark Books, 2004.

Powell, J. *Track and Field Fundamentals for Teacher and Coach.*, 4th ed. Champaign, IL: Stipes Publishing, 1987.

Rogers, J. *USA Track and Field Coaching Manual.* Champaign, IL: Human Kinetics, 2000.

Wallace, E. *Track and Field Coaches Guide: Practice Techniques and Materials for Building an Effective Program for Success in Every Event.* Englewood Cliffs, NJ: Prentice-Hall, 1999.

Chapter 27

1. Shewman, B. *Volleyball Centennial—The First 100 Years.* Indianapolis: Masters Press, 1995.

2. Ibid.

3. Ibid.

4. Ibid.

5. Summers, D. *The Sports-Book—The Games, The Rules, The Tactics, The Techniques.* New York: DK Publishing, 2007.

Further References

American Volleyball Coaches Association. *Volleyball Skills and Drills.* Champaign, IL: Human Kinetics, 2006.

Bertoli, J. *Volleyball Skills and Drills.* Terre Haute, IN: Wish Publishing, 2004.

Crisfield, D., and Monteleone, J. *Winning Volleyball for Girls.* New York: Checkmark Books, 2009.

Dearing, J. *Volleyball Fundamentals—A Better Way to Learn the Basics.* Champaign, IL: Human Kinetics, 2003.

Gozansky, S. *Volleyball Coaches Survival Guide—Practical Techniques and Materials for Building an Effective Program and a Winning Team*. Paramus, NJ: Parker Publishing, 2001.

Henry, C., and Corcoran, J. *Volleyball—Playing with Your Head at Any Height*. Terre Haute, IN: Wish Publishing, 2005.

Howard, R. E. *An Understanding of the Fundamental Techniques of Volleyball*. Needham, MA: Allyn & Bacon, 1995.

Kenny, B., and Gregory, C. *Volleyball Steps to Success*. Champaign, IL: Human Kinetics, 2006.

Kus, S. *Coaching Volleyball Successfully*. Champaign, IL: Human Kinetics, 2004.

Lenberg, K. (ed.). *Volleyball Skills and Drills*. Champaign, IL: Human Kinetics, 2006.

Neville, W. *Coaching Volleyball Successfully*. Champaign, IL: Human Kinetics, 1990.

Neville, W. *Serve It Up: Volleyball for Life*. Mountain View, CA: Mayfield Publishing, 1992.

Scates, A. *Winning Volleyball*. Dubuque, IA: Brown and Benchmark Publishers, 1993.

Scates, A., and Linn, M. *Complete Conditioning for Volleyball*. Champaign, IL: Human Kinetics, 2003.

Shondell, D., and Reynaud, C. (eds.). *The Volleyball Coaching Bible*. Champaign, IL: Human Kinetics, 2002.

Waite, P. *Aggressive Volleyball*. Champaign, IL: Human Kinetics, 2009.

Wise, M. *Volleyball Drills for Champions*. Champaign, IL: Human Kinetics, 1999.

Chapter 28

1. Geogebuer, T. Weightlifting in General. http://users.pandora.be/tom.goegebuer/weightlifting.htm (accessed December 15, 2004).

2. Jackson, A. See Chapter 42 in *Weightlifting in Sports and Recreational Activities*. New York: McGraw-Hill Educational Division, 2003.

Further References

Allsen, P. *Strength Training: Beginners, Body Builders, and Athletes*, 5th ed. Dubuque, IA: Kendall/Hunt, 2009.

Baechle, T. R., and Earle, R. W. *Essentials of Strength and Conditioning*. Champaign, IL: Human Kinetics, 2000.

Baechle, T. R., and Earle, R. *Fitness Weight Training*, 2nd ed. Champaign, IL: Human Kinetics, 2005.

Baechle, T. R., and Groves, B. R. *Weight Training, Steps to Success*, 3rd ed. Champaign, IL: Leisure Press, 2006.

Beckwith, K. *Weight Training*. Dubuque, IA: Kendall/Hunt, 2008.

Brown, L. *Strength Training*. Champaign, IL: Human Kinetics, 2007.

Cane-Johnson, D., Cane, J., and Glickman, J. *The Complete Idiot's Guide to Weight Training*, 2nd ed. New York: Penguin Group, 2005.

Darden, E. *The New High Intensity Training*. New York: Rodale, 2004.

Fahey, T. *Basic Weight Training for Men and Women*, 7th ed. New York: McGraw-Hill, 2010.

Faigenbaum, A., and Westcott, W. *Youth Strength Training*. Champaign, IL: Human Kinetics, 2009.

Faigenbaum, A., and Wescott, W. *Strength and Power for Young Athletes*. Champaign, IL: Human Kinetics, 2000.

Fleck, S. J., and Kraemer, W. J. *Designing Resistance Training Programs*. Champaign, IL: Human Kinetics, 1997.

Groves, B. *Power Lifting*. Champaign, IL: Human Kinetics, 2000.

Hesson, J. *Weight Training for Life*. Belmont, CA: Wadsworth, 2009.

Johnson, M. *Weightlifting and Conditioning Exercises*, 3rd ed. Dubuque, IA: Eddie Bowers, 2000.

Neporent, L., and Archer, S. *Weight Training for Dummies*. Hoboken, NJ: Wiley Publishing, 2006.

Sandeler, D. *Weight Training Fundamentals*. Champaign, IL: Human Kinetics, 2003.

Shepard, G. *Bigger, Stronger, Faster*, 2nd ed. Champaign, IL: Human Kinetics, 2009.

Smith, C., and Jones, D. *Conditioning and Weight Training*, 3rd ed. Dubuque, IA: Kendall/Hunt, 2001.

Stone, M., Stone, M., and Sands, W. *Principles and Practices of Resistance Training*. Champaign, IL: Human Kinetics, 2007.

Stoppani, J. *Encyclopedia of Muscle & Strength*. Champaign, IL: Human Kinetics, 2006.

Chapter 29

1. Feuerstein, G. *Yoga: The Technology of Ecstasy*. Los Angeles: Jeremy P. Tarcher, 1989.

2. Birkel, D., and Edgren, L. "Hatha Yoga: Improved Vital Capacity of College Students." *Alternative Therapies*, 6, no. 6, pp. 55–63, 2000.

3. Desai, M., and Desai, G. *Yoga Unveiled: The Evolution and Essence of a Spiritual Tradition* (DVD). www.yogaunveiled.com.

4. Ibid.

5. Ornish, D. *Dr. Dean Ornish's Program for Reversing Heart Disease*. New York: Ballentine Books, 1996.

6. Carrico, M. "Contraindications of Yoga." *Idea Health & Fitness Source*, November–December 1998, pp. 34–41.

7. Iyengar, B. K. S. *Light on Yoga* (revised edition). New York: Schocken Books, 1977.

8. Leonard, G. *Mastery: The Keys to Success and Long-Term Fulfillment*. New York: Plume, 1991.

9. Kramer, J. "Yoga as Self-Transformation." *Yoga Journal*, May 1980.

10. Schiffmann, E. *Yoga: The Spirit and Practice of Moving into Stillness*. New York: Pocket Books, 1996.

11. Farhi, D. *Yoga Mind, Body & Spirit*. New York: Henry Holt, 2000.

12. Couch, J. *The Runner's Yoga Book*. Berkeley, CA: Rodmell Press, 1999.

13. Schiffman, op. cit.

14. Couch, op. cit.

15. Schiffman, op. cit.

16. Couch, op. cit.

17. Schlosberg, S. and Neporent, L. *Fitness for Dummies*. Hoboken, NJ: Wiley Publishing, Inc., 2011.

18. Ibid.

19. Herman, E. *Pilates for Dummies*. Hoboken, NJ: Wiley Publishing, Inc., 2002.

20. Ibid.

21. Isacowitz, R. *Pilates*. Champaign, IL: Human Kinetics, 2006.

22. Chabut, L. *Core Strength for Dummies*. Hoboken, NJ: Wiley Publishing, Inc., 2009.

23. Isacowitz, R., op. cit.

24. Isacowitz, R., op. cit.

25. Isacowitz, R., op. cit.

26. Isacowitz, R., op. cit.

27. Isacowitz, R., op. cit.

28. Herman, op. cit.

29. Isacowitz, R., op. cit.

30. Isacowitz, R., op. cit.

31. Herman, op. cit.

32. Isacowitz, R., op. cit.

Further References

Anderson, S. *Yoga: Mastering the Basics*. Honesdale, PA: Himalayan Institute Press, 2008.

Bermsa, D. *Yoga Games for Children: Fun and Fitness Postures, Movements and Breath*. Alameda, CA: Hunter House, 2003.

Birch, B. *Power Yoga—The Total Strength and Flexibility Workout*. New York: Simon & Schuster, 1995.

Brown, C. *The Yoga Bible*. London, UK: Godsfield Press, 2003.

Budilovsky, J., Adamson, E., and Flynn, C. *The Complete Idiot's Guide to Yoga*, 4th ed. New York: Penguin Group, 2006.

Calhoun, Y. *Create a Yoga Practice for Kids*. Santa Fe: Sunstone Press, 2006.

Christensen, A. *The American Yoga Association Beginner's Manual*. New York: Fireside, 2002.

Craig, C. *Pilates on the Ball*. Rochester, VT: Healing Arts Press, 2001.

Dykema, R. *Yoga for Fitness and Wellness*. Belmont, CA: Thompson, 2006.

Feuerstein, G., and Payne, L. *Yoga for Dummies*, 2nd ed. Foster City, CA: I.D.G. Books, 2010.

Fraser, T. *Total Yoga*. New York: Sterling Publishing, 2007.

Fraser, T. *Yoga Bliss*. New York: Sterling Publishing, 2007.

Fronske, H. *Teaching Cues for Sport Skills for Secondary School Students*, 3rd ed. San Francisco: Benjamin Cummings, 2005.

Gerstein, N. *Guiding Yoga's Light: Lessons for Yoga Teachers*. Champaign, IL: Human Kinetics, 2008.

Hagen, A. *The Yoga Face*. New York: Penguin Group, 2007.

Hessel, J. *Pilates Basics*. Emmaus, PA: Rodale Press, 2003.

Lyon, D. *The Complete Book of Pilates for Men*. New York: Harper Collins Publishers, Inc., 2005.

Kurland, Z. *Morning Yoga Workouts*. Champaign, IL: Human Kinetics, 2007.

Kraftsow, G. *Yoga for Wellness*. New York: Penguin/Arkana, 1999.

Schatz, M. P. *Back Care Basics: A Doctor's Gentle Yoga Program for Back and Neck Pain Relief*. Berkeley, CA: Rodmell Press, 1992.

Siler, B. *Your Ultimate Pilates Body Challenge*. New York, NY: Random House, 2006.

Stanmore, T. *The Pilates Back Book*. Beverly, MA: Quayside Publishing Group, 2002.

Swenson, D. *Ashtanga Yoga: The Practice Manual*. Sugar Land, TX: Ashtanga Yoga Productions, 1999.

Tardent, H. *Beautiful Pilates*. Camberwell, Australia: Penguin Group, 2005.

Ungaro, A. *Pilates Body in Motion*. New York: DK Publishing, 2002.

Van Kooten, V. *From Inside Out—A Yoga Notebook from the Teachings of Angela & Victor, I and II*. Berkeley, CA: Ganesha Press, 2000.

Chapter 30
CANOEING AND KAYAKING

Further References

American Canoe Association. *Canoeing*. Champaign, IL: Human Kinetics, 2009.

Dillon, P, and Oyen, J. *Kayaking*. Champaign, IL: Human Kinetics, 2009.

Glickman, J. *The Kayak Companion*. North Adams, MA: Storey Books, 2003.

Gordon, H. *Canoeing Made Easy: A Manual for Beginners with Tips for the Experienced*. Old Saybrook, CT: Globe Pequot Press, 1992.

Gordon, H. *The Complete Book of Canoeing*, 3rd ed. Old Saybrook, CT: Globe Pequot Press, 2001.

Hutchinson, D. *Expedition Kayaking*. Guilford, CT: Globe Pequot Press, 2007.

Jacobsen, C. *Canoeing and Camping Beyond the Basics*, 2nd ed. Old Saybrook, CT: Globe Pequot Press, 2000.

Johnson, S. *Sea Kayaker's Handbook*. Camden, ME: Ragged Mountain Press, 2002.

Mattos, B. *Kayaking and Canoeing for Beginners*. London: Anness Publishing, 2007.

Rounds, J. *Basic Canoeing: All the Skills You Need to Get Started*. Basic How-to Guides. Mechanicsburg, PA: Stackpole Books, 2003.

Rounds, J. *Basic Kayaking*. Mechanicsburg, PA: Stackpole Books, 2005.

Stuhaug, D. *Kayaking Made Easy: A Manual for Beginners with Tips for the Experienced*, 2nd ed. Old Saybrook, CT: Globe Pequot Press, 1998.

Stuhaug, D. *The Complete Idiot's Guide to Canoeing and Kayaking*. New York: Penguin Group, 2004.

Swenson, A. *L. L. Bean Canoeing Handbook*. New York: Lyons Press, 2000.

CROSS-COUNTRY SKIING

1. REI: Snow Sports Expert Advice, Cross-Country Skiing: Glossary, http://www.rei.com/learn/expert-advice/crosscountry-skiing-glossary.html (accessed October 20, 2012)

Further References

Caldwell, J. *The New Cross-Country Ski Book*, 8th ed. Lexington, MA: Stephen Greene Press, 1987.

Cazeneuve, B. *Cross-Country Skiing: A Complete Guide*. A Trailside Series Guide. New York: W. W. Norton, 1995.

Gaskill, S. *Fitness Cross-Country*. Fitness Spectrum Series. Champaign, IL: Human Kinetics, 1997.

Gullion, L. *Nordic Skiing*. Champaign, IL: Human Kinetics, 1993.

Older, J. *Cross-Country for Everyone*. Mechanicsburg, PA: Stackpole Books, 1998.

Petersen, P., Lovett, R. A., and Morton, J. *The Essential Cross-Country Skier: A Step-by-Step Guide*. Camden, ME: Ragged Mountain Press/McGraw-Hill, 2000.

Sheahan, C. *Cross-Country Skiing: A Complete Guide*. New York: Sports Illustrated Winners Circle, 1988.

Vives, J. *Backcountry Skier*. Champaign, IL: Human Kinetics, 1999.

INDOOR CLIMBING

1. http://www.traversewall.com/reasons_build.shtml (accessed September 16, 2012).

2. http://en.wikipedia.org/wiki/Indoor_climbing (accessed September 3, 2012).

3. http://www.indoorclimbing.com (accessed September 2, 2012).

4. http://en.wikipedia.org/wiki/Climbing_wall (accessed September 3, 2012).

5. http://www.pecentral.org/store/msmanual/climbingchapter.html (accessed September 2, 2012).

6. indoorclimbing.com (accessed September 2, 2012) op. cit.

7. traversewall.com/reasons_build.shtml (accessed September 16, 2012) op. cit.

8. en.wikipedia.org/wiki/Climbing_wall (accessed September 3, 2012) op. cit.

9. http://www.indoorclimbing.com/Climbing_Technique.html (accessed September 2, 2012).

10. Ibid.

Further References

Stiehl, J. and Chase, D. *Traverse Walls 68 Activities On and Off the Wall*. Champaign, IL: Human Kinetics. 2008.

SKIN DIVING

Further References

Barsky, S. M. *A Simple Guide to Snorkeling Fun*. Flagstaff, AZ: Best Publishing, 1999.

Berger, K. *Scuba Diving*. A Trailside Guide. New York: W.W. Norton, 2000.

Coleman, C. *The Certified Diver's Handbook: The Complete Guide to Your Own Underwater Adventures*. Columbus, OH: International Marine/Ragged Mountain Press, 2004.

Graver, D. K. *Scuba Diving*, 3rd ed. Champaign, IL: Human Kinetics, 2003.

Jackson, J. *Complete Diving Manual*. Camden, ME: McGraw-Hill, 2005.

Joiner, J. (ed.). *NOAA Diving Manual: Diving for Science and Technology*, 4th ed. Flagstaff, AZ: Best Publishing, 2001.

Maas, T., and Sipperly, D. *Freedive*. Ventura, CA: Blue Water Free Divers, 1998.

Newman, J. *Scuba Diving and Snorkeling for Dummies*. New York: Wiley Publishing, Inc., 1999.

Orr, D., and Douglas, E. *Scuba Diving Safety*. Champaign, IL: Human Kinetics, 2007.

SKATEBOARDING

1. Brooke, M. *The Concrete Wave: The History of Skateboarding*. Toronto, Ontario: Warwick Publishing, 2005.

2. Ibid.

3. Werner, D. with Badillo, S. *Skateboarder's Start-up: A Beginner's Guide to Skateboarding*. San Diego: Tracks Publishing, 2000.

Further References

Badillo, S. with Werner, D. *Skateboarding: Book of Tricks*. San Diego: Tracks Publishing, 2003.

D'Arcy, S. and Marshall, P. *Freestyle Skateboarding Tricks*. Buffalo, NY: Firefly Books Inc., 2010.

Freimuth, J. *Extreme Skateboarding Moves*. Behind the Moves Series. Mankato, MN: Capstone Press, 2000.

Goodfellow, E. *Street Skateboarding: Flip Tricks*. San Diego: Tracks Publishing, 2005.

Goodfellow, E. *Street Skateboarding: Endless Grinds and Slides*. San Diego: Tracks Publishing, 2005.

Gutman, B. *Skateboarding: To the Extreme*. New York: St. Martin's Press, 1997.

Gutman, B. *The Wild and Exciting World of Skateboarding*. New York: Tor Books, 2001.

Hocking, J. *Skateboarding Half-Pipes, Ramps, and Obstacles*. New York: Rosen Publishing Group, 2006.

Mullen, R. *The Mutt—How to Skateboard and Not Kill Yourself*. New York: HarperCollins, 2004.

Werner, D. with Badillo, S. *Skateboarder's Start-up: 14 Tricks You Should Know*. San Diego, CA: Tracks Publishing, 2000.

Werner, D., and Badillo, S. *Skateboarding: New Levels, Tips and Tricks for Serious Riders*. San Diego: Tracks Publishing, 2002.

Werner, D., and Badillo, S. *Skateboarding: Book of Tricks*. Chula Vista, CA: Tracks Publishing, 2003.

SNOWBOARDING

1. Carlson, J., and Gross, M. M. (series eds.). *Snowboarding: A Woman's Guide*. Camden, ME: Ragged Mountain Press, 1998.
2. Bennett, J., Downey, S., and Arnell, C. *The Complete Snowboarder*, 2nd ed. New York: McGraw-Hill, 2000.
3. Ibid.
4. Ibid.
5. Ibid.
6. Ibid.
7. Carlson, op. cit.

Further References

Gifford, C. *Snowboarding*. New York: DK Publishing, 2007.

Goldman, G. *Snowboarding*. Mechanicsburg, PA: Stackpole Books, 2001.

Gutman, B. *Snowboarding*. New York: Tor Books, 2000.

Hart, L. *The Snowboard—A Guide for All Boarders Book*. New York: W.W. Norton, 1997.

Howe, S. *Sick: A Cultural History of Snowboarding*. New York: St. Martins Press, 1998.

Kleh, C. *Snowboarding Skills: The Back to Basics Essentials for All Levels*. Tonawanda, NY: Firefly Books, 2004.

Lurie, J., and Clarke, J. (photographer). *Fundamental Snowboarding*. Minneapolis: Lerner Publications Company, 1995.

Martin, D., and Diehl, M. *No-Fall Snowboarding*. New York: Simon and Schuster, 2005.

McNab, N. *Go Snowboard*. New York: DK Publishing, 2006.

Older, E. *Snowboarding*. Mechanicsburg, PA: Stackpole Books, 1999.

Ryan, K. *The Illustrated Guide to Snowboarding*. Dallas: Master's Press, 1998.

SNOWSHOEING

1. Savignano, P. *Snowshoeing*. Basic Essential Series. Guilford, CT: Globe Pequot Press, 2001.
2. Prater, G., and Felkley, D. (eds.). *Snowshoeing: From Novice to Master*, 5th ed. Seattle: Mountaineer Books, 2002.
3. Ibid.
4. Savignano, op. cit.

Further References

Griffin, S. *Snowshoeing*. Mechanicsburg, PA: Stackpole Books, 1998.

McDougall, L. *The Snowshoe Handbook*. Short Hills, NJ: Burford Books, 2000.

Olmsted, L. *Snowshoeing: A Trailside Guide*. New York: W. W. Norton, 1997.